Gamilaraay, Yuwaalaraay, & Yuwaalayaay DICTIONARY

Includes

G/Y/Y to English Dictionary
English to G/Y/Y Word Lists
Learner's Guide

Compiled and edited by
Anna Ash, John Giacon and Amanda Lissarrague

Main Gamilaraay and Yuwaalaraay informants:
Arthur Dodd, Greg Fields, Ted Fields, Peter Lang, Fred Reece and Ginny (Jenny) Rose

IAD PRESS
Alice Springs

First published by IAD Press in 2003
IAD Press
PO Box 2531
Alice Springs NT 0871
ph: 08 8951 1334
fax: 08 8952 2527
email: sales@iad.edu.au

© Yuwaalaraay Language Program, Walgett 2003

This book is copyright. Apart from any fair dealing for the purposes of private study, research, criticism or review, as permitted under the *Copyright Act 1968*, no part may be reproduced by any process without written permission. Please forward all enquiries to IAD Press at the address above.

National Library of Australia Cataloguing-in-Publication data

   Gamilaraay/Yuwaalaraay/Yuwaalayaay dictionary.

   ISBN 1 86465 051 6.

   1. Gamilaraay language—Dictionaries—English. 2. English language—
   Dictionaries—Gamilaraay. 3. Yuwaalaraay language—Dictionaries—English.
   4. English language—Dictionaries—Yuwaalaraay. I. Lissarrague, Amanda, 1958– .
   II. Ash, Anna. III. Giacon, John.

   499.1503

Production by Bruderlin MacLean Publishing Services
Cover illustrations by Warren Mason
Cover photo by Dayle Green
Maps by Brenda Thornley
Printed by Southwood Press, Sydney

IAD Press is assisted by the Commonwealth Government through the Australia Council, its arts funding and advisory body.

Gamilaraay, Yuwaalaraay, & Yuwaalayaay DICTIONARY

Foreword

Yaama nginday, dhagaan, baawaa ngay!

As Principal of the Australian Institute of Aboriginal and Torres Strait Islander Studies, and — perhaps more importantly — as a Gamilaraay man, I am well aware of the significance and centrality of language to our culture, our identity and our future as Aboriginal and Torres Strait Islander peoples.

As Indigenous Australians our language sustains us, informs us and unites us. It also clearly differentiates us from others in a very special and unique way. Loss and threatened loss of our language has been at the heart of many of the negative aspects of black/white relations in Australia since colonisation. It has served to exacerbate many of the racial and cultural problems experienced between Indigenous and non-Indigenous Australians. However, it is pleasing to note that — driven by both Indigenous and non-Indigenous community concerns and interests — a groundswell of action at the community level is gathering impetus across Australia.

Such positive actions and projects address the issue of language loss as part of a strong language revival movement. These initiatives enable previously dormant or threatened languages to be transformed into 'living' languages which, over time, may be reclaimed by their communities and language speakers — young and old alike.

These Indigenous language initiatives are to be supported and encouraged. This project, the *Gamilaraay, Yuwaalaraay & Yuwaalayaay Dictionary*, is part of just such an initiative. It has involved a diverse group of committed people, both Indigenous and non-Indigenous, who share common values and objectives. A special mention must go to those elders who have worked tirelessly to keep our language alive, and worthy of particular mention are Uncle Ted Fields, Auntie Rose Fernando and Auntie Daphne Jarret. Also vital to language revival are a group of younger Indigenous people who are committed to learning and teaching the languages. I also take this opportunity to acknowledge the invaluable contribution of the linguists Anna Ash and Amanda Lissarrague. Worthy of special mention, however, is the commitment, effort and influence of Brother John Giacon, whose involvement in this initiative is simply the latest aspect of his many years of support for language revival.

We hope that this project will generate a greater interest in and appreciation of the many Indigenous Australian languages currently in use, or being revived, across the nation. Such recognition can only add value to the cultural lives of all Australians and contribute towards the proper acknowledgment of the place, in the fabric of the nation, of the languages and cultures of the *first* Australians.

Gaba yanaya, bamba guwaala Gamilaraay, Yuwaalaraay!

Russ Taylor, Principal
Australian Institute of Aboriginal and Torres Strait Islander Studies
Canberra ACT

Contents

Foreword v
Preface ix
Acknowledgements x

An Introduction to Gamilaraay, Yuwaalaraay and Yuwaalayaay 1
    The purpose of this book..1
    The Gamilaraay and Yuwaalaraay people..1
    The Gamilaraay and Yuwaalaraay family of languages 5
    The sounds of Gamilaraay and Yuwaalaraay...6
    Relationship words 10
    The sources of information for the dictionary and learner's guide 12
    References and resources 14

THE DICTIONARY 17

Using the Dictionary 19

Gamilaraay/Yuwaalaraay/Yuwaalayaay *to* English Dictionary......................25
Gamilaraay/Yuwaalaraay/Yuwaalayaay *to* English New Word List..............160
English *to* Gamilaraay/Yuwaalaraay/Yuwaalayaay Word List 161
Gamilaraay/Yuwaalaraay/Yuwaalayaay *to* English Word List by Topic........213

THE LEARNER'S GUIDE 255

Chapter One: Getting Started...257
    How to use this learner's guide...257
    Talk it! 258
    Abbreviations and source references 258
    Simple sentences 259

Chapter Two: Suffixes (word endings)..264
    What is a suffix?..264
    Some common GY suffixes...264
    Suffixes and noun phrases 272
    Some other suffixes 272
    Knowledge suffixes 278
    Clitics...280
    Other possible suffixes..283

Chapter Three: Pronouns 286
    Bound pronouns..292
    Question pronouns..293
    Inclusive–exclusive, and related topics...293

Contents continued

    Zero pronouns 294
    Determiners/demonstratives and place words..................................294
    Linking words 300
Chapter Four: Verbs 302
    What is a verb? 302
    Simple verb stems, simple verb endings 302
    Transitive and intransitive verbs 302
    Verb classes 303
    Progressive endings 305
    Complex stems 312
    Change of verb class 319
    Relative verb endings...320
Chapter Five: Questions, Negatives, Time..322
    Questions...322
    Other question words 325
    Negatives 326
    Time words 328
Chapter Six: Sentences and Particles...330
    Language rules for sentences 330
    Sentences: Joining parts, style 332
    Other particles 333
    Reduplication 335

Appendixes 337
    1. Glossary of terms 337
    2. Summaries 340

Preface

This dictionary and learner's guide provides a substantial introduction to what is currently known of the Gamilaraay, Yuwaalaraay and Yuwaalayaay languages. (The word Yuwaalaraay is often used to refer to both Yuwaalaraay and Yuwaalayaay, and so the three languages may be referred to as Gamilaraay–Yuwaalaraay, or GY for short.) It is primarily written for those Gamilaraay and Yuwaalaraay people who are interested in relearning their language. Written grammars and dictionaries are not the best way to learn a language but sadly, for many Australian languages, they are the only way to learn most of the language.

This book is based on historical material and some current knowledge. It responds to a growing interest in language among GY people. Recent programs have seen an upturn in the use of GY language, where previously the story had been one of ongoing decline.

Language revival involves simultaneous processes of maintenance and development. If the original language is to be maintained there must be a thorough understanding of that language — or at least as thorough an understanding as the resources allow. If a language is to grow, it must be a language that can be used in this world, a language that has words for today. This book shows some of the words and rules of traditional GY, and some of the adaptations it is making to a new world.

There are two main sections to the book. The 'word' section includes the dictionary and word lists, and is largely about individual words. The learner's guide is an introduction to some aspects of the grammar of the languages. The learner's guide explains many of the features in the dictionary's example sentences. It shows how complex words are formed from simpler words and how words are put together into sentences.

Many people have contributed to the book — from those who gave information for word lists in the 1840s to those who checked proofs. My thanks go to all of them. On each revision of the work, additions, improvements and corrections have been made. Any suggestions for further changes are welcome and will be a valuable contribution to the next edition.

There are a number of groups involved in GY revival. They meet as the 'Gamilaraay/Yuwaalaraay Languages Network'. For further information, contact:

Yuwaalaraay Language Program　　　　　　　　Ph 02 6828 1060
St Joseph's Primary School
PO Box 125
Walgett NSW 2832

Lightning Ridge Central School　　　　　　　　Ph 02 6829 0511

Toomelah–Boggabilla: Boggabilla Central School　Ph 07 4676 2104

Goodooga Central School　　　　　　　　　　Ph 02 6829 6257

Coonabarabran High School　　　　　　　　　Ph 02 6842 1099

JG 2003

Acknowledgements

This book has grown out of the work of the Yuwaalaraay Language Program at Walgett, and that of other programs. The primary foundation of these programs is the ongoing work of elders to maintain and revive language. The support of others in the Gamilaraay–Yuwaalaraay community builds on this. The linguists, administrators and others provided some of the skills necessary for this revival. Many of those who have contributed are listed below, though space does not allow the details of their contributions to be spelled out. However, three people deserve special mention. Anna Ash worked on this project for over two years. She brought skill, experience and a commitment to quality and accuracy to the work. Without her involvement and commitment the project would be much impoverished and would certainly not be finished at this time. Amanda Lissarrague also brought similar qualities for the months she worked on the project. Ian Sim voluntarily spent many hours proofreading. His unique knowledge, gained around Goodooga in the 1950s, and his thorough approach have much enhanced the book.

Compilers

Anna Ash
John Giacon (Co-ordinator)
Amanda Lissarrague

Main Gamilaraay and Yuwaalaraay informants

Arthur Dodd
Greg Fields
Ted Fields
Peter Lang
Fred Reece
Ginny (Jenny) Rose

Other Gamilaraay and Yuwaalaraay informants

June Barker
Mary Brown
Vic Chapman
(Bulliga) Helen and
    daughter Mrs Dixon
Charlie Dodd
Burt Draper
Hannah Duncan
Rose Fernando
Granny Green

Harry Hall
Harry Hippi/Murray
Daphne Jarrett
Ron McIntosh
Linda Miller
Florence Munro
Grace Munro
Ted Murphy
Ada Murray
George Murray

Leila Orcher
Arthur Pitt
Bill Reid
George Rose
Mary Russel
Ernie Sands
Jack Sands
Jo Trindall
Pearl Trindall
Willie Willis

The above people have contributed information since around 1950. Unfortunately, most of the earlier records do not name the Gamilaraay or Yuwaalaraay person who provided the information.

Database

The FileMaker Pro computer database was designed by Tim Scott.

Proofreading

Ian Sim
Sylvia Haworth
Moy Hitchen
Marlene Scrimgeour

Other assistance

Peter Austin
Brett Baker
John Brown
Therese Carr
Vic Chapman
R M Dixon
Libby Fitzgerald
Karen Flick
Helen Fraser
Cliff Goddard
Moy Hitchen
Emily Knight
Meg Leathart
David Nathan
Nick Reid
Ian Sim
Liz Smith
Priscilla Strasek
Peter Thompson
Corinne Williams

Support

School of Languages, Cultures and Linguistics at the University of New England
Murdi Paaki ATSIC region
NSW Department of Education and Training
Catholic Schools Office, Armidale
Christian Brothers, New South Wales
St Joseph's Primary School, Walgett

Funding

The main source of funds was the Aboriginal and Torres Strait Islander Commission. Other funds were provided by:

NSW Department of Education and Training
Catholic Schools Office, Armidale
Walgett RSL Club
Walgett Sports Club
Lightning Ridge Bowling and Sports Club

An Introduction to Gamilaraay, Yuwaalaraay and Yuwaalayaay

The purpose of this book

This dictionary and learner's guide aims to provide a comprehensive list of Gamilaraay/Yuwaalaraay/Yuwaalayaay (GY) words and to show how they have been used and can be used. Over recent years there has been growing interest in reviving GY languages. There are a number of language programs, generally school based, and also individuals relearning the languages. Since knowledge within the community is often limited, people have been getting information from historical sources and recently produced word lists.

Unfortunately, the older word lists (those prepared prior to around 1960) can be difficult to use due to the large number of differing and inconsistent spelling systems. Further, it is not very easy to actually get hold of them. The word lists produced in more recent years — such as those by Austin (1993), Williams (1980) and Giacon (1998) — use a consistent spelling system, but provide limited information about each word. They are still largely word lists — with one GY word corresponding to one English word — rather than being actual dictionaries.

The dictionary section of this book contains much more information on the range of meanings a word may have, as well as grammatical and cultural information and examples of usage. As well as drawing on the written historical material it makes considerable use of the Yuwaalaraay tapes which have recently been transcribed (see page 13), providing us with a number of new words and broader information about previously recorded words.

The source material for each entry is contained in a computer database to facilitate further work, and also allows the basis for each entry to be easily reviewed. A website associated with the dictionary is being created (www.yuwaalaraay.org) so that additions and changes can be easily obtained. A CD ROM is being planned which will enable people to hear many words as they were spoken by fluent speakers.

The Gamilaraay and Yuwaalaraay people

The Gamilaraay and Yuwaalaraay people have walked their lands for thousands of years. The Gamilaraay area consists of around 75 000 km^2 of largely flat, black-soil country, with a number of major rivers and many smaller watercourses. The Nandewar Ranges, including Mount Kaputar, stand out from the surrounding country. The land is higher in the east, with the rivers flowing west into what is now called the Darling River (see maps on page 2).

The traditional boundaries of the Gamilaraay language are not exactly known. While we do know that other Gamilaraay dialects (including Guyinbaraay, Waalaraay,

An introduction to Gamilaraay, Yuwaalaraay and Yuwaalayaay

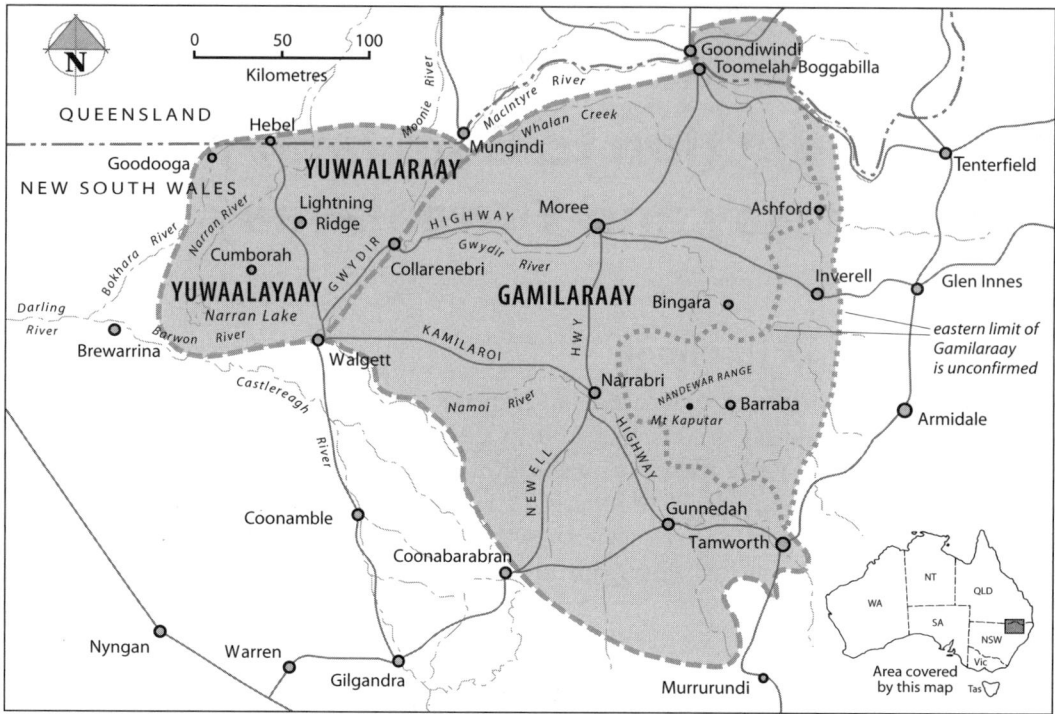

The approximate area covered by Gamilaraay, Yuwaalaraay and Yuwaalayaay languages. (Adapted from Austin et al, 1980, and Horton, 1994; there are some discrepancies about the GY area in the sources, most notably regarding the eastern limits of the language.)

Some neighbouring Aboriginal languages of Gamilaraay, Yuwaalaraay and Yuwaalayaay.

Wirriyaraay and Gawambaraay) were part of the Gamilaraay area, it is unclear whether the Yuwaalaraay language–speaking area was part of the Gamilaraay area or totally separate.

The most powerful figure in Gamilaraay belief is Baayami, the Creator. Other spirits and creators include Garriya, who is often depicted as a crocodile. As people walked the land they sang the songs and told the stories of the actions of these beings on that land. There were stories and songs about every bend in the river and every prominent feature. (Some stories are still told, such as that associated with Boobera Lagoon, near Boggabilla.)

Much of the Gamilaraay people's food came from plants (such as grass seeds, yams and gums) and animals (such as the macropods and possums). The rivers were a major part of Gamilaraay life, providing water and other food, such as fish, ducks, yabbies and an abundance of plant life.

Plants were also the source of many medicines and other useful materials. Bark was used to make canoes, toys and shelters, and kurrajong bark was used for rope. Spears and other tools were made from wood and gums. Many parts of an animal were used: possum skins were decorated and used as rugs, while other skins were used to carry water; kangaroo and emu sinews were used for rope; bones had various uses, including as personal jewellery.

The cultural life of the Gamilaraay included many events and celebrations. Regular *buurra* ceremonies ('bora' in English), at which young men went through the stages of initiation, brought people from many areas together to meet, sing and dance. The wise men, the *wiringin*, had major roles in the *buurra*, and in many other situations, such as curing illness, 'pointing the bone' at wrongdoers and in making rain.

Gamilaraay artwork included the decorations on artefacts and possum skins, carved trees around ceremonial areas, initiation scars and other similar scars. The people were painted and used bird feathers as decorations at corroborees. There were many songs, and special ceremonies for funerals.

The Gamilaraay people moved around a lot, their movements often governed by the supply of food and water. But the rivers, so important to Gamilaraay life and culture, were also the most attractive part of the country for whites. The arrival of sheep and cattle — and guns — meant that many of the traditional food sources vanished. By the mid-nineteenth century many of the Gamilaraay lived on sheep stations and much of the traditional way of life had gone. Disease, loss of lands, food and freedom, and massacres (such as the one at Myall Creek) had a huge impact.

Maintaining their rich cultural life became more and more difficult as the number of Gamilaraay dwindled and the opportunity to practise ceremonies was severely restricted by white society. By around 1900 it is likely that Gamilaraay numbers were at their lowest, reduced from around 6000 people to several hundred. The expectation of those in government and in much of white society was that Aboriginal people would simply disappear or be absorbed into mainstream culture.

That did not happen. Despite, or perhaps even because of, the weight of the laws and prejudice against them, the Gamilaraay people began to increase in both number and independence. Gamilaraay identity has remained strong, and today Gamilaraay culture continues to grow and develop. It includes elements of traditional culture, but also new elements.

The increase in the use of the Gamilaraay language is just one element of that growth and of renewed Gamilaraay identity. Uncle Ted Fields, a Yuwaalaraay speaker and one of the most important contributors to this book, is testament to the resilience of GY culture. He tells part of his story below.

Yaama, Gayaa ngaya nginaayngu dhurraandaay dhayndi ngay.
Hello, I am glad to write for you about my people.

I am a Yuwaalaraay man who has lived in the Yuwaalaraay area most of my life. My story is like that of many others.

I was born near Lightning Ridge and spent my first three or four years on Angledool Mission, near the Queensland border. Many Yuwaalaraay people lived on Government-controlled missions, where all things traditional were banned. When my mother died I was taken to live with my Granny Laura Hall at Yerranbah Shed. In May 1936 the mission was closed. Trucks turned up and most of the people were taken to another mission, at Brewarrina, about 200 km away. Some had already fled to other camps. People from lots of other nations — Muruwari, Ngiyampaa, Wangkangurra, Wangaaybuwan and others — were also taken to this mission.

Later I was living with other Yuwaalaraay people on the Angledool Mission site so I could go to school. Already many people did not know about corroborees and other parts of the culture.

At Bre Mission we were forbidden to speak our languages. *Dhaadhaa* Bill Boney pretended not to hear the English commands and was always singing and talking Yuwaalaraay. My grandmother, Laura Hall, couldn't understand much English at all, and when the manager's wife came to do the house inspections her husband acted as translator.

We used to move about over the country. Old Bill Kennedy was one who knew where there would be food at different times — sometimes along the river or on the black country or in the sandhills or on the red ridges — and people would move about to get it. There are also story lines along the country, such as the *Gali Gurunha* story that goes from Gingie, near Walgett (Ngiyampaa country) to Cumborah (Yuwaalaraay). The Narran River, and the Narran River story, finish at Narran Lake, where people from many different nations would come to corroboree and feast on the birds, shellfish and other food that was plentiful there at times. Many of the old people were fluent in four, five or more languages because they mixed with all the other groups.

Life has changed a lot. Many men, like my father, worked as stockmen and drovers. There were good times. There were also tensions. I went to gaol for my involvement in the Freedom Rides and other civil rights activities. Aboriginal people were moved around by the government, and moved around themselves, and so lots of the old structures were lost. We are still learning some things about living in this new world.

Baayami gulamalabadhaay nginaaynya.
May Baayami care for you.

The Gamilaraay and Yuwaalaraay family of languages

Gamilaraay and Yuwaalaraay mainly come from an area of what is now called New South Wales. The area is roughly bounded by Walgett, Goodooga, Mungindi, Goondiwindi, Ashford, Tamworth, Murrurundi and Coonabarabran. These two languages are very similar in their grammars and share many words, with around 70% of the words being the same. There were many dialects and languages which made up this group, but because so little information has been recorded it is difficult to be specific about the differences and about the areas belonging to each dialect and language. In the west of the area speakers fluent in Yuwaalaraay were alive much later than in the east — where Gamilaraay was spoken — and so much more is known about Yuwaalaraay.

There are also many words which are similar in Gamilaraay and Yuwaalaraay. For example, in some words an *r* in the Gamilaraay word is left out in the equivalent Yuwaalaraay word (so the word for 'hand', *mara*, becomes *maa*, and that for 'dingo', *marayn*, becomes *maayn*). More often it becomes a *y*, as in *maaru*, *maayu* 'well', *muru*, *muyu* 'nose' and *biruu*, *biyuu* 'hole'. You will see many more such pairs in the dictionary. They are even more obvious in the word lists.

As mentioned above, Yuwaalaraay and Yuwaalayaay are very similar, and so for most of this book we have simply said 'Yuwaalaraay' when referring to both languages. The name can be used in two ways: it can be used to mean Yuwaalaraay as distinct from Yuwaalayaay, but it can also be used to refer to the whole Yuwaalaraay and Yuwaalayaay area. The name 'Yuwaalayaay' refers to a language recorded in the Goodooga–Narran River area. Earlier records have 'Yuwaalayaay' as the name of the language used along the Narran River, though Fred Reece used the name Yuwaaliyaay, and his recordings are a major source of information. However, the two names almost certainly refer to the one dialect or language.

Gamilaraay/Yuwaalaraay/Yuwaalayaay are closely related to other languages which cover a band from north to south through New South Wales. These languages all have their word for 'no' as the first part of their name and the suffix for 'having' as the second. Thus, the people who have the word *gamil* for 'no' are known as the Gamil-araay. Similarly, those using *yuwaal* are the Yuwaal-araay, Yuwaal-ayaay and Yuwaal-iyaay (though these days the word for 'no' is shortened to *waal*), *wangaay* is used by the Wangaay-buwan, *wirray* is used by the Wira-djuri and *wayil* by the Wayilwan. Gamilaraay/Yuwaalaraay are less closely related to languages on the east coast and further to the west, but there are some similarities. In fact, there are quite a few features which are shared by most — if not all — of Australia's 250 or so Indigenous languages.

The sounds of Gamilaraay and Yuwaalaraay

The best way to learn the sounds of GY is to get hold of a CD or tape and to listen while looking at a written version of the words. Resources such as these are listed on pages 14 and 15 of this book.

GY uses many sounds which are also used in English and others which are not. These will be described below. Our mouths and ears are trained to the language(s) we know, so you may have to get used to making new sounds and noticing differences that you didn't notice before.

Because the spelling system for GY is fairly new it is a lot more consistent and so a lot easier to read than English. Generally, there is only one letter or pair of letters for each sound. In English the pronunciation of many words has changed over the centuries but the spelling has not, and so the spelling system is inconsistent and quite difficult to learn. (Think of the different sounds represented by 'ough' in 'plough', 'through' and 'bought'.) In GY there has not been time for the pronunciation of words to change, so the spelling system is very friendly, and does not take long to get used to.

The GY sounds that are similar to English include the three vowels *a*, *i* and *u*, and the consonants *l*, *m*, *n*, *r*, *w* and *y*. In GY (and in most Aboriginal languages) there is little or no distinction between the sounds made by English 'b' or 'p'. You can use either, but we have chosen to use the letter *b* in GY spelling. Similarly there is no distinction between 'd' and 't' (we have used *d*) or between 'g' and 'k' (we have used *g*).

Look at the pronunciation guide opposite to get a better idea of all the sounds of GY. The following provides some background information.

Vowels

Vowels are sounds that can be made continuously with the mouth fairly open. There are three vowels in GY, and they are written *a*, *i* and *u*. When the sound is made for a longer period it is called a long vowel, and these are written *aa*, *ii* and *uu*. There is some variation in the way vowels are pronounced. Vowels are particularly influenced by the sounds immediately before or after them. So *a* is often like the 'u' in the English word 'cut', but is different after *w*, when it often sounds like 'o' in 'got'.

In some cases the difference between long and short vowels is important because it makes a difference to the meaning of the word. In the words below, vowel length affects the meaning of the word:

milan	one
milaan	a type of yam
dhu-rri	will spear
dhuu-rri	will crawl
yili	lip
yiili	savage

The GY word *gabaa* is used by some old people for 'white person', and they use *gaba* for 'good'. Some young people do not know the 'good' meaning of *gaba* and use *gaba* to mean 'white person'. This is an example of a language changing so that you no longer need to make a sound distinction.

At times vowel length does not seem to make a difference to the meaning. In some of the recordings the word for rock is pronounced as both *maayama* and *mayama*.

Pronunciation rules

The following is a brief introduction to pronunciation rules. It is largely adapted from Peter Austin (1993). Note well that two letters (such as *dh*, *ng* and *dj*) can be used to represent one sound, as in the English words 'ele**ph**ant' or '**th**ink'.

GY spelling	Similar English sound
a	short vowel, as in 'cut', but sounds like 'o' in 'got' after *w*
aa	long vowel, as in 'father'
i	short vowel, as in 'pin'
ii	long vowel, as in 'peel'
u	short vowel, as in 'put'
uu	long vowel, as in 'cool'
ay	as in 'bay' or 'hay'
aay	as in 'my' or 'buy' (but sometimes said 'oy', as in 'boy')
b	between English 'b' and 'p', or can sound like either
d	between English 'd' and 't', or can sound like either
g	between English 'g' and 'k', or can sound like either
dh	like English 'd' but with the tip of your tongue between your teeth
m	the same as in English
n	the same as in English
ng	a single or 'one' sound, as in si**ng**er (not 'two' sounds, as in finger)
nh	like English 'n' but with the tip of your tongue between your teeth
ny	as in o**ni**on
dj	sometimes sounds like **J**ohn, or as in bu**dg**e, and even like 'ch' in 'catcher'
l	the same as in English
r	like 'r' in English 'run', but with the tongue tip turned back
rr	a 'rolled' 'r', as some Scottish or German people say it. Often, at the end of a word, it can sound like the 'd' in 'bed'
w	the same as in English, though *wu* at the start of a word is mostly pronounced like *u*
y	the same as in English, though *yi* at the start of a word is mostly pronounced like *i*

New sounds and spellings

There are some sounds that people who only speak English have difficulty learning to distinguish and find hard to make. These include *dh*, *nh*, *rr* and also *ng* at the start of a word.

 Remember that *ng* is always one 'soft' sound, as in 'singer'. If you see *ngg* then this is two sounds together (*ng* and *g*) and so has a 'hard' pronunciation, more like English 'finger'. A full stop between the letters *n* and *g* (*n.g*) means that there are two distinct sounds (*n* and *g*), not one, as in *ng*.

It is a good idea to practise these by yourself somewhere — in the shower or when driving or walking. You can practise *ngi* by saying 'singingingingingi . . ', and then gradually dropping the 'si' at the start. For *nga* say 'singanganga . . .' and once again try to drop the 'si'. Another way to learn to say *ng* at the beginning of a word is to put the tip of your tongue behind your bottom teeth. For *rr* try to make machine gun or engine noises.

The GY sounds *nh* and *dh* are made with the tongue in the same position between your teeth. When a *nh* is followed by a *dh* the *nhdh* is simplified and written *ndh*. This is **not** an *n* followed by a *dh*. Similarly *nydj* is written *ndj*.

The sounds *b*, *dh*, *d*, *dj* and *g* are called 'stop' sounds. They are made by closing off the air flow, then letting it go quickly. The sounds *m*, *nh*, *ny*, *n* and *ng* are called 'nasal' sounds. They are made by closing off the air flow through the mouth, and releasing the air through the nose. Try saying them while holding your nose. The sounds *d*, *n*, *l* and *rr* are all made with the tongue in the same place: the tip of the tongue is on the ridge behind the upper teeth.

To recap, here are a few examples of GY pronunciation:

gagil	bad	sounds like	***guggil***
walaay	camp	sounds like	***wol-eye***
wamba	mad	sounds like	***womba***
yinarr	woman	sounds like	***inarr*** or ***inud***
wuulaa	bearded dragon	sounds like	***oohlaa***

GY words can begin with *b*, *m*, *dh*, *nh*, *g*, *ng*, *w* and *y* (though a small number of words may begin with *dj* and *ny*). GY words can end with *a*, *aa*, *i*, *ii*, *u*, *uu*, *n*, *l*, *rr* and *y*. One exception recorded is *maang*, meaning 'message stick'. This could well be a borrowed word, possibly from Wiradjuri, since that language uses a final *ng*.

Stress patterns

GY has patterns for stressing or emphasising parts of a word. The stressed part of the word is emphasised or said a bit louder, and maybe for a bit longer. In English the first syllable of 'happy' is stressed, but in 'beside' it is the second syllable that is stressed.

 A syllable is a part of a word which contains a vowel, such as ri-ver, ca-stle, ju-ven-ile. In GY each syllable begins with a consonant and contains one vowel, such as: *ga-ba, wam-ba*.

For the great majority of words in GY, the rules are as follows. Firstly you need to work out where the main emphasis goes. When there are single vowels only in the word, the emphasis falls on the first syllable. Thus, **gaba**, **guni** and **wambanhiya**. However, when there are double vowels in the word they are emphasised. Thus, **bubaa**, **dhaadhaa**, *birralii* and **yaama**.

The second step is to work out the lesser emphasis. This occurs on the syllables two to the left or right of the main emphasis. The underlining shows the lesser emphasis:

wamban<u>hi</u>ya   <u>bi</u>*rralii*   <u>bu</u>*rrulaa*

Some exceptions to the simple rules

The examples given below are all exceptions to the main rules. (You might be better off ignoring this short section on exceptions if you do not already understand the simple bits well.) It is likely that rules can be formulated to explain these finer points of pronunciation, but so far they have not been formulated.

When words are made up of different parts joined together (compound words) the stress pattern often follows that of the original main word, not the resulting compound word. As mentioned earlier, the name Gamilaraay is made up of two parts, the word *gamil* meaning 'no' and the ending *-araay* meaning 'having'. In old material the stress is on the first and last syllable — **Ga**mila**raay** — but many people now put the stress on the second syllable and say the word Ga**mil**araay. In some words *ay* is emphasised in the same way as a long vowel, such as in *ngaayaybaay*. It may be that *ay* should be regarded as being equivalent to a long vowel.

Words with three short syllables are emphasised on the first and third syllable. For instance, *yulu-gi* is 'will dance', and the stress is **yu**lu-<u>gi</u> (primary stress in bold, secondary stress underlined). However, in the word *yulu-gi-gu*, 'in order to dance', the stress is sometimes different, with the primary stress on the second syllable. There is a related rule in the Wangaaybuwan language (Donaldson 1980, p 40). There may also be other rules and sub-rules which tell which parts of a word to stress, but this area needs further work.

Elision and modification

Elision and modification are processes where adjacent words, or parts of words, influence one another.

Elision is the process where parts of words near one another are left out. The following is not intended to be a full treatment of elision in GY, more to bring it to the learner's attention. English examples of elision include the shortening of 'I am' to 'I'm' and 'do not' to 'don't'. Even greater contractions can take place, such as 'going to' becoming 'gonna' and 'what did you' becoming 'wadja'.

In GY *ngaya* 'I' is often said as *ngay* before words starting with *y* or *ng*, so that *ngaya yanaa-y* 'I will go' can be said *ngay' yanaa-y* and *ngaya ngarra-y* 'I saw', can be said *ngay' ngarra-y*. Similarly, *nhama* 'that' often drops the final *a* before words starting with *b*, so that *nhama birray* 'that boy' can be said *nham' birray*.

Sometimes the sounds are influenced by the words that go before or after them, and this is called modification. There are some patterns in the modification of sounds, but it is not totally consistent. Also the variation tends to be shown in the spelling of suffixes and prefixes, but not in the spelling of words. Consider the English words **im**possible, **il**legal, **in**accurate and **ir**regular: the prefix (meaning 'not') changes. But when you say 'in Darwin', 'in this', 'in Italy' the 'n' can be slightly different in each case (feel where your tongue is) but the spelling stays the same.

Some GY words also change, depending on the words before or after them. The word *nhama* 'that' and other words that begin with *nh* are sometimes pronounced with an initial *ny* (like *nyama*) after words ending in *i* and *y*. Thus *maadhaay nhama* 'that dog' can be pronounced *maadhaay nyama*. However, this is not shown in the spelling of *nhama*.

Modification is often seen in GY suffixes. The variation in suffix form is well illustrated in the tables in the section on suffixes in the learner's guide (page 262). Some changes happen regularly. Word final *n* is often followed by a suffix beginning in *d* and word final *i* or *y* is often followed by a suffix form beginning with *dj*, and word final *l* is often followed by a suffix form beginning with a vowel. However these variations in the suffix forms are not universal, and one speaker will sometimes use different forms after the one word.

Relationship words

There are many relationship words in the dictionary, generally translated by English words such as mother, father, cousin and so on. However, the meaning of these GY words in traditional society was very different from the meaning of the English words because of the way GY society worked — the relationships between people were in many aspects very different from the ones we are used to today. What follows is a very brief introduction to the GY relationships system, pointing out some of those differences. It also shows how the meaning of some GY words has changed.

The recorded knowledge of many GY relationship terms is incomplete. The two main sources used here are *Kamilaroi and Kurnai* (Fison & Howitt 1880) and *Yuwaalayaay: The Language of the Narran River* (Sim 1999). Fison points out that, even when he was writing, many tribes or language groups had decreased greatly in number, and that knowledge was being lost. Further, some knowledge was kept secret or not imparted to non-Aboriginal researchers, and because the system was so unfamiliar to the European system they had great difficulty in understanding it. As Fison says (p 59), 'After years of inquiry into this . . . I am hopelessly puzzled.'

The main difference between European relationship terms and GY ones is that European terms are based on individual relationships while GY terms are based upon the groups to which an individual belongs.

Many details about social organisation are shown in the tables which follow. Each GY person belonged to one of the two moieties, and to a moiety subdivision. Each person also had a number of totems. One person's totems might include the emu, a particular star, a plant or plants, a wind and other things as well. Each person also belonged to one social class and also to one 'blood' group. When meeting a person the first thing to be found out was the person's meat (totem) and social class.

Type of classification	Group name		Group name	
Moiety	*Yanguu*		*Wudhurruu*	
Moiety subdivisions	*Magula* *Bumbira*		*Magula* *Bumbira*	
Totems	emu kangaroo frog galah etc.		wallaby duck goanna kookaburra etc.	
Social classes (Marriage classes)	Male *Gambuu* *Yibaay*	Female *Buudhaa* *Yibadhaa*	Male *Marrii* *Gabii*	Female *Maadhaa* *Gabudhaa*
Blood	*guwaygaliyarr* light blood		*guwaymadhan* heavy blood	

So a *Yanguu* woman is either *Magula* or *Bumbira*, belongs to some of the totems listed in that column, and is either *Buudhaa* or *Yibadhaa*. It is not clear what her 'blood classification' will be, whether *guwaygaliyarr* or *guwaymadhan*. A final division is into *giinbaligal*, the 'scaly tribe' (reptiles and fish), *dhurrun.gal* the 'furry tribe' and *dhigayaa* 'birds'. It is not clear how this relates to other classifications. A person's moiety, moiety subdivision and totems were the same as their mother's.

Marriage was determined by totem (meat) and social class. The totem rules about marriage were very strict. You could not marry someone of your own totem — death was the penalty. However, sometimes marriages which transgressed the social class rules would be accepted. As well as marriage it would be expected that the classifications affected other areas of life. (In some parts of the Northern Territory a person has obligations to look after people who are their classificatory uncles and aunts.) The correct marriage relationships, according to social class, are given below.

			Children	
			Male	Female
Gabii	must marry	*Yibadhaa*	*Gambuu*	*Buudhaa*
Marrii	must marry	*Buudhaa*	*Yibaay*	*Yibadhaa*
Gambuu	must marry	*Maadhaa*	*Gabii*	*Gabudhaa*
Yibaay	must marry	*Gabudhaa*	*Marrii*	*Maadhaa*

Relationship terms

Firstly, some examples of how relationship terms were used. *Bubaa* is 'father'. A *Buudhaa* (or *Gambuu*) has a *Gabii* father and she refers to all *Gabii* men as 'father'. She must marry a *Marrii* man, and she can use the term *guliirr*, 'partner', when speaking to any *Marrii* man. Qualifying terms such as 'little father' were used to distinguish blood father from classificatory father when needed.

There was a mother-in-law 'avoidance rule', so mother-in-law and son-in-law did not speak. So, for instance, any *Gabii* man has a *Buudhaa* mother-in-law and he does not speak to any *Buudhaa* women.

Some terms were also reciprocal, i.e. two people used the same word to speak to each other. For example, *garrimaay* is used by a son-in-law to speak of his mother-in-law and by the mother-in-law to speak of her son-in-law. The one word is used for the English 'grandfather' and 'grandson' — *dhaadhaa* — but only when it is the daughter's son that is referred to. In fact *dhaadhaa* can be used to refer to other senior people of the same class as one's *dhaadhaa*. Currently, however, *dhaadhaa* is used to refer to both grandfathers.

Since mother's father and father's father are of two different classes (for a *Maadhaa* woman they are *Gambuu* and *Marrii*) two different words were used for grandfather: *dhaadhaa* and (possibly) *dhilaagaa*.

While one's totem (emu, kangaroo, goanna etc.) is inherited from the mother, one's *Ngurrambaa* (traditional land) is inherited from the father.

The classification system above was used over large areas of Australia, and Fred Reece says that a Yuwaalaraay person meeting someone from the far north of Queensland would firstly ask them their 'meat', and would then know how to relate. This was especially important if the two were a man a woman.

▎The sources of information for the dictionary and learner's guide

Knowledge about these languages has come from Gamilaraay and Yuwaalaraay people, but only a small part is from present-day people. Most of what is now known about the language is from recordings and written records made over many years. A fluent speaker is someone who can talk about a wide range of topics using their language. This means that they know a large range of words (typically about 10 000) and can create many types of sentences and sequences of sentences. It seems probable that the last fully fluent Yuwaalaraay speakers died around the 1950s, and for Gamilaraay some time earlier. Since then the passed-down knowledge has steadily decreased.

The causes of this sad decline in language knowledge and use include the deaths of many Gamilaraay and Yuwaalaraay people in the early stages of colonisation, the anti-Aboriginal practices of various governments and other parties, the antagonism towards Aboriginal languages by the wider non-Indigenous community, the movement of people to different language speaking areas and the dominance of English. The decline in language knowledge began soon after Europeans arrived in the area. Arthur Dodd — a significant contributor to the grammar and dictionary — was born in 1890, and says his sisters did not learn the language. Fred Reece, another contributor, was also born in 1890, and rarely used the language in his adult life.

The ideal way to learn a language is to listen to fluent speakers, to imitate them, and to learn from them with questions such as, 'Is this right', or, 'How would you say this?' For Gamilaraay/Yuwaalaraay this is not possible. The main ways to find out about GY is to listen to recordings and to look at historical sources, with some knowledge coming from the current GY speakers.

Most of the cultural knowledge in the dictionary comes from local sources; however, some information, particularly that concerning plant life is from general references. References can be checked in the database.

Recordings and information from language speakers

Recordings were made of Fred Reece and Arthur Dodd in the 1970s. These are very valuable sources, since they record much that is not found in other sources. They are by far the most valuable source of information about pronunciation. Many other rules about the languages have also been discovered from analysis of these recordings. Because they are records of fairly fluent speakers, it is also possible to work out much new grammatical information from them. There are about fifty hours of these tapes. Fred Reece spoke Yuwaaliyaay, but had not used it for many years. He knows a lot but at times says, 'There is a word for that' or 'There is a way of saying that, but I can't remember it.' Arthur Dodd spoke Yuwaalaraay and was reasonably fluent. However, it seems that his everyday languages were Wayilwan–Ngiyambaa and English. He also spoke Gamilaraay. These men were mainly recorded by Janet Mathews and Corinne Williams.

There are also other recordings, such as those made by Stephen Wurm in the 1950s, but these are shorter and contain much less grammatical material.

Some of the speakers who contributed to the book (either from recordings, written materials or directly) are:

Mary Jane Cain, who lived from 1844 to 1929. She was a very strong leader among the Aboriginal people at Coonabarabran and was referred to as the Queen of her people. She had nine children and was very politically active, her work resulting in the establishment of Burra Bee Dee Mission. She recorded a number of Gamilaraay place names in the district.

Arthur Dodd, who made many tapes in the 1970s at Gingie near Walgett. He made tapes of Ngiyambaa and Yuwaalaraay. He was born on Dungalear Station in 1890. His mother was Yuwaalaraay and his father white.

Greg Fields, born at Angledool, NSW, was a long time resident of the Goodooga district. He was a Yuwaalaraay man who worked on many properties around the area. He died in 1957. His son, Ted, has been a major force in Yuwaalaraay language revival.

Ted Fields is a Yuwaalaraay man born in 1930 who has lived in Walgett for many years and has been a driving force behind language revival.

Fred Reece was born in 1890 and made many tapes in the 1970s at Lightning Ridge. His grandparents were Muruwari and he probably learnt Yuwaaliyaay (probably the same as Yuwaalayaay) at Bangate Station.

Ian Sim worked in the Goodooga area as a surveyor in the 1950s. He made written records of a considerable amount of material, mainly from Mrs Ginny Rose, Mr Willie Willis, Mrs Bindi West and Mr Greg Fields.

Ginny Rose, a Yuwaalayaay woman, was born at Nee Nee, Queensland, in 1880. Mrs Rose's Indigenous name was Dhaaygaliyaawaay, meaning 'rising up', to commemorate her birth during the floods of that period. She and Willie Willis lived at Goodooga in the 1950s.

Willie Willis, born at Willamurra Station, Queensland, in 1890, was a resident of the Goodooga district for 50 years. He was a Guwamu man and very knowledgeable in matters of law.

Historical sources and written materials

Since about 1840 people have been writing wordlists, phrases, sentences and language rules for GY, and there are many of these documents available in libraries and archives. The main works include those of the Rev. William Ridley (published 1870s), the surveyor R H Matthews (around 1900), K Langloh-Parker (1905), G Laves (1930s), Stephen Wurm (from the 1950s) and Ian Sim (recorded in the 1950s, published in 1999). Langloh-Parker's books also include many stories and descriptions of the customs of the Yuwaalayaay. They were written on the basis of what she learnt while living at Bangate, a property between Lightning Ridge and Goodooga.

The most important recent documents have been Peter Austin's *Dictionary of Gamilaraay* (1993), which contains about 500 words; and Corinne Williams' *A Grammar of Yuwaalaraay* (1980). Williams' book has about 1500 words and also provides much more grammar of Yuwaalaraay or Gamilaraay than anything before it.

John Giacon's own work has been mainly in Yuwaalaraay, and within that is based on the recordings of Fred Reece and Arthur Dodd. Therefore, this work will reflect that bias, and his lesser familiarity with other sources.

A final source has been new words created by language programs. There are a small number of these words and they have been approved by the elders associated with the programs.

Most of cultural knowledge in the dictionary comes from local sources. Some information, particularly that concerning plant life, is from general references. The main publicly available resources are listed below. Some are available online at Aboriginal Studies Electronic Data Archive (ASEDA), held at the Australian Institute of Aboriginal and Torres Strait Islander Studies. The ASEDA web site address is www.coombs.edu.au/SpecialProj/ASEDA.html. Some resources may also be available as data files from John Giacon, email address jgiacon@ozemail.com.au.

▎References and resources

Austin, P 1993, *A Reference Dictionary of Gamilaraay*, La Trobe University, Melbourne.

Austin, P & David N (no date), *Kamilaroi/Gamilaraay Web Dictionary*. On the internet at: http://coombs.anu.edu.au/WWWVLPages/AborigPages/LANG/GAMDICT/GAMDICT.HTM.

Austin, P, Williams, C & Wurm, S 1980, 'The Linguistic Situation in North-Central New South Wales', in B Rigsby & P Sutton (eds), *Papers in Australian Linguistics No 13*, Pacific Linguistics, Canberra, pp 167–80.

Dixon, R M W (unpub.), Tape and word list, Australian Institute of Aboriginal and Torres Strait Islander Studies, Canberra.

Donaldson, T 1980, *Ngiyambaa: The language of the Wangaaybuwan*, Cambridge University Press, Cambridge.

Fields, T 1995–2002, *Yuwaalarray Wordlist*, transcribed by John Giacon. Available at ASEDA and from Giacon.

Fison, L & Howitt, A W 1967, *Kamilaroi and Kurnai*, Anthropological Publications, Oosterhout N.B. (First published in 1880.)

Giacon, J (ed)1998, *Yuwaalaraay/Gamilaraay Wordlist*, Walgett High School Yuwaalaraay/Gamilaraay Language Program, Walgett.

Horton, D (ed) 1994, *The Encyclopaedia of Aboriginal Australia,* vols 1 & 2, Aboriginal Studies Press, Canberra.
Langloh-Parker, K 1953, *Australian Legendary Tales*, Angus & Robertson, Sydney.
—— 1905, *The Euahlayi Tribe*, Archibald Constable & Co, London.
Laves, G (no date), *Kamilaroi/Yualarai language cards and notebook*, Australian Institute of Aboriginal and Torres Strait Islander Studies, Canberra.
Mathews, J (unpub.), Tape recordings of elicitations with Arthur Dodd and Fred Reece, made in 1970 and held by the Australian Institute of Aboriginal and Torres Strait Islander Studies, Canberra. Transcript available from ASEDA and John Giacon.
Mathews, R H 1902, 'Languages of Some Native Tribes of Queensland, New South Wales and Victoria: Yualeai' in *Journal of the Royal Society of New South Wales*, vol. 36, pp. 135–90.
—— 1903, 'Languages of the Kamilaroi and other Aboriginal Tribes of New South Wales', in *Journal of the Royal Anthropological Institute*, vol. 33, pp. 259–83.
Milson, Mrs. c1840, *Kamilaroi Vocabulary*, held in the Mitchell Library, Sydney. MS MlLA 1668, CY Reel 2355.
O'Rourke, M J (1997), *The Kamilaroi Lands*, published by the author, Canberra.
Reay, M 1949, 'Native Thought in Rural New South Wales' in *Oceania*, no. XX, vol. 2, December, pp 89–228.
Ridley, Rev. W 1875, *Kamilaroi and other Australian Languages*, Government Printer, Sydney.
Sim, I (ed J Giacon) 1999, *Yuwaalayaay: The Language of the Narran River*, Walgett High School, Walgett.
Thompson, P (unpub.), Gamilaraay Words, manuscript produced in 1998.
Walgett Yuwaalaraay and Gamilaraay Language Program 2002, *We Are Speaking Gamilaraay & Yuwaalaraay*, Coolabah Publishing, Tamworth.
Williams, C (unpub.), Tape recordings of elicitations with Arthur Dodd and Fred Reece, made in 1970 and held by the Australian Institute of Aboriginal and Torres Strait Islander Studies, Canberra. Transcript available from ASEDA and John Giacon.
—— 1980, *A Grammar of Yuwaalaraay*, Pacific Linguistics, Series B, No. 74, Australian National University, Canberra.
Wurm, S (no date), Field Notes and Tapes, held at the Australian Institute of Aboriginal and Torres Strait Islander Studies, Canberra.

A longer list of references is available from the language program at Walgett.

The Dictionary

Using the Dictionary

▎A language revival dictionary

There are many types of dictionaries, but this is a language revival dictionary and, as such, it has a number of special characteristics. Current speakers of Gamilaraay and Yuwaalaraay (GY) know a relatively small number of words, and so information has largely come from historical sources. The number of words in those sources, and information about their use, is clearly limited. Therefore, many entries will be incomplete or will include some educated guesswork.

A second point about this kind of dictionary is that people using it will often have no other source of information about the language, and will be speakers of English as their first language. It is easy then for people to expect GY to be like English, but there are many differences that people need to be aware of. The dictionary contains numerous example sentences, and is followed by a learner's guide, both of which show many of the distinctive features of GY.

Some decisions have been made during the compilation of this dictionary which we hope will assist in language revival. In general, a standard 'form' has been adopted for words. The form of a word is its spelling or sound. For example, the spelling of the word for 'pelican', *gulayaali*, has also been recorded as *guliyali* and *guliyaali* in recent lists. The form with the best evidence (often the tape recording of a speaker) has been adopted. At times there are a number of words in the old sources each giving the same English translation. For instance, both *gaay* and *gaya* are given for 'language' but *gaya* is found in only one source. Having two words is likely to cause confusion and will not help in the process of language revival, so only *gaay* is included in the dictionary. In other cases two or more words have been included, since they are all found a number of times.

The amount of knowledge we have about individual words varies considerably. The form of the word *gaba* is definite. Its main meaning is 'good', and that is also definite. There are other uses of the word — for 'pretty', 'sweet' and so on — which are rarely found and so are not as certain. It is likely that only a limited range of meanings was recorded for any given word. A word could, therefore, have many more uses or meanings than previously thought. An example of a word with a large range of meanings is *binggi,* which was recorded as meaning 'needle', 'nail', 'pin', 'small sharp thing'. There are also words which have been found only once, such as *baanmal*, 'betrothal of babies', and so are less certain. Then there are also words like *gandawali*, 'cover', whose form is uncertain. It was written as *gûndawulla* in Mathews (1903). Based on other words Mathews has recorded, the spelling *gandawala* (the command form of the verb) is a good guess of the sounds he is representing, but one cannot be certain.

So the reliability of the form and meaning of the words varies. However, for language revival to go ahead people need definite words with clear meanings that they can use, and that is what this dictionary aims to give. Where there is a high degree of uncertainty this is mentioned in the entry. Also, words found in only one source are labelled 'one source'.

Recommended words

Some entries include the phrase 'This is the recommended word'. This generally happens when there are a number of words with one English translation, but one word is more common than the others and its meaning clearer. Even when the phrase 'This is the recommended word' is not used you will need to be careful in which words you choose to use when there are a number of possibilities. If there is a word that is more common, it is the one to use. Other words with the same meaning are there for information rather than for use. The more common word is recommended since having one word will make revival easier. For instance *buyuma*, *mirri* and *maadhaay* are all Yuwaalaraay words for 'dog' but *maadhaay* is the recommended word because it is most common in the sources.

New words

Any living language creates new words. GY people created the words *dhimba*, 'sheep', and *wilbaarr*, 'wheeled vehicle', relatively soon after the arrival of non-Aboriginal people. However, as the use of GY declined, no new words were created for many years. In recent years some new words have been created, for instance, the meaning of *wiyayl*, 'echidna quill', has been extended to 'pen' or 'pencil', and new words for numbers have been created. New words are needed so that GY can be used to talk about everyday things (telephones, plastic, jet planes etc.) but the process needs to be approached with caution so as to be as true as possible to the traditional patterns of GY. The tendency for people who only speak English is to modify GY so that it fits an English pattern, and this can also happen with the creation of new words. A small number of recently created new words are included in the dictionary. Gamilaraay and Yuwaalaraay people have decided that it is better for recently developed words to be treated separately, so they are in a separate list on page 160, following the main body of the dictionary.

A number of words in the dictionary are marked by an asterisk (*). These words are hypothesised forms, that is, what is presented is believed to be the correct form of the word, although there is no direct evidence.

Restricted words

A very small number of restricted words have been omitted entirely from the dictionary. Other restricted words are listed in the body of the dictionary, but do not include a definition. Gamilaraay and Yuwaalaraay people have decided that it is not appropriate for information about this word to be openly circulated. If you think you have a good reason to know more about this word, you can contact the Yuwaalaraay Language Program (contact details page vii) or consult the database used to produce the dictionary.

Why three languages?

There are several reasons for having three languages in one dictionary. The languages are very closely related — in the linguistic sense they are all dialects of a single language. Yuwaalaraay (shortened to YR), Yuwaalayaay (YY) and Gamilaraay (GR) share around 70% of their words, and the grammars are very similar. YR and YY are the most thoroughly documented language groups, having Williams' detailed grammar and word list of 1500 items (1980). GR has fewer words and less grammatical evidence.

As part of language revival it has been suggested that if one language lacks a word, then it can be borrowed from another language to fill the gap. This has been approved at meetings of the Gamilaraay/Yuwaalaraay Languages Network. GR, for instance, has no word for 'look for', so speakers have borrowed the YR and YY words. Conversely, there is no recorded YR or YY word for 'door', but a GR word, *girrinil*, exists. This could easily and usefully be used by YR and YY people.

A comparison of the three languages and a review of the sources has led to some words being rediscovered. These words have not been included in recent word lists. For example, *dhuurranmay* means 'leader' or 'chief' in YR and YY according to the word lists of Ian Sim and Ted Fields, but it wasn't until Reverend Ridley's 1875 word list was rechecked against these that there was good evidence for the existence of *dhuurranmay* in GR.

The database contains around 1720 YR words, of which 540 are 'rediscovered' in that they did not appear in recent word lists. There are 1750 YY words, of which 330 are 'rediscovered'. Evidence for the new words comes mainly from the tapes, Ted Fields and Ian Sim. Of the 1000 GR words, over 300 are 'rediscovered' words, in that they did not appear in recent word lists or dictionaries. Evidence for these new words comes mainly from the historical records of the Reverend Ridley, R H Mathews, Gerhardt Laves, Mrs Milson and Stephen Wurm, and from the more recent research of Peter Thompson.

The future

A dictionary has a certain life span, and with luck there will be a revised edition of this dictionary relatively soon. As research continues on the historical sources of GY, mistakes will undoubtedly be found, decisions revised and additional material uncovered, and so changes will be needed. Further, if language revival continues, new words will continue to be made so that new things can be talked about. Inevitably, since work for this dictionary has been based in the Walgett area, more words from there have been recorded. Now more words could well be recorded from other areas.

Corrections and additions to the word base of this dictionary of GY will be available on a forthcoming Yuwaalaraay website (www.yuwaalaraay.org). Information on Gamilaraay can also be found at:
http://coombs.anu.edu.au/WWWVLPages/AborigPages/LANG/GAMDICT/GAMDICT.HTM

How to use the dictionary

Before illustrating the layout of the dictionary it is important to point out again that GY is often very different from English and it is easy to use GY words 'incorrectly'. This is not to discourage people from using GY — that is the only way to learn it — but to warn you that *some* things you say may need to be changed later as your knowledge of the language increases.

Here are just a few examples of how GY (and other Aboriginal languages) are different from English. Firstly, they have 'dual' pronouns, meaning that there are special words for 'we: two people', 'you: two people' and, usually, for 'they: two people'. (For a fuller explanation of dual pronouns, see page 284 in the learner's guide.) Secondly, one word can often have a number of meanings. While this happens in English too (e.g. 'hit' has many uses, as in 'hit the dog', 'hit song', 'hit town' and 'hit 50 km'), the meanings are often grouped differently in GY. The one GY word *winanga-y* can mean 'think', 'know', 'understand' and 'remember' (and is related to *bina*, 'ear'). Another word, *dhurri*, is used for 'spear', 'stab', 'poke' and 'write'. Many Aboriginal languages have words that parallel these two. In English we say 'Do you want *a* drink?', using a noun. In GY the way to ask this is to say 'Do you want *to* drink?', using a verb. The message is to expect GY to be different.

The sections of the dictionary

To make the dictionary easier to use, the information about words is included in three sections: GR/YR/YY to English, English to GR/YR/YY word list, and English to GR/YR/YY word list by topic. The first section is the main part of the dictionary and contains detailed information about the words. The second section, English to GR/YR/YY (also referred to as the word list) contains English words in alphabetical order. This is the section you must use if you have an English word and you want the GR/YR/YY equivalent. It also has the languages that the word applies to and its part of speech. The third section, the 'word list by topic' or 'thesaurus' section, groups all the words according to their meaning. This may be useful for teachers and students who want to focus on a particular area for example 'emus' or 'verbs of motion'. Remember to exercise caution when using these last two sections: they contain very limited information about words, so before using words refer to the main body of the dictionary or you could find yourself misusing a word.

This book also includes an introductory grammar, or learner's guide, which points out many of the features seen in the example sentences. There is a pronunciation guide on page 7 which explains the spelling system used.

Layout of the main entries

Headwords are largely in English alphabetical order, but this is not completely strict as related words are usually grouped under a headword. The digraphs *dh*, *nh*, *ng*, *ny* and *rr* are treated as sequences of two letters. Each entry can have the following parts:

1. **Headwords** in bold.
2. **Language codes** indicate in which language the word occurs (YR = Yuwaalaraay, YY = Yuwaalayaay, and GR = Gamilaraay).
3. **Part of speech** indicates the grammatical category of the word. Some are definite — such as a

Using the dictionary

verb — while others are harder to define as the word is used in several ways, hence they may be described as 'adjective, adverb'. Parts of speech often do not match up exactly across languages (a noun phrase in GY may equate to an English adjective). As most learners will be English speakers we have used the English part of speech in many cases.

4. **Definitions** are numbered 1, 2, 3 etc. if there is more than one.
5. **Scientific names** are given for plants and animals wherever possible.
6. **Language codes.** If meanings are restricted to particular languages, this is also shown.
7. **Also** '*x*' indicates commonly occurring variations of the headword, often spellings that have been used in previously published word lists.
8. **General comments** contain any relevant non-linguistic information of a cultural, historical or biological nature.

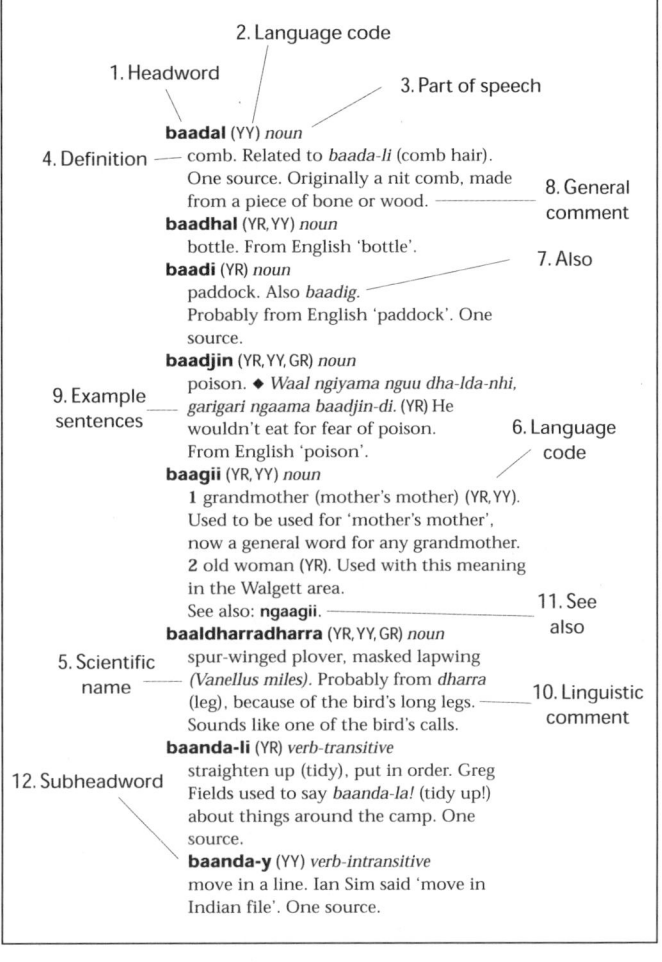

9. **Example sentences** are given in GY followed by a language code and the English translation. Words in brackets in the English translation may not occur in the GY sentence but are provided for a smooth translation. Some sentences have been simplified.
10. **Linguistic comments** include information on the following areas: grammar; the parts of words (morphemes); whether the word is rare or common; variations in the way it occurs; whether it has been recently developed; and the geographical area in which it is used. Often there are synonyms, and wherever possible one word is recommended. The phrase 'one source' indicates that there was only one source of evidence for the word, so it is less well supported. The phrase 'form uncertain' indicates that the word has been recorded in several different but related ways (that is, with different pronunciations or spellings). The phrase 'based on' is used when one word is thought to be derived from one or more other words. Again the relationship is not always certain; one could relate the word *gayiyabarra* to the suffix *-barra*, but a more likely relationship is with *barra*, 'thread'. The phrase 'used in' (some GY areas) means that the word is currently used by GY people.
11. **See also** points out related words including synonyms.
12. **Subheadwords** are related or derived from the headword. They are also in bold like the headword, but are not outdented. They may include all the above information.

Source people

Often the entries give the source of a quote or word, e.g. 'Fred Reece said . . .' Brief details of these people are given in the Introduction on page 13.

Other information about the entries

Example sentences

Most of the example sentences have been taken from tape transcripts, but a small number are from less reliable written sources. At times the sentences have been simplified or irregular uses changed so that they are more easily understood.

Species and placenames

The status of this information varies considerably. Generally, the plant and animal names are reliable, and where not this is shown in the entry. However, it is not always possible to know how a name was used. It could, for instance, refer to a number of closely related species (as does the English word 'cockatoo') or it might refer to only one stage of a species. This sort of detail was not always recorded. Many placenames are clearly GY words. However, there are often many derivations proposed for any one placename, so these should be treated with some caution. Some placenames are included to show that the origin is a GY word, even if no 'meaning' has been recorded for that word.

FileMaker Pro database

The written version of the dictionary was developed using a FileMaker Pro (FMP) database designed by Tim Scott. The database contains fields such as 'headword', 'part of speech', 'material copied from earlier sources' and 'comments'.

The database includes information about any number of historical sources for a particular word. One can check where the information for any dictionary entry comes from. Also, evidence for the many decisions about word spelling or whether a word is to be included can be checked.

The FMP database generated the three sections of the dictionary: GY *to* English, English *to* GY word list, and English *to* GY word list by topic. Those with the necessary expertise will also be able to use FMP to conduct particular searches and to generate other sets of data.

For further information about the database contact the language program at Walgett.

A CD of the dictionary is on the drawing board. It is hoped that it will have the information that is in the book, but also sound files of many of the words, and other useful material.

Gamilaraay/Yuwaalaraay/Yuwaalayaay *to* English Dictionary

Aa

-aaba-li (YR, YY) *suffix*
all. ◆ *Giirr nhama maadhaay-u dhinggaa dha-l-aaba-y.* (YR) The dog ate all the meat. ◆ *Giirruu ngaama ganunga birralii-gal banaga-w-aaba-lda-nhi.* (YR) All the boys (they) ran away.
The completive suffix is attached to verbs to indicate that the action is being done 'to all' or 'by all'. See Learner's Guide.

-araay (GR) *suffix*
with, having. Occurs in the language name Kamilaroi, *Gamil-araay* (no-having); so 'the language that has *gamil* (for no)'. For more information, see **-Baraay**.

-awaa (YR, YY) *suffix*
habitual. This suffix is found on a small number of verbs and gives the name of something that 'habitually or always does the action', e.g. *wungay-awaa* (dive-habitual) the name of the great black cormorant who is always diving. See Learner's Guide.

-ayla-y (YR) *suffix*
before, yesterday. This suffix is added to verbs to indicate that the action took place in the past, and translates as 'before' or 'yesterday'. See Learner's Guide.

Bb

-Baa (YR, YY, GR) *suffix*
1 time of. Occurs in *yaay-baa* (sun-baa) meaning 'summer' and *dhandarr-aa* (frost-aa) meaning 'winter'.
2 place of. Occurs in *walaay-baa* (camp-place of) meaning 'a person's country or home place'. ◆ *Gayaay-baa-ga ngiyani yanaa-waa-nha.* (YR) We are walking through a sandy place.
This suffix is attached to nouns; overall it conveys a meaning something like English 'context'. Some uses of *-baa* are not fully understood. Sometimes used to form adjectives, as in *dhalay-baa* (sharp) from *dhalay* (tongue), and *gurru-baa* (deep) from *gurru* (hole). Variant form is *-aa*. See Learner's Guide.

baa (YY) *noun*
hip. One source.

baa-y (YR, YY) *verb-intransitive*
1 hop (YR, YY). ◆ *Giirr nhama bunbun baa-nhi maayama-ga.* (YR) The grasshopper hopped over the stone.
2 jump (YR, YY). ◆ *Nhama bandaarr-giirr baa-y-la-nha.* (YR) He's jumping like a kangaroo.
3 stamp (YR). ◆ *Giirr ngiyama baa-y-la-nhi manduwii-dhalibaa dhayn-galgaa.* (YR) The men were stamping without any boots on.
4 flap (YR). ◆ *Giirr guduu baa-y-la-nhi ngiyarrma ganuu-ga.* (YR) The fish were flapping in the canoe.

baabi-li (YR, YY, GR) *verb-intransitive*
1 stay (YR, YY, GR). ◆ *Minyaaya-nda baabi-li?*

(GR) Where will you stay?
2 sleep (YR, YY, GR). ◆ *Ngurray yarral-a baabi-la-nha.* (GR) A black snake is sleeping on the stone.
3 camp (GR).
This is a rare word in YY and YR. There is limited evidence for a related form *baaba-y* (sleep).

baada-li (YY) *verb-transitive*
comb (hair). One source.

baadal (YY) *noun*
comb. Related to *baada-li* (comb hair). One source. Originally a nit comb, made from a piece of bone or wood.

baadhal (YR, YY) *noun*
bottle. From English 'bottle'.

baadi (YR) *noun*
paddock. Also *baadig*.
Probably from English 'paddock'. One source.

baadjin (YR, YY, GR) *noun*
poison. ◆ *Waal ngiyama nguu dha-lda-nhi, garigari ngaama baadji-di.* (YR) He wouldn't eat for fear of poison.
From English 'poison'.

baagii (YR, YY) *noun*
1 grandmother (mother's mother) (YR, YY). Used to be used for 'mother's mother', now a general word for any grandmother.
2 old woman (YR). Used with this meaning in the Walgett area.
See also: **ngaagii**.

baalaraan (YR, YY) *noun*
leopardwood flowers.
Another meaning, according to Fred Reece, is 'cypress-pine smoke or pollen'.

baaldharradharra (YR, YY, GR) *noun*
spur-winged plover, masked lapwing (*Vanellus miles*). Probably from *dharra* (leg), because of the bird's long legs. Sounds like one of the bird's calls.

baaluu (YR, YY) *noun*
moon. The moon is thought of as male, 'the Moon Man', and plays a very important role in Indigenous spiritual beliefs around Australia. ◆ *Giirr-nha wanda dhurra-l-uwi-nyi baaluu-dhi.* (YY) The whitefellas came back from the moon (talking about the Apollo 11 mission).
See also: **gilay**.

baama (YY) *noun*
cloud. Ian Sim said this is the word for any cloud. One source. See also: **gundaa**.

baamagaaliyan (YY) *noun*
white ant, termite. One source.

baaman (GR) *noun*
1 father's sister.
2 mother's brother's wife.
3 mother's mother's brother's daughter.
This is a relationship term. It is not clear if it refers to a relationship between two women, or between a man and a woman. For a man, all women were in one of four relationships: sister, mother, mother-in-law and potential spouse. His aunty (father's sister) was of the same social section as his mother-in-law. For example, for a *Marrii* man, they are both *Yibadhaa*. For the *Marrii* man, the other woman referred to above is also *Yibadhaa*. See Introduction.

baan (YR, YY, GR) *noun*
mistletoe, snotty gobbles (*Amyema* spp.). A parasitic plant which grows on trees and has small, gluey, very tasty fruit. Known as 'snotty gobbles' because of the sticky fruit. The leaves are used to treat sores: they are boiled in water and the liquid is drunk or applied to wounds. The berries contain a moderate amount of energy and water, some protein and fat, and are a good source of vitamin C.

baandjil (YY) *noun*
mistletoe bird (*Dicaeum hirundinaceum*). Talking about this bird may not have been allowed. This may be because *baan* (mistletoe) was thought to hide spirit children. From *baan* (mistletoe).

baanda-li (YR) *verb-transitive*
straighten up (tidy), put in order. Greg Fields used to say *baanda-la!* (tidy up!) about things around the camp. One source.

baanda-y (YY) *verb-intransitive*
move in a line. Ian Sim said 'move in Indian file'. One source.

baanduu (YR, YY, GR) *noun*
horse fly. Also called march fly.

baan.giirr (YR, YY) *noun*
1 black-tailed native hen (*Gallinula*

ventralis). This is a rare word, the common word is *gulguwi*. One source.
2 Bangate. A large property between Lightning Ridge and Goodooga, where Langloh-Parker lived; it is named after the native hens there.

baanmal (YY) *noun*
betrothal of babies. May be related to *baan* (mistletoe) which was thought to hide spirit children. One source.

baarra-y (YR, YY) *verb-intransitive*
1 crack. ◆ *Gawu baarra-nhi.* (YY) The egg cracked.
2 split. ◆ *Giirr nhama maayama baarra-nhi.* (YR) The rock split.
3 burst.

baarrama-li (YR, YY) *verb-transitive*
1 tear off, pull off, strip off. ◆ *Garruugii-dju ngay yulay baarrama-y bawurra-dhi.* (YY) My uncle tore the skin off the kangaroo. ◆ *Baarrama-li-laa ngiyani dhunbil maayawa-li-gu man.garr.* (YY) Then we will tear the sinews, to sew the bag.
2 tear. ◆ *Baarrama-li ngaya gi-yaa-nha bayagaa.* (YY) I am going to tear the clothes.
From *baarra-* (burst, crack, split) and *-ma-li* (suffix that makes a transitive verb).

baarray-rri (YR, YY, GR) *verb-transitive*
1 split (YR, YY, GR). ◆ *Baarray-na dhuu!* (YY) Split the wood!
2 burst, bust (YR, YY).
3 crack (YR, YY).
There is some evidence that this verb is *-rri* class, and other evidence which suggests *-li* class. The *-rri* class is more common and is recommended.

baarrgiin (YR) *noun*
hermit. Ted Fields said it was used in the instance of a person who works for months on their own in the bush; also called a 'bush rat'. One source.

baawaa (YR, YY, GR) *noun*
older sister, sister. *Bawa* has also been recorded and used recently; *baawaa* is the recommended word for 'sister'. *Baawaadhi* (my sister) is sometimes pronounced 'boyandi'.

Baawan (YY, GR) *placename*
Barwon River. ◆ *Baawan-gu ngaya yanaa-waa-nha.* (YY) I am going to the Barwon. Ridley recorded the meaning as 'great, wide, awful (River)'.

baawul (YR, YY) *noun*
chicken. From English 'fowl'. See also: **djigin**.

baaya (YY) *noun*
hairy melon *(Cucumis melo)*. Also called Ulcardo melon and cucumber. This was an important food; the rind is bitter so the contents are squeezed out.

baaya-li (YR, GR) *verb-transitive*
1 crack between teeth (YR). Arthur Dodd said '*Baaya-lda-nha* — that's when you're cracking a peanut in your mouth'.
2 bite off (YR). ◆ *Giirr nguu baaya-y.* (YR) He bit (it) off.
3 chop (GR).
See also: **yii-li**.

baayama-li (YR, YY) *verb-transitive*
spin. ◆ *Baayama-laa-nha-nga ngaya gawu, gaba burrulaa girran dhuu-ga.* (YY) I'm spinning the egg now, (got) good ashes on the fire.
Ted Fields said that this is what you do to an emu egg before cooking it. You spin it and toss it up in the air, then lay it on the ashes or coals. When it is cooked the egg will stand up on the rounder point.

baayamal (YR, YY) *noun*
black swan *(Cygnus atratus)*. From *Baayami* (the creator or supreme being); see the Black Swans story in Langloh-Parker.

baayamba (YR) *noun*
friend, mate. The recommended word is *maliyaa*.

Baayami (YR, YY, GR) *noun, placename*
1 Byame, God (YR, YY, GR). Also *Baayaami*. According to Langloh-Parker, women and uninitiated men were not allowed to use the word *Baayami*, instead they used *buwadjarr* (father) to talk about the Creator or Supreme Being. Ian Sim said that *bubaa* (father) was used instead of *Baayami*.
2 Byamee (GR). Locality on the Tamworth–Gunnedah road.

baayan (YR, YY, GR) *time adverb*
soon. Seems to be used in the same way as *yilaa* (soon, directly) and at this stage may

baayangali

be regarded as a synonym, with perhaps more of an implication of a causal relationship (because of this . . .), rather than the sequential meaning of *yilaa*. Also occurs as *baayan-duul*.

baayanbuu (GR) *time adverb*
immediately. From *baayan* (soon) and the hypothesised suffix *-buu* (all/totally). One source.

baayandhu (YR) *time adverb*
later on. Good for use in farewells — 'see you *baayandhu*'. Based on *baayan* (soon).

baayangali (YR) *noun*
nature. Ted Fields said this is the natural order of things, 'this is how things work'. One source.

baaybal (YR, YY) *noun*
frog. Arthur Dodd used *baaybal* as a general word for any frog. Possibly also refers to the salmon-striped frog (*Limnodynastes salmini*). ◆ *Giirr nguuma, birralii-djuul-u baaybal bayama-y, dha-li-gu.* (YR) The boy caught the frog to eat.

baaybuu (YR, YY, GR) *noun*
pipe. From English 'pipe'.

baaydjarr (YR, YY) *exclamation*
hey! An expression of surprise.

baayl (GR) *noun*
axe mark. Probably related to *baaya-li* (chop). One source.

baaylirrma-li (YR) *verb-transitive*
boil. From English 'boil'.

baayna (GR) *noun*
1 father. The recommended word for 'father' is *bubaa*.
2 wife's mother's brother.
For a man, these two relations would belong to the same social section.

babaaluma-y (YR, YY) *verb-intransitive*
jump into water (game). A game played by jumping into water with splashes.
◆ *Babaaluma-ya gungan-da!* (YY) Jump into the water!

babadhi (YY, GR) *noun*
restricted word. See p 20 for more information.

babarra (YR, YY) *noun*
1 brown and yellow snake (YR, YY). Ted Fields has told the story of when the two *babarra* fought and their boomerangs cut the top off a hill, leaving a flat ridge that is now known as Cumborah knob.
2 Babarra (YR). A ridge on the Walgett–Cumborah road where the two *babarra* fought with boomerangs. See also: **bubarraa**.

babarrabiin (YR, YY) *noun*
gidgee flowers. *Babarra* may be another word for the gidgee tree.

babarrngaan (YY) *noun*
river bug. Also called toad bug, it was thought to predict floods by moving to high ground. Possibly the slater. One source.

babi (YY) *noun*
spangled grunter (fish) (*Madigania*). Name may be from, or the origin of, the common name 'bobby'.

babuligaarr (YR, YY) *noun*
hotel. From English 'public house'.

baburr (YR, YY, GR) *noun*
1 foot (YR, YY, GR). ◆ *Baburr ngay bayn gi-yaa-nha.* (YY) My feet are getting sore.
2 footprint (YY).
Rarely used in GR and YR. See also: **dhina**.

badha (YR, YY, GR) *noun, adjective*
1 sandalwood tree, budda tree (*Eremophila mitchellii*) (YR, YY). Ted Fields said that the leaves are used for smoking people and places, including children who have misbehaved, the houses of the dead, and as a mosquito repellant. They are also boiled in water to make a medicine with many uses, often used for bathing sores. If a woman cannot conceive they made a long fire, put *badha* over it, and the woman slept on the hot *badha*. The wood is used for *bundi* (club, waddy).
2 bitter, sour (YR, YY, GR).

badha gali (YR) *noun*
new word. See p 160 for more information.

badha-y (YR) *verb-transitive*
give a hiding. ◆ *Giirr badha-nhi nguu nhama birralii-djuul.* (YR) He gave the boy a hiding.

-badhaay (YR, YY) *clitic*
might (would you). ◆ *Buma-li-badhaay ngaya nginunha.* (YR) I might hit you.
◆ *Bandaarr-badhaay nguu ngaama bilaa-yu*

dhu-rri. (YR) He might spear a kangaroo.
◆ *Warra-ya-badhaay.* (YR) Stand up.
This clitic is added to the first word of a sentence. In some cases it means 'might' or softens a command, but the meaning is unclear in many cases. Also occurs as *badhaayaa*, a combination of *badhaay* and *-Yaa*. This is sometimes translated 'must'.

Badhara Walaay (GR) *placename*
mountain on Namoi River. It was said that spirits live there. Based on *walaay* (camp). One source.

badhii (GR) *noun*
grandmother (mother's mother). Sources also give this as 'mother's mother's brother', but it is unlikely that one word means both 'mother's mother' and 'mother's mother's brother'. This is a rare word, the common word is *baagii*. See also: **waabi**.

badhuul (YR, YY) *noun*
1 mother-in-law's brother (YR, YY).
2 son-in-law (YY).
This word probably refers to a woman's relations, since in that case both people are of the same section; so for a *Buudhaa* both are *Gabi*.

badi (YR, YY) *noun*
1 fish trap. Ted Fields said it is a fence made of branches built across a gully to catch fish as a flood goes down.
2 fence.

badi ganaay (YR) *noun*
gate. From *badi* (fence) and *ganaay* (opening). One source.

badjigal (YR) *noun*
bicycle. From English 'bicycle'. One source.

badjin (YR, YY) *adjective*
small, little. ◆ *Badjin garra-la muyaan.* (YY) Cut the branch up small.
Also occurs as *badjin-duul* (little one).

badjinbal (YY) *adverb*
gradually. To describe an action, as in 'little by little'. One source.

badjindi (YY) *noun*
shorty, tiny. Nickname for anything small. One source.

badjin maadha (YR, YY) *noun*
overseer. This term comes from sheep and cattle stations, where the manager or owner was the *burrul maadha* (big boss) and the overseer was second in charge. From *badjin* (little) and *maadha* (master).

baga (YR, GR) *noun*
river bank. ◆ *Bundaa-nhi ngaam' birralii-djuul, baga-dhi ngiyarrma.* (YR) The boy fell from the river bank.
Possibly a form of *bagay*.

bagaan (YR, GR) *noun*
1 older sister (YR, GR). Mathews said 'older sister, before puberty'. According to Austin, adult males must avoid their elder sisters and not talk to them. Tindale recorded this meaning for Upper Barwon dialect.
2 younger sister (GR). The recommended word is *baawaa* (sister).

bagaarr (YR) *noun*
short cut. One source.

bagaay (YR) *noun*
shearing handpiece. One source.

bagabaga (YY) *noun*
emu chick (striped). Possibly based on *bagan* (stripe); the name therefore means something like 'striped'. See also: **barrgay**.

bagabagaali (YR) *noun*
musk duck *(Biziura lobata)*.

bagal (YY) *noun*
1 plate fungus.
2 plate. Used to refer to any round object. One source, some uncertainty about source language.

bagala (YR, YY, GR) *noun, placename*
1 leopardwood tree *(Flindersia maculosa)* (YR, YY, GR). A medium-sized tree with spotted or mottled bark. Fred Reece said that it was good for toothache. People would scrape the sappy part off the root bark and put it in hollow teeth. Ted Fields said 'to cure toothache, bake the root till it is hot then bite on it'.
2 Bukkulla (GR). Location.

Bagaldii (GR) *placename*
Bugaldie. Location between Barradine and Coonabarabran.

bagan (YR, YY) *noun*
stripe. Longitudinal (up and down) stripe.

baganbagan (YY) *adjective*
striped. For example, a butcher's apron.

baganbi (YY) *noun*
striped skink. Probably *Ctenotus robustus*.

bagandi (YR, YY, GR) *noun*
native cat, quoll *(Dasyurus geoffroii)*. The western quoll. Fred Reece saw them. Now extinct in the area but still found in Western Australia.

bagay (YR, GR) *noun*
1 river. ◆ *Gaayli gubi-y-la-y bagay-dha.* (GR) The children will be swimming in the river. ◆ *Mari yana-waa-nha bagay-gu guya ganma-li-gu.* (GR) The men are going to the river to catch fish.
2 creek.
Also *bagaay*.

Bagaybaraay (GR) *placename*
Boggabri. From *bagay* (creek) and *-baraay* (with, having).

Bagaybila (GR) *placename*
Boggabilla. Based on *bagay* (creek).

bagi (YY) *noun, placename*
1 white pipeclay.
2 Boggy Ridge. Place near Angledool; once called Buggy Ridge, now known as Boggy Ridge.

bagii (GR) *noun*
bad spirit. A short old man with a bald head and a fat stomach; he comes to the camps and eats all the meat without cooking it. One source.

bagiluu (YY) *noun*
cottonbush *(Maireana aphylla)*. Spiny shrub to one metre. Recorded as a woman's name.

bagu (YR, GR) *noun*
gliding possum. Probably the squirrel glider *(Petaurus norfolcensis)* which occurs further west than other possibilities, the greater glider *(Petauroides volans)* or the sugar glider *(Petaurus breviceps)*.

bagurr (YR, YY) *noun*
waist.

bal (YR, YY, GR) *noun*
nardoo *(Marsilea drummondii)*. A fern with leaves like four-leaf clovers that grows on low-lying ground; the spores, produced in woody containers the size of a wheat grain, can be gathered for food. Arthur Dodd said 'we put it on a big flat stone, crush it with a little flat stone, pour water with it, mix it up like dough, cook it in the ashes'.
One source. See also: **nhaadhuu**.

-bala (YR, YY) *clitic*
contrast. ◆ *Ngaya gugirrii-biyaay, nginda-bala gugirrii-dhalibaa.* (YY) I'm stronger than you (I'm strong, you're weak).
◆ *Gundhuwundhuu birray-djuul, ngayagay-bala gaba.* (YY) The boy (is) stubborn, the others (are) good. ◆ *Gaba-bala nhama dhaymaarr, gagil-bala nhalay dhaymaarr.* (YY) That ground (is) good, this ground (is) bad. ◆ *Maniila-y ngaya gi-yaa-nha, ngindaay-bala nguwalay yilawa-ya gaarrimay-a.* (YY) I'm going hunting, you all stop in the camp.
This suffix is known as a 'clitic', which means that it can be attached to different parts of speech. It is usually found at the beginning of a sentence or clause. It often marks a comparison between two things but the full range of meanings is not understood. See Learner's Guide.

balaa (YY, GR) *noun, adjective*
1 white (YY, GR).
2 clear alcohol (YY). It appears that the meaning has been extended from 'white' to include 'clear alcohol'.
See also: **banggabaa**.

balabalaa (YR, YY, GR) *noun*
butterfly. Originally the name for the white butterfly; now a general name for any butterfly. From *balaa* (white).

baladi (YR, YY) *noun*
saw. Also anything with a serrated jagged edge. Probably from *bal* (nardoo plant) because of the jagged edge of the plant's leaves.

balal (YR, YY, GR) *adjective, placename*
1 dry, empty, bare (YR, YY, GR). Possibly also 'clean'.
2 thirsty (YR, YY, GR).
3 Pallal (GR). One source for this meaning.

balal giniy (YY) *noun*
dead tree. From *balal* (dry) and *giniy* (tree).

balal muyaan (YY) *noun*
dead tree. From *balal* (dry) and *muyaan* (tree).

balam (YR) *noun*
  milky fluid. In milk thistle. Probably based on *balaa* (white). One source. See also: **balamba**.
balamba (YR, YY, GR) *noun*
  milk thistle *(Lactuca serriola)*. Fred Reece said that *balamba* leaves can be eaten when young, but are no good when old. Also called prickly lettuce, it is a thistle-like weed with yellow flower heads. Probably based on *balaa* (white) because of the white fluid it exudes.
balandharr (YY) *noun*
  head hair. This is a rare word, the common word is *dhaygal*.
balanhii (YR) *noun*
  cooler, fridge. A charcoal cooler — water dripped through the charcoal walls. One source. Possibly based on *nhii* (shortened form of *nhigii* — coals).
Balarangawul (GR) *placename*
  mountain on Namoi River. It was said that spirits lived there. One source.
balawagarr (GR) *noun*
  bearded dragon, frilled lizard *(Amphibolurus barbatus)*. The bearded dragon is commonly known as the frilled lizard in NSW, the real frill-necked is in Queensland and the Northern Territory. There are two types of bearded dragon (both large) and a river lizard which has a smaller 'beard'. See also: **dharri**.
balima (YR, YY) *noun*
  1 heaven, sky camp. A specific spot in the sky world. *Gunagala* is more like the English 'heaven'.
  2 place far away. This is a euphemism for 'as far from human affairs as possible'. Also *bulima*.
baliyaa (YR, YY) *adjective*
  cold.
balu (YR, YY, GR) *adjective*
  dead. Also *balun*. Also used in relation to fires. ◆ *Giirr nhama balu wii gi-nyi.* (YR) The fire is out.
  Related to *balu-gi* (die).
balu-gi (YR, YY, GR) *verb-intransitive*
  1 die (YR, YY, GR). ◆ *Yilaalu buwadjarr balu-gi.* (GR) Later (my) father will die.
  2 go out (fire) (YR, YY). ◆ *Dhuu ngay balu-waa-nha.* (YY) My fire is going out (dying).
balubuma-li (YY, GR) *verb-transitive*
  kill. From *balu* (dead) and *buma-li* (hit, kill).
baluburra-li (YR, YY) *verb-transitive*
  put out (extinguish). ◆ *Giirr ngaya baluburra-li.* (YR) I will put (the fire) out. Based on *balu* (dead). There are a number of similar words with this meaning including *baluwa-li*, *balubunma-li* and *baluburranba-li*.
balumbaluu (YY, GR) *adjective*
  weak. Also *barumbalu*. Probably based on *balu* (dead). Fred Reece doubts whether this is a general word, he uses it of a weak wind.
baluun (YR, YY) *noun, placename*
  1 great egret *(Ardea alba)* (YR, YY).
  2 Ballone (place and river) (YY).
Baluunbilyan (YR, YY) *placename*
  Bollonbillion. A waterhole at Angledool. From *baluun* (egret) and *bilyan* (waterhole), so 'Egret Waterhole'.
baluwaa (YR, YY, GR) *adverb*
  1 slowly, steadily (YR, YY, GR). ◆ *Baluwaa yanaa-waa-ya!* (YY) Walk slowly!
  2 quietly (YR, YY). ◆ *Giirr ngiyani nginunha winanga-li, gaay guwaa-lda-ndaay baluwaa.* (YY) We will listen to you, (if you) speak quietly.
  The basic meaning of *baluwaa* is 'with little energy'. Its translation changes slightly depending on the meaning of verbs following it, e.g. *baluwaa gudhuwa-y* (burn with little energy/smoulder); *baluwaa dhama-y* (gently rain/drizzle); *mayrraa baluwaa buuli-y* (wind easing up) and *baluwaa wiima-li* (carefully put down).
baluwaal (YY) *adverb*
  never. One source.
baluwa-li (YY) *verb-transitive*
  put out (extinguish). ◆ *Baluwa-la dhuu!* (YY) Put the fire out!
bama-li (YR, YY, GR) *verb-transitive*
  1 squash. ◆ *Bama-la nhama dhuyu maayama-gu.* (YY) Squash that snake with a stone.
  2 knead. ◆ *Dhuwarr bama-la!* (GR) Knead the bread!

bamba (YR, YY, GR) *adverb*
  1 hard (with force) (YR, YY, GR). ◆ *Yaama nginda bamba banaga-y?* (YR) Will you run hard? ◆ *Giirr ngaya bamba buma-y maadhaay.* (YR) I hit the dog hard.
  2 loudly (YR, YY). ◆ *Birralii-djuul-u bamba buwadjarr gaga-laa-nhi.* (YR) The little girl called out loudly to her father.
  3 very (YR, YY). ◆ *Giirr ngaya-laa yaluu bamba yiili gi-gi.* (YR) I'll get very angry again.
  The basic meaning of *bamba* is 'with lots of energy'. It changes slightly depending on the meaning of verbs following it, e.g. *bamba ngarra-li* (look carefully, stare), *bamba dha-li* (eat heartily) and *bamba dhanduwi-y* (sleep soundly).

bamba bayama-li (YY) *verb phrase*
  squeeze. From *bamba* (strongly, hard) and *bayama-li* (hold).

bamba ngami-li (GR) *verb phrase*
  stare. From *bamba* (strongly, hard) and *ngami-li* (look at).

bamba ngarra-li (YR, YY) *verb phrase*
  1 stare. ◆ *Garriya nganha bamba ngarra-lda-ya!* (YY) Don't stare at me!
  2 watch carefully. ◆ *Bamba dhaymaarr ngarra-laa-ya ngandabaa-dhi!* (YR) Watch (carefully) the ground for snakes!
  From *bamba* (strongly, hard) and *ngarra-li* (look at).

bambugal (GR) *noun*
  1 fingers.
  2 toes.
  Rare word, possibly including *-gal* (many).

bambul (YR, YY, GR) *noun*
  native orange tree *(Capparis mitchellii)*. A small tree with large white flowers, and fruit that is yellowish when ripe. This tree is important in the Boobera Lagoon story. Locally known as 'bumble'; it is thought to be a 'woman's tree', used to cure 'woman's itch' and other women's illnesses. The leaves are boiled in water and drunk to cure venereal disease. The fruit offers only moderate energy, water, and carbohydrate compared with other fruits, but is a good source of vitamin C and thiamine.

bambulngiyan (YR, YY) *noun*
  native orange tree flowers. Based on *bambul* (native orange tree) and *-(b)iyan*. See Learner's Guide.

bambuy (GR) *noun*
  1 father-in-law.
  2 son-in-law.
  One source.

bana (YR, YY, GR) *noun, placename*
  1 lean meat (YR, YY, GR).
  2 body (GR). An old source records *bana* as 'body' in contrast to *dhuwi* (soul).
  3 Bunna (YY). Waterholes near Goodooga and Wee Waa. One source.
  4 cannibal (YY). One source.

banaga-y (YR, YY, GR) *verb-intransitive*
  1 run (YR, YY, GR). ◆ *Waal nhama yarraaman banaga-waa-nha.* (YR) The horse is not running. ◆ *Minyaarru ngay maadhaay banaga-nhi?* (YY) Where did my dog run to?
  2 flow (water) (YR, YY). ◆ *Gungan wugawa nhama banaga-waa-nha.* (YY) That flood water is flowing.
  3 drive (YY). ◆ *Nhama-dhaay-nga wadjiin, wilbaa-ya banaga-waa-nha.* (YY) Here's that white woman, driving in the motor car.

banay (YR, YY, GR) *adjective*
  new word. See p 160 for more information.

banbandhuluwi (YR, YY, GR) *noun*
  crested bellbird *(Oreoica gutturalis)*. Banbandhuluwi sounds like the bird's five-note call.

bandaarr (YR, YY, GR) *noun*
  grey kangaroo *(Macropus giganteus)*. This is the eastern-grey kangaroo; it was eaten but the red kangaroo was preferred.
  ◆ *Bandaarr bilaa-yu nhama ngaya dhu-nhi.* (GR) I speared the kangaroo.
  Also the name of an unidentified star. Now the common word for 'kangaroo'.

Bandaarra (GR) *placename*
  Bundarra. A town west of Armidale. From

bandaarr (grey kangaroo) and probably *-aa* (place of).

bandi (YY) *noun*
punty bush *(Senna eremophila)*. This is a shrubby plant with golden cup-shaped flowers, and long many-seeded pods. They are used as a purgative to treat constipation. The English word 'punty' may not be from Yuwaalayaay since there are similar words in other Aboriginal languages.

bandibandi (YY) *noun*
diarrhoea. Probably related to *bandi* (punty bush).

bandiyal (YY) *noun*
saltbush. Also called thorny saltbush; a variable shrub, upright or spreading with some branches ending in spines; silver-grey leaves. Probably *Rhagodia spinescens*.

bandjalbarri (YR) *noun*
restricted word. See p 20 for more information.

bandji (YR) *noun*
bottom. Probably a Gunggari word. One source.

bandu (YR, YY) *adjective*
dirty. ◆ *Bandu nhama ngulu.* (YR) He's (got) a dirty face.

-ban.gaan (GR) *suffix*
very, really. One source. See also *-wan.gaan* (very, really — YR, YY).

ban.gul (YR, YY, GR) *noun*
echo, chopping noise.

bangalaa (GR) *noun*
dark. This is a rare word, the common word is *buluuy*. One source. Form uncertain.

bangga (YR, YY) *adjective*
white. Also *banggaa*. This is the form found in compound words, e.g. *birribangga* (little pied cormorant); the common word for 'white' is *banggabaa*.

banggabaa (YR, YY, GR) *noun, adjective*
1 white (YR, YY, GR).
2 clear alcohol (YR).
3 methylated spirits (YR).
Possibly from *banggaa* (white) and *-baa* (place of, time of).

banggadha-y (YR, YY) *verb-intransitive*
float. ◆ *Garril nhama banggadha-y-la-nha gungan-da.* (YY) The leaves are floating on the water.

See also: **dhangga-y**.

banggul (YR) *noun*
money. Also *ban.gu*. Used in some YR, GR areas. Recommended usage is *banggul* (money) and *yarral* (coins).

bangu (YR) *noun*
wing. Also occurs in *bangu badi* meaning the 'wing' leading into a sheepyard or fishtrap. This is a rare word the common word is *bungun* (wing, arm).

banhaayal (YR, YY) *noun*
house fly. Name for any fly.

bani (YR, YY) *noun*
front. ◆ *Bani-dja ngaya yanaa-waa-nha.* (YY) I am walking in front.

banigan (YR) *noun*
cup. From English 'pannikin'. *Gaala* is now used for 'mug'.

banma-li (GR) *verb-transitive*
help. One source. Form uncertain.

banngala (YR) *noun*
black bream.

banuwa (YR, YY) *noun*
black soil. In the west of the area the distinction between the black and red soil is important, with differences in vegetation, animals and other features, e.g. the black soil is hard to dig, so burials are on red soil which is often sandy.

bara-y[1] (YR, YY) *verb-intransitive*
fly ◆ *Giirr nhama bara-waa-nha dhigayaa.* (YR) The bird is flying.

bara-y[2] (GR) *verb-intransitive*
jump, hop. Form uncertain. Possibly *baaraay*.

baragi-y (YR, YY) *verb-intransitive*
fly around, fly in circle. ◆ *Giirr nhama dhigayaa bara-gi-la-nhi.* (YR) The birds were flying around.
From *bara-* (fly) and *-gi-y* (hypothesised suffix meaning 'around').

baraa (GR) *noun*
perch (unidentified fish).

-Baraay (GR) *suffix*
with, having. Variant forms are *-baraay*, *-araay*. This suffix is attached to nouns, meanings include accompaniment (e.g. with mum), property (e.g. with hair/hairy) and weak instrumental (e.g. walked with a stick). The variant also occurs in the

language name Kamilaroi, *Gamil-araay* (no-having); so 'the language that has *gamil* (for no)'. The ending is often used to form new words, particularly placenames such as Boggabri, *Bagay-baraay* (creeks-having). See also: **-araay**. See Learner's Guide.

barabin (YR, YY, GR) *noun*
semen. *Barambang* (semen) is a word used in Walgett, it may be from the Wangaaybuwan language.

baramay (GR) *adjective*
worn out. One source.

baranggal (YR, YY) *noun*
ankle. Possibly from English 'ankle'. The recommended word for 'ankle' is *ngawurr*.

barawaa (YR, GR) *noun*
plains turkey, bustard. Good eating; now rare in the area. There is a story about the bustard and emu (see Arthur Dodd and Langloh-Parker). See also: **gumbulgaban**.

barayamal (GR) *noun*
black swan *(Cygnus atratus)*. This is the recommended word for the black swan. See also: **burrunda**.

barigan (YR) *noun*
nepine *(Capparis lasiantha)*. This word is commonly used in Walgett, possibly originally *barrigan*. See **guwiibirr** for more information.

baril (GR) *noun*
barrel, bucket. From English 'barrel'.

bariyan (GR) *noun*
younger sister. Mathews wrote 'after puberty', Tindale and Wurm recorded this form for the upper Barwon River dialect. The recommended word is *baawaa* (sister).

Bariyan Ngama (GR) *noun*
Pleiades (stars). From *bariyan* (younger sister) and *ngama* (father's sister); the name may be just *bariyan*. This is rare, the common name is *miyaymiyaay*.

-barra (YR, YY) *suffix*
people from. This suffix is used to refer to the inhabitants of a place, e.g. *Nhungga-barra* (belonging to the country of the kurrajong tree), and *Garrii-barra* (belonging to the country of the orchid). The *Nhunggabarra* were the people who lived around Narran Lake and Narran River.

barra (YR, YY) *noun*
1 thread, filament. Anything very thin or fine.
2 split.
Related to *barra-li* (sharpen).

barrabarraa (YY) *adjective*
split open. From *barra* (a split).

barra-li (YR, YY, GR) *verb-transitive*
sharpen. ◆ *Waal nhama barra-la!* (YR) Don't sharpen it!

Barrali Mugulbaa (YR) *placename*
sharpening-tools place. Place with sharpening grooves in the rock, north of Lightning Ridge, near Wiidhalibaa. Based on *barra-li* (sharpen), *mugu* (blunt) and *-baa* (place of, time of). One source.

barra-y (GR) *verb-intransitive*
fly. The word for 'fly' was previously listed in GR as *barra-gi*, which is now thought to be more closely related to *baragi-y* (fly around). There is conflicting evidence as to whether this verb is *y* class or *gi* class, compare Wiradjuri *barra-y*.

barraay (YR, YY, GR) *adverb*
fast, quickly. ◆ *Barraay-bala nginda guwaa-lda-nha.* (YR) You talk too fast. ◆ *Barraay, yanaa-y gi-yaa-nha ngaya.* (YY) Quickly, I'm going to go. ◆ *Barraay ngaya yanaa-waa-nha.* (YY) I am walking quickly. ◆ *Yaama ngay guliirr barraay dhurra-l-uwi-y?* (YY) I wonder will my husband come home early (quickly)?

barraay milu gimbi-li (YR) *verb phrase*
wink. ◆ *Ngaama bubaay-djuul-u ngaama barraay mil-u gimbi-y ngaama burrul-bidi dhayn.* (YR) The little man winked at the big man.
From *barraay* (quickly) and *mil-u* (eye-with) and *gimbi-li* (do). *Milabi-li* is the recommended word for 'wink'.

barraaywan (YY) *time adverb*
immediately. Possibly from *barraay* (fast, quickly) and *-wan* (prominent feature).

barrabandu (YR, YY) *exclamation*
shame!, oh no! According to Ted Fields, people say this when they or someone else makes a mistake or drops something. It's not making fun, more like saying 'bad luck'. Also used when you change your mind. One source.

barrabarruun (YR, YY) *noun*
quail *(Coturnix* spp.*)*.

barran (YR, YY, GR) *noun, placename*
1 boomerang (YR, YY, GR).
2 Burren Junction (GR).

barranbaa (YR, YY) *noun, placename*
1 brigalow wattle *(Acacia harpophylla)* (YR, YY). A medium- to large-sized wattle which grows in large thickets known as 'brigalow scrub'.
2 location (YR). A place for collecting timber for *barran* (boomerangs) near Goodooga. Probably from *barran* (boomerang) and *-baa* (place of, time of).

barranbuu (YR) *noun*
nickname. Said to refer to an old stockman who had bow legs. Based on *barran* (boomerang) and, possibly, *buyu* (leg). One source.

barran.giiba (YR) *noun*
boomerang maker. From *barran*. One source.

barran.giirr (YY) *adjective*
new moon. Used to describe the moon in its early phase. From *barran* (boomerang) and *-giirr* (like, similar to). One source.

barranbarraan (YR, YY) *noun*
millipede. Possibly a nickname, from *barran* (boomerang) because of its many legs shaped like boomerangs. Also *barranbarraa*.

barranda (YR) *noun*
verandah. From English 'verandah'.

barrangga (GR) *noun*
ground parrot (red-rumped parrot). There is no word recorded for the common red-rumped parrot *(Psephotus haematonotus)*, nor any bird in this area commonly known as a ground parrot. In these circumstances it is appropriate to use this word, recorded as 'ground parrot', for the red-rumped parrot which is common and spends a lot of time on the ground.

barrawan¹ (YY) *noun*
golden bandicoot. Probably *Isodon auratus*. Once widespread, Langloh-Parker said it was extinct on the Narran before 1900. Possibly from *barra* (thread) because of the unusual 'guard hairs' over the fur. One source.

barrawan² (YY) *noun*
type of sedge. Probably a species of *Lepidosperma* or *Schoenus*. Sedges are rush or grass-like plants that grow in wet areas.

barrawaraay (YY) *noun*
sugar ant. One source.

barrgabarrga (YR, YY) *noun*
wood duck *(Chenonetta jubata)*. Also called maned duck.

barrgay¹ (YY) *noun*
flowering lignum, lignum fuchsia *(Eremophila polyclada)*. A stiff shrub with large white flowers. Fred Reece said that nectar can be sucked from the flowers.

barrgay² (YR, YY, GR) *noun*
emu chick. Older than *bagabaga*, and when the chick's stripes have gone. Fred Reece said an emu chick is '*barrgay* when half grown till full grown'.

barrgin (YY) *noun*
dusk. One source.

barriga (YR, YY, GR) *adjective*
new word. See p 160 for more information.

barriindjiin (YR, YY, GR) *noun*
peewee, magpie-lark *(Grallina cyanoleuca)*.

barrin (YR, YY) *noun*
baked soil. The red pieces of baked earth which are made in ground ovens. These are used, when hot, to put inside kangaroos and emus to help them cook.

barringgu (YR) *noun*
friend, mate. ◆ *Yaama barringgu?* (YR) How are you mate, friend? One source.

barriyay (GR) *noun*
window. One source. Form uncertain.

bawa¹ (YR) *noun*
older sister. This is now commonly used for 'sister'. See also: *baawaa*.

bawa² (YR, YY, GR) *noun*
back (body part). In some Australian Aboriginal languages, there is a link between body parts and the sign language for kin relations, compare *bawa* (older sister).

bawadhi (GR) *place adverb*
behind. From *bawa* (back) and *-dhi* (source). May also be used in the form

bawa-dha (back-at). One source. Form uncertain. The part of speech is also uncertain; it may be a suffixed noun.

Bawa³ (YY) *placename*
waterhole name. On the Walgett–Lightning Ridge road. One source.

bawanngaa (YR, YY) *noun*
granddaughter.

bawi-li (YR, YY, GR) *verb-transitive*
1 sing (YR, YY, GR). ◆ *Giirr ngaama burrulaa-gu dhayn-du bawi-lda-nhi.* (YR) All the men were singing.
2 praise (GR). One source for this meaning.

bawurra (YR, YY, GR) *noun*
1 red kangaroo *(Macropus rufus)* (YR, YY, GR). This was a favourite food. Now common in the western part of Gamilaraay territory. 'Blue flyer' is another name for the female red kangaroo. ◆ *Bawurra nhama dhayn-du buma-y.* (YY) The man killed that red kangaroo.
2 jackeroo, stockman (YY). One source for this meaning.

bayaal (YR) *adjective*
next. One source.

bayaarr (YR, YY) *noun*
greenhead ant.

baya (GR) *noun*
1 clothes.
2 cloth. Ridley wrote 'fur' or 'cloth'.

bayagaa (YR, YY) *noun*
clothes. ◆ *Bayagaa ngaya wagirrbuma-li.* (YR) I will wash the clothes.

bayama-li (YR, YY) *verb-transitive*
1 catch. The verb *bayama-li* includes the meaning 'catch with hands', while *yinabi-li* (catch) is used more generally.
◆ *Maayama nhama birralii-dju bayama-y.* (YY) The child caught a stone.
2 hold. ◆ *Bamba dhuyu bayama-lda-ya wuyu!* (YY) Hold the snake tight around the neck!

bayama-y (YR) *verb-intransitive*
be caught. Used in the context of 'they all got caught in the net'. A change in verb class from *-li* to *-y*. See Learner's Guide. One source.

bayangurr (YY) *noun*
young. A young bird or animal.
◆ *Bayangurr bawurra.* (YY) A baby or young red kangaroo.
Possibly from *baayan* (soon).

bayn (YR, YY, GR) *noun, adjective*
sore. ◆ *Waala ngaya warra-y-la-nha, dhina ngay bayn gi-nyi.* (YR) I can't stand, my foot is sore. ◆ *Bigibila-gu wamu-gu nhama gaba gimbi-li bayn nhama nginu.* (YY) Porcupine fat will make that sore of yours good (better).

Bayn Gabilaa (YR) *placename*
Piangobla. Ted Fields said it meant something like 'take away a sick person'. Possibly based on *bayn* (sick), the form of second word is uncertain. Another possible derivation was said to be *bayangurr bulaarr* (two young ones) because of some watercourses or waterholes there.

baynyi (YY) *noun*
ripple. Such as ripples made by fish. One source.

bibaaya (YY) *noun*
fruit bat, flying fox *(Pteropus scapulatus)*. Known as 'man's friend'; to hurt it was thought of as 'picking a fight' with the other sex.

bibi (YR, YY) *noun*
brown treecreeper *(Climacteris picumnus)*. Also called woodpecker. One of the bird's calls is 'bi-bi-bi . . . '. Known as 'woman's friend'; to hurt it was thought of as 'picking a fight' with the other sex.

bibil (YR, YY, GR) *noun*
bimble box tree *(Eucalyptus populnea)*. English 'bimble' is probably from *bibil*. Large-sized tree, also called poplar gum.

bibirrgaa (YR, YY) *noun*
pig. From English 'pig'. As with many introduced animals a number of similar words exist for pig e.g. *bigurr, biguun*.

bibu (YY) *noun*
dillon bush *(Nitraria billardieri)*. Also called wild grape, it is a spreading shrub with fruit which is purple or red when ripe. See also: **mugiyala**.

-bidi (YR, YY, GR) *suffix*
big. ◆ *Buma-y nguu buyabuya-dhuul dhayn wamu-bidi-dju.* (YY) The big fat fellow hit the little bony fellow.
Usually adds the meaning 'big' to a person or thing, e.g. *dhayn-bidi* (man-big). Commonly occurs in *burrul-bidi* (big-big) with the meaning 'very big, great big'; *wamu-bidi* (fat-big) meaning 'big fat' and *malaa-bidi* (tree-big) meaning 'tree'. Adds the meaning 'really' to a quality, e.g. *yiiliyan-bidi* (really savage).

bidjaay (YR, YY) *noun*
1 mud. ◆ *Bundaa-nhi ngaya, bulilbulil-a bidjaay-a.* (YY) I fell in the slippery mud.
2 paint. Refers to ochre and other earth materials used as body paint.

bidjaaybiyaay (YY) *adjective*
muddy. From *bidjaay* (mud) and *-biyaay* (with, having).

bidjaay balaa (YY) *noun*
white paint. Ian Sim said it is a type of white paint made from gypsum or lime. From *bidjaay* (mud, paint) and *balaa* (white).

bidjaaymamal (YY) *noun*
fairy martin *(Hirundo ariel)*. The nest is made from mud, often under bridges or eaves. From *bidjaay* (mud) and *mama-li* (stick).

bidjal (YR, YY) *noun*
tree bark.

bidjaraay (YR, YY) *noun*
rag. Probably from English 'bits of rag'.

bidjiirr (YR) *noun*
new word. See p 160 for more information.

bidjun (YR, YY, GR) *noun*
middle. ◆ *Bidjun-da garra-la!* (YY) Cut it in the middle!

bigal (GR) *noun*
navel, bellybutton. This is a rare word, the common word is *wirrigaal*.

bigan (YY) *noun*
law. One source.

biganbiyaay (YY) *adjective*
lawful. From *bigan* (the law) and *-iyaay* (with, having), so 'with, according to the law'. One source.

bigibila (YR, YY, GR) *noun*
porcupine, echidna *(Tachyglossus aculeatus)*. A popular food. Arthur Dodd said that porcupine was his meat and his mother's meat, and they did eat it. It was killed by hitting it just in front of the quills, then put on the fire until hot, so that the quills came out easily. He said it tastes just like a pig: good, sweet meat. There is a story about how the porcupine got its quills (see Williams, Langloh-Parker). It is said that porcupine fat was used as hair oil. See also: **marrawal**.

biginini (YY) *noun*
foal. From 'piccaninny' (little one, child).

biguun (GR) *noun*
pig. From English 'pig'.

bii (YR, YY) *noun*
chest.

biiba (YR, YY, GR) *noun*
1 paper (YR, YY, GR).
2 note (paper money) (YY).
3 letter (YR). As in a letter that you write to someone.
From English 'paper'.

biibabiiba (YR, YY) *noun*
book.

biibaya (YR, YY) *noun*
broombush *(Melaleuca uncinata)*. Medium-sized shrub with yellow flowers. Today, branches are cut and dried for use in brush fences.

biibii (YY) *noun*
cow's paper gut. Probably from English 'paper' or 'bible' and refers to the omasum, found in the guts of ruminants (sheep, cattle, goats, deer etc.), which 'looks like a book'. One source.

biibin (YY) *noun*
hooded robin *(Melanodryas cucullata)*. Feared and avoided because of its calling out at night; believed to be a 'bad spirit'. Hearing its call is supposed to cause a type of wasting sickness, and children's ears were stopped at night to prevent this.

biidjinma-li (YR) *verb-transitive*
win. Possibly from English 'beat' and *-ima-li* (suffix added to English verbs). One source.

biila (YY) *noun*
    daddy. Familiar or fond name as in English 'dad' or 'daddy'. The recommended word for 'dad' is *bubaa*. One source.

biilaa (YR, YY) *noun*
    shoulder blade.

biilara (GR) *noun*
    shoulder blade.

biimba-li (YR, YY) *verb-transitive*
    sweep. ◆ *Biimba-la dhaymaarr!* (YY) Sweep (that) ground!

biimbal (YY) *noun*
    broom, brush. Name for anything used to sweep. Related to *biimba-li* (sweep).

biirr (YR, YY) *adjective*
    one. The standard form is *biyarr*; the recommended word is *milan* (one).

biirra-li (YR, YY) *verb-transitive*
    skin. ◆ *Biirra-li ngaya gi-yaa-nha bawurra.* (YY) I'm going to skin (that) red kangaroo.

biirra gawugaa (GR) *noun*
    bald head. Based on *biirra-li* (skin) and *gawugaa* (hair).

biirrnga (YR, YY, GR) *noun*
    bony bream *(Nematalosa)*. Fred Reece said 'the bony bream is no good, he's got lots of bones'.

biirruun (YR, YY) *noun*
    swift (a bird). Probably the fork-tailed swift *(Apus pacificus)* or white-throated needletail *(Hirundapus caudacutus)*. Fred Reece said it 'comes before a storm'.

biiwan (YY) *noun*
    orphan (motherless child). Probably from *bii* (chest) and *-wan* (prominent feature).

biiwanbiiwan (YY) *noun, adjective*
    1 black-faced woodswallow *(Artamus cinerus)*.
    2 puffed out.
    3 boastful, bragging. From *bii* (chest) and *-wan* (prominent feature). Also *biyawan*.

biiwanma-li (YY) *verb-transitive*
    puff out chest. According to Ian Sim *biiwanma-li* means 'to inflate or puff out the chest' and possibly also means 'to spread out the arms'.

biiwii (YR, YY) *noun*
    sand goanna *(Varanus gouldii)*.

biiyalaa (YY) *noun*
    1 father.
    2 mother's sister's husband. These men are all of the same social section. This is a rare word, the common word is *bubaa*.

-bil (YR, YY, GR) *suffix*
    covered with, with a lot of. As in Boggabilla, *Bagaay-bil-a* (creeks-having a lot of-at); so, place full of creeks.
    ◆ *Nhulaan-bil ngaama ngaaluurr, waala ngaya bayama-lda-nha.* (YY) That fish is slimey, I can't hold it. ◆ *Dhaymaarr-bil ngay ngaay gi-nyi.* (YR) My mouth got full of dirt (has lots of dirt).
    This suffix is attached to nouns, it can turn a noun into an adjective, e.g. *mirril-bil* (snot-with a lot of) meaning 'snotty', and *gungan-bil* (water-with a lot of) meaning 'wet'. There is some evidence for the variants: *-bilaa*, *-bilay* and *-bilaay*.

bilaan (YY) *noun*
    alternative name. *Garriya* was usually referred to by a *bilaan*; three were recorded: *Dhuyuburrul* (big snake), *Gungandhi* (water meat); and Greg Fields used *Galigurraynaa* or *Galigurraynwaa* (affinity with water, water seeker). The *Garriya* was said to be 'full of water'. When the *Garriya* brothers were slain at *Buman.garriya*, the water gushing out created the Narran Lake. Some of the names recorded for supernatural creatures may be *bilaan*. ◆ *Bilaan nhama Gungandhi.* (YY) The name for that thing (is) *Gungandhi*. One source.

bilaarr (YR, YY, GR) *noun*
    1 spear. ◆ *Bandaarr bilaarr-u nhama ngaya dhu-nhi.* (GR) I speared the kangaroo with a spear.
    2 swamp oak, belah tree *(Casuarina cristata)*. The English verb 'spear' is translated as 'pierce with a spear', *bilaa-yu dhu-rri* in YR and YY.

bilabilaa (YY) *adjective*
    parallel. Probably based on a word *bilaa* (meaning unknown); compare also *bilaarr* (spear).

Bilaga (GR) *placename*
Pilliga. Based on *bilaarr* (swamp oak, belah tree) and *ga* (an abbreviation of *gawugaa* — head); said to mean 'head of swamp oak'. One source.

Bilambulaa (YY) *placename*
waterhole name. One source. A waterhole south-east of Cumborah, mentioned in the Cumborah Knob story. Said to be Plumbolar in English.

bilay (YR, YY, GR) *noun*
red-winged parrot (*Aprosmictus erythropterus*).

bilba (YR, YY) *noun*
bilby (*Macrotis lagotis*). Fred Reece said they were common in the Yuwaalayaay area in the early 1900s. Possible source of English 'bilby'. See also: **dhuluun.gayaa**.

bilga (YY) *adjective*
thin, bony. This is a rare word, the common word is *buyabuya*.

bilgin (YR, YY, GR) *noun*
splinter, piece, fragment. Also *bilginda*.

bilidjuu (YR, YY) *noun*
black-fronted plover (*Charadrius (Elseyornis) melanops*). Also *birridjuul*. Also called sandpiper and black-fronted dotterel; used as a nickname for a kid with skinny legs.

biligiyaan (YR, YY) *noun*
billycan. From English 'billycan'.

biliirr (YR, YY, GR) *noun*
red-tailed black cockatoo (*Calyptorhynchus banksii*). Has a big part in the story of how the animals got fire and the birds got their colours.

biliirrman (YY) *noun*
policeman. From English 'policeman'. See also: **maawulaaldaanga, gandjibal**.

bilum (YR, YY) *noun*
1 black stripe (YR, YY).
2 melon (YR). Ted Fields said it is a little melon (2–3 cm diameter) with a black stripe on it.
One source.

bilumbilum (YR, YY) *noun*
zebra finch (*Taeniopygia bichenovii*). The zebra finch has two black stripes on its cheeks; this word has also been used for the double-barred finch which has two black stripes on its chest.
From *bilum* (black stripe).

bilyan (YR, YY) *noun*
waterhole. This refers to a waterhole in a river.

bina (YR, YY, GR) *noun*
ear. In most Aboriginal societies the ear is seen as the instrument or seat of intelligence and perception. Therefore, there are many words and expressions based on ear: *binaal* (well behaved); *winanga-y* (think, from *bina-nga-y*); and *bina muurr gi-gi* (forget). This is a rare word in YY where the common word is *wudha*. See also: **manga**.

bina bina (GR) *noun*
restricted word. See p 20 for more information.

binadhiwuubiyan (YR, YY) *noun*
legless lizard, slow worm (*Pygopodida*). Arthur Dodd's comments indicate that this may be based on *bina* (ear) and *wuu-gi* (go into).

bina guraarr (GR) *noun*
rabbit. From *bina* (ears) and *guraarr* (long).

bina guwaal (YR) *adjective*
upset, nervous. Also *wudha guwaal*. From *bina* (ears) and *guwaa-li* (talk); compare the English 'hearing voices/things'. One source.

binamayaa (YR, YY) *noun*
large saltbush (*Atriplex nummularia*). Shrub growing to 3m with bluish-grey leaves; seeds are prolific and can be ground into flour and made into damper. Probably from *bina* (ear) because of the leaf shape.

bina muurr (YR, YY, GR) *adjective*
deaf. From *bina* (ear) and *muurr* (full, blocked, blunt). See also: **muga bina, muga wudha, mugu bina**.

binangarrangarra (YY) *noun, adjective*
1 teacher of the law.
2 clever, intelligent.
Based on *bina* (ear) and *ngarrangarra-li* (mind, look after). One source.

binanggal (YY, GR) *noun*
restricted word. See p 20 for more information.

binaal (YR, YY, GR) *adjective*
well behaved, well mannered. ◆ *Binaal gi-nyi.* (YY) (He) got well behaved. Probably based on *bina* (ear).

binaal bunma-li (YR, YY) *verb-transitive*
quieten, soothe, calm, settle down. Also *binaal burranba-li*. From *binaal* (well behaved) and *bunma-li* (make).

binda-y (YR, YY, GR) *verb-intransitive*
hang. For example, a child hanging on the breast, a flying fox roosting, and something, such as fruit or meat, hanging from a tree. ◆ *Binda-y-la-nha dhinggaa.* (YR) The meat is hanging up.

bindama-li (GR) *verb-transitive*
hang up. From *binda-* (hang) and *-ma-li* (suffix that makes a transitive verb). This is a rare word, the common word is *bindaybi-li*.

bindaybi-li (YR, YY, GR) *verb-transitive*
1 hang up (YR, YY, GR). ◆ *Bindaybi-la malawil-a.* (YR) Hang (it) up in the shade.
2 tie up (YR). ◆ *Giirr ngaya-laa maadhaay ngaama bindaybi-l-ngayi-y.* (YR) I'll tie that dog up tomorrow.
From *binda-y* (hang) and *-bi-li* (verb suffix).

bindamula (YR) *noun*
cactus. One source.

bindawu (GR) *noun*
muscle. One source.

bindiyaa (YR, YY, GR) *noun*
1 prickle (YR, YY, GR). Also *bindayaa*. ◆ *Giirr nhama bindayaa dhuma-y nhama ngay dhina-dhi.* (GR) I have already taken the prickle out of my foot.
2 prickly plant (YY). Used for 'roly-poly' or 'tumbleweed'.
3 roly-poly spirit (YY). One source mentions mythological 'roly-poly' men who spear people to death.
Probably means any prickle, and has been borrowed into English with more limited meaning 'bindi-eye'.

bindiyaabiyaay (YY) *adjective*
prickly, thorny. From *bindiyaa* (prickle) and *-biyaay* (with, having).

bin.gal (YR, YY) *noun*
fish fin.

bin.gawin.gal (YR, YY) *noun*
needlewood tree (*Hakea leucoptera, H. tephrosperma*). This shrub is associated with fire and water. The roots are a water source; a water carrier is called *bin.guwi*. In a story, the first fire was hidden in its seed capsules; traces of the fire are a red and white down on the flower and leaf. Nectar can be eaten from the flowers. The form of this word is uncertain, there is some evidence for *binggawinggal*.

bin.guwi (YR, YY, GR) *noun*
coolamon. Any canoe-shaped wooden vessel.

binggi (YY) *noun*
1 small sharp things.
2 needle.
3 nail.
4 pin.
Name for anything small and sharp, including the barbs on a spear. Also occurs in *binggi barra-biyaay* (needle and/with thread).

biraman (GR) *noun*
1 brother-in-law (sister's husband).
2 brother-in-law (wife's brother).
These two relations would be in the same social section, e.g. for a *Marrii* man, they are both *Gambuu*.

biramba (GR) *noun*
plover. Species uncertain. One source.

biri (GR) *noun*
chest.

biridji (GR) *place adverb*
in front. From *biri* (chest) and *-dji* (from/source). May also be used in the form *biri-dja* (chest-at). One source. Form uncertain. The part of speech is also uncertain; it may be a suffixed noun.

biridja (GR) *noun, placename*
1 flea.
2 Breeza. Town, 40 km south of Gunnedah.
One source.

birra (YY) *noun*
axe handle. See also: **Birrangulu**.

birraa[1] (YR, YY) *noun*
1 whitewood tree (*Atalaya hemiglauca*) (YR,

YY). A small tree with smooth pale bark. Ted Fields said it has edible *dhani* (gum) and the leaves can be chewed.
2 Birrah (YY). A station (property) south of Angledool.

birraawiin (YR, YY) *noun*
whitewood flowers. Based on *birraa* (whitewood tree) and *-(b)iyan*. See Learner's Guide.

birraa² (GR) *noun*
grub. Probably the grub found in *birraa* (whitewood tree) roots.

birraala (YY, GR) *noun*
musk duck *(Biziura lobata).*

birralii (YR, YY) *noun*
1 child. ◆ *Birralii-djuul-u nhama giniy gama-y.* (YR) The boy broke the stick.
◆ *Birralii-gal-u nhama maadhaay buma-y.* (YR) The children hit the dog.
2 baby. ◆ *Giirr-nga ngay gulii-yu birralii gaanga-nhi.* (YY) My wife had the baby all right.
Often used to translate 'boy' or 'girl'. Unlike many other nouns it often has the suffix *-gal* (many) attached; *-gal* is very rarely used on other words.

birraliidjuul *noun*
baby. From *birralii* (baby) and *-djuul* (little, one).

birran.gaa (YR) *noun*
stone axe, tomahawk. Also *birringgaa*. Arthur Dodd said that it's 'just like a tomahawk with a handle on it, made of stone'. See also: **dhamiyaa**.

Birrangulu (YR, YY) *noun*
Byame's wife. One of the two wives of *Baayami*, the other being *Ganhanbili*. *Birrangulu* is said to have had a long thin face. In the Guwamu language *Birrangula* is a name of the Creator. From *birra* (axe handle) and *ngulu* (forehead), so 'face like an axe handle'.

birray (YR, YY, GR) *noun*
1 boy (YR, YY, GR).
2 son (YY). Use with this meaning may be a recent development. Often occurs in *birray-djuul* (boy-little, one); meaning 'little boy' or 'boy'. The common meaning today is 'boy' but the word was previously used for 'uninitiated boy'.

birraybirraay (YR, YY, GR) *noun*
1 Orion's belt (stars). A group of stars.
2 boys.
The plurals *birray-galgaa* and *birray-gal* occur once each on the tapes; the plural *birraybirray* formed by reduplication, is rarely used.

birrga (YR, YY) *noun*
bogong moth grub. Arthur Dodd said: '*Birrga* — you dig them out of the ground, I seen people eating them, just pull them out of the hole with a hook or tie wire, kill them and chuck them in the fire, they cook in no time, get them out and down they go.' To locate the grub, the hunter smells the hole to see whether the grub is still in the ground.

birrgabirrga (YR) *noun*
peewee, magpie-lark *(Grallina cyanoleuca).* This is a rare word, the common word is *barriindjiin*. One source.

birribangga (YR, YY, GR) *noun*
little pied cormorant *(Phalacrocorax melanoleucos).* Also called black and white shag; in a story, he painted himself white on the front. Based on *biri* (chest, GR) and *banggabaa* (white).

birridul (YR, YY) *noun*
pistol. From English 'pistol'.

birriyan (YY) *noun*
little plains lizard.

birru (YY) *noun*
clever man's stick. The stick used by *wiringin* (clever men) to project power and 'throw the light'. Said to be 'like a walking stick', it is one of three sticks, the others being the smaller dance stick and the bigger funeral stick. See also: **wii muyaan**.

birrubirruu (YR, YY) *noun*
rainbow bee-eater *(Merops ornatus).* Said to be a 'clever bird', that was once a *wiringin* (clever man). When the birds flocked, it was said that 'the doctors are meeting', as clever men used to meet periodically.
From *birru* (*wiringin*'s stick) because the bird has two long central feathers which

biruu¹

were thought to resemble a clever man's stick. The name is similar to the bird's call. The name may also be related to the GR word *biruu* (hole). The bird nests in a hole in the ground or a bank. A number of bird names make sense in a number of ways, such as, as a story, the features of the bird, and its call.

biruu¹ (GR) *noun*
long way.

biruu² (GR) *noun*
hole. May have the same range of meanings as *biyuu* (YR, YY) (hole, cave, grave).

biruubaraay (GR) *adjective*
hollow. From *biruu* (hole) and *-baraay* (with, having).

biya (YY) *noun*
whistling kite *(Milvus sphenurus)*. One source.

biyaagaarr (YR, YY) *noun*
brown falcon *(Falco berigora)*. Also *biyaagaarrgaarr*. Said to come from the bird's cackling call.

-Biyaay (YR, YY) *suffix*
with, having. Variant forms are *-biyaay*, *-iyaay*. ◆ *Yaama-nda maayama-biyaay?* (YR) Have you got any money? ◆ *Dhaymaarr gungan-biyaay.* (YR) The ground is wet (with water). ◆ *Dhayn yanaa-waa-nha bilaarr-iyaay.* (YR) A man is walking along with spears.
The variant occurs in the language name *Yuwaal-iyaay* (no-having); so 'the language that has *(yu)waal* (for no)'. This suffix is attached to nouns. It has two main functions: to add the idea of 'with, having' to the noun, as in *ngaaluurr-biyaay* (with a fish); or to change it into an adjective, as in *biyuu-biyaay* (hole-having) 'hollow'; *guliirr-iyaay* (spouse having) 'married'; *dhandarr-iyaay* (frost-having) 'grey headed'; and *yuul-iyaay* (vegetable-having) 'full of food'. Yuwaalaraay speakers also sometimes used *-baraay* or *-araay* to express this meaning. See also: **-iyaay**.

biyaduul (YR, YY) *adjective*
alone. Possibly from *biyarr* (one) and *-dhuul* (little, one).

biyaga (YR, YY, GR) *noun*
tobacco. ◆ *Giirr nhama birralii-djuul-u biyaga buubi-lda-nhi, ngaama nguu gagil dhaygal gi-nyi.* (YR) The boy was smoking tobacco, he got a headache.
From English 'tobacco'.

-biyal (YR, GR) *suffix*
only, just. ◆ *Ngaya-biyal.* (YR) It's only me. ◆ *Bulaarr-biyal nhama-nha yanaa-y-la-nha.* (YR) (There were) only two walking about. Has been recorded as *-bil*. Probably related to *biyarr* (one).

biyal (GR) *noun*
knuckle. One source.

-(b)iyan (YR, YY) *suffix*
flower of, fruit of. Also *-iyan*. This suffix is added to various words for trees to indicate the flower or fruit of the tree, e.g. *yarraanbiin* (river gum flowers). The endings which convey the meaning 'flower of' have a number of similar, but slightly different forms; *-(b)iyan* is the hypothesised original form. See Learner's Guide.

biyarr (YR, YY) *adjective*
one. Also *biirr*. The recommended word is *milan* (one).

biyarruu (YR, YY) *noun*
same one. From *biyarr* (one). The suffix *-uu* may mean 'absolutely the very one', so *biyarruu* could be used of a place, time, or person, although we only have evidence for it meaning 'the same place'.

biyarrbirr (YR) *noun*
native banana yam. The tubers on *gaagulu* (native banana vine). One source.

biyay (YR) *exclamation*
enough! One source.

biyuu¹ (YR, YY) *noun*
long way. Also *biyu*. ◆ *Biyuu-gu ngay maadhaay yanaa-nhi.* (YY) My dog has gone a long way (away).

biyuugu yanaa-y (YY) *verb phrase*
avoid. From *biyuu-gu* (long way-movement to) and *yanaa-y* (walk, go).

biyuu² (YR, YY) *noun*
1 hole (YR, YY). ◆ *Ganadhaa nhama biyuu wanda-gu dhaymaa-ya mawu-nhi.* (YY) The white man dug a deep hole in the ground.
2 cave (YR).

3 grave (YR).

biyuubiyaay (YY) *adjective*
hollow. ◆ *Biyuu-biyaay nhama muyaan.* (YY) That's a hollow tree.
From *biyuu* (hole) and *-biyaay* (with, having).

Biyuulbarra (YY) *placename*
Peelborough waterhole. East of Lightning Ridge. Based on *biyuu* (hole) and *-barra* (place of). One source.

biyuurra-li (YR) *verb-transitive*
roll. ◆ *Ngaya-badhaay gi-yaa-nha nginunha biyuurra-li.* (YR) I am going to roll you (in the burrs).

biyuurra-y (YR) *verb-intransitive*
roll (self). ◆ *Ngaama-nga waan wii-dja wana-ngiili-nyi ngiyarrma-nga biyuurra-nhi.* (YR) The crow threw himself on the fire and rolled there.
A change in verb class from *-li* to *-y*. See Learner's Guide.

biyuurragi-y (YR) *verb-intransitive*
roll about/around. ◆ *Bamba ngaama-nga waan gindama-nhi, yalagiirrmawu waama-nha biyuurragi-la-nhi wii-dja.* (YR) The crow laughed so hard, then because of that he was rolling around in the fire. (From a story).
From *biyuurra-* (roll) and *-gi-y* (hypothesised suffix meaning 'around'). See Learner's Guide.

buba (GR) *noun*
biceps. One source.

bubaa (YR, GR) *noun*
father. Probably related to *buwadjarr* (father); the recommended word for 'dad' is *bubaa*. Used in some YR, GR areas.

bubaay (YR) *adjective*
small, little. Also *bubay*. Often occurs as *bubaay-djuul* (small-little, one) with the same meaning.

bubarraa (YR, YY) *noun*
fighting boomerang. In a story, the giant yellow and brown snakes (*babarra*) threw a fighting boomerang which cut off the top of a hill and created a flat ridge (*Babarra*). See also: **babarra**.

bubudhala (YR, YY) *noun*
emu tail. The big bunch of feathers at the back of an emu.

budhagalagala (YY) *noun*
whiskered tern (*Chlidonias hybrida*). Also called little seagull.

budhal (YR, YY) *noun*
toy club (waddy). See also: **garril budhal**.

budhanbaa (YR, YY) *noun*
black duck (*Anas superciliosa*).

budhi (YR, YY, GR) *noun*
1 body hair.
2 pubic hair.

budhu-li (YR, GR) *verb-transitive*
drive. Used of horse and cart. ◆ *Garriya nhama budhu-lda-ya! Giirruu nginunha-laa wanda-gu yanaaynbi-li.* (YR) Don't drive that! The white man will sack you.
This is the only *l* class verb whose stem ends in *u*. It may be an error.

budhun (YY) *noun*
pudding. From English 'pudding'. One source.

budhuulgaa (YR, YY) *noun*
white-faced heron, blue crane (*Egretta novaehollandiae*).

budidaa (YR) *noun*
potato. Also *burridhaa*. From English 'potato'.

budjigarr (YR, YY) *noun*
cat. ◆ *Budjigarr nhama yanaa-waa-nha.* (YY) Cats are walking along.
From English 'pussycat'. As with many introduced animals a number of similar words exist for 'cat'.

budun (YR) *noun*
taboo. Specifically a camp where someone has died. One source.

buganma-li (GR) *verb-transitive*
prepare. One source. Form uncertain.

bugalaa (YR, YY) *noun*
testicles, balls. This is the form of the word now commonly used. See also **buugalaa**.

bugarru (YR, YY) *noun*
tree for storing poison sticks.

Bugayirra (YY) *placename*
Bokhara River.

bugiyaa (YR) *noun*
poison stick, poison bone. One source.

bugu (YR, YY) *noun*
fighting club, big club. Ian Sim said 'a knob-headed club'.

bul (YY) *noun*
saw. This is a rare word, the common word is *baladi*. One source.

-bula (YR, YY) *suffix*
also, too. ◆ *Bayagaa nguungu ngaya wagirrma-lda-nhi, dhuwarr-bula ngaya nguungu wuu-nhi, dhinggaa-bula.* (YY) I used to wash his clothes, I used to give him bread too, meat too. ◆ *Ngulu-gu ngaya bundaa-nhi, dhaymaarr-bil ngay ngaay gi-nyi, mil-bula.* (YY) I fell on my face and got my mouth full of dirt, my eyes too. This suffix is similar to *bulaarr* (two).

bula (GR) *noun*
bullock. From English 'bullock'. One source.

bulaadjal (YY) *adjective*
only two. From *bulaarr* (two).

bulaangaa (YY) *adjective*
pair. Possibly from *bulaarr* (two). One source.

bulaangu (YR, YY) *noun*
twins. Form uncertain, possibly from *bulaarr* (two) and *-nguu* (he/she).

bulaarr (YR, YY, GR) *adjective*
two.

bulaarra (GR) *adverb*
twice. From *bulaarr* (two).

bulaarrbulaarr (YY, GR) *adjective*
four. An older word, from *bulaarr* (two). The recommended word is *buligaa* (four).

bulaarruu maa (YY) *adjective*
ten. An older word, based on *bulaarr* (two) and *maa* (hand). The recommended word is *banay* (ten).

bulaawa (YR, YY) *noun*
flour. From English 'flour'.

bulabul (YY) *noun*
native gooseberry. Probably 'ground cherries' *(Physalis)*, the fruits of some species can be used for jam.

bulamin (GR) *noun*
angophora (apple tree). Probably *Angophora floribunda*; similar to a eucalyptus tree. Form uncertain.

bulanggiin (YR, YY, GR) *noun*
blanket. ◆ *Guwima-li gi-yaa-nha ganugu bulanggiin yaay-a.* (YY) They are going to dry their blankets in the sun. From English 'blanket'. There are a number of versions of this word including: *bulanggi, bulanggiirr* and *bulaanggiin*. This often happens with borrowed words.

bulawaa (YR, YY) *noun*
emu pair. At breeding times emus are often seen in pairs. From *bulaarr* (two).

bulawulaarr (YR) *adjective*
four. An older word, from *bulaarr* (two). The recommended word is *buligaa* (four).

bulaybulay (YR, YY) *noun*
blue bonnet (bird) *(Northiella haematogaster)*.

bulayrr (YR, YY, GR) *adjective*
warm. ◆ *Ngaya bulayrr.* (YY) I am warm.

bulga (YR, YY) *noun*
crucifix frog *(Notaden bennettii)*. Also called holy cross toad or Catholic frog. It has a series of dots in a cross shape on its back.

bulgirran (GR) *noun*
bull. Possibly from English 'bull'. One source.

buli-y (YR, YY) *verb-intransitive*
slip. ◆ *Buli-nyi nginda dhaymaa-ya.* (YY) You slipped on the ground.

buligaa (YR, YY, GR) *adjective*
four. Possibly related to *buligaa* Jack, a man who had lost a finger. This is the recommended word.

bulii (YR, YY, GR) *noun*
flea.

buliirra-li (YR, YY) *verb-intransitive*
breathe. ◆ *Waala ngaya buliirra-lda-nha.* (YY) I can't breathe.

buliirral (YR, YY, GR) *noun*
breath. ◆ *Ngaya buliirral-dhalibaa.* (YY) I've got no breath.

buliirral ganaay (YY) *adjective*
short of breath. From *buliirral* (breath) and *ganaay* (shallow).

buliirral wanda (YR, YY) *noun*
wind gust. Breeze that springs up out of nowhere. From *buliirral* (breath) and *wanda* (ghost), so 'ghost breath'.

bulilbulil (YR, YY) *adjective*
slippery. ◆ *Dhaymaarr nhama bulilbulil gi-nyi.* (YR) The ground is slippery. Related to *buli-y* (slip).

buliyaagu (YR, YY, GR) *time adverb*
morning. ◆ *Warra-y-ngayi-nyi ngaya buliyaagu.* (GR) I got up this morning. Words like 'morning' are rarely used; the meaning is conveyed by using a different verb suffix, such as *-ngayi-y*.

buliyaarr (YR, YY) *noun*
water weed. Possibly 'pondweeds' *(Potamogeton)*. Ian Sim said it is a massive floating waterweed with no flower.

buluba-li (YR, YY) *verb-transitive*
cover. Also *bulumba-li*. ◆ *Milan nhama gawu buluba-y dhinawan-du.* (YY) The emu covered up one egg there.

buluba-y (YR, YY) *verb-intransitive*
cover (self), be covered. ◆ *Giirr ngaya gi-yaa-nha buluba-y.* (YR) I'm going to cover (myself) up.
A change in verb class from *-li* to *-y*. See Learner's Guide.

bulubama-li (YR, YY) *verb-transitive*
cover. ◆ *Minya-dhu-waa nhama bulubama-la dhinggaa, nhuwi nhama-laa gi-gi.* (YY) Cover that meat with something or else it will go bad.
The difference in meaning between *buluba-li* and *bulubama-li* is not understood. Slightly different verbs such as these two probably have differences in meaning that are currently lost.

bululuwi (YR, YY, GR) *time adverb*
evening. Fred Reece said 'it is like afternoon . . . but not dark'.

bulumburr (YR, YY) *noun*
native tomato *(Solanum esuriale)*. Yellow berries eaten raw, cooked or dried.

bulunbulun (YR, YY) *noun*
1 mulga parrot *(Psephotus varius)* (YR, YY). In most historical records *bulunbulun* is defined as 'green parrot' which does not identify the species. Ian Sim identified it as the mulga parrot, and Fred Reece said 'people use *bulunbulun* for the ringneck, but the ringneck's real name is *nhan.garra*'.
2 ringneck parrot (YR, YY). This is a currently used meaning but is not recommended.
3 two stars (YY). Called 'the two sisters'; they lead the Southern Cross in a traditional story.

buluurr (YR, YY, GR) *noun*
tawny frogmouth *(Podargus strigoides)*. An owl-like bird. Arthur Dodd said the bird's call sounded like 'they're all asleep tonight, Jim, they're all asleep tonight, Jim'. Fred Reece said 'the frogmouth sits like a dry spout, *buluurr* is the noise he makes'.

buluuy (YR, YY, GR) *noun, adjective*
1 night. ◆ *Dhama-y yilaa buluuy-a.* (YY) It's going to rain at night.
2 black. ◆ *Buluuy-bala nhama waan.* (YR) The crow is black.
3 dark. ◆ *Ngali buluuy-a yanaa-nhi.* (YY) We two went there in the dark.

Buluuy Nhaaybil (GR) *placename*
Blue Knobby. Volcanic tor near North Star (outside Moree) which has many dark rock faces. Also location near Upper Norton. Based on *buluuy* (black) and, perhaps, *nhaayba* (knife), due to the appearance of the rock faces. The similarity between *buluuy* and English 'blue' has lead to the inaccurate English name.

buma-li (YR, YY, GR) *verb-transitive*
1 hit. ◆ *Giirr ngaya bamba buma-y maadhaay.* (YR) I hit the dog really hard.
2 kill. ◆ *Ngaandu gi-yaa-nha nhama buma-li ngandabaa?* (YR) Who is going to kill this brown snake?
Possibly the original meaning was based on *maa* (hand), but the verb can be used to talk about new situations like 'hit with a car'.

buma-y (YR) *verb-intransitive*
be hit. A change in verb class from *-li* to *-y*. This verb is not fully understood and needs further investigation.

bumala-y (YR, GR) *verb-intransitive*
fight. ◆ *Waal ngali yaluu buma-la-y.* (YR) We won't fight again.

Gamilaraay/Yuwaalaraay/Yuwaalayaay *to* English Dictionary

bumal

This is the reciprocal form of *buma-li* (hit, kill), literally 'hit each other', and is used to mean 'fight'.

Bumaay (GR) *placename*
Boomi. From *buma-y* (hit).

Buman Garriya (YY) *placename*
location. A place on the Narran Lake where *Baayami* the Creator ambushed and killed the *Garriya* brothers, thereby creating the lake. Based on *buma-li* (hit, kill-past) and *garriya* (crocodile).

bumal (YR, YY) *noun*
1 hitting thing. Name for anything that is used for hitting something.
2 hitting stick.
3 hammer. As in *binggi bumal-iyaay* (nails and/with hammer).
Related to *buma-li* (hit, kill).

bumaldaay (YY) *noun*
hit man, thug. This form has been recorded, but is not recommended for use because the way it is used in sentences (i.e. which suffixes it can have) is not understood. Related to *buma-li* (hit, kill).

bumbaali-y (YR) *verb-intransitive*
jump in. Form is uncertain, it occurs only once on the tape sources. See also: **babaaluma-y**.

Bumbira (YY) *noun*
social group. Every type of living thing, every species, every totem, is divided into two types: *Magula* and *Bumbira*. This may be based on a distinction between 'large' and 'small' in all animals. It has been said that *Magula* people are thought of as more important than *Bumbira* people. People inherit this from their mother. See also: **Magula**.

buna (YR) *noun*
fly. Name for any fly. Used in some YR, GR areas. One source.

bunbarr (YR, YY) *noun*
rosewood, bunnary tree *(Alectryon oleifolius,* syn. *Heterodendrum oleifolium)*. This is a small tree with blue-grey to silver-green leaves; also called bullock bush because it has been used for stockfeed. However it can be poisonous to stock and is also called poison tree.

bunbarrayn (YR, YY) *noun*
rosewood fruit.

bunbul (YR, YY) *noun*
meeting place. Also the name of this particular type of meeting which involves men of a certain status discussing 'private business'. It is strictly off limits to everyone else. One source calls it the 'little bora ring'.

bunbun (YR, YY, GR) *noun*
grasshopper. Name for any grasshopper; also a nickname for a very active child. Ted Fields said that 'holy *bunbun*' (an expression of surprise) was brought to Walgett around 50 years ago by Jack Ryan (*buligaa* Jack), a stockman from Cunnamulla, who died in Carinda.

bundaa-gi (YR, YY, GR) *verb-intransitive*
fall. ♦ *Gaayli nhama bundaa-gi.* (GR) The child will fall down.
♦ *Gabugaan ngay bundaa-nhi.* (GR) My hat fell (off).

bundaama-li (YR, YY, GR) *verb-transitive*
1 knock down. ♦ *Maadhaay-u nhama dhiil-u bilaarr bundaama-y.* (YR) The dog knocked the spear over with his tail.
2 push down. ♦ *Yiiliyanbaa-gu bundaama-y buyabuya-dhuul dhaymaa-ya.* (YY) The savage one pushed the thin one on the ground.
From *bundaa-* (fall) and *-ma-li* (suffix that makes a transitive verb).

bundabul (YR) *noun*
banded plover. Possibly banded lapwing plover *(Vanellus tricolor)*.

bundhabundha (YR, YY) *noun*
poison. Fred Reece said it was 'made out of ground up bones from dead bodies, if you had a set on someone you would sneak it into their food'. Possibly related to *bundaa-gi* (fall).

bundi (YR, YY, GR) *noun*
club. Long handled club or waddy with round knob on the end. Used now as a general word for 'club'.

bundul (YR) *noun*
    banana. The origin of this word is not known. One source.
bundurr (YR, YY) *noun*
    1 clever man's bag (YR, YY).
    2 spirit holder (YY). A container, bag, or hole in the ground, in which a *wiringin* imprisons a spirit when he catches it by magic. In this context it also means 'caught' or 'in the bag'.
bunduun (YR, YY) *noun*
    sacred kingfisher *(Todirhampus sancta)*.
bunduurraa (YR, YY) *noun*
    bark canoe.
bungun (YR, YY, GR) *noun*
    1 arm (YR, YY, GR). ◆ *Ngaya nginu-laa bungun gayma-li.* (YR) I'll twist your arm.
    2 wing (YR, YY, GR). ◆ *Bungun nhama dhigaraa-gu.* (GR) That is the wing of a bird. Also refers to the part of the emu wing close to the body. This part was eaten.
    3 branch (GR).
bunibuni (YY) *noun*
    duckweed. A small floating plant, possibly both common duckweed *(Lemna minor)* and small duckweed *(Spirodela pusilla)*; or perhaps a word for any low green plant, as it is in the Guwamu language.
bunma-li (YR, YY, GR) *verb-transitive*
    cause (a change). ◆ *Winambuu-gu nganha garigari bunma-y.* (YR) The little hairy men made me frightened. ◆ *Nguu nhama dhiil ngarribaa bunma-y.* (YR) He cocked his tail up (made it go up).
    This is a rare word, the common word is *burranba-li*.
bununggaa (YY) *noun*
    armband. A string tied around a man's arm, a symbol of some status, perhaps temporary as when involved in a ceremony. Based on *bungun* (arm).
bura (GR) *noun*
    bone.
    burabura (GR) *adjective*
        thin, bony. Reduplication of *bura* (bone).
buri (YR, GR) *noun*
    matches. Used in some YR, GR areas.
buribara (YR) *adjective*
    pregnant. Used in Walgett.

burra (YY) *noun*
    ruby saltbush *(Enchylaena tomentosa)*. Small shrub growing to 50 cm, with hairy silvery stems and narrow pale-green leaves. Flattish, red, berry-like fruits are sweet and succulent and can be eaten. It was also used as a green vegetable on Charles Sturt's expedition; it was found to be good for the prevention of scurvy. One source.

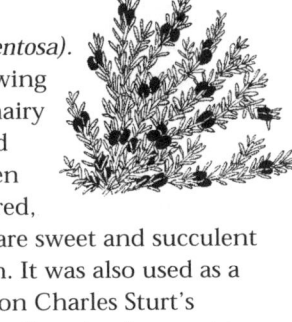

burra-li (YR) *verb-intransitive*
    begin. Ted Fields said it is used in the expression *burra-la yulu-gi* (let the festivities begin).
burraalga (YR, YY, GR) *noun*
    brolga, native companion *(Grus rubicundus)*. There is a brolga and emu story (see Dodd, Williams and Langloh-Parker). Ridley said the word comes from *burrul* (big or high) and *ga*, perhaps a short form of *gawugaa* (head). Possible source of English 'brolga'.
burraanban (YR, YY) *noun*
    frying pan. From English 'frying pan'.
burraay (YR) *noun*
    boy. This word is used in Walgett.
burraaydal (YR, YY) *noun*
    bridle. From English 'bridle'.
burrambuurra (YR, YY) *noun*
    initiation song. Based on *buurra* (initiation ceremony).
burran (YY) *noun*
    dust storm. One source.
burranba-li (YR, YY, GR) *verb-transitive*
    cause (a change). ◆ *Gagil-u ngaama gungan-du ngiyaninya bayn burranba-li.* (YR) This bad water will make us sick. ◆ *Giirr binaal burranba-la.* (YR) Make (the kids) be quiet. ◆ *Burrulaa nhama ngurrala-gu dhina ngiyaningu bayn burranba-y.* (YR) The stones hurt our feet (made our feet sore). Possibly related to *burra-li* (begin).
burranba-y (YR, YY) *verb-intransitive*
    become. ◆ *Giirr nhama gaba burranba-nhi.* (YR) He became well; (the boy) was pleased.

burranbaa

A change in verb class from *-li* to *-y*. See Learner's Guide.

burranbaa (YY) *adjective*
new. ◆ *Ganugu gaarrimay gaa-nhi burranbaa-gu dhaymaarr-gu.* (YY) They took the camp to new ground.
Related to *burranba-li* (cause a change). One source.

burran.gul (YR) *noun*
hollow tree. Also *murunggal*. This is a rare word, the common word is *ngadhul*. One source.

burrarra (YR, YY, GR) *noun*
bulrush (cumbungi) *(Typha sp.)*. Also *burara*. Water plant with rush-like leaves and spear-like flower spikes. The very new white to green shoots are gathered and eaten raw or cooked. It is said that the rhizomes or roots were ground to make a flour for damper, but also that they contain a toxic substance; leaves have been used for weaving mats and baskets, and the seed heads were once sold as pillow stuffing along the Murray.

burray (YR) *noun*
fart. Used in Walgett. One source.

burrbiyaan (YR) *noun*
body, self. Used in some YR, GR areas. One source.

burrgiyan (GR) *noun*
cat. From English 'pussycat'.

burrgulbiyan (YR, YY) *noun*
myrtle, turkey bush *(Myoporum deserti)*. Also called dogwood, an erect shrub with edible yellow fruit.

burrii (GR) *noun*
brigalow wattle *(Acacia harpophylla)*.

Burrigala (GR) *placename*
Brigalow Station; off the Coonabarabran–Coonamble road. Based on *burrii* (brigalow wattle); described as 'place of the *burrii*'. One source.

Burriiwarranha (YR, YY, GR) *placename*
Brewarrina. Probably from *burrii* (brigalow wattle) and *warra-nha* (standing); form is uncertain.

burriimaan (YR) *noun*
swagman. At big stations (e.g. Bangate) there was a camp or hut for the swagman; they would go to the station to work and collect food. One source.

burriin (YR, YY, GR) *noun*
1 shield, broad shield (YR, YY, GR). ◆ *Burriin nhama ngaya gimbi-y bagala-dhi.* (YY) I made this shield from leopardwood.
2 cover (YY). Anything used as a cover.
3 shame (YR). Used in Walgett, an expression used when someone makes a mistake or gets caught out (a Charlie Kennedy word).
Also *buriin*.

burrugarrbuu (YR, YY, GR) *noun*
magpie *(Gymnorhina tibicen)*. Also *gurrabuu*. The guardian of girls at puberty; when a girl first menstruates, women sing 'the magpie song' in a rite for her.

burruguu (YR) *noun*
time of creation, dreamtime. One source.

burrul (YR, YY, GR) *adjective*
big, much. ◆ *Burrul mayrraa dhurra-laa-nha.* (YR) A big wind is coming. ◆ *Giirr ngay ngaama gulii-yu burrul-bidi mangun.gaali bayama-y.* (YR) My husband caught a big goanna.
Often occurs as *burrul-bidi* (big-big) with the same meaning. Evidence for *burrul* in GR is weak.

burrul bina (GR) *adjective*
clever, wise. From *burrul* (big) and *bina* (ear). One source.

burrul burranba-li (YY) *verb-transitive*
raise (bring up). As in 'raise or bring up children'. From *burrul* (big) and *burranba-li* (cause to become). One source.

burrul gi-gi (YY) *verb phrase*
grow. From *burrul* (big) and *gi-gi* (be).

Burrul Gungan (YY) *placename*
Narran Lake. From *burrul* (big) and *gungan* (water). One source.

burrul maadha (YR, YY) *noun*
boss. Originally meant 'property manager', now refers to the boss of anything, e.g. a police chief, or manager of a company. From *burrul* (big) and *maadha* (master).

burrul ngambaa (YY) *noun*
aunt (mother's older sister). From *burrul*

(big) and *ngambaa* (mother).

burrulaa¹ (YR, YY, GR) *adjective*
many, a lot. ◆ *Burrulaa nhama mari ngarri-y-aaba-lda-nha.* (GR) Many people are sitting down.

burrulaabaa (YY) *noun*
leader. A man in a position of authority over others. Based on *burrulaa* (many). One source.

burrulaa garay (GR) *noun*
lot of talk. From *burrulaa* (many, a lot) and *garay* (words).

Burrulaa² (YY) *noun*
Creator (Byame). Also means 'great' or 'mighty', a name commonly used for the Creator in stories. See also: **Baayami**.

burruluu (GR) *noun*
fly.

burrumba-y (YR, YY) *verb-intransitive*
skip. This word was previously recorded as *burrumba-li*, but is more likely to be *burrumba-y*.

burrumbal (YY) *noun*
skipping game. Langloh-Parker described the game: They had a long rope with a man at each end to swing it. The skipper jumps in an ordinary way for a few rounds and then begins variations such as: taking thorns out of his feet, digging as if for larvae of ants, digging yams, grinding grass seed, jumping like a frog, doing a sort of cobbler's dance, striking an attitude as if looking for something in the distance, running out, snatching up a child and skipping with it in his arms, or lying flat down on the ground, rising and letting the rope slip under him.

burrumbi (YR) *noun*
corner. One source.

burrun (YR, YY) *noun*
type of moth. A common large grey species.

burrunda (GR) *noun*
black swan *(Cygnus atratus)*. This is a rare word, the common word is *barayamal*.

burrunggal (YR, YY) *noun*
coolabah tree grub. Possibly the grub of *burrun* (type of moth).

burruwi (YR, YY) *noun*
1 earthquake (YY). Said to be caused by the Creator trying to free his leg from under the earth. If he ever does, the world will end, or go back to the dreamtime, as it was before the great 'turn around'.
2 echo (YR, YY). Also a loud noise 'like thunder' which is a spirit manifestation and may be heard when someone dies.

buru (YR, YY, GR) *noun*
testicles, balls. ◆ *Waal ngaya gi-yaa-nha nginu buru wuu-rri.* (YR) I am not going to give you the testicles. (This is from the *guniibuu* (robin redbreast) story.) An abbreviation of *burugalaa*. Variant *buu* is used in Angledool.

burubiyaay (YY) *noun*
male. From *buru* (balls) and *-biyaay* (having). See also: **mandayaa**.

burugalaa (GR) *noun*
1 ball, ball game. See also: **buugalaa**.
2 testicles, balls.

burudha (GR) *noun*
bull ant. See also: **gabiyan**.

buruma (GR) *noun, placename*
1 dog. ◆ *Nginda dhii wuu-na buruma-gu!* (GR) You give the meat to the dog! Also like English 'chicken'.
2 Boorooma. Location where the Big Warrambool enters the main river on the Walgett–Brewarrina road.

buruwi-y (GR) *verb-intransitive*
rest, spell, ease up.

buu¹ (YR, YY) *noun*
testicles, balls. An abbreviation of *buugalaa*.

buu² (YR, YY) *noun*
1 base. Name for the bottom or base of objects.
2 bucket base.

buu³ (GR) *noun*
leaf.

buuba-li (GR) *verb-transitive*
fart, break wind.

buubi-li (YR, YY, GR) *verb-transitive*
1 blow. ◆ *Buubi-la nhama dhuu!* (YY) Blow that smoke!
2 smoke tobacco. ◆ *Garriya buubi-la!* (YR) Don't smoke (tobacco)!

buubili (GR) *noun*
cigarette. Related to *buubi-li* (blow, smoke tobacco). The recommended word is *mugu*.

buubiyala (YY) *noun*
blueberry (*Myoporum* spp. including *montanum*). Also called western boobialla, and *gii* (bitter) after the bitter taste of the blue/purple fruit; the name applies to more than one species.

buubumurr (GR) *noun*
platypus (*Ornithorhynchus anatinus*). One source.

buubuurrbu (YY) *noun*
pied butcherbird (*Cracticus nigrogularis*). One source.

buubuwin (YY) *noun*
emu decoy. The 'trumpet' or 'cornet' used to entice emus into an ambush. Possibly related to *buubi-li* (blow).

Buudhaa (YR, YY, GR) *noun*
1 women's social section (YR, YY, GR). Sometimes used in Walgett with meaning 'clever woman'. Marries *Marrii*, children are *Yibaay* (male) and *Yibadhaa* (female), brother is *Gambuu*.
2 meeting (YR). Meetings where presents are exchanged. One source for this meaning.
See also: **Gabudhaa, Maadhaa, Yibadhaa**.

buudhan (YY) *noun*
child (last). Last possible child of a woman. One source.

buudhi-rri (YY) *verb-transitive*
brush (with leaves). ◆ *Buudhi-rri ngaya gi-yaa-nha garril-u.* (YY) I'm going to brush him over with leaves now, (knock the ashes off him). One source.

buudhu-rri (YR) *verb-transitive*
put fire out. Arthur Dodd used this verb in relation to the story about why the crow is black. ◆ *Nhama biyuurra-waa-nhi, nguu wii ngaama buudhu-rraa-nhi.* (YR) He was rolling along, he was putting that fire out. Possibly related to *dhu-rri* (pierce). Many verb roots are made up of a number of elements. This verb is probably made up of *dhu-* with either *bu-* (to do with hitting) or *buu-* (to do with breath).

buugalaa (YR, YY) *noun*
1 ball, ball game. Langloh-Parker described the game as follows: all of one *dhii* (totem), both men and women, are partners. The ball, made of sewn-up kangaroo skin, is thrown in the air; whoever catches it goes with their side into the middle, the other circling round. The ball is again thrown in the air, and if one of the circle outside the centre ring catches it, then all his side goes into the middle, the others circling round, and so on. The totem keeping it longest wins.
2 testicles, balls.
Now generally pronounced 'bugala'.

buugiin (YR, YY) *noun*
tree sucker.

buugudaguda (YR, YY, GR) *noun*
spotted nightjar (*Eurostopodus argus*). Also called 'rainbird'. *Buugudaguda* sounds like the bird's call.

buul¹ (YR, YY, GR) *noun*
jealousy. Also occurs in *buul warra-y* (jealousy-stand), meaning 'be jealous, have envy'.

buularaay (GR) *adjective*
jealous. From *buul* (jealousy) and *-araay* (with, having).

buuliyaay (YR, YY) *adjective*
jealous. From *buul* (jealousy) and *-iyaay* (with, having).

buul² (YY) *noun*
tree knot. A knot or lump in wood or a stick.

buulbuul (YY) *adjective*
knotty, lumpy. Of, e.g. a tree or stick.

buuldirran (YR) *noun*
ram. Possibly from English.

buuli-y (YR, YY) *verb-intransitive*
blow. ◆ *Mayrraa nhama dhaay gungan-di buuli-yaa-nha.* (YY) There's a wind blowing this way from the water.

buulii (YR, YY, GR) *noun*
whirlwind. Ted Fields said that the whirlwind can hold a *malimali* (spirit) and may be something to be worried about; sometimes people would break branches and go into the *buulii* to stop it. Related to *buuli-y* (blow).

buumadhayaa (YR) *noun*
fox. Possibly from *buyuma* (dog) and

dhayaa (brother, GR).

buumayamayal (YR, YY) *noun*
fly-catcher lizard. Appears in a story, associated with the original creation of the sky, part of which he owns; children were not to interfere with this lizard, because he could cause the sky to fragment and fall. Possibly *Cryptoblepharus*. Possibly based on *buma-li* (hit, kill).

buunggal (YR, YY, GR) *noun*
native potato. Possibly *Microtis* (ground orchids).

buunhu (YR, YY) *noun*
grass. Name for any grass.

buunhuumayuu (YR, YY) *adjective*
grassy. Based on *buunhu* (grass). The derivation of this word is not fully understood.

buurr (YR, YY, GR) *noun*
1 string, rope (YR, YY, GR). Originally made from kurrajong bark, now general word for any string or rope. String used for making nets etc.
2 fishing line (YR, YY, GR).
3 hair-string belt (GR).

buurra (YR, YY, GR) *noun*
1 initiation ceremony, bora. Fred Reece said that the boras were secret: 'You don't say what you saw there, I never seen it, but I heard them singing the songs before going away, they go away for a month or two, they are supposed to be a man then, they learn the secrets.'
2 bora ground, initiation ground. It is said that it is a large ring, around 25 m in diameter. Possible source of English word 'bora'. Based on *buurr* (belts used in ceremony).

buurrabang (YY) *noun*
bora ground. The 'public' ground at the bora; perhaps the name of the 'big ring' there. The final *-ng* was not used in Yuwaalayaay, this word may be borrowed from Wiradjuri.

buurrabiyaay (YY) *noun*
boy at initiation. From *buurra* (bora) and *-biyaay* (with, having). One source.

buurra-li (YR, YY) *verb-transitive*
pluck, pull out. ◆ *Giirr ngaama gundiirr buurra-lda-nhi.* (YR) (He) is plucking those emu feathers. ◆ *Yiiliyanbaa-gu nhama buurra-y dhaygal buyabuya-dhuul-i dhaygal-i.* (YY) The cranky (woman) pulled the hair out of the bony one's head.
Possibly related to *buurra* (initiation ceremony) in which boys are 'plucked' or taken from their mothers.

buurraan (YR, YY, GR) *noun*
vein.

buurrbaa (GR) *noun*
fully initiated man. Probably based on *buurr* (string, rope) and *-baa* (place of, time of). This was an informal name, there were also a series of 'status names' given at each stage of initiation. These are not known. One source.

buurrii (GR) *noun*
sister. Austin notes that adult males must avoid their elder sisters, and not talk to them. It is uncertain whether this word was used for an older or younger sister. The recommended word is *baawaa* (sister).

buurrma-li (YR, YY) *verb-transitive*
pull. A rare verb, probably related to *buurra-li* (pluck, pull out).

buurrngan (YR, YY) *noun*
meat ant. They are important in the story about the *bigibila* getting its quills.

buuwan (YY) *noun*
black paint. One source.

buuwarran (YY) *noun*
pipe. As in a 'water' or 'gas' pipe.

buuway (YR, YY) *noun*
grey teal duck *(Anas gibberifons)*.

buuwayamba (YY) *noun*
bough shed, shade house. Ian Sim said this is a borrowed word in common use.

buuwi-y (YR, YY) *verb-intransitive*
rest, spell, ease up. ◆ *Buuwi-y ngaya gi-yaa-nha.* (YY) I am going to have a spell.

buuwirr (GR) *noun*
smallpox. One source. Form uncertain.

buuyan (YR) *noun*
heat.

buuyawiya-li (YY) *verb-transitive*
tell. ◆ *Nginda buuyawiya-la barraay wana gimbi-li.* (YY) You tell (him) to do it quickly!
This is a rare word, the common word is

dhubaanma-li. One source. See also: **buyawila-li**.

buuybuuy (GR) *noun*
pennyroyal, river mint *(Mentha satureiodes)*. The leaves, when dried and boiled, make a kind of tea.

buwaarr (YR) *noun*
board. From English 'board'. One source.

buwabiila (YR) *time adverb*
afterwards. One source.

buwabil (YR, YY) *noun*
possessions. Was used of a swag or belongings.

buwabildhalibaa (YR, YY) *adjective*
poor. From *buwabil* (possessions) and *-dhalibaa* (without).

buwabuwa (YY) *adjective*
loose, rattling. Also *buwanbuwan*. Used, e.g. of a loose fence post. One source.

buwadjarr (YR, YY, GR) *noun*
father. According to Langloh-Parker, women and uninitiated men were not allowed to use the word *Baayami* to talk about the Creator, instead they used *Buwadjarr* to talk about the Creator Spirit. Sometimes pronounced 'boy-jarr'; *bubaa* (dad) is a less formal term.

buwama-li (YR, YY) *verb-transitive*
shake down. As in 'rattle or shake down fruit from a tree'. ◆ *Ngaandu ngay gawu buwama-y?* (YR) Who shook my eggs (out of the nest)?
One source. See also: **dhirranba-li**.

buwarr (YR) *noun*
sacred things.

buwarrgaa (YR, YY) *noun*
dead person's things.

buwawa-li (YY) *verb-transitive*
attack. ◆ *Buwawa-li gi-yaa-nha ngaya nginunha.* (YY) I am going to attack you. One source.

buwi-y (YR, GR) *verb-transitive, intransitive*
smell. ◆ *Giirr ngaama nguu dhinggaa buwi-nyi.* (YR) He smelt the meat. ◆ *Giirruu ngaama gaba buwi-y-la-nhi dhinggaa.* (YR) That meat smelt good.

buya (YR, YY) *noun*
bone.

buyabuya (YR, YY) *adjective*
thin, bony. *Buri-buri* is sometimes used in Walgett. See also: **bilga**.

buyaduul (YR, YY) *adjective*
short. Possibly from *buya* (bones) and *-duul* (little, one).

buyal (GR) *noun*
mother-in-law (wife's mother). An avoided relation. Reay (1945, p 310) said 'until about 1895 a man wishing to speak to his mother-in-law could go part of the way to her camp and then turn back. He could then address her by shouting in the direction in which he was facing, and had to speak loudly in order that all his wife's relatives could hear what he was saying'. See also: **garrimaay**.

buyawila-li (YR) *verb-transitive*
make (force). Also *buyawira-li*. ◆ *Nhama ngambaa-gu buyawila-y nhama gungan ngawu-gi-gu.* (YR) The mother made (him) drink the water.
One source. The form of this verb is uncertain.

buyu (YR, YY, GR) *noun*
lower leg, calf of leg, shin. Commonly used now for the whole leg.

buyu wayawaya (YY) *adjective*
bandy legged. From *buyu* (leg) and *wayawaya* (bent, crooked).

buyudhurrungiili (YR, YY) *noun*
white-faced heron, blue crane *(Egretta novaehollandiae)*. Probably based on *buyu* (legs) and *dhurrun* (hair), so 'little hairy legs'. From a story about a woman with very hairy legs.

buyuga (YR, YY) *noun*
bull ant *(Myrmecia)*.

buyuma (YR) *noun*
dog. ◆ *Buyuma-gu nhama nginunha yii-y.* (YR) That dog bit you.
See also: **mirri, maadhaay**.

buyumadhuul (YR) *noun*
glutton. From *buyuma* (dog) and *-dhuul* (one), so 'greedy like a dog'.

buyuwaalwaal (YY) *noun*
black-winged stilt *(Himantopus himantopus)*. Said to be 'all leg and bark' due to its long legs and 'yelping' call. From *buyu* (leg) and *waalwaal* (bark).

Dd

-dha-y¹ (YR, YY, GR) *suffix*
eating. Added to the main verb to indicate that the action of the main verb is associated with eating. e.g. *buma-dha-y* (hit-eating-past) means 'hit after eating'. This is a recently defined GY suffix and needs further work.

-dha-y² (YR, YY, GR) *suffix*
each other (reciprocal suffix for *-rri* class verbs).

-dha-y³ (YR, YY, GR) *suffix*
regular progressive suffix for *-rri* class verbs.

dha-li (YR, YY, GR) *verb-transitive*
eat. ◆ *Nhama garaarr dhimba-gu dha-lda-nha.* (GR) The sheep is eating the grass. ◆ *Yaama nginda burrul dha-y?* (GR) Did you eat enough?

dhaa-rri (GR) *verb-transitive*
have sex, make love.

dhaadal (YR, YY) *noun*
saddle. From English 'saddle'.

dhaadhaa (YR, YY) *noun*
1 grandfather (mother's father).
2 grandson (daughter's son).
Commonly used today as 'grandfather', this word illustrates the different way Aboriginal people saw relationships, grandfather and grandson would be the same class/social section. A *Marrii* man would have a *Gambuu* as mother's father and as daughter's son.
See also: **dhilaagaa**.

dhaadharr (YR, YY, GR) *noun*
1 bark hut (YR, YY, GR). Also a slab of bark.
2 tin canoe (YR). Used in Walgett and Brewarrina. One source for this meaning.

dhaadhiirr (YR, YY, GR) *noun*
red-backed kingfisher (*Todirhamphus pyrrhopygia*). At Goodooga, was the name of the red backed kingfisher; possibly the sacred kingfisher elsewhere.

dhaal (YR, YY, GR) *noun*
1 cheek.
2 jaw, jawbone. Also *badhal*.

dhaala-gi (YR, YY) *verb-intransitive*
feel sick, be sick. ◆ *Dhaala-gi ngaya gi-yaa-nha.* (YY) I'm going to be sick. Previously listed as *dhaalu-gi*.

dhaalan (YY) *noun*
1 pronunciation, accent. ◆ *Gaay gagil dhaalan.* (YY) Badly pronounced talk.
2 tune, intonation.
Probably based on *dhalay* tongue. One source. Also *dhaalanaay*.

dhaaliyaay (YR, YY) *noun*
fish net. Fred Reece said that it was made from kurrajong bark, and some, which were not as good, were made from 'straw'. Possibly from *dhaal* (jaw bone) and *-iyaay* (with, having), from the shape of the net.

dhaamba (YR, YY) *noun*
damper. From English 'damper'.

-DHaan (YR, YY, GR) *suffix*
good at. Also *-daan*, *-djaan*. Occurs in *dhi-dhaan* (meat-good at) meaning 'good hunter'.

dhaan (YR, YY) *place adverb*
sideways, to the side. ◆ *Dhaan bundaa-gi gi-yaa-nha.* (YY) It's going to fall sideways.

dhaandhaan (YY) *adjective*
staggering. One source.

dhaandiyaay (YR, YY) *adjective*
leaning. Used to describe, e.g. a leaning tree. From *dhaan* (sideways, to the side) and *-iyaay* (with, having). One source.

dhaarri-y (YR) *verb-intransitive*
disappear. One source.

dhaarrin.gaarrin (YR, YY) *noun*
nankeen night heron (*Nycticorax caledonicus*). This word has less evidence, the recommended word is *dharrun*.

dhaay (YR, YY, GR) *place adverb*
this way, to here. Towards speaker.
◆ *Dhaay yana-ya!* (GR) Come here! ◆ *Dhaay gaa-nga nhama bandaarr!* (GR) Bring that kangaroo here! ◆ *Minyaaya-nda dhaay yanaa-waa-nhi?* (YR) Where were you coming from?
Often occurs in a two-word phrase where the first word is a place word e.g. *ngaarrima dhaay* 'there to here' — (coming) here from there.

Dhaay Galiyawaay (YY) *verb phrase*
name (climbing this way). Mrs Ginny Rose was born at Nee Nee, Queensland, in 1880. Her Yuwaalayaay name, *Dhaay galiyawaay*, refers to her birth during the floods of that time, when the water level was rising. From *dhaay* (this way) and *galiya-waa-y* (climbing).

dhabi-y (YR, YY, GR) *verb-intransitive*
1 be quiet. Fred Reece said: 'If I was sneaking along (hunting) and you were a kid following me, I'd say "*Dhabi-ya!*", because the emu might hear you.'
◆ *Dhabi-ya nginda!* (YY) You be quiet!
2 be still. ◆ *Waal ngaama-nha dhabi-y-la-nha.* (YR) It won't keep still.
Also *dhabii-y*.

dhabima-li (YR, YY, GR) *verb-transitive*
leave alone. ◆ *Dhabima-la nganha!* (YY) Leave me alone!
From *dhabi-* (be quiet, be still) and *-ma-li* (suffix that makes a transitive verb).

dhabilga (GR) *noun*
belt. One source. Form uncertain. Ridley said it was worn with pendants around the waist.

dhabirra-y (YY) *verb-intransitive*
roll down a bank. One source.

dhabiyaan (YR, YY, GR) *adjective*
quiet. Based on *dhabi-y* (be quiet).

dhadha-li (YR, YY, GR) *verb-transitive*
taste. ◆ *Dhadha-la nhama dhinggaa!* (YY) Taste that meat!

dhadha-y (YR, YY) *verb-intransitive*
taste. ◆ *Giirruu nhama dhinggaa gaba dhadha-y-la-nhi.* (YR) That meat tasted good. A change in verb class from *-li* to *-y*. See Learner's Guide.

dhadhaal (YR) *adjective*
grey. Form uncertain.

dhadhalurraa (YR, YY) *noun*
grey-crowned babbler (*Pomatostomus temporalis*). Also called 'pine babbler'.

dhadhin¹ (YY) *noun*
shade, shadow. Of a tree or other non-human things. See also: *malawil*.

dhadhin² (YR) *place adverb*
south.

dhaga (YR) *noun*
mess, rubbish. Also *dhagaarr*. One source. Used in some YR, GR areas.

dhagaan (YR, YY, GR) *noun*
1 brother (YR, YY, GR). Some sources say 'older brother'. This word is found referring to other relationships where the two people are of the same social section, such as a woman's daughter's daughter, or a woman's sister's daughter's daughter (e.g for a *Buudhaa*, both these are also *Buudhaa*).
2 cousin (YY).
See also *galumaay* (younger brother).

dhagaay (YR, YY, GR) *noun*
golden perch, yellowbelly (*Plectroplites ambiguus*).

dhagadhaal (YR) *noun*
shovel. Possibly from English 'shovel'. One source.

dhagin (YR, YY) *noun*
socks. From English 'stocking'.

dhaguway (YR, YY) *noun*
noisy friar bird (*Philemon corniculatus*). Also called 'leather head'.

dhal (GR) *noun*
salt. Also *dhalbil*. From English 'salt'.

dhala (YR, YY) *noun*
eye dirt (sleep).

dhalaa (GR) *question word*
where? ◆ *Dhalaa ngay yuundu?* (GR) Where is my axe? ◆ *Dhalaa-nda yana-waa-nha?* (GR) Where are you going? ◆ *Dhalaa gi-gi?* (GR) Where will (you) be?
Dhalaanda is a short way of saying *Dhalaa nginda?* (Where are you?).

dhalagal (GR) *noun*
bearded dragon, frilled lizard (*Amphibolurus barbatus*).

dhalan (GR) *noun*
grasstree (*Xanthorrhoea australis*). The flower nectar, shoots and base of leaves can be eaten; the tall straight stems of the flower spikes can make light spear shafts.

dhalandjaa (YY) *noun*
fuchsia. Fred Reece said they also call it 'honeysuckle' and used to suck the nectar out of the flowers; it is dangerous to sheep. Possibly *Eremophila maculata*.

dhalay (YR, YY, GR) *noun, exclamation*
1 tongue (YR, YY, GR).
2 finished! (YR). According to Ted Fields

this was said when you've finished eating. One source.
3 cheeky! (YR). Used with this meaning in Lightning Ridge.

dhalaybaa (YR, YY) *adjective*
sharp. Refers to things like spears and claws. ◆ *Dhalaybaa nhama wiyayl.* (YY) The quills are sharp.
Probably based on *dhalay* (tongue) and *-baa* (place of, time of).

dhalaybidi (YR) *adjective*
talkative. ◆ *Garriya bamba gaay guwaa-lda-ya, giirruu nginda dhalay-bidi, bamba dhugay gaay guwaa-lda-nha.* (YR) Stop talking, you're talkative, you're always talking.
From *dhalay* (tongue) and *-bidi* (big).

dhalaydhalibaa (YR, YY) *adjective*
dumb (speechless). Also *dhalaydjalibaa*.
From *dhalay* (tongue) and *-dhalibaa* (without).

dhalayndjaa (YR) *noun*
native carrot. Ian Sim said it has a pink flower, the red taproot was cooked and eaten; probably a species of geranium. Possibly based on *dhalay* (tongue).

dhalbin (YR) *noun*
medicine. Used for Bex and Aspro, and perhaps any medicine. Possibly based on *dha-li* (eat) or English 'tablet'. One source.

-dhalibaa (YR, YY, GR) *suffix*
without, lacking. ◆ *Gundaa-dhalibaa nhama gunagala.* (YY) The sky (is) without clouds. ◆ *Buunhu-dhalibaa dhaymaarr.* (YR) The ground (is) without grass.
This suffix is attached to nouns. Also occurs in the placename *Wii-dhalibaa* (fire/firewood-without); *buwabil-dhalibaa* (possessions-without) meaning 'poor'; *giyal-dhalibaa* (fear-without) meaning 'shameless'; and *dhalay-dhalibaa* (tongue-without) meaning 'dumb'. Possibly also a word, e.g. Thalaba (location 30 km east of Walgett) and Ridley recorded it as a word meaning 'destitute'. Ted Fields said it was a separate word e.g. *wii dhalibaa* (dead fire). See Learner's Guide.

dhaliman (YR) *noun*
Chinese man. Used in some YR, GR areas. One source. See also: **mil binggarr**.

dhaluraa (YR, YY) *noun*
white-browed woodswallow (*Artamus superciliosus*). Also called 'blue martin'. Said to include the masked woodswallow, (*A. personatus*) which flocks with it. Langloh-Parker calls them 'tree manna-bringing birds'.

dhama-li (YR, YY, GR) *verb-transitive*
feel, touch. ◆ *Giirr ngaya nhama dhama-laa-nha galiya-waa-ndaay nganundi buyu-ga barranbarraan.* (YR) I can feel the centipede which is climbing my leg.

dhama-y (YR, YY) *verb-transitive*
rain. ◆ *Giirruu dhama-waa-nha yalagiyu.* (YR) It's raining right now.
The verb 'rain' in the Wangaaybuwan language is transitive. In the absence of information for YR and YY, *dhama-y* is listed as transitive. See also: **yuuyuu bundaa-gi**.

dhamarr (YR, YY, GR) *noun*
bronzewing pigeon (*Phalps chalcoptera*).

dhambi (YR) *adjective*
short. Occurs only once on the tapes.

dhambidjuul (YR) *adjective*
short. From *dhambi* (short) and *-djuul* (little, one).

dhamiyaa (YR, YY) *noun*
tomahawk. Probably from English 'tomahawk'. See also: **giirrgal**.

dhamu (YR, YY) *noun*
pigweed (*Portulaca oleracea*). Succulent ground cover with small yellow flowers and small capsules containing many small black seeds. Seeds can be ground into a paste and cooked like a damper. Leaves, stems and roots can be eaten; contains valuable amounts of protein, water, fibre and minerals.

dhanbadhanba (YY) *noun*
1 mud hornet. Possibly also an unidentified bird (a swallow or martin) that builds a mud nest.
From the Guwamu word *dhanba* (mud).

dhandarr (YR, YY, GR) *noun*
1 frost.
2 ice.

dhandarraa (YR, YY, GR) *noun*
winter. From *dhandarr* (frost, ice) and *-aa* (place of, time of). Possibly also a

placename, Dandara, west of Tamworth.

dhandarriyaay (YR, YY) *adjective*
grey haired. From *dhandarr* (frost, ice) and *-iyaay* (with, having).

dhanduwi-y (YR, YY) *verb-intransitive*
1 sleep (YR, YY). ◆ *Dhanduwi-nyi nhama dhaymaa-ya.* (YR) (He) slept on the ground.
2 lie (down) (YR, YY). ◆ *Giirr ngaya gi-yaa-nha dhanduwi-y.* (YR) I'm going to lie down.
3 camp, stop, stay (YR, YY). ◆ *Ngiyarrma ngaya gi-yaa-nha dhanduwi-y-la-y.* (YR) I'm going to camp there.
4 live (YR). ◆ *Minyaaya ngama nginu ngambaa-dhi dhanduwi-y-la-nhi?* (YR) Where did your mother live?
See also: *yuwarra-y*.

dhanduwiyma-li (YR) *verb-transitive*
put someone to bed. ◆ *Giirruu yinarr-duul-u nhama birralii wagirrbama-lda-nhi, waama-nga dhanduwi-y-ma-y.* (YR) The woman washed the baby then put it to sleep.
From *dhanduwi-y* (sleep) and *-ma-li* (suffix that makes a transitive verb).

dhan.gaay (YR, YY) *noun*
puddle. Rainwater lying on the ground.

dhan.galaadhil (GR) *noun*
grey shrike-thrush (*Colluricincla harmonica*). Also known as the messenger or mailman bird.

dhan.galan.gaa (YR) *adjective*
covered, disguised. For example, covered in bushes as when disguised for hunting emus. One source. Form uncertain.

dhan.gal (YR, YY) *noun*
shelly log. A log that is disintegrating or rotting, and leaving concentric 'shells'.

dhan.gayan.gan (YR, YY) *noun*
ironwood (*Acacia excelsa*). Small tree with drooping leaves and hard wood.

dhan.gurr (YR, YY, GR) *adjective*
lame, crippled. Used of legs or arms.

dhan.gurrama-y (YR) *verb-intransitive*
dance (make a corroboree). Langloh-Parker said of corroborees that 'women form the orchestra, the men are the dancers, as a rule, though women do on occasions take part too. [There are two dances . . .] one is a sort of in and out movement of the knees, while keeping the feet close together. Another which they call 'shivering of the chest', a sort of drawing in and out of their breath, causing a vibratory motion'. Arthur Dodd translated this verb as 'shake a leg'.
◆ *Gaba nhama ganunga dhan.gurrama-y-la-nha.* (YR) They (are) all dancing well.

dhanga (YR, YY, GR) *noun*
heel.

dhangga-li (YR) *verb-transitive*
skip. For example, to skip a rock or a mussel shell across water. Related to *dhangga-y* (float).

dhangga-y (YR, YY) *verb-intransitive*
1 float (self) (YR). ◆ *Giirr ngiyama gungan-da dhangga-waa-nhi.* (YR) He was floating on the water.
2 swim on surface (YY).
Also *dhan.ga-y*. A change in verb class from *-li* to *-y*. See Learner's Guide. See also: *banggadha-y*.

dhanggalma-li (YR) *verb-transitive*
float. ◆ *Giirr ngaya ngiyarrma gungan-da dhanggalma-y ngay ganuu.* (YR) I floated my canoe in the water.
From *dhangga-* (float) and *-ma-li* (suffix that makes a transitive verb). One source.

dhanggaal (YR, YY) *noun*
1 small waterhole. Occurs in the placenames Dungle and Dungle Ridge, between Collarenebri and Angledool.
2 lagoon.

dhanggal (YR, YY, GR) *noun*
large mussel.

Dhanggaliirr (YR) *placename*
Dungalear. A large property between Walgett and Lightning Ridge that was previously located on the river. Possibly based on *dhanggal* (mussel), thought to mean 'many mussels'.

Dhanggalamandjiirr (YY) *placename*
location. Mentioned in a story about Lightning Ridge. This place is in the dry country between Cumborah and the Barwon River and is therefore unlikely to be related to *dhanggal* (large mussel).

dhanggaluwi (YR) *noun*
water weed. A red floating weed, on the Narran and Warrego rivers. Possibly *Azolla filiculoides*.

dhanggi-li (GR) *verb-intransitive*
lie, tell a lie. Previously written as 'dhangi-li'. One source.

dhanggiwa-li (YY) *verb-transitive*
deceive, trick. Related to *dhanggi-li* (lie, tell a lie). One source.

dhanggiway (YR) *noun*
trick (sleight of hand). Possibly related to *dhanggiwa-li* (deceive, trick). One source.

dhanggima-li (YY) *verb-transitive*
soak. ◆ *Dhanggima-li nhama gi-yaa-nha bayagaa yina-yu.* (YY) The woman is going to soak the clothes.

dhani (YR, YY) *noun*
1 tree gum (YR, YY). Gum is eaten, used to seal things, and used in ceremonies. The gum from wattle trees can be eaten straight from the tree in balls like toffee, or melted in warm water to make a jelly. It can be soaked in water with something sweet like honey, manna or flower nectar.
2 glue (YR).

dhanibanban (YY) *noun*
dollar bird *(Eurystomus orientalis)*. Greg Fields said the name means 'the eater of gum' *(dhani)*. The red beak is said to be coloured from eating tree gum.

dhaniyaa (YR, YY) *noun*
silver wattle *(Acacia decora)*. Also called western golden wattle, this medium-sized tree has powder on the leaves and small branches giving it a silvery look; it has pale lemon flowers. The name also refers to the edible gum *(dhani)*.

dhanmurr (YR, YY) *noun*
burial ground, cemetery.

dharaa (YR) *noun*
crowd, big mob. One source.

dharayan (GR) *noun*
large hailstone.

dhariil (GR) *noun*
reed. Possibly common reed *(Phragmites australis)*. May have been used for making bags or baskets.

Dhariilaraay (GR) *placename*
Tarilarai. From *dhariil* (reeds) and *-araay* (with, having). Also Tareelaroi, east of Moree.

Dhariilduul (GR) *placename*
Drilldool. From *dhariil* (reed) and *-duul* (little, one).

dharra (YR, YY, GR) *noun*
1 thigh, leg (YR, YY, GR).
2 creek (GR).
3 tree branch (GR).
It is common to extend the words for body parts to geographical features, so *dharra* can be confidently used to mean 'creek' and 'branch' in all three languages.

dharrabilay (YY) *noun*
long-legged insect. Insect that creeps around at night. Also a general name for anything with especially long legs; and a nickname for a long-legged person. Based on *dharra* (thigh, leg) and *-bil* (having a lot of).

Dharramalan (GR) *noun*
spirit. Described by Greenway as the mediator between man and Byamee. Also called 'the voice of Byamee at the bora'. Based on *dharra* (thigh, leg) and *maal* (one), as the spirit had only one leg.

dharramudhu (YY) *noun*
restricted word. See p 20 for more information.

Dharrawaawul (YR, YY) *placename*
Terewah. Ted Fields said that this was a common meeting place. From *dharra* (leg, thigh) and *waawul* (narrow), so named because it was on a branch of the Narran Lake, not the main body of water. May be the origin of *Dharriwaa* now used as a name for Narran Lake.

dharraa[1] (YY, GR) *noun*
flaking bark. Possibly related to *dhaadharr* (bark hut).

dharraabiin (YY) *noun*
manna (on bark). This word was given as referring to the manna found on bark. Manna occurs as small, round, white objects on bark and leaves. It is a sugary substance that is made by insects, and can be eaten raw or mixed with wattle gum and dissolved in water. Manna also occurs as a sugary substance that runs down and crystallises, e.g on the sugarwood bush. Based on *dharraa* (tree bark) and *-(b)iyan*. See Learner's Guide.

dharraa[2] (YR, YY, GR) *adjective*
drunk.

dharraadhaandhaan (YY) *adjective*
staggering drunk. From *dharraa* (drunk) and *dhaan* (sideways, to the side). One source. See also: **dhaandiyaay**.

dharraan.gilaay (YR, YY, GR) *adjective*
drunk. Possibly from English 'drunk'.

dharraawaa (YY) *noun*
bigamist. A person who has 'married' when not free to do so under the law. Possibly from *dhaa-rri* (have sex, GR) and *-awaa* (habitual).

dharragarra (YR) *noun*
platypus *(Ornithorhynchus anatinus)*. May be a borrowed word since platypus is unknown in the area. One source.

dharran¹ (YR, YY) *noun*
forked stick. Used to hold tents up or generally as a prop.

dharran² (GR) *noun*
type of frog. One source.

dharrarr (GR) *noun*
rib.

dharrawu-li (YR, GR) *verb-intransitive*
come back, return. ◆ *Dhaay dharrawu-la!* (GR) Come back this way!
See also: **dhurraluwi-y**.

dharrawuluwi-y (YR, YY) *verb-intransitive*
come back, go back, return.
◆ *Dhuwinba-la nhama dhamiyaa, yilaa ngaya-laa dharrawu-l-uwi-y.* (YR) You plant (hide) that tomahawk, directly I'll be coming back.
From *dharrawu-li* and *-uwi-y* (suffix that means 'back').

dharrawurra (YR, YY, GR) *noun*
trousers. Also *dharrawidil*. Possibly from English 'trousers' or *dharra* (leg, thigh).

dharrday (YY) *noun*
native mandarine *(Capparis loranthifolia)*. Also called narrow-leaf bumble. Has edible, smooth-skinned fruit. Similar to *bambul* (native orange tree) but smaller and more spiny. Thought of as a woman's tree. The form is uncertain (because of the unusual '*rrd*' combination).

Dharrgabala (YR) *placename*
location. A place where people with *dharrgadharrga* (venereal disease) went — near Warrengulla on Coocoran Lake. There is high ground in the middle of the lake which is thought to be a bora ground.

dharrgadharrga (YR) *noun*
venereal disease. It is thought that one cure is to warm up *badha* leaves, chew and swallow them. The urine becomes green as a result. This word is used in some YR, GR areas.

dharri (GR) *noun*
bearded dragon, frilled lizard *(Amphibolurus barbatus)*.

dharrii (YY) *noun*
seed cake. Made out of *dhunbarr* (grass seed). One source.

dharringarra (YR, YY) *noun*
thunder cloud.

dharriwa (YR) *noun*
lemonwood. One source.

Dharriwaa (YR) *placename*
Narran Lake. One source.

dharrun (YR, YY, GR) *noun*
nankeen night heron *(Nycticorax caledonicus)*. Thought of as a bad character, to be avoided. When this bird flocks, it is said to be a sign of bad weather, and trouble brewing.

dharruwii (YR, YY) *noun*
grey shrike-thrush *(Colluricincla harmonica)*. Also called postman bird; it was said to carry bad news, e.g. of death. Langloh-Parker gives this as the name of a bird whose description fits the blue-faced honeyeater, and she says 'in it is embodied some dead woman's spirit'.

dhawaarrii (YY) *noun*
blue crowfoot *(Erodium crinitum)*. Fred Reece said that crowfoot grows on the black ground, having big, snappy stalks, and people used to eat it like lettuce or celery.

dhawadha (YR, YY, GR) *adjective*
new word. See p 160 for more information.

dhawudjarrdalmu (GR) *noun*
magpie goose *(Anseranas semipalmata)*. One source. Form uncertain.

dhawuma-li (YR, YY, GR) *verb-transitive*
cook in a hole (roast). A fire is lit in a hole or hollow and after it has burned down, food is placed in the ashes, then covered over with dirt to roast. Fred Reece said that this word refers to the act of covering up with dirt: 'If I'm telling you to cook him, you put him in the hole and I tell you *dhawuma-la-nga* when it comes to covering him up.' ◆ *Dhawuma-li ngaya gi-yaa-nha-nha girran-da.* (YY) I'm going to cook, roast (him) in the ashes.
From *dhawun* (earth, ground, dirt) and *-ma-li* (suffix that makes a transitive verb). See also: **yilama-li**.

dhawun (GR) *noun*
1 earth, ground, dirt.
dhawunbaraay (GR) *adjective*
dirty. From *dhawun* (dirt) and *-baraay* (with, having).
dhawunma (GR) *noun*
burial ground, cemetery. Based on *dhawun* (ground, earth).

dhawurraa (YR) *noun*
white ochre. Used for body painting.

dhawurran (YR, YY) *noun*
older sister. The recommended word is *baawaa* (sister).

dhaya-li (YR, YY, GR) *verb-transitive*
1 ask (YR, YY, GR).
2 beg (GR).

dhayaamba-li (YR, YY) *verb-transitive*
whisper. ◆ *Miimii, bina-ga nganunda ngaama dhayaamba-la!* (YR) Miimii, whisper to me, in (my) ear!
The person being whispered to is marked by the locative (to/at/on) case. See also: **maaya-li**.

dhayaaminyaa (YY) *noun*
Children's python *(Liasis childreni)*. One common name is still 'Children's python', but its scientific name is now Stimson's python *(Antaresia Stimsoni)*.

dhayaanduul (YR) *noun*
teacher. One source. See also: **dhiirral**.

dhayaanmaa (YR) *noun*
Sunday school. One source.

dhayaarr (YR) *noun*
bark sheet. One source.

dhaya (YR, YY, GR) *noun*
older brother. A variety of definitions are given including 'eldest brother' and 'half-brother'; also occurs in *dhaya-dhi* (my elder brother). This is a rare word, the common word is *dhagaan*.

dhayan (YR, YY) *noun*
large hailstone.

dhayarr (YY) *noun*
jew lizard.

dhaygal (YR, YY, GR) *noun*
1 head (YR, YY). ◆ *Ngay dhaygal baarra-y-nhi.* (YR) My head split (open).
2 head hair (YR, YY, GR). ◆ *Dhaygal dhurra-laa-nha.* (YR) (Your) hair is growing.

dhaygalbaarrayn (YR, YY) *noun*
Darling lily *(Crinum flaccidum)*. Has large white trumpet-shaped flowers. Arthur Dodd said 'it has a big potato underneath — can't eat them — *dhaygalbaarrayn, dhaygal* means your head, and if you eat that it will split it (give you a headache), that's why they name it that way'. The name is also said to come from the seeds which look like a 'split head'. Based on *dhaygal* (head) and *baarray-rri* (split).

dhaygal gaya-y (YY) *verb phrase*
headache. ◆ *Dhaygal ngay gaya-waa-nha.* (YR) My head is turning (I have a headache). From *dhaygal* (head) and *gaya-y* (turn).

dhaygaliyaay (YR, YY) *adjective*
clever. From *dhaygal* (head) and *-iyaay* (with, having).

dhaygaluwi (YR, YY) *noun*
pillow. Based on *dhaygal* (head) and *-uwi* (back).

dhaylngulu (YR) *adjective*
good-looking. This is a rare word, the common word is *gaba ngulu*. One source.

dhaymaarr (YR, YY) *noun*
1 earth, ground, dirt.
2 home. Where someone lives, or is from.

dhaymaadhi (YY) *noun*
ground-dwelling animals. To talk generally about flesh food that needs to be dug up, you would say, 'Let's go hunting *dhaymaadhi-gu* (for ground meat).' To specify burrowing frogs you would add *'yuwayaa'* (any frog). One source. Possibly *dhaymaarrdhi*.

dhayn (YR, YY) *noun*
1 Aboriginal man. ◆ *Dhuyu-gu nhama dhayn yii-y.* (YR) The snake bit the man.
◆ *Bulaa-yu dhayn-du dhinggaa dha-lda-nha.* (YR) Two men are eating meat.
2 Aboriginal person. ◆ *Waal guwaa-la dhayn-da!* (YR) Don't talk to any blackfellas!
◆ *Bilaa-yu ngaya dhu-nhi dhayn.* (YY) I speared a blackfella.

dhayndalmuu (YR, YY) *noun*
1 messenger (YR, YY). A special *wiringin* who brings messages from *Baayami*; Billy Rook was thought to be the last one around Walgett.
2 priest (YR). Used in Walgett.
3 counsellor (YR). Used in Walgett.
Based on *dhayn* (man).

dhayurr (YR, YY) *noun*
large grindstone. Lower millstone or grinding dish. See also: *giba*.

-Dhi¹ (YR, YY, GR) *suffix*
1 from. ◆ *Giirr nhama dhigayaa bara-nhi dhayn-di.* (YR) The birds flew from the man.
◆ *Giirr ngaama birralii-djuul banaga-nhi yinarr-i.* (YR) The little child ran away from the woman.
2 because of. Indicates the cause or reason for an action, including the source of a fear. ◆ *Bamba dhaymaarr ngarra-laa-ya ngandabaa-dhi.* (YR) Look hard (carefully) at the ground for snakes. ◆ *Giirr ganunga gaba gi-yaa-nha dhinggaa-dhi.* (YR) They are nice and full (good) because of the meat.
◆ *Giyal ngaya gi-la-nhi maadhaay-dji yiiliyanbaa-dhi.* (YR) I was frightened of the savage dog.
3 circumstance. Includes other unexplained uses. In the following example the *ngadhul* (hollow) is followed by the circumstantial suffix.
◆ *Nhaadhiyaan-bidi nhama ngadhul-bidi ngiyarrma nguu ngaama birralii-djuul guwaa-y, wuu-gi-gu ngiyarrma ngadhul-i.* (YR) He told the boy to go into the big hollow in the big log.
The source/circumstantial suffix is attached to nouns. Variant forms are *-dhi, -i, -di, -dji*. See Learner's Guide.

-dhi² (YR, YY, GR) *suffix*
possessor (family member). This is the best explanation of this suffix but does not explain all its uses. An example that supports this meaning is: ◆ *Giirr ngaama ngay ngambaa-dhi balu-nhi.* (YR) My mother died.
This suffix is used to indicate the 'possession' of a family member, indicating 'my, your, his, her, their' mother etc. Often occurs on family terms such as *bubaa* (father). Sim comments that this is probably related to *dhii* (totem). As an optional term it would naturally tend to be used most by someone using relationship terms for their 'own side' (moiety).

dhibayuu (YR, YY, GR) *noun*
1 Australasian shoveler duck *(Anas rhynchotis)*.
2 whistling duck. A number of sources have this definition, but this may be an error based on the name 'whistling duck' being used for both species.
Form uncertain.

dhibi (YY) *noun*
red-kneed dotterel *(Erythrogonys cinctus)*.

dhidhilan (GR) *noun*
sparks.

dhigadhiga (YR) *adjective*
bold, cheeky. Used to describe cheeky children. Possibly based on English 'cheeky'. One source.

dhigaraa (GR) *noun*
bird. A general name for any bird.
◆ *Bungun nhama dhigaraa-gu.* (GR) This is the wing of a bird.

dhigayaa (YR, YY) *noun*
1 bird (YR, YY). A general name for any bird.
2 feathered tribe (YY). The feathered tribe refers to birds as a group; it is one of three types of animals, others being the scaly and furry tribes. Also refers to people and totems.

dhigun (YR, YY, GR) *noun*
bird's topknot. Refers to the topknot on cockatoos and pigeons. The cockatoo topknot was valued as a decoration on ornaments used in dance and ceremony.

The cockatoo was sometimes called *dhigundi*, perhaps a general term for all birds with topknots.

dhii¹ (YR, YY, GR) *noun*
1 meat. Name for all meat foods. ◆ *Nginda dhii wuu-na buruma-gu!* (GR) You give the meat to the dog!
Shortened form of *dhinggaa*.
2 meat (totem). Primarily a totemic animal or plant inherited from one's mother, but totems also include many other things, e.g. sun, moon, stone, water, smoke and wind. Mathews said: 'A man's totem is supposed to watch over his welfare, and forewarn him of the designs of his enemies. If any of his friends are away in a different part of the tribal territory, and sickness or death overtakes them, or they meet with a serious accident, his totem appears in sight, by which he knows there is something wrong.' Fred Reece said 'if I come to a camp and there's a lot of dark fellas I tell them my meat straight away'.
3 animal.
Shortened form of *dhinggaa*.

dhiidhaan (YR, GR) *noun*
good hunter. Based on *dhii* (meat, animal).

dhiidjuul (GR) *noun*
piece of meat. From *dhii* (meat) and *-djuul* (little, one).

dhiiyaanmaa (YR) *noun*
heaven. The exact meaning is uncertain, but something like 'mother's place in heaven'. This is a rare word, the common word is *balima*. Based on *dhii* (totem). One source.

dhii² (YR, YY, GR) *noun*
tea. ◆ *Yaama nginda nhama dhii-nginda?* (YR) You want any of this tea?
From English 'tea'.

dhii garril (YR, YY) *noun*
tea leaves. From *dhii* (tea) and *garril* (leaf).

dhii man.garr (YR) *noun*
new word. See p 160 for more information.

dhiiburruu (YY) *noun*
velvet potato bush *(Solanum ellipticum)*. Also called wild gooseberry; a low prickly shrub with purple flowers and greenish edible berry.

dhiidja-li (YR, YY) *verb-transitive*
lick.

dhiidjalaa (YR) *noun*
crawler. A polite way of saying someone is 'sucking up' to another person. Probably related to *dhiidja-li* (lick). One source.

dhiidjiinbawaa (YR, YY) *noun*
soldier bird, miner bird *(Manorina spp.)*. Also *dhiidjiibawaa*. Arthur Dodd said the name sounds like the bird's 'dhii dhii' call. Two very similar species are found in the area: yellow-throated miner *(Manorina flavigula)* (illustrated) and noisy miner *(Manorina melanocephala)*.

dhiil¹ (YR, YY) *noun*
1 wilga *(Geijera parviflora)*. A small tree with bell-shaped white flowers and aromatic leaves. The leaves were used as medicine.
2 sacred tree. Wilga leaves are used in burial ceremonies, see *yilbin*.

dhiil² (YR, YY) *noun*
tail. ◆ *Guyaarr bawurra-gu dhiil, guyaarr gi-gi-la-nhi.* (YY) The kangaroo's tail was very long.
Probably from English 'tail'.

dhiilgulay (YR, YY) *noun*
bird trap. Ted Fields said it is a bird trap, made from two sticks and a net; it is set on swamps for ducks, and on Mitchell grass for parrots.
From *dhiil* (wilga tree) and *gulay* (net).

Dhiilgulaybaa (YR) *noun*
bird-trapping place. From *dhiilgulay* (bird trap) and *-baa* (place of, time of). One source.

dhiilguwin (GR) *noun*
native potato. Possibly velvet potato bush *(Solanum ellipticum)*.

dhiin (GR) *noun*
elbow.

dhiinaa (YR, YY, GR) *noun*
brood comb. Also known as bee bread, it contains the young bees and was relished as a delicacy.

dhiinbaay (YR, YY) *noun*
1 yamstick. The common word for yamstick is *ganay*.
2 ceremonial boomerang. Long and narrow, pointed at both ends with engraved designs.

dhiinbi-y (YR) *verb-intransitive*
dive. Compare *wunga-y* (dive, duck under). One source.

dhiinbin (YR, YY, GR) *noun*
Australasian grebe, diver (bird) *(Tachybaptus novaehollandiae)*. Probably related to *dhiinbi-y* (dive).

dhiinyaan (YR, YY) *noun*
sow thistle *(Sonchus oleraceus)*. Also called yellow or milk thistle, the young leaves and shoots can be eaten, but may be bitter.

dhiinyaay (YR, YY, GR) *noun*
silver ironbark *(Eucalyptus melanophloia)*. Grows on ridges, has a straight trunk with deeply furrowed bark.

dhiiriil (GR) *noun*
seed or grass necklace. One source.

dhiirra-li (YR) *verb-transitive*
teach. ◆ *Garriya dhiirra-la!* (YR) Don't teach (him)!
There are only two occurrences of this verb with this meaning, one is *-y* class and the other is *-li* class. The recommended use is *-li* class.

dhiirra-y (YR, YY, GR) *verb-transitive*
1 know. ◆ *Miimii, yaama-nda dhiirra-y-la-nha gawubarray?* (YR) Miimii, do you know of any stars? ◆ *Waal ngiyani dhiirra-y-la-nha nhama dhayn.* (YY) We don't know these men.
2 remember. ◆ *Yaama-nda dhiirra-y-la-nha nhama dhayn?* (YR) Do you remember the people?
A change in verb class from *-li* to *-y*. See Learner's Guide.

dhiirral (YR) *noun*
teacher. Probably related to *dhiirra-li* (teach). This word is from two recent sources. This process (adding *l* to the verb stem) is common for forming the names of things, e.g. *bumal* (hammer), but is not found elsewhere for forming the names of people. Investigation is continuing on how to form words such as 'teacher'.

dhiirralbidi (YR) *noun*
school principal. From *dhiirral* (teacher) and *-bidi* (big).

dhiirrma-li (YR, YY) *verb-transitive*
leave alone.

dhiiyaan (YR) *noun*
family. Based on *dhii* (totem). A person of the same bloodline or matrilineal totem is called *dhiiyaan-da* (family-in/locative). Used in some YR, GR areas.

dhila-y (YR, YY) *verb-intransitive*
sneak, creep. ◆ *Waal ngangunda dhila-waa-ya!* (YR) Don't sneak up on me! ◆ *Giirr ngaama dhayn-duul dhila-waa-nhi bandaarr-gu.* (YR) The man sneaked up on the kangaroo.
The one being sneaked up to is marked with locative (to, at, on) or allative (movement to) case.

dhilaagaa (YR, YY) *noun*
1 grandfather (father's father). Langloh-Parker said 'an elderly man of the same totem as person speaking to or of him'.
2 great-uncle (mother's mother's brother).
3 senior man (respected elder).
Also *dhilaa*.

dhilay-rri (YR, YY) *verb-transitive*
1 push away (YR, YY). ◆ *Dhilay-nhi nhama dhayn-du yinarr-duul.* (YY) The man pushed the small woman away. ◆ *Dhilay-rri ngaya gi-yaa-nha buunhu dhinawan-di.* (YY) I am going to push the grass off the emu.
2 throw out (YR). ◆ *Garriya dhilay-dha-ya!* (YR) Don't throw it out!

dhimba (YR, YY, GR) *noun*
sheep. ◆ *Nhama garaarr dhimba-gu dha-lda-nha.* (GR) The sheep is eating the grass. Possibly from English 'jumbuck'.

Dhimbambaraay (GR) *placename*
Timbumburi Creek. From *dhimba* (sheep) and *-baraay* (with, having).

dhina (YR, YY, GR) *noun*
1 foot (YR, YY, GR). Langloh-Parker said that a foot sign, e.g. on a tree, means that people are to follow. ◆ *Giirr nhama bindiyaa dhuma-y nhama ngay dhina-ga.* (GR) I have already taken the burr out of my foot.
2 footprint, tracks (YR, YY, GR). Only used

for things with feet; see also *gay* (snake track).
3 toe (GR). There is limited evidence for this meaning; compare *mara* (hand) which is also used for 'finger'. See also: **baburr**.

dhinabarra (YY) *noun*
mythical beings (type of). Also *dhinabarradha*. Spirits with bird-like feet. From *dhina* (foot) and *barra* (split).

dhinagarral (YY) *noun*
poison. Said to be made from various substances, including ground up human bones and black yam; given in food. *Dhinagarral* is the actual killing agent for a magic projectile, *dhinagarralawaa*, 'thrown' by a *wiringin* (clever man). From *dhina* (feet) and *garra-li* (cut); because it was said to cut the feet out from under the victim.

dhinagarralawaa (YY) *noun*
death stone. Possibly from *dhina* (feet), *garra-li* (cut) and *-awaa* (habitual), so '(the stone) that cuts people's feet out from under them'. See also: **wuyugarralawaa**.

dhinawan (YR, YY, GR) *noun*
emu *(Dromaius novaehollandiae)*. The story of emu and brolga tells how emu lost its wings; also see the story of how the echidna got its quills. Emu is an important food, both meat and eggs are eaten. It is said that emu oil was used in cold weather to protect people's skins. From *dhina* (foot) and *-wan* (prominent feature).

dhina yulu (GR) *noun*
toenail. From *dhina* (foot) and *yulu* (nail).

dhinayal (YR) *noun*
pins and needles. One source. Probably based on *dhina* (foot).

dhinba-li (YY) *verb-transitive*
singe. ◆ *Dhinba-lda-nha dhayn-du bawurra, dhurrun gaylama-li-gu.* (YY) The men always singe the kangaroo, to burn the hair off.

dhinbay (YR, YY) *noun*
fighting boomerang.

dhinbirr (YR, YY, GR) *noun*
knee.

dhinbiya warra-y (YR, YY) *verb phrase*
kneel. From *dhinbi-ya* (knee-on) and *warra-y* (stand), so 'stand on your knees'.

dhindi (YY) *noun*
fishing spear. A short heavy spear, used to spear fish underwater. When the water is clear, the hunter swims underwater along the river banks looking for fish.

Dhindirrina (YY) *placename*
waterhole name. On the Narran River, near the NSW–Queensland border. Possibly based on *dhindi* (fishing spear).

dhindiirr (YR, YY) *noun*
tin dish. From English 'tin dish'.

dhindu (YR) *noun*
mouse. Originally a particular species; now any small mouse-like animal.

dhinggaa (YR, YY) *noun*
1 meat. ◆ *Yilama-la nhama dhinggaa!* (YY) Cook that meat!
2 meat (totem). ◆ *Minya nginda dhinggaa?* (YR) What is your meat? Fred Reece said: '*Minya dhinggaa?* [What meat?] . . . you couldn't marry who you like, you had to be a certain sort of meat, like an animal, goanna, kangaroo, emu or porcupine.'

dhinggal (YR) *noun*
1 seed.
2 foetus.
One source.

dhinmirr (YY, GR) *noun*
eyebrow. Also *dhinmil*.

dhiriya (GR) *noun, adjective*
1 old man.
2 first finger. Pointer finger.
3 old.
4 grey.

dhirra (YR, YY) *adverb*
flash. This word seems to have a range of related meanings such as 'confidently', 'noticeably', 'restlessly', 'fidgety' and 'quickly'. *Dhirra* possibly meant 'teeth' in an older version of the language, or may be borrowed from a neighbouring language. May relate to *dhirra-li* (wake up, awake).

dhirrabil (YY) *adjective*
smiling.

dhirrabuu (YR) *adjective*
very flash.

dhirradhirra (YY) *adjective*
flash, showy. Said to mean 'always showing their teeth'.

dhirragal (YY) *adjective*
teeth on edge. The physical sensation that happens when you bite on something sour.

dhirra-li (YR) *verb-intransitive*
wake up, awake. ◆ *Yalagiirrmawu-bala ngaama ganunga dhirra-laa-y.* (YR) They will wake up then.

dhirranba-li (YR, YY, GR) *verb-transitive*
shake. ◆ *Dhirranba-la nhama muyaan dhuwarr bundaa-gi-gu.* (YY) Shake that tree, so the fruit will fall.

dhirranba-y (YR, YY) *verb-intransitive*
1 shake (YR, YY). ◆ *Gagil nhama maalaabidi, dhirranba-y-la-nha.* (YR) That tree is no good, it's shaking.
2 shiver (YR). ◆ *Dhirranba-y-la-nha nhama dhayn.* (YR) That man is shivering.
3 wag (YR). ◆ *Giirr nhama dhiil dhirranba-y-la-nha maadhaay-gu.* (YR) The dog's tail is wagging.
4 rattle (YR). ◆ *Mubal ngay dhirranba-y-la-nha.* (YR) My stomach is rattling (it's empty).
A change in verb class from -*li* to -*y*. See Learner's Guide.

dhirridhirri (YR, YY, GR) *noun*
1 willy wagtail *(Rhipidura leucophrys)* (YR, YY, GR). The name relates to the bird's call. Ian Sim said that this bird was not liked very much.
2 troublemaker (YY).
3 nosey person (YY).
'Troublemaker' and 'nosey person' are derived meanings. Also *dhirriirrii*.

dhirrin (YY) *noun*
high ground. Above flood level, out of the water. One source.

dhirrinbaa (YR) *noun*
bad-weather camp. On high ground. Possibly from *dhirrin* (high ground) and -*baa* (place of, time of). One source.

dhirrindjal (YR, YY) *adjective*
numb. As in when you get pins and needles.

dhiyaagarra (YR) *noun*
bed. Related to *dhiyaagarra-li* (prepare a bed — YY, GR).

dhiyaagarra-li (YY, GR) *verb-transitive*
1 prepare a bed (YY, GR). ◆ *Dhiyaagarra-la!* (GR) Make the bed!
2 spread (GR).

dhiyaagarri (GR) *noun*
1 blanket.
2 bedroll.
Probably related to *dhiyaagarra-li* (prepare a bed).

dhiyama-li (YR, YY, GR) *verb-transitive*
pick up, lift up. ◆ *Wirri ngaya gi-yaa-nha dhiyama-li warangana-biyaay.* (YY) I am going to pick up the coolamon with honey in it. ◆ *Ngaandu gi-yaa-nha ngay dhiinbaay dhiyama-li?* (YY) Who is going to get (pick up) my yamstick? ◆ *Yaama nguu-nga nhama maayama dhiyama-li?* (YY) Can he lift up the stone?
From *dhiya-* (lift up) and -*ma-li* (suffix that makes a transitive verb). There are no occurrences of **dhiya-y* (lift up, intransitive) but *dhiya* is found in other verbs which refer to lifting up something, e.g. *dhiyarra-li*.

dhiyarra-li (YR, YY) *verb-transitive*
dip, scoop. ◆ *Bamba ngaya yilawa-y-la-nhi gungan dhiyarra-li-gu, nhaadhiyaan gama-nhi, bundaa-nhi ngaya gungan-da.* (YY) I sat straight down to scoop up water, the log broke and I fell in the water.
From **dhiya-* (lift up) and **-rra-li* (hypothesised verb suffix).

dhu-rri (YR, YY, GR) *verb-transitive*
1 spear, stab (YR, YY, GR). ◆ *Bilaa-yu ngaya bandaarr dhu-nhi.* (YR) I speared a kangaroo.
2 sting (YR, YY, GR). ◆ *Muundhuu-yu nganha dhu-nhi.* (YY) A hornet stung me.
3 poke (with pointed object) (YR, YY). ◆ *Dhu-na nhama dhinawan!* (YY) Poke that emu!
4 tap (YR). ◆ *Giirr ngaama ngaya dhu-rraa-nhi dhaymaarr ganay-u ngay.* (YR) I tapped the ground with my yamstick.
5 have sex, make love (YR, YY).
6 write (YR). ◆ *Nhama nguu biiba dhu-dha-nha.* (YR) He's writing that letter.
7 carve (YR). ◆ *Giirr ngaya nhama-li barran*

dhu-dha-nhi. (YR) I carved that boomerang. The basic meaning of *dhu-rri* is something like 'pierce' or 'push against with a sharpish object'; so it is used to translate words like 'spear, poke, (bee) sting, and (mosquito) bite'. Many Aboriginal languages have a similar word with a similar range of meanings.

dhuba-y (YR, YY, GR) *verb-intransitive*
point. ◆ *Garriya dhuba-ya!* (YY) Don't point!

dhubaanma-li (YR, YY, GR) *verb-transitive*
tell about. ◆ *Miimii, yaama ngaya nginunda dhubaanma-y buma-la-ngindaay dhayn?* (YR) Miimii, did I tell you about the men who were fighting?
Probably from *dhuba-y* (point).

dhubaay (YR) *noun*
1 old woman. Respectful term for an older woman.
2 midwife, nurse.
3 wife.
Also *dhubay*. Used in Walgett.

dhubayan (YY) *noun*
tattletale, dobber. Related to *dhuba-y* (point).

dhubayn (YR) *noun*
body, spirit (human), self. Used in some YR, GR areas, mainly to mean 'body'. One source.

dhubi-li (YR, YY, GR) *verb-transitive*
spit. ◆ *Dhubi-y nguu ngaama maayama.* (YR) He spat that stone out.

dhubi-y (YR, YY) *verb-intransitive*
stoop. ◆ *Dhubi-ya, dhiyama-la nhama maayama!* (YY) Stoop down and pick up that stone! This is a rare word, the common word is *dhuli-y*.

dhubil (YY) *noun*
spit. Related to *dhubi-li* (spit).

dhuga (YR, YY, GR) *noun*
sugar. From English 'sugar'.

dhugaadjuul (YR) *noun*
little one. Not recommended for use, a better word is *bubaaydjuul*.

dhugaaga ngambaa (YY) *noun*
aunt (mother's younger sister). Related to *dhugaadjuul* (little) and *ngambaa* (mother).

dhugaalubaa (YR, YY) *noun*
shrimp. Some people including Fred Reece use *giidjaa* for shrimp.

dhugaay (YR, YY) *adjective*
small, little. The more common term is *bubaay*.

dhugay (YR, YY) *adverb*
always. Also *dhugaay*. ◆ *Dhugay nhama dhayn dhanduwi-y-la-nha.* (YY) That man is always sleeping.

dhula (GR) *noun*
scorpion.

dhulan (YR, YY) *noun*
black wattle *(Acacia salicina)*. Also called cooba, and native or broughton willow, this medium-sized tree has drooping willowy branches. As with all acacias, the gum can be collected from cuts in the bark and soaked with honey or manna to make a sweet drink. Acacia seeds are very nutritious, with higher protein and fat contents than wheat or rice; the gum has a lot of fibre. There is variation across wattle trees, some gums and seeds are better to eat than others.

dhuli (YY) *adjective*
1 bent over.
2 arched, bowed.
Related to *dhuli-y* (bend down, lean over).

dhuli-y (YR, YY, GR) *verb-intransitive*
1 bend down, stoop (YR, YY, GR). ◆ *Giirr nguu dhuli-y-la-nhi dhiyama-li-gu bulanggiin.* (YR) She bent down to pick up the blanket.
2 lean over (YR). ◆ *Giirr ngaama maalaa-bidi gaawaa-ga ngaama dhuli-y-la-nha.* (YR) There was a tree leaning over the water.

dhulii (YR, GR) *noun*
sand goanna *(Varanus gouldii)*. See also: **biiwii**.

dhulirra-li (YR, YY, GR) *verb-intransitive*
drip. ◆ *Gungan ngaama dhulirra-lda-nha.* (YR) The water is dripping. Possibly related to *dhuli-y* (bend down, lean over).

dhulirral (YY) *noun*
water drops. Related to *dhulirra-li* (drip).

dhulu (GR) *noun*
  1 tree.
  2 stick.
  3 message stick. Bucknell described one message stick as 'about seven inches long, and three quarters of an inch wide at the bottom, tapering to about half an inch at the top, it is flat, with the sides slightly rounded off, being about one third of an inch thick down the centre, and has markings on both sides of it'. See also: **maang**.

dhulu buurra (YY) *noun*
  bora message stick. From *dhulu* (stick) (GR) and *buurra* (bora). One source.

dhuluuma-y (YR) *verb-intransitive*
  thunder. ◆ *Nhama dhuluumaa-waa-nha.* (YR) It's thundering. ◆ *Yilaa-laa dhama-y. Nhama-laa dhuluumaa-waa-nha.* (YR) It will rain soon. It's thundering now.

dhuluumay (YR, YY, GR) *noun*
  thunder. Two types of thunder are recognised: a sharp, cracking thunder is said to be made by *Nalgalgan* or *Ngululgan* (Guwamu language) the 'thunder man' who has 'clappers' on his arms. This spirit was known 'right through', that is, over a wide area. Low muttering thunder is said to be the voice of the Creator. Related to *dhuluuma-y* (thunder).

dhuluun.gayaa (YR, YY) *noun*
  bilby. Ian Sim said it may be based on *dhulu* (stick) because the bilby carries its tail up stiffly like a stick when running; *gayaa* may relate to the bilby's preference for sandy country, *gayaay*. See also: **bilba**.

dhuma-li (GR) *verb-transitive*
  1 take out. ◆ *Giirr nhama bindiyaa dhuma-y nhama ngay dhina-ga.* (GR) I have taken the burr out of my foot.
  2 open. This verb can also be used to mean 'open', e.g. open a door.

dhumadhuma (YR, YY) *noun*
  smallpox. One source.

dhumbaay (YR) *noun*
  drawing stick. Ted Fields said that each person had a *dhumbaay*, a stick two to three feet long, used to 'express things', e.g. to draw things on the ground. One source.

dhumbil (YR) *adjective*
  full, humped. Also *dhumbi*. ◆ *Giirr ngaya mubal dhumbil gi-nyi.* (YR) My stomach got full. ◆ *Giirr ngaama bigibila-bala dhumbil bawa.* (YR) The porcupine has a humped back.

dhumbun (GR) *noun*
  restricted word. See p 20 for more information.

dhun (YY, GR) *noun*
  1 penis.
  2 tail.
  Word used to refer to other things that hang down.

dhunbarra (YY) *noun*
  welcome swallow *(Hirundo neoxena)*. From *dhun* (tail) and *barra* (split).

dhunbarran (GR) *noun*
  initiation-ground pathway. The pathway, around 250 m long, connecting the two rings of an initiation ground. Previously written *dhanbarran*.

dhun.gayrra (YR, YY) *noun*
  lightning, chain lightning. Perhaps a compound of *dhun* (tail). See also: **murrumay**.

dhunbarr (YR, YY) *noun*
  grass seed. A name for any grass seed ready for grinding. Seeds can be ground between stones and baked like damper in ashes. Possibly to do with fairy grass. Possibly from *dhun* (tail, hanging thing); grass hangs down when heavy with seed.

dhunbil (YR, YY) *noun*
  sinew. ◆ *Dhunbil nguu gi-yaa-nha dhuwima-li dhinawan-di buyu-dhi.* (YR) He is going to pull the sinews from the emu's leg. ◆ *Yabi-la nhama dhinawan-gu dhunbil.* (YY) Twist that emu sinew.

dhunbiliyaay (YY) *adjective*
  strong, sinewy. Refers to people or animals. From *dhunbil* (sinew) and *-iyaay* (with, having).

dhunbilyabi (YY) *noun*
  sinew string. From *dhunbil* (sinew) and *yabi-li* (twist, plait). One source.

dhuni (YR, YY) *noun*
  sun. This is a rare word, the common word is now *yayaay*.

dhunidjuni (YR, YY) *noun*
Jacky Winter (bird) (*Microeca leucophaea*).

dhuningarraay (YR, YY) *adjective, noun*
1 old. ◆ *Dhuningaraay-u dhayn-du gaba gaay guwaa-lda-nhi.* (YY) The old men spoke (the language) well.
2 old person. One source for this meaning.
Probably based on *dhuni* (sun) and *-araay* (with, having). May be a Wiradjuri/Wangaaybuwan word with *-ng* before the suffix *-araay*, so 'someone having many suns'.

dhuniya (YR, YY) *noun*
daylight. Recommended word.

dhunmidjirr (YY) *noun*
bush rat. Possibly long-haired rat (*Rattus villosissimus*).

dhura-li (GR) *verb-transitive*
make noise. One source. Form is uncertain, may be *dhurra-li*.

dhuradhuraba-li (YR) *verb-transitive*
tap. Arthur Dodd used this word to talk about tapping the ground with his stick to see if there was a hollow below in which a goanna was hiding. Possibly 'dhurradhurraba-li'. The reduplicated form of *dhura-li* (make noise) has this particular meaning.

dhural (YR) *noun*
noise, sound.

dhurra-li¹ (YR, YY, GR) *verb-transitive*
make (construct). ◆ *Yilaalu nhama barran dhurra-li.* (GR) (He) will make a boomerang later.
This is a rare word, the common word is *gimbi-li* (YR, YY) and *gimubi-li* (GR).

dhurra-li² (YR, YY, GR) *verb-intransitive*
1 come (YR, YY, GR). Often used about people, it is also used with different events associated with the body: *giyal dhurra-li* (itch will come, i.e. will be itchy); *nguluurr dhurra-li* (tears will come, i.e. will cry). Arthur Dodd used this verb to talk about a dog's tongue 'hanging (coming) out' and fingernails 'growing (coming) out'.
◆ *Bulaarr ngaama dhayn walaay-gu dhurra-y.* (YR) The two men came to the camp.
◆ *Giirr-bala ngaama bamba guway dhurra-y.* (YR) A lot of blood came out.
2 rise (sun/moon) (YR, YY, GR). ◆ *Yaraay nhama dhurra-laa-nha.* (GR) The sun is rising. ◆ *Bamba nhama yinarr dhaala-nhi, yaay dhurra-lda-ndaay.* (YY) The woman was very sick at sunrise (when the sun rose).
3 grow (YR). ◆ *Giirr malga ngaama dhurra-lda-nha gumbugan-da.* (YR) That mulga grows there at that sandhill.

dhurraaba-li (YR) *verb-transitive*
make come out. Also *dhurraanma-li*. This verb is also found in the expressions *gaawil dhurraaba-li* (make vomit) and *guway dhurraanma-li* (make bleed). ◆ *Giirr nguu ngaama dhayn-gu yiya dhurraaba-y.* (YR) He knocked the man's teeth out. From *dhurra-* (come) and *-ba-li* (verb suffix).

dhurraami-li (YR, YY) *verb-transitive*
wait (for). ◆ *Dhurraami-li ngaya gi-yaa-nha nginunha.* (YY) I am going to wait for you. From *dhurra-* (come) and *-mi-li* (verb suffix possibly to do with *mil* eye/seeing).

dhurraluwi-y (YR, YY, GR) *verb-intransitive*
come back, return. ◆ *Yilaa ngaya-laa dhurra-l-uwi-y!* (YR) I will come back later! From *dhurra-* (come) and *-l-uwi-y* (back).

dhurrabal (GR) *noun*
road. Related to *dhurra-li* (come). This is a rare word, the common word is *yuruun*.

dhurradhurraa (YY) *adjective*
untidy, all over the place. One source.

dhurralbuu (YR) *noun*
south-west wind. A hot wind that precedes thunderstorms and light showers, warning of a dry season ahead. One source.

dhurrandhurran (YR, YY) *noun*
north wind.

dhurran.gali (YR) *noun*
children's game. A kid's game of 'tip' played in the water. Related to *gali* (water). One source.

dhurrawaay (GR) *noun*
kangaroo rat. Probably rufous bettong (*Aepyprymnus rufescens*).

dhurrin¹ (YR, YY) *adjective*
1 raw. Of meat.
2 green (unripe).

dhurrin² (YR, YY) *adjective*
greedy.

dhurriwuudhaay (YR, YY) *noun*
lover.

dhurriya-y (YR) *verb-intransitive*
ride, e.g a horse. One source. Form uncertain.

dhurrubuu (YR) *noun*
1 starling.
2 unknown bird. Ted Fields said it is one of the birds that guides you when you are lost, saying *dhurrubuu* (follow me). One source.

dhurrulawaa (YR, YY, GR) *noun*
water weed. Also *dhurrarrawaa*. Fred Reece said that it is a long rope-like weed with a yellow flower.

dhurrun (YR, YY, GR) *noun*
1 fur, wool.
2 hair. This refers to animal hair and people's body hair.

Dhurrunbandaay (YY) *placename*
Dirranbandi. Said to be to do with *dhurrun.gal* (hairy caterpillars) and *baanda-y* (move in Indian file).

dhurrundhurrun (YY) *adjective*
hairy, furry. From *dhurrun* (hair).

dhurrun.gal (YR, YY) *noun*
1 hairy caterpillar (*Ochrogaster lunifer*) (YR, YY). Also called processionary caterpillar. These caterpillars follow each other along in a line. This is also the name for their bag nest.
2 furry tribe (YY). The furry tribe refers to hairy animals as a group; it is one of three types of animals, others being the scaly and the feathered tribes. Also refers to people and totems.
From *dhurrun* (hair) and *-gal* (group, mob).

dhuru (GR) *noun*
snake. Name for any snake.

dhuruyaal (GR) *adjective*
1 right-handed.
2 right (not left).

dhuu (YR, YY, GR) *noun*
1 smoke (YR, GR).
2 fire (YY).

dhuubaarr (YR, YY) *noun*
1 funeral smoke. Fred Reece said that *dhuubaarr* is the smoke used in burial ceremonies. Everybody shifts camp when somebody dies, then a couple of women go around at sundown with fire in some sticks or bushes and smoke every camp out. He said 'That's how they sing that song: *dhuubaarr-ba marrabaa*.'
2 fine rain.
Related to *dhuu* (smoke). See also: **wuyugil** (smoke).

dhuumuyu (YY) *adjective*
blackened, smoked. Based on *dhuu* (smoke). One source.

dhuu-rri (YR, YY, GR) *verb-intransitive*
crawl. This verb is also used to express slow movement, such as 'kangaroos crawling along' and 'thieves sneaking about'. ◆ *Birralii-djuul ngaama-laa dhuu-rri, waal ngindaay ngarrangarra-lda-ndaay.* (YR) The baby might crawl away if you all don't watch him.

dhuubuu (YR, YY, GR) *noun*
soap. From English 'soap'.

dhuudhinma-li (YR) *verb-transitive*
shoot. ◆ *Maayrr-laa nhalay bandaarr gi-gi, giirr nhama wanda-gu dhuudhinma-l-aaba-y.* (YR) There will be no more 'roos here, the white man shot them all out.
From English 'shoot' and *-ima-li*.

-DHuul (YR, YY, GR) *suffix*
1 little, small (YR, YY, GR). Variant forms are *-dhuul, -djuul, -duul*. ◆ *Buma-la nhama birralii-djuul.* (YR) Hit that little child.
◆ *Milan-duul ngali bayama-y dhagaay.* (YR) We caught one little perch.
2 one (YR, YY).
This suffix is attached to nouns, it has a wide range of meanings.

dhuuraay (GR) *noun*
1 flame.
2 light.

dhuurran (YY) *adjective*
knowledgeable. Also *dhuurrandhuurran*. One source.

dhuurranmay (YR, YY, GR) *noun*
leader, chief, boss. Also *dhuurranmaay*. 'The top man'; top of its group or kind, can be applied to any group of things. Ted Fields said they lead the corroboree and

hunting party.
dhuurranmay waa (YY) *noun*
boss shell. Believed to be the 'alligator' shell, that is, a piece of Garriya's egg, made into a pendant and worn by the 'top men'. From *dhuurranmay* (chief, leader) and *waa* (shell). One source.
dhuurrguu (YR) *adjective*
relaxed. One source.
dhuurrma-li (YR, YY) *verb-transitive*
shift, drag. ◆ *Dhuurrma-la nhama nhaadhiyaan!* (YY) Shift that log! Based on *dhuu-* (crawl) and *-ma-li* (suffix that makes a transitive verb). Sometimes used to translate 'pull'.
dhuuyaal (YR, YY) *adjective*
1 right-handed. Ian Sim said 'right hand side'.
2 right (not left).
dhuuyaay (YR, YY) *noun*
1 flame.
2 light.
3 firestick.
Possibly from *dhuu* (fire) and *yaay* (sun).
dhuwa (YR) *adjective*
grey. One source. This word is uncertain.
dhuwadhuul (YR) *noun*
grey one. Probably from *dhuwa* (grey) and *-dhuul* (little, one). One source. This word is uncertain.
dhuwaanbay (YY) *noun*
channel-billed cuckoo (*Scythrops novaehollandiae*). Identification is uncertain. Ian Sim said it is also called the death bird and is feared because it is thought to warn of a death. It rarely appears but will sit in the tallest trees and call day and night. Also recorded as *dhiyanbay*.
dhuwaarrgaa (YR) *noun*
thunder. Ted Fields described it as a clap of thunder in mid-winter that tells the hibernating goannas and other reptiles to turn over, so that they do not lie on the same side all winter. One source.
dhuwadi (YR, YY, GR) *noun*
shirt. From English 'shirt'.
dhuwarr (YR, YY, GR) *noun*
1 bread (YY). When talking about food it was common to talk of *dhuwarr* for vegetable food or bread and *dhinggaa* for meat, using these two words for 'food' rather than just one. ◆ *Mari-dhu dhuwarr nhama ngay gaarrama-y.* (GR) That man stole my bread. ◆ *Dhuwarr dhaay gaa-nga dha-li-gu!* (GR) Bring the bread here to eat!
2 vegetable food (YR, YY, GR). Name for various starchy root foods, e.g. tar vine root and yams.
Also occurs in *baadjin dhuwarr* (poison food).
dhuwi (YR, YY, GR) *noun*
1 soul, spirit (human) (YR, YY, GR). A person's dream spirit that travels about at night.
2 heart wood (GR). As in the heart or centre of the tree.
3 inside (GR). For example, 'inside the hut'. Greenway translated *dhuwi* as 'smoke, spirit, heart, central life'.
dhuwigalinmal (YR, YY) *noun*
clamorous reed warbler (*Acrocephalus stentoreus*). The bird's singing at night is said to be catching someone's dream spirit and singing it 'up to heaven'; a sign of a death occurring, this bird was feared and hated, and was killed whenever possible. Based on *dhuwi* (soul, spirit) and probably *galiya-y* (climb).
dhuwi-y (YR, YY) *verb-transitive*
stick into. ◆ *Giirr nganunda dhina-ga burrulaa-gu bindiyaa-gu dhuwi-nyi.* (YR) Lots of bindi-eyes are sticking into (my) foot. ◆ *Muyaan-du nganha dhuwi-nyi maa-dhi.* (YY) A stick stuck into my hand.
dhuwima-li (YR, YY) *verb-transitive*
1 remove, take out (YR, YY). ◆ *Mubal-laa dhayn-du dhuwima-li, yilama-li-gu.* (YY) Then the man will take out the guts, to cook it. ◆ *Dhuu ngaya gi-yaa-nha gimbi-li, bigibila ngaya gi-yaa-nha wiyayl dhuwima-li.* (YY) I'm going to make a fire (to clean the porcupine), I'm going to take the quills out of the porcupine.
2 take off (clothes) (YY). ◆ *Bayagaa dhuwima-la!* (YY) Take your clothes off! It may be that the verb form *dhuwima-y* is more appropriate for 'removing something from oneself'.
dhuwinba-li (YR, YY) *verb-transitive*
hide (plant). Also *dhurrinba-li*. ◆ *Minyaaya*

ngaama dhinggaa birralii-gal-u dhuwinba-y? (YR) Where did the children hide that meat?
'Plant' is another word for 'hide' in the GY area. Has also occurred as *dhuwinbaluwi-y* (hide again).

dhuwinba-y (YR) *verb-intransitive*
hide (self). ◆ *Nguu ngiyarrma yurrul-a dhuwinba-nhi.* (YR) He hid in the bushes.
A change in verb class from *-li* to *-y*. See Learner's Guide.

dhuwindhuwi (YY) *noun*
sparks.

dhuwiyuwiy (YR, YY) *noun*
black ant.

dhuyu (YR, YY) *noun*
snake. Name for any snake. ◆ *Dhuyu-gu nhama dhayn yii-y.* (YR) The snake bit the man.

dhuyubagan (YR) *noun*
bandy bandy snake *(Vermicella annulata)*. From *dhuyu* (snake) and *bagan* (stripe). One source.

dhuyugarral (YR, YY) *noun*
earthworm. From *dhuyu* (snake) and *garra-li* (cut).

dhuyumanga (YR) *noun*
python. From *dhuyu* (snake) and *manga* (ear). Name for any python; Ted Fields said the name comes from its wide head which makes it look as if it has ears.

dhuyul (YR, YY, GR) *noun*
hill, high ground. Also *dhuyuul, dhuuyul*.

dhuyuldhuyul (YY) *adjective*
hilly. From *dhuyul* (hill).

djigin (YR) *noun*
chicken. From English 'chicken'. See also: **baawul**.

djiibirrirr (YY) *noun*
grey-fronted honeyeater *(Lichenostomus plumulus)*. One of only a few words that begin with *dj-*, all these words are from recent sources.

djulu (YY) *noun*
1 dirt (debris). Fine debris left on the ground after heavy rain.
2 sawdust.
One source.

Gg

-Ga (YR, YY, GR) *suffix*
1 in, at, on. Indicates the place where something is; also called the locative case suffix. ◆ *Birralii garungga-nhi gaawaa-ga.* (YY) The boy drowned in the river.
◆ *Minyaaya ngaya-laa nginunha ngarra-li? Gugurruwan-da.* (YY) Where will I see you? At the Coocoran Lake. ◆ *Giirr ngaya dhinggaa yilama-y dhuu-ga nginda gimbi-ndaay* (YY) I cooked the meat on the fire that you made.
2 to (dative). Occasionally used to mean 'giving to'; usually the *-gu* (owner suffix) is used. The locative/dative suffix is attached to nouns and adjectives. Variant forms are *-ga, -da, -a, -dja, -dha, -ya*. See Learner's Guide.

gaa-gi (YR, YY, GR) *verb-transitive*
1 take (YR, YY, GR). ◆ *Nhama bandaarr gaa-waa-nhi walaay-gu.* (GR) They took the kangaroo to the camp.
2 bring, fetch (YR, YY, GR). *Dhaay gaa-gi* (here — bring) can be used to make it clear that the meaning is 'bring' (not 'take' or 'carry'). ◆ *Ngaaluurr ngaarrima dhaay gaa-nga!* (YY) Bring that fish here!
3 carry (YR, GR). ◆ *Bandaarr bulaarr mari-dhu gaa-waa-nhi.* (GR) Two men carried the kangaroo.
4 wear (YR). ◆ *Dhayn-du guudii gaa-gi-la-nhi.* (YR) The man wore a coat.
5 own, have (YR, YY, GR).
See also: **wamba-li**.

gaaguwi-y (YR, YY) *verb-transitive*
bring back, take back. ◆ *Gaa-g-uwi-ya nhama birralii-djuul ngambaa-ngun-da nguungu.* (YR) Take the child back to his mother.
From *gaa-* (take, bring, fetch, carry) and *-g-uwi-y* (verb suffix meaning 'back').

gaabiin (YR, YY, GR) *noun*
carbeen *(Eucalyptus tessellaris)*. Arthur Dodd said 'he's very near like a gum tree, they call him *gaabiin* . . . he grows so high . . . on the sandhills, not along the river

here.' Common around Moree and Narrabri. Has a short stocking of dark grey bark around the base and then smooth pale bark on the rest of the trunk. Possible source of English 'carbeen'.

gaabu (YR) *exclamation*
hush! One source.

gaadhaay (YR) *noun*
ghost. Used in some YR, GR areas. One source. May originally be a Wangaaybuwan word.

gaadhal (YR) *noun*
parrot (feeding). Ted Fields said it means an adult parrot feeding its young, perhaps from the sound it makes. One source.

gaadhii (YR) *noun*
1 sister. This is a rare word, the common word is *baawaa*.
2 grandmother (mother's mother). This is a rare word, the common word is *baagii*. The two definitions of *gaadhii* are probably due to the fact that a particular woman's grandmother (on their mother's side) and also that woman's sister are both classified as belonging to the same social section. So this word may actually mean, for a woman, 'another woman in my social section'. Due to the respect given to older people, it is unlikely that someone would refer to an older person using this term.

gaagul (YR) *noun*
young kurrajong root.

gaagulu (YR, YY) *noun*
native banana (*Marsdenia australis*). The flowers, leaves and young pods are eaten raw, while mature brown pods are roasted in the coals. Ted Fields said they are a long yam on a green vine, and are good if you're thirsty. Roots are roasted, pounded with rocks to separate the flesh from the tough inner core, and only the skin and flesh is eaten. See also: **giban**.

gaala (YR) *noun*
1 tin mug, mug. Currently used as 'mug', see also *banigan* (cup). Ted Fields said it was a homemade tin 'pint' made out of a tin can and wire.
2 can (tin can).

gaalan (GR) *noun*
type of ant. There is conflicting evidence about this word. It has been used to refer to meat ants, black ants and sugar ants.

gaalanha (YR, YY) *conjunction*
and. This is a rare word. Form uncertain.

-gaali (YR, YY) *suffix*
group of two. This suffix is added to nouns to indicate that there is a group of two, e.g. *wirri-gaali* (bowl-group of two) is a nickname for goats, after the goat's udder which looks like two bowls.

gaali (YR, YY) *pronoun*
they (two people — doer to).

gaalinha (YR, YY, GR) *pronoun*
they (two people — doer/done to). Rarely used.

gaalinga (YR, YY, GR) *pronoun*
they (two people — doer/done to). Rarely used.

gaalingu (YR, YY, GR) *pronoun*
1 their (two people).
2 to them (two people). This is only used when something is 'given to' or 'done for' them (two people). *Gaalingunda* is used for 'movement to' them (two people). Also *ngurugaalingu*.

gaalingunda (YR, YY, GR) *pronoun*
to/at/on them (two people).

gaalingundi (YR, YY, GR) *pronoun*
from them (two people).

-gaalu (YR) *suffix*
pretend. ◆ *Giirr ngaama birralii-gal yulu-gi-la-nhi ngaama walaay-gaalu-ga.* (YR) The children were playing (in) a pretend house (cubby house).
Added to nouns to indicate that the thing is not real, it is make-believe.

gaanba-li (YR) *verb-transitive*
wipe. ◆ *Yaama-nda nhama ngamu gaanba-li ngulu-dhi nguungu?* (YR) Will you wipe the milk from his face?

gaanga-y (YR, YY, GR) *verb-transitive, intransitive*
1 give birth (YR, YY, GR). ◆ *Giirr ngay gulii-yu birralii gaanga-nhi.* (YR) My wife had (gave birth to) the baby.
2 lay egg (YR, YY). ◆ *Giirr nguuma gawu gaanga-nhi wiidhaa-gu.* (YR) The bowerbird laid eggs there.
3 be born (YR, YY). ◆ *Yilaalu gumbugan-da gaanga-nhi ngaya.* (YR) Long ago I was born

on the sandhill.

gaarra-li (YR, YY, GR) *verb-transitive*
rub. ◆ *Bawa ngama ngay gaarra-la!* (YR) Rub my back! ◆ *Guway-u nhama gaarra-la yulay dhinawan-gu!* (YR) Rub the emu skin with blood!

gaarra-y (YR, YY, GR) *verb-intransitive*
paint (self) (YR). ◆ *Giirr ngaya gi-yaa-nha gaarra-y yulugi-gu.* (YR) I'm going to paint (myself) for the corroboree.
The basic meaning of this verb is to 'rub your own body'. It involves a change in verb class from *-li* to *-y*. See Learner's Guide.

gaarrama-li (GR) *verb-transitive*
steal. Also *garrama-li*. ◆ *Mari-dhu dhuwarr nhama ngay gaarrama-y.* (GR) That man stole my bread.

gaarri-y (YR, YY) *verb-intransitive*
1 get down (YR, YY). ◆ *Baluwaa ngaya gaarri-yaa-nhi muyaan-di.* (YY) I was getting down very slowly from the tree.
2 spill, drip, leak (YR, YY). ◆ *Gungan gaarri-nyi.* (YR) The water spilled. ◆ *Giirr nhama gungan maalaa-bidi-dji gaarri-y-la-nha.* (YR) Water is dripping from the trees.
◆ *Gungan nhama gaarri-y-la-nha.* (YY) Water is leaking there.
3 go down, set (moon/sun) (YY). ◆ *Baaluu gaarri-yaa-nha.* (YY) (The) moon is setting.
◆ *Dhuni gaarri-nyi.* (YY) (The) sun set.
The most common word for 'set' is *wuu-gi*. Also *gaari-y*.

gaarrima-li (YR, YY) *verb-transitive*
1 spill. ◆ *Giirr ngaama nguu gungan gaarrima-y.* (YR) He spilt the water.
2 pour.
From *gaarri-* (spill, drip, leak) and *-ma-li* (suffix that makes a transitive verb).

gaarrimay (YY) *noun*
1 camp.
2 nest.
See also: *walaay*.

gaawaa (YR, YY) *noun*
1 river (YR, YY). ◆ *Giirr ngaya ngaama gaawaa-gu yanaa-y.* (YR) I will go to the river.
2 deep water (YR). ◆ *Ngiyarrma ngaya wunga-y-la-nhi, gaawaa-ga.* (YR) I was swimming here in the deep water.
See also: *gaawal*.

gaawal (YR, YY, GR) *noun, placename*
1 creek (YR, YY, GR). Ian Sim said it was also possibly a watercourse, swamp or drainage line.
2 lagoon (YR, YY, GR).
3 Cowal (YY). Location.

Gaawalbaa (YY) *placename*
Cowelba. On the Collarenebri–Angledool road. From *gaawal* (creek) and *-baa* (place of, time of).

gaawi-li (YR, YY, GR) *verb-transitive*
vomit, spew, regurgitate. ◆ *Birralii-dju ngay gaawi-y gungan nginda wuu-ndaay nguungu.* (YY) My kiddy puked up the water that you gave him.

gaawil (YR, YY) *noun*
vomit. From *gaawi-li* (vomit).

gaay¹ (YR, YY) *noun*
1 word. Occurs with the verb *guwaa-li* (talk, speak). ◆ *Gaay guwaa-la nganunda.* (YY) Talk to me.
2 message. ◆ *Yaama nguuma dhirridhirri-dju nginu, maayu, gaba gaay guwaa-lda-nha?* (YR) Does that willy wagtail tell you a good message?
3 language. ◆ *Ngaya gi-yaa-nha gaay guwaa-li dhayn-gu gaay-a.* (YY) I am going to talk in Aboriginal people's language.
4 story. ◆ *Giirr nhama birralii-gal-u, winanga-lda-nhi nhama ngaandu-waa gaba gaay guwaa-lda-ndaay.* (YR) These kids, they listened to someone who was telling good stories.

gaay gawaa-y (YR, YY) *verb phrase*
mimic, imitate speech. From *gaay* (word, language) and *gawaa-y* (follow).

gaay giirruu (YY) *exclamation*
true words! From *gaay* (word) and *giirruu* (absolutely, too right).

gaayaa wana-gi (YR) *verb phrase*
talk. ◆ *Giirr ngiyani-luu winanga-lda-nha nhama gaayaa wana-gi-la-ndaay.* (YR) We can hear them talking.
This is a rare phrase, the common word is *guwaa-li*. Possibly from *gaay* (word, speech) and *wana-gi* (throw), so 'throwing words around'.

gaay² (GR) *noun, adjective*
1 small, little.

2 child.
Also occurs as *gaay-djuul* (small-little, just, one) and *gaayndjuul*.

gaayli (GR) *noun*
child. From *gaay* (child, small).

gaaynggal (GR) *noun*
baby. Possibly originally a plural based on *gaay* (child, small) and *-gal* (many). Also found as *gaaynduul* which is probably a singular form.

gaaynmara (GR) *noun, adjective*
1 child.
2 small, little.
From *gaay* (small, child).

gaba[1] (YR, YY, GR) *adjective, adverb*
1 good, well. ◆ *Giirruu ngaya gaba ngarra-lda-nha.* (YY) I can see well. ◆ *Gaba-dhuul nhama maadhaay.* (YY) That's a good little dog. ◆ *Gaba nhama yinarr.* (YR) She's a good woman.
2 all right, correctly. ◆ *Giirr gaay ngali gaba guwaa-laa-nha.* (YY) We are talking all right.
3 well (healthy).
Gaba can qualify both nouns and verbs. It has a wide range of meanings, including 'pleasant', 'nice', 'wholesome', 'glad', 'happy', 'honest', 'sweet', 'tender' (as in meat), and 'fresh' (as in water). Sometimes occurs as *gaba-dhuul* (good-little, just, one) meaning 'good one, good person'; and *giirr gaba* (right).

gababala (YR, YY) *adjective*
better. ◆ *Gaba-bala ngay barran.* (YR) My boomerang is better (than yours).
From *gaba* (good) and *-bala* (contrast).

gaba binaal (YR, YY) *adjective*
peaceful, well mannered. Based on *gaba* (good) and *bina* (ear).

gaba dhaygal (YY) *adjective*
clever. Level headed. From *gaba* (good) and *dhaygal* (head).

gaba guuyay (YR, YY) *adjective*
good mood. ◆ *Yaama nginu gaba guuyay?* (YR) Are you (in a) good mood?
From *gaba* (good) and *guuyay* (mood). Sometimes used to translate 'happy'.

gabangaarr (YR) *adjective, adverb*
nicely. Probably based on *gaba* (good). One source.

gaba ngulu (YR, YY) *adjective*
good-looking. From *gaba* (good) and *ngulu* (face).

gaba[2] (GR) *noun*
hill, mountain range.

gabaa (YR, GR) *noun*
white man. Possibly from English 'government'. Some people now say it *gaba*, older people generally use *gaba* for 'good'. See also: **wanda**.

gaban (YR, YY) *noun*
lung.

gabanbaa (YR, YY, GR) *adjective*
light (not heavy). ◆ *Gabanbaa nhama maayama.* (YY) That's a light stone. Probably based on *gaba* (good) and *-baa* (place of, time of).

gabanma-li (YR) *verb-transitive*
heal. Based on *gaba* (good, well) and *-ma-li* (suffix that makes a transitive verb), so 'make well'. One source. See also: **maayuma-li**.

gabarraa (YR, YY) *noun*
sacred stone. A crystal used by *wiringin* (clever men) for such things as healing and magic.

gabi (YR) *noun*
new word. See p 160 for more information.

Gabii (YR, YY, GR) *noun*
men's social section. A person's marriage division (and also their meat/totem) determined who they should marry. *Gabii* marries *Yibadhaa*, children are *Gambuu* (male) and *Buudhaa* (female), sister is *Gabudhaa*. Possible source of the surname 'Cubby'. See also: **Marrii, Gambuu, Yibaay**.

gabinya (GR) *noun*
boy. ◆ *Gabinya yarraan-gu galiya-waa-nha.* (GR) The boy is climbing the gum tree. See also: **birray**.

gabirr (YR) *noun*
cabbage. From English 'cabbage'.

gabirra (YY) *noun*
waterlily (*Nymphoides crenata*). Has round leaves up to 10 cm and yellow fringed flowers.

gabiyan (GR) *noun*
bull ant. See also: **burudha**.

Gabudhaa

Gabudhaa (YR, YY, GR) *noun*
women's social section. Marries *Yibaay*, children are *Marrii* (male) and *Maadhaa* (female), brother is *Gabii*. See also: **Buudhaa, Yibadhaa, Maadhaa**.

gabugaan (GR) *noun*
hat. ◆ *Gabugaan ngay bundaa-nhi.* (GR) My hat fell off.
This is a rare word, the common word is *gabundi*.

gabundi (YR, YY, GR) *noun*
1 hat (YR, YY, GR). Originally a type of head cover, possibly worn by men, 'like a tea cosy'.
2 lid, top (YY).

gaburran (YR, YY, GR) *noun*
1 top (YR, YY, GR). ◆ *Ngaama walaay waan-gu maalaa-bidi-dja, ngarribaa gaburran-da.* (YR) The crow's nest (is) in the tree, up there on top.
2 high place (YR). ◆ *Giirruu, dhuu ngaama ngarribali gaburran-gu dhurra-y.* (YR) The smoke rose high over there.
See also: **ngarribaa**.

gabuul (YR, YY) *noun*
mother louse. Also *gabuu*.

gadha (YY) *noun*
little red lizard.

gadhaa (YR) *noun*
cheeky. An affectionate term used in some YR, GR areas. One source.

gadhabal (GR) *exclamation*
wonderful!

gadhamayawa-li (YR, YY) *verb-transitive*
hide. ◆ *Garriya nhama money gadhamayawa-la!* (YY) Don't hide the money!
This is a rare word, the common word is *dhuwinba-li*. The difference between these verbs is not understood. The form of this verb is uncertain.

gadharra (YY) *noun*
little corella *(Cacatua sanguinea)*. Possibly a Guwamu word.

gadharrgadharr (YR, YY) *adjective*
torn, ragged.

gadhiigurrii (YY) *noun*
poison stick, poison bone. Langloh-Parker said that it is smaller than *guuyarra* and is used against women.

gadhuu (YR) *noun*
1 male echidna.
2 echidna ant sack. A bag-like part of the intestines of various animals, including echidna, goanna and turkey. It is like a bird's crop. It is not poisonous in *bigibila*. When an echidna is prepared for eating, the ant sack is removed, so that the meat does not taste of ants (formic acid). In the goanna it is a 'poison bag'. Ted Fields said that when you kill a goanna you should immediately pull the tongue and the bag out.
3 ant nest.
Used in some YR, GR areas.

gadibundhu (YR, YY) *noun*
1 quinine tree *(Alstonia constricta)* (YR, YY). Also known as Peruvian; the name is said to relate to *gadi* (bitter) perhaps in another language.
2 quinine bark (YR). Ted Fields said that the bark of the roots is boiled to make a very bitter liquid useful for diabetes and many other illnesses. The liquid is used to cure infectious sores, though it is very severe on the skin.

gadjigadji (YR) *noun*
re-growth. Lots of little trees, about 2–4 m tall, that have grown up after a flood. This word indicates that there may be an unrecorded word, *gadji* (sapling). One source.

gadjul (YR) *noun*
car spring. Leaf of a car spring used to dig out rabbits, echidnas and other animals. This replaced the traditional wooden *ganay*. One source.

gaga-li (YR, YY, GR) *verb-transitive*
call, shout (at), yell (at), sing out.
◆ *Birralii-djuul-u bamba buwadjarr gaga-laa-nhi.* (YR) The little girl called her father loudly. ◆ *Giirr gaga-y ngaya nginunda.* (YY) I called out to you. ◆ *Bamba nguu gaga-laa-nha.* (YY) He's singing out loudly.
◆ *Ngaandu nganha gaga-laa-nha?* (YY) Who is calling me?

gagalarrin (YR, YY) *noun*
pink cockatoo, Major Mitchell cockatoo *(Cacatua leadbeateri)*. Also *gagalay*. Possible source of English 'Cocklarina'.

gagan.gagan (YR, YY) *adjective*
many coloured. This word indicates that there may be an unrecorded word, *gagan*.

gagarr (YR, YY) *noun*
1 moss.
2 rubbish, leaf litter.

gagil (YR, YY, GR) *adjective, adverb, placename*
1 bad, no good (YR, YY, GR). ◆ *Gagil-wan.gaan ngaama dhadha-y-la-nhi.* (YR) That tasted really bad. ◆ *Gagil nhama gungan.* (YR) That's bad water.
2 Coghill (GR). Ridley said 'bad, nasty (water)'.
Gagil has a wide range of meanings, including 'naughty', 'horrible', 'sore', 'sick', 'jealous' and 'stale'. Sometimes occurs in *gagil-dhuul* (bad — little, one) meaning 'unhappy' or 'bad one, bad person'.

gagilbiyal (YR) *adjective*
sorry. Based on *gagil* (bad) and, possibly, *-biyaay* (with, having). One source.

gagil dhaygal (YR) *noun*
headache. From *gagil* (bad) and *dhaygal* (head).

gagil guuyay (YY) *adjective*
bad mood. From *gagil* (bad) and *guuyay* (mood). Sometimes used to translate 'jealous'.

gagil ngulu (YR, YY) *adjective*
ugly. ◆ *Garriya nhama gagil ngulu dhayn, gaay guwaa-lda-ya.* (YR) Don't talk to that ugly man.
From *gagil* (bad) and *ngulu* (face).

gagilaarriin (YY) *noun*
carbeen flowers. See also: **gaabiin**.

-gal (YR, YY) *suffix*
1 many (little things) (YR, YY). ◆ *Giirr nhama birralii-gal-u bawi-lda-nhi.* (YR) The children were singing.
2 group, mob (YY). Added to *dhurrun* (fur) and *giinbal* (scales) to indicate a class of living things: *dhurrun.gal* (furry group, mob) and *giinbaligal* (scaled group, mob). The suffix *-gal* is used mainly for young people, especially *birralii-gal* (child-many) and for little things. It is also known as the diminutive plural suffix. The suffix *-galgaa* can be attached to any other noun to indicate 'more than one'.

galaanbi-li (YR, YY) *verb-transitive*
scrape. ◆ *Galaanbi-la nhama barran!* (YY) Scrape that boomerang!

galaarr (YR, YY) *question word*
how? Also *gulaarr*. ◆ *Galaarr-nda bundaa-nhi muyaan-di?* (YY) How did you fall off the tree? ◆ *Giirr ngaama bandaarr, bayn dhina, baa-waa-nhi, galaarr-aa nhama dhina gi-nyi.* (YR) The kangaroo is there, hopping along with a sore foot, (I) don't know what happened to his foot.
Sometimes translated as 'what'. The recommended word for 'how?' is *gulaarr*.

galaarr gi-gi (YR, YY) *verb phrase*
1 what to do? ◆ *Miimii, galaarr nginda gi-gi ngandabaa-gu nginunha yii-ldaay?* (YR) Miimii, what will you do if a snake bites you? ◆ *Galaarr ngiyani gi-yaa-nha gi-gi gungan-gu?* (YY) What are we going to do for water?

galaay (YR) *exclamation*
speak of the devil! Ted Fields said that this is used when you are speaking of someone and they appear. One source.

galalu (GR) *noun*
currawong. Possibly pied currawong (*Strepera graculina*). This word is recorded as 'magpie', but there is the common word *burrugarrbuu* (magpie), so this is recommended as a word for currawong, for which no name has been recorded.

galambiirr (YR) *adjective*
greedy. One source. See also: **dhurrin**[2].

galan (YY) *noun*
blister.

galan.galaan (YR, YY) *noun*
native spinach (*Tetragonia tetragonioides*). Also called New Zealand spinach, it is a succulent trailing plant with triangular leaves and greenish yellow flowers. Young shoots can be eaten cooked or raw. Ian Sim said that the name may relate to watery blisters on the plant.

galariin (YR, YY, GR) *noun*
coolabah flowers.

Galariinbaraay (YY, GR) *placename*
Collarenebri. From *galariin* (coolabah blossoms) and *-baraay* (with, having).

galawu (YR, YY) *question word*
when? Also *galaawuu, gulawu, gulaawuu.*

galay

◆ *Galawu nginda dhaay yanaa-nhi.* (YR) When did you come here?
These forms are likely to be related to the two forms *gulaarr* and *galaarr* (how).

galay (YR, YY, GR) *adjective*
new word. See p 160 for more information.

galduman (YR) *noun*
brother. Also *garraman*. Used in some YR, GR areas. One source.

-galgaa (YR, YY) *suffix*
many. ◆ *Dhuwinba-y ngaama nguu wii dhayn-galgaa-dhi.* (YR) She hid the fire from the people.
The suffix *-galgaa* can be attached to any noun to indicate 'more than one', while the suffix *-gal* is only used for young people, especially *birralii-gal* (child-many), and small things. Use of this plural marker is not obligatory.

galgalbanaa (YR, YY) *noun*
burrowing frog *(Neobatrachus sudelli)*. This frog contains water, and was used for food.

galgandi (YR) *noun*
flying fox (made of rope/wire). Used for carrying material, e.g. across a river. One source.

galgarriirr (YR, YY) *noun*
black-headed monitor *(Varanus tristus)*. Sometimes called the pink goanna because the male turns a dirty pink colour during the mating season.

gali (GR) *noun*
1 water.
2 rain.
3 tear.
Also used in some YR areas. See also: **yuuyuu**.

galibaay (GR) *noun*
red-bellied black snake *(Pseudechis porphyriacus)*. Sometimes called water snake. Form uncertain. Probably from *gali* (water).

galibaraay (GR) *adjective*
full of water, wet. From *gali* (water) and *-baraay* (with, having).

Gali Gurunha (YR) *noun, placename*
1 creation spirit. Ted Fields said: 'In the dreamtime *Gali Gurunha* lived at Gingie, and some of the warriors coming back from the Narran River came on dry times, and had no water. *Gali Gurunha* dug the underground river from the Barwon to Cumborah Springs. We believe *Gali Gurunha* created the spring to save the warriors, this is not tradition but history.'
2 waterhole at Gingie. A spirit and the deep hole in the river where he lives. This hole is near Gingie mission, just west of Walgett.
Based on *gali* (water — GR). This name has been written many ways, including *Gali Gurunaa, Gali Gurranaa* and *Gali Gurrna*; however Gingie is in Ngiyambaa country, and in that language *Gali Gurunha* means 'the water is going in' which is consistent with the story.

Galimandi (YR) *placename*
Kalmundi Station. A property on the Collarenebri road (24 miles from Walgett). There is an old camp just up the river from there. From *gali* (water — GR).

galimaramara (GR) *noun*
flock bronzewing *(Phaps histrionica)*. From *gali* (water) and *mara* (hand); probably due to the unusual way the bird lands on water.

galindjari (YR, YY) *noun*
honey drink. A drink made from water and honey. One source said it may contain pituri. Based on *gali* (water — GR).

galingin (YR, GR) *adjective*
thirsty. From *gali* (water) and *-ngin* (wanting).

galinmay (YR, YY) *noun*
water bag. Made from animal skin, probably carpet snake. Probably based on *gali* (water — GR). One source.

galimingaa (YR, YY, GR) *noun*
grandson.

galinggaa (YR, YY, GR) *noun*
sheep intestines (small). Also *galinggali(ng)*. Highly prized as food. Ted Fields said that *galinggaa* are the edible small intestines of the sheep; also known as 'curly guts' they are green when full, so it is better to leave the sheep for a few days before killing it, so they are brown and better to eat.

galiya-y (YR, YY, GR) *verb-intransitive*
1 climb (YR, YY, GR). ◆ *Giirruu ngaya gungandi galiya-nhi.* (YR) I climbed from the river. ◆ *Bawa-ga ngay nhama bulii galiya-waa-nha.* (YY) Fleas are climbing on my back. ◆ *Maadhaay-u nganha gaawaa-nhi, ngaya-bala-dha muyaan-di galiya-nhi.* (YY) The dog chased me and I climbed up the tree. ◆ *Waala-nga galiya-y-la-nhi maayama-bidi-dji.* (YY) He couldn't climb up the big stone.
2 rise (sun/moon) (YR, YY). ◆ *Gundaa nhama galiya-waa-nha, yiiyuu gi-yaa-nha bundaa-gi.* (YY) The clouds are coming up (rising), the rain is going to fall. ◆ *Ngarra-y ngaya baaluu galiya-ngindaay.* (YY) I saw the moon rising.
In one instance on the tapes the verb is used transitively. The object being climbed is most commonly marked with the source suffix, but at times has no suffix. The reasons for the variation are not clear and this verb needs further work.

galuma-li (YR, YY) *verb-transitive*
care for. Form uncertain.

galumaay (YR, YY, GR) *noun*
younger brother. Sources include various comments such as 'before *buurra*' and 'after *buurra*'. ◆ *Galumaay-u wii garra-ldanha.* (GR) My brother is cutting firewood. See also *dhagaan* (brother).

galuuba (YR, YY, GR) *noun*
clover *(Trigonella suavissima)*. A low herb of the pea family, it was eaten by the explorer Thomas Mitchell who said it was delicious, as tender as spinach, and kept its green colour when boiled. From English 'clover'.

gama-li (YR, YY, GR) *verb-transitive*
1 break (YR, YY, GR). ◆ *Giirruu ngaya gama-y nhama bilaarr.* (YR) I broke the spear.
2 block (deflect) (YR). ◆ *Burrul-bidi-dju ngaama dhayn-du bilaarr wana-nhi, ngumbala-nga bubaay-djuul-u gama-nhi.* (YR) The big man threw the spear, the small man blocked it.

gama-y (YR, YY) *verb-intransitive*
break. ◆ *Giirr nhama bilaarr gama-nhi.* (YR) The spear broke.
A change in verb class from *-li* to *-y*. See Learner's Guide.

gamaal (YY) *noun*
taboo. Specifically a camp where someone has died. It was said that some tree carvings were called *gamaal* meaning that someone died there. Possibly related to *gama-li* (break, block).

gamaama-li (YR, YY) *verb-transitive*
rub. This is a rare word, the common word is *gaarra-li*. The difference between these verbs is not understood.

gambaal (YR, YY, GR) *noun*
silver bream, sooty grunter. Sometimes called *baayamala(n)*, because in the original 'turning', when species were given their non-human forms, this fish was favoured by *Baayami* by being allowed to partly keep the power of speech.

gambaay (YR, YY) *noun*
1 sister-in-law (YR, YY). Ginny Rose said that in a story, emu and turkey call each other *gambaay* (sister-in-law).
2 sweetheart (YR). This term was only recorded between women.

gambada (YY) *noun*
scarf. From English 'comforter'.

gambadhuul (YR) *noun*
group of emus. Consisting of the father and chicks. One source.

gambigambi (YY) *noun*
type of moth. A big grey moth that flies at night. Also *gambima*. One source.

gambu (YR, YY) *noun*
stone axe, tomahawk.

Gambuu (YR, YY, GR) *noun*
men's social section. A person's marriage division (and also their meat/totem) determined who they should marry. *Gambuu* marries *Maadhaa*, children are *Gabii* (male) and *Gabudhaa* (female), sister is *Buudhaa*. A possible source of the surname 'Combo'. See also: **Marrii, Gabii, Yibaay**.

gamidjina (YY) *noun*
surveyor. The derivation is unknown, and may actually be a nickname based on *dhina* (foot). One source.

gamil (GR) *particle*
1 no, not.
2 didn't, don't, won't. ◆ *Gamil ngaya*

Gamilaraay

nginu buruma buma-y. (GR) I didn't hit your dog.
Occurs at the beginning of phrases.

gamil maaru (GR) *adverb*
badly, carelessly, not right. From *gamil* (no, not) and *maaru* (well, carefully).

gamila (GR) *particle*
can't, couldn't. Based on *gamil* (no, not). See also *waala* (YR, YY).

gamilgaa (GR) *question word*
why not? Based on *gamil* (no, not). See also *waalgaa* (YR). One source.

gamilu (GR) *particle*
1 hold on, not yet.
2 before.
From *gamil* (no, not) and *-u* (time suffix).

Gamilaraay (YR, YY, GR) *noun*
1 Gamilaraay tribe.
2 Gamilaraay language. ◆ *Gamilaraay nginda guwaa-lda-nha.* (GR) You are speaking Gamilaraay.
From *gamil* (no) and *-araay* (with, having); that is, having *gamil* for 'no'. Older speakers generally put the emphasis on the first syllable. 'Kamilaroi' and 'Gamilaroi' are two common spellings. It has been spelt many other ways.

gamiyan (YR, YY) *noun*
aunt (father's sister). This is a rare word, the common word is *walgan*.

gamugamuu (YR, YY) *noun*
1 maggot.
2 blowfly.

gamugamuubiyaay (YR, YY) *adjective*
fly-blown. From *gamugamuu* (maggot, blowfly) and *-biyaay* (with, having).

gana (YR, YY, GR) *noun*
liver. Also *ganha*. ◆ *Gagil ngay gana gi-nyi.* (YY) My liver got bad.

gana garraa (YR) *adjective*
cranky, shitty. Based on *gana* (liver). One source.

gana garranba-li (YY) *verb phrase*
contradict. Possibly from *gana* (liver) and *garranba-li* (push, shove).

gana walingay (YY) *adjective*
sad. From *gana* (liver) and *walingay* (lonely, sulky).

ganagiil (YR) *adjective*
sad. Probably based on *gana* (liver).

ganaay¹ (YR) *noun, adjective*
1 opening.
2 open.

ganaay² (YR, YY, GR) *adjective*
shallow.

ganadhaa (YR, YY) *adjective*
deep. ◆ *Ganadhaa gungan. Ganadhaa biyuu.* (YY) Deep water. Deep hole.

ganagaa (YR) *noun*
wart.

ganal (GR) *noun*
common ant.

ganalay (YY) *noun*
plains grass *(Astrebla* spp.). Probably Mitchell grass, it was dried on racks in the sun and the seeds were gathered, ground and made into damper; large quantities were stored.

ganandhaal (YY, GR) *noun*
darter, long-necked shag *(Anhinga melanogaster)*. Also known as snake bird.

ganangganaa (YR, YY) *noun*
type of beetle. There is conflicting evidence about this word: it has been used to refer to the green lacewing, the cockroach and a flat black beetle. It is said that the beetle emits a bad smell when crushed.

ganay (YR, YY, GR) *noun*
yamstick, digging stick.
◆ *Nhama nguungu guliirr yanaa-waa-nha, ganay-biyaay.* (YR) His wife is walking with her yamstick.
This is the women's digging stick; it is pointed at one end and used for digging up sand goannas, other game and plants.

ganayanay (YR, YY) *noun*
supplejack tree *(Ventilago viminalis)*. The roots and bark mashed and soaked in water are good for rheumatism, swellings, cuts, sores and toothache. Also said to restore hair in bald men.

gandaadhaay (YY) *noun*
stranger. Greg Fields thought that originally this meant coming from beyond the 'big' river, that is, the Darling River. Probably from *gandaarr* (other side of the river — YR).

gandaarr (YR, YY, GR) *noun*
   other side of river. ◆ *Giirr ngaya gubi-nyi gandaarr-gu.* (YY) I swam to the other side.

gandawa-li (GR) *verb-transitive*
   cover. One source.

gandjarra (YR) *noun, adjective*
   1 best.
   2 champion. See also: **wii**.

gandjibal (YR, YY, GR) *noun*
   policeman. ◆ *Giirr-nha gandjibal-u gaay guwaa-lda-nha dhayn-da.* (YY) The policeman is talking to the men now. From English 'constable'.

ganduwi (YR, YY) *noun*
   1 one male emu. A male emu, when by itself.
   2 bachelor.

gan.garra (YY) *noun*
   tree martin *(Hirundo nigricans)*. Locally called the white-back swallow because of its rump. One source.

ganhaga (YR, YY) *noun*
   underneath, below. As in 'the area below something'.

ganhan (YY) *noun*
   pigweed *(Portulaca oleracea)*. Succulent ground cover with small yellow flowers and small capsules containing many small black seeds. Seeds can be ground into a paste and cooked like a damper. Leaves, stems and roots can be eaten; contains valuable amounts of protein, water, fibre and minerals. See also: **dhamu**.

Ganhanbili (YY) *noun*
   Byame's wife. One of two, the other being Birrangulu. Based on *ganhan* (pigweed).

ganma-li (GR) *verb-transitive*
   1 catch. ◆ *Mari yana-waa-nha bagaay-gu guya ganma-li-gu.* (GR) The men are going to the river to catch fish.
   2 hold. ◆ *Ganma-la nhama buruma!* (GR) Hold on to the dog!

ganu (YR, GR) *adjective*
   all.

ganugu (YR, YY, GR) *pronoun*
   they (more than two people — doer to).

ganunga (YR, YY, GR) *pronoun*
   they (more than two people — doer/done to).

ganungawu (YR, YY) *adjective, pronoun*
   1 all.
   2 whole.
   3 everything.
   Based on *ganu* (all) and *-wu* (all).

ganungu (YR, YY, GR) *pronoun*
   1 their (more than two people). ◆ *Bulanggiirr ganungu banggadha-nhi gungan-da.* (YY) Their blankets floated in the water.
   2 to them (more than two people). This is only used when something is 'given to' or 'done for' them (more than two). *Ganungunda* is used for 'movement to' them (more than two). ◆ *Wuu-na ganungu.* (YY) Give (it) to them.

ganungunda (YR, YY, GR) *pronoun*
   to/at/on them (more than two people). ◆ *Guwiinbaa-ga nhama dhinawan ganungunda dhurra-y.* (YR) The emus came close to them.

ganungundi (YR, YY, GR) *pronoun*
   from them (more than two people). ◆ *Bandaarr ngaama baa-nhi ganungundi.* (YR) The kangaroo hopped away from them.

ganurran (YY) *noun*
   fourteen or fifteen emus.

ganuu (YR) *noun*
   canoe. From English 'canoe'. The recommended word is *bunduurraa*.

ganuurr (GR) *noun*
   red kangaroo *(Macropus rufus)*. Probably used in the east of the area. See also: **bawurra**.

gara-li (GR) *verb-transitive*
   answer.

garaarr (GR) *noun*
   grass. Name for any grass. ◆ *Nhama garaarr dhimba-gu dha-lda-nha.* (GR) The sheep are eating the grass. Possibly from English 'grass'.

garaay (GR) *noun*
   1 sand.
   2 louse nit.

garaay dhuyul (GR) *noun*
   sandhill. From *garaay* (sand) and *dhuyul* (hill, high ground).

garaayaa (YR, YY) *noun*
   restless flycatcher (*Myiagra inquieta*). Call is like a 'razor grinder', a whirring hiss. Is said to be a woman's spirit. When the bird hovers close to the ground it is said to be 'looking for yams', like a woman searching the ground. Possibly related to *garaay* (sand).

gararrngan (GR) *noun*
   caterpillar, grub. One source.

garawi-li (GR) *verb-transitive*
   pelt, throw at. Also *gaarawi-li*. For more information see *gayawi-li*.

garay (GR) *noun*
   word. Also *gari*. ◆ *Burrulaa nhama garay guwaa-lda-nha.* (GR) Many people are talking (words).

garaydhalibaa (GR) *adjective*
   silent. From *garay* (word) and *-dhalibaa* (without).

garigari (YR, YY, GR) *adjective*
   afraid, frightened.

garima-li (YR) *verb-transitive*
   spin (eggs). ◆ *Giirruu ngiyani-luu-nga ngaarrma dhinawan-gu gawu garima-lda-nhi.* (YR) We spun the emu eggs. One source.

garra (YR, YY, GR) *noun, placename*
   1 crack, gap (YR, YY, GR). Any crack in the ground or gap in trees; also a split, crack or saw cut in wood. Perhaps also used to mean a long lagoon.
   2 Gurah (GR). A long lagoon around 70 km north of Moree.
   The word *garra* is very frequently used to form other words. It is probably based on *garra-li* (cut).

Garrabilaa (YY) *placename*
   location. Ian Sim, writing in Goodooga, said this was a placename 'up north', so called because the ground cracks there 'run the same way'. From *garra* (cracks) and *bilaa* (parallel).

Garradhuul (YY) *placename*
   location. From *garra* (cracks) and *-dhuul* (little, one).

garragali (YY) *noun*
   planigale (rat-like marsupial). Like a little rat; lives in *garra* (ground cracks); in a story, said to be *wambanhiiya* (cousin) to *bagandi* (native cat). Probably either paucident planigale (*Planigale gilesi*) or narrow-nosed planigale (*P. tenuirostris*).

garragarraa (YY) *adjective*
   1 cut, mown, clipped.
   2 shaved.
   Based on *garra-li* (cut).

garragarraandi (YR, YY) *noun*
   prickly gecko. A small, thick-tailed gecko, aggressive and vocal. Probably *Heteronotia binoei*. Greg Fields said that it makes the mirage seen in warm weather, and that people were afraid of it because it was originally a great doctor. Named because it lives in *garra* (cracks).

garran.garra (YY) *noun*
   drought. One source. Possibly based on *garra* (cracks), which appear during droughts.

garra-li (YR, YY, GR) *verb-transitive*
   cut. ◆ *Nguuma dhayn-duul-u nhama bandaarr garra-laa-nha nhaayba-gu.* (YR) The man is cutting the kangaroo up with a knife. ◆ *Giirr ngaama garra-ngiili-nyi.* (YR) That one cut himself. ◆ *Nginda nhama wii garra-la wii-gu!* (GR) You cut the firewood for the fire!

garra-y (YR, YY) *verb-intransitive*
   1 be cut. ◆ *Baburr nguu buma-y maayama-ga, bundaa-nhi-nya, dhinbirr nguungu garra-nhi maayama-ga.* (YY) He hit his foot on a rock, (he) fell, his knee was cut on the rock.
   2 choke. ◆ *Garriya yalagiirrma garra-waa-ya!* (YR) Don't choke like that! ◆ *Garra-nhi nhama birralii-djuul dhinggaa dha-lda-ndaay.* (YR) The boy choked while eating meat.
   This verb is not fully understood and needs further work. A change in verb class from *-li* to *-y*. See Learner's Guide.

garraagaa (YR, YY, GR) *noun*
   crane (bird).

garrabi-y (YY) *verb-intransitive*
   be full of food. ◆ *Giirr ngaya garrabi-nyi.* (YY) I am full (not hungry). One source.

garragarraan (YR) *noun*
   straight river. Ted Fields said it is a straight stretch of river with high banks,

suitable for setting nets to catch ducks. One source.

garralan (GR) *noun*
sword. From *garra-li* (cut).

Garrali (YY) *placename*
location. Ian Sim said it is a place on the Narran River where, in a story, the hero 'cut across, from one point to another in a straight line', instead of following a winding path.

garran (YR) *noun*
quarrel, row. Probably related to *garranba-li* (push, shove). One source.

garranba-li (YY) *verb-transitive*
push against, shove. One source.

garran.garraan (YY) *adjective*
1 tight, stuck tight.
2 constipated.
Probably related to *garranba-li* (push, shove).

garrangay (YR, YY, GR) *noun*
duck. Name for any duck.

garrarana (YR) *noun*
1 bullroarer.
2 dragonfly.
Used in some YR, GR areas. One source. See also: **murrumanamanaa**.

garrarr (YR, YY) *noun*
tree frog (one type). Possibly *Litoria nasuta*. A small grey frog with long legs and a sharp nose.

garrawa-li (YY) *verb-transitive*
keep, retain, store. ◆ *Garrawa-la!* (YY) Keep it! One source.

garrawal (YR, YY) *noun*
shop, store. According to Ian Sim, this word is related to *garrawa-li* and means 'a place where things are kept'.

Garrawila (GR) *placename*
Garrawila. Mary Jane Cain said it was where a big battle had been fought.

Garrawilingaay (YR) *placename*
Currawillinghi. The name of a property near Hebel where there are lots of rabbit burrows. Probably based on *garra* (crack).

garrawirr (GR) *noun*
ringtail possum (*Pseudocheirus peregrinus*). The ringtail is not a typical Western Plains animal but is usually found in the eastern ranges. One source.

garrayarray (YY) *noun*
native peach (*Ehretia membranifolia*). Possibly based on *garra* (crack) and *-araay* (with, having); or a reduplicated form.

garrbaali (YR, YY) *noun*
shingleback lizard (*Trachydosaurus rugosus*).

garri-y (GR) *verb-intransitive*
stop, cease doing. See also: **garriya**².

garriguwin.guwin (YY) *noun*
grey butcherbird (*Cracticus torquatus*). See also: **guwaaydjidji**.

garrii (YR, YY) *noun*
black orchid (*Cymbidium canaliculatum*). Also called wild arrowroot and tree orchid, it grows in the forks or hollow spouts of gum trees. The fruit and the bulbs can be eaten; the bulbs are very starchy but can be grated or pounded and the starch washed out. It can be used as a medicine.

Garriibarra (YY) *noun*
orchid country people. According to Ginny Rose and Greg Fields, the *Garriibarra* might have originally been a group of YY speakers from somewhere on the eastern side of YY territory. From *garrii* (tree orchid) and *-barra* (people from).

garriil (GR) *adjective*
cold. ◆ *Ngaya garriil.* (GR) I am cold.

garril (YY, GR) *noun*
leaf.

garril budhal (YY) *noun*
game with toy club. Langloh-Parker said of the game: 'If a bush is not at hand, a bushy branch of a tree is stuck up. The men arm themselves with *budhal* or miniature waddies, then stand a few feet behind the bush, which varies from five to eight feet or so in height. They throw their *budhal* in turn; these have to skim through the top of the bush, which seems to give them fresh impetus instead of slackening them. The distance they go beyond is the test of a good thrower; over three hundred yards is not unusual.' Probably from *garril* (leaf) and *budhal* (toy club).

Garrilgarril (YR) *placename*
location. A shady fishing spot possibly on

garrimaay

Currawillinghi (Garrawilingaay) Station. From *garril* (leaf). One source.

garrimaay (YR, YY, GR) *noun*
1 mother-in-law (wife's mother) (YR, YY, GR).
2 son-in-law (woman's daughter's husband) (YR, YY, GR).
3 grandmother (father's mother) (GR). This term probably has to do with the avoidance relationship that existed between these relations. An avoidance relationship was part of social law, it was not to do with whether individuals liked each other or not. For more information, see *buyal*.

Garriya¹ (YR, YY) *noun*
crocodile. Sometimes known as the 'alligator', *Garriya* is the mythical giant creative serpent, which made the rivers and lakes. It is associated with water and rain, and is represented in the night sky by a dark shape along the Milky Way. To speak this name aloud, especially near water, is said to be dangerous because he might hear you. In autumn and winter, when his sky form is most extensive to the north, *Garriya* is said to stand up (*dhuyuwarra*); in the spring he goes away. There appears to be no association between *Garriya* and rainbows, although his eyes are said to be rainbow-like (coloured and striped). They project a 'coloured light' up through the water. This serves as a warning to ordinary people, but as a beacon to *mali* (clever men's spirits) who get magic from him. It is said that *Garriya* has a kind of foot, and can 'stand up to look at the country'.

garriya² (YR, YY, GR) *particle*
don't, stop. ◆ *Garriya nhama ngay nhaayba gaa-nga!* (GR) Don't take my knife!
◆ *Garriya gaarrima-la gungan.* (YY) Don't spill the water. ◆ *Garriya gaay guwaa-la!* (YY) Stop talking!
This is stronger than *gamil* or *waal*. It occurs at the beginning of sentences and is the most common way of giving a negative command. It is the imperative (command) form of the underlying verb *garri-y* (stop). It is followed by an imperative form of the verb.

garriyawu (YR, YY) *exclamation*
wait a while! ◆ *Nguwama garriyawu!* (YR) Wait there!
From *garriya* (don't, stop).

garru (YY) *noun*
fur cloak. One source.

garrul (YR) *noun*
halo around moon or sun. One source.

garruu (YR, YY, GR) *noun*
1 uncle (mother's brother).
2 father-in-law.
This is the common word for 'uncle'. These two relations would be in the same social section. Also occurs as *garruugii*.

garruuyal (YY) *noun*
sandalwood tree grub.

garruwi (YY, GR) *noun*
sandalwood tree (*Eremophila mitchellii*). This is a rare word, the common word is *badha*.

garungga-y (YR, YY) *verb-intransitive*
drown. ◆ *Birralii garungga-nhi gaawaa-ga.* (YY) (The) boy drowned in the river.

garunggama-li (YR) *verb-transitive*
drown. ◆ *Bulaa-yu dhayn-du bayama-y nhama bandaarr waama gungan-da garunggama-y.* (YR) Two men caught that kangaroo then drowned him in the river. From *garungga-* (drown) and *-ma-li* (suffix that makes a transitive verb).

gawaa-y (YR, YY) *verb-transitive*
chase, follow, drive. ◆ *Maadhaay-u nganha gawaa-nhi ngaya-bala muyaan-di galiya-nhi.* (YY) The dog chased me and I climbed up the tree. This verb means both 'chase' and 'follow', as in: 'fish following deep water' and 'kookaburra and lizard following pelican to discover her secret fire'. It also means to 'drive' as in 'drive an animal or a bird along'.

gawarrawarr (YR, YY, GR) *adjective*
green. Also recorded as 'blue'.

gawarrgay (YR, YY) *noun*
spirit emu. This is the Coal Sack, a dark emu-shaped patch in the night sky, near the Southern Cross, which is said to be a spirit emu. Ginny Rose said that its nest is similar to an emu's but the eggs are pure white, and its generally 'upside down'

stance in the sky during autumn and winter relates to the (earthly) emu's breeding cycle. Also a featherless emu which lives underwater and hates people, and is highly feared. Thought to be related to *Garriya* and to live in the same deep waterholes.

gawaruurr wanaayal (YY) *noun*
blowfly *(Calliphoridae)*. Possibly from *gawarrawarr* (green) and *banhaayal* (bush fly). One source. See also: **gamugamuu**.

gawu (YR, YY, GR) *noun*
1 egg (YR, YY, GR). ◆ *Buumadhayaa-gu nhama gawu dha-lda-nha baaldharradharra-gu.* (YR) The fox is eating the plover's eggs.
2 brain (YR, YY).
3 insect (YR, YY, GR).
Also *gabu*.

gawubaa (YR) *noun*
egg yolk. From *gawu* (egg) and *-baa* (meaning uncertain in this word).

gawugalgaa (YY) *noun*
insects. A name for any swarm of small insects, e.g. as seen around a lamp at night, or a cloud of midges. From *gawu* (insect) and *-galgaa* (many).

gawubarray (YR, YY) *noun*
star.

Gawubuwan Gunigal (GR) *placename*
Boobera Lagoon or MacIntyre River. One source. Form uncertain.

gawugaa (GR) *noun*
1 head.
2 head hair.
Possibly from *gawu* (brain) and *-ga* (at) so, 'where the brain is'.

gawun (YR, YY) *noun*
orphan (fatherless child).

gawuwildhaa (YR) *noun*
western bloodwood *(Eucalyptus opaca)*. Possibly means 'rambling' or 'wandering aimlessly' due to the curling branches. One source.

gay (YR, YY) *noun*
snake track. Snake tracks were carefully avoided as treading on one was thought to cause skin sores; the cart tracks of the early European explorer Mitchell were thought to be a giant snake track.

gaya-li (YR, YY) *verb-transitive*
answer. ◆ *Waal gaya-lda-ya!* (YR) Don't answer!

gaya-y (YR, YY) *verb-intransitive*
turn, turn over, twist. ◆ *Gaya-ya, nhamunda dhanduwi-ya!* (YY) Turn over and lie on your ribs! ◆ *Dhaygal ngay gaya-waa-nha.* (YY) My head is turning (I have a headache).
Related to *gaya-li*. A change in verb class from *-li* to *-y*. See Learner's Guide.

gayaa (YR, YY, GR) *adjective*
1 happy (YR, YY, GR). ◆ *Gayaa nhama maadhaay gi-yaa-nha.* (YR) This dog will be happy.
2 pleased (YR, YY).
3 proud (YR, YY).

gayaandhi (YR) *noun*
peacekeeper. Possibly from *gayaa* (happy).

gayaangay (YY) *noun*
five or six emus. One source.

gayaay[1] (YR, YY) *noun*
1 sand (YY).
2 louse nit (YR, YY).

gayaayaan (YY) *noun*
sandhill. From *gayaay* (sand). See also: **gumbugan**.

gayaay[2] (YR, YY, GR) *adjective*
sexy, randy.

gayaayabi-li (YR, YY, GR) *verb-transitive*
restricted word. See p 20 for more information.

gayadharri (YR) *noun*
monster, freak. Animals which are unusual, e.g. a camel. One source.

gayalaay (YY) *noun*
tabooed woman's camp. One source.

-gayaluu (YY) *suffix*
inhabitants of, dweller in. Also *-gaali*, *-gali*. This suffix is added to the place word, e.g. *Narran-gayaluu* (Narran-inhabitants) meaning people of the Narran River; and *garra-gali* (cracks-dweller in) meaning an animal that lives in ground cracks. One source.

gayandaay (YR, YY) *noun*
1 bora spirit (YR, YY). The leading spirit at the *buurra* (bora) is said to be the father-in-law to all people. *Gayamay* (or *Gayami*), is his wife who is mother-in-law to all

people. On earth they appear as the rainbow: the upper band of colours is the man; the lower band is his wife. In the Guwamu language these spirits are *Ngardbana* and his wife *Ngardgirigan*.
2 bullroarer (YY). The sound of the bullroarer is *Gayandaay*'s voice, calling the young men to be initiated.
3 brother-in-law (YR, YY). Ted Fields said that a boy was handed over to *Gayandaay* at the *buurra* ceremony. It was perhaps a person or the place where they put a young boy when he became a man.

gayarr (YY) *noun*
back of knee. One source.

gayarra-gi (YR, YY, GR) *verb-transitive*
search for, look for. Also *gayrra-gi*. ◆ *Giirr ngaya-nga gayarra-gi-la-nha ngambaa-dhi ngay.* (YR) I am looking for my mother.

gayarra-y (YR, YY, GR) *verb-intransitive*
1 turn around, revolve (YR, YY, GR). Also used to mean 'change direction', e.g. 'The wind changed direction.' ◆ *Birralii-djuul bandaarr-giirr gayarra-nhi.* (YR) The child turned around like a kangaroo.
2 turn into, transform (YR, YY). ◆ *Yinarr gayarra-nhi burraalga.* (YY) The woman turned into a brolga.
3 tangle up (YR). ◆ *Giirr ngaama dhunbil gayarra-nhi.* (YR) The sinews got all tangled up.

gayawi-li (YR, YY) *verb-transitive*
1 pelt, throw at. The 'thing thrown' has the 'using' (instrumental) suffix. ◆ *Giirruu ngaama birray-djuul-u maayama-gu gayawi-lda-nhi ngaama garrangay.* (YR) The boys were throwing stones at the ducks.
◆ *Gayawi-li ngaya gi-yaa-nha nginunha bugalaa-gu.* (YY) I am going to pelt you with the ball.
2 point bone, kill. Used with *guuyarra* (ceremonial bone). ◆ *Wiringin-du nhama guuyarra-gu gayawi-y.* (YY) The witchdoctor pointed the bone (at him).
Also *gaayawi-li*. See also: **wana-gi**.

gayga (YY) *noun*
budda pea *(Aeschynomene indica)*. Also known as kath sola, this is a shrub of the legume or bean family, having yellow flowers and producing pith, the substance used to make pith helmets, fishing floats and rafts.

gaygay (YR, YY, GR) *noun*
catfish *(Tandanus tandanus)*. Possibly from *gayn* (scraper) because of the smooth scaleless skin.

gayiya (YY) *noun*
spider. Name for any spider. One source.

gayiyabarra (YY) *noun*
spider web. From *gayiya* (spider) and *barra* (thread). One source.

gayla-y (YR, YY) *verb-intransitive*
1 burn. ◆ *Giirr nhama dhinggaa gayla-nhi.* (YR) The meat is burnt.
2 cook. ◆ *Giirruu ngaya baayama-laa-nha, waalu nhama gayla-nhi gawu.* (YY) I'm spinning it up all right now, but the egg's not cooked yet.

gaylama-li (YR, YY) *verb-transitive*
burn. ◆ *Garriya ngaama dhinggaa gaylama-la!* (YR) Don't burn that meat!
From *gayla-* (burn) and *-ma-li* (suffix that makes a transitive verb). See also: **gudhuwa-li, gundaawa-li**.

gayliyaay (YR, YY) *adjective*
1 good-hearted, kind.
2 generous.
Form is uncertain but probably includes *-iyaay* (with, having).

gayma-li (YR, YY) *verb-transitive*
1 stir. ◆ *Gayma-la nhama budhun.* (YY) Stir the pudding.
2 twist. ◆ *Buyu-dhi nhama gayma-la dhunbil dhuwima-li-gu.* (YY) Twist the sinew to get it out of the leg.
3 turn. ◆ *Gayma-la nhama nhaadhiyaan.* (YY) Turn that log over.
Probably from *gaya-* (turn, twist) and *-ma-li* (suffix that makes a transitive verb). Also *gayama-li*.

gayn (YR, YY) *noun*
scraper. A tool, often an old boomerang, used to push, scrape, and smooth down coals for cooking. Related to *gaynma-li* (scrape).

gaynda (YY) *noun*
carpenter's plane. Or anything used to smooth things. From *gayn* (fire rake).

gayn.gayn¹ (YY) *adjective*
1 smooth.
2 calm.

gayn.gayn² (YR, YY) *noun*
native lime *(Eremocitrus glauca)*. Also known as desert lime, desert lemon, and native cumquat. This spiny shrub of the citrus family has a round, yellow, edible fruit which can be used in marmalade and drinks.
It is unusual to have a one-syllable word repeated in this way.

gaynma-li (YY) *verb-transitive*
1 smooth off.
2 scrape.
3 calm.
Related to *gayn* (scraper). One source.

gayrr (YR, YY, GR) *noun*
name. ◆ *Ngaandi nginda gayrr?* (YR) What's your name?

gayrriyaay (YY) *adjective*
1 named.
2 well known.
From *gayrr* (name) and *-iyaay* (having).

gayrra (YR) *noun*
new word. See p 20 for more information.

gayrragumbirri (YR) *noun*
new word. See p 20 for more information.

gayrrba-li (YR, YY) *verb-transitive*
name. ◆ *Gayrrba-la dhayn!* (YY) Name that man! From *gayrr* (a name) and *-ba-li* (verb suffix associated with making sound).

-gi (YR, YY, GR) *suffix*
future tense suffix for *-gi* class verbs.
◆ *Ngawu-gi gulawuliil-u.* (YY) The topknot pigeon will drink.

gi-gi (YR, YY, GR) *verb-intransitive*
1 be, become (get) (YR, YY, GR). ◆ *Yuulngin ngaya gi-nyi.* (GR) I am (got) hungry. ◆ *Giirr ngaya bayn gi-gi-la-nhi.* (YR) I was sick.
◆ *Minya-nginda-nda gi-gi-la-nha?* (YR) What do you want? (What do you lack?)
◆ *Waal-bala ngaya garigari gi-gi-la-nha.* (YR) I don't get frightened.
2 going to (do something) (YR, YY). When used in this context, the form of this verb is always *gi-yaa-nha* or *gi-yaa-nhi*. ◆ *Giirr ngaya gi-yaa-nha dhanduwi-y.* (YR) I am going to lie down. ◆ *Giirr gi-yaa-nha nguu gaarrima-li.* (YR) He is going to spill it.

◆ *Giirruu nhama dhayn-dhuul buyabuya gi-yaa-nha.* (YR) The small man is getting (going to be) bony/thin.
3 goes to (leads) (YR). ◆ *Walaay-gu ngay nhama yuruun gi-yaa-nha.* (YR) This road goes to my camp.
In many cases the English verb 'be' (is, was etc.) is not translated by *gi-gi* but by a verb suffix, e.g. *yanaa-waa-nha* 'is walking', or another verb, e.g. *dhinawan dhuyul-a warra-y-la-nha* 'the emu is (standing) on the hill'. See Learner's Guide.

giba (YR, YY) *noun*
small grindstone. Arthur Dodd said it is used for grinding seeds and sharpening tools. See also: **dhayurr**.

giban (YR, YY) *noun*
native banana yam *(Marsdenia australis)*. Arthur Dodd said that *gaagulu* is the vine that *giban* grows on: you follow the vine, find one the size of a tennis ball joined onto another one, you dig further and get one the size of your head; 'When you eat them you wouldn't know when to knock off. Sweet.' Fred Reece said: '*Giban* is a big potato — there were some at the Three Mile (at Lightning Ridge), vine run up the tree, with fruit . . . dig down, and you get one then another, all full of water. They only grow in certain parts, in patches, grow as big as grapefruit, all white as snow, full of water, eat them raw, taste earthy, and all water — a bit sweetish.'

gibaylandhi (GR) *adverb*
formerly. One source. Form uncertain.

gidjarray (YR, YY) *noun*
twelve apostle bird *(Struthidea cinerea)*. Also *gidjiyarray*. Fred Reece called this bird lousy Jack, and said it was the first to make friends with you in the bush.

gidjarri (YR) *adjective*
nervous. One source.

gidjigidji (YR) *noun*
armpit. One source.

gidjigidjiba-li (YR, YY) *verb-transitive*
tickle. ◆ *Baburr ngaya-laa nginu gidjigidjiba-li.* (YY) I will tickle your feet.

gidjiirr

Related to *gidjigidji* (underarm) and *-ba-li* (verb suffix).

gidjiirr (YR, YY, GR) *noun, adjective*
1 gidgee *(Acacia cambagei)* (YR, YY, GR). Large wattle tree, sometimes known as stinking wattle due to the leaves giving off a strong smell when rain is approaching or when wet.
2 yellow ochre (YR).
3 yellow (YR).
Possible source of English 'gidgee'.

gidjirrgidjirr (YR, YY, GR) *adjective*
yellow. From *gidjiirr* (gidgee tree) because of its yellow flowers.

gidjirrigaa (YR, YY, GR) *noun*
1 budgerigar *(Melopsittacus undulatus)* (YR, YY, GR).
2 star (a particular star) (YY). A yellowish star in the north, opposite the Southern Cross: possibly Arcturus.
Possibly from *gidjirr* (yellow). Possible source of English 'budgerigar'.

gigirrgigirr (YR, YY) *noun*
west wind.

gigirrma-li (YR, GR) *verb-transitive*
kick. Also *gigima-li*. ◆ *Bamba nguu buwadjarr nguungu gigirrma-y.* (YR) He kicked his father hard.
From *gig* ('kick') and *-irrma-li* (suffix added to English verbs).

giguwi (YR, YY, GR) *noun*
1 sneeze (YR, YY, GR).
2 hiccup (YR, YY). ◆ *Giguwi nhama dhu-dha-nhi ngiyarrma.* (YR) He had hiccups.

giguwi dhu-rri (YR, YY) *verb phrase*
1 sneeze (YR, YY). ◆ *Giguwi dhu-na!* (YY) Sneeze!
2 hiccup (YR).
From *giguwi* (sneeze, hiccup) and *dhu-rri* (poke etc.). This has also been written as one word: *giguwidhu-rri*.

gigwidjil (YR) *noun, placename*
1 red soil. Ted Fields said it is claypan or 'hard red' country.
2 Kigwigil. Property west of Walgett. Said to come from *gii guwiigaa* meaning 'there are lots of termite nests'. A paddock on Bangate Station had a similar name. One source.

gii (YR, YY, GR) *noun, adjective*
1 heart (YR, YY, GR).
2 gall bladder (YY).
3 bitter (YY).
4 blueberry (common name) (YY). Another name for *buubiyala* (blueberry) due to the bitterness of its fruit.

giibaabu (YR, YY) *time adverb*
early morning. Ted Fields said 'before sun up'.

giidjaa (YR, YY, GR) *noun*
1 ant (any, black) (YR, YY, GR).
2 shrimp (YR, YY).
Some evidence for the meaning 'black ant', but probably can mean any ant.

giidjuugiidjuu (YY) *adverb*
constant. To describe an action that is ongoing or repetitious. One source.

giidjuwaa (YY) *adjective*
green. This is a rare word, the common word is *gawarrawarr*.

giigal (YR, YY) *noun*
scab.

giigaliyaay (YR, YY) *adjective*
scabby. From *giigal* (scabs) and *-iyaay* (with, having).

gii-gi (YR, YY) *verb-intransitive*
itch. ◆ *Gii-gi-la-nha ngay bungun.* (YY) My arm is itching. Form uncertain.

Giiguradjin (YY) *placename*
Narran Lake. Refers to a northern part of the lake. Said to be from *gii Garriya-djin* meaning 'the *Garriya* created this'.

giil (YR, YY, GR) *noun*
1 piss, urine (YR, YY, GR).
2 beer (YR, YY). Compare Australian English slang 'piss' (alcohol).
Also, probably only in recent times, *giili*.

giili-y (YR, GR) *verb-intransitive*
urinate, piss. ◆ *Giirr nhama birralii-djuul giili-nyi napkin-da.* (YR) That baby pissed in his pants (his nappy).

giinba-li (YR, YY) *verb-transitive*
scale. ◆ *Giinba-la nhama ngaaluurr!* (YY) Scale that fish!

giinbal (YR, YY, GR) *noun*
scales. Of fish, snakes and lizards.

giinbaligal (YY) *noun*
scaly tribe. The scaly tribe refers to reptiles and fish as a group; it is one of three types of animals, others being the furry and the feathered tribes. Also refers to people and totems. Based on *giinbal* (scales) and *-gal* (group, mob).

giinbay (GR) *noun*
small mussel. Also *giinbaay*.

giinbaywarraymal (YY) *noun*
seagull, silver gull *(Larus novaehollandiae)*. From *giinbay* (mussel — GR) and *warrayma-li* (send); so 'sender/bringer of mussels', from a story. See also: **maanggiiwarraywarraymal**.

giindjuu (YR) *noun*
bone marrow. This word is probably related to *gindjul* with something like 'slime' being the common meaning.

giin.gii (YR, YY) *noun, placename*
1 bubble, froth (YR, YY).
2 frog eggs (YR, YY).
3 Gingie (YR). Site of an old mission, now a village just outside Walgett. Named because of the froth on the river there during floods.
Also *giigii*.

giiri-gi (GR) *verb-intransitive*
itch. One source. Form uncertain.

-giirr (YR, YR, GR) *suffix*
like, similar to. ◆ *Giirr nhama bubaay gilay dhurra-laa-nha, barran-giirr.* (YR) That new moon is rising, (it's) like a boomerang.
◆ *Bamba nham banaga-y-la-nha, yarraaman-giirr.* (YR) He runs fast, like a horse.
Probably related to *giirr* (really, truly), this suffix is added to nouns. Also occurs in *yuluwirri-giirr maayama* (rainbow-like stone), meaning 'opal'.

giirr (YR, YY, GR) *particle*
really, truly. ◆ *Giirr ngaya guwaa-y, giirr.* (YR) I did tell, really.
When said by itself, *giirr* means 'right' or 'true'. Occurs mainly at the beginning of sentences. Its exact meaning is unclear but is usually translated as 'really', also 'certainly' or 'indeed'.

giirr maaru (GR) *exclamation*
well done!, good job! From *giirr* (really, truly) and *maaru* (well, carefully).

giirr maayu (YR, YY) *exclamation*
well done!, good job! ◆ *'Giirr maayu' ngaya guwaa-y.* (YY) I said 'well done'.
From *giirr* (really, truly) and *maayu* (well, carefully).

giirrnga (YY) *exclamation*
that's enough! From *giirr* (right) and *-nga* (now). One source.

giirruu (YR, YY, GR) *particle*
absolutely, too right. From *giirr* (really, truly) and *-uu* (all), which makes the statement stronger than if *giirr* is used. Arthur Dodd translates *giirruu dhalaybaa* as 'terrible sharp'.

giirra-li (GR) *noun*
wake up. One source. Form uncertain.

giirray (GR) *noun*
crayfish.

giirrgal (YY) *noun*
tomahawk. Also *girrgal*. ◆ *Dhaay nhama ngay giirrgal wuu-na.* (YY) Give (me) my tomahawk.
See also: **dhamiyaa**.

giiyan (YY, GR) *noun*
centipede.

giiyanma-li (YR, YY, GR) *verb-transitive*
frighten. ◆ *Ngambaa, dhagaan-du nganha giiyanma-lda-nha.* (YY) Mother, my brother is frightening me.
From *giyal* (afraid) and *-ma-li* (suffix that makes a transitive verb). Possibly *giyanma-li*.

-gi-la-y (YR, YY, GR) *suffix*
regular progressive suffix for *-gi* class verbs. ◆ *Giirr ngambaa-gu birralii-djuul nhima-y, waal yu-gi-la-y-gu.* (YR) The mother pinched the little boy, (so he) wouldn't cry. ◆ *Maadhaay-u yu-gi-la-nha.* (YY) The dog is howling.

gilaa (YR, YY, GR) *noun*
galah *(Cacatua roseicapilla)*. Possible source of English 'galah'.

gilaan.garra (YR, YY) *noun, placename*
1 Darling pea (YR, YY). Shrubby bush to 2 m with purple-pink pea-like flowers.
2 location (YY). A place down the river from Bangate Station.

gilay (YR, GR) *noun*
moon. See also: *baaluu*.

gilgaay (YR) *noun*
shallow waterhole. Used for a place where water lies in a paddock after rain, not a waterhole in the river. A common word around many parts of Australia. One source.

gilgal (YY) *noun*
small waterhole. Used in Goodooga for the small round waterholes found in hard-pan country, often surrounded by dense grass. One source.

gilgulba-rri (YR, YY) *verb-intransitive*
come out, emerge. ◆ *Gilgulba-na!* (YY) Come out! Ted Fields said that this refers to a snake, goanna or possum coming out of a hole. The form of this verb is uncertain.

-gili (YR, YY) *suffix*
side (location). Words with this suffix indicate on which side something happened, e.g. *ngaarrigili* (other side), *ngawugili* (this side) and *ngarribaagili* (above).

giligili (YR) *adjective*
upset. Ted Fields said it is used, for example, of a horse that is upset as the saddle is being put on. One source.

giliin (YR) *adjective*
clean. From English 'clean'.

giluu (YR, YY) *noun*
aunt (father's sister). This is a rare word, the common word is *walgan*.

gima (GR) *noun*
marsupial mouse. This word could now be used as a general term for 'marsupial mouse'.

gimbi-li (YR, YY) *verb-transitive*
1 do. ◆ *Giirr-bala nhama nguu maayu gimbi-lda-nha.* (YR) He is doing it very carefully.
2 make (construct). ◆ *Yaluu ngaya-laa buurr gimbi-li* (YY) I am going to make another fishing line.

gimiyandi (GR) *time adverb*
yesterday. One source.

gimubi-li (GR) *verb-transitive*
1 do.
2 make (construct).

See *gimbi-li* for more information.

gindama-y (YR, YY, GR) *verb-intransitive*
laugh. The one being laughed at is marked by the 'source' case. ◆ *Gugurrgaagaa gindama-nhi nganundi.* (YR) The kookaburras laughed at me. ◆ *Giirruu nhama birralii-djuul gindama-la-nhi maadhaay-dji.* (YR) The children were laughing at the dog.

gindarragaa (YR) *adjective*
funny. Probably related to *gindama-y* (laugh). One source.

Gindhayndaamuwi (YY) *noun*
son of Byame. One source. Form uncertain.

gindjul (YR) *noun*
1 diarrhoea.
2 snail slime/track.

gindjulgarra (YR, YY) *noun*
snail. Probably based on *gindjul* (slime).

gindjulmaan (YR) *noun*
crayfish colon. The visible 'shit bag'. Probably based on *gindjul* (slime). One source.

gindjurra (GR) *noun*
frog. This is a rare word, the common word is *yurayaa* (any frog).

giniirr (YR, YY) *noun*
evil spirit. Also *giniirrginiirr*. A spirit who calls out his name at night; the 'bogeyman'. Used currently in some YR, YY, GR areas.

ginilgarriya (YY) *noun*
ceremonial log. A log, shaped and painted to represent *Garriya* (a crocodile) and used in ceremonies to bring and to stop rain. It was kept in a secluded place. The ceremonies were said to include men riding on the crocodile's back, to bring rain, and shovelling hot coals into the crocodile's open mouth, to stop rain. From *giniy* (stick, tree) and *Garriya* (crocodile).

giniy (YR, YY) *noun*
1 stick.
2 tree. Used in Walgett.

giniybaal (YR) *noun*
corner post. For example, the corner post of a fence. Based on *giniy* (stick).

giniybarra (YR) *noun*
tree spirit. Ted Fields said it is the name of

a tree spirit at Miralwin. From *giniy* (tree) and *barra* (people from). One source.

giniy waal (YR) *noun*
dead wood. From *giniy* (tree) and *waal* (no). One source.

giniy walingay (YR, YY) *noun*
unusual tree. Any tree growing out of its normal environment, away from others of its species; said to be sad or grieving at being separated from its own kind. From *giniy* (tree) and *walingay* (lonely, sulky).

girraa (YR, YY) *noun*
leaf.

girran.girraa (YR, YY) *noun, placename*
1 leaves (YR, YY).
2 location (YY). A place on the Narran River, up from Angledool.
One of the few words that form a plural by reduplication. Seems to have the meaning 'bunch' or 'mass of leaves' rather than just many leaves which is *burrulaa girraa*. Also *girraan.girraa*.

Girrawiin (YR, YY) *placename*
Girrawheen. A National Park near Wallangarra on the NSW–Queensland border. Thought to mean 'place of flowers'. Possibly based on *girraa* (leaf) and *-(b)iyan*. See Learner's Guide.

girrabirrii (YR, YY, GR) *noun*
long-necked turtle (*Chelodina longicollis*).

girran (YR, YY, GR) *noun*
ashes.

girrandhaal (YR) *noun*
rake. Based on *girran* (ashes). One source.

girranbiiyan (YY) *noun*
sandhill wattle (*Acacia ligulata*). Ian Sim said that it is a type of silver wattle; the wood ash was used, possibly for medicinal purposes. The seeds can be ground and roasted for damper; and the grubs in the roots can be eaten. The bark can be boiled or soaked, and drunk as cough medicine and for dizziness, nerves and fits. Sick people can be 'smoked' with the leaves.

girray (YR, YY) *noun*
battle.

girraybaa (YY) *noun*
battle ground. From *girray* (battle) and *-baa* (place of, time of).

girribal (YR, YY, GR) *noun*
riddle. A form of riddle or question/answer game which was a popular pastime. Langloh-Parker said: 'Riddles play a great part in their social life, and he who knows many is much sought after. (They are) little songs describing the things to be guessed, whose peculiarities the singer acts as he sings — a sort of one-man show, pantomime in miniature, with a riddle running through it.

'For example: What is it that says to the floodwater, "I am too strong for you, you cannot push me back?" Answer: *guduu* (codfish).

'What is it that says, "You cannot help yourself; you will have to go and let me take your place; you cannot stay when I come?" Answer: the grey hairs in a man's beard to the black ones.

' "If a man hide himself so that his wife could not see him, and he wanted her to know where he was, yet had promised not to speak, laugh, cry, sneeze, cough, nor move his hands nor feet, how could he do so?" Answer: whistle.

' "The strongest man cannot stand against me. I can knock him down, yet I do not hurt him. He feels better for my having knocked him down. What am I?" Answer: sleep.

' "I am not water, yet all who are thirsty, seeing me, come toward me to drink, though I am no liquid. What am I?" Answer: a mirage.

' "What is it that goes along the creek, across the creek, underneath it, and along it again, and yet has left neither side?" Answer: The yellow-flowering creeping water-weed.

' "Here I am, just in front of you. I can't move; but if you kick me I will knock you down, though I will not move to do it." Who says this? Answer: a stump that anyone falls over.

' "You cannot walk without me, yet you grease your body and forget me and let me crack, even though, but for me, you could neither walk nor run." Who says that? Answer: someone's feet.'

girrigirri

Another example: What animals are these: the first says: 'Friend, how can you see from the side?' The second animal replies: 'And how can you see, looking from the nose?' Answer: *yin.ga* (crayfish) and *ngalaagaa* (crab).

girrigirri (YR) *adjective*
noisy. According to one source, this expression is used in *girribal* (the riddle game). After the riddle asker gives the clues, they call out *'Girrigirri?'* (guess what?). Related to *girriinba-li* (make noise).

girriinba-li (YR) *verb-transitive*
make noise. Also *giliinba-li*. ◆ *Giirr nhama girriinba-lda-nha birralii-gal-u.* (YR) The children are making a lot of noise.

girrinil (GR) *noun*
door.

girrinya (YY) *noun*
daughter-in-law. One source.

girruu (YY) *noun*
well, soak, spring.

giwiirr (GR) *noun*
Aboriginal man. This word has been largely replaced by *mari* (Aboriginal man, Aboriginal person).

giyaan (YR) *noun*
tin can. From English 'can'. One source. See also: **gaala**.

giyal (YR, YY, GR) *adjective*
afraid, frightened. Possibly based on *gii* (heart).

giyaldhalibaa (YR, YY) *adjective*
shameless, no shame. From *giyal* (afraid) and *-dhalibaa* (without).

giyalgil (YR) *adjective*
sour. One source.

giyalgiyal (YR, YY) *adjective*
itchy.

giyarral (YY) *noun*
cattle, bullock. Also *giyarrdal*. From English 'cattle'.

giyawaan (YR, YY) *noun*
kurrajong bark. This is the inner fibre, when stripped and ready for making nets and string bags.

giyiirr (YY) *noun*
coolabah tree gum. The gum from coolabah trees can be eaten straight from the tree in balls like toffee, or melted in warm water to make a jelly. It can be soaked in water with something sweet like honey, manna or flower nectar. One source.

-Gu^1 (YR, YY, GR) *suffix*
1 doer to. Variant forms are *-gu, -dhu, -du, -u, -dju, -yu*. This suffix (also called the ergative suffix) is attached to the name of the person or thing that is doing an action to someone or something else. ◆ *Buyuma-gu nhama nginunha yii-y.* (YR) The dog bit you. ◆ *Dhuyu-gu nganha yii-y.* (YY) A snake bit me.
2 do with. This suffix (also called the instrumental suffix) indicates an instrument, weapon, tool or other thing that is being used. ◆ *Giirr nganha nguuma giniy-u buma-y.* (YR) He hit me with a stick. The ergative/instrumental suffix is attached to nouns and adjectives. See Learner's Guide.

-gu^2 (YR, YY, GR) *suffix*
1 movement to. Indicates movement towards the thing named. Also known as the 'allative suffix'. ◆ *Giirr nguu yanaa-nhi gaawaa-gu.* (YR) He went to the river.
2 purpose. Indicates the purpose, or reason for an action. Also known as the 'purposive suffix'. ◆ *Warangana-gu ngaya garra-y ngaama maalaabidi.* (YR) I cut the big tree for honey.
3 belonging to. Indicates that something belongs to someone, e.g. 'the girl's dog'. Also known as the 'genitive suffix'.
◆ *Dhinawan-gu dhunbil.* (YR) Emu's sinew.
4 for. Indicates when someone does something for someone else. Also known as the 'benefactive suffix'. ◆ *Yina-yu nhama dhuu gimbi-y birralii-gu.* (YR) The woman made a fire for the child.
The form of this suffix does not change.

-gu^3 (YR, YY, GR) *suffix*
purpose verb suffix. Indicates the purpose or reason for doing something. ◆ *Ngay-bala nhama wuu-na bilaarr dhalaybaa, bandaarr ngaya dhu-rri-gu.* (YR) Give me that sharp spear, so I can spear the kangaroo.
◆ *Dhuu gi-yaa-nha ngali gimbi-li, ngaaluurr yilama-li-gu.* (YY) We are going to make a fire, to cook the fish. ◆ *Yanaa-y gi-yaa-nha*

ngaya, bayagaa ngay ngaawa-y-gu. (YY) I am going to walk now, to look for my clothes. ◆ *Dhirranba-la nhama muyaan, dhuwarr bundaa-gi-gu.* (YY) Shake that tree, so the fruit will fall.
This suffix always follows the future (verb) suffix. See Learner's Guide.

guba (YR) *noun*
koala *(Phascolarctos cinereus).*

gubadhu (YR, YY, GR) *noun*
diamond dove *(Geopelia cuneata). Gubadhu* sounds like the bird's call.

gubi-y (YR, YY, GR) *verb-intransitive*
swim. ◆ *Guya nhama gubi-yaa-nha.* (GR) The fish is swimming. ◆ *Yaama nginda gubi-y-la-nha gaawaa-ga?* (YY) Can you swim the river?
See also: **wunga-y**.

gubigala (YY) *noun*
currant bush, warrior bush *(Apophyllum anomalum).* This is a rare word, the common word is *wayaarra*. One source.

Gubiyaandaa (YR) *placename*
location. Near Goodooga. Probably based on *gubi-y* (swim).

gubiyaay (YY, GR) *noun*
orchid. Probably the edible bulb of a yellow orchid, known around Mungindi as 'goobi-eye'.

gubiyalanhay (YR) *noun*
chasings, tip. A chasing game played in the water. Based on *gubi-y* (swim). One source. See also: **dhurran.gali**.

guburra (GR) *noun*
initiated youth. Probably based on *buurra* (bora).

guburruu (YR, YY, GR) *noun*
swamp box *(Eucalyptus largiflorens).* Also called black box or river box, a medium-large sized tree growing on river flats and low-lying areas, where flooding occurs.

Guburruubaa (YR) *placename*
location. From *guburruu* (swamp box) and *-baa* (place of, time of).

guda (YY, GR) *noun*
koala *(Phascolarctos cinereus).*

gudhurr (GR) *noun*
belt. One source.

gudhurru (GR) *noun*
small club. One source. Maybe related to *gudhurr* (belt).

gudhuwa-li (YR, YY, GR) *verb-transitive*
burn. This verb also means 'cook'.
◆ *Garriya ngaama dhinggaa gudhuwa-la!* (YR) Don't burn the meat!
See also: **gundaawa-li, gaylama-li**.

gudhuwa-y (YR, GR) *verb-intransitive*
1 burn (YR). ◆ *Giirruu nhama birralii-djuul gudhuwa-nhi wii-dja.* (YR) The baby was burnt on the fire. ◆ *Giniy nhama gudhuwa-y-la-nha.* (YR) That stick is burning.
2 be hot (YR, GR). ◆ *Girran nhama gudhuwa-waa-nha.* (YR) Those ashes are hot.
◆ *Gudhuwa-waa-nha ngaya.* (YR) I am hot.
3 burn with pain (YR). ◆ *Ngama bandaarr dhina ngaama gudhuwa-y-la-nha.* (YR) That kangaroo('s) foot is burning (hurting).
4 cook (YR). ◆ *Giirr ngaama bandaarr gudhuwa-nhi.* (YR) The kangaroo is cooked.
A change in verb class from *-li* to *-y*. See Learner's Guide.

gudhuwan (YY) *noun*
cook. Related to *gudhuwa-li* (burn). Also occurs in *gaba gudhuwan* (good cook). One source.

gudiny (YY) *noun*
little (hairy) people. Ted Fields said this is a Goodooga word; *-ny* is a common ending on 'secret language' words but not in standard GY. See *winambuu* (YR) for more information.

gudjibaal (YR) *noun*
proud (nickname). One source.

gudugaa (YR, YY) *noun*
type of yam. An unknown species.

guduu (YR, YY, GR) *noun*
1 Murray cod *(Maccullochella macquariensis)* (YR, YY, GR). ◆ *Nginda bayama-y ngaama guduu-bidi.* (YR) You caught a big cod. Kay Kneale said that *guduu* was rolled in mud, cooked in a fire and covered with coals until the mud hardened. When cooked, the mud was peeled off to separate the flesh from the scales and guts.
2 fish (YR). Limited support for the general meaning 'fish'.

Guduuga (YR, YY) *placename*
Goodooga. Probably based on *guduu* (cod) and *-ga* (at).

gugal (YY) *noun*
pure honey. One source.

gugan (YR) *noun*
half-caste. One source.

gugil (YR, YY, GR) *noun*
dew.

gugirrii (YR, YY) *noun*
sinew. Also *gundiirri*.

gugirriibiyaay (YR, YY) *adjective*
strong. Used, e.g. of tea. From *gugirrii* (sinews) and *-biyaay* (with, having).

gugirriidhalibaa (YR, YY) *adjective*
weak. From *gugirrii* (sinews) and *-dhalibaa* (without).

gugul (YY) *noun*
branch. One source.

gugumadharraa (YR, YY) *noun*
land yam (*Parsonsia eucalyptophylla*). Also *gaguulmadharraa*. Also called black yam, this vine has a poisonous, dark-coloured tuber or yam. Children are warned against confusing this plant with *gaagulu* (bush banana) which it slightly resembles when young.

gugun.gugun (YR, YY) *noun*
policeman fly (*Asilidae*).

gugurrgaagaa (YR, YY, GR) *noun*
kookaburra (*Dacelo novaeguinea*).

Gugurruwan (YR, YY) *noun, placename*
1 birthing tree. Ted Fields said that there is one on Dungalear Station. In a story, a wife of *Baayami* bore a child, or menstruated there.
2 Coocoran Lake. Near Lightning Ridge.

gula (YR, YY) *noun*
1 fork in tree.
2 fork (cutlery). Ian Sim said it is also forked objects, but not a forked stick.

gulaagul (YY) *noun*
water hollow in tree. A water-holding tree, ironbark or box, with a split in the fork and a hollow below the fork. After rain, this hollow would be full of water for a long time. The tree was known by the mark which the overflow made down the trunk, discolouring the bark. Based on *gula* (tree fork). One source.

gulaban (YR) *noun*
seat. Ted Fields said it is a seat made out of *gula* (a fork in a tree) and a wheat bag.

gula-li (YR, YY, GR) *verb-transitive*
bark. ◆ *Maadhaay-u nhama gula-lda-nha.* (YY) The dog is barking.

gulaanbali (YR) *noun*
pelican (*Pelecanus conspicillatus*). The recommended word is *gulayaali* because it is in all three languages.

gulaarr (YR, GR) *question word*
how? ◆ *Gulaarr gi-yaa-nha nhama-nda ngandabaa buma-li?* (YR) How are you going to kill that snake?
This is the recommended word, *galaarr* (how?) also occurs.

gulaay (YR, YY) *noun*
1 log bridge (YR, YY). For example, across a creek.
2 stool, bench (YR).

gulabaa (YR, YY, GR) *noun*
coolabah tree (*Eucalyptus coolibah* ssp. *arida*). This is a medium-sized tree that grows in watercourses and depressions and has a very hard timber. Branches and leaves can be used to stun fish in waterholes, but may need to be left overnight, and used for cooking emu in a ground oven. The leaves are boiled in water and sweetened with honey; this liquid is drunk to relieve colds and whooping cough. Flour can be made from the seeds: branches are broken off and laid on a claypan, the seed capsules will open after five days, and the debris is collected and winnowed. Seeds can then be soaked, cleaned, dried and ground, and the resulting paste eaten. The roots may be tapped for water and the inner bark can be beaten and applied as a poultice for snake bite and severe headache. Possibly from *gula* (tree fork) and *-baa* (place of, time of). Possible source of English 'coolabah'.

gulagama-li (YR, YY) *verb-transitive*
embrace, hold, cuddle. ◆ *Gulagama-la nhama birralii!* (YY) Cuddle the baby! *Gulagama-li* and its variant *gulama-li* has a general meaning of 'put your arms around'. Ted Fields said that you would do it to a distressed person, to reassure them. Possibly this verb only refers to children, as it is similar to the first part of the word

gulumaldhaay (foster parent). Perhaps based on *gula* (tree fork).

gulagarranba (YR) *noun*
comeback boomerang. Possibly related to *gula* (fork in tree).

gulal (YR, YY) *noun*
headband. See also: **ngulugaayrr**.

gulawularr (YR) *noun*
sweetbread. Ted Fields said it is a part of the sheep intestines on the *mubal* (stomach). Form uncertain.

gulawuliil (YR, YY, GR) *noun*
topknot pigeon *(Ocyphaps (Geophaps) lophotes)*. Also *gulawiliil*. Also called crested pigeon. It is thought that the name relates to the forked shape (*gula*) of the head in profile.

gulay (YR, YY, GR) *noun*
1 net bag (YR, YY, GR). Originally a net sling used to carry a baby on the mother's back. The word is now used for anything similar, e.g. a string shopping bag.
2 fish net (GR).
3 goanna eggs (YR). The string of eggs laid by a goanna.

gulayaali (YR, YY, GR) *noun*
pelican *(Pelecanus conspicillatus)*. Based on *gulay* (net bag), from a story.

gulbirr (YR, GR) *adjective*
1 few (YR).
2 some (YR, GR).

gulbiyaay (YR) *exclamation*
welcome! Also *gulbiyay*, *gulbiyaanha*. One source.

gulgulay (YY) *noun*
golden wattle. The timber is tough and close grained, it is a rich source of tannin, and the gum can be eaten. Possibly *Acacia pycnantha*.

gulguu (YR, YY) *adjective*
strange. Only occurs twice, in *gulguu giniy* (bent tree) and *gulguu mari* (strange man).

gulguwi (YR, YY, GR) *noun*
black-tailed native-hen *(Gallinula ventralis)*. The Culgoa River may be named after this bird, which was very common on the river.

guli (YY, GR) *noun, placename*
1 river grass (native millet) *(Panicum decompositum)* (YY, GR). Refers to the grass and the seed. Mitchell wrote the following while he travelled along the Narran: 'panicum . . . a grass whereof the seed ('Cooly') is made by the natives into a kind of paste or bread. Dry heaps of this grass that had been pulled espressly [sic] for the purpose of gathering the seed, lay along our path for many miles. I counted nine miles along the river, in which we rode through this grass only, reaching to our saddle-girths, and the same grass seemed to grow back from the river, at least as far as the eye could reach through a very open forest. I had never seen such rich natural pasturage in any other part of New South Wales. Still it supplied the bread of the natives; and these children of the soil were doing everything in their power to assist me, whose wheels would probably bring the white man's cattle into it.'
2 grain (YY, GR).
3 Goolhi (GR). Station west of Gunnedah. Also *gulu*.

gulibaa (YR, YY, GR) *adjective*
three.

guligal (YR, YY) *noun*
1 bee droppings (YR, YY). Fred Reece said '*guligal* are droppings from the bees, if there is a nest it can fall in one little area and you know there is a nest in the tree'.
2 Coorigel (YY). As in Coorigel Springs (at Angledool); this name has also been recorded as *gawurragiil*, *gurraagal* or *gurragiil*, said to be 'all the same'.

guliirr (YR, YY, GR) *noun*
spouse, husband, wife. ◆ *Guliirr-nginda ngaya.* (YR) I want a wife (or husband).

guliirraraay (GR) *adjective*
married. From *guliirr* (husband, wife) and -*araay* (with, having).

guliirrdhalibaa (YR, YY, GR) *adjective*
1 widowed.
2 unmarried.
From *guliirr* (husband, wife) and -*dhalibaa* (without).

guliirriyaay (YR, YY) *adjective*
married. From *guliirr* (husband, wife) and *-iyaay* (with, having).

guliman (YR, GR) *noun*
1 coolamon.
2 dish. Word for any dish.
Widely used in English. This word might come from *guli* (river grass/native millet); coolamons are used in seed collection and processing.

gulimugarr (YR, YY) *noun*
goat-head burr *(Tribulus terrestris)*. Also called cat-head, it is a three-pronged prickle or thorn.

guliyaan (YR) *adjective*
new, strange. There is a story about Oxley coming to the area that uses *guliyaan* which may mean 'strange', 'strange people' or 'new'. One source. Form uncertain.

gulu (YY) *noun*
lump. One source.

gulumaldhaay (YR, YY) *noun*
foster parent. This word has been recorded, but is not recommended for use because the way it is used in sentences is not understood. Possibly from *galuma-li* (care for).

gulun (YY) *noun*
widow, widower. This is a rare word, the common word is *guliirrdhalibaa* (widowed). One source.

gulungguluu (YR, YY) *adjective*
rotten. Occurs in *gulungguluu giniy* (rotten log).

gulurr (GR) *noun*
waist.

guluu (YY) *noun*
butcherbird. This is a rare word. See also: **garriguwin.guwin, guwaaydjiidjii** and **buubuurrbu**.

gum (YR) *noun*
methylated spirits. One source. This word is commonly used in Walgett.

gumaay (YR, YY, GR) *noun*
water rat.

gumawuma (YR, YY, GR) *noun*
small dragon lizard.

gumay (GR) *noun*
lip. See also: **yili**.

gumba (YY) *adjective*
flinty (very hard).

gumbadhaa (YR, YY) *noun*
1 iron.
2 machinery.
From *gumba* (flinty, very hard) and *-dhaa* (associated with).

gumbadhina (YY) *noun*
hard foot; nickname for someone who is a good walker or roams around a lot. From *gumba* (very hard) and *dhina* (foot).

gumbi (YR) *noun*
water weed. Ted Fields said it has nutty, edible, grape-like fruit and grey-green felt-like leaves like clover, which float on water, and small yellow flowers. One source.

gumbilgal (YR, GR) *noun*
bark container. Also *gumbilgaa*. Used for drinking. Also refers to the bark which is used to make a canoe.

gumbirri (GR) *noun*
brain.

gumbiyaa (YR) *noun*
horseshoe. Probably based on *gumba* (flinty, very hard — YY). One source.

gumbu (YR, YY) *noun*
corroboree ground. Raised up above the surrounding area.

gumbubudhuu (YR, YY) *noun*
wrestling game. Langloh-Parker described wrestling as a great *buurra* time entertainment. Family clans played against other clans. A *Yibaay* (social section) man for example, will go into a ring and place a *maadji* (painted stick) with a bunch of feathers at the top. In will run a *Gabii* (social section) man who tries to make off with the stick; the two then wrestle. Into the ring will go others of each side, wrestling in their turn. The side that finally throws the most men and gets the *maadji* wins. Before wrestling matches begin people grease their bodies to make them slippery.

gumbugan (YR, YY, GR) *noun*
1 sand.
2 sandhill.

gumbul (YR, YY) *noun*
bottom, bum. ◆ *Guwaymbarra gumbul*

nguu ngarranma-y. (YR) He showed (his) red backside.

gumbulgaban (YR, YY) *noun*
plains turkey, Australian bustard (*Ardeotis australis*). From *gumbul* (bottom) and *gaban* (light). Possibly to do with turkey's mating display.

Gumbulgabanbaa (YR, YY) *placename*
location. A waterhole on the Narran River, near old Bangate Station bridge. There were lots of plains turkeys west of old Bangate Station. From *gumbulgaban* (plains turkey) and *-baa* (place of, time of).

gumi (YR, YY, GR) *noun*
native tomato (*Solanum coactiliferum*). Grows in areas where water lies, such as claypans. Refers to the plant and the fruit. Fred Reece said that there are two sizes: the big one is *guduugumi*, the small one is *gumi*. They grow to around 20 cm high, with yellow fruit that is not sweet, so its better if you cook it, roast it in ashes, so that it gets soft and has a nice taste. There were acres of them in the black soil country, the ground would be yellow with them, like marbles, but they haven't been seen in big numbers for years. Also called felted nightshade.

gumil (YR, YY) *noun*
woman's armlet.

gumilaa (YR, YY, GR) *noun*
possum-fur loincloth. Fred Reece said that it is a possum skin worn around the front and back, not a belt. Possibly related to *gumil* (armlet).

guna (YR, YY, GR) *noun*
faeces, shit.

gunadha (YR, YY) *noun, adjective*
1 boggy ground.
2 boggy. ◆ *Gunadha-wan.gaan nhama dhaymaarr.* (YR) The ground (was) very boggy.
From *guna* (faeces, shit).

gunagalaa (YR, YY, GR) *noun*
toilet. Based on *guna* (shit). Used currently in some areas.

gunagunaa (YY) *adjective*
1 brown. Any brownish colour.
2 dirty, disgusting.
One source.

gunambaal (YR) *noun*
darter, long-necked shag. For more information see *gunambaay* (GR) and *ganandhaal* (YY).

gunambaay (GR) *noun*
1 wood duck (nickname). This and similar words turn up a number of times with related meanings, and the common element seems to be *guna*. Used of cormorants and wood ducks.
2 water bird. A general name for any water bird that leaves lots of *guna* (shit, droppings) in one spot.
It is common in a number of languages to have words based on *guna* as names of such water birds.

Gunambil (GR) *placename*
Coonamble. From *guna* (faeces) and *-bil* (having a lot of).

guna-gi (YR) *verb-intransitive*
defecate, shit.

gunaba (GR) *noun*
initiation ground. Mathews states it is the smaller bora ring, around 15 m in diameter. The secret part of the ceremony takes place in the *gunaba* (sometimes called '*Baayami*'s ground') and, under penalty of death, no uninitiated person or woman is allowed to see it.

Gunabarabin (GR) *placename*
Coonabarabran.

gunagala (YR, YY, GR) *noun*
1 sky.
2 heaven.

gundaa (YR, YY, GR) *noun*
cloud.

gundaawa-li (YR, YY) *verb-transitive*
burn (with a lot of flame). This word is used if fire is burning a lot of things or a large area, as in a bush fire. ◆ *Gundaawa-la nhama buunhu!* (YY) Burn that grass!

gundal

See also: **gudhuwa-li, gaylama-li**.
gundaawa-y (YR) *verb-intransitive*
burn (with a lot of flame). ◆ *Buwadjarr-gu ngay ngaama gundhi gundaawa-nhi.* (YR) My father's house burnt (down).
A change in verb class from *-li* to *-y*. See Learner's Guide.

gundal (GR) *noun*
bread. ◆ *Mari-dju gundal nhama dha-lda-nha.* (GR) The man is eating the bread.
This is a rare word, the common word is *dhuwarr*.

gundhi (YR, YY, GR) *noun*
1 house (YR, YY, GR). May have originally meant a bark shelter. ◆ *Nhama gundhi-dja ngarri-la-nha.* (GR) He is sitting in the house.
2 stringybark gum tree (YY). An unidentified eucalypt.

Gundhimayan (GR) *placename*
Condamine River. From *gundhi* (house) and *mayan* (waterhole); said to mean 'house on the stream'. One source.

gundhilgaa (YR) *noun*
town. From *gundhi* (house). One source.

gundhuwundhuu (YR, YY) *adjective*
1 stubborn.
2 selfish.
3 sulky.
Also *gundhuwundhuul*.

gundiirr (YR, YY) *noun*
emu feather.

gun.gan (YR) *noun*
wound. One source.

gun.giyan (YR, YY) *noun*
manna. Arthur Dodd said: '*Gun.giyan*, you see him on the river, when the wind blow the leaves down you'll see lots of round, white spots on it, just like a pain tablet, aspirin, and its round and you open them and taste them, its sweet like sugar.'
Possibly includes *-(b)iyan*. See Learner's Guide.

gun.gun (YR, YY) *adjective*
afraid, frightened. ◆ *Gun.gun ngaya gi-nyi.* (YY) I got frightened.
Used in some YR, GR areas.

gungan (YR, YY) *noun*
water.

gunganbiyaay (YR, YY) *adjective*
wet. ◆ *Dhaymaarr nhama baliyaa, gunganbiyaay.* (YR) The ground is cold and wet.
From *gungan* (water) and *-biyaay* (having). Also occurs as *gungan-bil* (water-having lots).

gungurima (GR) *noun*
halo around moon.

gunha (YR, YY) *noun*
scorpion.

gunharr (YR, YY, GR) *noun*
kangaroo rat. Original sources say 'kangaroo rat', but it is probably a bettong *(Bettongia)*. See the story about the making of fire (Arthur Dodd, Langloh-Parker). Some thought of the kangaroo rat as a very promiscuous animal, the name *gunharr* was applied to a young woman who was a 'run-around'.

gunhugunhu (YR, YY, GR) *noun*
cold, cough.

gunhugunhu dhu-rri (YR, YY, GR) *verb phrase*
cough. ◆ *Waal ngaya gunhugunhu dhu-nhi.* (YR) I didn't cough (so much).
From *gunhugunhu* (a cough) and *dhu-rri* (spear, poke etc.).

guni (GR) *noun*
native bee.

gunidjaa (YR, YY, GR) *noun, placename*
1 orphan (motherless child) (YR, YY, GR).
2 black-faced cuckoo-shrike (YR, YY). The grey bird with a black face is like a child covered in clay or ash, mourning its dead parent or mother. Arthur Dodd said: '*Gunidjaa* — you can hear them naming themselves like that.'
3 Gunnedah (GR). There are several possible derivations for this placename. See also *ganadhaa* (deep) and *Gunudha*. From *guni* (mother) and *-djaa*, probably short for *-dhalibaa/-djalibaa* (without).

gunidjarr (YR, YY, GR) *noun*
1 mother.
2 aunt (mother's sister).
3 female.
See also: **gunii**.

gunidjarrbaa (YR, YY, GR) *noun*
female.
From *gunidjarr* (mother) and *-baa* (place

of, time of). Probably used to talk about animals and humans.

gunidjarr baburr (YY, GR) *noun*
big toe. Also *gunidjarrba*. From *gunidjarr* (mother) and *baburr* (foot). It is possible that other similar expressions were not recorded e.g., **gunidjarr dhina* (big toe — YR, YY, GR).

gunidjarr maa (YR, YY) *noun*
thumb. From *gunidjarr* (mother) and *maa* (hand, finger). The expression 'mother-hand' for 'thumb' is used in other Australian Aboriginal languages. It is possible that other similar expressions were not recorded, e.g. **gunidjarr mara* (thumb — GR).

gunii (YR, YY, GR) *noun*
1 mother. Ridley said that children call out to their mother '*gunii!*'. This is probably the vocative form which is used when talking to someone. It is probably an abbreviation of *gunidjarr*. Also *guni* which is commonly used today.
See also: **ngambaa**.
2 aunt (mother's sister).

guniibuu (YR, YY) *noun*
robin redbreast *(Petroica goodenovii)*. Also called red-capped robin. Based on *gunii* (mother) and *buu/buru* (testicles); according to a story told by Arthur Dodd, this is what the bird says (see Williams and tapes).

gunimaa (YR) *noun*
mother earth. Ted Fields said it means 'mother land or mother earth'. Based on *gunii* mother. One source.

guniinii (YR, YY, GR) *noun*
queen native bee.

guniyal (GR) *noun*
plain, flat.

gunmi-li (YR) *verb-transitive*
look at (greedily). Uncle Ted Fields translates this word as 'cadging, look at something with a greedy look, a wanting look in the eye'. One source.

gunu (YY) *noun, placename*
1 lime gypsum.
2 Goonoo. Said to be a place west of Goodooga.
Also *gunuwaa*.

Gunu Gunu (GR) *placename*
Goonoo Goonoo. From *gunu* (lime).

gunubingaa (YR, YY, GR) *noun*
nephew (sister's son).

Gunudha (GR) *placename*
Gunnedah. Commonly thought of as 'place of white stone', this town name may be based on *gunu* (lime gypsum). See also **Gunidjaa**.

gunugayngaa (YR, YY, GR) *noun*
niece (sister's daughter).

gunyamurr (YR, YY) *noun*
east wind.

guraarr (GR) *adjective*
1 long.
2 tall.
Also *guraarraala*.

guraay (GR) *adverb*
slowly. Also *guraaybaa*. ◆ *Guraay yana-ya!* (GR) Walk slowly!

gurabi (GR) *noun*
curlew, bush thick-knee *(Burhinus grallarius)*. One source. See also: **wuruyan**.

gurayn (GR) *noun*
flower.

guri (GR) *noun*
emu apple tree, gruie *(Owenia acidula)*. One source. See also: **guwi**.

guriya (GR) *noun*
backbone, spine.

gurra (YR, GR) *noun*
huntsman spider. Form is uncertain, may be *garra*. Also a general word for any spider; see also *gayiya* (any spider).

gurra-li (YR) *verb-transitive*
consume all. (Of the food or drink.) Arthur Dodd also translated this verb as '(He) cleaned it all up.' ◆ *Ngaya ngaama gurra-y dhulii biyaduul-u.* (YR) I ate all the goanna myself (alone). ◆ *Giirr ngaya-laa ngaama gurra-li.* (YR) I'll drink it all up.

gurraari (GR) *noun*
white cypress pine *(Callitris glaucophylla)*. Possibly refers to any cypress pine. See *gurraay* for more information.

gurraay (YR, YY) *noun*
white cypress pine *(Callitris glaucophylla)*. Can be a large tree, its softwood timber is known for its resistance to termite attack. The leaves are ground and boiled in water,

gurragurra

which is used in the treatment of sores and scabies and can be rubbed on the chest, like Vicks Vaporub. Also can be used for smoking sick people. Possibly *gurraay* refers to any cypress pine. See also: **yilbin**.

gurragurra (YY) *noun*
waterlily. Possibly swamp lily *(Ottelia ovalifolia)*. Has floating oval leaves and white three-petalled flowers.

gurriyaa (YR) *noun*
wax-lipped orchid *(Glossodia major)*. One source.

gurru (YR, YY, GR) *noun, adjective*
1 hole. Name for any hole including graves, cooking holes and potholes and 'crab holes', a naturally occurring hole in black soil, over 50 cm wide; also any little depression in the ground. ◆ *Giirr-nha dhinawan gayla-nhi, gurru-dhi ngiyani-laa dhuwima-li, dha-li-gu.* (YY) The emu is cooked, we will get him out from the hole to eat him.
2 grave. ◆ *Giirr ngiyani yanaa-waa-nha wuyugil-iyaay, burrulaa-nga dhayn yanaa-waa-nha gurru-gu.* (YY) We (all) are going with the smoke, many men are walking to the grave.
3 round. One source for this meaning.

gurrugaawal (YR) *noun*
marsh. Probably based on *gurru* (hole) and *gaawal* (creek, lagoon). One source. Form uncertain.

gurrugurru[1] (YY) *adjective*
very deep.

gurrumayuu (YY) *noun*
holey country. Based on *gurru* (hole). One source.

gurruubaa (YR, YY, GR) *adjective*
deep. Based on *gurru* (hole) and *-baa* (place of, time of).

gurruga baabay (YY) *(?)*
woman's camp. This expression was used to refer to the place away from the main camp where a woman stayed when she was menstruating or giving birth. It is not clear whether this expression involves a verb or not. Possibly *gurru-ga baabi-li* or from a variant of *baabi-li*. One source.

gurrugurru[2] (YR, YY) *adjective, pronoun*
everything, all. See also **ganungawu**, **burrulaa**.

gurrulay (YR, YY) *noun, placename*
1 river wattle (YR, YY). This tree is similar to black wattle *(Acacia salicina)*, but more slender; it grows on inland watercourses, often with river red gums. Also called river cooba. The *dhani* (gum) is eaten and the seed pods can be roasted and the seeds eaten. The wood is hard, and the bark is used for making string when kurrajong is not available.
2 Gurly Station (YY).

gurrulayngayn (YR, YY) *noun*
river wattle flowers. Based on *gurrulay* (river wattle).

gurruubi-li (YY) *verb-transitive*
swallow. One source. See also: **wuwi-li**.

gurruwan (YR, YY) *noun*
restricted word. See p 20 for more information.

gurruway (YR) *noun*
temporary waterhole. A waterhole next to a sandhill/lunette of sand, e.g. 48 km north of Walgett on the Lightning Ridge road, where there was a hotel. Probably based on *gurru* (hole). One source.

guru (GR) *noun*
western barred bandicoot *(Perameles bougainville)*.

gurugun (YR, GR) *noun*
peaceful dove *(Geopelia placida)*. 'Gurugun' sounds like the bird's call.

guudii (YR, YY) *noun*
coat. From English 'coat'.

guugaarr (YR, YY) *noun*
tree goanna *(Varanus varius)*. Also *guugaa*. Perhaps a Wangaaybuwan word.

guuguu (YR, YY) *noun*
dead relative. Ted Fields said that this name is used instead of the dead person's name, which should not be spoken. Fred Reece said, '*Guuguu* is a man who died, you don't want to mention his name, it might be a relation and you say: poor old *guuguu*.'
It is common for Aboriginal languages to have a word with this use.

guulaabi-y (YR) *verb-intransitive*
warm up. ◆ *Ngaya wii wiima-y, maa guulaabi-y-la-nha.* (YR) I made a fire, my hands were warming up.
*Guulaabi-li (warm something up) may also exist. So there may be a change in verb class from *-li* to *-y*. See Learner's Guide.

guulay (YR, YY, GR) *adjective*
new word. See p 160 for more information.

guuma-li (YR) *verb-transitive*
collect, gather. Also *guruma-li*. ◆ *Nhama birralii-djuul-u wugan guuma-laa-nha.* (YR) The boy is gathering sticks.

guuma-y (YY) *verb-intransitive*
hide, plant (self). ◆ *Guuma-y-la-nha ganunga nginundi.* (YY) They are planting/hiding from you.
The person being hidden from is marked by the 'from' (source) case.

guumay (GR) *noun*
ground orchid. This word is used in Coonabarabran.

guunay (YY) *noun*
dirge, funeral song. One source.

guurrama-li (YY) *verb-intransitive*
resist, stand strong. *Guurrama-la!* (stand firm, don't be pushed over!) is a rallying cry. One source.

guurrguurr (YY) *noun*
boobook owl *(Ninox novaeseelandiae)*. One source.

guurrman (YR, YY, GR) *noun*
leech. Also used as a nickname for children when they keep hanging on to their mother's skirt.

guuwarr (YR, YY, GR) *noun*
red ochre. Possibly from *guway* (blood).

guuwiyaay (YY) *noun*
mythological warrior enemies. Langloh-Parker said that these were enemies who came to attack, but when they threatened the camp dog with death, they were turned into large rocks of great beauty, striped and marked and coloured, like men painted for ceremony, and which are now found on one of the mountains near Beemery.

guuya-li (YR, YY, GR) *verb-intransitive*
shine. ◆ *Yaay-dha nhama nginu wilbaarr guuya-lda-nha.* (YY) Your car is shining in the sun.

guuyaa (YR, YY) *noun*
backbone, spine.

guuyaarrma (YY) *noun*
persistent rain. One source.

guuyal (GR) *noun*
shine. Related to *guuya-li* (shine).

guuyalaraay (GR) *adjective*
shiny.

guuyay (YR, YY, GR) *noun*
mood, humour.

guwa (YR, YY, GR) *noun*
fog, mist.

guwan.guwan (YR) *adjective*
foggy. From *guwa* (fog).

guwaa (GR) *noun*
hornet.

guwaa-li (YR, YY, GR) *verb-transitive*
1 talk (to), speak (to). 'Talk' usually occurs as *gaay guwaa-li* (words — talk). When 'talking to' or 'telling something to' someone, the one being talked to is marked with the dative case. ◆ *Gaay guwaa-la nganunda.* (YY) Talk to me.
◆ *Dhugay nhama yina-yu gaay guwaa-lda-nha.* (YY) The woman is always talking.
2 tell. When 'tell' means 'command' the one commanded is in 'done to' form.
◆ *Ngaandu nginunha guwaa-y yanaa-y-gu?* (YR) Who told you to go?
3 say. ◆ *Gulaanbali-dju guwaa-y 'ngaayaybaay'.* (YR) Pelican said 'yeah, all right'.
4 make (someone do something). *Guwaa-li* is also used to translate 'make someone do something', e.g. 'I made him behave himself.' ◆ *Giirr ngaama ngambaa-gu guwaa-y birralii-djuul warra-y-gu.* (YR) Mother made the children get up. See also: **dhubaanma-li**.

guwaala-y (YR) *verb-intransitive*
converse (talk to each other). From *guwaa-* (talk) and *-la-y* (each other). The reciprocal form of *guwaa-li* (talk) is used to say 'converse'.

guwaaybaa (YY) *adverb*
slowly. This is a rare word, the common word is *baluwaa*.

guwaaydjiidjii (YR, YY) *noun*
grey butcherbird *(Cracticus torquatus)*. From *guwaay* (says) and *djiidjii* (bird call).

guwadhaa (YR, YY, GR) *noun*
quandong *(Santalum acuminatum)*. Refers to the tree and the fruit. These small trees have edible red fruit, which may be a bit sour but can be made into jam. Like other sandalwoods, these trees are root parasites, getting their nutrients through sucker-like attachments to host plants. Fruit stones are cracked to get at the kernel which can be eaten raw, or pounded for the oil which is used as a moisturiser. The dried fruit can be pounded into a paste. The kernel is very high in energy, protein and fat; the fruit is high in water and carbohydrates. Ridley said that the stone or seed was used as an ornament.

guwarray (YY, GR) *noun*
restricted word. See p 20 for more information.

guway (YR, YY, GR) *noun*
blood. Many other words are formed using *guway*.

Guwaybila (YR, YY) *noun*
planet Mars. Based on *guway* (blood).

guwaybuyan (YY) *noun*
skeleton spirit. A hairless, red, skeleton-like spirit; Ginny Rose said 'he's just bones'. From *guway* (blood) and *buya* (bone).

Guwayda (YR, YY) *placename*
Gwydir River. Probably based on *guway* (blood); said to mean 'place or river of red (banks)'. One source.

guwaygalaa (GR) *noun*
red soil.

guwaygaliyarr (YR, YY, GR) *noun*
light blood group. This is a two-way social division, with matrilineal inheritance, that is, it is inherited through a person's mother. The other social group is *guwaymadhan* (dark blood). Relates to the creation by *Baayami* of the first people from the ground, 'low down' and 'high up'. Possibly based on *guway* (blood) and *galiya-y* (climb, rise).

guwaymadhan (YR, YY, GR) *noun*
heavy blood group. From *guway* (blood) and *madhan* (heavy). See *guwaygaliyarr* for more information.

guwaymbarra (YR, YY, GR) *adjective*
red. As in *mil guwaymbarra* (red-eyed from crying). Based on *guway* (blood).

guwi (YR, YY) *noun*
emu apple tree, gruie *(Owenia acidula)*. Also *gurruuwi*. A shrub or small tree with round fruit which is red when ripe. The fruit makes a cordial or jam; emus like to eat the fruit.

guwiibirr (YR, YY) *noun*
nepine *(Capparis lasiantha)*. Common in the west, nepine is a low, spiky shrub or climbs up trees. Yellow passionfruit-like fruit ripen in autumn. The fruit can be eaten, and honey from flowers can be used as a remedy for coughs. The plant, including roots, can be soaked and the water applied to swellings, snake bites, insect bites and stings.

guwiigaa (YR, YY) *noun*
termite mound. This word refers only to nests of termites.

guwiin (YR, YY, GR) *noun, adjective*
close, near. The form *guwiin* occurs in the sources only once, so the recommended word is *guwiinbaa*.

guwiinbaa (YR, YY, GR) *noun, adjective*
close, near. ◆ *Ganay nhalay ngay wi-y-la-nha dhaymaa-ya, guwiinbaa-ga nhama birralii-djuul-a.* (YR) My yamstick is lying on the ground near the little boy.
◆ *Guwiinbaa maadhaay ngay dhanduwi-y-la-nhi.* (YY) My dog was sleeping close by. From *guwiin* (close, near) and *-baa* (place of, time of).

guwiinbarraan (YR) *noun, adjective*
close to a fire, around a fire. Based on *guwiinbaa* (close, near).

guwiinba-li (YR, YY) *verb-intransitive*
come near. ◆ *Dhigayaa nhama guwiinba-laa-nha.* (YY) The bird is coming near (us).

guwiirr (YR) *adjective*
sweet. One source.

guwiirra (YR) *noun*
1 manna. Ted Fields said this refers to the manna on gum leaves.
2 sweetheart. One source.
3 mallee willow *(Pittosporum phylliraeoides)*. Also called butter bush, it is a small tree with inedible, very bitter, yellow fruits. One source. From *guwiirr* (sweet).

guwiirr gungan (YR) *noun*
new word. See p 160 for more information.

guwiirr widja (YR) *noun*
new word. See p 160 for more information.

guwiirrnga-li (YR) *verb-transitive*
love (be sweet on). Probably from *guwiirr* (sweet). One source.

guwilii (YR) *noun*
tent. One source.

guwima-li (YY) *verb-transitive*
spread out to dry. Also *guwiba-li*. It is difficult to be certain about the exact meaning of this verb. Fred Reece uses it in four sentences which involve 'putting' clothes or blankets out to dry in the sun.
◆ *Guwima-la ngay bayagaa yaay-dha.* (YY) Put my clothes out in the sun to dry. One source.

guwin (YY) *noun*
grey colour or shape. Widely used word for ghost. Ginny Rose used a word something like *guwingabulaa* about a place near Goodooga Reserve where 'the two girls' are said to appear.

guwinii (YR) *noun*
yellow ochre. Used in some YR, GR areas. One source.

guwinyarri (YY) *noun*
white-bellied sea eagle *(Haliaeetus leucogaster)*.

guwiya (YR) *noun*
fish. Name for any fish. Arthur Dodd said it is a Wangaaybuwan word. Used in some YR, GR areas. *Guya* (fish) may be a simplified version of this word.

guya (GR) *noun*
fish. Also *guwiya*. Name for any fish.
◆ *Guya nhama gubi-yaa-nha.* (GR) The fish is swimming. ◆ *Mari yana-waa-nha bagaay-gu guya ganma-li-gu.* (GR) The men are going to the creek to catch fish.

guyaarr (YR, YY) *adjective*
1 long.
2 tall.
Also *guyaarraala*.

guyan (YR) *adjective*
shy. One source.

guyayn (YR, YY) *noun*
flower. Name for any flower.

guuyarra (YR, YY) *noun*
poison bone. Said to be used by *wiringin* (clever men) for killing by pointing; its preparation and use involved a set of rituals and procedures. ◆ *Wiringin-du nhama guuyarra-gu gayawi-y.* (YY) The clever man pointed the bone to him.
Used with *gayawi-li* (point bone).

guyu (YR, YY) *noun*
western barred bandicoot *(Perameles bougainville)*.

guyungan (YR, YY, GR) *noun*
own. ◆ *Yinarr-bala yuurrma-y guyungan-da.* (YY) The women will corroboree on their own. Form uncertain.

Ii

-ili (YY) *suffix*
little (affectionate). Added to kin terms or names, e.g. *dhagaan-ili* (older brother-little); *Ganhan-b-ili* (pigweed-little: the name of one of the Creator's wives). Ian Sim said that it is an affectionate term, compare English 'Johnny' and John.

-iyaay (YR, YY) *suffix*
with, having. Occurs in the language name *Yuwaal-iyaay* (no-having); so 'the language that has *(yu)waal* (for no)'. For more information, see *–biyaay*.

Ll

-la (YR, YY, GR) *suffix*
command suffix for *-li* class verbs. ◆ *Gaay guwaa-la!* (YY) Speak!

-la-y (YR, YY, GR) *suffix*
each other (reciprocal suffix for *-li* class verbs). ◆ *Giirr ngali-nya ngarra-la-y.* (YR) We will see each other. ◆ *Giirr ngaama bulaarr birralii-djuul buma-la-y-la-nha.* (YR) The two boys are fighting with each other.
The reciprocal suffix is attached to verbs to indicate that the action is being done to 'each other'.

-laa (YR, YY) *clitic*
then. ◆ *Maayrr dhinggaa walaay-dja. Giirr ngiyani-laa yanaa-y maniila-y bandaarr-gu.* (YR) There's no meat in the camp. Then we will go and hunt for kangaroos. ◆ *Girribal ngali-laa guwaa-li.* (YY) We'll tell some riddles directly.
Often added to the first or second word of the sentence/phrase. Fred Reece sometimes translates *-laa* as 'directly'. The meaning of this suffix is not fully understood. See Learner's Guide.

-laa-y (YR, YY, GR) *suffix*
moving progressive suffix for *-li* class verbs. ◆ *Yilaalu ngaama gilay dhurra-laa-y.* (YR) Soon the moon will be rising. ◆ *Yaay dhurra-laa-nha.* (YY) The sun is coming up.

-lda-y (YR, YY, GR) *suffix*
regular progressive suffix for *-li* class verbs. ◆ *Wagi nhama nguu guwaa-lda-nha.* (YY) He's telling a lie.

-ldaay (YR, YY, GR) *suffix*
relative suffix for *-li* class verbs. ◆ *Guwaa-la nganunda buma-ldaay nginunha ngaandu-waa.* (YR) Tell me if anyone hits you.

-Vli-y (YR, YY, GR) *suffix*
benefactive suffix for *-li* class verbs. 'V' indicates that the previous vowel is lengthened. ◆ *Giirr ngaya nginu yilama-a-li-nyi nhama, dha-li-gu-nda.* (YR) I cooked that for you to eat.

-li (YR, YY, GR) *suffix*
future tense suffix for *-li* class verbs. ◆ *Giirr*

ngaya wiima-li. (YR) I will put (it) down. This verb suffix occurs in the future form of *-li* class verbs, e.g. *garra-li* (will cut).

-luu (YR, YY) *suffix*

all possible. Also *-lu, -uu, -buu, -wu, -yu(u)*. ◆ *Ngiyani-yuu gimbi-li.* (YR) We'll all do it. ◆ *Nhaadhiyaan nhama ngali-yu dhiyama-li.* (YY) We'll both pick up that log. The meaning and form is not fully understood. See Learner's Guide.

Mm

-ma (YR, GR) *suffix*

known information. ◆ *Minya-ma?* (YR) What is it?
Possibly indicates 'you know (so how about you tell me)' as in *yaama* (question word). This is a tentative definition.

-ma-li (YR, YY, GR) *suffix*

make (something) happen. ◆ *Giirruu ngaya gi-yaa-nha nginunha dhanduwi-y-ma-li.* (YR) I am going to make you go to sleep.
The causative suffix is attached to verbs to indicate that the action is being 'made to happen'. Also used to form GY verbs from English verbs; the process is generally: English verb + *i/irr* + *ma-li* as in *gigirrmali* (kick). See Learner's Guide.

ma-y (YR) *verb-intransitive*

1 be on top. ◆ *Giirr nhama-nha ma-y-la-nha nhaadhiyaan-da.* (YR) He's there, on top of the log.
2 be up. As in 'up in a tree'.
Found only in the progressive forms *ma-y-la-nha, ma-y-la-nhi* or with the relative (verb) suffix *ma-y-la-ndaay*. The form of this word is uncertain, it is also heard as *maaya-y, maya-y* and *maa-y*.

maa (YR, YY, GR) *noun, adjective*

1 hand (YR, YY). Langloh-Parker said that a hand sign, e.g. on a tree, shows which way people have gone.
2 finger (YR, YY). Also occurs once in *maa-galgaa* (finger-plural, fingers).
3 five (YR, YY, GR). The meaning 'five' has recently been adopted; a number of Aboriginal languages have used the word for 'hand' to also mean 'five'.
4 totem (YY). Langloh-Parker said that marks called *maa* on rugs and weapons tell who made them and where they belong. The *maa* for the *dhinawan* (emu) clan is an arrow head pointing downwards; to particularise which branch of that *maa*, there would be painted a kurrajong leaf, so telling it belonged to a *dhinawan* of the kurrajong tribe and country.

maa buma-y (YR, YY) *verb phrase*
clap hands. From *maa* (hand) and *buma-y* (hit self). ◆ *Giirruu yinarr-galgaa-gu-bala ngaama maa buma-y-la-nhi.* (YR) The women were clapping their hands.

maagu (YR) *noun*
restricted word. See p 20 for more information.

maadha (YR, YY, GR) *noun*
boss, master. ◆ *Nhama ngaya yanaa-waa-nha maadha-gu.* (GR) I am going to the boss.
From English 'master'.

Maadhaa (YR, YY, GR) *noun*
women's social section. Marries *Gambuu*, children are *Gabii* (male) and *Gabudhaa* (female), brother is *Marrii*. See also: **Buudhaa, Yibadhaa, Gabudhaa**.

maadhaabulaa (YY) *noun*
spoonbill (*Platalea* spp.). Probably applies to both the royal spoonbill (*Platalea regia*) and the yellow-billed spoonbill (*P. flavipes*).

maadhaay (YR, YY) *noun*
dog. This is the recommended word for 'dog'. See also: **buyuma, mirri, buruma**.

maadji (YY) *noun*
feathered stick. A painted stick with a bunch of feathers at the top, used in *gumbubudhuu*, wrestling performed at a *buurra*. One source.

maadjirr (YR, YY) *noun*
matches. From English 'matches'.

maal (GR) *adjective*
one.

maala (GR) *adverb*
once. From *maal* (one).

maalaabidi (YR) *noun*
big tree. General word for any large tree. *Maalaa* is occasionally used by itself.

maamaa (YR) *noun*
father's mother. This is a rare word, the common word for grandmother is *baagii*.

maambiyaa (YR, YY) *noun*
tree spirit. Said to appear, day or night, when the weather is very windy and overcast.

maamii (YR, YY) *noun*
1 old woman (YR, YY).
2 lactating female (YR). Used of humans and animals. Possibly from English 'mummy' or 'ma'am'.

maamuu (YR) *noun*
wing noise. Usually to do with ducks. One source.

Maandhi (YR) *placename*
lake name. South of Grawin waterhole. One source.

maang (GR) *noun*
message stick. The *-ng* at the end of the word suggests that *maang* was borrowed from another language. See also: **dhulu**.

maanggii (YR, YY) *noun*
small mussel. In a story, the seagull is the bringer of *maanggii*.

maanggiiwarraywarraymal (YR, YY) *noun*
seagull, silver gull (*Larus novaehollandiae*). Based on *manggii* (mussels) and *warrayma-li* (send); so 'sender/bringer of mussels', from a story. See also: **giinbaywarraymal**.

maarama (GR) *noun*
stone.

maaru (GR) *adverb*
well, carefully.

maaruma-li (GR) *verb-transitive*
fix, heal, make better. ◆ *Wiringin nhama maaruma-li.* (GR) The clever man will fix/heal (him).
From *maaru* (well, carefully) and *ma-li* (suffix that makes a transitive verb), so 'make well'.

maawulaaldaanga (YY) *noun*
policeman. The derivation probably involves *maa* (hand) and *yulaa-li* (tie up), but the actual derivation of this form is not understood. See also: **biliirrman, gandjibal**.

maaya (YR) *exclamation*
hey!

maaya-li (YR, YY, GR) *verb-transitive*
whisper. The difference between *maaya-li* and *dhayaamba-li* is not understood. See also: **dhayaamba-li**.

maayaal (YR, YY, GR) *noun*
myall tree (*Acacia pendula*). Medium-sized tree with rough bark and drooping leaves; a good fodder tree. Possible source of English 'myall'.

maayal (YR, YY, GR) *noun*
crowfoot. Probably *Erodium crinitum*. Ted

Fields said it is good to eat.

maayama (YR, YY) *noun*
1 stone.
2 money.
This is a rare word for 'money', the more common words are *banggul* and *yarral*. Also *mayama*.

maayamabaa (YY) *noun*
stony place. From *maayama* (stone) and *-baa* (place of, time of).

maayamamayuu (YY) *adjective*
stony. Based on *maayama* (stone).

maayama yuluwirrigiirr (YR, YY) *noun*
opal. From *maayama* (stone), *yuluwirri* (rainbow) and *-giirr* (like).

maayama-li (YY) *verb-transitive*
make by hand. Ian Sim said that this word means to mould or fashion, e.g. to shape dough into loaves. One source.

maaydja (YR) *adjective*
free. As in 'costs nothing'. From *maarr* or *maayrr* (nothing). One source.

maayn (YR, YY) *noun*
dingo (*Canis familiaris dingo*).

maayndjul (YR) *adjective*
very good, tempting. Commonly used in Walgett of things you like, so 'tasty', 'pleasant' or 'enjoyable'.

maayrr (YR, YY) *particle*
no, none. Also *maarr*. ◆ *Maayrr nhalay bandaarr, gi-gi-la-nhi.* (YR) There were no kangaroos here. ◆ *Maarr ngaaluurr gaawaa-ga.* (YY) (There's) no fish in the river. Occurs at the beginning of sentences and is used with nouns (not verbs), usually followed by the noun it modifies. Also used in expressions like *maarr-wan.gaan* (no, none-very) meaning 'nothing at all'. There is limited evidence that *maayrrngay* means 'no more'.

maayu (YR, YY) *adverb*
well, carefully. ◆ *Giirr-bala nhama nguu maayu bilaarr garra-lda-nha, maayu gimbi-lda-nha.* (YR) He is cutting the spear carefully, making (it) carefully. ◆ *'Giirr maayu' ngaya guwaa-y.* (YY) I said 'well done'. ◆ *Giirr ngaya maayu dhanduwi-y-la-nha.* (YY) I always sleep well.

maayuma-li (YR) *verb-transitive*
fix, heal, make better. From *maayu* (well, carefully) and *ma-li* (suffix that makes a transitive verb), so 'make well'. One source. See also: **gabanma-li**.

mabu (YR, YY, GR) *noun*
beefwood tree (*Grevillia striata*). Medium-sized tree with rough dark bark and cream flowers. It is said that beefwood gum was given to children to make them strong and was also used for swollen knees. A hole is made in the ground, some coals put in, then beefwood leaves and then the gum on top. The hole is covered with bark and a hole is cut in the bark, big enough for the knee to be steamed.

mabun (YR, YY) *noun*
1 thigh.
2 gully, creek.
Body-part words are often used to refer to geographic and other features, compare *bungun* (arm, wing, branch).

madhamadha (YR, YY, GR) *adjective*
1 rough, bumpy. Used to describe surfaces, such as roads.
2 knotty.

madhanbaa (YR, YY, GR) *adjective*
heavy. Possibly from *madhan* (heavy) and *-baa* (place of, time of). However, *madhan* occurs in the sources only once, so the recommended word is *madhanbaa*.

madhanmadhan (YY) *adjective*
very heavy. Too heavy to move or lift.

madhay (YY) *noun*
native parsnip (*Trachymene glaucifolia*). Also called native carrot, it is said that the root can be eaten raw or cooked.

madja (YR, YY, GR) *exclamation*
sorry! ◆ *Madja, waala-badhaay nhama ngaya wamba-li!* (YY) Sorry, I can't carry them all!
A general expression of disappointment, a bit like Australian English 'bugger!' or 'oh dear!'.

madjagurra (YR, YY) *exclamation*
oh dear! Also *madjagaa, madjagaarr*. Also means something like 'bugger' or 'damn'; and an expression of disbelief, as in 'it's hard to believe that' or 'really?'.

magal (YR, YY) *noun*
stone knife. Also described as a chisel, it is made from a wooden handle with a sharp stone, used to shape wooden objects.

Magarrawayaa (YY) *placename*
Muckerawa (waterhole). On the Narran River above Wilby.

Magula (YY) *noun*
social group. Every type of living thing, every species, every totem, is divided into two types: *Magula* and *Bumbira*. This may be based on a distinction between 'large' and 'small' in all animals. It has been said that *Magula* people are thought of as more important than *Bumbira* people. People inherit this from their mother. One source. See also: **Bumbira**.

mala (YR, GR) *noun*
1 fork.
2 bottom, bum.
3 restricted word. See p 20 for more information.
The main meaning seems to be 'fork', as in the 'fork of a tree' or anything that branches into two, as the body branches into two legs; so bottom and bum are derived meanings. See also: **gumbul**, **yanggal**.

malagan (YR, YY, GR) *noun*
1 teenage girl (YR, YY, GR).
2 restricted word. See p 20 for more information.

malawil (YR, YY) *noun, placename*
1 human shadow (YR, YY). It is current knowledge that people didn't tread on the shadows of elders.
2 shadow spirit (YY).
3 location (YY). *Malawil* is a place on the Narran River, near Angledool, so called 'because of the shadows there'; also refers to the spirit that lives there. Ginny Rose said that *Malawil* was the name of the *Garriya* waterhole, upstream from Bollonbillion.

malga (YR, YY) *noun*
mulga (*Acacia aneura*). Small tree, 5–10 m with silver-grey leaves and yellow rod-shaped flowers. The seeds can be roasted and ground for damper. Some accounts say that the seed is soaked first. Others, that the seeds are ground into a coarse flour, mixed into a paste and eaten raw. The trees can have many waxy red growths that can be pounded up and mixed in water to be drunk as tea. All acacia seeds are rich in nutrients, with higher energy, protein and fat than crops such as wheat and rice. Possible source of English 'mulga'.

maliga (YR, YY) *noun*
spitfire grub. Larva of the sawfly, a kind of wasp that lays its eggs on eucalypt leaves.

malimali (YR, YY) *noun*
1 clever man's spirit (YR, YY). Spirit belonging to the *wiringin* (Aboriginal clever man or healer); in astral or spirit form he acts, travels, and visits the spirit world.
2 person's spirit (YR).
Also *mali*.

maliyaa (YR, YY) *noun*
friend, mate. See also: **mamal**.

maliyan (YR, YY, GR) *noun*
1 wedge-tailed eagle (*Aquila audax*) (YR, YY, GR). In several stories, including one with the bowerbird.
2 long-necked turtle (*Chelodina longicollis*) (YR). Rare usage. Arthur Dodd said that this turtle is 'stinking' and people don't eat it.
3 policeman (YR). Rare usage.
See also: **girrabirrii**.

Maliyan.gaalay (YR, YY) *noun*
Morning Star, Venus (planet). Based on *maliyan* (eagle).

Maliyangarr (YY) *noun*
ancestral eagle man. An ancestral being mentioned in a story. Based on *maliyan* (eagle).

malu (YY, GR) *adjective*
1 quiet.
2 tired.
This is a rare word, the common word is *yinggil* (tired).

mama-li (YR, YY, GR) *verb-transitive*
stick.

mama-y (YR) *verb-intransitive*
  stick. ◆ *Nhama gilaa, guway mama-nhi.* (YR) That galah, the blood was stuck (on it). A change in verb class from *-li* to *-y*. See Learner's Guide. One source.

mamaay (GR) *noun*
  grandmother (father's mother). This is a rare word, the common word is *badhii*.

mamal (YR, YY) *noun*
  friend, mate. This is a rare word, the common word is *maliyaa*.

mamaldhalibaa (YR, YY) *adjective*
  1 alone, friendless (YR, YY).
  2 unique (YY). When used of a thing or object, it means that there is not another one like it.
  From *mamal* (friend, mate) and *-dhalibaa* (without).

mamalmamal (YY) *adjective*
  sticky. Related to *mama-li* (stick).

mambul (YR) *noun*
  knife. Ted Fields said this refers to a long knife, e.g. a machete. One source.

man.ga (YR) *noun*
  new word. See p 160 for more information.

man.gaman.ga (YR, YY, GR) *adjective*
  1 wide.
  2 flat. ◆ *Giirruu yalagiirrma-wu, ngaarrma-nha dhaygal nguungu, man.gaman.ga burranba-y, nguuma, ganay-u.* (YR) Then (she) made his head flat, with the yamstick.

man.garr (YR, YY, GR) *noun*
  1 bag (YR, YY, GR). Arthur Dodd said 'any bag or sack'. Ian Sim said it was originally a skin bag used for storage and carrying; now a name for any bag. ◆ *Wiima-la nhama man.garr.* (YY) Put that bag down.
  2 pouch (kangaroo) (YR, YY). Also can be used for the pouch of any marsupials.

manbu (YY) *adjective*
  flat. One source. See also: **man.gaman.ga**.

mandarray (YY) *noun*
  mouse. Unidentified species. See also: **dhindu**.

manday[1] (YR) *noun*
  1 penis.
  2 testicles.
  Used in some YR, GR areas. A slang word.

mandayaa (YR, YY, GR) *noun*
  male. Based on *manday* (penis) and *-aa* (place of, time of). Probably used to talk about animals and humans.

manday[2] (YR, YY, GR) *noun*
  series of steps (sequence). Steps cut in trees to climb the tree. Also used in relation to a particular type of public recital of placenames in sequential order. This was known as 'telling the country', and a skilled recital of geography in full and correct order, 'from the top to the bottom', was highly admired. ◆ *Buli-nyi ngaya manday-dji.* (YY) I slipped off the step (in the tree).

mandaymanday (YY) *adjective, adverb, noun*
  1 sequentially. One thing after another.
  2 string of stars. A string of small stars in the northern sky where the tree rat climbed up; in the story about the tree of *maliyan*, the wedge-tailed eagle.
  From *manday* (series of steps), so 'step by step'. Previously written *mandimandi*.

mandhii (YY) *noun*
  special uncle. For a man, it refers to any *garruu* (classificatory uncle) who is the same *dhii* (totem) as him; that is, a man who is one generation older and of the same matrilineal totem.

mandhiigan (YY) *noun*
  initiation guardian. This term referred to a boy's personal guardian during initiation, who was chosen from a group of people who were *mandhii* to the boy. A boy's *mandhiigan* was said to look after him and ensure that his totem was properly represented; they were also said to balance the power of the 'other side', that is, the other moiety. *Mandhiigan* had the responsibility for making sure the initiation was properly carried out. From *mandhii* (special uncle).

mandha (YR, GR) *noun*
  1 bread (YR, GR).
  2 food, tucker (YR).

mandhamandha (YR) *noun*
  unleavened bread. Made without baking powder. From *mandha* (bread). One source.

mandhu (GR) *noun*
  moustache.

Mandiwaa

Mandiwaa (YY) *placename*
location. Also *Mandiwawu*. Based on *manday* (step, generation level).

mandjaarr (YR) *noun*
bunch. As in a bunch of grapes. One source.

manduwii (YR, YY, GR) *noun*
boot, shoe. Ian Sim said it was originally a 'slipper' worn when burrs were troublesome. Possibly a borrowed word.

manga (YR) *noun*
ear. Used with this meaning in Walgett. See also: **bina**.

Mangalaalaa (YR) *placename*
creek name. A creek near Boorah Tank, 29 miles from Walgett on the Walgett–Lightning Ridge road. One source.

mangalaarr (YR, YY) *noun*
Yuurrila's tree. This is the *mingga* (spirit haunted tree) in which *Yuurrila* resides. Munggilah is the name of a nearby waterhole on the Narran River below old Bangate Station.

mangan (YR, YY) *noun*
woma (snake) *(Aspidites ramsayi)*. Arthur Dodd said it might be 'a snake as thick as my leg; he's not very long, and he's harmless'.

manggaay (GR) *noun*
shingleback lizard *(Trachydosaurus rugosus)*.

manggarraan (YR, YY. GR) *noun*
black kite *(Milvus migrans)*. Also called the fork-tailed kite.

mangun.gaali (YR, YY, GR) *noun*
tree goanna *(Varanus varius)*. Name for tree goanna when in its banded phase, that is when it has wide bands of black and yellow on body and tail. Also called black goanna and lace monitor. Fred Reece said 'he's a spotted goanna with stripes — he painted himself'. It is said that goanna oil was used for pains in the head and stiffness.

maniila-y (YR, YY) *verb-intransitive*
1 go hunting. This verb is used in two types of sentences such as: 'I'm going hunting' or 'I'm going hunting for kangaroo', in which case the animal being hunted is marked with the purposive case.
◆ *Giirr ngaya-laa maniila-y.* (YR) I'm going hunting.
2 hunt. ◆ *Maniila-y ngaya gi-yaa-nha bawurra-gu.* (YY) I'm going to hunt for kangaroo.
3 find, look for. ◆ *Ngindaay maniila-waa-ya guduu-gu.* (YR) You all (go ahead) and find some fish.

manuma-li (YR, YY) *verb-transitive*
steal. ◆ *Giirr nhama maadhaay-u bura manuma-y.* (YR) The dog stole some bones.

manumadhaay (YR, YY) *noun*
thief. Related to *manuma-li* (steal). The rules for the derivation and use of this word are uncertain.

mara (GR) *noun*
1 hand.
2 finger.

mara buma-y (GR) *verb phrase*
clap hands. From *mara* (hand) and *buma-y* (hit self).

maraay (YR, YY) *noun*
clear area, camp area. Also *maraaya*. Also known as 'box hollows' because they are surrounded by box trees. A low area which gets swampy after rain, is grass covered and surrounded by coolabah trees which are scarred. There are several *maraay* near Narran Lake and along the ridge running towards Angledool; there is one on Moordale Station. Thought to be *Baayami*'s footprints.

marama-li (GR) *verb-transitive*
make by hand. From *mara* (hand) and *-ma-li* (suffix that makes a transitive verb).

maran (YR, YY) *noun*
ancestors. Any ancestors who go more than three generations back — which is as far back as kinship terms apply.

mararra (GR) *noun*
bridled nail-tail wallaby *(Onychogalea fraenata)*. A very early source has *marawirra*, probably from *mara* (hands) and *wirra-li* (twist), which could describe the strange turning movement of the wallaby's arms when hopping quickly.

marawanda (YY) *noun*
red-tailed phascogale. Possibly *Phascogale calura*, a small, meat eating, nocturnal, tree climbing marsupial. Possibly

originally a Gamilaraay word, from *mara* (hand) and *wanda* (ghost, but perhaps in this word, 'white'), due to its white forepaws. One source.

marayn (GR) *noun*
dingo *(Canis familiaris dingo)*.

marayrr (GR) *particle*
no, none.

marayrrdhuul (GR) *noun*
childless woman. From *marayrr* (no, none) and *-dhuul* (one). One source.

mari (GR) *noun*
1 Aboriginal person. ◆ *Burrulaa nhama mari.* (GR) (There are) many people over there.
2 Aboriginal man. ◆ *Nhama mari dhaay yana-y.* (GR) The man will come here. ◆ *Nhama mari-dhu gagil buruma ganma-lda-nha.* (GR) The man is holding the bad dog. Widely used in Aboriginal English. English spelling *murri*. Pronounced 'mardi' by some (with the tongue curled back). See also: **giwiirr**.

marrabaa (GR) *adjective*
1 good.
2 well.
This is a rare word, the common word is *gaba*.

marra gi-gi (GR) *verb phrase*
rejoice, celebrate. From *marrabaa* (good, well) and *gi-gi* (be).

marragula (YR, YY) *place adverb*
to here (nearby). Also *marragulay*. ◆ *Giirr nhama-nha ngaarrigulay marragula baa-y-la-nhi.* (YR) He was hopping that way and this way.

marrama (YR, YY, GR) *place adverb*
there (close). ◆ *Marrama nguungu gundhi.* (YY) There (is) his house.
Possibly based on *mara* (hand GR). It seems likely that this word is used to refers to things that are visible.

marramarrama-li (GR) *verb-transitive*
praise. Based on *marrabaa* (good, well) and *-ma-li* (suffix that makes a transitive verb). One source.

marramba-li (YR) *verb-transitive*
1 wrap up. Also *marranba-li*. ◆ *Buluuy ngaama baliyaa gi-nyi, ngiyarrma nguu birralii-djuul ngaama marramba-y bulanggiin-da.* (YR) The night was cold and she wrapped the baby in a blanket.
2 cover up. ◆ *Giirruu ngaya nhama marranba-y.* (YR) I will cover it over.

marramba-y (YR) *verb-intransitive*
be wrapped. Also *marranba-y*. ◆ *Birralii-djuul bulanggiin-da marranba-y-la-nhi.* (YR) The baby was wrapped up in a blanket. A change in verb class from *-li* to *-y*. See Learner's Guide. One source.

marran (YR, YY) *noun*
spleen.

marrawal (GR) *noun, placename*
1 porcupine, echidna *(Tachyglossus aculeatus)*. Ridley said it was also called *dhalay-dhalay* (tongue); this may have been a nickname based on its long tongue.
2 Murrawal. Location south of Coonabarabran. One source. See also: **bigibila**.

marrgamarrgaay (YR, YY, GR) *noun*
trapdoor spider.

marrgin (YR, YY, GR) *noun*
gun. From English 'musket'.

marriga (YR) *noun*
car. Also *mariga*. From English 'motor car'. See also: **wilbaarr**.

Marrii (YR, YY, GR) *noun*
men's social section. A person's marriage division (and also their meat/totem) determined who they should marry. *Marrii* marries *Buudhaa*, children are *Yibaay* (male) and *Yibadhaa* (female), sister is *Maadhaa*. Probably related to the common surname 'Murray'. See also: **Gabii, Gambuu, Yibaay**.

mawu-gi (YR, YY, GR) *verb-transitive*
1 dig. This verb is used to talk about digging cooking holes, graves, digging for yams and other underground animals, and for goannas digging themselves into the ground. ◆ *Mawu-nga nhama dhaymaarr!* (YY) Dig up that ground!
2 scratch. ◆ *Mawu-ngiili-nyi ngaya.* (YY) I scratched myself.

mawurr (YR, YY) *noun*
mimosa bush *(Acacia farnesiana)*. Medium- to large-sized shrub with spiny stems and strongly perfumed, golden ball flowers.

Seeds can be eaten green, as beans.

mawurrngiyan (YY) *noun*
mimosa bean pods. Based on *mawurr* (mimosa bush) and *-(b)iyan* (fruit of). See Learner's Guide. One source.

mayaarr (YR) *noun*
bee's wax, wax spout. Arthur Dodd said: 'The bees are working, they put some wax around, and they call this wax *mayaarr*, that's how they find the nest in the winter time. When the bees are not working, they are sealed in.'

mayabi-li (YR, YY, GR) *verb-transitive*
1 put up. ◆ *Nguwama mayabi-la malawil-a.* (YR) Here, put it up in the shade.
2 hang up. ◆ *Dhinggaa ngaya gi-yaa-nha mayabi-li.* (YY) I am going to hang the meat up.
Probably based on *ma-y* (be up) and *bi-li* (verb suffix).

mayabuu (YR, YY) *adverb*
still (continuing).

mayan (GR) *noun*
waterhole, creek.

mayarra (YR, YY) *noun*
bridled nail-tail wallaby *(Onychogalea fraenata)*. Also *mayrra*. Once common on the slopes and plains to the west of the Great Dividing Range, the bridled nail-tail wallaby may now survive only in a small population near Dingo in central Queensland. The common wallaby these days is the swamp wallaby.

mayrra (YR, YY) *noun*
little girl. Also *mayarray*. This is a rare word, the common word is *miyay*.

mayrraa (YR, YY, GR) *noun*
wind.

mayuubiyuu (YY) *noun*
redbill, swamp hen. Probably purple swamp hen *(Porphyrio porphyrio)*.

-mi-y (GR) *verb suffix*
ironic imperative. This is not recorded in recent information, but Ridley (1875) called it the 'ironic imperative'. He spelt it 'gowaalmia', meaning 'speak if you dare'. It is now spelt *guwaa-l-mi-ya*. One source.

midi (YY) *noun*
missus, mistress. Lady of the house. Probably from the English.

midjirr (YR, YY, GR) *noun*
umbrella bush. Also called miljee, the seeds can be eaten raw.

midjul (YR) *noun*
bone. A bone after the meat and perhaps the marrow has been eaten. *Buyuumidjul* is the leg bone of an animal, with edible marrow. 'Mitchell bone' means 'shoulder blade' in Walgett. This is a rare word, the common word is *buya*. One source.

miidja (YY, GR) *noun*
water bag. Made from a carpet python skin.

miimi (GR) *noun*
sister. The recommended word is *baawaa* (sister).

miimii[1] (YR) *noun*
1 old woman. Used with this meaning in Walgett.
2 grandmother. Probably from *miimii* (grandmother — Wangaaybuwan language).

miimii[2] (YR, YY) *noun*
1 river's edge (YR, YY).
2 edge (YY).

miinba-y (YR, YY) *verb-transitive*
ask for. The person being asked is marked by the source or the dative case. The use of this verb is not properly understood.
◆ *Garriya nganundi miinba-la-ya!* (YR) Don't ask me for anything! ◆ *Waal nganunda miinba-nhi.* (YR) (He) didn't ask me.
See also: **dhaya-li**.

miinma-li (YR, GR) *verb-transitive*
pull. ◆ *Miinma-la maadhaay-gu dhiil!* (YR) Pull the dog's tail!

miirrmiirr (YY) *adverb*
backwards. The meaning of this word is not fully understood. One source.

mil (YR, YY, GR) *noun*
eye. There are some derived words, e.g. the placename *Milduul* (Mildool), thought to be named because of eye-like marks in the rocks there.

milabi-li (GR) *verb-intransitive*
wink. From *mil* (eye) and *-bi-li* (verb suffix). One source.

mil binggarr (GR) *noun*
Chinese man. Possibly means 'narrow eyes'. One source.

mil buluuy (YR) *noun*
black eye. From *mil* (eye) and *buluuy* (black).

mil guway (YY) *noun*
bloodshot eye. From *mil* (eye) and *guway* (blood).

milgumilgu (YY) *adjective*
alert, watchful. Based on *mil* (eye).

mil warra (YY) *noun*
swollen eye. From *mil* (eye) and *warra-y* (stand, swell).

milu gawaa-y (YY) *verb phrase*
watch. From *mil-u* (eye-with) and *gawaa-y* (follow), so 'follow with the eye'.

mila (GR) *noun*
hip. One source.

milaan (YR, YY, GR) *noun*
yam (water ribbons) *(Triglochin procera)*. Grows in billabongs with small tubers forming on the roots; these can be eaten raw or cooked. Has ribbon-like leaves that float on the water's surface.

Milaanbaa (YR) *placename*
waterhole name. A waterhole near the Walgett–Lightning Ridge road, about 30 km north of Walgett. From *milaan* (yam-water ribbons) and *-baa* (place of, time of).

milambaraay (YR, GR) *noun*
cow. Based on English 'milk' and *-baraay* (with, having) meaning 'milk-having'.

milambiyaay (YY) *noun*
cow. Based on English 'milk' and *-biyaay* (with, having) meaning 'milk-having'.

milamilaa (YY) *adjective*
shrunken (shrivelled). *Ngamu milamilaa* is the name of mythical women who have tiny breasts. One source.

milan¹ (YR, YY) *adjective*
one. The recommended word for 'one'.

milanburr (YR, YY) *adjective*
first again. Used of the horse which usually led the rest of the mob into the yards; *milanburr* (he's first again). Based on *milan* (one). This word is not fully understood.

milandjal (YY) *adjective*
only one. Based on *milan* (one).

milanduul (YY) *adjective*
alone, only one. From *milan* (one) and *-duul* (little, one).

milan² (YY) *noun*
melon. From English 'melon'.

milan³ (YR, GR) *noun*
close, near. ♦ *Giirr ngaya-la bandaarr wii milan-da wiima-y.* (YR) I put the kangaroo down near the fire.
This may actually be a suffix. The limited GR evidence suggests this word can be used in relation to 'time' as well as 'space', e.g. 'close/near to daylight'.

milanhay (YR) *noun*
eel. One source.

milaya (YY) *noun*
kangaroo rat (bettong). Possibly referred to the burrowing bettong *(Bettongia lesueur)*, which is now not found in the area.

Milaygiin (GR) *noun*
a spirit. A spirit with no hair, and with immense nails which he inserts in people. One source.

milbaawaay (YR, YY) *noun*
jumper ant. Possibly from *mil* (eye) and *baa-waa-y* (will be jumping).

milbarawaay (GR) *noun*
jumper ant. Possibly from *mil* (eye) and *bara-waa-y* (will be jumping).

milbay (GR) *noun*
curlew. This is a rare word, the common word is *wuruyan* (curlew, bush thick-knee).

Milduul (YR, YY) *placename*
Mildool. Probably named because of marks in the rock or ground, that resemble eyes. Located between Angledool and Hebel in *Nhunggabarraa* territory. *Baayami* made a cave there for the warriors to rest and hunters camped there. From *mil* (eye) and *-duul* (little, one).

milgin (YR) *noun*
milk. From English 'milk'.

Mili (GR) *placename*
Millie Station. A property south-west of Moree. Ridley said it means 'white pipeclay (silicate of magnesia)'. One

milimamal

source. See also **milimili**.

milimamal (GR) *noun*
swallow. Unknown species. Based on *milimili* (mud) and *mama-li* (stick), so 'mud sticker'. One source.

milimili (GR) *noun*
mud. Ridley said 'pipeclay'.

minan (YY) *noun*
milky weed *(Euphorbia drummondii)*. Also called caustic weed and flat spurge. Its milky sap has been used for treating sores of different kinds. It was also used in a drink to treat genital diseases, and in Queensland to treat snakebite.

mindjarru (YR, YY) *noun*
yellow tit, weebill (bird) *(Smicrornis brevirostris)*. This bird is in a story about how the porcupine got its quills.

mingga (YR, YY, GR) *noun*
spirit-haunted tree. One source says it is usually a tree, but can be other things, e.g. a rock; so the basic meaning may be 'spirit home'. Also described as a ghost ground or burial place, a secret place in the bush, inhabited by ghosts.

minya (YR, YY, GR) *question word*
what? ◆ *Minya nhama?* (YR) What's that? ◆ *Minya nginda dhinggaa?* (YR) What is your meat?

minyadhi (YR, YY) *question word*
why?, why not? ◆ *Minya-dhi nganundi banaga-nhi?* (YR) Why (did you) run away from me?
From *minya* (what) and *-dhi* (source) as in 'what caused it?'.

minyagaa (YR, YY) *pronoun*
something. ◆ *Minya-gaa ngaarrima-dhaay yanaa-waa-nha.* (YY) There's something coming there.
From *minya* (what) and *-gaa* (some). Used to talk about unknown things. After *minya* and a few other words, *-gaa* is used instead of *-waa*.

minyagu (YR, YY, GR) *question word*
why (what for)? ◆ *Minya-gu nginda dhaay yanaa-nhi?* (YY) What did you come here for?
From *minya* (what) and *-gu* (purpose).

minyama (YR, GR) *question word*
what? ◆ *Minya-ma ngaama, barriindjiin-yaa ngaama?* (YR) What kind (of bird is) that, a peewee maybe?
Based on *minya* (what?) and the suffix *-ma* which seems to mean that the person being asked knows the answer. However, *-ma* may be better defined in future. *Minyama* is rarely used, *minya* is the common form.

minyaminyabal (GR) *pronoun*
everything. Based on *minya* (what?).

minyaminyagaa (YR) *pronoun*
everything. ◆ *Ngaama bubaay-djuul-u, birralii-djuul-u, dhuwarr-dhinggaa dha-ldaay, minyaminyagaa dha-y.* (YR) The little child who was eating, ate everything.
Based on *minya* (what?) and *-gaa* (some).

minyangay (YR, YY, GR) *question word*
how many? ◆ *Minyangay nginu birralii-gal?* (YR) How many children do you have?
Based on *minya* (what?), the meaning of *-ngay* is not known.

minyaarr (YR, YY, GR) *question word*
which? ◆ *Minyaarr birralii nguuma dhayn-duul-gu?* (YR) Which children belong to the little man?

minyaarru (YR, YY) *question word*
where (to)? ◆ *Minyaarru ngay maadhaay banaga-nhi?* (YY) Where did my dog run to? ◆ *Minyaarru nginda yanaa-waa-nha?* (YY) Where are you going?
Based on *minyaarr* (which). See also: **minyaaya**.

minyaarruwaa (YR) *place adverb*
to somewhere. From *minyaarru* (where to).

minyaarruwaayaa (YR) *place adverb*
don't know where to. ◆ *Banaga-nhi ngaama ganunga minyaarru-waayaa.* (YR) They ran to somewhere, don't know where.
From *minyaarru* (where to) and *-waayaa* (don't know).

minyaaya (YR, YY) *question word*
where (at)? ◆ *Minyaaya nginda?* (YR) Where are you? ◆ *Minyaaya ngay guliirr?* (YY) Where (is) my missus?
Probably from *minyaarr* (which). See also: **minyaarru**.

minyaaya dhaay (YR, YY) *question word*
where (from)? ◆ *Minyaaya dhaay, ngindaay yanaa-waa-nha?* (YR) Where are you (more

than two people) coming from? From *minyaaya* (where at) and *dhaay* (this way).
minyaayawaa (YR) *place adverb*
at somewhere. From *minyaaya* (where at).
minyaayawaayaa (YR) *place adverb*
don't know where at. ◆ *Yaluu ngiyarrma ganunga minyaaya-waayaa yanaa-waa-nha.* (YR) They're going somewhere again (I don't know where).
From *minyaaya* (where at) and *-waayaa* (don't know).
mirii (GR) *noun*
star.
mirii yanan (GR) *noun*
shooting star. Based on *mirii* (star), *yana-y* (go). One source.
mirraal (YR, YY, GR) *adjective*
new word. See p 160 for more information.
mirri (YR, GR) *noun*
dog. Used to be rare in YR, but found in names such as *Mirriwuula*, and now widely used to refer to dogs. See also: **maadhaay, buyuma**.
Mirriwuula (YR, YY) *noun*
spirit dog. Mythical giant ancestor of the dingo; subject of song and story; said to now be in the sky and the water; represented in the night sky by a dark area in the Milky Way. Ted Fields said *Mirriwuula* lives at *Mirrigana*, a deep hole in the Namoi River near the Namoi village. Based on *mirri* (dog) (YR, GR).
mirrii (YR, YY) *noun*
drooping currant, native cherry *(Exocarpus cupressiformis)*. Looks a bit like a conifer or pine tree and has an edible fruit stem.
mirril (YR, YY, GR) *noun*
mucus, snot.
mirrindjaa (GR) *noun*
shrimp.
mirringamu (YR, YY, GR) *noun*
jagged spear. Sometimes described as 'multibarbed', may have been used for both hunting and fighting. Possibly from *mirri* (dog) and *ngamu* (breast).
mirriraa (GR) *noun*
lignum *(Meuhlenbeckia cunninghamii)*. One source. For more information see *mirriyaa*.

mirriyaa (YR, YY) *noun*
lignum *(Meuhlenbeckia cunninghamii)*. Almost leafless shrub, with small yellowish flower, grows in thick clumps on low-lying ground. Also *mirrii* in Langloh-Parker.
Mirriyaabarra (YY) *noun*
lignum country people. Ian Sim said that according to Ginny Rose and Greg Fields, *Mirriyaabarra* was probably the name of a group of Yuwaalayaay speakers who originally lived somewhere 'down south on the flat country'. From *mirriyaa* (lignum) and *-barra* (people from). Also *mirriibarra* in Langloh-Parker.
mirrun (YY) *noun*
emu net. Long net of light rope, used to catch emus.
miyaay (YR) *exclamation*
okay! (satisfactory). Ted Fields said it means 'it will pass', 'it will do' or 'not bad' — used about food and probably other things. One source.
miyay (YR, YY, GR) *noun*
1 girl (YR, YY, GR). Up to puberty. Often occurs in *miyay-djuul* (girl-little, just, one); meaning 'little girl' or 'girl'.
2 daughter (YY). Use with this meaning may be a recent development. Currently the common word for girl, with meaning extended to older age. One plural form is *miyaymiyaay* (girls).
miyaymiyaay (YR, YY, GR) *noun*
1 little girl (YR, YY).
2 Seven Sisters (stars), Pleiades (stars) (YR, YY, GR). A group of stars which occur in a story. Many Aboriginal peoples have stories which involve these sisters/stars.
3 mallee willow *(Pittosporum phylliraeoides)* (YR, YY). Also called butter bush, it is a small tree with inedible, very bitter, yellow fruits. The name is said to refer to the brightly coloured seeds.
From *miyay* (girl). Both *miyay-djuul* and *miyaymiyaay* are used for 'little girl' and 'little girls'. *Miyay-djuul* is the more common and if the plural is to be shown *miyay-djuul-galgaa* is recommended. The plural is generally not marked.

mubal (YR, YY, GR) *noun*
stomach, belly, guts. ◆ *Mubal bayn gi-nyi.* (GR) (My) stomach is sore.

mubal dhiyama-li (YY) *verb phrase*
gut. From *mubal* (stomach) and *dhiyama-li* (lift up). The more common expression is *mubal dhuwima-li*.

mubal dhuwima-li (YR, YY) *verb phrase*
gut. From *mubal* (stomach) and *dhuwima-li* (take out, remove). This is the usual expression for 'gut'.

mubal muurra-y (YY) *verb phrase*
be full of food. From *mubal* (stomach) and *muurra-y* (be full). One source.

mubalyaal (YY, GR) *adjective*
pregnant. From *mubal* (stomach) and *yaal* (false).

mubirr (YR, YY, GR) *noun*
1 initiation scars, cicatrices (YR, YY, GR). Arthur Dodd said that initiation scars were cut into men's upper arms and chest with mussel shells; you were 'not a man unless you got cut up like that — women got them too, on the breast'. Fred Reece said that old men had three or four scars on the shoulders and little ones all the way down the back. ◆ *Giirr nhama burrul dhayn mubirr-biyaay.* (YR) The big man has scars (on his chest).
2 carving, engraving (YR, YY).
3 mark, writing (YY).
4 scar (YY).

mubirr dhu-rri (YY) *verb phrase*
1 write.
2 carve.
From *mubirr* (carving) and *dhu-rri* (poke). One source.

mudhay (YR, YY, GR) *noun*
brushtail possum *(Trichosurus vulpecula)*. A favourite food species. Fred Reece said that when they cooked possum it was plucked like a chicken. They also carried honey and probably water in possum skins. It is said that possum fat was used for hair oil.
◆ *Gabinya mudhay-gu galiya-waa-nha.* (GR) The boy is climbing for possums. Possibly also the name of a star.

mudhi (YR, YY) *noun*
old man, old friend. Respectful term of address. Perhaps used of a childhood friend in later life. Used in some YR, GR areas.

mudhu (YR, YY) *noun*
inside. According to Ted Fields, *dhaay yanaa-ya, mudhu-gu* (come here, inside) was said to people as they came to the camp. ◆ *Mudhu-gu ngaama wuu-nhi.* (YR) He went inside.

mudhun (YY) *noun*
secret name. Also *mundhun*. It was said that in the old days many things such as *Garriya* (the crocodile) had a secret name. See also: **bilaan**.

muga (YR, YY, GR) *adjective*
1 blind (YR, YY, GR).
2 blunt (YR, YY).
The adjective *muga* is used with both *mil* (eye) and *bina* (ear) to give expressions for 'blind' and 'deaf'. Also *mugu*.

muga bina (YR, GR) *adjective*
deaf. From *muga* (blunt) and *bina* (ears). See also: **mugu bina, bina muurr**.

muga wudha (YY) *adjective*
deaf. Also *mugu wudha*. From *muga* (blunt) and *wudha* (ear). See also: **mugu bina, bina muurr**.

mugaadhaa (YR, YY) *noun*
marthaguy burr.

mugarr (YR, YY, GR) *noun*
kidney.

mugarrabaa (YR, YY) *noun*
magpie *(Gymnorhina tibicen)*. This is a rare word, the common word is *burrugarrbuu*.

mugi-li (YY) *verb-transitive*
mix. Possibly based on English 'mix'. One source.

mugiin.gaa (YR, YY) *noun*
sandfly.

mugiyala (YR) *noun*
dillon bush *(Nitraria billardieri)*. Also called wild grape, it is a spreading shrub with fruit which is purple or red when ripe. One source. See also: **bibu**.

mugu[1] (GR) *adjective*
blunt.

mugu bina (YR, YY, GR) *adjective*
deaf.

mugu² (YR) *noun*
cigarette. Pronounced 'muku'.

mula (YR, YY) *noun, adjective*
1 boil.
2 swelling.
3 pus.
4 soft, weak. Used to deride or put down the opposition in football.

mulabiyaay (YR) *adjective*
kind. From *mula* (soft, weak) and *-biyaay* (with, having). One source.

mulamula (YR, YY, GR) *adjective*
soft.

mulama (YR) *noun*
colon. Ted Fields said it is the last bit of the guts before the anus. This word is used in Angledool. One source.

mulan (YY) *noun*
half, part. Also a section, or a piece of something.

mulandha (GR) *noun*
far side. One source.

mulaydjalbii (YY) *noun*
skylark. Possibly rufous songlark or brown songlark *(Cinclorhamphus)*. One source.

mulindjal (YY, GR) *noun*
rufous whistler *(Pachycephala rufiventris)*. Also *mulimuli*. Ian Sim said the familiar name is *mulimuli*.

muluumay (YY) *noun*
type of plant. Possibly a tall sedge.

mumumbaay (GR) *noun*
squatter pigeon *(Geophaps scripta)*. One source. Form uncertain.

mundharr (GR) *noun*
death adder *(Acanthopis antarcticus)*.

mundimundi (YR, YY, GR) *adjective*
spotted.

mundimundi dhuwarr (YY) *noun*
brownie (cake). From *mundimundi* (spotted) and *dhuwarr* (bread).

munggal (YY, GR) *adjective*
only. Form and meaning is uncertain. The recommended word is *yiyal*.

mungin (YR, YY, GR) *noun*
mosquito.

mungin.gagalawaa (YR, YY) *noun*
pallid cuckoo. Arthur Dodd said 'they call out 'kaakaakaakaakaa', like that, in the morning'. Based on *mungin* (mosquito), *gaga-li* (call) and *-awaa* (habitual) because the bird is said to call up mosquitoes when it arrives each spring.

Mungungulu (YY) *placename*
waterhole name. On the Narran River below Nullawa; probably refers to a wide point of land there. From *mungumungu* (wide) and *ngulu* (forehead).

munhi (YR, YY, GR) *noun*
louse, lice.

Munhibarabin (YY, GR) *noun*
spirit. Greenway said that this spirit is the wife of *Dharramalan*. *Munhibarabin* is in charge of the instruction and supervision of women, for women may not see or hear *Dharramalan* on pain of death. Langloh-Parker called her the 'spirit sister-in-law'. Possibly from *munhi* (egg, actually 'louse') and *barabin* (semen).

munun (YR, YY) *noun*
emu spear. Fred Reece said: 'The only way to trap emu was to surround a mob at a drinking place, or eating, and sneak up in a circle. You could also wait near water or get up a tree nearby with a *munun*, the emu spear, and spear him, or you can hide if there is plenty of rubbish in the water, or in the lignum [shrub]. The emu comes back to the same place to drink as long as he is not disturbed. They mostly come between 10 and 11 for water in summer time. You paint yourself so they can't smell you, and use the big long spear so you can reach him. He won't run very far before he will drop.'

muraabi (YR) *noun*
crayfish claw. One source.

muraay (GR) *noun*
white cockatoo, sulphur-crested cockatoo *(Cacatua galerita)*.

muramin (YY) *noun*
kurrajong bark. The name for the bark before the inner fibres are stripped out for string etc. One source.

muran (YR, YY) *noun*
dark (before dawn). The very dark time just before the sun rises.

murraagu (YR, YY) *noun*
   man-like spirit. Seen during the day, said to have the power to 'turn', that is assume other forms and to turn thrown weapons back against the thrower.

murraan.gali (YR, YY) *noun*
   corroboree leader.

murragal (YR, YY) *noun*
   bird trap. Ted Fields used to make these traps at Angledool for birds, including parrots; they consist of parallel strings tied between two tea-tree sticks which are very springy.

murrambagan (YY) *noun*
   mother's mother's mother. One source.

murrawa (YR) *noun*
   lizard (nickname). Ted Fields said it is the nickname of a fidgety little lizard and means something like 'quick but crooked'. One source.

murrgu (YR, YY, GR) *noun*
   swamp oak, belah tree (*Casuarina cristata*). See the widow story in Langloh-Parker. A large 'she-oak' tree with dark grey-black bark. Also called 'desert oak'.

murrgugal (YR) *noun*
   belah tree swamp. From *murrgu* (belah tree) and *gal* (many). One source.

murrgumurrgu (YR, YY) *noun*
   ibis (*Threskiornis molucca, T. spinicollis*). Refers to both types of common ibis: the black (straw-necked) and the white. The name is said to come from the long, hanging feathers on the bird's neck, which are like the leaves of the *murrgu* (she-oak tree).

Murrgu Walaay (YR) *placename*
   Swamp Camp. A campsite on the highway north of Lightning Ridge, with belah trees. A story tells that people died and became the trees. From *murrgu* (swamp oak) and *walaay* (camp).

murrguwidjuwii (YR) *noun*
   belah wood sparks. Based on *murrgu* (belah tree), *wii* (fire) and *dhuwindhuwi* (sparks). One source.

murrila (YR, YY) *noun*
   rocky ground/ridge.

murru (YR, YY, GR) *noun*
   bottom, bum. See also: **gumbul, mala**.

murrubidi (YR) *adjective*
   lucky. Also *murrumbiirr*. Used, for example, when someone wins a lot at cards. Based on *murru* (bottom) *-bidi* (big), so 'arsey'. *Ngiibidi* may be a stronger term.

Murrudhi Gindamalaa (YR, YY) *noun*
   planet Venus. Also called the Evening Star, from a story about an old man who laughed at an old woman's bum, and was banished from the land. Now when that star changes colour, he is said to be still laughing. Based on *murru* (bum), *-dhi* (source) and *gindama-y* (laugh), so 'laughing at the bum'. Possibly *murrudhi gindamawaa*.

murrubi (YR, YY) *noun*
   death adder (*Acanthopis antarcticus*). See also: **wularr**.

murrula (YR, YY, GR) *noun*
   pointed club. Plain club for killing game.

murrumanamanaa (YR, YY) *noun, placename*
   1 dragonfly (*Anisoptera*) (YR, YY). Based on *murru* (club); the insect waves its tail like a club.
   2 bullroarer (YR).
   3 Mirramanar Station (YR). On the Walgett–Cumborah road. Ted Fields said this is an old campsite; there was water in the sand in the old river channel, and people used to put hollow logs in the sand to create a well. The area is rich in food. Another source says there is a location, 'Murramiknaa', midway between Walgett and Cumborah, thought to come from *muramin* (kurrajong bark).

murrumay (YR, YY, GR) *noun*
   1 thunder. ◆ *Yalagiirrmawu ngaama, ganunga dhanduwi-nyi, winanga-lda-y ganugu murrumay.* (YR) They slept until they heard the thunder.
   2 lightning. ◆ *Murrumay-u buma-y muyaan.* (YY) Lightning struck the tree. This is a rare word, the common words are *dhuluumay* (thunder) and *dhun.gayrra* (lightning).

murrun (YR, YY, GR) *adjective*
   alive. Also occurs as *murrun-baa*.

murrunbaa (YR, YY) *adjective*
   another, other. ◆ *Murrunbaa nhama yinarr dhaay yanaa-waa-nha, wadhi-dhi.* (YY)

Another woman is coming here, from the bush.
Possibly from *murrun* (alive) and *-baa* (place of, time of).

murrundunmali (GR) *noun*
colon (descending). One source.

murrurwalingay (YR, YY) *adjective*
stale. Possibly from *walingay* (lonely, sulky).

muru (GR) *noun*
1 nose.
2 beak.
3 point. One source for this meaning.

muru biruu (GR) *noun*
nostril. From *muru* (nose) and *biruu* (hole).

Murungamildaa (YY) *noun*
mythical tribe. Langloh-Parker said 'a tribe who had no eyes and saw through the nose'. Possibly from *muru* (nose) and *ngami-li* (see).

muruwaa (YY) *noun*
turpentine bush *(Eremophila sturtii)*. Also *muruwaal*. May have been soaked in water as a medicinal bath, and applied to sores.

muuliyaay (YR, YY) *noun*
magic stone. When Ted Fields and his father were camped at Currawilinghi Station a magic stone appeared one morning when they went down for water; it warned of a big flood which came soon after. It moved out of the water by itself, was black and about 10 cm long. This word includes the suffix *-iyaay* (with, having) which suggests that another word, **muul*, may mean magic.

muundhuurr (YR, YY) *noun*
wasp, hornet. This is probably the mud-dauber wasp, a large solitary wasp preying on spiders and caterpillars.

muurr (YR, YY, GR) *adjective*
1 full, blocked.
2 blunt.
It is used with body parts to create idioms, e.g. *bina muurr* (deaf).

muurr gi-gi (YR, YY, GR) *verb phrase*
forget. Ian Sim recorded the phrase *bina muurr gi-gi* which literally means 'ear becoming blocked'. ◆ *Muurr ngaya gi-nyi, minyaaya-waayaa ngaya manduwii ngay wiima-y.* (YR) I forgot, I don't know where I put my boots.
From *muurr* (full, blocked, blunt) and *gi-gi* (be). See also: **bina**.

muurra-li (YY) *verb-transitive*
fill.

muurra-y (YY) *verb-intransitive*
fill. As in 'the bucket will fill up'. A change in verb class from *-li* to *-y*. See Learner's Guide.

muurrguu (YR, YY) *noun*
barking owl *(Ninox connivens)*. Its call is a dog-like double bark.

muuwi (YY) *adjective*
stranger to corroboree. Ian Sim said this described a person who has not seen or been instructed in a particular 'spirit song' corroboree. One source.

muwan (GR) *noun*
greenhead ant. One source. Form uncertain.

muwi-li (GR) *verb-transitive*
shut. One source.

muyaan (YR, YY) *noun*
1 tree. General word for any tree.
◆ *Galiya-ya nhama muyaan!* (YY) Climb (up) that tree!
2 stick. ◆ *Muyaan nhama banggadha-laa-nha gungan-da.* (YY) There's a stick floating on the water.
3 branch. ◆ *Nhay-bil nhama muyaan, gagil.* (YY) That branch has lots of knots, (it's) bad.

muyaay (YR, YY) *noun*
1 white cockatoo, sulphur-crested cockatoo *(Cacatua galerita)* (YR, YY).
2 pointers of Southern Cross (YY).

muyawa-li (YR, YY) *verb-transitive*
sew. Also *maayawa-li*. ◆ *Giirr-bala nhama ngaya muyawa-y dhunbil-u.* (YR) I sewed it with sinews. See also: **nhinga-li**.

muyu (YR, YY) *noun*
nose.

muyudhaa (YY) *noun*
nostril. Based on *muyu* (nose).

muyu waa (YY) *noun*
nose bone/shell. From *muyu* (nose) and *waa* (shell).

muyumul (YR) *adjective*
two-faced. One source.

muyuwa-li (YR, YY) *verb-transitive*
duck (in water).

Nn

-na (YR, YY, GR) *suffix*
command suffix for *-rri* class verbs.
◆ *Wuu-na nguungunda dhinggaa!* (YY) Give (the) meat to him!

-nda (YR, YY, GR) *suffix*
you (one person — doer/doer to).
◆ *Dhalaa-nda yana-waa-nha?* (GR) Where are you going? ◆ *Minya-nda nhama ngarra-y?* (YR) What did you see? ◆ *Waalaa-nda ngaama dhinggaa dhuwinba-y?* (YR) Didn't you plant (hide) that meat?
This pronoun suffix is the second part of *nginda* (you).

-ndaali (YR, YY, GR) *suffix*
you (two people — doer/doer to).
◆ *Garriya-ndaali yanaa-ya.* (YR) Don't you two come.
This pronoun suffix is the second part of *ngindaali* (you two).

-ndaay¹ (YR, YY, GR) *suffix*
you (more than two people — doer/doer to). ◆ *Garriya-ndaay maaya-la.* (YR) Don't you all whisper.
This pronoun suffix is the second part of *ngindaay* (you, more than two).

-ndaay² (YR, YY, GR) *suffix*
relative suffix for *-li* and *-rri* class verbs.
◆ *Giirr ngaama birray-djuul-u buma-y ngaama miyay-djuul yu-gi-la-ndaay.* (YR) The boys hit the girl who was crying.

-nga¹ (YR, YY) *clitic*
1 now (YR, YY). ◆ *Giirr-nga ngay mil gaba gi-nyi.* (YY) My eyes are all right now. The suffix *-nga* is not fully understood.
2 then (YR, YY). ◆ *Barraay-badhaay nhama dha-la, yanaa-y-gu ngali-nga.* (YR) Eat it up quickly, we'll go then.
3 or (YY). ◆ *Yinarr-nga yuurray.* (YY) A woman or a man.

-nga² (YR, YY, GR) *suffix*
command suffix for *-gi* class verbs.
◆ *Gungan ngawu-nga!* (YY) Have a drink! (Drink the water!)

-n.giili-y (YR, YY, GR) *suffix*
benefactive suffix for *-gi* class verbs. ◆ *Giirr ngaya nginu gaa-n.giili-nyi.* (YR) I brought it for you. ◆ *Giirr ngaya birralii-gu gaa-n.giili-y.* (YR) I will bring it for the child.

'naa-y (YR, YY) *verb-intransitive*
go, come, walk. ◆ *Giirr ngaya 'naa-nhi Galariinbiyaay-a* (YY) I went to Collarenebri.
A relaxed way of saying *yanaa-y*.

ngaa (YR, YY, GR) *particle*
yes. ◆ *Ngaa, giirr ngaya yilama-y burrulaa.* (YY) Yes, I cooked a lot.
The recommended word for 'yes' in YR and YY.

ngaawawu (YR, YY) *exclamation*
that's right! Based on *ngaa* (yes) and, perhaps, *-wu* (all), so a strong or emphatic 'yes'.

ngaayaybaay (YR) *exclamation*
okay! all right! ◆ *Ngaayaybaay, waal nginda nganunda guwaa-li.* (YR) All right, you won't tell me.
Probably based on *ngaa* (yes). A useful word that is often used by many people.

ngaagii (YR, YY) *noun*
grandmother (father's mother). See also: **baagii**.

ngaaluurr (YR, YY) *noun*
fish. Name for any fish. ◆ *Ngali gaawaa-gu yanaa-waa-nha ngaaluurr bayama-li-gu.* (YY) We are going to the river to catch fish.

ngaamba (YY) *noun*
fellow, fella, bloke. One source.

ngaambi-li (YR) *verb-transitive*
trade, swap. This word could be used for 'buy'. One source. Form uncertain.

ngaambiyan (YR) *noun*
give-and-take paddock. Ted Fields said that this was the name of a paddock on the Narran River at Bangate Station; the fences crossed the river so that stock from paddocks on both sides could get to water. One source.

ngaan (YR) *question word*
what? Ted Fields said *ngaan* is used when people do something unexpected or change their mind.

ngaana (YY) *pronoun*
who? (doer/done to). ◆ *Ngaana nginda?* (YY) Who are you? ◆ *Ngaana nginda gayrr?* (YY) What's your name?

The more common word is *ngaandi*.

ngaanawaa (YY) *pronoun*
someone (doer/done to). From *ngaana* (who, doer/ done to) and *-waa* (some). The more common word is *ngaandi-yaa*.

ngaanbanaa (GR) *noun*
cockatoo (possibly corella) *Cacatua sanguinea*. Sources do not specify which of the white cockatoos this refers to, but possibly the corella since the white cockatoo is *muraay*.

ngaandi (YR, YY, GR) *pronoun*
who? (doer/done to). When asking someone's name *ngaandi* is used, in this case it translates as English 'what?'.
◆ *Ngaandi nginda gayrr?* (YR) What is your name? ◆ *Ngaandi nhama dhayn?* (YR) Who is that man? ◆ *Ngaandi nginda ngarra-y?* (YR) Who did you see?
Also *ngaana* (YY).

ngaandingaandi (YR) *common expression*
what's-a-name. Probably used like English 'you know, old what's-his-name', when a person forgets someone's name. From *ngaandi* (who?). One source.

ngaandiyaa (YR, YY) *pronoun*
someone (doer/done to). ◆ *Ngaandi-yaa dhaay dhurra-laa-nha.* (YR) Someone is coming. ◆ *Ngaandi-yaa dhaay yanaa-waa-ndaay bagaarr nhama-nha yanaa-y.* (YR) When someone was coming this way he would 'go the short cut'.
From *ngaandi* (who, doer/ done to) and *-yaa* (some, variant of *-waa*).

ngaandu (YR, YY, GR) *pronoun*
who? (doer to). ◆ *Ngaandu gi-yaa-nha ngay dhiinbaay dhiyama-li?* (YY) Who is going to get my yamstick? ◆ *Ngaandu bandaarr buma-y?* (GR) Who hit the kangaroo?
Occurs at the beginning of sentences.

ngaanduwaa (YR, YY, GR) *pronoun*
someone (doer to). ◆ *Ngaandu-waa nginunha gaga-lda-nha.* (YY) Someone is calling you.
From *ngaandu* (who, doer to) and *-waa* (some).

ngaanngu (YR, YY, GR) *pronoun*
1 whose? ◆ *Ngaanngu nhama bilaarr?* (YR) Whose is that spear? ◆ *Ngaanngu bilaarr nginda gaa-nhi?* (YY) Whose spear did you take?
2 to who? This is only used when something is 'given to' or 'done for' someone. There is a different word for 'movement to who'.
Occurs at the beginning of sentences.

ngaannguwaa (YR, YY, GR) *pronoun*
someone's. ◆ *Ngaanngu-waa nhama malawil.* (YR) There's someone's shadow.
From *ngaanngu* (whose?) and *-waa* (some).

ngaanngunda (YR, YY, GR) *pronoun*
to who? This includes the dative ending *-ngunda*.

ngaanngundawaa (YR, YY, GR) *pronoun*
to someone. ◆ *Ngaya-laa nginunha wuu-rri ngaanngunda-waa.* (YR) I will give you to someone else.
From *ngaanngunda* (to who?) and *-waa* (some).

ngaanngundi (YR, YY, GR) *pronoun*
from who? This includes the source ending *-ngundi*.

ngaanngundiyaa (YR, YY, GR) *pronoun*
from someone. ◆ *Guway-biyaay nhama bilaarr nginu, ngaanngundi-yaa nhama dhurra-y.* (YR) Your spear has blood on it that came from someone.
From *ngaanngundi* (from who?) and *-yaa* (some, variant of *-waa*).

ngaarr (GR) *adjective, adverb*
hard, strong.

ngaarri (YR, YY, GR) *place adverb*
there, over there. ◆ *Ngaarri, nhama.* (YR) He (is) over there.

ngaarribiyan (YR) *place adverb*
north.

ngaarribu (GR) *time adverb*
very long ago. Possibly from *ngaarri* (there) and either *-u* (time suffix) or *buu* (all, totally).

ngaarriga (YY) *adjective*
opposite moiety. A person who belongs to the 'other side' of the moiety division.

ngaarrigili (YR, YY, GR) *noun*
other side. ◆ *Giirr ngaya-nha ngarra-y ngaarri-gili-gu yanaa-waa-ndaay.* (YR) I saw him going to the other side.
Used to refer to the 'other side' of things, such as a river, humpy or tree. Includes suffix *-gili* (side) and has been recorded

with the suffixes -*dja* (at), -*gu* (to) and -*dhi* (from).

ngaarrigulay (YR, YY, GR) *place adverb*
over there (that way). ◆ *Ngaarrigulay yanaa-waa-ya wila-y-gu nginda.* (YR) Go over there to sit down. ◆ *Ngaarrigulay ngarra-la!* (YY) Look over that way!
Probably refers to a direction, not a place. This word is sometimes used to indicate 'a long way'.

ngaarrima (YR, YY, GR) *place adverb*
over there. ◆ *Giirruu ngaama birralii-gal yulu-gi-la-nha ngaarrima.* (YR) The children are playing over there.

ngaarrimali (YR) *place adverb*
over there (that way). ◆ *Ngaarri-ma-li ngarra-la.* (YR) Look over there.
Possibly from *ngaarri* (there), -*ma* (unanalysed suffix) and *-li* (hypothesised direction suffix).

ngaarringaarri (YR, GR) *place adverb*
right over there. ◆ *Yilaa nguu ngarra-y ngaarringaarri-nga bulaarr-nga.* (YR) Soon he saw those two right over there.
From *ngaarri* (there, over there).

ngaarrma (YR, YY) *demonstrative*
that. ◆ *Bawurra ngaya ngaawa-waa-nha ngaarrma nginda ngarra-ndaay.* (YY) I am looking for that kangaroo you saw.
The standard form is *nhama*. See Learner's Guide.

ngaawa-y (YY) *verb-transitive*
1 search for, look for. ◆ *Ngaawa-y ngaya gi-yaa-nha yarraaman.* (YY) I'm going to look for (my) horse.
2 find. ◆ *Giirr ngaya ngaawa-nhi bugalaa.* (YY) I found the ball.
See also: **gayarra-gi**.

ngaay (YR, YY, GR) *noun*
1 mouth (YR, YY, GR).
2 opening, entrance (YR, YY).
Also means 'rim', as in the rim of a bucket or cup.

ngaay gaya-li (YR, YY, GR) *verb phrase*
kiss. ◆ *Garriya nhama ngaay gaya-la maadhaay!* (YY) Don't kiss that dog!
From *ngaay* (mouth) and *gaya-li* (answer — YR, YY). See also: **ngayaga-li**.

ngaaybu (YY) *adjective*
full. Also *ngabu*. Perhaps from *ngaay* (mouth) and –*bu* (all).

ngabi (YY) *noun*
grey snake (*Hemiaspis damelii*). Also *ngabil*.

ngadaa (YR, YY, GR) *place adverb*
1 down, down there (YR, YY, GR). ◆ *Ngadaa dhuli-ya!* (YR) Bend down!
2 under (YR, YY). ◆ *Giirr nguu ngadaa nhaadhiyaan-da ngarra-y.* (YR) She looked under the log.
3 west (sundown) (YR, YY).

ngadaa dhuni (YY) *noun*
mid-afternoon. Ian Sim said 'about 4pm'.
From *ngadaa* (down) and *dhuni* (sun).

ngadaali (YR, YY) *place adverb*
downwards. ◆ *Ngadaa-li nguu bara-nhi.* (YR) He flew down. ◆ *Ngadaa-li nginda yanaa-waa-ndaay, maayu ngarra-laa-ya mangun.gaali-badhaay-nda ngarra-li.* (YR) When you're going downhill, watch out for (any) goannas you might see.
Possibly from *ngadaa* (down) and *-li* (hypothesised direction suffix). Indicates motion downwards.

ngadaamali (YR) *place adverb*
downstream. ◆ *Ngadaamali-nga banaga-nhi.* (YR) He ran downstream.

ngadaluwi-y (YY) *verb-intransitive*
squat. ◆ *Gurrugurru ngada-l-uwi-nyi.* (YY) Each one squatted back down.
From *ngadaa* (down) and -*l-uwi-y* (suffix that indicates 'back'). One source.

ngadhan.gaa (YR) *particle*
thought (suppose). ◆ *Ngadhan.gaa nguu ngaama guduu bayama-y.* (YR) I thought she caught a fish.
Occurs at the beginning of sentences and has only been translated as 'I thought'.

ngadhul (YR, YY, GR) *noun*
1 hollow tree. ◆ *Nhama dhayn-du, dhulii, dhuwima-y, ngama ngadhul-i.* (YR) The man took the goanna from the hollow tree.
2 tree stump. A stump from a tree dying and rotting, not a stump from a tree cut down. Only refers to a dead tree.

ngaduwi (YR, YY) *noun*
gundabluie wattle (*Acacia victoriae*). Has small leaves, 2–3 cm; good stock fodder.

ngagan (YR, YY) *noun*
chin.

ngalaagaa (YR, YY) *noun*
    crab. Fred Reece said '*ngalaagaa* . . . lives in swamp, digs down, he's good to eat and you get water from the hole; he tastes like crayfish'.
ngali (YR, YY, GR) *pronoun*
    we (two people — doer/doer to). Also occurs as *ngali-luu* (both of us).
ngaliman (YR, YY) *adverb*
    almost, nearly. Also *nhaliman*. ◆ *Buli-nyi ngaya gungan-da, ngaliman ngaya garungga-nhi.* (YY) I slipped in the water and I nearly drowned.
ngalingu (YR, YY, GR) *pronoun*
    1 our (two people). ◆ *Biyuu-ga nhama walaay ngalingu.* (YR) Our (two people) house is a long way away.
    2 to us (two people). ◆ *Yaama nginda dhinggaa wuu-rri ngalingu?* (YY) Will you give meat to us two? This is only used when something is 'given to' or 'done for' us two. *Ngalingunda* is used for 'movement to' us two.
ngalingunda (YR, YY, GR) *pronoun*
    to/at/on us (two people).
ngalingundi (YR, YY, GR) *pronoun*
    from us (two people). ◆ *Dhigayaa nhama bara-nhi ngalingundi.* (YY) The bird flew away from me and you.
ngalinya (YR, YY, GR) *pronoun*
    us (two people — done to). ◆ *Giirr nginda ngalinya buma-y muyaan-du.* (YR). You hit the two of us with a stick.
ngalirr (YY, GR) *noun*
    umbilical cord. One source. Form uncertain.
ngama (GR) *noun*
    father's sister.
Ngamaay (GR) *placename*
    Namoi River. Ridley said that this may be based on the 'ngamai tree (a variety of the acacia)' or *ngamu* (breast) because the river is curved like a woman's breast.
ngamawidhalbaa (YR) *noun*
    colon. Ted Fields said it is the last bit of the guts before the anus. Word used in Walgett. One source.
ngambaa (YR, YY, GR) *noun*
    1 mother.
    2 aunt (mother's sister). The word is generally not used with the meaning 'aunt' today. Sometimes occurs as *ngambaadhi*.
ngami-li (GR) *verb-transitive*
    1 see. ◆ *Ngaya nhama bandaarr ngami-lda-nhi.* (GR) I saw (was seeing) a kangaroo.
    2 look. ◆ *Yilaalu ngaya ngami-li buruma.* (GR) Later I will look at this dog.
    3 watch. ◆ *Nhama ngalinya ngami-lda-nha.* (GR) (They) are watching us two.
ngamilma-li (GR) *verb-transitive*
    teach. Based on *ngami-* (see) and *ma-li* (ending that makes a transitive verb), so 'make see'. Most Aboriginal languages use words associated with 'ear' for 'teach' and so the authenticity of this word is questionable. One source.
ngamu (YR, YY, GR) *noun*
    1 breast.
    2 breastmilk.
ngamugaa (YR) *noun*
    restricted word. See p 20 for more information.
ngamurrawarray (GR) *noun*
    restricted word. See p 20 for more information.
ngamu-gi (YR, YY, GR) *verb-transitive*
    suck, suckle. Has been found referring to a baby at the breast, or sucking the poison from a snakebite. From *ngamu* (breast).
ngamulngamul (YR, YY) *noun*
    ripple, wave. Possibly based on *ngamu* (breast), from the shape.
ngamuma-li (YR) *verb-transitive*
    milk a cow. From *ngamu* (breast, breastmilk) and *-ma-li* (suffix that makes a transitive verb). One source.
ngamumbirra (YR, YY) *noun*
    native plum *(Santalum lanceolatum)*. Also called sandalwood. It has small edible fruit, powdery blue-green leaves and aromatic wood. Fred Reece said that the fruit is nice to eat, having a stone like a cherry, and is black when ripe. Emus love

to eat it. The timber is also oily and may have been used for making fire by rubbing it. The kernel is pounded into a paste and rubbed on sore areas. Bark shavings are soaked and the liquid is rubbed on itchy areas. Leaves and bark are soaked in water, which is drunk as a purgative to cause diarrhoea. The outer wood is soaked in water which is used for 'sickness of the chest'. The roots are soaked in water which is used to treat rheumatism and to refresh the body. Leaves are burnt to drive away mosquitoes, and people smoke themselves and their babies to gain strength for long trips. The berry has a high water content, and some protein, fat and energy.

Ngamumbirrabaa (YY) *placename*
location. From *ngamumbirra* (wild plum) and *-baa* (place of, time of).

ngamurr (GR) *noun*
daughter. This is a rare word, the common word is *miyay*.

ngana (YY) *noun*
grass windbreak, grass hut. Ian Sim said it is made from long grass sods placed in a line and woven together. See also *nhanu* (bower — YR). These words may be related.

nganangana (YR, YY) *noun, adjective, adverb*
1 cork. The material and cork for a bottle.
2 floating, buoyant. Also used of the 'floating' flight of certain birds: *bara-y nganangana* (will fly in a floating manner).

nganawayngaa (YY) *noun*
grandchild (son's child). One source.

nganbi-y (YR, YY) *verb-intransitive*
lean. ◆ *Giirr dhayn-duul ngaama maalaabidi-dja nganbi-y-la-nha.* (YY) The man is leaning up against that tree.

nganbima-li (YR) *verb-transitive*
lean. ◆ *Dhiyama-y ngaya ngaama ngay ganay waama ngaya-nga nganbima-y maalaa-bidi-dja.* (YR) I picked up my yamstick then leant it against a tree. From *nganbi-* (lean) and *-ma-li* (suffix that makes a transitive verb), so 'make lean'.

nganbirr (YY, GR) *adjective, adverb*
1 crosswise, across. Also *nganbi*. Used to describe things that are 'across' something, e.g. in English 'the bridge across the river'.
2 non-marriageable (woman). A person is *nganbirr* when they are ineligible as a marriage partner, because they are in the wrong social section. This was not an absolute prohibition; irregular marriages were reluctantly recognised. Based on *nganbi-y* (lean). See also: **ngan.gi**.

nganbinganbi (YY) *adverb*
to and fro. As in a saw cutting wood across the grain, or something thrown this way and that, or to the left and right. Based on *nganbirr* (crosswise, across).

nganda (YR, YY, GR) *noun*
1 tree bark (YR, YY, GR).
2 tin (YR, YY). As in roofing tin and anything else made of tin, including cans. The meaning of *nganda* may have been extended to 'tin' because both bark and tin are used for roofing.
3 canoe (GR). ◆ *Nganda nhama baga-dha wila-y.* (GR) A canoe will stop on the river bank.

ngandanganda (YY) *adjective*
shiny, reflective, glittering. From *nganda* (tin).

ngandabaa (YR, YY, GR) *noun*
1 king brown snake (*Pseudechis australis*) (YR, YY, GR). Also called mulga snake.
2 snake (YR). Only one source uses *ngandabaa* as the general word for 'snake'. See *dhuyu/dhuru* (any snake).

ngandan (YY, GR) *noun*
type of fish.

ngandirr (YR, GR) *noun*
steep bank. Also *nganggil* (YY).

ngan.gi (YY, GR) *noun*
non-marriageable woman. A woman that a man cannot marry because, while she is of the right section, she is still 'too closely' related. This was an absolute prohibition on marriage to prevent incest. One source. See also: **nganbirr**.

nganggil (YY) *noun*
steep bank.

nganha (YR, YY, GR) *pronoun*
me (done to). ◆ *Buruma-gu nganha yii-li.* (GR) The dog will bite me.

nganunda (YR, YY, GR) *pronoun*
to/at/on me. ◆ *Gaay guwaa-la nganunda.*

(YY) Talk to me. ◆ *Yiili-bala ngarunda nhama dhayn gi-nyi maayama ngaya wana-ngindaay.* (YY) The man got cranky with me because I threw the stone. ◆ *Dhaay-nda nganunda wuu-rri.* (YR) You will give it to me. This pronoun is sometimes used for 'giving to', but the more usual pronoun is *ngay*.

ngarundi (YR, YY, GR) *pronoun*
from me. ◆ *Garriya nganundi miinba-la-ya.* (YR) Don't ask me (for anything). ◆ *Yanaa-ya nganundi.* (YY) Go away from me. ◆ *Nguuwi nganundi dhurra-laa-nha.* (YY) I am sweating (sweat is coming from me).

Nganundi Gindamalaa (GR) *noun*
planet Venus. From *nganundi gindamalaa* (he laughs at me), also *nginundi gindamalaa* (he laughs at you). See also: **Murrudhi Gindamalaa**.

nganuwaay (GR) *noun*
potential spouse (for a man). This meant a woman of the right social section and often a 'second cousin'. For instance for a *Marrii* man the right class for marriage is *Buudhaa*. Examples of potential spouses include: mother's cross-cousin's daughter; mother's mother's brother's son's daughter.

Ngara (YY) *noun*
social group. One side of a twofold division of all species, which had some significance in marriage regulation. The name of the other side was not recorded.

ngaragay (GR) *conjunction*
and, another.

ngarra-li (YR, YY) *verb-transitive*
1 see. ◆ *Giirr ngaya nginunha ngarra-y.* (YY) I saw you.
2 look. ◆ *Dhuyu ngarra-la!* (YY) Look at the snake!
3 watch. ◆ *Giirr ngaya nginunha ngarra-lda-y.* (YR) I will watch you.

ngarra-y (YR, YY) *verb-intransitive*
look. This use of the verb only occurs in the progressive forms *ngarra-y-la-nha* and *ngarra-y-la-nhi.* ◆ *Giirruu nhama bunbun-giirr ngarra-y-la-nha.* (YR) He looks like a grasshopper. ◆ *Gagil nhama ngulu ngarra-y-la-nha.* (YY) (His) face looks bad.
A change in verb class from -*li* to -*y*. See Learner's Guide.

ngarrala-y (YR) *verb-intransitive*
court. ◆ *Giirr nhama bulaarr-nha ngarra-la-y-la-nha.* (YR) Those two are courting. From *ngarra-li* (see, look, watch) and -*la-y* (each other), with a special use to indicate 'courting'.

ngarrangarra-li (YR, YY) *verb-transitive*
mind, look after. ◆ *Yaama nginda ngay maadhaay ngarrangarra-lda-y?* (YR) Will you mind my dog?
The reduplicated form of *ngarra-li* (look, see, watch) has this particular meaning. See Learner's Guide.

ngarranma-li (YR, YY) *verb-transitive*
show. ◆ *Nhama nguungunda barran ngarranma-la!* (YR) Show the boomerang to her!
From *ngarra-* (see, look) and -*ma-li* (suffix that makes a transitive verb).

ngarraadhaan (YR, YY) *noun*
bat. Name for any small bat. Known as 'man's friend'. Possibly from *ngarra-li* (see) and -*dhaan* (good at).

ngarraagulay (YR) *place adverb*
over there (other side). Also *ngarraagula*. This often occurs in the phrase *ngaarrigulay ngarraagulay*, meaning something like 'this way and that'. The basic meaning of *ngarraagulay* might be 'to the other place'. See Learner's Guide.

ngarraga-li (YY) *verb-transitive*
feel sorry for someone, pity someone. Based on *ngarragaa* (poor, pitiful). One source.

ngarragaa (YR, YY, GR) *exclamation, adjective*
1 poor (helpless), pitiful. Often occurs in *ngarragaa-dhuul* (poor — little, just, one); meaning 'poor fellow' or 'poor little fellow'. ◆ *Dhigayaa ngarragaa-dhuul.* (YY) Poor little bird.
2 silly. Ted Fields that if *ngarragaa* is said in a certain tone it can mean a 'poor type of person'.
3 alas!, oh dear!
Still in common use. Also *naragaa*.

ngarrala (YR, YY, GR) *noun*
large locust.

ngarrama (YR) *noun*
birthplace spirit. Spirit who looks after the

ngurrambaa (birthplace). One source.

ngarran¹ (YR, YY, GR) *noun*
dawn. ◆ *Dhinawan nhama ngay buma-y, ngarran-da.* (YR) I killed an emu at dawn. Probably from *ngarra-li* (see).

ngarran² (YY) *noun*
medicine bush (fuschia). Rounded shrub with spotted flowers. Possibly (*Eremophila maculata*).

ngarrawidhalba (YR) *noun*
father-in-law. This is a rare word, the common word is *garruu* (father-in-law).

ngarrdanma-li (YY) *verb-transitive*
make mouth water. Possibly from *-dha-y* (suffix to do with eating) and *ma-li* (suffix that makes a transitive verb).

ngarri-y (GR) *verb-intransitive*
sit. ◆ *Nhama gundhi-dha ngarri-y-la-nha.* (GR) He is sitting in the house.
This verb was previously listed as *ngarri-li* but has been re-analysed as *ngarri-y*.

ngarribaa (YR, YY, GR) *place adverb*
1 up, high. This word can also be used to mean 'above, up there'. ◆ *Nhama maayu dhigayaa bara-waa-nha ngarribaa gunagala-ga.* (YR) The bird is flying high in the sky.
2 east.

  ngarribaa bidjunda (YY) *noun*
  midday. From *ngarribaa* (up) and *bidjun-da* (middle-at).

  ngarribaa dhuni (YY) *noun*
  mid-morning. Ian Sim said 'about 10 o'clock'. From *ngarribaa* (up) and *dhuni* (sun).

  ngarribaagili (YR) *place adverb*
  above. From *ngarribaa* (up) and *-gili* (side).

  ngarribaali (YR, YY) *place adverb*
  upwards. ◆ *Giirr dhuu ngaama dhurra-y ngarribaali gaburran-gu.* (YR) The smoke rose upwards towards the top.
  Possibly from *ngarribaa* (up, high) and **-li* (hypothesised direction suffix). This is the opposite of *ngadaali* (motion downwards).

ngaru-gi (GR) *verb-transitive*
drink.

ngawi-y (YY) *verb-intransitive*
smell. ◆ *Gaba nhama ngawi-y-la-nha.* (YY) It smells good.

ngawil (YR, YY) *noun*
emu bush (*Eremophila longifolia*). Medium-sized tree with drooping branches and tubular, red-spotted, white flowers.

ngawingawi (YY) *noun*
pennyroyal, river mint (*Mentha satureiodes*). Also *ngawilngawil*. This peppermint smelling herb which grows on the banks of creeks is used in various ways. Soaked in water, it was drunk as a blood purifier, and it was also heaped into a pillow for anyone suffering from sleeplessness. Probably from *ngawi-y* (smell).

ngawu-gi (YR, YY) *verb-transitive*
drink. ◆ *Nhama birralii-djuul-u gungan ngawu-gi-la-nha.* (YR) The little boy is drinking the water.

ngawurr (YY, GR) *noun*
ankle.

ngay¹ (YR, YY, GR) *pronoun*
1 my. ◆ *Nhama ngay gundhi.* (GR) That is my house. ◆ *Guliirr nhama ngay.* (YY) That's my husband/wife.
2 to me. ◆ *Gaba-dhuul nhama maadhaay, ngay wuu-na.* (YY) That's a good little dog, give it to me. ◆ *Giirr nhama ngay buwadja-yu wuu-nhi, bilaarr.* (YR) My father gave it to me, the spear.
This is only used when something is 'given to' or 'done for' me. *Nganunda* is used for 'movement to' me.

ngay² (YR, YY) *noun*
grub hook. Stick, barb or hook for removing guts before cooking.

  ngaydju dhiyama-li (YY) *verb phrase*
  hook out (grub). From *ngay-dju* (hook-with) and *dhiyama-li* (pick up, lift up), another word for this is *dhuwima-li* (take out).

ngaya (YR, YY, GR) *pronoun*
I. ◆ *Buluuy-a ngaya yanaa-nhi.* (YY) I went in the dark.

ngayaga (YR, YY, GR) *place adverb*
behind. ◆ *Nhama ngay maadhaay banaga-waa-nha ngayaga nganunda.* (YR) My dog is running behind me.

ngayaga-li (YR, YY) *verb-transitive*
kiss. Form uncertain. Possibly related to *ngaay* (mouth).

ngayagay (YR) *conjunction*
and, another. ◆ *Yilaa ngaya-laa burrulaa*

dhinggaa dhaay gaa-g-uwi-yaa-y, mudhay ngayagay, mangun.gaali ngayagay. (YR) Soon I'll bring back a lot of meat, and possum and goanna. ◆ *Giirr ngaya ngarra-y minya-gaayaa; giirr ngaya ngaama ngandabaa ngarra-y nguuma ngayagay yina-yu ngandabaa ngarra-y.* (YR) I saw something; I saw a brown snake there (and) the woman saw a brown snake (too). ◆ *Yaama nginda ngayagay yugal bawi-lda-y?* (YR) Will you sing another song?

This word can link two unrelated things, compared to *yaluu* which means 'more of the same'. See also: **-bula** (also, too).

ngayarray (YR) *adjective*
speckled. One source.

ngaybaan (GR) *noun*
nepine *(Capparis lasiantha)*. See *guwiibirr* for more information.

-ngayi-li (YR) *suffix*
all day, on-going, habitual. This suffix is added to verbs to indicate that the action continued all day, or that the action is ongoing or habitual. See Learner's Guide.

-ngayi-y (YR, YY) *suffix*
yesterday (recent past), tomorrow (near future). ◆ *Gama-l-ngayi-nyi ngaama nguu bilaarr nguungu.* (YR) He broke his spear yesterday. ◆ *Giirr ngaya-laa ngarra-l-ngayi-y.* (YR) I will look (for it) tomorrow.

This suffix is added to verbs and expresses recent past and near future. The suffixed verb is *-y* class. See Learner's Guide.

ngaymbuwan (YR, YY) *noun*
saucepan. Possibly from English 'iron pan'.

ngayrrngayrr (YR, YY) *noun*
green tree frog *(Litoria caurulea)*. The name comes from the frog's call.

ngayu-gi (YR, YY) *verb-transitive*
tread on, trample. ◆ *Ngayu-nhi ngaya dhuyu.* (YY) I trod on a snake.

ngayuun (YR, YY) *noun*
camel melon *(Citrullus lanatus)*. Fred Reece said it is a big oval melon that is very good to eat. Also called green melon.

ngibaay (GR) *exclamation*
strange! One source.

ngiilay (YR, YY, GR) *place adverb*
from here. ◆ *Yanaa-ya ngiilay, garriya-bala nguwalay wila-y-la-ya!* (YR) Go away from here, don't stop here!
Indicates movement away from the speaker.

-ngiili-y (YR, YY) *suffix*
oneself. ◆ *Buma-ngiili-nyi ngaya dhaygal-a giirrgal-u.* (YY) I hit myself on the head with my tomahawk.
The reflexive suffix is attached to verbs to indicate that the action is being done to oneself. See Learner's Guide.

ngiirr (GR) *noun*
eyebrow.

ngiirrma (GR) *place adverb*
there. Possibly an alternative form of *ngiyarrma* (YR).

nginaalingu (YR, YY, GR) *pronoun*
1 your (two people).
2 to you (two people). This is only used when something is 'given to' or 'done for' you (two people). *Nginaalingunda* is used for 'movement to' you (two people).
◆ *Ngaya-bala nginaalingu bilaarr wuu-nhi.* (YR) I gave the spears to you two.

nginaalingunda (YR, YY, GR) *pronoun*
to/at/on you (two people).

nginaalingundi (YR, YY, GR) *pronoun*
from you (two people).

nginaalinya (YR, YY, GR) *pronoun*
you (two people — done to).

nginaayngu (YR, YY, GR) *pronoun*
1 your (more than two people).
◆ *Nginaayngu bayn ngambaa-dhi gi-nyi.* (YR) Your mother is sick (talking to three or more people).
2 to you (more than two people). This is only used when something is 'given to' or 'done for' you (more than two). *Nginaayngunda* is used for 'movement to' you (more than two). ◆ *Ngiyani, bilaarr nginaayngu wuu-nhi.* (YR) We gave the spears to all of you.

nginaayngunda (YR, YY, GR) *pronoun*
to/at/on you (more than two people).

nginaayngundi (YR, YY, GR) *pronoun*
from you (more than two people). ◆ *Giirr nhama ganunga banaga-y nginaayngundi.* (YR) They will run away from all of you.
◆ *Waal ngaya-laa yaluu dhinggaa manuma-lda-y, nginaayngundi.* (YR) I'll never steal

nginaaynya

meat again from you fellows.

nginaaynya (YR, YY, GR) *pronoun*
you (more than two people — done to).

-nginda (YR, YY, GR) *suffix*
wanting. Also *-ngin, -ngindi*.
◆ *Dhinggaa-nginda ngaya.* (YR) I want meat.
◆ *Guliirr-nginda ngaya.* (YR) I want a wife (or husband).
Also used in *yuul-ngin* (hungry) and *gungan-nginda* (thirsty).

nginda (YR, YY, GR) *pronoun*
1 you (one person — doer/doer to).
◆ *Yaama nginda?* (YR) How are you? ◆ *Biiba nginda dhu-dha-nha.* (YR) You are writing a letter.
An alternative form is the bound pronoun *-nda*.

ngindaali (YR, YY, GR) *pronoun*
you (two people — doer/doer to). An alternative form is the bound pronoun *-ndaali*.

-ngindaay (YR, YY, GR) *suffix*
relative suffix for *-y* and *-gi* class verbs.
◆ *Yaama-nda winanga-y-la-nha bidjaay-a bundaa-ngindaay?* (YY) Do you remember when you fell in the mud?
See also: *-ndaay, -ldaay*.

ngindaay (YR, YY, GR) *pronoun*
you (more than two people — doer/doer to). An alternative form is the bound pronoun *-ndaay*.

ngininnginin (YR, YY) *noun*
small locust, cicada. Form uncertain.

nginu (YR, YY, GR) *pronoun*
1 your (one person). ◆ *Nhama nginu guliirr.* (GR) That is your wife. ◆ *Banaga-ya ngambaa-ngun-da nginu.* (YR) Run to your mother.
2 to you (one person). This is only used when something is 'given to' or 'done for' you (one person). *Nginunda* is used for 'movement to' you (one person). ◆ *Giirr, badjin ngaya nginu wuu-rri.* (YY) I'll give you a little bit.

nginunda (YR, YY, GR) *pronoun*
to/at/on you (one person). ◆ *Giirr ngaya waal nginunda guwaa-y.* (YR) I didn't tell you. ◆ *Giirr ngaya nginunda yiili gi-gi-la-nha.* (YR) I am wild (angry) with you.
◆ *Yilaa ngaya nginunda maayu bawi-lda-y.*

(YR) Soon I will sing well for you.

nginundi (YR, YY, GR) *pronoun*
from you (one person). ◆ *Guuma-y-la-nha ngaya nginundi.* (YY) I am hiding from you.
◆ *Waal ngaya giyal gi-la-nha nginundi.* (YY) I am not frightened of you.

nginunha (YR, YY, GR) *pronoun*
you (one person — done to).

ngiyani (YR, YY, GR) *pronoun*
we (more than two people — doer/doer to). Also occurs as *ngiyani-luu* (all of us).

ngiyaningu (YR, YY, GR) *pronoun*
1 our (more than two people). ◆ *Nhalay ngiyaningu bilaarr.* (YR) These are our spears.
2 to us (more than two people). This is only used when something is 'given to' or 'done for' us (more than two). *Ngiyaningunda* is used for 'movement to' us (more than two). ◆ *Yaama-nda ngiyaningu nhama guduu wuu-dha-y?* (YR) Will you be giving us the cod?

ngiyaningunda (YR, YY, GR) *pronoun*
to/at/on us (more than two people).
◆ *Ngay guliirr yanaa-nhi dhaay ngiyaningunda.* (YR) My husband walked towards us. This pronoun is sometimes used for 'giving to', but the more usual pronoun is *ngiyaningu*. ◆ *Giirr ngiyaningunda dhinggaa nguu wuu-nhi.* (YY) He gave us some meat.

ngiyaningundi (YR, YY, GR) *pronoun*
from us (more than two people).
◆ *Ngiyaningundi bara-nhi.* (YR) (It) flew away from us.

ngiyaninya (YR, YY, GR) *pronoun*
us (more than two people — done to).

ngiyarrma (YR, YY) *place adverb*
there. Also *ngiyama, ngiima*. ◆ *Giirruu ngaama dhaymaarr walanbaa gi-nyi, ngiyarrma nguu waala mawu-gi-la-nhi.* (YR) The ground was hard, he couldn't dig there. This word was often transcribed 'ngiima' in YY.
Generally refers to the time, place or thing already mentioned. See Learner's Guide.

ngubi (GR) *noun*
chest. This is a rare word, the common word is *biri*.

ngudjiin (YR, YY) *noun*
eyelash.

ngulawaa (YY) *noun*
good season. One source.

ngulu (YR, YY, GR) *noun*
1 face (YR, YY, GR).
2 forehead (YR, YY, GR).
3 point (YY, GR). Any geographical feature of a long narrow shape, e.g. a point of land sticking out into a river.
4 surface (GR). As in 'surface of the water'.

ngulugaayrr (YR, YY, GR) *noun*
headband (plaited). A narrow net painted red and worn as a headband. Based on *ngulu* (face, forehead).

nguluumanbuu (YY) *noun*
flat-headed gudgeon (a fish). Said to be 'cousin' to the cod; it looks a bit like a small cod. Based on *ngulu* (head) and *manbu* (flat).

Nguluwawul (YY) *placename*
Nullawa. A place on the Narran River. A bluff, with steep abrupt sides. From *ngulu* (forehead, face) and *waawal* (narrow).

Nguluyuundu (YY) *noun*
axe-face spirit. Willie Willis said this is a mythical being whose forehead is an axe blade. From *ngulu* (face, forehead) and *yuundu* (axe).

nguluurr (YR, YY) *noun*
tear.

ngunmal (YY, GR) *noun*
yard, enclosure. An enclosed area, e.g. a yard in a fish trap. ◆ *Nginda wubarra-la ngunmal-a!* (GR) You pen (it) up in the yard!

ngunuugaa (YR, YY, GR) *noun*
elbow.

ngurrala (YR) *noun*
stone. This is a rare word, the common word is *maayama*. One source.

ngurrambaa (YR, YY) *noun*
birthplace, family land. A man's land which he inherits from his father, and to which his spirit returns when he dies if the correct funeral rites are held. A man's ownership of his *ngurrambaa* is determined by birth and does not depend on him occupying the place or visiting it, although that was the usual custom. Possibly from *ngurra* (camp — Wangaaybuwan language) and *-baa* (place of, time of).

ngurran.gali (YR, YY) *noun*
sitting emu. An emu sitting anywhere, whether on its nest, drinking or sharpening its beak. Possibly related to the Wangaaybuwan word *ngurruy* (emu).

ngurray (YY, GR) *noun*
black snake. Possibly spotted black snake or blue-bellied black snake *(Pseudechis guttatus)*.

ngurrgun (YY) *noun*
husky voice. ◆ *Ngurrgun ngaya gi-nyi gaay guwaa-lda-ndaay burrulaa.* (YY) I'm getting a husky voice from talking too much.

ngurru (GR) *noun*
night. The more common word is *buluuy*.

ngurrugu (YR, GR) *time adverb*
tomorrow. From *ngurru* (night).

ngurruula-y (YR, YY) *verb-transitive*
snore. ◆ *Bamba wanda-gu ngurruula-nhi.* (YY) The white man snores terribly.

nguru (GR) *pronoun*
he, she (doer/doer to).

ngurugaali (GR) *pronoun*
they (two people — doer to).

nguruma (GR) *noun*
spirit-haunted stone. One source. Form uncertain.

*ngurunga (GR) *pronoun*
her, him (done to). This is the hypothesised form based on *nguru* (him, her) and the pronoun pattern. The usual way of saying 'him/her — done to' is *nhama* or its variants, or an abbreviation *-nha*.

ngurungu (GR) *pronoun*
1 her(s), his.
2 to her, him. This is only used when something is 'given to' or 'done for' him or her. *Ngurungunda* is used for 'movement to' him or her.

*ngurungunda (GR) *pronoun*
to/at/on him/her. The hypothesised form based on *nguru* (him, her) and the pronoun pattern.

*ngurungundi (GR) *pronoun*
from him/her. The hypothesised form based on *nguru* (him, her) and the

pronoun pattern.

nguruwi (GR) *noun*
sweat.

nguu¹ (YR, YY) *pronoun*
he, she (doer/doer to). ◆ *Dhinggaa nguu dha-lda-nha.* (YR) He is eating meat. ◆ *Giirr ngaama nguu wii wiima-y.* (YR) She (doer to) made a fire. ◆ *Giirr nguu gaarrima-y.* (YY) He (doer to) did spill it.

nguu² (YR, YY) *noun*
swamp paperbark, tea-tree *(Melaleuca adnata)*. Bushy shrub or small tree, with white 'bottle-brush' like flowers.

nguuguuba-li (YR) *verb-transitive*
1 chew. ◆ *Giirr nhama nguu nguuguuba-y.* (YR) He chewed it (the meat) all up.
2 sip. ◆ *Baluwaa nguuguuba-lda-ya bubaay, garriya-bala bamba ngawu-nga!* (YR) Slowly sip a little bit, don't drink too much!

nguuluwi (YR, YY) *noun*
tadpole.

nguuma¹ (YR) *demonstrative*
that, those. ◆ *Giirr-bala nguuma bubaay-galgaa-gu birralii-gal mudhay dha-lda-nhi.* (YR) Those small children had eaten the possum. ◆ *Waala nguuma bandaarr dhu-dha-nha bilaa-yu.* (YR) That person can't spear kangaroos with a spear.
This demonstrative can also be used instead of 'he', 'she', 'it', 'that one' and 'they'. The rules for the use of this word are uncertain. See Learner's Guide.

nguuma² (YY) *noun*
spirit-haunted stone. One source.

nguunga (YR, YY) *pronoun*
her, him (done to). The usual way of saying 'him/her done to' is *nhama* or its variants, or an abbreviation, *-nha*.

nguungu (YR, YY) *pronoun*
1 her(s), his. ◆ *Nhalay nguungu gundhi.* (YY) Here's his house. ◆ *Dhina nguungu ngaama bayn.* (YR) Her feet were sore.
2 to her, him. This is only used when something is 'given to' or 'done for' him or her. *Nguungunda* is used for 'movement to' him or her. ◆ *Nguungu wuu-nhi dhinggaa.* (YR) (They) gave meat to her/him.

nguungunda (YR, YY) *pronoun*
to/at/on him/her. ◆ *Nhama-nga burrulaa dhayn warra-y-la-nhi guwiinbaa-ga nguungunda.* (YR) A lot of people were standing at (around) her.

nguungundi (YR, YY) *pronoun*
from him/her. ◆ *Banaga-waa-nha bamba dhayn nguungundi.* (YY) The man is running quickly away from him. ◆ *Gaa-nga nguungundi dhinggaa.* (YY) Take that meat away from him.

nguuwi (YR, YY) *noun*
sweat. ◆ *Nguuwi nganundi dhurra-laa-nha.* (YY) I am sweating (sweat is coming from me).
Possibly *nhuwi* (rotten, stinking).

nguwa (YR, YY, GR) *place adverb*
here. ◆ *Yiyal ngaya dhurra-y nguwa nginda gaay guwaa-lda-ndaay.* (YR) I just came here when you were talking.

nguwagili (YR, YY) *noun*
this side. Also *ngagili*. Used to refer to 'this side' of things, such as a river, humpy or camp. ◆ *Nguwa-gili-dja walaa-dha ngay wila-ya!* (YR) Sit on this side of my camp! Based on *nguwa* (here) and *-gili* (side). Has been recorded marked with the locative case.

nguwalay (YR, YY) *place adverb*
here (hereabouts). ◆ *Yaama ngaya nguwalay yilawa-y nginunda?* (YY) Can I stop here with you?

nguwama (YR, YY) *place adverb*
there. ◆ *Warra-ya nguwama.* (YY) Stand there. ◆ *Nguwama ngaama birralii-djuul-u dhubi-lda-nhi, dhaymaa-ya.* (YR) The boy spat here, on the ground.
This word is not fully understood: it is based on *nguwa* (here) but is usually translated 'there'.

nguwa-li (YR, YY) *verb-transitive*
fold, roll up. Could be used for 'rolling up your swag'. Form uncertain.

nguwan.nguwan (YY) *adjective*
folded, wrapped. Also *nguwanguwa*. From *nguwa-li* (fold, roll up).

-nha¹ (YR, YY) *suffix*
that. ◆ *Giirr ngaya nhama-nha wii buubi-lda-nha.* (YR) I am putting (blowing) out that fire. ◆ *Gayaa-nha gi-nyi, guliirr nguungu dhurra-y.* (YY) He was happy, his wife came.

This suffix is probably a shortened form of *nhama* (that) and is sometimes translated 'he', 'she' or 'those'. It is not to be confused with the verb suffix *-nha*. It occurs as *-nya* after word final *-i* or *-y*. This suffix is not fully understood.

-nha² (YR, YY, GR) *suffix*
present progressive verb suffix. ◆ *Waal ngaya winanga-y-la-nha.* (YR) I don't remember. ◆ *Gaba nhama maadhaay, waal nguu yii-lda-nha.* (YY) That's a good dog, he isn't biting. ◆ *Yina-yu nhama bawi-laa-nha.* (YY) The women are singing.

nhaadhiyaan (YR, YY) *noun*
log.

nhaadhuu (YR, YY, GR) *noun*
nardoo *(Marsilea drummondii)*. Thought to be borrowed from another language, the recommended GY word is *bal*. See *bal* for more information.

nhaagal (YY) *noun*
bora-ground spirit. One source.

nhaal (GR) *noun*
type of yam.

nhaamanhi (YR) *noun*
sweet dough. Flour, water and sugar were mixed to make this dough which people ate as children. One source.

nhaan (YR) *exclamation*
expression of surprise. Sometimes translated 'oops'. One source. Form uncertain.

nhaanma-li (YR, YY) *verb-transitive*
drop. ◆ *Bugalaa ngaya nhaanma-y.* (YY) I dropped the ball.

nhaayba (YR, YY, GR) *noun*
knife. Also *nhaaybu*. From English 'knife'.

nhalawilbayn (YR) *noun*
reflection. Ted Fields said this is a person's reflection in the water. One source.

nhalay (YR, YY, GR) *demonstrative*
1 this. ◆ *Giirruu nhalay dhaymaarr mulamula gi-nyi.* (YR) This ground is soft.
2 here. ◆ *Dhaay yanaa-ya, milaan nhalay.* (YY) Come here, here's a yam. ◆ *Nhalay ngay birralii dhuu-rraa-nha.* (GR) My baby is crawling here.
The meaning of *nhalay* seems to be that the object or place is nearby and usually visible. At times it is used in contrast to *nhama* (that). Also *nhali, ngalay*.

nhalganhalga (YR, YY, GR) *noun*
cow horn.

nhama (YR, YY, GR) *demonstrative*
1 that, the. ◆ *Gagil nhama yinarr.* (YR) That woman is bad. ◆ *Guwaa-la-badhaay nhama wana-gi-gu dhinggaa nhuwi.* (YR) You tell him to go and throw that stinking meat away. ◆ *Minyaaya ngaama dhinggaa birralii-gal-u dhuwinba-y?* (YR) Where did the children plant (hide) that meat? ◆ *Wamu nhama dhayn; wamu nhama wanda.* (YY) That blackfella (is) fat; that whitefella (is) fat. ◆ *Guliirr nhama ngay yanaa-waa-nha.* (YY) That's my missus walking along.
2 there. ◆ *Wanda nhama bara-waa-nha.* (YY) A white man is flying there.
This demonstrative can stand in for pronouns like 'he', 'she' and 'it'. It can also mean 'that one', 'those ones'. Ted Fields said it can be a warning '(look at) that!'. The variant *nyama* is expected following words ending in *-y* and *-i*. Before words beginning in *b-*, and especially before suffixes, *nhama/ngaama* is often said *nham/ngaam* (e.g. *nham bulaarr*). Also *ngaama, nguuma, nguumu* and *ngaamu*. These may actually be different words whose precise use is now not clear.

nhama dhaay (YR) *exclamation*
look out! From *nhama* (that) and *dhaay* (to here), so 'that's coming towards us'.

nhamali (YR) *demonstrative*
that, the. Also *nhamalay*. ◆ *Bandaarr nhama-li-nga baa-waa-nha.* (YR) The kangaroo is hopping along now.
The difference between this and *nhama* is not understood.

nhamun (YR, YY, GR) *noun*
rib.

nhamurra-li (YR, YY) *verb-transitive*
bury. ◆ *Nhamurra-la nhama maadhaay!* (YY) Bury that dog!

nhamurra-y (YR, YY) *verb-intransitive*
be buried. This verb only occurs in the progressive forms *nhamurra-y-la-nha* and *nhamurra-y-la-nhi*. ◆ *Mawu-nga nhama dhaymaarr, maadhaay nhama-nha nhamurra-y-la-nha.* (YY) Dig up that

ground, there's a dog buried there. A change in verb class from *-li* to *-y*. See Learner's Guide.

nhan (YR, YY, GR) *noun*
back of neck. Also called nape (of neck). Possibly also 'neck'.

nhan.garra (YR, YY) *noun*
ringneck parrot *(Barnardius barnardi)*. Based on *nhan* (neck) and *garra* (cut).

nhangana (GR) *noun*
boot, shoe. ◆ *Nhangana nhama gagil.* (GR) This shoe is bad.
See also: **manduwii**.

nhangi (YR) *noun*
old woman. Used in some YR, GR areas. One source.

nhaniguurr (YR, YY, GR) *noun*
goat. From English 'nanny-goat'.

nhanu (YR) *noun*
bower. As in the nest or 'playground' of the bowerbird. See also *ngana* (grass windbreak, hut — YY). These words may be related. One source.

nhanuwaaydji (YR) *noun*
grandchild, son's or daughter's child. This is a rare word, the common words are *dhaadhaa* and *bawanngaa*. One source.

Nharibaraay (GR) *placename*
Narrabri. Possibly from **nhari* (hypothesised cognate of *nhay* — knot in tree in YR, YY) and *-baraay* (with, having).

nharran (YY) *adjective, placename*
1 skinny. Pearl Trindall said that 'Narran gutted' was used to describe skinny people; this may be connected to the name of the river. Another source states that it is colloquial Australian English.
2 Narran River. The meaning of this name is uncertain. Greenway said that *Narran* was used to describe a river: 'Nerang or Noorong: small or nearer to [not going so far round], as opposed to Coolgoa [far off, going a long way round and then rejoining].' Ian Sim said that it was pronounced 'Nharrin'.

nhayamban (GR) *noun*
iron pot. Probably based on English 'iron pan'. One source.

nhay (YR, YY) *noun*
tree knot.

-nhi (YR, YY, GR) *suffix*
past tense suffix for *-y*, *-gi* and *-rri* class verbs. ◆ *Giirr ngaya ngaama bilaa-yu dhu-nhi bandaarr.* (YR) I speared a kangaroo with a spear.

nhigii (YR, YY, GR) *noun*
coals.

nhii (YR, YY) *noun*
charcoal.

Nhiinhii (YY) *placename*
Nee-Nee. From *nhii* (charcoal).

nhiibi (GR) *noun*
grey snake *(Hemiaspis damelii)*.

nhiigiliirr (YR, YY) *noun*
necklace. From English 'necklace'.

nhiirruu (YY) *noun*
1 burial bark. ◆ *Dhayn-du yanaa-y nhiirruu garra-li-gu, giirrgal-u.* (YY) The man goes out to cut burial bark, with a tomahawk.
2 coffin.
Also *miirru*.

nhiiyanhiiya (YR) *adjective*
very fond. One source.

nhima-li (YR, YY, GR) *verb-transitive*
pinch. ◆ *Birralii-dju nhama gi-yaa-nha yinarr-duul nhima-li.* (YY) The boy is going to pinch that girl.

nhimalnhimal (YR, YY) *adjective*
spiteful. Based on *nhima-li* (pinch).

nhimaylii (YR, YY) *noun*
young echidna. Also used as a girl's name.

nhimin (GR) *noun*
1 kurrajong tree *(Brachychiton populneus)*. Evergreen tree to 20 m high with bell-shaped flowers, cream to reddish-brown inside; leaves can be used for fodder.
2 rope. Made from the bark of kurrajong trees. See also: **nhungga**.

nhinay (YR, YY) *noun*
native melon.

nhinga-li (YY, GR) *verb-transitive*
sew.

nhingal (YY, GR) *noun*
bone needle. Piece of bone made into an awl.

nhingil (YR, YY, GR) *noun*
small saltbush *(Atriplex holocarpa)*. It is said that for irritations of the skin, dwarf saltbush twigs are heated and the hot ends are placed on the irritated part.

nhirrin (YR, YY, GR) *noun*
side. ◆ *Bubaay-galgaa-bala ngaama nhirrin-da dhanduwi-y-la-nha.* (YR) The little (kangaroos) were lying on their side.

nhulaan (YR, YY) *noun*
slime.

nhulaanbil (YY) *adjective*
slimey. Also *nhulaanhulaan.* From *nhulaan* (slime) and *-bil* (with lots of).

nhunduu (YR, YY, GR) *adjective*
1 blunt.
2 tasteless, unsweetened. Commonly used in Walgett for unsugared tea. Also *ngundu*.

nhunduwaa (YY) *adjective*
thick. ◆ *Gaba nhama nhunduwaa dhadhin.* (YY) That's a good thick shade.
One source. Probably from *nhunduu*.

nhungga (YR, YY) *noun*
kurrajong tree *(Brachychiton populneus)*. Evergreen tree to 20 m high with bell-shaped flowers, cream to reddish-brown inside; leaves can be used for fodder. Seeds can be baked and eaten, but great care must be taken to remove the poisonous hairs surrounding the seeds in the pod. The roots of large kurrajong trees can be tapped for water during droughts, while the yam-like roots of the young plants can be eaten. The inner bark is used for rope, the seeds are used as a coffee substitute, and the gum can be eaten.

Nhunggabarra (YY) *noun*
kurrajong-country people. Ian Sim said that *Nhunggabarra* was well known as the name of a main southern group of Yuwaalayaay speakers. Ginny Rose and Greg Fields thought that the *Nhunggabarra* originally lived around Narran Lake, south of Cumborah. Older people knew about the recent history of one group of *Nhunggabarra* who settled at Bangate Station after white occupation (and were written about by Langloh-Parker).
From *nhungga* (kurrajong tree) and *-barra* (people from).

nhuubala (GR) *adjective*
new. Probably from English 'new fellow'.

nhuunma-li (YY, GR) *verb-transitive*
milk a cow. Ridley gave the meaning as 'draw out with the hands'.

nhuwi (YR, YY, GR) *adjective*
1 rotten.
2 smelly, stinking.
Possibly the same word as *nguuwi* (sweat).

nhuwigu buma-li (YR) *verb phrase*
kill (stone dead). From *nhuwi-gu* (smelly/stinking-purpose) and *buma-li* (hit, kill). To make it clear that the meaning is 'kill', not just 'hit', the expression *nhuwigu buma-li* can be used.

nhuwiwan (YY) *noun*
1 stinky.
2 western grey kangaroo (nickname) *(Macropus fulginosus)*.
From *nhuwi* (rotten, smelly) and *-wan* (prominent feature).

nhuyu-gi (YR) *verb-transitive*
chastise. Ted Fields said 'to chastise a child, often by smoking it'. One source. Form uncertain.

-nyi (YR, YY, GR) *suffix*
past-tense suffix for *-y* and *-gi* class verbs (after *i*). ◆ *Giirr ngaya gaba dhanduwi-nyi.* (YY) I did have a good sleep.

nyii (YR, GR) *noun*
anus. Also *nyiidjuul*. One source said *ngii*.

nyiinmay (GR) *noun*
penis head.

nyiinmaya (GR) *noun*
foreskin.

Pp

pickima-li (YR) *verb-transitive*
pick. From English *pick* and *-ma* (suffix that makes a transitive verb). Not recommended for use but included to illustrate how word formation changed as the use of GY declined. The use of *-ima-li* to form GY verbs is common, but the retention of the English sounds as in 'pick' is not.

Rr

-rraa-y (YR, YY, GR) *suffix*
regular progressive suffix for *-rri* class verbs. ◆ *Yilaa nhama-laa dhuu-rraa-y, birralii-djuul.* (YR) Soon the baby will be able to crawl.

-rri (YR, YY, GR) *suffix*
future-tense suffix for *-rri* class verbs.
◆ *Badjin ngaya nginu wuu-rri.* (YY) I'll give you a bit.
This verb suffix occurs in the future form of *-rri* class verbs, e.g. *wuu-rri* (will give).

Uu

*-u (YR) *suffix*
time. There are a lot of time words that use the suffix **-u*. See Learner's Guide.

-uwi (YR, YY, GR) *suffix*
back. This suffix can be added to nouns to extend or change the meaning, e.g. *dhaygal-uwi* (head-back) meaning 'pillow' and *bumal-uwi* (instrument for hitting-back) meaning 'hammer'.

-uwi-y (YR, YY) *suffix*
back. ◆ *Giirr ngiyani yanaa-w-uwi-nyi walaay-gu.* (YR) We (all) went back to the camp. ◆ *Waal ngaama-laa dhaay dharrawu-l-uwi-y.* (YR) He will not come back. ◆ *Giirr ngaama nhaadhiyaan-da ngaama birralii-djuul wila-w-uwi-nyi.* (YR) The boy sat back against the log.
This suffix can be added to verbs to mean 'back'.

Ww

wa-li (YR, YY) *verb-transitive*
put in. ◆ *Mudhay nhama nguu man.ga-ya wa-y.* (YY) He put the possum in the bag.

wa-y (YR, YY) *verb-intransitive*
be in, be inside. ◆ *Dhina-bala wa-y-la-nha manduwii-dja.* (YR) (Your) foot is inside the boot. ◆ *Dhinawan ngaama wa-y-la-nhi man.ga-ya nguungu.* (YR) The emu was in his bag. ◆ *Yaluu ngaarrma-nga bilaarr wa-y-la-nha mubal-a nguungu.* (YR) The spear was still sticking into his stomach.
Only occurs in the progressive forms *wa-y-la-nha* and *wa-y-la-nhi*. A change in verb class from *-li* to *-y*. See Learner's Guide.

-waa-y (YR, YY, GR) *suffix*
moving progressive suffix for *-y* and *-gi* class verbs. ◆ *Barraay-badhaay yanaa-waa-ya!* (YR) Come quickly! ◆ *Giirr ngaya wana-waa-nha nhama maayama.* (YR) I am throwing a stone. ◆ *Nhama ngaya yana-waa-nha walaay-gu.* (GR) I am going to the camp. ◆ *Minyagu yana-waa-nhi?* (GR) Why did you come?

-Waa (YR, YY) *suffix*
some. Variant forms are *-waa, -aa, -gaa, -yaa*. ◆ *Warra-ya minyaaya-waa.* (YR) Stand somewhere else. ◆ *Ngarraagula minyaarru-waa yanaa-ya.* (YR) Go somewhere else, over there. ◆ *Ngaana-waa nhama-dhaay yanaa-waa-nha.* (YY) Someone is coming there. ◆ *Ngaandu-waa ngalingu bigibila manuma-y.* (YY) Somebody shook (stole) our porcupine.
The suffix *-Waa* is added to question words and question pronouns, and indicates that the identity of the person or thing is unknown or of no particular interest. It is like the 'some' in English 'someone', 'somebody', 'somewhere', 'somehow', but is occasionally translated 'I don't know . . . '. See also: **minya-gaa** (something) and **minyaminyagaa** (everything). See Learner's Guide.

waa[1] (YR, YY, GR) *noun*
1 shell (YR, YY, GR). Name for any shell.

2 shell chest pendant (YR, YY). Sea shells, traded from the coast, were rare and highly prized ornaments, worn by men on special occasions. Mussel shells were common.

waa² (YR, YY, GR) *exclamation*
expression of praise.

waa-li (GR) *verb-transitive*
throw. ◆ *Nhama mari-dhu bilaarr waa-lda-nha.* (GR) The man is throwing a spear. ◆ *Nginda mudhay waa-la wii-dha!* (GR) You throw the possum on the fire!

waabi (GR) *noun*
1 grandmother (mother's mother). Marries *dhaadhaa*.
2 mother's mother's brother. This is a rare word, the common word is *baagii*. It is an unusual kinship term because it refers to a female and male. It may be wrongly recorded.

waagaan (GR) *noun*
little crow *(Corvus bennetti)*. See also: *waaruu*.

waagiyan (YR, YY) *noun*
little crow *(Corvus bennetti)*.

waaguu (YR, YY) *noun*
hide and seek game.

waal (YR, YY) *particle*
1 no, not. ◆ *Waal, waal ngaya ngarra-y.* (YR) No, I didn't see (it). ◆ *Waal, maayrr dhuwarr.* (YY) No, (I have) no bread.
2 didn't, don't, won't. ◆ *Waal gimbi-la.* (YR) Don't do it. ◆ *Waal ganunga dhaay yanaa-nhi.* (YR) They didn't come this way. ◆ *Waal guwaa-la.* (YY) Don't talk (about it). ◆ *Minya? Waal ngaya winanga-y.* (YY) What? I didn't hear. ◆ *Waal, waala ngaya gubi-y-la-nha.* (YY) No, I can't swim. ◆ *Waal nhama birralii-gal-u dhinggaa dha-lda-nha.* (YY) The kids won't eat meat.
A word expressing negation, denial or refusal. To say something doesn't exist or is not present, use the suffix *-dhalibaa* (without), as in *wii-dhalibaa* (firewood-without, or no firewood). *Waal* also occurs in *waal ngaanduwaa* (no someone), so 'no-one'. *Waal* may come from *yuwaal*: compare the language name *Yuwaal-araay* (no-having), that is, the language that has *yuwaal* for 'no'.

waala (YR, YY) *particle*
can't, couldn't. ◆ *Nhalay-bala gagil gungan, waala ngiyani ngawu-gi.* (YR) This is bad water, we can't drink it. ◆ *Waala ngaya buliirra-lda-nha.* (YY) I can't breathe.
Based on *waal* (no, not).

waalgaa (YR) *question word*
why not? ◆ *Waal-gaa ngaama dhayn-duul dhaay yanaa-waa-nhi nguwalay?* (YR) Why didn't the man come here?
Based on *waal* (no, not). One source.

waal maayu (YY) *adverb*
badly, carelessly, not right. ◆ *Waal ngaya maayu gaa-waa-nhi, birralii-djuul nhama ngaya wamba-laa-ndaay.* (YY) I could not carry (the wood) well, because I was carrying the baby.
From *waal* (no, not) and *maayu* (well, carefully, right). See also: **maayu**.

waal ngaanduwaa (YR) *pronoun*
no one (doer to). ◆ *Buubi-y ngaama nguu wii, waal ngaanduwaa ngarra-li-gu.* (YR) She blew the fire out, so no-one would see it. This is made up of two words *waal* (no, not) and *ngaanduwaa* (someone).

waalu (YR, YY) *particle*
1 hold on, not yet. ◆ *Waalu, winanga-y ngaya gi-yaa-nha.* (YY) Hold on, I am going to think. ◆ *Waalu gimbi-la dhuu!* (YY) Don't make the fire yet!
2 before. ◆ *Dhuwarr birralii-dju dhaymaa-ya wana-nhi, gaa-nga nguungundi waalu nguu dha-ndaay!* (YY) The baby threw his bread on the ground, take it from him before he eats it!
From *waal* (no, not) and **-u* (hypothesised time suffix). Also *waaluu*.

waalwaal (YY) *noun*
dog bark.

waama (YR, YY) *particle*
because, therefore. ◆ *Warra-y-ma-y ngaya waama muyaan-da, bidjaay-bil ngaya gi-nyi.* (YY) I stood it up against the tree because I was all covered in mud.
The meaning of this word is not fully understood. See Learner's Guide.

waan¹ (YR, YY, GR) *noun*
crow, Australian raven *(Corvus coronoides)*. ◆ *Buluuy-bala nhama waan.* (YR) (He's) black, that crow.

A 'clever' bird who carries his magic in a 'doctor's bag' around his neck; that is, the feather throat 'pouch'.

waan² (YR, YY) *noun*
work. ◆ *Waan-gu-nha yanaa-nhi gundhi-gu.* (YY) Going to work at the station.
From English 'work'.

waanda (YR) *adverb*
first. ◆ *Nginda waanda wunga-waa-ya!* (YR) You dive first!
Possibly a suffix; there may be other meanings. One source.

waaraal (GR) *noun*
pup.

waaruu¹ (GR) *noun*
grandson (son's son).

waaruu² (YR, GR) *noun*
crow, raven. General word for any crow or raven. *Waaruu* became black because he rolled in a fire to put it out — in a story about getting fire and birds getting their colours.

waawul (YR, YY) *adjective*
narrow.

waay (YY) *noun*
mud catfish. One source.

waaya (YR, YY) *noun*
wire. From English 'wire'.

-Waayaa (YR) *suffix*
don't know. Variant forms -waayaa, -yaayaa, -aayaa, -gaayaa. ◆ *Ngaandu-waayaa nhaanma-y.* (YR) I don't know who dropped it. ◆ *Birralii-djuul nhama-nga yu-gi-la-nhi, minya-dhi-yaayaa.* (YR) The baby is crying now, (I) don't know why. ◆ *Waala ngaama ngaya ngarra-y, minyaaya-waayaa ngaama dhayn-duul gi-nyi.* (YR) I can't see him, (I) don't know where that man is.
◆ *Giirr birralii-gal yanaa-nhi gayarra-gi-gu ngaama yarraaman, minyaarru-waayaa ngaama yarraaman yanaa-nhi.* (YR) The children went to look for the horse, they didn't know where that horse went.
◆ *Galawu nginda dhurra-l-uwi-yaa-nha dhaay? Galawu-waayaa.* (YR) When are you going to come back this way again? (I) don't know when.
This suffix is usually translated as 'don't know' and is only attached to question words, e.g. *ngaandu-waayaa* (don't know who), *minyadhi-yaayaa* (don't know why), *minyaaya-waayaa* (don't know where), *minyaarru-waayaa* (don't know where to) and *galawu-waayaa* (don't know when). An irregular form is *minya-gaayaa* (don't know what).

waayaal (YR, YY) *noun*
pup.

wabu (YR, YY, GR) *noun*
river bend.

wabuwi (GR) *noun*
weather spirit. Mrs Milson wrote: 'He was the greatest spirit of all; he commands the seasons and weather, his residence is in the North, and water springs up all round him of a blood colour . . . his status is immense, and so great a veneration have the Blacks for him that if another tribe or black speaks irreverently of him the punishment of death ensues, he changes his residence to the skies, and whenever he died the world will be destroyed by huge rocks which fall from Heaven. Mulla Mulla [Mala Mala] his wife lives in the South . . . when she dies, darkness rests upon the earth till her husband removes it. She presides over the night, he over the day.' One source.

wadhaagudjaaylwan (YY) *noun*
birth spirit. One source. Form uncertain.

wadhagii (YR) *noun*
secret. One source.

wadhi (YY) *noun*
bush. ◆ *Wadhi-gu ngiyani yanaa-nhi.* (YY) We walked into the bush.

wadhu (YR) *noun*
cave. One source.

wadhuurr (YR, YY, GR) *noun*
windbreak. Also *wadhuul*. Fred Reece said: 'A *wadhuurr* is made out of bushes, if you are going to camp the night, you pick a good old wilga tree, especially on a frosty night or if there is a heavy dew. You make a good fire and a windbreak to block the wind, and put bushes underneath you, break some boughs off, make a good bed for yourself so you won't break your hip on the hard ground . . . that's a *wadhuurr*.'
◆ *Wadhuurr warrayma-la!* (YY) Build a windbreak!

wadjiin (YR, YY, GR) *noun*
white woman. From English 'white gin'.

wagaaygaali (YY) *noun*
Richard's pipit *(Anthus novaeseelandiae)*. One source.

wagarraa (YR, YY) *noun*
1 club (throwing stick) (YR, YY).
2 bark throwing stick (YR). Arthur Dodd said that they were cut out of trees in the shape of a bat. Probably used in games and contests.

wagi¹ (YR, YY) *noun*
1 plain, open ground. ◆ *Ngaarrma-nga wagi-dja wila-y-la-nha.* (YR) He's there sitting down on the plain.
Open ground, away from the cover of trees.
2 outside. ◆ *Giirr ngaama nguu wagi-gu yanaa-nhi.* (YR) He went outside.

wagibaa (YR, YY) *noun*
plain, open (treeless) country. From *wagi* (plain) and *-baa* (place of, time of).

wagibaa dhaygal (YR, YY) *adjective*
bald. ◆ *Waal-bala ngaya wagibaa dhaygal.* (YY) I'm not bald headed.
From *wagibaa* (plain) and *dhaygal* (hair).

wagimal (YY) *noun*
plains rat. Lives on the plain; said to be now gone from the country. Based on *wagi* (plain).

wagiwagi (YR, YY) *noun*
1 plain, open (treeless) country (YR, YY).
2 Richard's pipit *(Anthus novaeseelandiae)* (YY). Possibly a nickname for Richard's pipit; from *wagi* (plain, open ground).

wagi² (YR, YY) *noun, adjective*
1 lie. ◆ *Wagi nhama wadjiin-du guwaa-lda-nha.* (YY) That white woman is telling a lie.
2 pretend, gammon. Ian Sim said it was also the name of a children's game, like charades.

wagirrbuma-li (YR, GR) *verb-transitive*
wash. Also *wagirrbama-li*. ◆ *Giirr ngaya gi-yaa-nha nhama birralii-djuul wagirrbuma-li.* (YR) I'm going to wash the baby.

wagirrbuma-y (YR) *verb-intransitive*
wash (self). ◆ *Yaama nginda wagirrbuma-nhi?* (YR) Did you wash yourself?
A change in verb class from *-li* to *-y*. See Learner's Guide.

wagirrma-li (YR, YY) *verb-transitive*
wash. Also *wagirrba-li*. ◆ *Gaawaa-gu ngaya yanaa-waa-nhi bayagaa wagirrma-li-gu.* (YY) I went to the river to wash (my) clothes. One source. See also: **wagirrbuma-li**.

wagirrma-y (YY) *verb-intransitive*
wash (self). ◆ *Wagirrma-nhi ngaya.* (YY) I washed myself. ◆ *Ngulu wagirrma-ya!* (YY) Wash (your) face!
A change in verb class from *-li* to *-y*. See Learner's Guide.

wagun (YR, YY, GR) *noun*
brush turkey *(Alectura lathami)*.

wala (YR, YY) *noun*
Australian kestrel, nankeen kestrel *(Falco cenchroides)*.

walaay (YR, YY, GR) *noun*
1 camp. ◆ *Nhama ngaya yana-waa-nha walaay-gu.* (GR) I am going to the camp. ◆ *Nhama bandaarr gaa-waa-nha walaay-gu.* (GR) They are taking the kangaroo to the camp.
2 humpy. A shelter, like a little hut.
3 nest, e.g. a bird nest or catfish nest.

walaaybaa (YR, YY, GR) *noun*
home, home country. A person's country or home place. From *walaay* (camp) and *-baa* (place of, time of).

walan (YR, YY) *adjective*
1 hard, solid.
2 tough. As in, 'tough meat'.

walanbaa (YR, YY) *adjective*
1 hard, solid. ◆ *Giirruu ngaama dhaymaarr walanbaa.* (YR) The ground was hard.
2 strong. ◆ *Walanbaa ngaya dhayn.* (YY) I am a strong man.
3 tough. ◆ *Giirruu nginu dhinggaa, walan-bala nginu dhinggaa, walanbaa, ngay-bala gaba.* (YR) Your meat is really tough, by comparison my meat is good.
From *walan* (hard) and *-baa* (place, time of). See also: **gugirriibiyaay**.

walanbaa gungan (YR) *noun*
rum. From *walanbaa* (hard) and *gungan* (water). One source.

walanbarruu (YR, YY) *noun*
claypan. *Walanbarruu* refers to the 'scalded' (burnt) claypan, where nothing grows. From *walan* (hard).

walanduurr (YY) *adjective*
hard-hearted. From *walan* (hard). One source.

Walan.gala (YY) *placename*
Walangala. A place near Lightning Ridge, said to mean 'hard ground' or 'place'. There is also a property 'Warrengulla'. From *walan* (hard).

walan.gumba (YY) *noun*
1 hard ground. Also used to describe 'flinty' ground.
2 hard thing.
From *walan* (hard) and *gumba* (flinty, very hard).

walarr (YR, YY, GR) *noun*
shoulder.

walawala (GR) *noun*
storm. One source.

walban (YR, YY, GR) *noun*
1 trough. Ian Sim said it was originally a wooden container, possibly used for water.
2 bucket.

walgan (YR, YY) *noun*
1 mother-in-law (husband's mother).
2 aunt (any), aunt (man's father's sister). A man's father's sister ('aunt' in English) is also a classificatory mother-in-law, and the term *walgan* is found as both 'aunt' and 'mother-in-law'. These days *walgan* is used in the same way as the English word 'aunt'.

walindja-li (YR) *verb-intransitive*
be lonely. ◆ *Giirruu nhama-laa birralii-djuul walindja-lda-y ngambaa-dhi nguungu yanaa-ngindaay.* (YR) The baby will be lonely when his mother goes away.
One source. See also: **walingay**.

walingay (YR, YY) *adjective*
1 out of place.
2 lonely, sulky.
The term *walingay* is used to describe a range of negative emotions, occuring in compounds such as *murrurwalingay* (stale) and *gana walingay* (sad). Also *walindjal*.

waluubaal (YR, YY, GR) *noun*
tree lizard. Also called sleepy lizard and tree skink *(Egernia striolata)*. Fred Reece said that it is about 6–8 inches long and lives in the bark of trees.

waluwarr (YY) *adjective*
wide, spread out.

waluwarr bunma-li (YY) *verb phrase*
make bigger, spread out. From *waluwarr* (wide, spread out) and *bunma-li* (make). Also *waluwarr burranba-li*. One source.

wamara (YR, YY) *noun*
spear thrower (woomera). Widely used in English. Possible source of English 'woomera'.

wamba (YR, YY, GR) *adjective*
1 mad, crazy.
2 stupid, silly.
3 eccentric.
This word is still widely used.

Wamba (YY) *noun*
Canopus (star). The Wamba story tells that 'he went mad and is running away', the two green parrot sisters chased him across the sky. An associated phrase is *wamba bagaarr banagawaanha*, from *wamba* (mad), *bagaarr* (shortcut) and *banaga-y* (run). One source.

wamba-li (YR, YY, GR) *verb-transitive*
carry. ◆ *Bilaarr nhama nguu wamba-laa-nha wala-ya.* (YY) He's carrying the spear on his shoulder.

wamban (YY) *noun*
baby. Examples include *wamban birray* (baby boy) and *wamban miyay* (baby girl).

wambanhiiya (YR, YY) *noun*
cousin.

wambin (YY) *noun*
breastplate. Probably made out of woven string to protect the chest. See also: **wirrgun**.

wamburr (YY) *noun*
western grey kangaroo *(Macropus fuliginosus)*. Also *wambuurra*. Also called black-faced kangaroo. People called it 'scrubber' and 'stinker' as it was the least acceptable kangaroo meat. One source. See also: **nhuwiwan**.

Wamburra (YY) *placename*
Womborah. Location in the Goodooga district. From *wamburr* (western grey kangaroo) and probably *-aa* (place of). One source.

wamu (YR, YY, GR) *noun, adjective*
fat. ◆ *Wamu nhama dhayn.* (YY) He (is) a fat man.

wamuwaa (YY) *noun*
small brown ant.

-wan (YR, YY) *suffix*
prominent (big). Used mainly in names of animals and birds, *-wan* means 'with a big or prominent feature': e.g. *dhina-wan* (foot-prominent feature) 'emu'; *nhuwi-wan* (stink-prominent feature) 'stinker', nickname for the western grey kangaroo. See Learner's Guide.

wana (YR, YY, GR) *particle*
let (something happen). ◆ *Wana nguu buma-li nhama dhinawan.* (YR) Let him kill that emu.
When *wana* is in a sentence, the verb is in the future form. Probably related to *wanagidjay* (stop it) and *wana-gi* (throw, leave).

wana-gi (YR, YY) *verb-transitive*
1 throw, pitch. ◆ *Giirr nhama birralii-djuul-u nhama maayama wana-nhi maadhaay-a.* (YR) The child threw a stone at the dog.
2 leave. Ted Fields said that this verb is used to mean 'leave', as in 'when a man leaves his wife' or when you run out on somebody, and 'leave them to look after themselves'. See also: **gayawi-li**.

wana-y (YY) *verb-intransitive*
perch, roost. This verb is used to talk about birds. One source.

wanaa (YY, GR) *particle*
mustn't. Followed by the imperative form of verb. Can be used as an exclamation meaning 'don't do that!'.

wanaal (YY, GR) *noun*
taboo, forbidden. For example, when someone is not allowed to eat a certain food. ◆ *Ngaya wanaal guduu.* (GR) Cod (is) taboo (for me).

wanagidjay (YR, YY) *exclamation*
stop it! Probably based on *wana* (let something happen).

wanba (YR, YY) *noun*
sloping river bank.

wanda (YR, YY, GR) *noun*
1 ghost, spirit.
2 white man.
See also: **gabaa**.

wandhala (GR) *noun*
eaglehawk. Possibly the black falcon *(Falco subniger)*.

-wan.gaan (YR, YY) *suffix*
very, really. ◆ *Giirruu nhama birralii-djuul yuulngindi-wan.gaan gi-gi-la-nhi.* (YR) The boy was very hungry. ◆ *Gaba-wan.gaan ngaama dhadha-y-la-nhi dhinggaa.* (YR) That meat tasted really good.
Also used in expressions like *maarr-wan.gaan* (no, none-very) meaning 'nothing at all', *miimii-dja-wan.gaan* (river bank-at-very) meaning 'right to the river bank', and *gandjarra-wan.gaan* (champion-very) meaning 'the best champion'.

wangal (YR, YY, GR) *noun*
woman's possum-fur belt. Also *wangan*. Also described as a possum-wool string.

wangali (GR) *noun*
afterbirth. Form is uncertain, possibly based on *wangal*, as it is said that a woman giving birth had a possum-fur body belt wrapped tightly around her. One source.

wanggal (YR, YY) *noun*
toy roller. A child's toy made by putting wire through a tin and putting stones in the tin. When pulled it rolls and rattles.

wanggalay (YR, YY) *noun*
1 game with discs and spears.
2 bark discs. Langloh-Parker described *wanggalay* as follows: a number of men arm themselves with *widjuwidju* (toy spears), 1–2 m long. Two men take the *wanggalay* (pieces of bark), either squared or rounded and about 40 cm in diameter, and stand about 50 m from each other. First one and then the other throws their piece of bark, which rolls swiftly along the ground past the other men who try to spear it. He who hits the most wins the game. The old men scored well.

wangga-y (YY) *verb-intransitive*
roll. This verb is used to describe the movement of such things as cars and carts that move along by the rolling of their wheels.

wanggama-li (YR, YY) *verb-transitive*
roll. ◆ *Wanggama-la-nha.* (YY) Keep it rolling (to a horse pulling a cart). ◆ *Dhaan wanggama-la-nha.* (YY) Roll it over to one side.

From *wangga-* (roll) and *-ma-li* (suffix that makes a transitive verb). One source.

wanggarra-y (YR) *verb-intransitive*
be lost. One source.

wanggarrama-li (GR) *verb-transitive*
lose. One source.

wanggii (YY) *noun*
barn owl *(Tyto alba)*. One source.

wan.guy (GR) *noun*
wallaby.

wara (GR) *noun*
left. Form is uncertain, but probably the basis of *waragaal* (left-handed, left).

waragaal (GR) *adjective*
1 left-handed.
2 left.

warawara (GR) *adjective*
crooked, bent. Probably from *wara* (left).

waraba (GR) *noun*
short-necked turtle *(Chelodina expansa)*.

warangana (YR, YY) *noun*
1 bee.
2 honey. This is the common word for honey. ◆ *Giirr ngaya burrulaa warangana.* (YR) I have a lot of honey.

warra-y (YR, YY, GR) *verb-intransitive*
1 stand. ◆ *Yinarr nhama warra-y-la-nha.* (YY) The woman is standing there.
2 stand up, get up. ◆ *Warragil warra-ya!* (YY) Stand up straight! ◆ *Warra-ya, yaay dhurra-laa-nha.* (YY) Get up, the sun is rising.
3 swell. ◆ *Mula nhama warra-nhi.* (YY) The boil swelled up there.

warrayma-li (YR, YY, GR) *verb-transitive*
1 build, put up (YR, YY, GR). ◆ *Giirruu ngaya gaba-dhuul gaarrimay warrayma-y.* (YY) I built (put up) a good little camp.
2 stand up (YR, YY). ◆ *Dhiyama-la nhama ngay giirrgal, warrayma-la muyaan-da.* (YY) Pick up my tomahawk and stand it up against that tree.
3 send (YR, YY). ◆ *Garriya warrayma-la!* (YR) Don't send (it)!
4 raise (bring up) (YR). ◆ *Gaba ngaya maadhaay yilaalu warra-y-ma-y.* (YR) I raised a good dog long ago.

From *warra-y* (stand) and *-ma-li* (suffix that makes a transitive verb).

warraynga-y (YR) *verb-intransitive*
get up. ◆ *Garriya warraynga-ya!* (YR) Don't get up yet!
From *warra-y* (stand). Form is uncertain, may be *warrayma-y* or *warraynha-y*.

warragil (YR, YY, GR) *adjective, adverb*
straight, true. ◆ *Buyabuya-dhuul nhama dhayn warragil warra-y-la-nhi.* (YY) The bony fellow stood up straight. ◆ *Warragil ngay bilaarr.* (YY) My spear is straight.
Possibly related to *warra-y* (stand).

warrala (YR, YY) *noun*
brown snake. One of two species of 'thin' brown snake found in western NSW; probably the western brown snake *(Pseudonaja nuchalis)*.

warrambul (YR, YY, GR) *noun*
1 watercourse (overflow channel) (YR, YY, GR). The name is used to refer to overflow channels which have water only during flood times. The name is used on road signs, e.g. Big Warrambool.
2 Milky Way (YR, YY).

warran (YR, YY, GR) *noun*
1 tree butt, tree trunk.
2 tree root.
3 end. The thick or butt end of anything.
Probably based on *warra-y* (stand).

warranggal (YR, YY, GR) *adjective*
strong, powerful. May refer to someone or something that is important or influential, e.g. a person, river or magic stone. Possibly from *warra-y* (stand). One source.

warrawarra (YY) *adjective*
standing. For example, a whirlwind is said to 'stand up'.

warrawilbaarru (YR, YY) *noun*
whirlwind spirit. Women at Bangate Station, seeing a *buulii* (whirlwind) coming, would call out to the kids, and people would get *bibil* branches to break it up. Related to *warra-y* (stand) and *wilbaarr* (whirlwind spirit).

warray (GR) *noun*
type of yam.

warrayaa (YR, YY) *adjective*
lost.

warrayaa yanaa-y (YY) *verb phrase*
be lost. From *warrayaa* (lost) and *yanaa-y* (go).

warraymbaa (YR) *noun*
workplace. Related to *warrayma-li* (build) and *-baa* (place of, time of), so 'where things are built'. One source.

warrgiiba (YR, YY) *noun*
cook. ◆ *Guyaarr yinarr gaba warrgiiba.* (YY) The tall woman is a good cook.

warringaay (YY) *noun*
nut grass (*Cyperus* spp.) Also *warruungan*. This is probably the bush onion which has corms or bulbs the size of shallots on the end of shallow roots. Eaten raw or cooked, the corms may be stored underground; they have a tough husk that is removed before eating.

warru (GR) *adjective*
wide, spread out. One source. Form uncertain.

warrul (YR, YY, GR) *noun*
1 worker bee.
2 bee's nest.
3 honey.
The word now commonly used in YR and YY for honey is *warangana*.

warruma-li (GR) *verb-transitive*
spread out. One source. Form uncertain.

warrungan (YY) *noun*
bullfrog. The name comes from its call — 'warrung'. Possibly *Cyclorama* spp.

warruwi (GR) *noun*
pathway. One source.

wawal (GR) *noun*
echo. The more common word is *ban.gul*. One source. Form uncertain.

waya¹ (YR, YY) *noun*
left. Form is uncertain, but probably the basis of *wayagaal* (left-handed, left).
wayagaal (YR, YY) *adjective*
1 left-handed.
2 left.
wayawaya (YR, YY) *adjective*
crooked, bent.

waya² (YY) *noun*
tree snake. Possibly green tree snake (*Dendrelaphis punctulata*).

wayaarra (YR, YY) *noun*
currant bush, warrior bush (*Apophyllum anomalum*). Also called native or wild grape, it is typically 2–3 m tall.

wayal (YR) *noun*
snake track. One source.

wayamaa (YR, YY, GR) *noun*
1 old man (YR, YY, GR).
2 old things (YR). Also used to talk about old kangaroos and old dogs, could probably also be used for other old things.

wayamba (YR, YY) *noun*
short-necked turtle (*Chelodina expansa*). The short-necked turtle was eaten, while *girrabirrii* (long-necked turtle) was not.

waygal (YR, YY) *noun*
woven bag. Woven out of reeds.

waylurr (YR) *noun*
slime. This is a rare word, the common word is *nhulaan*.

wayuwaal (YR, YY) *noun*
man's belt. Ginny Rose said this was also the name of a woven headband for men.

wayway (YR, YY) *noun*
1 large oval fungus (*Polyporus mylitta*) (YR, YY). According to Langloh-Parker, people were not supposed to touch these. Another source used this word for native bread, an edible fungus that tastes like boiled rice and is found near rotten trees and underground.
2 little humpy (YR). Like a windbreak.

wi-y (YR, GR) *verb-intransitive*
lie. ◆ *Minya-bala nhalay maayama wi-y-la-nha dhaymaa-ya?* (YR) What sort of stone (is) this, lying on the ground?
This verb is usually used with non-living things. It occurs only in progressive (regular) forms.

widja (YR) *noun*
bread. This is a rare word, used in some YR, GR areas. The common word is *dhuwarr*.

widjuwidju (YY) *noun*
toy spear. Actually sharpened sticks used in the *wanggalay* game. One source.

wii (YR, YY, GR) *noun, adjective*
1 fire (YR, YY, GR). ◆ *Nginda mudhay waa-la wii-dha!* (GR) You throw the possum on the fire!
2 firewood (YR, YY, GR). ◆ *Galumaay-dhu wii garra-lda-nha.* (GR) My brother is cutting

firewood.
3 light (YR, YY, GR).
4 clever (YR, YY).
5 bobby fish (YR, YY). A little fish about 3 cm long.
6 spirit light (YY). The light or fire within the *wiringin* (clever man). This power can be demonstrated or projected in various ways, e.g. through a magic bone, stone or stick. The 'fire' is an energy like electricity.

wii muyaan (YR, YY) *noun*
clever man's stick. Ian Sim said this was a loose name for the *birru* (clever man's stick) which was used to project power and 'throw the light'. From *wii* (fire, clever person) and *muyaan* (stick).

wiibiyaay (YR, YY) *noun, adjective*
1 firestick (YR). A flaming stick used as a torch, e.g. green spinifex or pine bark.
2 hot (YY). From *wii* (fire) and *-biyaay* (with, having).

wiimbirru (YY) *noun*
game with leaf and fire. Langloh-Parker described *wiimbirru* as a favourite fireside game. A big fire was made of leafy branches. Each player got a dry coolabah leaf, warmed it until it bent a little, then placed it on two fingers and hit it with one finger into the current of air, caused by the flame, which lifted it up. Everyone flicked their leaves at the same time, and anxiously watched whose would go the highest. Each watched his leaf descend, caught it, and began again. Based on *wii* (fire). One source. Form uncertain.

wiinhii (YR, YY) *noun*
coals. Based on *wii* (fire) and *nhii* (charcoal). See also: **nhigii**.

Wii Waa (GR) *placename*
Wee Waa. Based on *wii* (fire); the derivation of *waa* is not understood.

Wii Warra (YR, YY) *placename*
Wee Warra Plain. A place north of Cumborah; the meaning, 'fire standing up', comes from a story in which the plain was set alight and the flames rose high. Related to *wii* (fire) and *warra-y* (stand).

wii wiima-li (YR, GR) *verb phrase*
make a fire, light a fire. ◆ *Giirr ngaya nhama wii wiima-y* (YR) I have made the fire.
From *wii* (fire) and *wiima-li* (put). See also: **wulanabi-li**.

wiibi-li (GR) *verb-intransitive*
be sick. ◆ *Nhama mari wiibi-lda-nha.* (GR) That man is sick.
Possibly from *wii* (fire) and *-bi-li* (verb suffix) or *wi-y* (lie down).

wiibidi (YR, YY) *noun*
gecko, tree dtella *(Gehyra variegata)*. Possibly from *wii* (fire) and *-bidi* (big).

wiibil (GR) *adjective*
sick. Related to *wiibi-li* (be sick).

wiidhaa (YR, YY, GR) *noun*
spotted bowerbird *(Chlamydera maculata)*. The bowerbird is in a story about a fight, where the wedge-tailed eagle threw the bowerbird onto a fire. A 'clever' bird that still keeps his collection of magic stones. The bones and other items that the bowerbird collects are thought to be the magic charms of the *wiringin* (clever man). Based on *wii* (fire) and, possibly, *-dja* (at, on).

wiidhaga (YR, YY) *noun*
bachelor's camp. Possibly named after the bowerbird's bower which he decorates to attract a mate. From *wiidhaa* (bowerbird) and *-ga* (at, on).

Wiidhalibaa (YR, YY, GR) *placename*
Weetalibah. The name for several localities, including Ted Fields' birthplace near Bangate Station. Also spelt 'Wytaliba'. From *wii* (fire, firewood) and *-dhalibaa* (without), so 'place without fire or firewood'. May have had an associated meaning: 'no domestic hearth' or 'no partner', as in *dhayn wiidhalibaa* 'poor bloke, has to look after himself'.

wiigun (YR) *noun*
back log. A large log put at the back of a fire. One source.

wiigunma-li (YR) *verb-transitive*
stoke. A general meaning is seen in

wiigunma-la! (stoke the fire!); it also means to push the two ends of the *wiigun* (back log) together when the middle had burnt out. One source.

wiigurrun.gurrun (YR, YY) *noun*
white-winged triller *(Lalage tricolor)*. The name is like the bird's call; Arthur Dodd said that you can hear it 'in the middle of the night, singing out like that, *wiigurrun.gurrun.gurrun*'. Also called summer bird.

wiila-y (YR, YY, GR) *verb-transitive*
whistle. Also the 'whistling' call of spirits. ◆ *Dhigayaa-gu wiila-nhi.* (YY) The bird whistled. ◆ *Wiila-nhi nguu.* (YY) He whistled.

wiiluun (YR) *noun*
1 dribble.
2 slime.

wiima-li (YR, YY, GR) *verb-transitive*
put down. ◆ *Wiima-la nhama!* (YR) Put it down! ◆ *Minyaaya ngaama ngay dhamiyaa wiima-y?* (YR) Where did they leave (put) my tomahawk?
From *wi-* (lie down) and *-ma-li* (suffix that makes a transitive verb).

wiima-y (YR) *verb-intransitive*
put (on self). Arhur Dodd used this verb when talking about women putting mussel shells on their heads. It could be used to refer to make-up.
A change in verb class from *-li* to *-y*. This verb is not used for 'putting on clothes', see *wuu-gi*. See Learner's Guide. One source.

wiirra-li (YR, YY) *verb-transitive*
1 shave. ◆ *Wiirra-la nhama birralii!* (YY) Shave that child!
2 shear.

wiirra-y (YR, YY) *verb-intransitive*
shave (self). ◆ *Wirra-y ngaya gi-yaa-nha ngulu.* (YY) I'm going to shave (my) face.
A change in verb class from *-li* to *-y*. See Learner's Guide.

wiiwambin (YY) *noun*
red-browed pardalote *(Pardalotus rubricatus)*. From *wii* (fire) and *wambin* (breastplate), to do with the yellow spot on its chest.

wiiwiimal (YY) *noun*
body-snatching spirit. Also described as a red spirit that flies down and grabs people like an eagle.

wiiyuu (YR) *noun*
1 chough *(Corcorax melanorhamphus)*. A symbol of peace. *Wiiyuu* is like the bird's call.
2 red-eyed spirit. Seen at night.

wila-y (YR, GR) *verb-intransitive*
1 sit (YR). ◆ *Wila-y ngaya gi-yaa-nha.* (YR) I'm going to sit down.
2 stay, stop, live (YR, GR). ◆ *Minyaaya nginu ngaama dhaymaarr, minyaaya-nda wila-y-la-nha?* (YR) Where's your country, where do you stop?
3 ride (YR). ◆ *Giirr ngaama birralii-djuul maayu wila-waa-nhi bawa-ga gulay-a.* (YR) The baby had a good ride on (his mother's) back, in the net bag.

wilaarrdaa (YR, YY) *noun*
north wind.

wilay (YY) *noun*
snake bean *(Ryncharrhena quinquepartita)*. Also called climbing purple star, it is a climbing vine which has a thin green bean.

wilbaarr (YR, YY) *noun*
1 car. Name for any wheeled vehicle. Some say that *wilbaarr* is from the English 'wheelbarrow'; but it may not be as it is also in the name *Warrawilbaarru*, a feared spirit which travels in whirlwinds; he spins or 'goes like a wheel'.
2 cart.
3 whirlwind spirit.

wilgi (YR, YY) *noun*
1 cane grass *(Eragrostis australasica)* (YR, YY). The seed may have been ground up with water to make damper.
2 Wilkie (YY). Name of a property.

wilgu (YY) *noun*
ceremonial stick. A painted stick topped with a bunch of feathers; carried and planted in the ground in some ceremonies. Used as a badge or symbol of authority and to mark a 'power' or 'business' area. One source.

wilidhubaay (YR) *noun*
pink-eared duck *(Malacorhynchus membranaceus)*.

wiligabuul (YY) *noun*
pink-eared duck *(Malacorhynchus membranaceus)*.

winambuu (YR) *noun*
little (hairy) people. Arthur Dodd said: 'Nobody knows where they live, but they come there, if you come to a quiet place, nobody about, might be them two little fellas come along, one fella with a big belly, sticking out, another little fella, little thin fella, and they'll start talking to you there then, they talk about a lot of things, and they turn around trying to make you mad . . . take you away, make you do what they want you to do, make you silly.'

winanga-li (YR, YY, GR) *verb-transitive*
1 hear. ◆ *Giirr ngaya nginunha winanga-lda-nha.* (YR) I hear you.
2 listen. ◆ *Winanga-la nganha!* (YR) Listen to me!

winanga-y (YR, YY, GR) *verb-transitive*
1 understand (YR, YY, GR). ◆ *Yaama nginda winanga-y-la-nha?* (YY) Do you understand?
2 know (YR, YY, GR). ◆ *Waal ngaya nhama winanga-y-la-nha.* (YR) I don't know that (man). ◆ *Waal nguu winanga-y-la-nha galaarraa-nda bilaarr gimbi-ldaay.* (YR) He doesn't know how you made the spear.
3 remember (YR, YY, GR). ◆ *Yaama-nda winanga-y-la-nha gaba ngaaluurr ngiyani bayama-ldaay?* (YY) Do you remember those good fish we caught? ◆ *Waala ngaya winanga-y-la-nha.* (YY) I can't remember (I forget).
4 think (YR, YY, GR). ◆ *Waalu, winanga-y ngaya gi-yaa-nha.* (YY) Hold on, I'm going to think. ◆ *Giirruu ngay birralii-dju winanga-y-la-nha nhama nguu dhigayaa buma-li gi-yaa-nha barran-du.* (YR) My kids think (believe) that he is going to hit that bird with a boomerang.
5 love (YR). ◆ *Giirr nhama ganungu ngambaa-gu winanga-w-aaba-lda-nha.* (YR) Their mother loves them all.
There are some English words (know, think, love) translated as both *winanga-li* and *winanga-y*. It is not understood why the same meanings occur with both classes of the verb. It may be because this fine level of difference is lost as the language is no longer spoken regularly. For the present it is recommended that *winanga-y* be used to translate these, since it is the form that is used slightly more often in the sources. The English words 'remember' and 'understand' are overwhelmingly or exclusively translated by *winanga-y*. More may be found out about *winanga-li/winanga-y* as similar pairs are studied in related languages.

wiraarr (GR) *noun*
cockatiel, quarrian *(Nymphicus hollandicus)*.

wirayl (GR) *noun*
echidna quill. One source has *wirayla* (porcupine, echidna).

wiringin (YR, YY, GR) *noun*
Aboriginal doctor, clever man. Has powers to cure illness or perform magic.
◆ *Wiringin-du nhama maaruma-li.* (GR) The clever man will fix (him).

wirra (GR) *noun*
restricted word. See p 20 for more information.

wirra-li (GR) *verb-transitive*
twist. Also *wirrabi-li*.

wirraa (YR, YY) *noun*
fish intestines. The 'gut-ball' that is removed after cooking.

wirraa-y (YR, YY, GR) *verb-intransitive*
limp, hobble. ◆ *Wirraa-waa-nha-nga milan yinarr.* (YY) One woman was limping.
◆ *Yalbala wirraa-waa-ya!* (YY) Pretend (you're) limping!

wirralaa (GR) *question word*
when? Form is very uncertain, may be *wirru* (ending in *-u*, which is more typical of time words).

wirrgun (YR, YY) *noun*
chest protector, breastplate. Probably originally part of men's ceremonial decoration. The word could be used for 'waistcoat'.

wirri (YR, YY) *noun*
1 small coolamon (YR, YY). Fred Reece said

that a *wirri* is a bark dish or a bowl cut out of a tree, made for carrying honey.
2 plate (YR). Meaning extended by Walgett Language Program.

wirribula (GR) *noun*
goat. Based on *wirri* (small coolamon) and *bulaarr* (two), from the shape of the udder. See also: **nhaniguurr, wirrigaali**.

wirrigaali (YY) *noun*
goat. May be a nickname, derived from the shape of the goat's udders which look like two oval bowls. From *wirri* (small coolamon) and *-gaali* (a group of two), from the shape of the udder. See also: **nhaniguurr**.

wirribiiyan (YY) *noun*
young woman. Possibly from *wirri* (small coolamon) and *bii* (chest). This is a rare word, another word is *malagan* (teenage girl). One source.

wirrigaal (YR, YY, GR) *noun*
navel, bellybutton.

wirriil (GR) *noun*
feather. This is a rare word, the common word is *yadhaarr*.

wirrilaa (YR, GR) *noun*
brush turkey *(Alectura lathami)*.

wirringgaa (YR, GR) *noun*
Aboriginal woman, married woman. The common word is *yinarr*.

wirrun (YR, YY) *noun*
1 juice, gravy. The 'gravy' or liquid from a grub and other foods.
2 soup, sauce.

wirrunbiyaay (YY) *adjective*
juicy. From *wirrun* (juice, gravy) and *-biyaay* (with, having).

wirrwirr (YY) *noun*
striated pardalote *(Pardalotus striatus)*. *Wirrwirr* sounds like 'widwid', one of the bird's calls.

wiwurra (YR, YY, GR) *adjective*
new word. See p 160 for more information.

wiya-gi (GR) *verb-transitive*
cook. ◆ *Bandaarr nhama wiya-gi.* (GR) (We) will cook the kangaroo.
There may be a related verb, *guwiya-gi*, but evidence is uncertain.

wiyaarr (YR, YY) *noun*
cockatiel, quarrian *(Nymphicus hollandicus)*.

wiyal (YR) *adjective*
crooked. Also *wiil*. Occurs in *giniy-wiyal* (any crooked tree). One source. See also: **wayawaya**.

wiyalwiyal (YR) *adjective*
all over the place. From *wiyal* (crooked). One source.

wiyay (YR, YY) *noun*
chip. Name for any chip, e.g. of wood or stone.

wiyaybaa (YR, YY) *noun, adjective*
1 stranger, foreigner.
2 strange, odd.
Also *wiyaybal*.

wiyayi-li (YY) *verb-transitive*
remove quills. This verb is rare, the common expression is *wiyayl dhuwima-li* (remove quills).

wiyayl (YR, YY) *noun*
1 echidna quill. ◆ *Dhalaybaa nhama wiyayl.* (YY) The quills are sharp.
2 pen, pencil. Meaning extended by Walgett Language Program.

wubarra-li (GR) *verb-transitive*
pen up. Refers to pushing animals into an enclosure. ◆ *Yaama nginda wubarra-y dhimba?* (GR) Did you pen up the sheep? One source.

Wubi Wubi (YY) *placename*
name of a sacred mountain. Said to lie to the north, and to 'touch the sky'; the 'jumping off point' for spirits leaving the earth.

wubu¹ (YR, YY) *noun*
mushroom. Includes red tree fungus.

wubuubiyaay (YR, YY) *adjective*
mouldy. Based on *wubu* (mushroom) and *-biyaay* (with, having).

wubu² (YR) *noun*
sparrow. One source.

wubun (YR, YY) *noun*
blue-tongue lizard *(Tiliqua scincoides)*.

wudha (YY, GR) *noun*
ear. This is a rare word in GR, the common word is *bina*.

wudha muurr (YY) *adjective*
forgetful. From *wudha* (ear) and *muurr* (full, blocked, blunt).

wudhugaa (YR, YY, GR) *noun*
tar vine *(Boerhavia diffusa)*. Fred Reece said: '*Wudhugaa* grows in summertime on the black ground. You get a big carrot root, cook it and eat it, very nice . . . cook it in the bottom of a hole — and on the bottom of the hole put grass on the coals. Have all the vegetables clean, put them on the green grass, put grass on top of them and put coals from another fire on top of the grass again and put the dirt on top, make it airtight if you can.'

Wudhurruu (YY, GR) *noun*
moiety name. All things and people were divided into two groups or moieties. The name of the *Marrii/Gabii* moiety is *Wudhurruu*. People of the *Wudhurruu* group married people of the *Yanguu* group. Thought to include the totems wallaby, duck, goanna, kookaburra, possum, red snake, carpet snake, and kangaroo (and others). There were ten primary totems in each moiety. See also: **Yanguu**.

wugalwugal (YY) *noun*
four emus. One source.

wugamaabaydaa (YR, YY, GR) *noun*
black-breasted kite *(Hamirostra melanosternon)*. Also called the black-breasted buzzard. In a story, this bird and *maliyan* (eagle) are said to be cousins. Ian Sim said the bird eats emu eggs — it either breaks them in the nest or breaks a hole in the egg and carries it away.

wugan (YR, YY, GR) *noun*
1 wood. Light branches or fine kindling wood. Mostly used to talk about firewood.
2 sticks.

wugan.galgaa (YR) *noun*
kindling. ◆ *Giirr ngaama nguu, gulbirr ngaarrma man.ga-ya gaa-gi-la-nhi wugan-galgaa.* (YR) She carried some kindling in a bag.
From *wugan* (wood) and *-galgaa* (many).

wugawa (YR, YY, GR) *noun*
flood. ◆ *Wugawa nhama dhurra-laa-nha.* (GR) A flood is rising.

wugi (YY) *noun*
flood peak. When the flood is at its highest. One source.

wula-li (YR, YY, GR) *verb-intransitive*
blaze. ◆ *Giirr-nga wula-laa-nha dhuu.* (YY) The fire is blazing (now).
The form of this word is uncertain.

wulan (YR, YY, GR) *adjective*
blazing. Occurs in *wii wulan* (a blazing fire).

wulanabi-li (YR, YY, GR) *verb-transitive*
light (fire/lamp). ◆ *Garriya wulanabi-la!* (YR) Don't light the fire! ◆ *Giirr ngaya wii wulanabi-y.* (YR) I lit the fire.
Based on *wula-* (blaze) and *(-na)-bi-li* (verb suffix). See also: **wii wiima-li**.

wularr (YY) *noun*
fierce snake *(Parademansia microlepidota)*. Also *wularra*. Known locally as tiger snake and taipan. Willie Willis said that the tiger snake, black snake and death adder were originally the Moon Man's dogs and are represented by three stars together (probably in Sagittarius) which are waiting for him to 'cross the water'.

Wularraba (YY) *placename*
location. A place near Lightning Ridge where an ancestral snake was killed and became a hill. Based on *wularr* (fierce snake) and *-baa* (place of, time of).

wulbul (YY) *noun*
1 bendy stick.
2 stock whip. The use of *wulbul* has been broadened to include this meaning.

wulbuldaan (YY) *noun*
tree branch game. Langloh-Parker described the game as follows: a low overhanging branch of a tree is chosen, and as many as it will bear, old and young, men and women, straddle it; and holding on to the higher overhanging branches, they swing up and down with as much spring as they can get out of the branch they are on. Probably from *wulbul* (bendy stick) and *dhaan* (sideways) or *-dhaan* (good at).

wulbul yaal (YR) *noun*
stick horse. Probably from *wulbul* (bendy stick) and *yaal* (a lie).

wulbul yiya (YY) *noun*
cracker on a whip. The little piece of leather or string at the end of a stockwhip that helps make the whip crack or make a loud noise. From *wulbul* (whip) and *yiya* (tooth).

wulbuwulbu (YY) *adjective*
flexible, bendy.

wulul (YY) *noun*
noise. For example, the sound of ducks flying.

wululgal (YR, YY) *noun*
noisy mob. A derogatory or insulting word. From *wulul* (noise) and *-gal* (many).

wululuu (YY, GR) *noun*
whistling duck. Probably plumed whistling duck *(Dendrocygna eytoni)*.

wumbala (YR) *noun*
echidna crop. One source. See also: **gadhuu**.

wun.ga-li (GR) *verb-intransitive*
return.

wun.guwi (YR, YY, GR) *noun*
1 Adam's apple, throat (YR, YY, GR).
2 passage, cattle race (YY). The meaning has been broadened from 'throat' to also mean a 'passage' or 'race', as in 'cattle race/chute'.

wunga-y (YR, YY) *verb-intransitive*
1 bathe, paddle. *Wunga-y* and *gubi-y* mean two different things. *Gubi-y* means 'proper swimming, with the feet off the ground'. *Wunga-y* means 'to paddle about in the water, standing on the bottom'. Fred Reece used the old English word 'bogey' instead of 'paddle'. ◆ *Wunga-y ngaya gi-yaa-nha.* (YY) I'm going to have a paddle.
2 dive, duck under. ◆ *Wunga-y ngaya gi-yaa-nha maanggii-gu.* (YY) I'm going to dive for some mussels.
See also: **gubi-y, dhiinbi-y**.

wungala (YR, YY) *noun*
witchetty grub, whitewood grub.

wungayawaa (YR, YY) *noun*
great black cormorant *(Phalacrocorax carbo)*. From *wunga-y* (dive) and *-awaa* (habitual), so, 'a bird that is always diving'.

wurranin (YR) *noun*
cradle. One source.

Wurrawaadhiyan (YR) *noun, placename*
1 battle spirit.
2 location. On the Walgett–Collarenebri road.
Possibly based on *wuurraa* (battle). One source.

wurrugaa (YR) *noun*
owner.

wurrumay (GR) *noun*
son. Form uncertain.

wurrun (YR, YY) *noun, adjective*
1 swelling.
2 swollen.
Also *wurrurr*.

wuru (GR) *noun*
1 throat.
2 neck. Probably the front of the neck, compare *nhan* (back/nape of neck).
See also: **wun.guwi**.

wuruga (GR) *noun*
calf of leg.

wurumal (GR) *noun*
sleepy lizard. Probably the stumpy lizard or blue-tongue lizard.

wurunga-y (GR) *verb-intransitive*
dive. See also the cognate *wunga-y* (dive — YR, YY) which has more information.

wurungayawaa (GR) *noun*
great black cormorant. Related to *wurunga-y* (dive).

wurungga-li (YR) *verb-intransitive*
peep (peek). Transitivity is uncertain. One source.

wurunggal (YR) *noun*
peephole. Ted Fields said it was a spy hole; for example, a peephole that you make in a hollow tree to let the light shine on chicks in the nest. Related to *wurungga-li* (peep). One source.

wuruyan (GR) *noun*
curlew, bush thick-knee *(Burhinus grallarius)*. See also: **gurabi**.

wuu (YY) *noun*
hook. One source.

wuu-gi (YR, YY) *verb-intransitive*
1 go into. This verb refers to the act of going into a place, or putting oneself into an enclosed space or clothes. The name of the place gone into is marked with various case suffixes, the choice of which is not

fully understood. ◆ *Dhama-ngindaay barraay ngaama wuu-gi ngiyarrma-nga man.ga-ya.* (YR) He'll get into that pouch quickly when it rains. ◆ *Giirr nhama biyuu-dhi wuu-nhi.* (YR) He went into the hole. ◆ *Mudhu-gu ngaama wuu-nhi.* (YR) He went inside.
2 go down, set (moon/sun). This is the common word for 'set (moon/sun)'.
◆ *Yaay wuu-waa-nha.* (YY) The sun is going down. ◆ *Gungan nhama wuu-waa-nha.* (YY) The water is going down. ◆ *Giirr yayaay wuu-waa-ngindaay yalagiirrmawu ngaya dhurra-laa-nhi walaay-a.* (YR) When the sun was setting (at sunset) I arrived at the camp.
3 dress self. One source for this definition. This use of *wuu-gi* indicates that 'she put herself into the clothes'. ◆ *Bayagaa-dhi nguu yaluu wuu-nhi balal gi-ngindaay.* (YY) She put her clothes on again when they were dry. See also: **wuuma-li**.

wuu-rri (YR, YY, GR) *verb-transitive*
give. ◆ *Dhuwarr-bala ngaya nguungu wuu-nhi.* (YY) I gave him bread too. ◆ *Dhayn-gu dhinggaa wuu-na!* (YY) Give (some) meat to the man!
The person being given something generally has the *-gu* suffix; pronouns are in owner/genitive case.

wuurriyala-y (GR) *verb-transitive*
barter. From *wuu-rri* (give) and *-la-y* (each other). One source.

wuurrma-li (YY) *verb-transitive*
send. Possibly from *wuu-rri* (give) and *ma-li* (suffix that makes a transitive verb).

wuudalay (YY) *noun*
rain-making stone. A smooth flat stone placed in a waterhole by a *wiringin* (clever man) during the rain-making ritual; interfering with it causes much rain. One source.

wuulaa (YR, YY) *noun*
bearded dragon, frilled lizard *(Amphibolurus barbatus)*. Also known as the jew lizard in some old sources. The bearded dragon is commonly known as the frilled lizard in NSW, the real frill-necked is in Queensland and the Northern Territory.

wuulaabila-y (YR) *verb-intransitive*
sunbake. Possibly from *wula-li* (blaze) or *wuulaa* (bearded dragon) and *-bi-la-y* (verb suffix).

wuuli-y (YR) *verb-intransitive*
swoop down. One source.

wuulman (YR) *noun*
old man. Probably from English 'old man'. A related word is *wuulbila* (old fellow).

wuuma-li (YY) *verb-transitive*
dress someone. ◆ *Gaba-dhi nhama bayagaa-dhi wuuma-la birralii-gal.* (YY) Dress your kids with good clean clothes.
From *wuu-* (go into) and *-ma-li* (suffix that makes a transitive verb).

wuumaa (YY) *noun*
bora messenger. One source. Form uncertain.

wuumi-li (YR) *verb-intransitive*
peep (peek). ◆ *Giirr ngaama wuumi-lda-nha man.ga-ya ngambaa-dhi nguungu.* (YR) He's peeping out from his mother's pouch. Form uncertain.

wuurraa (YR) *noun*
battle. This is a rare word, the common word is *girray*. One source.

wuuyan (YR, YY) *noun*
curlew, bush thick-knee *(Burhinus grallarius)*. This bird calls out at night.

wuuyuu (YR, YY, GR) *noun*
chough *(Corcorax melanorhamphus)*. Also called white-winged chough. *Wuuyuu* sounds like the bird's call. Ted Fields said that this bird, with its red eye, is a symbol of peace; also the name for a red-eyed spirit seen at night.
Also occurs as *wiiyuu*, although this variant is not recommended.

wuwi-li (YY) *verb-transitive*
swallow. ◆ *Wuwi-la dhinggaa!* (YY) Swallow that meat!
See also: **gurruubi-li**.

wuyu (YR, YY) *noun*
1 throat.
2 neck. Probably the front of the neck, compare *nhan* (back/nape of neck).

wuyubuluuy (YR, YY) *noun*
black snake. Possibly from *wuyu* (neck) and *buluuy* (black). See also: **wularr**.

wuyugarralawaa (YY) *noun*
death stone. A special stone, which when 'thrown' will lodge in the victim's throat and suffocate them. Possibly from *wuyu* (throat), *garra-li* (cut) and *-awaa* (habitual). See also: **dhinagarralawaa**.

wuyugi-li (YY) *verb-transitive*
smoke (ceremonial). Used in ceremonies, associated with cleansing. One source.

wuyugil (YR, YY) *noun*
1 ceremonial smoke. Sometimes used for ritual smoking. Fred Reece described how *wuyugil* was used as a punishment: 'They make sandalwood smoke with them green bushes. They put them all together, the bunchy ones, make a fire in it, chuck the coals in it, they can rig it in such a way that the coals won't fall out. They put it down on the ground, get the blooming kid, bring him up and hold his head in it. When they go to smoke him they bloomin well half choke him, he don't like it and he won't want it again, it makes him behave himself.' *Dhayn-du nhama nhiirruu wamba-li gurru-gu, wuyugil-a nhama-laa gaa-waa-y.* (YY) The men will carry the burial bark to the grave, taking it in (through) the ceremonial smoke.
2 smoke.

Yy

-y (YR, YY, GR) *suffix*
past tense suffix for *-li* class verbs.
◆ *Dhuyu-gu nganha yii-y.* (YY) A snake bit me. ◆ *Giirr ngaya dha-y dhii nhama.* (GR) I have already eaten the meat.

-y (YR, YY, GR) *suffix*
future tense suffix for *-y* class verbs.
◆ *Yilaa ngali yanaa-y.* (YY) We will go soon. This verb suffix occurs in the future form of *-y* class verbs, e.g. *banaga-y* (will run). It also occurs in the past tense form of *-li* class verbs, e.g. *guwaa-y* (talked). This can cause some confusion initially.

-y-la-y (YR, YY, GR) *suffix*
regular progressive suffix for *-y* class verbs.
◆ *Waala ngaya dhanduwi-y-la-nhi.* (YR) I could not sleep. ◆ *Gaarrimay-a ngaya-laa yilawa-y-la-y.* (YY) I will be sitting down at the camp.

-ya (YR, YY, GR) *suffix*
command suffix for *-y* class verbs. ◆ *Dhaay yanaa-ya ngambaa!* (YY) Come here mother!

-Yaa (YR, YY) *suffix*
1 must, might (YR, YY). ◆ *Giirr-yaa murrumay dhurra-li.* (YR) We might have a storm. ◆ *Waal-bala ngaya winanga-y-la-nha, bamba-yaa ngaya dhanduwi-nyi.* (YR) I don't remember, I must have been sleeping soundly.
2 either . . . or (YR). ◆ *Nhama-yaa birralii-gal-u, manuma-y, maadhaay-u-yaa dha-y.* (YR) Either the kids have taken (it), or the dogs have eaten (it).
Variant forms are *-yaa, -aa*. This may be best described as a 'probability' suffix, it can be attached to many types of words and is usually translated 'must', 'probably' or 'might'. The meaning of this suffix is not fully understood. See Learner's Guide. There is another *-yaa* which is a variant of *-Waa* meaning 'unknown' (someone, somewhere).

-yaa-y (YR, YY, GR) *suffix*
moving progressive suffix for *-y* and *-gi* class verbs (after *-i*). ◆ *Gaba gi-yaa-ya!* (YR)

Be good! ◆ *Guya nhama gubi-yaa-nha.* (GR) The fish are swimming.

yaa (YR, YR) *exclamation*
steady on! (YR). Ted Fields said it is an exclamation like 'wake up, you are going too far'. One source.

yaadha (YY) *noun*
day. Based on *yaay* (sun) and *-dha* (at/in, an irregular form of the place suffix). Recommended word.

yaaga-y (YR, YY) *verb-intransitive*
moan. ◆ *Garriya yaaga-y-la-ya!* (YR) Don't make that noise! Possibly *yaaga-li*. Possibly related to *yagaay* (ouch).

yaal (YR, YY, GR) *noun, adjective*
1 lie (YR, YY, GR). ◆ *Gamil ngay yaal guwaa-lda-nha, giirruu.* (GR) I am not telling a lie.
2 pretend, false (YR).

yaal dhanggi-li (GR) *verb phrase*
lie, tell a lie. From *yaal* (a lie) and *dhanggi-li* (tell a lie). One source.

yaama (YR, YY, GR) *question word, exclamation*
1 question word. ◆ *Yaama-nda nhama ngay wuu-rri?* (GR) Will you give that to me? *Yaama* is found at the beginning of sentences, and creates a 'yes-no' question. *Yaama nginda* (will you) is often shortened to *yaamanda*. ◆ *Yaama nginda guliirr-iyaay?* (YR) Do you have a partner? ◆ *Yaama nginda yanaaynbi-li nhama maadhaay?* (YR) Will you let that dog go? ◆ *Yaama-nda ngarra-y?* (YY) Did you see anything?
2 hello, greetings. This is a modern use of the word. ◆ *Yaama maliyaa!* (YR) Hello friend/mate! In Gamilaraay it also occurs as *Yaamagara nginda?* (How are you?).

yaamagaa (YR, YY) *question word*
whether, if. ◆ *Giirr ngaama nguu dhinggaa dhadha-wa-y-la-nhi yaama-gaa gaba.* (YR) He tasted the meat to see if it was good. One source.

yaamagara (GR) *question word*
hello, greetings. ◆ *Yaamagara nginda?* (GR) How are you?
This may be related to the Wangaaybuwan word *yamagarra* which literally means 'how are you feeling?'. Some people also say *yaamagarruu*, literally 'how are you uncle?', but used more generally, not just with uncles. This may be a corruption of *yamagarra*.

yaamarra (YR, YY) *noun*
sheaf of grass seed. It is unclear whether this is a general term or refers to a specific species.

yaambul (YR, GR) *adjective, exclamation*
1 silly, mad. The meaning is uncertain: older sources have *yambuli* (old woman), while people today use it to mean 'silly', 'mad'.
2 pretending! It means 'you're joking/pretending!'.

yaambuwiirr (YR, YY) *noun*
pretend fight. Langloh-Parker said: one man defends himself with a bark shield from the bark toy boomerangs that others throw; the old men usually win.

yaarrbin (YR) *noun*
1 gate post.
2 hitching rail.
One source.

yaarri-y (GR) *verb-intransitive*
1 go down, set (moon/sun).
◆ *Yaraay nhama yaarri-yaa-nha.* (GR) The sun is setting. ◆ *Gilay nhama yaarri-yaa-nha.* (GR) The moon is setting.
2. spill, drip, leak.
This verb is probably the Gamilaraay equivalent of *gaarri-y*.

yaarrima-li (GR) *verb-transitive*
1 spill.
2 pour.
From *yaarri-* (spill) and *-ma-li* (suffix that makes a transitive verb). One source.

yaarrngan (YR, YY) *noun*
wave, splash.

yaay (YR, YY) *noun*
sun. This is related to *yayaay* (sun).

yaaybaa (YR, YY) *noun*
summer. Based on *yaay*, a variant of *yayaay* (sun) and *-baa* (place of, time of).

yaayngarralgaa (YY) *noun*
clock, watch. Based on *yaay* (sun) and *ngarra-li* (looking). One source.

yaaya-li (YR, YY) *verb-transitive*
chop. ◆ *Yaaya-li ngaya gi-yaa-nha nhaadhiyaan.* (YY) I am going to chop the log.

yabaa (YR, YY, GR) *noun*
carpet python *(Morelia spilotes)*.

yabi-li (YR, YY) *verb-transitive*
1 twist, plait (YY). Fred Reece said that sinew when dried out was used for string. First it was washed and softened, then the women twisted it on their thighs to make a line. Kangaroo-skin blankets were sewn with sinews from the kangaroo's tail or from the emu's leg. There is a big sinew at the back of the emu's leg, with two or three strands. They teased it out into little threads, and they twisted it up into a line, like a rope. It is very strong when twisted very tight. It was used to make nets and bags and other things. ◆ *Yabi-la nhama dhinawan-gu dhunbil!* (YY) Twist that emu sinew!
2 kiss (YR, YY). See also: **ngaay gaya-li**.

yabil (YY) *noun*
large bark vessel. One source.

yadhaarr (YR, YY, GR) *noun*
feather, down (of birds). Feathers or down of any bird except the emu. It is said that bird down was used to stop bleeding.

yadhaba-li (GR) *verb-transitive*
sharpen.

yadhala (GR) *adjective*
sharp. Also *yadha*.

yagaay (YR, YY, GR) *exclamation*
hey!, look!, ouch! An expression of fright or hurt. Probably related to *yaaga-y* (moan). *Yagaay* or similar words are used across much of Australia as an exclamation of surprise and distress.

yala-y (YR, YY) *verb-intransitive*
follow. Form is uncertain, possibly *yalaa-y* or *yila-y*. This is a rare word, the common word is *gawaa-y*.

yalaa (YR, YY) *noun*
jail. ◆ *Yalaa-ga nginaalinya wa-li.* (YY) (He) will put you two in jail.

yalaayn (YR) *noun*
fishing line. From English 'line'. This is a rare word, the common word is *buurr*.

yalabiyaay (YR) *adjective*
not with it. Ted Fields said this means something like 'you're lost' or 'you're having me on'. Possibly from *yaal* (a lie) and *-biyaay* (with, having).

yalagidhaay (YR) *place adverb*
right around. As in something 'turned/went right around'. ◆ *Yalagidhaay ngaama dhurra-y.* (YR) It (boomerang) came right around.
Possibly related to *yalagiirr(ma)* (like this) and *dhaay* (to here).

yalagiirrma (YR, GR) *adverb*
1 like that, in that manner (YR, GR).
◆ *Garriya nhama bilaarr gaa-gi-la-ya yalagiirrma.* (YR) Don't carry the spear like that.
2 because (consequence) (YR). Sometimes translated 'that is why' or 'therefore'.
◆ *Yayaay-badhaay ngama ngarribaa gunagala-ga ngiyarrma gudhuwa-y-la-nhi yalagiirrma ngiyani malawil-a wila-y-la-nhi.* (YR) The sun was burning high up in the sky, that's why we were sitting in the shade. ◆ *Garriya gimbi-lda-ya yalagiirrma buma-li ngaya nginunha.* (YR) Don't do (that) because I will hit you.
Possibly a compound *yalagiirr-ma*.

yalagiirrmawu (YR) *time adverb*
at that time, then. The meaning and function of this word is not clear. It seems to have a time reference, and was also used to translate 'before' as in 'the children watched the dancing before they fell asleep'. It occurs in sentences with two clauses. ◆ *Dhinawan nhama gaarra-la guway-u, yulay gaarra-la, yalagiirrmawu ngiyani biyuu-ga wa-li, dhawuma-li-gu.* (YR) Rub that emu with blood, rub the skin, then we'll put him in the hole and cook (him). ◆ *Wana nhama yayaay dhurra-ldaay, yalagiirrmawu nginunha ngaya ngarra-li.* (YR) Let the sun come up, then I'll see you.
◆ *Buluuy-a ngaya dhanduwi-nyi, yalagiirrmawu-bala ngaya-nga yuwa-ya ngarra-lda-nhi gagil dhayn.* (YR) I went to sleep, then in my sleep I saw a bad man.
From *yalagiirrma* (like that/in that manner) and *-wu* (time suffix).

yalagiyu (YR) *time adverb*
now.

yalbala (YR, YY) *particle*
gammon, pretend. Also *yala, yalabala*. Ted Fields said it also occurs in *yalbala yiya*

(false teeth) and *wanda nhama yalbala mil* (that whitefella's got a false eye). ◆ *Yalbala nhama bandaarr, baa-y-la-nhi.* (YR) That (is) a pretend kangaroo, hopping. ◆ *Yalbala wirraa-waa-ya!* (YY) Pretend to limp! Occurs at the beginning of sentences. Probably from *yaal* (a lie, pretend, false) and *-bala* (contrast).

yaliwunga (GR) *adverb*
always. Form uncertain.

yaluu (YR, YY, GR) *particle*
again. Also occurs in *ngaama yaluu* (at the same time). ◆ *Garriya gaarrima-la yaluu gungan!* (YR) Don't spill the water again! Usually occurs at the beginning of sentences, sometimes translated as 'still'. Like many *yal-* words, this may contain a simplified form of *yiyal* (just, only); *yaluu* may also include *-u* (time). The meaning of this word is not fully understood. See Learner's Guide.

yaluuyaluu (YY) *adjective*
same, copied. Also *yalyualu, yalulu*. From *yaluu* (again). One source.

yambiyan (YY) *noun*
kangaroo-tooth ornament. Made from the teeth fixed in gum. One source.

yambuli (GR) *noun*
old woman. Previously also written *yambi*.

yana-y (GR) *verb-intransitive*
1 go. ◆ *Dhalaa-nda yana-waa-nha?* (GR) Where are you going?
2 come. ◆ *Dhaay yana-ya!* (GR) Come here! ◆ *Minya-gu yana-waa-nhi?* (GR) What did you come for?
3 walk.

yanaa-y (YR, YY) *verb-intransitive*
1 go. ◆ *Buluuy-a ngaya yanaa-nhi.* (YY) I went there in the dark (at night).
2 come. ◆ *Dhaay yanaa-ya!* (YY) Come here!
3 walk. ◆ *Buluuy-a ngaya gi-yaa-nha yanaa-y.* (YY) I am going to walk in the dark (at night).
Also occurs in the shortened form, *'naa-y*.

yanaawuwi-y (YR, YY) *verb-intransitive*
go home, go back. ◆ *Galawu gi-yaa-nha-nda yanaa-w-uwi-y?* (YY) When are you going to go home?
From *yanaa-* (go, come) and *-w-uwi-y* (suffix that means 'back').

yanaaynbi-li (YR, YY) *verb-transitive*
1 release, let go (YR, YY). ◆ *Yanaaynbi-la maadhaay!* (YY) Let the dog go!
2 sack (YR). ◆ *Giirruu nginunha-laa wanda-gu yanaaynbi-li.* (YR) The white man will sack you.
From *yanaa-* (go) and *(n)-bi-li* (verb suffix).

yanbiyaay (YY) *noun*
healer's totem. A totem belonging to some *wiringin*, it makes a whistling sound. Langloh-Parker said that the *wiringin* must never eat it or they will die. Any injury to a *yanbiyaay* hurts the man himself. The *wiringin*, if in danger, has the power to assume the shape of his *yanbiyaay*. Women are sometimes given a *yanbiyaay*.

yanggal (YR, YY, GR) *noun*
vagina.

yanggiidjaa (YR, GR) *noun*
handkerchief. From English 'handkerchief'.

Yanguru (GR) *noun*
moiety name. For more information see *yanguu*.

Yanguu (YY) *noun*
moiety name. All things and people were divided into two groups or moieties. The name of the *Yibaay/Gambuu* moiety is *Yanguu*. People of the *Yanguu* group married people of the *Wudhurruu* group. Thought to be made up of galah, emu, kangaroo, frog (and probably others). See also: **Wudhurruu**.

yanguuwii (YR, YY) *noun*
sacred fire. Possibly a fire kept burning at a bora ceremony, managed by the *Yanguu* moiety. From *Yanguu* (moiety name) and *wii* (fire).

yaraay (GR) *noun*
sun. See also: **yayaay**.

yaraaybaa (GR) *noun*
summer.

yaraadha (GR) *noun*
day, daytime. Probably based on *yaraay* (sun) and *-dha* (at/in).

yaraay dhurra-li (GR) *verb phrase*
sunrise. From *yaraay* (sun) and *dhurra-li* (rise).

yaraay warra-y (GR) *verb phrase*
eclipse of sun. From *yaraay* (sun), *warra-y*

yaray

(stand). One source.

yaray (GR) *noun*
sheep intestines (large). Highly prized as food; cooked and eaten.

yarayawu (GR) *noun*
sickness spirit. Spirit with four eyes who is thought to cause all sickness, he takes a large bag and gets into it when cold. One source. Form uncertain.

yarigin (YR) *adjective*
thirsty.

yarraadharr (YR, YY) *noun*
piece of bark. Fred Reece described it as 'bark thrown to scare ducks — like a little bat'. It scares the flying ducks, which dive to water level and fly into the net stretched across the waterway.

yarraaman (YR, YY, GR) *noun*
horse. There are many variant forms, e.g. *yarraman, yaraaman* and *yirraamaan.* Similar words are used for 'horse' in many Aboriginal languages.

yarraan (YR, YY, GR) *noun*
1 river red gum tree *(Eucalyptus camaldulensis)* (YR, YY, GR). ◆ *Gabinya yarraan galiyawaa-nha.* (GR) The boy is climbing the river red gum. Typically a large, gnarled, wide-spreading tree which grows along rivers and billabongs.
2 Southern Cross (stars) (YR).

yarraanbiin (YY) *noun*
river gum flowers. Based on *yarraan* (river gum) and *-(b)iyan.* See Learner's Guide.

yarraangan (YR, YY, GR) *noun*
gum tree grub. Mathews said 'edible grub of gum tree'. Based on *yarraan* (river gum).

yarragaa (YR, YY, GR) *noun*
spring wind. Possibly 'spring'.

yarral (YR, YY, GR) *noun*
1 stone (GR). ◆ *Ngurray yarral-a baabi-lanha.* (GR) A snake is sleeping on the stone.
2 money (coins) (YR, YY, GR). Recommended usage is *banggul* (money) and *yarral* (coins).

Yarralaraay (GR) *placename*
Yalaroi. From *yarral* (stone) and *-araay* (with, having).

Yarralduul (GR) *placename*
Yarralduul. From *yarral* (stone) and *-duul* (little, one). Location south of Burren Junction.

yarran (YR) *noun*
yarran wattle *(Acacia homalophylla).* Small tree, 7–10 m high, timber is dark brown and solid, used for making tools and weapons such as *barran* (boomerangs).

Yarranbaa (YY) *placename*
Yeranbah. From *yarran* (yarran wattle) or *yarraan* (river red gum), and *-baa* (place of).

yarrarr (YR) *noun*
rice. Possibly from English 'rice'. One source.

yarray (YR, YY, GR) *noun*
1 beard, whiskers. Also anything that looks like whiskers.
2 moustache.
Also occurs as *yaray* probably due to the influence of English.

yarraybiyaay (YY) *noun*
boy at puberty. From *yarray* (beard, whiskers) and *-biyaay* (with, having).

yarrbun (YR, YY) *adjective*
very tired, exhausted. Arthur Dodd said 'gone in the legs'.

yarrbun maa (YY) *adjective*
clumsy. Also *yarrban.* From *yarrbun* (very tired) and *maa* (hand).

yarrin (YY) *noun*
water current.

yarudhagaa (GR) *noun*
matrilineal totem. The matrilineal totem was a basic totem, other totems could be given to a person. Since *dhii* is also 'matrilineal totem', *Yarudhagaa* may have a special meaning which is no longer known. One source.

yawa-li (YR, YY) *verb-transitive*
track. ◆ *Yawa-la nhama bigibila, nhama nguungu baburr dhaymaa-ya.* (YY) Track that porcupine, that's his foot(print) on the ground.

yawi (YR, YY) *noun*
person's spirit. A person's soul or spirit; said to hang around the body for three days after death; visible as a light at night. When a spirit goes up into the sky world, there is said to be a noise like thunder, which is the spirit 'ladder' they used dropping back to earth. People would say 'the ladder has dropped', meaning the spirit has gone for good. Perhaps used in English 'yowi'.

yawi buliirral (YY) *noun*
spirit breath. From *yawi* (person's spirit) and *buliirral* (breath).

yawu (YR, GR) *particle*
yes. Ted Fields said *yawu* can be used when answering the phone.

yawurr (GR) *noun*
small berry. Dipped in honey and eaten.

yaya-li (YR, YY) *verb-transitive*
tell off, scold. Also *djaya-li*. ◆ *Giirr ngaya-nha yaya-y.* (YR) I just roused on him.
◆ *Giirr-nga nguu yaya-laa-nha.* (YY) She's rousing now.

yayala-y (YR, YY) *verb-intransitive*
quarrel. Also *yayla-y*. ◆ *Giirr ngali dhinggaa-nginda yaya-la-y-la-y.* (YR) We will quarrel about the meat.
From *yaya-* (tell off, scold) and *-la-y* (reciprocal suffix), so 'scold each other'.

yayaay (YR, YY) *noun*
sun. The sun is said to be female.
◆ *Giibaabu ngali yanaa-y, yayaay dhurra-ldaay.* (YR) We will go early in the morning, when the sun rises.
In compounds, *yayaay* sounds like *yaay*, e.g. *yaaybaa* (summer).

yaydja (YR) *noun*
skin cracks. Cracks that people get in their feet, especially after running around in mud and water. One source.

Yibaay (YR, YY, GR) *noun*
men's social section. A person's marriage division (and also their meat/totem) determined who they should marry. *Yibaay* marries *Gabudhaa*, children are *Marrii* (male) and *Maadhaa* (female), sister is *Yibadhaa*. Possible source of the surnames 'Hippai' and 'Hippett'. See also: **Marrii, Gabii, Gambuu**.

Yibadhaa (YR, YY, GR) *noun*
women's social section. Marries *Gabii*, children are *Gambuu* (male) and *Buudhaa* (female), brother is *Yibaay*. See also: **Buudhaa, Maadhaa, Gabudhaa**.

yii (YR) *exclamation*
hey! One source.

yii-gi (YY) *verb-intransitive*
shiver. ◆ *Yii-gi-la-nha ngaya.* (YY) I am shivering.

yii-li (YR, YY, GR) *verb-transitive*
bite. ◆ *Garriya nhama yii-la!* (GR) Don't bite him! ◆ *Dhuyu-gu nganha yii-y.* (YY) A snake bit me.
Also used of something, e.g. chilli, having 'a bite'.

yiil (YY) *noun*
small pigweed *(Portulaca filifolia)*. Also called slender pigweed, it is a 'hairy' species of pigweed; cottony fluff of its long hairs could be used for decoration. See also: **ganhan, dhamu**.

yiilaman (YR) *noun*
shield. A thick shield about 30 cm long and 15 cm wide, made of a light wood such as kurrajong, used to 'slant off' or deflect spears or block boomerangs. Possibly borrowed from another language.

yiilay (YR, YY) *noun, adjective*
1 hop bush *(Dodonea viscosa* ssp. *angustissima)* (YR, YY). Ian Sim said it is so called 'because its got a bite . . . it is the bite that cures you' — used medicinally.
2 ripe (YY). Used only once with this meaning on the tapes, sometimes *gaba* (good) is used for 'ripe'. ◆ *Giirr-nga nhama yiilay gi-nyi guwi.* (YY) That emu apple is really ripe.
3 cooked (YY).

yiili (YR, YY, GR) *adjective*
angry. ◆ *Ngaya nginundi yiili.* (GR) I am angry with you. ◆ *Yiili ngaya gi-nyi.* (YY) I got angry.
Also *yiilay*, so possibly the same word as *yiilay* (hop bush, cooked, ripe). See also: **yiiliyanbaa**.

yiili burranba-li (YR, YY) *verb phrase*
annoy, make someone angry. From *yiili* (angry) and *burranba-li* (make).

yiilinhi (GR) *noun*
war. From *yiili* (angry). One source. Form uncertain.

yiiliyanbaa (YR, YY) *adjective*
1 angry (YR, YY).
2 savage (YR, YY).
Based on *yiili* (angry) and *-baa* (place of, time of). It is sometimes translated as Aboriginal English 'wild'. See also: **yiili**.

yiiliyanbaa wanda (YY) *noun*
spirits of the lower world. From *yiiliyanbaa* (angry) and *wanda* (ghost, spirit). One source.

yiiliyiili (YR, YY) *adjective*
peppery, spicy. From *yiili* (angry).

yiiliyiiliyan (YY) *noun*
angry person. Someone who is aggressive or 'looking for a fight'. From *yiili* (angry). One source.

yiindal (YY, GR) *noun*
swamp grass. There are two types: fine and coarse; they grow on the edges of swamps and are eaten by emus.

yiirriirr (YR, YY) *noun*
mirage.

yiiy (YR) *exclamation*
listen! Ted Fields said it means something like 'there you are' or 'I told you that'. One source.

yilaa (YR, YY, GR) *time adverb*
1 soon, directly. ◆ *Dhuwinba-la nhama dhamiyaa, yilaa ngaya dharrawu-l-uwi-y.* (YR) You hide that tomahawk, directly I'll be coming back for it.
2 recently. ◆ *Yilaa ngiyama dhama-nhi, dhaymaarr-bala gungan-biyaay.* (YR) It rained recently, the ground (is) wet.
The basic meaning is 'within a little time' in the past or future; sometimes used to translate English 'then'. Often the shortened form *-laa* is attached to a nearby word, e.g. *ngaya-laa* (I-soon). Generally *yilaa* occurs first in a phrase or sentence. Also occurs as *yilaal*.

yilaa buluuya (YY) *noun*
tonight. Based on *yilaa* (soon) and *buluuy-a* (night-at).

yilaadhu (GR) *time adverb*
1 now (immediately).
2 today.
Based on *yilaa* (soon, directly). May mean *right now*.

yilaalu (YR, YY, GR) *time adverb*
1 long ago. Ian Sim said *yilaalu* was often used to start a story; compare this with the English 'once upon a time . . .'
2 long time later. From *yilaa* (soon, recently). The basic meaning is 'at a long time' in the past or future. Also *yilambu* in Gamilaraay.

yilaambiyal (GR) *noun*
beginning. Based on *yilaa* (soon) and *biyal* (just). One source.

yilaan.gaal (YY) *adjective*
1 fresh. As in 'fresh meat'.
2 new. This is a possible meaning. From *yilaa* (soon, recently).

yilama-li (YR, YY) *verb-transitive*
cook. ◆ *Ngiyarrma-nga bulaa-yu ngaama guduu yilama-y.* (YR) Those two cooked the fish.
This is the general word for 'cook' and also means 'cook on coals'. See also: **dhawuma-li**.

yilama-y (YR) *verb-intransitive*
cook. ◆ *Giirr dhinggaa yilama-nhi.* (YR) The meat cooked.
A change in verb class from *-li* to *-y*. One source.

yilambu (GR) *time adverb*
long ago. Based on *yilaa* (soon, recently). This is a rare word, the common word is *yilaalu*.

yilawa-y (YY) *verb-intransitive*
1 sit. ◆ *Ganunga yilawa-y-la-nha gaarrimay-a.* (YY) They are all sitting in the camp.
2 stay, stop, live. ◆ *Yilawa-ya nguwalay, yilaal nginda yanaa-w-uwi-y.* (YY) Stop here (for a while), soon you can go back home.

yilbin (YY) *noun*
leaves used for burying. Fred Reece said that *yilbin* leaves are from *gurraay* (cypress pine) and *dhiil* (wilga tree), they are used for burying people: 'We put a lot of it down first, then put the coffin on top of them.' These leaves were not used for other things, such as holding food.

yili (YR, YY, GR) *noun*
1 lip (YR, YY, GR).

2 gills (YY).
See also: **gumay**.

yiluwidi (YR) *adjective*
blue. One source.

yin.ga (YR, YY) *noun*
crayfish.

yinabi-li (YR, YY, GR) *verb-transitive*
1 fish, catch fish. ◆ *Garriya nguwalay yinabi-lda-ya!* (YR) Don't catch (fish) here!
2 catch with instrument. ◆ *Giirr ngaya biyarr bandaarr maadhaay-u yinabi-y.* (YR) I caught one kangaroo with the dog. Also occurs in *ngaaluurr dhaaliyay-biyaay yinabi-li* (catch fish with a net). The expression *ngaaluurr yinabi-li* has been used for 'catching fish with a line'.

yinabil (GR) *noun*
hook. One source.

yinarr (YR, YY GR) *noun*
Aboriginal woman. ◆ *Waal nhama yinarr banaga-nhi.* (YR) The woman didn't run. ◆ *Yina-yu nhama dhuu gimbi-y birralii-gu.* (YR) The woman made a fire for the child.

yinarraa (YR, YY) *noun*
senior lady (respected elder). Name for a very respected woman. Fred Reece said that people used to call Mrs Langloh-Parker *yinarraa* or head woman, 'like saying she was a lady . . . that's like the queen giving some lady a title'.

yinarraagalaa (YR, YY) *noun*
old woman. Based on *yinarr* (woman).

yinggil (YR, YY, GR) *adjective*
1 tired.
2 lazy.

yira (GR) *noun*
tooth.

yira murrun (GR) *noun*
young man. Refers to boys who are identified as ready to go through their first big bora. This expression refers to the practice of knocking out a tooth as part of initiation and presumably means a young man before the tooth has been removed. From *yira* (tooth) and *murrun* (alive).

yirrgayn (YR, YY) *adjective*
clear. As in grassless ground; Fred Reece said 'clean, no rubbish on it'.

yirrin (YR, YY, GR) *noun*
owlet nightjar *(Aegotheles cristatus)*. Fred Reece said: '*Yirrin* is a little grey bird, goes "girrin"; big as a soldier bird, lives in a hollow all day and comes out at night, he's got owl's eyes, a miniature owl.' Its familiar or pet name is *dhagaanili* (little older brother) because 'he helps the people'; apparently the only night-bird that people like, it gives warning of rainy weather coming by calling out during the day.

yiya (YR, YY) *noun*
1 tooth (YR, YY). Also used to refer to anything that looks like a tooth, including features of the landscape.
2 seed (YY).
3 peg (YY).
Here it is probable that the meaning has been extended from 'tooth' to 'seed' and 'peg'. This is a fairly common process in many languages.

yiyabiyaay (YR, YY) *noun*
firestick. From *yiya* (tooth) and *-biyaay* (with, having). This may refer to the glowing coal at the point of the stick.

yiyadhalibaa (YY) *adjective*
toothless. From *yiya* (teeth) and *-dhalibaa* (without).

yiya murrun (YY) *noun*
young man. From *yiya* (tooth) and *murrun* (alive). For more information see *yira murrun*.

yiyagungawuma (YR, YY) *noun*
small hailstone. Form is uncertain, possibly based on *yiya* (tooth).

yiyal (YR, YY, GR) *adverb*
just, only. ◆ *Yiyal yilawa-ya.* (YR) Just sit down (there). ◆ *Milanduul yiyal ngali bayama-y dhagaay.* (YR) We only caught one yellowbelly.

yiyaldu (GR) *particle*
furthermore. Based on *yiyal* (just, only).

yiyalgidjaay (YY) *noun*
fully initiated young man. Possibly based on *yiya* (tooth) and *gi-gi* (to be). The rules for using words made by adding *-djaay* to a verb are not clear. This was an informal name; there were a series of 'status names'

given at each stage of initiation which are not known. One source.

yu-gi (YR, YY, GR) *verb-intransitive*
cry, weep. ◆ *Giirruu nhama-la birralii-djuul yu-nhi bamba ngambaa-dhi nguungu balu-ngindaay.* (YR) The baby cried, when his mother died.

yubama-li (YR, YY) *verb-transitive*
make cry. ◆ *Nhama birralii yubama-la!* (YY) Make that little boy cry!
From *yu-* (cry), and *-bama-li* (verb suffix associated with emitting sound or speaking).

yuga-li (GR) *verb-intransitive*
celebrate. From *yugal* (song). One source.

yugal (YR, YY, GR) *noun*
song. ◆ *Garriya nhama bawi-lda-ya yugal.* (YR) Don't keep singing that song. ◆ *Gagil-bala nhama yugal, yaluu ngaama ngayagay yugal bawi-la.* (YR) That's a bad song, sing another song.

yugali (YY) *noun*
little song. The little song or rhyme was a teaching or memory aid, e.g. according to Ginny Rose, the dove story had a 'little song', which had as its themes: spots, eyes red from crying, and sore shins. These were a reminder of the story explaining how the dove got its colours and walking gait.

yugin (YR, YY) *noun*
1 father. This is a rare word for 'father', the more common words are *bubaa* and *buwadjarr*.
2 uncle (father's brother).
Compare this with *garruu* (originally — mother's brother) who is a different section from *yugin* (father's brother). Also *yuginya*.

yulaa-li (YR, YY, GR) *verb-transitive*
1 tie up. ◆ *Yulaa-li gi-yaa-nha ngaya nginunha.* (YR) I am going to tie you up.
2 knot.

yulaanbi-li (YR, YY) *verb-transitive*
tangle. The form of this verb is uncertain.

Yulanbay (YR) *noun*
spirit. Spirit in the waterhole at Namoi village, where the reeds are tangled. Possibly related to *yulaanbi-li* (tangle).

yulanbiirr (YR) *noun, placename*
1 tangle. Ted Fields said it can refer to a tangle of grass moving in the water that can drown animals, e.g. at Boobera Lagoon.
2 waterhole name. Eight miles from Walgett on Come By Chance Road. Ted Fields said it was a spirit waterhole. When the water was clear you could see the tangled weed.
Probably from a variant form of *yulaanbi-li* (tangle). One source.
Also *Yulambiirr*.

yulama (GR) *noun*
wallaroo (*Macropus robustus*).

yulay (YR, YY, GR) *noun*
skin.

yuli (YR, YY, GR) *adjective*
new word. See p 160 for more information.

yulu (YR, YY, GR) *noun*
1 nail, fingernail, toenail (YR, YY, GR).
2 claw (YR, YY, GR).
3 scratch (claw mark) (YY).

yulumara (GR) *noun*
fingernail. From *yulu* (nail) and *mara* (hand). One source.

Yuluwaya (YR, YY) *noun*
long-nailed spirit. Also *yuluway*. A spirit with long sharp fingernails, which are used to spear people. Based on *yulu* (nail, claw).

yulu-gi (YR, YY, GR) *verb-intransitive*
1 play. ◆ *Giirr nhama bulaarr birralii-djuul yulu-gi-la-nhi.* (YR) The (two) babies were playing.
2 dance. This verb can also be used to mean 'corroboree'. ◆ *Yaama ngindaay yulu-gi?* (YR) Will you (all) dance? Langloh-Parker describes two popular dance styles: one has an in-and-out movement of the knees, while keeping the feet close together (elsewhere called 'shake-a-leg'). The other was called 'shivering of the chest', a sort of drawing in and out of the breath, causing a vibratory motion.
3 gamble.

yuluumaarraa (YY) *noun*
bogong moth grub. To locate the grub, the hunter scrapes away surface litter, revealing the grub's hole. They then smell the hole, or 'pop' the hole with a finger, to tell whether the grub is still in the ground. The grub is hooked out with a long piece of *gurrulay* (river wattle) bark, or a piece of wire.

yuluurrinma-li (YR) *verb-transitive*
lose. Also *yuluurrima-li*. ◆ *Giirr nhama biya-yu dhayn-du bilaarr yuluurrinma-y.* (YR) One man lost his spear.
Possibly from English 'lose'.

yuluwirri (YR, YY, GR) *noun*
rainbow.

yumbu (YR) *adjective*
1 cry-baby. ◆ *Giirruu nhama birralii-djuul yumbu.* (YR) That kid (is a) cry-baby
2 cranky.
Possibly related to *yumbuy* (fatherless boy).

yumbuy (YR, YY) *noun*
orphan (fatherless boy).

yumu (YR, YY) *noun*
spotty river gum tree *(Eucalyptus obtusa)*. Similar to *yarraan* (river red gum), but *yumu* tends to have darker blue-grey leaves and a more rounded bud.

yundiyundi (YY) *noun*
wren. General and familiar name for three wrens: the splendid fairy-wren *(Malurus splendens)*; the variegated fairy-wren *(M. lamberti)*; and the white-winged wren *(M. leucopterus)*.

yungiirr (YR, YY) *noun*
spoilt child, cry-baby. Also occurs as *yungiirrbidi* (big cry-baby), based on *yu-gi* (cry) and *-bidi* (big). ◆ *Gagil nhama birralii-gal, yungiirr-bidi.* (YY) That kid is bad, a big cry-baby.

yurabirr (YR, YY) *noun*
rabbit. From English 'rabbit'.

yurayaa (GR) *noun*
any frog. Possibly also a burrowing frog.

Yuriyuri (YR) *placename*
location. Said to mean 'a place of many trees', east of Walgett. One source.

yurraamu (YR, YY, GR) *noun*
1 rum (YR, YY, GR). Name for alcoholic spirits (not beer).
2 wine (YR).
From English 'rum'.

yurrandaali (GR) *noun*
tree goanna *(Varanus varius)*. Name for tree goanna when in its spotted phase. See also: **mangun.gaali**.

yurringga-li (YR) *verb-transitive*
push. ◆ *Garriya nganha yurringga-la!* (YR) Don't push me!

yurrugu (YR) *noun*
rope. Possibly from English 'rope'. One source.

yurrul (YR, YY, GR) *noun*
1 bush, scrub (YR, YY, GR). Also occurs as *yurrul-aa* (scrub-place of). *Yurrul* refers to an area of thick vegetation, not just one plant. ◆ *Wii nhama gudhuwa-laa-nha yurrul-a.* (GR) A fire is burning in the scrub.
2 seed (YR). A seed used for a float on fishing lines, may be from kangaroo grass. One source.

yurrun (YR, YY, GR) *noun*
scar. Word for any scar, compared with *mubirr* (initiation scar).

yuru (GR) *noun*
cloud. This is a rare word, the common word is *gundaa*.

yuruun (YR, YY, GR) *noun*
road. Also *yurruun*. Fred Reece said it is from English 'road'.

yuu (YR, YY, GR) *noun*
dust.

yuuga-y (YY) *verb-intransitive*
gush out, spurt. As of floodwater. One source.

yuul (YR, YY, GR) *noun*
1 vegetable food. Now used for any food.
2 food.

yuularaay (GR) *adjective*
full of food, sated, satisfied. From *yuul* (food) and *-araay* (with, having).

yuuliyaay (YR, YY) *adjective*
full of food, sated, satisfied. From *yuul* (vegetable food) and *-iyaay* (with, having).

yuulngin (YR, YY, GR) *adjective*
hungry. Also *yuulngindi*. ◆ *Yuulngin ngaya gi-la-nhi.* (YY) I was hungry.
From *yuul* (food) and *-ngin* (wanting).

yuulbaarra-y (YY) *verb-intransitive*
be astonished. Form is uncertain, but

possibly includes *baarra-y* (crack, split, burst). One source.

yuuliin (YY) *noun*
dogwood flowers.

yuumbu (YR) *adjective*
numb. ◆ *Giirr ngaya maa nhalay yuumbu gi-nyi.* (YR) My hands were numb (I couldn't feel anything).
One source. See also: **dhirrindjal**.

yuundu (YR, YY, GR) *noun*
1 stone axe, tomahawk.
2 axe.

yuurra-gi (YR) *verb-intransitive*
move. This is a rare word, the common word is *yanaa-y* (go, walk).

yuurraa (YR, YY, GR) *noun*
dogwood, eurah *(Eremophila bignoniiflora)*. Ted Fields said that the leaves are boiled for drinking. Also said to be used for coughs and colds, and for making anything that needed to be springy.

yuurraa-li (YR) *verb-transitive*
cover up. ◆ *Girran-du nhama yuurraa-la.* (YR) Cover it with ashes.
Form uncertain. This verb is not as common as *buluba-li* and the difference between these two verbs is not understood.

yuurrambi-li (YR) *verb-transitive*
wag, wave. One source. Based on *yuurra-* (move) and *-bi-li* (verb suffix).

yuurray (YR, YY) *noun*
1 initiated man.
2 important man.
3 Aboriginal man.

yuurri (YR) *noun*
woman spirit. This spirit described as a beautiful small woman with long black hair. If a drover's camp is dirty she will clean the camp, but if the drover has a woman in the camp she will smash things up out of jealousy.

Yuurrila (YY) *noun*
spirit. A spirit, described as an old man with huge staring eyes, long hair and a black bark drape, that appeared in about 1895 to Alice Dixon at Bangate Station. She was not 'strong enough' to receive its song message, so the message was received by the *wiringin* Gingerbeer Billy. This song message and the story of his appearances became a famous and very serious corroboree. *Yuurrila* lives in a *mingga* (spirit-haunted tree) called *Mangilaarr*. Munggilah is the name of a nearby waterhole on the Narran River below old Bangate Station. There is a path to a nearby ridge called *Bubirra* where he takes the air at night. One source.

yuurrma-li (YY) *verb-transitive*
play with. ◆ *Waal nhama maadhaay yuurrma-lda-ya!* (YY) Don't play with that dog!
One source.

yuurrma-y (YR, YY) *verb-intransitive*
1 corroboree. ◆ *Giirr ngiyani yuurrma-nhi.* (YY) We had a corroboree.
2 play. ◆ *Yuurrma-y ngiyani gi-yaa-nha.* (YY) We are going to play.
A change in verb class from *-li* to *-y*. See Learner's Guide.

yuuruu (GR) *noun*
rain.

yuuwaanmi-li (YY) *verb-transitive*
lose. One source.

yuuwirr (YY) *noun*
armpit. Compare *gidjigidji* (underarm — YR). One source.

yuuyuu (YR, YY) *noun*
rain. Also *yiiyuu*.

yuuyuu bundaa-gi (YY) *verb phrase*
rain. ◆ *Gundaa-nga ngaama galiya-waa-nha yiiyuu gi-yaa-nha bundaa-gi.* (YY) The clouds are coming up, it's going to rain (rain will fall).
From *yuuyuu* (rain) and *bundaa-gi* (fall). This is rare, the more common word is *dhama-y* (rain).

Yuwaalaraay (YR, YY, GR) *noun*
1 Yuwaalaraay tribe.
2 Yuwaalaraay language.
From *yuwaal* (old word for 'no') and *-araay* (with, having); that is, having *yuwaal* for 'no'.

Yuwaalayaay (YR, YY, GR) *noun*
1 Yuwaalayaay tribe.
2 Yuwaalayaay language.
Based on *yuwaal* (old word for 'no') and *-ayaay* an irregular form of the suffix *-iyaay* (with, having); that is, having

yuwaal for 'no'.

Yuwaaliyaay (YY) *noun*
    1 Yuwaalayaay tribe.
    2 Yuwaalayaay language.
    Probably a variant of *Yuwaalayaay*. This is the language name that Fred Reece used.

yuwaarran (YR) *adjective*
    broken-hearted. One source.

yuwaba-y (YR, YY) *verb-transitive*
    hunt away, chase away. ◆ *Bandaarr nhama yuwaba-ya!* (YR) Chase the kangaroos away!

yuwagayrr (GR) *noun*
    ibis. One source. Form uncertain.

yuwanma-li (YR) *verb-transitive*
    put back, return. One source.

yuwarr (YR, YY) *noun*
    sleep. Related to *yuwarra-y* (go to sleep).

    yuwaya ngarra-li (YR, YY) *verb phrase*
    dream. ◆ *Yuwa-ya ngaya ngarra-y dhinawan banaga-waa-ndaay.* (YY) I dreamt about an emu running. (In my sleep I saw an emu running).
    From *yuwa-ya* (sleep-in, at) and *ngarra-li* (see).

    yuwaya wiima-li (YY) *verb phrase*
    dream. ◆ *Yuwa-ya ngaya wiima-y.* (YY) I dreamt.
    From *yuwa-ya* (sleep-in, at) and *wiima-li* (put down, leave). One source.

yuwarra-y (YR, YY) *verb-intransitive*
    go to sleep. ◆ *Yuwarra-y-la-nha nginda.* (YR) You're going to sleep. See also: **yuwarr**.

yuwayaa (YR, YY) *noun*
    any frog. Also *yuwaay*.

Gamilaraay/Yuwaalaraay/Yuwaalayaay *to* English
New Word List

badha gali (YR) *noun*
   beer. From *badha* (bitter) and *gali* (water). Word developed by Walgett Language Program.

banay (YR, YY, GR) *adjective*
   ten. Word developed by Walgett Language Program.

barriga (YR, YY, GR) *adjective*
   hundred. Word developed by Walgett Language Program, borrowed from Kaurna language.

bidjiirr (YR) *noun*
   biscuit. From English 'biscuit'. Word developed by Walgett Language Program, borrowed from Kaurna language.

dhawadha (YR, YY, GR) *adjective*
   thousand. Word developed by Walgett Language Program, borrowed from Kaurna language.

dhii man.garr (YR) *noun*
   tea bag. From *dhii* (tea) and *man.garr* (bag). Word developed by Walgett Language Program.

gabi (YR) *noun*
   coffee. From English 'coffee'. Word developed by Walgett Language Program.

galay (YR, YY, GR) *adjective*
   eight. Word developed by Walgettt Language Program.

gayrra (YR) *noun*
   electricity. From *dhan.gayrra* (lightning). Word developed by Walgettt Language Program.

   gayrragumbirri (YR) *noun*
   computer. From *gayrra* (electricity) and *gumbirri* (brain). Word developed by Walgett Language Program.

guulay (YR, YY, GR) *adjective*
   seven. Word developed by Walgett Language Program.

guwiirr gungan (YR) *noun*
   soft drink. From *guwiirr* (sweet) and *gungan* (water). Word developed by Walgett Language Program.

guwiirr widja (YR) *noun*
   cake, biscuit. From *guwiirr* (sweet) and *widja* (bread). Word developed by Walgett Language Program.

man.ga (YR) *noun*
   table. Word developed by Walgett Language Program from *man.gaman.ga* (flat).

man.gaman.ga (YR) *adjective*
   flat. See *mungumungu*.

mirraal (YR, YY, GR) *adjective*
   nine. Word developed by Walgett Language Program.

nguunguu (GR) *noun*
   may be another name for the barn owl. The word is possibly related to *nguu* (paperbark).

wirri (YR, YY) *noun*
   1 small coolamon (YR, YY). Fred Reece said that a *wirri* is a bark dish or a bowl cut out of a tree, made for carrying honey.
   2 plate (YR). Meaning extended by Walgett Language Program.

wiwurra (YR, YY, GR) *adjective*
   million. Word developed by Walgett Language Program, borrowed from Kaurna language.

wiyayl (YR, YY) *noun*
   1 echidna quill. ◆ *Dhalaybaa nhama wiyayl.* (YY) The quills are sharp.
   2 pen, pencil. Meaning extended by Walgett Language Program.

yuli (YR, YY, GR) *adjective*
   six. Word developed by Walgett Language Program.

English *to* Gamilaraay/Yuwaalaraay/Yuwaalayaay Word List

It is important to check the dictionary entry for more information about a word.

Aa

Aboriginal doctor *(noun)* .... wiringin YR, YY, GR
Aboriginal man *(noun)* .... dhayn, yuurray YR, YY
　　　　　　　　　　　　　　giwiirr, mari GR
Aboriginal person *(noun)* .... dhayn YR, YY
　　　　　　　　　　　　　　mari GR
Aboriginal woman *(noun)* ...... yinarr YR, YY, GR
　　　　　　　　　　　　　　wirringgaa YR, GR
above *(place adverb)* .... ngarribaagili YR
absolutely *(particle)* .... giirruu YR, YY, GR
accent *(noun)* .... dhaalan YY
across *(adjective, adverb)* .... nganbirr YY, GR
Adam's apple *(noun)* .... wun.guwi YR, YY, GR
afraid *(adjective)* .... garigari, giyal YR, YY, GR
　　　　　　　　　　　　　　gun.gun YR, YY
afterbirth *(noun)* .... wangali GR
afterwards *(time adverb)* .... buwabiila YR
again *(particle)* .... yaluu YR, YY, GR
alas! *(exclamation)* .... ngarragaa YR, YY, GR
alcohol *(noun)* .... yurraamu GR
alcohol (clear) *(noun)* .... balaa YY
　　　　　　　　　　　　　　banggabaa YR
alert *(adjective)* .... milgumilgu YY
alive *(adjective)* .... murrun YR, YY, GR
all *(adjective)* .... ganu YR, GR
　　　　　　　　　　　　　　ganungawu,
　　　　　　　　　　　　　　gurrugurru^2 YR, YY
all *(suffix)* .... -aaba-li YR, YY
all day *(suffix)* .... -ngayi-li YR
all over the place *(adjective)* ...... dhurradhurraa YY
　　　　　　　　　　　　　　wiyalwiyal YR
all possible *(suffix)* .... -Luu YR, YY
all right *(adjective, adverb)* .... gaba YR, YY, GR
all right! *(exclamation)* .... ngaayaybaay YR

almost *(adverb)* .... ngaliman YR, YY
alone *(adjective)* .... biyaduul,
　　　　　　　　　　　　　　mamaldhalibaa YR, YY
　　　　　　　　　　　　　　milanduul YY
also *(suffix)* .... -bula YR, YY
alternative name *(noun)* .... bilaan YY
always *(adverb)* .... dhugay YR, YY
　　　　　　　　　　　　　　yaliwunga GR
ancestors *(noun)* .... maran YR, YY
ancestral eagle man *(noun)* ...... Maliyangarr YY
and *(conjunction)* .... gaalanha YR, YY
　　　　　　　　　　　　　　ngaragay GR
　　　　　　　　　　　　　　ngayagay YR
angophora (tree) *(noun)* .... bulamin GR
angry *(adjective)* .... yiili YR, YY, GR
　　　　　　　　　　　　　　yiiliyanbaa YR, YY
angry person *(noun)* .... yiiliyiiliyan YY
animal *(noun)* .... dhii^1 YR, YY, GR
ankle *(noun)* .... baranggal YR, YY
　　　　　　　　　　　　　　ngawurr YY, GR
annoy *(verb phrase)* .... yiili burranba-li YR, YY
another *(adjective)* .... murrunbaa YR, YY
another *(conjunction)* .... ngaragay GR
　　　　　　　　　　　　　　ngayagay YR
answer *(verb-transitive)* .... gara-li GR
　　　　　　　　　　　　　　gaya-li YR, YY
ant (any, black) *(noun)* .... giidjaa YR, YY, GR
ant (black) *(noun)* .... dhuwiyuwiy YR, YY
ant (bull) *(noun)* .... burudha, gabiyan GR
　　　　　　　　　　　　　　buyuga YR, YY
ant (common) *(noun)* .... ganal GR
ant (greenhead) *(noun)* .... bayaarr YR, YY
　　　　　　　　　　　　　　muwan GR
ant (jumper) *(noun)* .... milbaawaay YR, YY
　　　　　　　　　　　　　　milbarawaay GR
ant (meat) *(noun)* .... buurrngan YR, YY
　　　　　　　　　　　　　　gaalan GR

English	Gamilaraay/Yuwaalaraay/Yuwaalayaay
ant nest *(noun)*	gadhuu YR
ant sack (echidna) *(noun)*	gadhuu YR
ant (small brown) *(noun)*	wamuwaa YY
ant (sugar) *(noun)*	barrawaraay YY
ant (type of) *(noun)*	gaalan GR
ant (white) *(noun)*	baamagaaliyan YY
anus *(noun)*	nyii YR, GR
arched *(adjective)*	dhuli YY
arm *(noun)*	bungun YR, YY, GR
armband *(noun)*	bununggaa YY
armlet (woman's) *(noun)*	gumil YR, YY
armpit *(noun)*	gidjigidji YR
	yuuwirr YY
around a fire *(noun, adjective)*	guwiinbarraan YR
ashes *(noun)*	girran YR, YY, GR
ask *(verb-transitive)*	dhaya-li YR, YY, GR
ask for *(verb-transitive)*	miinba-y YR, YY
astonished (be) *(verb-intransitive)*	yuulbaarra-y YY
at *(suffix)*	-Ga YR, YY, GR
at that time *(time adverb)*	yalagiirrmawu YR
attack *(verb-transitive)*	buwawa-li YY
aunt (any) *(noun)*	walgan YR, YY
aunt (father's sister) *(noun)*	gamiyan, giluu YR, YY
aunt (man's father's sister) *(noun)*	walgan YR, YY
aunt (mother's older sister) *(noun)*	burrul ngambaa YY
aunt (mother's sister) *(noun)*	gunii, gunidjarr, ngambaa YR, YY, GR
aunt (mother's younger sister) *(noun)*	dhugaaga ngambaa YY
Australasian grebe *(noun)*	dhiinbin YR, YY, GR
Australian bustard *(noun)*	gumbulgaban YR, YY
Australian kestrel *(noun)*	wala YR, YY
Australian raven *(noun)*	waan[1] YR, YY, GR
avoid *(verb phrase)*	biyuugu yanaa-y YY
awake *(verb-intransitive)*	dhirra-li YR
axe *(noun)*	yuundu YR, YY, GR
axe-face spirit *(noun)*	Nguluyuundu YY
axe handle *(noun)*	birra YY
axe mark *(noun)*	baayl GR
axe (stone) *(noun)*	birran.gaa YR
	gambu YR, YY
	yuundu YR, YY, GR

Bb

English	Gamilaraay/Yuwaalaraay/Yuwaalayaay
Babarra *(placename)*	Babarra YR
babbler (grey-crowned) *(noun)*	dhadhalurraa YR, YY
baby *(noun)*	birralii, birraliidjuul YR, YY
	gaaynggal GR
	wamban YY
bachelor *(noun)*	ganduwi YR, YY
bachelor's camp *(noun)*	wiidhaga YR, YY
back *(verb suffix)*	-uwi-y YR, YY
back (body part) *(noun)*	bawa[2] YR, YY, GR
back log *(noun)*	wiigun YR
back of knee *(noun)*	gayarr YY
back of neck *(noun)*	nhan YR, YY, GR
backbone *(noun)*	guriya GR
	guuyaa YR, YY
backwards *(adverb)*	miirrmiirr YY
bad *(adjective, adverb)*	gagil YR, YY, GR
bad mood *(adjective)*	gagil guuyay YY
bad spirit *(noun)*	bagii GR
bad-weather camp *(noun)*	dhirrinbaa YR
badly *(adverb)*	gamil maaru GR
	waal maayu YY
bag *(noun)*	man.garr YR, YY, GR
bag (clever man's) *(noun)*	bundurr YR, YY
bag (net) *(noun)*	gulay YR, YY, GR
bag (water) *(noun)*	miidja YY, GR
	galinmay YR, YY
bag (woven) *(noun)*	waygal YR, YY
baked soil *(noun)*	barrin YR, YY
bald *(adjective)*	wagibaa dhaygal YR, YY
bald head *(noun)*	biirra gawugaa GR
ball, ball game *(noun)*	buugalaa YR, YY
ball, ball game *(noun)*	burugalaa GR
Ballone (place and river) *(noun)*	baluun YY
balls *(noun)*	buu[1], bugalaa, buugalaa YR, YY
	buru YR, YY, GR
	burugalaa GR
banana *(noun)*	bundul YR
banana (native) *(noun)*	gaagulu YR, YY
banded plover *(noun)*	bundabul YR

English	Gamilaraay/Yuwaalaraay/Yuwaalayaay
bandicoot (golden) (noun)	barrawan[1] YY
bandicoot (western barred) (noun)	guru GR
	guyu YR, YY
bandy legged (adjective)	buyu wayawaya YY
Bangate Station (placename)	Baan.giirr YR, YY
bank (steep) (noun)	ngandirr YR, GR
	nganggil YY
bare (adjective)	balal YR, YY, GR
bark (verb-transitive)	gula-li YR, YY, GR
bark (burial) (noun)	nhiirruu YY
bark canoe (noun)	bunduurraa YR, YY
bark container (noun)	gumbilgal YR, GR
bark discs (noun)	wanggalay YR, YY
bark (flaking) (noun)	dharraa YY, GR
bark hut (noun)	dhaadharr YR, YY, GR
bark (kurrajong) (noun)	giyawaan YR, YY
	muramin YY
bark (piece of) (noun)	yarraadharr YR, YY
bark sheet (noun)	dhayaarr YR
bark throwing stick (noun)	wagarraa YR
bark (tree) (noun)	bidjal YR, YY
	nganda YR, YY, GR
barking owl (noun)	muurrguu YR, YY
barn owl (noun)	wanggii YY
barrel (noun)	baril GR
barter (verb-transitive)	wuurriyala-y GR
Barwon River (placename)	Baawan YY, GR
base, base of bucket (noun)	buu[2] YR, YY
bat (noun)	ngarraadhaan YR, YY
bat (fruit) (noun)	bibaaya YY
bathe (verb-intransitive)	wunga-y YR, YY
battle (noun)	girray YR, YY
	wuurraa YR
battle ground (noun)	girraybaa YY
battle spirit (noun)	Wurrawaadhiyan YR
be (verb-intransitive)	gi-gi YR, YY, GR
be astonished (verb-intransitive)	yuulbaarra-y YY
be born (verb-intransitive)	gaanga-y YR, YY
be buried (verb-intransitive)	nhamurra-y YR, YY
be caught (verb-intransitive)	bayama-y YR
be covered (verb-intransitive)	buluba-y YR, YY
be cut (verb-intransitive)	garra-y YR, YY
be full of food (verb phrase)	mubal muurra-y YY
be full of food (verb-intransitive)	garrabi-y YY
be hit (verb-intransitive)	buma-y YR
be hot (verb-intransitive)	gudhuwa-y YR, GR
be in/inside (verb-intransitive)	wa-y YR, YY
be lonely (verb-intransitive)	walindja-li YR
be lost (verb phrase)	warrayaa yanaa-y YY
be lost (verb-intransitive)	wanggarra-y YR
be on top (verb-intransitive)	ma-y YR
be quiet (verb-intransitive)	dhabi-y YR, YY, GR
be sick (verb-intransitive)	dhaala-gi YR, YY
	wiibi-li GR
be still (verb-intransitive)	dhabi-y YR, YY, GR
be up (verb-intransitive)	ma-y YR
be wrapped (verb-intransitive)	marramba-y YR
beak (noun)	muru GR
bean pods (mimosa) (noun)	mawurrngiyan YY
beard (noun)	yarray YR, YY, GR
bearded dragon (noun)	balawagarr, dhalagal, dharri GR
	wuulaa YR, YY
because (particle)	waama YR, YY
because (consequence) (adverb)	yalagiirrma YR
because of (suffix)	-DHi[1] YR, YY, GR
become (verb-intransitive)	burranba-y YR, YY
	gi-gi YR, YY, GR
bed (noun)	dhiyaagarra YR
bedroll (noun)	dhiyaagarri GR
bee (noun)	warangana YR, YY
bee droppings (noun)	guligal YR, YY
bee-eater (rainbow) (noun)	birrubirruu YR, YY
bee (native) (noun)	guni GR
bee (queen, native) (noun)	guniinii YR, YY, GR
bee (worker) (noun)	warrul YR, YY, GR
bee's nest (noun)	warrul YR, YY, GR
bee's wax (noun)	mayaarr YR
beefwood tree (noun)	mabu YR, YY, GR
beer (noun)	badha gali YR
	giil YR, YY
beetle (type of) (noun)	gananganaa YR, YY
before (particle)	gamilu GR
	waalu YR, YY
before (suffix)	-ayla-y YR
beg (verb-transitive)	dhaya-li GR
begin (verb-intransitive)	burra-li YR
beginning (noun)	yilaambiyal GR
behind (place adverb)	bawadhi GR
	ngayaga YR, YY, GR

belah tree

English	Gamilaraay/Yuwaalaraay/Yuwaalayaay
belah tree (noun)	bilaarr, murrgu YR, YY, GR
belah tree swamp (noun)	murrgugal YR
belah wood sparks (noun)	murrguwidjuwii YR
bellbird (crested) (noun)	banbandhuluwi YR, YY, GR
belly (noun)	mubal YR, YY, GR
bellybutton (noun)	bigal GR; wirrigaal YR, YY, GR
belonging to (suffix)	-gu² YR, YY, GR
below (noun)	ganhaga YR, YY
belt (noun)	gudhurr, dhabilga GR
belt (hair-string) (noun)	buurr GR
belt (man's) (noun)	wayuwaal YR, YY
belt (woman's/possum fur) (noun)	wangal YR, YY
bench (noun)	gulaay YR
bend down (verb-intransitive)	dhuli-y YR, YY, GR
bendy (adjective)	wulbuwulbu YY
bendy stick (noun)	wulbul YY
bent (adjective)	warawara GR; wayawaya YR, YY
bent over (adjective)	dhuli YY
berry (small) (noun)	yawurr GR
best (adjective)	gandjarra YR
betrothal of babies (noun)	baanmal YY
better (adjective)	gababala YR, YY
biceps (noun)	buba GR
bicycle (noun)	badjigal YR
big (adjective)	burrul YR, YY
big (suffix)	-bidi YR, YY, GR
big club (noun)	bugu YR, YY
big mob (noun)	dharaa YR
big toe (noun)	gunidjarr baburr YY, GR
big tree (noun)	maalaabidi YR
bigamist (noun)	dharraawaa YY
bilby (noun)	bilba, dhuluun.gayaa YR, YY
billycan (noun)	biligiyaan YR, YY
bimble box tree (noun)	bibil YR, YY, GR
bird (noun)	dhigaraa GR; dhigayaa YR, YY
bird (dollar) (noun)	dhanibanban YY
bird (mistletoe) (noun)	baandjil YY
bird trap (noun)	dhiilgulay, murragal YR, YY
bird-trapping place (noun)	Dhiilgulaybaa YR
bird (unknown) (noun)	dhurrubuu YY
bird's topknot (noun)	dhigun YR, YY, GR
Birrah (placename)	Birraa¹ YY
birth spirit (noun)	wadhaagudjaaylwan YY
birthing tree (noun)	Gugurruwan YR, YY
birthplace (noun)	ngurrambaa YR, YY
birthplace spirit (noun)	ngarrama YR
biscuit (noun)	bidjiirr, guwiirr widja YR
bite (verb-transitive)	yii-li YR, YY, GR
bite off (verb-transitive)	baaya-li YR
bitter (adjective)	badha YR, YY, GR; gii YY
black (adjective)	buluuy YR, YY, GR
black ant (noun)	dhuwiyuwiy YR, YY
black bream (noun)	banngala YR
black-breasted kite (noun)	wugamaabaydaa YR, YY, GR
black duck (noun)	budhanbaa YR, YY
black eye (noun)	mil buluuy YR
black-faced cuckoo-shrike (noun)	gunidjaa YR, YY
black-faced woodswallow (noun)	biiwanbiiwan YY
black-fronted plover (noun)	bilidjuu YR, YY
black-headed monitor (noun)	galgarriirr YR, YY
black kite (noun)	manggarraan YR, YY, GR
black orchid (noun)	garrii YR, YY
black paint (noun)	buuwan YY
black snake (noun)	ngurray YY, GR; wuyubuluuy YR, YY
black snake (red-bellied) (noun)	galibaay GR
black soil (noun)	banuwa YR, YY
black stripe (noun)	bilum YR, YY
black swan (noun)	baayamal YR, YY; barayamal, burrunda GR
black-tailed native hen (noun)	baan.giirr YR, YY; gulguwi YR, YY, GR
black wattle (noun)	dhulan YR, YY
black-winged stilt (noun)	buyuwaalwaal YY
blackened (adjective)	dhuumuyu YY
blanket (noun)	bulanggiin YR, YY, GR; dhiyaagarri GR
blaze (verb-intransitive)	wula-li YR, YY, GR

English	Gamilaraay/Yuwaalaraay/Yuwaalayaay	Source
blazing (adjective)	wulan	YR, YY, GR
blind (adjective)	muga	YR, YY, GR
blister (noun)	galan	YY
block (deflect) (verb-transitive)	gama-li	YR
blocked (adjective)	muurr	YR, YY, GR
bloke (noun)	ngaamba	YY
blood (noun)	guway	YR, YY, GR
blood group (heavy) (noun)	guwaymadhan	YR, YY, GR
blood group (light) (noun)	guwaygaliyarr	YR, YY, GR
bloodshot eye (noun)	mil guway	YY
bloodwood (western) (noun)	gawuwildhaa	YR
blow (verb-intransitive)	buuli-y	YR, YY
blow (verb-transitive)	buubi-li	YR, YY, GR
blowfly (noun)	gamugamuu	YR, YY
	gawaruurr wanaayal	YY
blue (adjective)	yiluwidi	YR
blue bonnet (bird) (noun)	bulaybulay	YR, YY
blue crane (noun)	budhuulgaa, buyudhurrungiili	YR, YY
blue crowfoot (noun)	dhawaarrii	YY
Blue Knobby (placename)	Buluuy Nhaaybil	GR
blue-tongue lizard (noun)	wubun	YR, YY
blue wren (noun)	yundiyundi	YY
blueberry (noun)	buubiyala	YY
blueberry (common name) (noun)	gii	YY
blunt (adjective)	muga	YR, YY
	mugu	GR
	muurr, nhunduu	YR, YY, GR
board (noun)	buwaarr	YR
boastful (adjective)	biiwanbiiwan	YY
bobby fish (noun)	wii	YR, YY
body (noun)	bana	GR
	burrbiyaan, dhubayn	YR
body hair (noun)	budhi	YR, YY, GR
body-snatching spirit (noun)	wiiwiimal	YY
Boggabilla (placename)	Bagaybila	GR
Boggabri (placename)	Bagaybaraay	GR
boggy (adjective)	gunadha	YY
boggy ground (noun)	gunadha	YR, YY
Boggy Ridge (placename)	Bagi	YY
bogong moth grub (noun)	birrga	YR, YY
	yuluumaarraa	YY
boil (noun)	mula	YR, YY
boil (verb-transitive)	baaylirrma-li	YR
Bokhara River (placename)	Bugayirra	YY
bold (adjective)	dhigadhiga	YR
Bollonbillion (placename)	Baluunbilyan	YR, YY
bone (noun)	bura	GR
	buya	YR, YY
	midjul	YR
bone (jaw) (noun)	dhaal	YR, YY, GR
bone marrow (noun)	giindjuu	YR
bone needle (noun)	nhingal	YY, GR
bone (poison) (noun)	guuyarra	YR, YY
bony (adjective)	bilga	YY
	burabura	GR
	buyabuya	YR, YY
bony bream (noun)	biirrnga	YR, YY, GR
Boobera Lagoon, MacIntyre R. (placename)	Gawubuwan Gunigal	GR
boobook owl (noun)	guurrguurr	YY
book (noun)	biibabiiba	YR, YY
boomerang (noun)	barran	YR, YY, GR
boomerang (ceremonial, fighting) (noun)	dhiinbaay	YR, YY
boomerang (comeback) (noun)	gulagarranba	YR, YY
boomerang (fighting) (noun)	bubarraa	YR, YY
boomerang maker (noun)	barran.giiba	YR
Boomi (placename)	Bumaay	GR
Boorooma (placename)	Buruma	GR
boot (noun)	manduwii	YR, YY, GR
	nhangana	GR
bora (noun)	buurra	YR, YY, GR
bora ground (noun)	buurra	YR, YY, GR
	buurrabang	YY
bora-ground spirit (noun)	nhaagal	YY
bora message stick (noun)	dhulu buurra	YY
bora messenger (noun)	wuumaa	YY
bora ring (little) (noun)	bunbul	YR, YY
bora spirit (noun)	gayandaay	YR, YY
boss (noun)	burrul maadha	YR, YY
	dhuurranmay, maadha	YR, YY, GR

English *to* Gamilaraay/Yuwaalaraay/Yuwaalayaay Word List

boss shell

English	Translation
boss shell (noun)	dhuurranmay waa YY
bottle (noun)	baadhal YR, YY
bottom (noun)	bandji YR
	gumbul YR, YY
	mala YR, GR
	murru YR, YY, GR
bough shed (noun)	buuwayamba YY
bowed (adjective)	dhuli YY
bower (noun)	nhanu YR
bowerbird (spotted) (noun)	wiidhaa YR, YY, GR
box tree (bimble) (noun)	bibil YR, YY, GR
boy (noun)	birray YR, YY, GR
	burraay YR
	gabinya GR
boy at initiation (noun)	buurrabiyaay YY
boy at puberty (noun)	yarraybiyaay YY
boys (noun)	birraybirraay YR, YY, GR
bragging (adjective)	biiwanbiiwan YY
brain (noun)	gawu YR, YY
	gumbirri GR
branch (noun)	bungun, dharra GR
	gugul YY
	muyaan YR, YY
bread (noun)	dhuwarr YR, YY, GR
	gundal GR
	mandha YR, GR
	widja YR
bread (unleavened) (noun)	mandhamandha YR
break (verb-intransitive)	gama-y YR, YY
break (verb-transitive)	gama-li YR, YY, GR
break wind (verb-transitive)	buuba-li GR
bream (black) (noun)	banngala YR
bream (bony) (noun)	biirrnga YR, YY, GR
bream (silver) (noun)	gambaal YR, YY, GR
breast (noun)	ngamu YR, YY, GR
breastmilk (noun)	ngamu YR, YY, GR
breastplate (noun)	wambin YY
	wirrgun YR, YY
breath (noun)	buliirral YR, YY
breathe (verb-transitive)	buliirra-li YR, YY
Breeza (placename)	Biridja GR
Brewarrina (placename)	Burriiwarranha YR, YY, GR
bridle (noun)	burraaydal YR, YY
bridled nail-tail wallaby (noun)	mararra GR
	mayarra YR, YY
Brigalow (placename)	Burrigala GR
brigalow wattle (noun)	burrii GR
	barranbaa YR, YY
bring (verb-transitive)	gaa-gi YR, YY, GR
bring back (verb-transitive)	gaaguwi-y YR, YY
broad shield (noun)	burriin YR, YY, GR
broken-hearted (adjective)	yuwaarran YR
brolga (noun)	burraalga YR, YY, GR
bronzewing (flock) (noun)	galimaramara GR
bronzewing pigeon (noun)	dhamarr YR, YY, GR
brood comb (noun)	dhiinaa YR, YY, GR
broom (noun)	biimbal YY
broombush (noun)	biibaya YR, YY
brother (noun)	dhagaan YR, YY, GR
	galduman YR
brother (older) (noun)	dhaya YR, YY, GR
brother (younger) (noun)	galumaay YR, YY, GR
brother-in-law (noun)	gayandaay YR, YY
	biraman GR
brown (adjective)	gunagunaa YY
brown and yellow snake (noun)	babarra YR, YY
brown falcon (noun)	biyaagaarr YR, YY
brown snake (noun)	warrala YR, YY
brown treecreeper (noun)	bibi YR, YY
brownie (cake) (noun)	mundimundi dhuwarr YY
brush (noun)	biimbal YY
brush turkey (noun)	wagun YR, YY, GR
	wirrilaa YR, GR
brush (with leaves) (verb-transitive)	buudhi-rri YY
brushtail possum (noun)	mudhay YR, YY, GR
bubble (noun)	giin.gii YR, YY
bucket (noun)	baril GR
	walban YR, YY, GR
bucket base (noun)	buu^2 YR, YY
budda pea (noun)	gayga YY
budda tree (noun)	badha YR, YY
budgerigar (noun)	gidjirrigaa YR, YY, GR
bug (river) (noun)	babarrngaan YY
Bugaldie (placename)	Bagaldii GR
build (verb-transitive)	warrayma-li YR, YY, GR
Bukkulla (placename)	Bagala GR
bull (noun)	bulgirran GR
bull ant (noun)	burudha, gabiyan GR
	buyuga YR, YY
bullfrog (noun)	warrungan YY

English	Gamilaraay/Yuwaalaraay/Yuwaalayaay
bullock (noun)	bula GR
	giyarral YR, YY
bullroarer (noun)	garrarana, murrumanamanaa YR
	gayandaay YY
bulrush (cumbungi) (noun)	burrarra YR, YY, GR
bum (noun)	gumbul YR, YY
	mala YR, GR
	murru YR, YY, GR
bumpy (adjective)	madhamadha YR, YY, GR
bunch (noun)	mandjaarr YR
Bundarra (placename)	Bandaarraa GR
Bunna (placename)	Bana YY
bunnary tree (noun)	bunbarr YR, YY
buoyant (adjective)	nganangana YR, YY
burial bark (noun)	nhiirruu YY
burial ground (noun)	dhanmurr YR, YY
	dhawunma GR
buried (be) (verb-intransitive)	nhamurra-y YR, YY
burn (verb-intransitive)	gayla-y YR, YY
	gudhuwa-y YR
burn (verb-transitive)	gaylama-li YR, YY
	gudhuwa-li YR, YY, GR
burn (with a lot of flame) (verb-intransitive)	gundaawa-y YR
burn (with a lot of flame) (verb-transitive)	gundaawa-li YR, YY
burn with pain (verb-intransitive)	gudhuwa-y YR
burr (goat-head) (noun)	gulimugarr YR, YY
burr (marthaguy) (noun)	mugaadhaa YR, YY
Burren Junction (placename)	Barran GR
burrowing frog (noun)	galgalbanaa YR, YY
burst (verb-intransitive)	baarra-y YR, YY
burst (verb-transitive)	baarray-rri YR, YY
bury (verb-transitive)	nhamurra-li YR, YY
bush (noun)	wadhi YY
	yurrul YR, YY, GR
bush rat (noun)	dhunmidjirr YY
bush thick-knee (noun)	gurabi, wuruyan GR
	wuuyan YR, YY
bustard (Australian) (noun)	barawaa YR, GR
	gumbulgaban YR, YY
butcherbird (noun)	guluu YY
butcherbird (grey) (noun)	garriguwin.guwin YY
	guwaaydjiidjii YR, YY
butcherbird (pied) (noun)	buubuurrbu YY
butterfly (noun)	balabalaa YR, YY, GR
Byame (noun)	Baayami YR, YY, GR
Byame's son (noun)	Gindhayndaamuwi YR, YY
Byame's wife (noun)	Birrangulu YR, YY
	Ganhanbili YY
Byamee (placename)	Baayami GR

Cc

English	Gamilaraay/Yuwaalaraay/Yuwaalayaay
cabbage (noun)	gabirr YR
cactus (noun)	bindamula YR
cake (noun)	guwiirr widja YR
calf of leg (noun)	buyu YR, YY, GR
	wuruga GR
call (verb-transitive)	gaga-li YR, YY, GR
calm (adjective)	gayn.gayn[1] YY
calm (verb-transitive)	binaal bunma-li YR, YY
	gaynma-li YY
camel melon (noun)	ngayuun YR, YY
camp (noun)	gaarrimay YY
	walaay YR, YY, GR
camp (verb-intransitive)	baabi-li GR
	dhanduwi-y YR, YY
camp area (noun)	maraay YR
camp (bachelor's) (noun)	wiidhaga YR
camp (bad-weather) (noun)	dhirrinbaa YR
camp (woman's) (verb phrase)	gurruga baabay YY
can (tin can) (noun)	gaala YR
cane grass (noun)	wilgi YR, YY
cannibal (noun)	bana YY
canoe (noun)	ganuu YR
	nganda GR
canoe (bark) (noun)	bunduurraa YR, YY
canoe (tin) (noun)	dhaadharr YR
Canopus (star) (noun)	Wamba YY
can't (particle)	gamila GR
	waala YR, YY
car (noun)	marriga YR
	wilbaarr YR, YY
car spring (noun)	gadjul YR
carbeen (noun)	gaabiin YR, YY, GR
carbeen flowers (noun)	gagilaarriin YY
care for (verb-transitive)	galuma-li YR, YY
carefully (adverb)	maaru GR
	maayu YR, YY
carelessly (adverb)	gamil maaru GR
	waal maayu YY
carpenter's plane (noun)	gaynda YY
carpet python (noun)	yabaa YR, YY, GR
carrot (native) (noun)	dhalayndjaa YR
carry (verb-transitive)	gaa-gi YR, GR
	wamba-li YR, YY, GR
cart (noun)	wilbaarr YR, YY
carve (verb phrase)	mubirr dhu-rri YY
carve (verb-transitive)	dhu-rri YR
carving (noun)	mubirr YR, YY
cat (noun)	budjigarr YR, YY
	burrgiyan GR
catch (verb-transitive)	bayama-li YR, YY
	ganma-li GR
catch fish (verb-transitive)	yinabi-li YR, YY, GR
catch with instrument (verb-transitive)	yinabi-li YR, YY, GR
caterpillar (noun)	gararrngan GR
caterpillar (hairy) (noun)	dhurrun.gal YR, YY
catfish (noun)	gaygay YR, YY, GR
catfish (mud) (noun)	waay YY
cattle (noun)	giyarral YY
cattle race (noun)	wun.guwi YY
caught (be) (verb-intransitive)	bayama-y YR
cause (a change) (verb-transitive)	bunma-li, burranba-li YR, YY, GR
cave (noun)	biyuu[2], wadhu YR
cease doing (verb-intransitive)	garri-y GR
celebrate (verb-intransitive)	yuga-li GR
celebrate (verb phrase)	marra gi-gi GR
cemetery (noun)	dhanmurr YR, YY
	dhawunma GR
centipede (noun)	giiyan YY, GR
ceremonial boomerang (noun)	dhiinbaay YR, YY
ceremonial log (noun)	ginilgarriya YY
ceremonial smoke (noun)	wuyugil YR, YY
ceremonial stick (noun)	wilgu YY
ceremony (initiation) (noun)	buurra YR, YY, GR
chain lightning (noun)	dhun.gayrra YR, YY
champion (noun)	gandjarra YR
channel-billed cuckoo (noun)	dhuwaanbay YY
charcoal (noun)	nhii YR, YY
chase (verb-transitive)	gawaa-y YR, YY
chase away (verb-transitive)	yuwaba-y YR, YY
chasings (noun)	gubiyalanhay YR
chastise (verb-transitive)	nhuyu-gi YR
cheek (noun)	dhaal YR, YY, GR
cheeky (adjective)	dhigadhiga YR
	gadhaa YR
cheeky! (exclamation)	dhalay YR

English	Gamilaraay/Yuwaalaraay/Yuwaalayaay
cherry (native) *(noun)*	mirrii YR, YY
chest *(noun)*	bii YR, YY
	biri, ngubi GR
chest protector *(noun)*	wirrgun YR, YY
chew *(verb-transitive)*	nguuguuba-li YR
chick (emu) *(noun)*	barrgay^2 YR, YY, GR
chicken *(noun)*	baawul YR, YY
	djigin YR
chief *(noun)*	dhuurranmay YR, YY, GR
child *(noun)*	birralii YR, YY
	gaay^2, gaayli, gaaynmara GR
child (last) *(noun)*	buudhan YY
childless woman *(noun)*	marayrrdhuul GR
children's game *(noun)*	dhurran.gali YR
children's python *(noun)*	dhayaaminyaa YY
chin *(noun)*	ngagan YR, YY
Chinese man *(noun)*	dhaliman YR
	mil binggarr GR
chip *(noun)*	wiyay YR, YY
choke *(verb-intransitive)*	garra-y YR, YY
chop *(verb-transitive)*	baaya-li GR
	yaaya-li YR, YY
chopping noise *(noun)*	ban.gul YR, YY, GR
chough *(noun)*	wiiyuu YR
	wuuyuu YR, YY, GR
cicada *(noun)*	ngininnginin YR, YY
cicatrices *(noun)*	mubirr YR, YY, GR
cigarette *(noun)*	buubili GR
	mugu^2 YR
circumstance *(suffix)*	-DHi^1 YR, YY, GR
clamorous reed warbler *(noun)*	dhuwigalinmal YR, YY
clap hands *(verb phrase)*	maa buma-y YR, YY
	mara buma-y GR
claw *(noun)*	yulu YR, YY, GR
claw (crayfish) *(noun)*	muraabi YR
claypan *(noun)*	walanbarruu YR, YY
clean *(adjective)*	giliin YR
clear *(adjective)*	yirrgayn YR, YY
clear alcohol *(noun)*	balaa YY
	banggabaa YR
clear area *(noun)*	maraay YR
clever *(adjective)*	burrul bina YR
	dhaygaliyaay, wii YR, YY
	binangarrangarra, gaba dhaygal YY
clever man *(noun)*	wiringin YR, YY, GR
clever man's bag *(noun)*	bundurr YR, YY
clever man's spirit *(noun)*	malimali YR, YY
clever man's stick *(noun)*	birru YY
	wii muyaan YR, YY
climb *(verb-intransitive)*	galiya-y YR, YY, GR
clipped *(adjective)*	garragarraa YY
clock *(noun)*	yaayngarralgaa YY
close *(noun)*	milan^3 YR, GR
close *(noun, adjective)*	guwiin, guwiinbaa YR, YY, GR
close to a fire *(noun, adjective)*	guwiinbarraan YR
cloth *(noun)*	baya GR
clothes *(noun)*	baya GR
	bayagaa YR, YY
cloud *(noun)*	baama YY
	gundaa YR, YY, GR
	yuru GR
cloud (thunder) *(noun)*	dharringarra YR, YY
clover *(noun)*	galuuba YR, YY, GR
club *(noun)*	bundi YR, YY, GR
club (big, fighting) *(noun)*	bugu YR, YY
club (pointed) *(noun)*	murrula YR, YY, GR
club (small) *(noun)*	gudhurru GR
club (throwing stick) *(noun)*	wagarraa YR, YY
clumsy *(adjective)*	yarrbun maa YY
coals *(noun)*	nhigii YR, YY, GR
	wiinhii YR, YY
coat *(noun)*	guudii YR, YY
cockatiel *(noun)*	wiraarr GR
	wiyaarr YR, YY
cockatoo (Major Mitchell, pink) *(noun)*	gagalarrin YR, YY
cockatoo (possibly corella) *(noun)*	ngaanbanaa GR
cockatoo (red-tailed black) *(noun)*	biliirr YR, YY, GR
cockatoo (sulphur-crested, white) *(noun)*	muraay GR
	muyaay YR, YY
cod (Murray) *(noun)*	guduu YR, YY, GR
coffee *(noun)*	gabi YR
coffin *(noun)*	nhiirruu YY
Coghill *(placename)*	Gagil GR
cold *(adjective)*	baliyaa YR, YY
	garriil GR
cold *(noun)*	gunhugunhu YR, YY, GR

Collarenebri

Collarenebri (placename) ....Galariinbaraay YY, GR
collect (verb-transitive) ....guuma-li YR
colon (noun) ....mulama, ngamawidhalbaa YR
colon (crayfish) (noun) ....gindjulmaan YR
colon (descending) (noun) ....murrundunmali GR
coloured (many) (adjective) ......gagan.gagan YR, YY
comb (noun) ....baadal YY
comb (hair) (verb-transitive) ....baada-li YY
come (verb-intransitive) ....dhurra-li² YR, YY, GR
    yanaa-y, 'naa-y YR, YY
    yana-y GR
come back (verb-intransitive) ....dharrawu-li YR, GR
    dharrawuluwi-y YR, YY
    dhurraluwi-y YR, YY, GR
come near (verb-intransitive) ...guwiinba-li YR, YY
come out (verb-intransitive) ......gilgulba-rri YR, YY
comeback boomerang (noun) ....gulagarranba YR
common ant (noun) ....ganal GR
computer (noun) ....gayrragumbirri YR
Condamine River (placename) ....Gundhimayan GR
constant (adverb) ....giidjuugiidjuu YY
constipated (adjective) ....garran.garraan YY
consume all (verb-transitive) ...gurra-li YR
contradict (verb phrase) ....gana garranba-li YY
contrast (clitic) ....-bala YR, YY
converse (talk to each other) (verb-intransitive) ....guwaala-y YR
Coocoran Lake (placename) ...Gugurruwan YR, YY
cook (noun) ....gudhuwan YY
    warrgiiba YR, YY
cook (verb-intransitive) ....gayla-y YR, YY
    gudhuwa-y, yilama-y YR
cook (verb-transitive) ....wiya-gi GR
    yilama-li YR, YY
cook in a hole (roast) (verb-transitive) ....dhawuma-li YR, YY, GR
cooked (adjective) ....yiilay YY
coolabah flowers (noun) ....galariin YR, YY, GR
coolabah tree (noun) ....gulabaa YR, YY, GR
coolabah tree grub (noun) ....burrunggal YR, YY
coolabah tree gum (noun) ....giyiirr YY
coolamon (noun) ....bin.guwi YR, YY, GR
    guliman YR
coolamon (small) (noun) ....wirri YR, YY

cooler (noun) ....balanhii YR
Coonabarabran (placename) ....Gunabarabin GR
Coonamble (placename) ....Gunambil GR
Coorigel (placename) ....Guligal YY
copied (adjective) ....yaluuyaluu YY
corella (little) (noun) ....gadharra YY
    ngaanbanaa GR
cork (noun) ....nganangana YR, YY
cormorant (great black) (noun) ....wungayawaa YR, YY
    wurungayawaa GR
cormorant (little pied) (noun) ....birribangga YR, YY, GR
corner (noun) ....burrumbi YR
corner post (noun) ....giniybaal YR
correctly (adverb) ....gaba YR, YY, GR
corroboree (verb-intransitive) ...yuurrma-y YR, YY
corroboree ground (noun) ......gumbu YR, YY
corroboree leader (noun) ....murraan.gali YR, YY
cottonbush (noun) ....bagiluu YY
cough (noun) ....gunhugunhu YR, YY, GR
cough (verb phrase) ....gunhugunhu dhu-rri YR, YY, GR
couldn't (particle) ....gamila GR
    waala YR, YY
counsellor (noun) ....dhayndalmuu YR
country (holey) (noun) ....gurrumayuu YY
court (verb-intransitive) ....ngarrala-y YR
cousin (noun) ....dhagaan YY
    wambanhiiya YR, YY
cover (noun) ....burriin YY
cover (verb-transitive) ....buluba-li YR, YY
    gandawa-li GR
cover (self) (verb-intransitive) ...buluba-y YR, YY
cover up (verb-transitive) ....bulubama-li YR, YY
    marramba-li, yuurraa-li YR
covered (adjective) ....dhan.galan.gaa YR
covered (be) (verb-intransitive) ....buluba-y YR, YY
covered with (suffix) ....-bil YR, YY, GR
cow (noun) ....milambaraay YR, GR
    milambiyaay YY
cow horn (noun) ....nhalgaṉhalga YR, YY, GR
cow's paper gut (noun) ....biibii YY
Cowal (placename) ....Gaawal YY
Cowelba (placename) ....Gaawalbaa YY
crab (noun) ....ngalaagaa YR, YY

English	Gamilaraay/Yuwaalaraay/Yuwaalayaay	Source
crack (noun)	garra	YR, YY, GR
crack (verb-intransitive)	baarra-y	YR, YY
crack (verb-transitive)	baarray-rri	YR, YY
crack between teeth (verb-transitive)	baaya-li	YR
cracker on a whip (noun)	wulbul yiya	YY
cracks (skin) (noun)	yaydja	YR
cradle (noun)	wurranin	YR
crane (blue) (noun)	budhuulgaa, buyudhurrungiili	YR, YY
crane (bird) (noun)	garraagaa	YR, YY, GR
cranky (adjective)	gana garraa, yumbu	YR
crawl (verb-intransitive)	dhuu-rri	YR, YY, GR
crawler (noun)	dhiidjalaa	YR
crayfish (noun)	giirray	GR
	yin.ga	YR, YY
crayfish claw (noun)	muraabi	YR
crayfish colon (noun)	gindjulmaan	YR
crazy (adjective)	wamba	YR, YY, GR
creation spirit (noun)	Gali Gurunha	YR
Creator (Byame) (noun)	Burrulaa[2]	YY
creek (noun)	bagay	YR, GR
	dharra, mayan	GR
	gaawal	YR, YY, GR
	mabun	YR, YY
creek name (placename)	Mangalaalaa	YR
creep (verb-intransitive)	dhila-y	YR, YY
crested bellbird (noun)	banbandhuluwi	YR, YY, GR
crippled (adjective)	dhan.gurr	YR, YY, GR
crocodile (noun)	Garriya[1]	YR, YY
crooked (adjective)	warawara	GR
	wayawaya	YR, YY
	wiyal	YR
crosswise (adjective, adverb)	nganbirr	YY, GR
crow (noun)	waan[1]	YR, YY, GR
	waaruu[2]	YR, GR
crow (little) (noun)	waagaan	GR
	waagiyan	YR, YY
crowd (noun)	dharaa	YR
crowfoot (noun)	maayal	YR, YY, GR
crowfoot (blue) (noun)	dhawaarrii	YY
crucifix frog (noun)	bulga	YR, YY
cry (verb-intransitive)	yu-gi	YR, YY, GR
cry (make) (verb-transitive)	yubama-li	YR, YY
cry-baby (adjective)	yumbu	YR
cry-baby (noun)	yungiirr	YR, YY
cuckoo (channel-billed) (noun)	dhuwaanbay	YY
cuckoo (pallid) (noun)	mungin.gagalawaa	YR, YY
cuckoo-shrike (black-faced) (noun)	gunidjaa	YR, YY
cuddle (verb-transitive)	gulagama-li	YR, YY
cup (noun)	banigan	YR
curlew (noun)	gurabi, milbay, wuruyan	GR
	wuuyan	YR, YY
currant bush (noun)	gubigala	YY
	wayaarra	YR, YY
currant (drooping) (noun)	mirrii	YR, YY
Currawillinghi (placename)	Garrawilingaay	YR
currawong (noun)	galalu	GR
current (water) (noun)	yarrin	YY
cut (adjective)	garragarraa	YY
cut (verb-transitive)	garra-li	YR, YY, GR
cut (be) (verb-intransitive)	garra-y	YR, YY

Dd

English	Gamilaraay/Yuwaalaraay/Yuwaalayaay
dad *(noun)*	bubaa YR, GR
daddy *(noun)*	biila YY
damper *(noun)*	dhaamba YR, YY
dance *(verb-intransitive)*	yulu-gi YR, YY, GR
dance (make a corroboree) *(verb-intransitive)*	dhan.gurrama-y YR
dark *(noun)*	bangalaa GR
	buluuy YR, YY, GR
dark (before dawn) *(noun)*	muran YR, YY
Darling lily *(noun)*	dhaygalbaarrayn YR, YY
Darling pea *(noun)*	gilaan.garra YR, YY
darter *(noun)*	ganandhaal YY, GR
	gunambaal YR
daughter *(noun)*	miyay YY
	ngamurr GR
daughter-in-law *(noun)*	girrinya YY
dawn *(noun)*	ngarran[1] YR, YY, GR
day *(noun)*	yaadha YY
	yaraadha GR
daylight *(noun)*	dhuniya YR, YY
daytime *(noun)*	yaraadha GR
dead *(adjective)*	balu YR, YY, GR
dead person's things *(noun)*	buwarrgaa YR, YY
dead relative *(noun)*	guuguu YR, YY
dead tree *(noun)*	balal giniy YY
	balal muyaan YY
dead wood *(noun)*	giniy waal YR
deaf *(adjective)*	bina muurr,
	mugu bina YR, YY, GR
	muga bina YR, GR
	muga wudha YY
death adder *(noun)*	mundharr GR
	murrubi YR, YY
death stone *(noun)*	dhinagarralawaa,
	wuyugarralawaa YY
deceive *(verb-transitive)*	dhanggiwa-li YY
deep *(adjective)*	ganadhaa YR, YY
	gurruubaa YR, YY, GR
deep water *(noun)*	gaawaa YR
defecate *(verb-intransitive)*	guna-gi YR
dew *(noun)*	gugil YR, YY, GR
diamond dove *(noun)*	gubadhu YR, YY, GR
diarrhoea *(noun)*	bandibandi YY
	gindjul YR
didn't *(particle)*	waal YR, YY
	gamil GR
die *(verb-intransitive)*	balu-gi YR, YY, GR
dig *(verb-transitive)*	mawu-gi YR, YY, GR
digging stick *(noun)*	ganay YR, YY, GR
dillon bush *(noun)*	bibu YY
	mugiyala YR
dingo *(noun)*	maayn YR, YY
	marayn GR
dip *(verb-transitive)*	dhiyarra-li YR, YY
directly *(time adverb)*	yilaa YR, YY, GR
dirge *(noun)*	guunay YY
Dirranbandi *(placename)*	Dhurrunbandaay YY
dirt *(noun)*	dhawun GR
	dhaymaarr YR, YY
dirt (debris) *(noun)*	djulu YY
dirty *(adjective)*	bandu YR, YY
	dhawunbaraay GR
	gunagunaa YY
disappear *(verb-intransitive)*	dhaarri-y YR
disguised *(adjective)*	dhan.galan.gaa YR
disgusting *(adjective)*	gunagunaa YY
dish *(noun)*	guliman YR
dish (tin) *(noun)*	dhindiirr YR, YY
dive *(verb-intransitive)*	dhiinbi-y YR
	wunga-y YR, YY
	wurunga-y GR
diver (bird) *(noun)*	dhiinbin YR, YY, GR
do *(verb-transitive)*	gimbi-li YR, YY
do *(verb-transitive)*	gimubi-li GR
do with *(suffix)*	-Gu[1] YR, YY, GR
dobber *(noun)*	dhubayan YY
doctor (Aboriginal) *(noun)*	wiringin YR, YY, GR
doer to *(suffix)*	-Gu[1] YR, YY, GR
dog *(noun)*	buruma GR
	buyuma YR
	maadhaay YR, YY
	mirri YR, GR
dog bark *(noun)*	waalwaal YY
dogwood *(noun)*	yuurraa YR, YY, GR
dogwood flowers *(noun)*	yuuliin YY
dollar bird *(noun)*	dhanibanban YY
don't *(particle)*	garriya[2] YR, YY, GR
	waal YR, YY
	gamil GR
don't know *(suffix)*	-Waayaa YR
don't know where at *(place adverb)*	minyaayawaayaa YR

don't know where to
 (place adverb) .... minyaarruwaayaa YR
door (noun) .... girrinil GR
double-barred finch (noun) ... bilumbilum YR, YY
dove (diamond) (noun) .... gubadhu YR, YY, GR
dove (peaceful) (noun) .... gurugun YR, GR
down, down there
 (place adverb) .... ngadaa YR, YY, GR
down (of birds) (noun) .... yadhaarr YR, YY, GR
downstream (place adverb) ...... ngadaamali YR
downwards (place adverb) .... ngadaali YR, YY
drag (verb-transitive) .... dhuurrma-li YR, YY
dragonfly (noun) .... garrarana YR
 murrumanamanaa YR, YY
drawing stick (noun) .... dhumbaay YR
dream (verb phrase) .... yuwaya ngarra-li YR, YY
 yuwaya wiima-li YY
dreamtime (noun) .... burruguu YR
dress self (verb-intransitive) ...... wuu-gi YR, YY
dress someone
 (verb-transitive) .... wuuma-li YY
dribble (noun) .... wiiluun YR
Drilldool (placename) .... Dhariilduul GR
drink (verb-transitive) .... ngaru-gi GR
 ngawu-gi YR, YY
drink (honey) (noun) .... galindjari YR, YY
drip (verb-intransitive) .... dhulirra-li YR, YY, GR
 gaarri-y YR, YY
 yaarri-y GR
drive (verb-intransitive) .... banaga-y YY
drive (verb-transitive) .... budhu-li YR, GR
 gawaa-y YR, YY
drooping currant (noun) .... mirrii YR, YY
drop (verb-transitive) .... nhaanma-li YR, YY
drought (noun) .... garran.garra YY
drown (verb-intransitive) .... garungga-y YR, YY
drown (verb-transitive) .... garunggama-li YR
drunk (adjective) .... dharraa², dharraan.gilaay YR, YY, GR
dry (adjective) .... balal YR, YY, GR
dry (spread out to)
 (verb-transitive) .... guwima-li YY
duck (noun) .... garrangay YR, YY, GR
duck (Australasian
 shoveler) (noun) .... dhibayuu YR, YY, GR
duck (black) (noun) .... budhanbaa YR, YY

duck (grey teal) (noun) .... buuway YR, YY
duck (in water)
 (verb-transitive) .... muyuwa-li YR, YY
duck (musk) (noun) .... bagabagaali YR
 birraala YY, GR
duck (pink-eared) (noun) .... wilidhubaay YR
 wiligabuul YY
duck under (verb-intransitive) ... wunga-y YR, YY
duck (whistling) (noun) .... dhibayuu YR, YY, GR
 wululuu YY, GR
duck (wood) (noun) .... barrgabarrga YR, YY
duckweed (noun) .... bunibuni YY
dumb (speechless)
 (adjective) .... dhalaydhalibaa YR, YY
Dungalear Station
 (placename) .... Dhanggaliirr YR
dusk (noun) .... barrgin YY
dust (noun) .... yuu YR, YY, GR
dust storm (noun) .... burran YY
dweller in (suffix) .... -gayaluu YY

Ee

each other (reciprocal
    -*li* class verbs) *(suffix)*............-la-y YR, YY, GR
each other (reciprocal
    -*rri* class verbs) *(suffix)*...........-dha-y YR, YY, GR
eagle (wedge-tailed) *(noun)* ...maliyan YR, YY, GR
eaglehawk *(noun)*...........................wandhala GR
ear *(noun)*..bina YR, YY, GR
    manga YR
    wudha YY, GR
early morning *(time adverb)*....giibaabu YR, YY
earth *(noun)*......................................dhawun GR
    dhaymaarr YR, YY
earthquake *(noun)*.........................burruwi YY
earthworm *(noun)*..........................dhuyugarral YR, YY
ease up *(verb-intransitive)*...........buruwi-y GR
    buuwi-y YR, YY
east *(place adverb)*........................ngarribaa YR, YY, GR
east wind *(noun)*............................gunyamurr YR, YY
eat *(verb-transitive)*.......................dha-li YR, YY, GR
eccentric *(adjective)*......................wamba YR, YY, GR
echidna *(noun)*................................bigibila YR, YY, GR
    marrawal GR
echidna ant sack *(noun)*............gadhuu YR
echidna crop *(noun)*.....................wumbala YR
echidna (male) *(noun)*.................gadhuu YR
echidna quill *(noun)*......................wirayl GR
    wiyayl YR, YY
echidna (young) *(noun)*...............nhimaylii YR, YY
echo *(noun)*......................................ban.gul YR, YY, GR
    burruwi YR, YY
    wawal GR
eclipse of sun *(verb phrase)*......yaraay warra-y GR
edge *(noun)*......................................miimii² YY
edge (river's) *(noun)*....................miimii² YR, YY
eel *(noun)*..milanhay YR
egg *(noun)*..gawu YR, YY, GR
egg (frog) *(noun)*...........................giin.gii YR, YY
egg yolk *(noun)*..............................gawubaa YR
eggs (goanna) *(noun)*..................gulay YR
egret (great) *(noun)*......................baluun YR, YY
eight *(adjective)*.............................galay YR, YY, GR
either . . . or *(suffix)*......................-Yaa YR
elbow *(noun)*...................................dhiin GR
    ngunuugaa YR, YY, GR

electricity *(noun)*...........................gayrra YR
embrace *(verb-transitive)*............gulagama-li YR, YY
emerge *(verb-intransitive)*..........gilgulba-rri YR, YY
empty *(adjective)*..........................balal YR, YY, GR
emu *(noun)*......................................dhinawan YR, YY, GR
emu apple tree *(noun)*................guri GR
    guwi YR, YY
emu bush *(noun)*..........................ngawil YY
emu chick *(noun)*..........................barrgay² YR, YY, GR
emu chick (striped) *(noun)*.......bagabaga YY
emu decoy *(noun)*.........................buubuwin YY
emu feather *(noun)*......................gundiirr YR, YY
emu net *(noun)*..............................mirrun YY
emu (one male) *(noun)*...............ganduwi YR, YY
emu pair *(noun)*.............................bulawaa YR, YY
emu (sitting) *(noun)*....................ngurran.gali YR, YY
emu spear *(noun)*..........................munun YR, YY
emu tail *(noun)*..............................bubudhala YR, YY
emus (4) *(noun)*.............................wugalwugal YY
emus (5 or 6) *(noun)*....................gayaangay YY
emus (14 or 15) *(noun)*................ganurran YY
emus (group of) *(noun)*...............gambadhuul YR
enclosure *(noun)*............................ngunmal YY, GR
end *(noun)*..warran YR, YY, GR
engraving *(noun)*..........................mubirr YR, YY
enough! *(exclamation)*.................biyay YR
entrance *(noun)*............................ngaay YR, YY
eurah *(noun)*...................................yuurraa YR, YY, GR
evening *(time adverb)*.................bululuwi YR, YY, GR
everything *(pronoun)*..................ganungawu,
    gurrugurru² YR, YY
    minyaminyagaa YR, GR
    minyaminyabal GR
evil spirit *(noun)*...........................giniirr YR, YY
exhausted *(adjective)*...................yarrbun YR, YY
expression of praise
    (exclamation)......................waa² YR, YY, GR
expression of surprise
    (exclamation)......................nhaan YR
eye *(noun)*..mil YR, YY, GR
eye (black) *(noun)*.........................mil buluuy YR
eye (bloodshot) *(noun)*................mil guway YY
eye dirt (sleep) *(noun)*.................dhala YR, YY
eyebrow *(noun)*..............................dhinmirr YY, GR
    ngiirr GR
eyelash *(noun)*................................ngudjiin YR, YY

Ff

English	Translation
face *(noun)*	ngulu YR, YY, GR
faeces *(noun)*	guna YR, YY, GR
fairy martin *(noun)*	bidjaaymamal YY
falcon (brown) *(noun)*	biyaagaarr YR, YY
fall *(verb-intransitive)*	bundaa-gi YR, YY, GR
false *(adjective)*	yaal YR
family *(noun)*	dhiiyaan YR
family land *(noun)*	ngurrambaa YR, YY
fan *(noun)*	dhirra mara YR
far side *(noun)*	mulandha GR
fart *(noun)*	burray YR
fart *(verb-transitive)*	buuba-li GR
fast *(adverb)*	barraay YR, YY, GR
fat *(noun, adjective)*	wamu YR, YY, GR
father *(noun)*	baayna GR
	biiyalaa YY
	bubaa YR, GR
	buwadjarr YR, YY, GR
	yugin YR, YY
father-in-law *(noun)*	bambuy GR
	garruu YR, YY, GR
	ngarrawidhalba YR
father's mother *(noun)*	maamaa YR
father's sister *(noun)*	baaman, ngama GR
feather *(noun)*	wirriil GR
	yadhaarr YR, YY, GR
feather (emu) *(noun)*	gundiirr YR, YY
feathered stick *(noun)*	maadji YY
feathered tribe *(noun)*	dhigayaa YY
feel *(verb-transitive)*	dhama-li YR, YY, GR
feel sick *(verb-intransitive)*	dhaala-gi YR, YY
feel sorry for someone *(verb-transitive)*	ngarraga-li YY
fella *(noun)*	ngaamba YY
fellow *(noun)*	ngaamba YY
female *(noun)*	gunidjarr, gunidjarrbaa YR, YY, GR
fence *(noun)*	badi YR, YY
fetch *(verb-transitive)*	gaa-gi YR, YY, GR
few *(adjective)*	gulbirr YR
fierce snake *(noun)*	wularr YY
fight *(verb-intransitive)*	bumala-y YR, GR
fight (pretend) *(noun)*	yaambuwiirr YR, YY
fighting boomerang *(noun)*	bubarraa, dhiinbaay YR, YY
fighting club *(noun)*	bugu YR, YY
filament *(noun)*	barra YR, YY
fill *(verb-intransitive)*	muurra-y YY
fill *(verb-transitive)*	muurra-li YY
fin (fish) *(noun)*	bin.gal YR, YY
finch (double-barred) *(noun)*	bilumbilum YR, YY
find *(verb-intransitive)*	maniila-y YR, YY
find *(verb-transitive)*	ngaawa-y YY
fine rain *(noun)*	dhuubaarr YR, YY
finger *(noun)*	maa YR, YY
	mara GR
finger (first) *(noun)*	dhiriya GR
fingernail *(noun)*	yulu YR, YY, GR
	yulumara GR
fingers *(noun)*	bambugal GR
finished! *(exclamation)*	dhalay YR
fire *(noun)*	dhuu YY
	wii YR, YY, GR
fire (light/make a) *(verb phrase)*	wii wiima-li YR, GR
fire (sacred) *(noun)*	yanguuwii YR, YY
firestick *(noun)*	dhuuyaay, yiyabiyaay YR, YY
	wiibiyaay YR
firewood *(noun)*	wii YR, YY, GR
first *(adverb)*	waanda YR
first again *(adjective)*	milanburr YR, YY
first finger *(noun)*	dhiriya GR
fish *(noun)*	guduu, guwiya YR
	guya GR
	ngaaluurr YR, YY
fish *(verb-transitive)*	yinabi-li YR, YY, GR
fish (bobby) *(noun)*	wii YR, YY
fish fin *(noun)*	bin.gal YR, YY
fish intestines *(noun)*	wirraa YR, YY
fish net *(noun)*	dhaaliyaay YR, YY
	gulay GR
fish trap *(noun)*	badi YR, YY
fish (type of) *(noun)*	ngandan YY, GR
fishing line *(noun)*	buurr YR, YY, GR
	yalaayn YR
fishing spear *(noun)*	dhindi YY
five *(adjective)*	maa YR, YY, GR
fix *(verb-transitive)*	maaruma-li GR
	maayuma-li YR

flaking bark

English	Gamilaraay/Yuwaalaraay/Yuwaalayaay
flaking bark (noun)	dharraa YY, GR
flame (noun)	dhuu YY
	dhuuraay GR
	dhuuyaay YR, YY
flash (adjective)	dhirradhirra YY
flash (adverb)	dhirra YR, YY
flash (very) (adjective)	dhirrabuu YR
flat (adjective)	man.gaman.ga YY, GR
	manbu YY
flat (noun)	guniyal GR
flat-headed gudgeon (a fish) (noun)	nguluumanbuu YY
flea (noun)	bulii YR, YY
	biridja GR
flexible (adjective)	wulbuwulbu YY
flinty (very hard) (adjective)	gumba YY
float (self) (verb-intransitive)	banggadha-y YR, YY
	dhangga-y YR, YY
float (verb-transitive)	dhanggalma-li YR
floating (adverb)	nganangana YR, YY
flock bronzewing (noun)	galimaramara GR
flood (noun)	wugawa YR, YY, GR
flood peak (noun)	wugi YY
flour (noun)	bulaawa YR, YY
flow (water) (verb-intransitive)	banaga-y YR, YY
flower (noun)	gurayn GR
	guyayn YR, YY
flower of (suffix)	-Biyan YR, YY
flowering lignum (noun)	barrgay[1] YY
flowers (carbeen) (noun)	gagilaarriin YY
flowers (coolabah) (noun)	galariin YR, YY, GR
flowers (dogwood) (noun)	yuuliin YY
flowers (gidgee) (noun)	babarrabiin YR, YY
flowers (leopardwood) (noun)	baalaraan YR, YY
flowers (native orange tree) (noun)	bambulngiyan YR, YY
flowers (river gum) (noun)	yarraanbiin YY
flowers (river wattle) (noun)	gurrulayngayn YR, YY
flowers (whitewood) (noun)	birraawiin YY
fly (noun)	banhaayal YR, YY
	buna YR
	burruluu GR
fly (verb-intransitive)	bara-y[1] YR, YY
	barra-y GR
fly around, fly in a circle (verb-intransitive)	baragi-y YR, YY
fly-blown (adjective)	gamugamuubiyaay YR, YY
fly-catcher lizard (noun)	buumayamayal YR, YY
fly (horse) (noun)	baanduu YR, YY, GR
fly (house) (noun)	banhaayal YR, YY
fly (policeman) (noun)	gugun.gugun YR, YY
flying fox (noun)	bibaaya YY
flying fox (made of rope/wire) (noun)	galgandi YR
foal (noun)	biginini YY
foetus (noun)	dhinggal YR
fog (noun)	guwa YR, YY, GR
foggy (adjective)	guwan.guwan YR
fold (verb-transitive)	nguwa-li YR, YY
folded (adjective)	nguwan.nguwan YY
follow (verb-transitive)	gawaa-y YR, YY
follow (verb-intransitive)	yala-y YR, YY
fond (very) (adjective)	nhiiyanhiiya YR
food (noun)	mandha YR
	yuul YR, YY, GR
food (vegetable) (noun)	dhuwarr YR, YY
	yuul YR, YY, GR
foot (noun)	baburr, dhina YR, YY, GR
footprint (noun)	baburr YY
	dhina YR, YY, GR
for (suffix)	-gu[2] YR, YY, GR
forbidden (noun)	wanaal YY, GR
forehead (noun)	ngulu YR, YY, GR
foreigner (noun)	wiyaybaa YR, YY
foreskin (noun)	nyiinmaya GR
forget (verb phrase)	muurr gi-gi YR, YY, GR
forgetful (adjective)	wudha muurr YY
fork (noun)	mala YR, GR
fork (cutlery) (noun)	gula YR, YY
fork in tree (noun)	gula YR, YY
forked stick (noun)	dharran[1] YR, YY
formerly (adverb)	gibaylandhi GR
foster parent (noun)	gulumaldhaay YR, YY
four (adjective)	bulaarrbulaarr YY, GR
	bulawulaarr YR
	buligaa YR, YY, GR
fox (noun)	buumadhayaa YR
fragment (noun)	bilgin YR, YY, GR
freak (noun)	gayadharri YR
free (adjective)	maaydja YR
fresh (adjective)	yilaan.gaal YY
friar bird (noisy) (noun)	dhaguway YR, YY
fridge (noun)	balanhii YR

friend (noun)	baayamba, barringgu YR
	maliyaa, mamal YR, YY
friendless (adjective)	mamaldhalibaa YR, YY
frighten (verb-transitive)	giiyanma-li YR, YY, GR
frightened (adjective)	garigari, giyal YR, YY, GR
	gun.gun YR, YY
frilled lizard (noun)	balawagarr, dhalagal, dharri GR
	wuulaa YR, YY
frog (noun)	baaybal YR, YY
	gindjurra GR
frog (any) (noun)	yurayaa GR
	yuwayaa YR, YY
frog (bull) (noun)	warrungan YY
frog (crucifix) (noun)	bulga YR, YY
frog eggs (noun)	giin.gii YR, YY
frog (Sudells' frog/burrowing) (noun)	galgalbanaa YR, YY
frog (type of) (noun)	dharran² GR
frog (type of tree frog) (noun)	garrarr YR, YY
frogmouth (tawny) (noun)	buluurr YR, YY, GR
from (suffix)	-DHi¹ YR, YY, GR
from here (place adverb)	ngiilay YR, YY, GR
front (noun)	bani YR, YY
frost (noun)	dhandarr YR, YY, GR
froth (noun)	giin.gii YR, YY
fruit bat (noun)	bibaaya YY
fruit of (suffix)	-Biyan YR, YY
fruit (rosewood) (noun)	bunbarrayn YR, YY
frying pan (noun)	burraanban YR, YY
fuchsia (noun)	dhalandjaa YY
full (adjective)	dhumbil YR
	muurr YR, YY, GR
	ngaaybu YY
full of food (adjective)	yuularaay GR
	yuuliyaay YR, YY
full of food (be) (verb-intransitive)	garrabi-y YY
full of food (be) (verb phrase)	mubal muurra-y YY
full of water (adjective)	galibaraay GR
fully initiated man (noun)	buurrbaa GR
fully initiated young man (noun)	yiyalgidjaay YY
funeral smoke (noun)	dhuubaarr YR, YY
funeral song (noun)	guunay YY
fungus (plate) (noun)	bagal YY
funny (adjective)	gindarragaa YR
fur (noun)	dhurrun YR, YY, GR
fur cloak (noun)	garru YY
furry (adjective)	dhurrundhurrun YY
furry tribe (noun)	dhurrun.gal YY
furthermore (particle)	yiyaldu GR

Gg

galah (noun) .... gilaa YR, YY, GR
gall bladder (noun) .... gii YY
gamble (verb-intransitive) .... yulu-gi YR, YY, GR
game with discs and
  spears (noun) .... wanggalay YR, YY
game with leaf and fire
  (noun) .... wiimbirru YY
game with toy club (noun) .... garril budhal YY
Gamilaraay (Gamilaroi)
  language, tribe (noun) .... Gamilaraay YR, YY, GR
gammon (adjective) .... wagi² YR, YY
gammon (particle) .... yalbala YR, YY
gap (noun) .... garra YR, YY, GR
Garrawila (placename) .... Garrawila GR
gate (noun) .... badi ganaay YR
gate post (noun) .... yaarrbin YR
gather (verb-transitive) .... guuma-li YR
gecko (noun) .... wiibidi YR, YY
gecko (prickly) (noun) .... garragarraandi YR, YY
generation level (noun) .... manday² YY
generous (adjective) .... gayliyaay YR, YY
get down (verb-intransitive) ..... gaarri-y YR, YY
get up (verb-intransitive) .... warra-y YR, YY, GR
                                                    warraynga-y YR
ghost (noun) .... gaadhaay YR
                                                    wanda YR, YY, GR
gidgee (noun) .... gidjiirr YR, YY, GR
gidgee flowers (noun) .... babarrabiin YR, YY
gills (noun) .... yili YY
Gingie (noun) .... giin.gii YR
girl (little) (noun) .... mayrra YR, YY
                                                    miyaymiyaay YR, YY
girl (teenage) (noun) .... malagan YR, YY, GR
Girrawheen (placename) .... Girrawiin YR
give (verb-transitive) .... wuu-rri YR, YY, GR
give a hiding
  (verb-transitive) .... badha-y YR
give-and-take paddock
  (noun) .... ngaambiyan YR
gliding possum (noun) .... bagu YR, GR
glittering (adjective) .... ngandanganda YY
glue (noun) .... dhani YR
glutton (noun) .... buyumadhuul YR

go (verb-intransitive) .... yanaa-y, 'naa-y YR, YY
                                                    yana-y GR
go back (verb-intransitive) .... yanaawuwi-y,
                                                    dharrawuluwi-y YR, YY
go down (moon/sun)
  (verb-intransitive) .... wuu-gi YR, YY
                                                    gaarri-y YY
                                                    yaarri-y GR
go home (verb-intransitive) ..... yanaawuwi-y YR, YY
go hunting (verb-intransitive) .. maniila-y YR, YY
go into (verb-intransitive) .... wuu-gi YR, YY
go out (fire)
  (verb-intransitive) .... balu-gi YY
go to sleep (verb-intransitive) .. yuwarra-y YR, YY
goanna eggs (noun) .... gulay YR
goanna (sand) (noun) .... biiwii YR, YY
                                                    dhulii YR, GR
goanna (tree) (noun) .... galgarriirr,
                                                    guugaarr YR, YY
                                                    mangun.gaali YR, YY, GR
                                                    yurrandaali GR
goat (noun) .... nhaniguurr YR, YY, GR
                                                    wirribula GR
                                                    wirrigaali YY
goat-head burr (noun) .... gulimugarr YR, YY
God (noun) .... Baayami YR, YY, GR
goes to (leads)
  (verb-intransitive) .... gi-gi YR
going to (do something)
  (verb-intransitive) .... gi-gi YR, YY
golden bandicoot (noun) .... barrawan¹ YY
golden perch (noun) .... dhagaay YR, YY, GR
golden wattle (noun) .... gulgulay YY
good (adjective) .... marrabaa GR
good (adjective, adverb) .... gaba YR, YY, GR
good at (suffix) .... -dhaan YR, YY, GR
good-hearted (adjective) .... gayliyaay YR, YY
good hunter (noun) .... dhiidhaan YR, GR
good job! (exclamation) .... giirr maaru GR
                                                    giirr maayu YR, YY
good-looking (adjective) .... gaba ngulu YR, YY
                                                    dhaylngulu YR
good mood (adjective) .... gaba guuyay YR, YY
good season (noun) .... ngulawaa YY
Goodooga (placename) .... Guduuga YR, YY
Goolhi (placename) .... Guli GR
Goonoo (placename) .... Gunu YY

English	Language
Goonoo Goonoo (placename)	Gunu Gunu GR
gooseberry (native) (noun)	bulabul YY
gradually (adverb)	badjinbal YY
grain (noun)	guli YY, GR
grandchild (son's child) (noun)	nganawayngaa YY
grandchild (son's or daughter's child) (noun)	nhanuwaaydji YR
granddaughter (noun)	bawanngaa YR, YY
grandfather (mother's father) (noun)	dhaadhaa YR, YY, GR
grandfather (father's father) (noun)	dhilaagaa YR, YY
grandmother (noun)	miimii¹ YR
	baagii YR, YY
grandmother (father's mother) (noun)	garrimaay, mamaay GR
	ngaagii YR, YY
grandmother (mother's mother) (noun)	baagii YR, YY
	badhii, waabi GR
	gaadhii YR
grandson (noun)	galimingaa YR, YY, GR
grandson (daughter's son) (noun)	dhaadhaa YR, YY, GR
grandson (son's son) (noun)	waaruu¹ GR
grass (noun)	buunhu YR, YY
	garaarr GR
grass (cane) (noun)	wilgi YR, YY
grass (fairy) (noun)	dhunbarr YR, YY
grass hut (noun)	ngana YY
grass (plains) (noun)	ganalay YY
grass seed (noun)	dhunbarr YR, YY
grasstree (noun)	dhalan GR
grass windbreak (noun)	ngana YY
grasshopper (noun)	bunbun YR, YY, GR
grassy (adjective)	buunhuumayuu YR, YY
grave (noun)	biyuu² YR
	gurru YR, YY, GR
gravy (noun)	wirrun YR, YY
great black cormorant (noun)	wungayawaa YR, YY
	wurungayawaa GR
great egret (noun)	baluun YR, YY
great-uncle (mother's mother's brother) (noun)	dhilaagaa YR, YY
greedy (adjective)	dhurrin² YR, YY
	galambiirr YR
green (adjective)	gawarrawarr YR, YY, GR
	giidjuwaa YY
green tree frog (noun)	ngayrrngayrr YR, YY
green (unripe) (adjective)	dhurrin YR, YY
greenhead ant (noun)	bayaarr YR, YY
	muwan GR
greetings (exclamation)	yaama YR, YY, GR
	yaamagara GR
grey (adjective)	dhadhaal, dhuwa YR
	dhiriya GR
grey butcherbird (noun)	guwaaydjiidjii YR, YY
grey colour/shape (noun)	guwin YY
grey-crowned babbler (noun)	dhadhalurraa YR, YY
grey-fronted honeyeater (noun)	djiibirrirr YY
grey haired (adjective)	dhandarriyaay YR, YY
grey kangaroo (noun)	bandaarr YR, YY, GR
grey one (noun)	dhuwadhuul YR
grey shrike-thrush (noun)	dhan.galaadhil GR
	dharruwii YR, YY
grey snake (noun)	ngabi YY
	nhiibi GR
grey teal duck (noun)	buuway YR, YY
grindstone (large) (noun)	dhayurr YR, YY
grindstone (small) (noun)	giba YR, YY
ground (noun)	dhawun GR
	dhaymaarr YR, YY
ground-dwelling animals (noun)	dhaymaadhi YY
ground (hard) (noun)	walan.gumba YY
ground (high) (noun)	dhirrin YY
ground orchid (noun)	guumay GR
ground parrot (noun)	barrangga GR
group (suffix)	-gal YY
group of emus (noun)	gambadhuul YR
group of two (suffix)	-gaali YR, YY
grow (verb-intransitive)	dhurra-li² YR
grow (verb phrase)	burrul gi-gi YY
grub (noun)	birraa², gararrngan GR
grub (bogong moth) (noun)	birrga YR, YY
	yuluumaarraa YY
grub (coolabah tree) (noun)	burrunggal YR, YY
grub (gum tree) (noun)	yarraangan YR, YY, GR
grub hook (noun)	ngay² YR, YY

grub (sandalwood tree)
   (noun) .... garruuyal YY
grub (spitfire) (noun) .... maliga YR, YY
grub (whitewood) (noun) .... wungala YR, YY
gruie (noun) .... guri GR
                                              guwi YR, YY
gully (noun) .... mabun YR, YY
gum (from coolabah tree)
   (noun) .... giyiirr YY
gum (from trees) (noun) .... dhani YR, YY
gum tree grub (noun) .... yarraangan YR, YY, GR
gum tree (river red) (noun) .... yarraan YR, YY, GR
gum tree (spotty river)
   (noun) .... yumu YR, YY
gun (noun) .... marrgin YR, YY, GR
gundabluie wattle (noun) .... ngaduwi YR, YY
Gunnedah (placename) .... Gunidjaa,
                                              Gunudha GR
Gurah (placename) .... Garra GR
Gurly Station (placename) .... Gurrulay YY
gush out (verb-intransitive) .... yuuga-y YY
gut (verb phrase) .... mubal dhiyama-li YY
                                              mubal dhuwima-li YR, YY
guts (noun) .... mubal YR, YY, GR
Gwydir River (placename) .... Guwayda GR
gypsum (lime) (noun) .... gunu YY

Hh

habitual (suffix) .... -awaa YR, YY
                                              -ngayi-li YR
hailstone (large) (noun) .... dharayan GR
                                              dhayan YR, YY
hailstone (small) (noun) .... yiyagungawuma YR, YY
hair (noun) .... dhurrun YR, YY, GR
hair (body, pubic) (noun) .... budhi YR, YY, GR
hair (head) (noun) .... balandharr YY
                                              dhaygal YR, YY, GR
                                              gawugaa GR
hair-string belt (noun) .... buurr GR
hairy (adjective) .... dhurrundhurrun YY
hairy caterpillar (noun) .... dhurrun.gal YR, YY
hairy melon (noun) .... baaya YY
half (noun) .... mulan YY
half-caste (noun) .... gugan YR
halo around moon (noun) ...... gungurima GR
halo around moon/sun
   (noun) .... garrul YR
hammer (noun) .... bumal YR, YY
hand (noun) .... maa YR, YY
                                              mara GR
handkerchief (noun) .... yanggiidjaa YR, GR
hang (verb-intransitive) .... binda-y YR, YY, GR
hang up (verb-transitive) .... bindama-li,
                                              bindaybi-li,
                                              mayabi-li YR, YY, GR
happy (adjective) .... gayaa YR, YY, GR
hard (adjective) .... walan, walanbaa YR, YY
hard (adjective, adverb) .... ngaarr GR
hard ground, hard thing
   (noun) .... walan.gumba YY
hard-hearted (adjective) .... walanduurr YY
hard (with force) (adverb) .... bamba YR, YY, GR
hat (noun) .... gabugaan GR
                                              gabundi YR, YY, GR
have (verb-transitive) .... gaa-gi YR, YY, GR
have sex (verb-transitive) .... dhaa-rri GR
                                              dhu-rri YR, YY
having (suffix) .... -baraay, -araay GR
                                              -biyaay, -iyaay YR, YY
he (doer/doer to) (pronoun) ... nguru GR
                                              nguu[1] YR, YY

English	Language	Dialect
head (noun)	dhaygal	YR, YY
	gawugaa	GR
head hair (noun)	balandharr	YY
	dhaygal	YR, YY, GR
	gawugaa	GR
headache (noun)	gagil dhaygal	YR
headache (verb phrase)	dhaygal gaya-y	YR
headband (noun)	gulal	YR, YY
headband (plaited) (noun)	ngulugaayrr	YR, YY, GR
heal (verb-transitive)	gabanma-li, maayuma-li	YR
	maaruma-li	GR
healer's totem (noun)	yanbiyaay	YY
hear (verb-transitive)	winanga-li	YR, YY, GR
heart (noun)	gii	YR, YY, GR
heart wood (noun)	dhuwi	GR
heat (noun)	buuyan	YR
heaven (noun)	balima	YR, YY
	dhiiyaanmaa	YR
	gunagala	YR, YY, GR
heavy (adjective)	madhanbaa	YR, YY, GR
heavy blood group (noun)	guwaymadhan	YR, YY, GR
heavy (very) (adjective)	madhanmadhan	YY
heel (noun)	dhanga	YR, YY, GR
hello (exclamation)	yaama	YR, YY, GR
	yaamagara	GR
help (verb-transitive)	banma-li	GR
her (pronoun)	ngurunga	GR
	nguunga	YR, YY
her(s) (pronoun)	ngurungu	GR
	nguungu	YR, YY
here (demonstrative)	nhalay	YR, YY, GR
here (place adverb)	nguwa	YR, YY, GR
	nguwalay	YR
here (hereabouts) (place adverb)	nguwalay	YY
hermit (noun)	baarrgiin	YR
heron (nankeen night) (noun)	dhaarrin.gaarrin	YR, YY
	dharrun	YR, YY, GR
heron (white-faced) (noun)	budhuulgaa, buyudhurrungiili	YY
hey! (exclamation)	baaydjarr	YR, YY
	maaya, yii	YR
	yagaay	YR, YY, GR
hey (wake up)! (exclamation)	yaa	YR
hiccup (noun)	giguwi	YR, YY
hiccup (verb phrase)	giguwi dhu-rri	YR
hide (verb-intransitive)	guuma-y	YY
hide (verb-transitive)	gadhamayawa-li	YR, YY
hide and seek game (noun)	waaguu	YR, YY
hide (plant) (verb-transitive)	dhuwinba-li	YR, YY
hide (self) (verb-intransitive)	dhuwinba-y	YR
high (place adverb)	ngarribaa	YR, YY, GR
high ground (noun)	dhirrin	YY
	dhuyul	YR, YY, GR
high place (noun)	gaburran	YR
hill (noun)	dhuyul	YR, YY, GR
	gaba²	GR
hilly (adjective)	dhuyuldhuyul	YY
him (done to) (pronoun)	ngurunga	GR
	nguunga	YR, YY
hip (noun)	baa	YY
	mila	GR
his (pronoun)	ngurungu	GR
	nguungu	YR, YY
hit (verb-transitive)	buma-li	YR, YY, GR
hit (be) (verb-intransitive)	buma-y	YR
hit man (noun)	bumaldaay	YY
hitching rail (noun)	yaarrbin	YR
hitting stick (noun)	bumal	YR, YY
hitting thing (noun)	bumal	YR, YY
hobble (verb-intransitive)	wirraa-y	YR, YY, GR
hold (verb-transitive)	bayama-li, gulagama-li	YR, YY
	ganma-li	GR
hold on (particle)	gamilu	GR
	waalu	YR, YY
hole (noun)	biruu²	GR
	biyuu²	YR, YY
	gurru	YR, YY, GR
holey country (noun)	gurrumayuu	YY
hollow (adjective)	biruubaraay	GR
	biyuubiyaay	YY
hollow tree (noun)	burran.gul	YR
	ngadhul	YR, YY, GR
home (noun)	dhaymaarr	YR, YY
	walaaybaa	YR, YY, GR
home country (noun)	walaaybaa	YR, YY, GR
honey (noun)	warangana	YR, YY
	warrul	YR, YY, GR
honey drink (noun)	galindjari	YR, YY
honey (pure) (noun)	gugal	YY
honeyeater (grey-fronted) (noun)	djiibirrirr	YY

English	Gamilaraay/Yuwaalaraay/Yuwaalayaay
hooded robin (noun)	biibin YY
hook (noun)	wuu YY
	yinabil GR
hook (grub) (noun)	ngay² YR, YY
hook out (grub) (verb phrase)	ngaydju dhiyama-li YY
hop (verb-intransitive)	baa-y YR, YY
	bara-y GR
hop bush (noun)	yiilay YR, YY
horn (cow) (noun)	nhalganhalga YR, YY
hornet (noun)	guwaa GR
	muundhuurr YR, YY
hornet (mud) (noun)	dhanbadhanba YY
horse (noun)	yarraaman YR, YY, GR
horse fly (noun)	baanduu YR, YY, GR
horse (stick) (noun)	wulbul yaal YR
horseshoe (noun)	gumbiyaa YR
hot (adjective)	wiibiyaay YY
hot (be) (verb-intransitive)	gudhuwa-y YR, GR
hotel (noun)	babuligaarr YR, YY
house (noun)	gundhi YR, YY, GR
house fly (noun)	banhaayal YR, YY
how? (question word)	galaarr, gulaarr YR, GR
how many? (question word)	minyangay YR, YY, GR
human shadow (noun)	malawil YR, YY
humour (noun)	guuyay YR, YY, GR
humped (adjective)	dhumbil YR
humpy (noun)	walaay YR, YY, GR
humpy (little) (noun)	wayway YR
hundred (adjective)	barriga YR, YY, GR
hungry (adjective)	yuulngin YR, YY, GR
hunt, go hunting (verb-intransitive)	maniila-y YR, YY
hunt away (verb-transitive)	yuwaba-y YR, YY
huntsman spider (noun)	gurra YR, GR
husband (noun)	guliirr YR, YY, GR
hush! (exclamation)	gaabu YR
husky voice (noun)	ngurrgun YY
hut (bark) (noun)	dhaadharr YR, YY, GR
hut (grass) (noun)	ngana YY

Ii

English	Gamilaraay/Yuwaalaraay/Yuwaalayaay
I (pronoun)	ngaya YR, YY, GR
ibis (noun)	murrgumurrgu YR, YY
	yuwagayrr GR
ice (noun)	dhandarr YR, YY, GR
if (question word)	yaamagaa YR, YY
imitate speech (verb phrase)	gaay gawaa-y YR, YY
immediately (time adverb)	baayanbuu
	barraaywan YY
important man (noun)	yuurray YR, YY
in (suffix)	-Ga YR, YY, GR
in (be) (verb-intransitive)	wa-y YR, YY
in front (place adverb)	biridji GR
inhabitants of (suffix)	-gayaluu YY
initiated man (noun)	yuurray YR, YY
initiated youth (noun)	guburra GR
initiation ceremony (noun)	buurra YR, YY, GR
initiation ground (noun)	buurra YR, YY, GR
	gunaba GR
initiation ground pathway (noun)	dhunbarran GR
initiation leader (noun)	mandhiigan YY
initiation scars (noun)	mubirr YR, YY, GR
initiation song (noun)	burrambuurra YR, YY
insect (noun)	gawu YR, YY, GR
insect (long-legged) (noun)	dharrabilay YY
insects (noun)	gawugalgaa YY
inside (noun)	dhuwi GR
	mudhu YR, YY
inside (be) (verb-intransitive)	wa-y YR, YY
in that manner (adverb)	yalagiirrma YR, GR
intelligent (noun)	binangarrangarra YY
intestines (fish) (noun)	wirraa YR, YY
intestines (large, sheep) (noun)	yaray GR
intestines (small, sheep) (noun)	galinggaa YR, YY, GR
intonation (noun)	dhaalan YY
iron (noun)	gumbadhaa YR, YY
iron pot (noun)	nhayamban GR
ironbark (silver) (noun)	dhiinyaay YR, YY, GR
ironwood (noun)	dhan.gayan.gan YR, YY
itch (verb-intransitive)	gii-gi YR, YY
	giiri-gi GR
itchy (adjective)	giyalgiyal YR, YY

Jj

jackeroo (noun)	bawurra YY
Jacky Winter (bird) (noun)	dhunidjuni YR, YY
jagged spear (noun)	mirringamu YR, YY, GR
jail (noun)	yalaa YR, YY
jaw, jawbone (noun)	dhaal YR, YY, GR
jealous (adjective)	buularaay GR
	buuliyaay YR, YY
jealousy (noun)	buul¹ YR, YY, GR
jew lizard (noun)	dhayarr YY
juice (noun)	wirrun YR, YY
juicy (adjective)	wirrunbiyaay YY
jump (verb-intransitive)	baa-y YR, YY
	bara-y² GR
jump in (verb-intransitive)	bumbaali-y YR
jump into water (game) (verb-intransitive)	babaaluma-y YR, YY
jumper ant (noun)	milbaawaay YR, YY
	milbarawaay GR
just (adverb)	yiyal YR, YY, GR
just (suffix)	-biyal YR, GR

Kk

Kalmundi (placename)	Galimandi YR
Kamilaroi language, tribe (noun)	Gamilaraay YR, YY, GR
kangaroo (grey) (noun)	bandaarr YR, YY, GR
kangaroo rat (noun)	dhurrawaay GR
	gunharr YR, YY, GR
kangaroo rat (bettong) (noun)	milaya YY
kangaroo (red) (noun)	bawurra YR, YY, GR
	ganuurr GR
kangaroo tooth ornament (noun)	yambiyan YY
kangaroo (western grey) (noun)	wamburr YY
kangaroo (western grey — nickname) (noun)	nhuwiwan YY
keep (verb-transitive)	garrawa-li YY
kestrel (Australian, nankeen) (noun)	wala YR, YY
kick (verb-transitive)	gigirrma-li YR, GR
kidney (noun)	mugarr YR, YY, GR
Kigwigil (placename)	Gigwidjil YR
kill (verb-transitive)	buma-li YR, YY, GR
	balubuma-li YY, GR
	gayawi-li YR, YY
kill (stone dead) (verb phrase)	nhuwigu buma-li YR
kind (adjective)	gayliyaay YR, YY
	mulabiyaay YR
kindling (noun)	wugan.galgaa YR
king brown snake (noun)	ngandabaa YR, YY, GR
kingfisher (red-backed) (noun)	dhaadhiirr YR, YY, GR
kingfisher (sacred) (noun)	bunduun YR, YY
kiss (verb)	yabi-li YR, YY
kiss (verb phrase)	ngaay gaya-li YR, YY, GR
kiss (verb-transitive)	ngayaga-li YR, YY
kite (black) (noun)	manggarraan YR, YY, GR
kite (black-breasted) (noun)	wugamaabaydaa YR, YY, GR
kite (whistling) (noun)	biya YY
knead (verb-transitive)	bama-li GR
knee (noun)	dhinbirr YR, YY, GR
knee (back of) (noun)	gayarr YY

English	Gamilaraay/Yuwaalaraay/Yuwaalayaay
kneel *(verb phrase)*	dhinbiya warra-y YR, YY
knife *(noun)*	mambul YR
	nhaayba YR, YY, GR
knife (stone) *(noun)*	magal YR, YY
knock down *(verb-transitive)*	bundaama-li YR, YY, GR
knot *(verb-transitive)*	yulaa-li YR, YY, GR
knot (tree) *(noun)*	buul² YY
	nhay YR, YY
knotty *(adjective)*	buulbuul YY
	madhamadha YR, YY, GR
know *(verb-transitive)*	dhiirra-y,
	winanga-y YR, YY, GR
knowledgeable *(adjective)*	dhuurran YY
knuckle *(noun)*	biyal GR
koala *(noun)*	guba YR
	guda YY, GR
kookaburra *(noun)*	gugurrgaagaa YR, YY, GR
kurrajong bark *(noun)*	giyawaan YR, YY
	muramin YY
kurrajong country people *(noun)*	Nhunggabarra YY
kurrajong tree *(noun)*	nhimin GR
	nhungga YR, YY

Ll

English	Gamilaraay/Yuwaalaraay/Yuwaalayaay
lacking *(suffix)*	-dhalibaa YR, YY, GR
lactating female *(noun)*	maamii YR
lagoon *(noun)*	gaawal YR, YY, GR
	dhanggaal YR, YY
lake name *(placename)*	Maandhi YR
lame *(adjective)*	dhan.gurr YR, YY, GR
land yam *(noun)*	gugumadharraa YR, YY
language *(noun)*	gaay YR, YY
large bark vessel *(noun)*	yabil YY
large grindstone *(noun)*	dhayurr YR, YY
large hailstone *(noun)*	dharayan GR
	dhayan YR, YY
large locust *(noun)*	ngarrala YR, YY, GR
large mussel *(noun)*	dhanggal YR, YY, GR
large oval fungus *(noun)*	wayway YR, YY
large saltbush *(noun)*	binamayaa YR, YY
later (long time) *(time adverb)*	yilaalu YR, YY, GR
later on *(time adverb)*	baayandhu YR
laugh *(verb-intransitive)*	gindama-y YR, YY, GR
law *(noun)*	bigan YY
lawful *(adjective)*	biganbiyaay YY
lay egg *(verb-transitive)*	gaanga-y YR, YY
lazy *(adjective)*	yinggil YR, YY, GR
leader *(noun)*	burrulaabaa YY
	dhuurranmay YR, YY, GR
leader (corroboree) *(noun)*	murraan.gali YR
leaf *(noun)*	buu³ GR
	garril YY, GR
	girraa YR, YY
leaf litter *(noun)*	gagarr YR, YY
leak *(verb-intransitive)*	gaarri-y YR, YY
	yaarri-y GR
lean *(verb-intransitive)*	nganbi-y YR, YY
lean *(verb-transitive)*	nganbima-li YR
lean meat *(noun)*	bana YR, YY, GR
lean over *(verb-intransitive)*	dhuli-y YR
leaning *(adjective)*	dhaandiyaay YR, YY
leave *(verb-transitive)*	wana-gi YR, YY
leave alone *(verb-transitive)*	dhabima-li YR, YY, GR
	dhiirrma-li YR, YY
leaves *(noun)*	girran.girraa YR, YY
leaves used for burying *(noun)*	yilbin YY

English	Translation
leech (noun)	guurrman YR, YY, GR
left (noun)	wara GR
	waya YR, YY
left, left-handed (adjective)	waragaal GR
	wayagaal YR, YY
leg (noun)	dharra YR, YY, GR
leg (calf of) (noun)	wuruga GR
leg (all, lower) (noun)	buyu YR, YY, GR
legless lizard (noun)	binadhiwuubiyan YR, YY
lemonwood (noun)	dharriwa YR
leopardwood flowers (noun)	baalaraan YR, YY
leopardwood tree (noun)	bagala YR, YY, GR
let go (verb-transitive)	yanaaynbi-li YR, YY
let (something happen) (particle)	wana YR, YY, GR
letter (noun)	biiba YR
lice (noun)	munhi YR, YY, GR
lick (verb-transitive)	dhiidja-li YR, YY
lid (noun)	gabundi YY
lie (noun)	wagi² YR, YY
	yaal YR, YY, GR
lie (verb-intransitive)	wi-y YR, GR
lie (down) (verb-intransitive)	dhanduwi-y YR, YY
lie (tell a) (verb phrase)	yaal dhanggi-li GR
lie (tell a) (verb-transitive)	dhanggi-li GR
lift up (verb-transitive)	dhiyama-li YR, YY, GR
light (noun)	dhuuraay GR
	dhuuyaay YR, YY
	wii YR, YY, GR
light a fire (verb phrase)	wii wiima-li YR, GR
light blood group (noun)	guwaygaliyarr YR, YY, GR
light (fire/lamp) (verb-transitive)	wulanabi-li YR, YY, GR
light (not heavy) (adjective)	gabanbaa YR, YY, GR
lightning (noun)	dhun.gayrra YR, YY
	murrumay YR, YY, GR
lignum (noun)	mirriyaa YR, YY
	mirriraa GR
lignum country people (noun)	Mirriyaabarra YY
lignum fuchsia (noun)	barrgay¹ YY
like (suffix)	-giirr YR, YY, GR
like that (adverb)	yalagiirrma YR, GR
lily (Darling) (noun)	dhaygalbaarrayn YR
lime gypsum (noun)	gunu YY
lime (native) (noun)	gayn.gayn² YR, YY
limp (verb-intransitive)	wirraa-y YR, YY, GR
lip (noun)	gumay GR
	yili YR, YY, GR
listen (verb-transitive)	winanga-li YR, YY, GR
listen! (exclamation)	yiiy YR
little (suffix)	-DHuul YR, YY, GR
little (adjective)	badjin, dhugaay YR, YY
	bubaay YR
	gaay, gaaynmara GR
little (affectionate) (suffix)	-ili YY
little bora ring (noun)	bunbul YR, YY
little corella (noun)	gadharra YY
little crow (noun)	waagaan GR
	waagiyan YR, YY
little girl (noun)	mayrra YR, YY
	miyaymiyaay YR, YY
little (hairy) people (noun)	gudiny YY
	winambuu YR
little humpy (noun)	wayway YR
little one (noun)	dhugaadjuul YR
little pied cormorant (noun)	birribangga YR, YY, GR
little plains lizard (noun)	birriyan YY
little red lizard (noun)	gadha YY
little song (noun)	yugali YY
live (verb-intransitive)	dhanduwi-y YR
	wila-y YR, GR
	yilawa-y YY
liver (noun)	gana YR, YY, GR
lizard (blue-tongue) (noun)	wubun YR, YY
lizard (fly-catcher) (noun)	buumayamayal YR, YY
lizard (jew) (noun)	dhayarr YY
lizard (little plains) (noun)	birriyan YY
lizard (little red) (noun)	gadha YY
lizard (nickname) (noun)	murrawa YR
lizard (shingleback) (noun)	garrbaali YR, YY
	manggaay GR
lizard (sleepy) (noun)	wurumal GR
lizard (small dragon) (noun)	gumawuma YR, YY, GR
lizard (tree) (noun)	waluubaal YR, YY, GR
locust (large) (noun)	ngarrala YR, YY, GR
locust (small) (noun)	ngininnginin YR, YY
log (noun)	nhaadhiyaan YR, YY
log bridge (noun)	gulaay YR, YY
log (shelly) (noun)	dhan.gal YR, YY
loincloth (possum fur) (noun)	gumilaa YR, YY, GR
lonely (adjective)	walingay YR, YY

English	Gamilaraay/Yuwaalaraay/Yuwaalayaay
lonely (be) *(verb-intransitive)*	walindja-li YR
long *(adjective)*	guraarr GR
	guyaarr YR, YY
long-nailed spirit *(noun)*	Yuluwaya YR, YY
long-necked shag *(noun)*	ganandhaal YY, GR
	gunambaal YR
long-necked turtle *(noun)*	girrabirrii YR, YY, GR
	maliyan YR
long time ago *(time adverb)*	yilaalu YR, YY, GR
	yilambu GR
long time later *(time adverb)*	yilaalu YR, YY, GR
long way *(noun)*	biruu¹ GR
	biyuu¹ YR, YY
look *(verb-intransitive)*	ngarra-y YR, YY
look *(verb-transitive)*	ngami-li GR
	ngarra-li YR, YY
look! *(exclamation)*	yagaay YR, YY, GR
look after *(verb-transitive)*	ngarrangarra-li YR, YY
look at (greedily) *(verb-transitive)*	gunmi-li YR
look for *(verb-intransitive)*	maniila-y YR, YY
look for *(verb-transitive)*	gayarra-gi YR, YY, GR
	ngaawa-y YY
look out! *(exclamation)*	nhama dhaay YR
loose *(adjective)*	buwabuwa YY
lose *(verb-transitive)*	yuluurrinma-li YR
	yuuwaanmi-li YY
lost *(adjective)*	warrayaa YR, YY
lost (be) *(verb-intransitive)*	wanggarra-y YR
lost (be) *(verb phrase)*	warrayaa yanaa-y YY
lot (a) *(adjective)*	burrulaa YR, YY, GR
lot of talk *(noun)*	burrulaa garay GR
loudly *(adverb)*	bamba YR, YY
louse *(noun)*	munhi YR, YY, GR
louse (mother) *(noun)*	gabuul YR, YY
louse nit *(noun)*	garaay GR
	gayaay¹ YR, YY
love *(verb-transitive)*	winanga-y YR
love (be sweet on) *(verb-transitive)*	guwiirrnga-li YR
lover *(noun)*	dhurriwuudhaay YR, YY
lower leg *(noun)*	buyu YR, YY, GR
lucky *(adjective)*	murrubidi YR
lump *(noun)*	gulu YY
lumpy *(adjective)*	buulbuul YY
lung *(noun)*	gaban YR, YY

Mm

English	Gamilaraay/Yuwaalaraay/Yuwaalayaay
machinery *(noun)*	gumbadhaa YR, YY
mad *(adjective)*	wamba YR, YY, GR
	yaambul YR, GR
maggot *(noun)*	gamugamuu YR, YY
magic stone *(noun)*	muuliyaay YR, YY
magpie *(noun)*	burrugarrbuu YR, YY, GR
	mugarrabaa YR, YY
magpie goose *(noun)*	dhawudjarrdalmu GR
magpie-lark *(noun)*	barriindjiin YR, YY, GR
	birrgabirrga YR
Major Mitchell cockatoo *(noun)*	gagalarrin YR, YY
make a fire *(verb phrase)*	wii wiima-li YR, GR
make better *(verb-transitive)*	maaruma-li GR
	maayuma-li YR
make bigger *(verb phrase)*	waluwarr bunma-li YY
make by hand *(verb-transitive)*	maayama-li YY
	marama-li GR
make come out *(verb-transitive)*	dhurraaba-li YR
make (construct) *(verb-transitive)*	dhurra-li¹ YR, YY, GR
	gimbi-li YR, YY
	gimubi-li GR
make cry *(verb-transitive)*	yubama-li YR, YY
make (force) *(verb-transitive)*	buyawila-li YR
make love *(verb-transitive)*	dhaa-rri GR
	dhu-rri YR, YY
make mouth water *(verb-transitive)*	ngarrdanma-li YY
make noise *(verb-transitive)*	dhura-li GR
	girriinba-li YR
make someone angry *(verb phrase)*	yiili burranba-li YR, YY
make (someone do something) *(verb-transitive)*	guwaa-li YR, YY, GR
make (something) happen *(suffix)*	-ma-li YR, YY, GR
male *(noun)*	burubiyaay YY
	mandayaa YR, YY, GR
male echidna *(noun)*	gadhuu YR
mallee willow *(noun)*	guwiirra YR
	miyaymiyaay YR, YY

mistletoe bird

English	Gamilaraay/Yuwaalaraay/Yuwaalayaay
man (Aboriginal) (noun)	dhayn, yuurray YR, YY
	giwiirr, mari GR
man (Chinese) (noun)	mil binggarr GR
man (fully initiated) (noun)	buurrbaa GR
man (important, initiated) (noun)	yuurray YR, YY
man-like spirit (noun)	murraagu YR, YY
man (old) (noun)	wayamaa YR, YY, GR
	wuulman YR
	dhiriya GR
man (white) (noun)	gabaa YR, GR
	wanda YR, YY, GR
man (young) (noun)	yira murrun GR
	yiya murrun YY
man's belt (noun)	wayuwaal YR, YY
mandarine (native) (noun)	dharrday YY
manna (noun)	gun.giyan YR, YY
	guwiirra YR
manna (on bark) (noun)	dharraabiin YY
many (adjective)	burrulaa YR, YY, GR
many (suffix)	-galgaa YR, YY
many (little things) (suffix)	-gal YR, YY
many coloured (adjective)	gagan.gagan YR, YY
mark (noun)	mubirr YY
married (adjective)	guliirraraay GR
	guliirriyaay YR, YY
married woman (noun)	wirringgaa YR, GR
Mars (planet) (noun)	Guwaybila YR, YY
marsh (noun)	gurrugaawal YR
marsupial mouse (noun)	gima GR
marthaguy burr (noun)	mugaadhaa YR, YY
masked lapwing (noun)	baaldharradharra YR, YY, GR
master (noun)	maadha YR, YY, GR
matches (noun)	buri YR, GR
	maadjirr YR, YY
mate (noun)	baayamba, barringgu YR
	maliyaa, mamal YR, YY
matrilineal totem (noun)	yarudhagaa GR
me (done to) (pronoun)	nganha YR, YY, GR
meat (noun)	dhii^1 YR, YY, GR
	dhinggaa YR, YY
meat ant (noun)	buurrngan YR, YY
	gaalan GR
meat (lean) (noun)	bana YR, YY, GR
meat (piece of) (noun)	dhiidjuul GR
meat (totem) (noun)	dhii^1 YR, YY, GR
	dhinggaa YR, YY
medicine (noun)	dhalbin YR
medicine bush (fuchsia) (noun)	ngarran^2 YY
meeting (noun)	buudhaa YR
melon (noun)	bilum YR
	milan^2 YY
melon (camel) (noun)	ngayuun YR, YY
melon (native) (noun)	nhinay YR, YY
men's social section (noun)	Gambuu, Yibaay, Gabii, Marrii YR, YY, GR
mess (noun)	dhaga YR
message (noun)	gaay YR, YY
message stick (noun)	dhulu, maang GR
message stick (bora) (noun)	dhulu buurra YY
messenger (noun)	dhayndalmuu YR, YY
methylated spirits (noun)	gum, banggabaa YR
mid-afternoon (noun)	ngadaa dhuni YY
mid-morning (noun)	ngarribaa dhuni YY
midday (noun)	ngarribaa bidjunda YY
middle (noun)	bidjun YR, YY, GR
midwife (noun)	dhubaay YR
might (suffix)	-Yaa YR, YY
might (would you) (clitic)	-badhaay YR, YY
Mildool (placename)	Milduul YR, YY
milk (noun)	milgin YR
milk a cow (verb-transitive)	ngamuma-li YR
	nhuunma-li YY, GR
milk (breast) (noun)	ngamu YR, YY, GR
milk thistle (noun)	balamba YR, YY, GR
milky fluid (noun)	balam YR
Milky Way (noun)	Warrambul YR, YY
milky weed (noun)	minan YY
million (adjective)	wiwurra YR, YY, GR
millipede (noun)	barranbarraan YR, YY
mimic (verb phrase)	gaay gawaa-y YR, YY
mimosa bean pods (noun)	mawurrngiyan YY
mimosa bush (noun)	mawurr YR, YY
mind (verb-transitive)	ngarrangarra-li YR, YY
miner bird (noun)	dhiidjiinbawaa YR, YY
mirage (noun)	yiirriirr YR, YY
Mirramanar Station (placename)	Murrumanamanaa YR
missus (noun)	midi YY
mist (noun)	guwa YR, YY, GR
mistletoe (noun)	baan YR, YY, GR
mistletoe bird (noun)	baandjil YY

mistress

English	Gamilaraay/Yuwaalaraay/Yuwaalayaay
mistress (noun)	midi YY
mix (verb-transitive)	mugi-li YY
moan (verb-intransitive)	yaaga-y YR, YY
mob (suffix)	-gal YY
moiety name (noun)	Wudhurruu YY, GR
	Yanguru GR
	Yanguu YY
moiety (opposite) (adjective)	ngaarriga YY
money (noun)	banggul YR
	maayama YR, YY
money (coins) (noun)	yarral YR, YY, GR
monitor (black-headed) (noun)	galgarriirr YR, YY
monster (noun)	gayadharri YR
mood (noun)	guuyay YR, YY, GR
moon (noun)	baaluu YR, YY
	gilay YR, GR
moon (halo around) (noun)	gungurima GR
	garrul YR
moon (new) (adjective)	barran.giirr YY
morning (time adverb)	buliyaagu YR, YY, GR
morning (early) (time adverb)	giibaabu YR, YY
Morning Star (noun)	Maliyan.gaalay YR, YY
mosquito (noun)	mungin YR, YY, GR
moss (noun)	gagarr YR, YY
moth (type of) (noun)	burrun YR, YY
	gambigambi YY
mother (noun)	gunii, gunidjarr, ngambaa YR, YY, GR
mother earth (noun)	gunimaa YR
mother-in-law (husband's mother) (noun)	walgan YR, YY
mother-in-law (wife's mother) (noun)	buyal GR
	garrimaay YR, YY, GR
mother-in-law's brother (noun)	badhuul YR, YY
mother louse (noun)	gabuul YR, YY
mother's brother's wife (noun)	baaman GR
mother's mother's brother (noun)	waabi GR
mother's mother's brother's daughter (noun)	baaman GR
mother's mother's mother (noun)	murrambagan YY
mother's sisters' husbands (noun)	biiyalaa YY
mouldy (adjective)	wubuubiyaay YR, YY
mountain on Namoi River (placename)	Badhara Walaay, Balarangawul GR
mountain range (noun)	gaba^2 GR
mouse (noun)	dhindu YR
	mandarray YY
mouse (marsupial) (noun)	gima GR
moustache (noun)	mandhu GR
	yarray YR, YY, GR
mouth (noun)	ngaay YR, YY, GR
move (verb-intransitive)	yuurra-gi YR
move in a line (verb-intransitive)	baanda-y YY
movement to (suffix)	-gu^2 YR, YY, GR
mown (adjective)	garragarraa YY
much (adjective)	burrul YR, YY
Muckerawa (waterhole) (placename)	Magarrawayaa YY
mucus (noun)	mirril YR, YY, GR
mud (noun)	bidjaay YR, YY
	milimili GR
mud catfish (noun)	waay YY
mud hornet (noun)	dhanbadhanba YY
muddy (adjective)	bidjaaybiyaay YY
mug (noun)	gaala YR
mulga (noun)	malga YR, YY
mulga parrot (noun)	bulunbulun YR, YY
Murrawal (placename)	Marrawal GR
Murray cod (noun)	guduu YR, YY, GR
muscle (noun)	bindawu GR
mushroom (noun)	wubu^1 YR, YY
musk duck (noun)	bagabagaali YR
	birraala YY, GR
musn't (particle)	wanaa YY, GR
mussel (large) (noun)	dhanggal YR, YY, GR
mussel (small) (noun)	giinbay GR
	maanggii YR, YY
must (suffix)	-Yaa YR, YY
my (pronoun)	ngay^1 YR, YY, GR
myall tree (noun)	maayaal YR, YY, GR
myrtle (noun)	burrgulbiyan YR, YY
mythical beings (type of) (noun)	dhinabarra YY
mythical tribe (noun)	Murungamildaa YY
mythological warrior enemies (noun)	guuwiyaay YY

Nn

English	Gamilaraay/Yuwaalaraay/Yuwaalayaay
nail (noun)	binggi YY
	yulu YR, YY, GR
name (noun)	gayrr YR, YY, GR
name (verb-transitive)	gayrrba-li YR, YY
name (alternative) (noun)	bilaan YY
name of a sacred mountain (placename)	Wubi Wubi YY
name (secret) (noun)	mudhun YY
named (adjective)	gayrriyaay YY
nankeen kestrel (noun)	wala YR, YY
nankeen night heron (noun)	dhaarrin.gaarrin YR, YY
	dharrun YR, YY, GR
nardoo (noun)	bal YR, YY, GR
	nhaadhuu YR, YY, GR
Narrabri (placename)	Nharibaraay GR
Narran Lake (placename)	Burrul Gungan, Giiguradjin YY
	Dharriwaa YR
Narran River (placename)	Nharran YY
narrow (adjective)	waawul YR, YY
native banana (noun)	gaagulu YR, YY
native banana yam (noun)	biyarrbirr YR
	giban YR, YY
native bee (noun)	guni GR
native carrot (noun)	dhalayndjaa YR
native cat (noun)	bagandi YR, YY, GR
native cherry (noun)	mirrii YR, YY
native companion (noun)	burraalga YR, YY, GR
native gooseberry (noun)	bulabul YY
native hen (black-tailed) (noun)	baan.giirr YR, YY
	gulguwi YR, YY, GR
native lime (noun)	gayn.gayn[2] YR, YY
native mandarine (noun)	dharrday YY
native melon (noun)	nhinay YR, YY
native orange tree (noun)	bambul YR, YY, GR
native orange tree flowers (noun)	bambulngiyan YR, YY
native parsnip (noun)	madhay YY
native peach (noun)	garrayarray YY
native plum (noun)	ngamumbirra YR, YY
native potato (noun)	buunggal YR, YY, GR
	dhiilguwin GR
native spinach (noun)	galan.galaan YR, YY
native tomato (noun)	bulumburr YR, YY
	gumi YR, YY, GR
nature (noun)	baayangali YR
navel (noun)	bigal GR
	wirrigaal YR, YY, GR
near (noun)	milan[3] YR, GR
near (noun, adjective)	guwiin, guwiinbaa YR, YY, GR
nearly (adverb)	ngaliman YR, YY
neck (noun)	wuru GR
	wuyu YR, YY
neck (back of) (noun)	nhan YR, YY, GR
necklace (noun)	nhiigiliirr YR, YY
necklace (seed or grass) (noun)	dhiiriil GR
Nee-Nee (placename)	Nhiinhii YY
needle (noun)	binggi YY
needle (bone) (noun)	nhingal YY, GR
needlewood tree (noun)	bin.gawin.gal YR, YY
nephew (sister's son) (noun)	gunubingaa YR, YY, GR
nepine (noun)	barigan YR
	guwiibirr YR, YY
	ngaybaan GR
nervous (adjective)	bina guwaal, gidjarri YR
nest (noun)	gaarrimay YY
	walaay YR, YY, GR
net bag (noun)	gulay YR, YY, GR
net (emu) (noun)	mirrun YY
net (fish) (noun)	dhaaliyaay YR, YY
	gulay GR
never (adverb)	baluwaal YY
new (adjective)	burranbaa, yilaan.gaal YY
	guliyaan YR
	nhuubala GR
new moon (adjective)	barran.giirr YY
next (adjective)	bayaal YR
nicely (adjective)	gabangaarr YR
niece (sister's daughter) (noun)	gunugayngaa YR, YY, GR
night (noun)	ngurru GR
	buluuy YR, YY, GR
nine (adjective)	mirraal YR, YY, GR
nit (louse) (noun)	garaay GR
	gayaay[1] YR, YY

English	Gamilaraay/Yuwaalaraay/Yuwaalayaay
no (particle)	gamil, marayrr GR
	waal, maayrr YR, YY
no good (adjective, adverb)	gagil YR, YY, GR
no-one (doer to) (pronoun)	waal ngaanduwaa YR
no shame (adjective)	giyaldhalibaa YR, YY
noise (noun)	dhural YR
	wulul YY
noise (chopping) (noun)	ban.gul YR, YY, GR
noise (make) (verb-transitive)	dhura-li GR
noise (wing) (noun)	maamuu YR
noisy (adjective)	girrigirri YR
noisy friar bird (noun)	dhaguway YR, YY
noisy mob (noun)	wululgal YR, YY
non-marriageable (woman) (noun)	ngan.gi, nganbirr YY, GR
none (particle)	maayrr YR, YY
	marayrr GR
north (place adverb)	ngaarribiyan YR
north wind (noun)	dhurrandhurran, wilaarrdaa YR, YY
nose (noun)	muru GR
	muyu YR, YY
nose bone/shell (noun)	muyu waa YY
nosey person (noun)	dhirridhirri YY
nostril (noun)	muru biruu GR
	muyudhaa YY
not (particle)	gamil GR
	waal YR, YY
not right (adverb)	waal maayu YY
	gamil maaru GR
not with it (adjective)	yalabiyaay YR
not yet (particle)	gamilu GR
	waalu YR, YY
note (paper money) (noun)	biiba YY
now (clitic)	-nga[1] YR, YY
now (time adverb)	yalagiyu YR
now (immediately) (time adverb)	yilaadhu GR
Nullawa (placename)	Nguluwawul YY
numb (adjective)	dhirrindjal YR, YY
	yuumbu YR
nurse (noun)	dhubaay YR
nut grass (noun)	warringaay YY

Oo

English	Gamilaraay/Yuwaalaraay/Yuwaalayaay
oak (swamp) (noun)	bilaarr, murrgu YR, YY, GR
ochre (red) (noun)	guuwarr YR, YY, GR
ochre (white) (noun)	dhawurraa YR
ochre (yellow) (noun)	gidjiirr, guwinii YR
odd (adjective)	wiyaybaa YR, YY
oh dear! (exclamation)	madjagurra YR, YY
	ngarragaa YR, YY, GR
oh no! (exclamation)	barrabandu YR, YY
okay! (exclamation)	ngaayaybaay YR
okay! (satisfactory) (exclamation)	miyaay YR
old (adjective)	dhiriya GR
	dhuningarraay YR, YY
old friend (noun)	mudhi YR, YY
old man (noun)	dhiriya GR
	mudhi YR, YY
	wayamaa YR, YY, GR
	wuulman YR
old person (noun)	dhuningarraay YR, YY
old things (noun)	wayamaa YR
old woman (noun)	baagii, dhubaay, miimii[1], nhangi YR
	maamii, yinarraagalaa YR, YY
	yambuli GR
older brother (noun)	dhaya YR, YY, GR
older sister (noun)	baawaa YR, YY, GR
	bagaan YR, GR
	bawa[1] YR
	dhawurran YR, YY
on (suffix)	-Ga YR, YY, GR
on-going (suffix)	-ngayi-li YR
on top (be) (verb-intransitive)	ma-y YR
once (adverb)	maala GR
one (adjective)	biirr, biyarr, milan[1] YR, YY
	maal GR
one (suffix)	-DHuul YR, YY
one male emu (noun)	ganduwi YR, YY
oneself (suffix)	-ngiili-y YR, YY
only (adjective)	munggal YY, GR
only (adverb)	yiyal YR, YY, GR
only (suffix)	-biyal YR, GR

English	Gamilaraay/Yuwaalaraay/Yuwaalayaay
only one *(adjective)*	milandjal, milanduul YY
only two *(adjective)*	bulaadjal YY
opal *(noun)*	maayama yuluwirrigiirr YR, YY
open *(adjective)*	ganaay¹ YR
open *(verb-transitive)*	dhuma-li GR
open ground *(noun)*	wagi¹ YR, YY
open (treeless) country *(noun)*	wagibaa, wagiwagi YR, YY
opening *(noun)*	ngaay YR, YY; ganaay¹ YR
or *(clitic)*	-nga¹ YY
orange tree (native) *(noun)*	bambul YR, YY, GR
orchid *(noun)*	gubiyaay YY, GR
orchid (black) *(noun)*	garrii YR, YY
orchid country people *(noun)*	Garriibarra YY
orchid (wax-lipped) *(noun)*	gurriyaa YR
Orion's belt (stars) *(noun)*	Birraybirraay YR, YY, GR
ornament (kangaroo tooth) *(noun)*	yambiyan YY
orphan (fatherless boy) *(noun)*	yumbuy YR, YY
orphan (fatherless child) *(noun)*	gawun YR, YY
orphan (motherless child) *(noun)*	biiwan YY; gunidjaa YR, YY, GR
other *(adjective)*	murrunbaa YR, YY
other side *(noun)*	ngaarrigili YR, YY, GR
other side of river *(noun)*	gandaarr YR, YY, GR
ouch! *(exclamation)*	yagaay YR, YY, GR
our (more than two people) *(pronoun)*	ngiyaningu YR, YY, GR
our (two people) *(pronoun)*	ngalingu YR, YY, GR
out of place *(adjective)*	walingay YR, YY
outside *(noun)*	wagi¹ YR, YY
over there *(place adverb)*	ngaarri, ngaarrima YR, YY, GR
over there (other side) *(place adverb)*	ngarraagulay YR
over there (that way) *(place adverb)*	ngaarrigulay YR, YY, GR; ngaarrimali YR
overseer *(noun)*	badjin maadha YR, YY
owl (barking) *(noun)*	muurrguu YR, YY
owl (barn) *(noun)*	wanggii YY
owl (boobook) *(noun)*	guurrguurr YY
owlet nightjar *(noun)*	yirrin YR, YY, GR
own *(noun)*	guyungan YR, YY, GR
own *(verb-transitive)*	gaa-gi YR, YY, GR
owner *(noun)*	wurrugaa YR

Pp

English	Gamilaraay/Yuwaalaraay/Yuwaalayaay
paddle (verb-intransitive)	wunga-y YR, YY
paddock (noun)	baadi YR
paint (noun)	bidjaay YR, YY
paint (black) (noun)	buuwan YY
paint (self) (verb-intransitive)	gaarra-y YR, YY, GR
pair (adjective)	bulaangaa YY
Pallal (placename)	Balal GR
pallid cuckoo (noun)	mungin.gagalawaa YR, YY
paper (noun)	biiba YR, YY, GR
parallel (adjective)	bilabilaa YY
pardalote (red-browed) (noun)	wiiwambin YY
pardalote (striated) (noun)	wirrwirr YY
parrot (feeding) (noun)	gaadhal YR
parrot (ground, red-rumped) (noun)	barrangga GR
parrot (mulga) (noun)	bulunbulun YR, YY
parrot (red-winged) (noun)	bilay YR, YY, GR
parrot (ringneck) (noun)	bulunbulun, nhan.garra YR, YY
part (noun)	mulan YY
passage (noun)	wun.guwi YY
pathway (noun)	warruwi GR
pathway (initiation ground) (noun)	dhunbarran GR
peaceful (adjective)	gaba binaal YR, YY
peaceful dove (noun)	gurugun YR, GR
peacekeeper (noun)	gayaandhi YR
peach (native) (noun)	garrayarray YY
peep (peek) (verb-intransitive)	wuumi-li, wurungga-li YR
peephole (noun)	wurunggal YR
peewee (noun)	barriindjiin YR, YY, GR / birrgabirrga YR
peg (noun)	yiya YY
pelican (noun)	gulaanbali YR / gulayaali YR, YY, GR
pelt (verb-transitive)	garawi-li GR / gayawi-li YR, YY
pen (noun)	wiyayl YR, YY
pen up (verb-transitive)	wubarra-li GR
pencil (noun)	wiyayl YR, YY
pendant (shell chest) (noun)	waa[1] YR, YY
penis (noun)	dhun YY, GR / manday[1] YR
penis head (noun)	nyiinmay GR
pennyroyal (noun)	buuybuuy GR / ngawingawi YR, YY
people from (suffix)	-barra YR, YY
peppery (adjective)	yiiliyiili YR, YY
perch (verb-intransitive)	wana-y YY
perch (golden) (noun)	dhagaay YR, YY, GR
perch (unidentified fish) (noun)	baraa GR
persistent rain (noun)	guuyaarrma YY
person (Aboriginal) (noun)	dhayn YR, YY / mari GR
person (old) (noun)	dhuningarraay YR, YY
person's spirit (noun)	dhuwi YR, YY, GR / malimali YY / yawi YR, YY
phascogale (red-tailed) (noun)	marawanda YY
Piangobla (placename)	Bayn Gabilaa YR
pick (verb-transitive)	pickima-li YR
pick up (verb-transitive)	dhiyama-li YR, YY, GR
piece (noun)	bilgin YR, YY, GR
piece of bark (noun)	yarraadharr YR, YY
piece of meat (noun)	dhiidjuul GR
pied butcherbird (noun)	buubuurrbu YY
pig (noun)	bibirrgaa YR, YY / biguun GR
pigeon (bronzewing) (noun)	dhamarr YR, YY, GR
pigeon (squatter) (noun)	mumumbaay GR
pigeon (topknot) (noun)	gulawuliil YR, YY, GR
pigweed (noun)	dhamu YR, YY / ganhan YY
pigweed (small) (noun)	yiil YY
Pilliga (placename)	Bilaga GR
pillow (noun)	dhaygaluwi YR, YY
pin (noun)	binggi YY
pinch (verb-transitive)	nhima-li YR, YY, GR
pine (white cypress) (noun)	gurraari GR / gurraay YR, YY
pink cockatoo (noun)	gagalarrin YR, YY
pink-eared duck (noun)	wilidhubaay YR / wiligabuul YY

English	Gamilaraay/Yuwaalaraay/Yuwaalayaay
pins and needles (noun)	dhinayal YR
pipe (noun)	baaybuu YR, YY, GR
	buuwarran YY
pipeclay (white) (noun)	bagi YY
piss (noun)	giil YR, YY, GR
piss (verb-intransitive)	giili-y YR, GR
pistol (noun)	birridul YR, YY
pitch (verb-transitive)	wana-gi YR, YY
pitiful (adjective)	ngarragaa YR, YY, GR
pity someone (verb-transitive)	ngarraga-li YY
place far away (noun)	balima YR, YY
place of (suffix)	-Baa YR, YY, GR
plain (noun)	guniyal GR
	wagi¹, wagibaa, wagiwagi YR, YY
plain pigeon (noun)	galimaramara GR
plains grass (noun)	ganalay YY
plains rat (noun)	wagimal YY
plains turkey (noun)	barawaa YR, GR
	gumbulgaban YR, YY
plait (verb-transitive)	yabi-li YY
planet Mars (noun)	Guwaybila YR, YY
planet Venus (noun)	Murrudhi Gindamalaa YR, YY
	Nganundi Gindamalaa GR
planigale (rat-like marsupial) (noun)	garragali YY
plant, hide (self) (verb-intransitive)	guuma-y YY
plant (prickly) (noun)	bindiyaa YY
plant (type of) (noun)	muluumay YY
plate (noun)	wirri YR
plate (noun)	bagal YY
plate fungus (noun)	bagal YY
platypus (noun)	buubumurr GR
	dharragarra YR
play (verb-intransitive)	yulu-gi YR, YY, GR
	yuurrma-y YR, YY
play with (verb-transitive)	yuurrma-li YY
pleased (adjective)	gayaa YR, YY
Pleiades (stars) (noun)	Bariyan Ngama GR
	Miyaymiyaay YR, YY, GR
plover (noun)	biramba GR
plover (banded) (noun)	bundabul YR
plover (black-fronted) (noun)	bilidjuu YR, YY
plover (spur-winged) (noun)	baaldharradharra YR, YY, GR
pluck (verb-transitive)	buurra-li YR, YY
plum (native) (noun)	ngamumbirra YR, YY
point (noun)	ngulu YY, GR
	muru GR
point (verb-intransitive)	dhuba-y YR, YY, GR
point bone (verb-transitive)	gayawi-li YR, YY
pointed club (noun)	murrula YR, YY, GR
pointers of Southern Cross (noun)	muyaay YY
poison (noun)	baadjin YR, YY, GR
	bundhabundha YR, YY
	dhinagarral YY
poison bone (noun)	guuyarra YR, YY
poison bone, poison stick (noun)	bugiyaa YR
	gadhiigurrii YY
poke (with pointed object) (verb-transitive)	dhu-rri YR, YY, GR
policeman (noun)	biliirrman, maawulaaldaanga YY
	gandjibal YR, YY, GR
	maliyan YR
policeman fly (noun)	gugun.gugun YR, YY
poor (adjective)	buwabildhalibaa YR, YY
poor (helpless) (adjective)	ngarragaa YR, YY, GR
porcupine (noun)	bigibila YR, YY, GR
	marrawal GR
possessions (noun)	buwabil YR, YY
possum (brushtail) (noun)	mudhay YR, YY, GR
possum fur loincloth (noun)	gumilaa YR, YY, GR
possum (gliding) (noun)	bagu YR, GR
possum (ringtail) (noun)	garrawirr GR
post (corner) (noun)	giniybaal YR
potato (noun)	budidaa YR
potato (native) (noun)	buunggal YR, YY, GR
	dhiilguwin GR
potential spouse (for a man) (noun)	nganuwaay GR
pouch (kangaroo) (noun)	man.garr YR, YY
pour (verb-intransitive)	yaarri-y YR
pour (verb-transitive)	gaarrima-li YR, YY
	yaarrima-li GR
powerful (adjective)	warranggal YR, YY, GR

praise

praise *(verb-transitive)* .... marramarrama-li, bawa-li GR
praise (expression of)
   (exclamation) .... waa² YR, YY, GR
pregnant *(adjective)* .... buribara YR
   mubalyaal YY, GR
prepare *(verb-transitive)* .... buganma-li GR
prepare a bed
   (verb-transitive) .... dhiyaagarra-li YY, GR
pretend *(adjective)* .... wagi² YR, YY
   yaal YR
pretend *(particle)* .... yalbala YR, YY
pretend *(suffix)* .... -gaalu YR
pretend fight *(noun)* .... yaambuwiirr YR, YY
pretending! *(exclamation)* .... yaambul YR, GR
prickle *(noun)* .... bindiyaa YR, YY, GR
prickly *(adjective)* .... bindiyaabiyaay YY
prickly gecko *(noun)* .... garragarraandi YR, YY
prickly plant *(noun)* .... bindiyaa YY
priest *(noun)* .... dhayndalmuu YR
prominent (big) *(suffix)* .... -wan YR, YY
pronunciation *(noun)* .... dhaalan YY
proud *(adjective)* .... gayaa YR, YY
pubic hair *(noun)* .... budhi YR, YY, GR
pudding *(noun)* .... budhun YY
puddle *(noun)* .... dhan.gaay YR, YY
puff out chest
   (verb-transitive) .... biiwanma-li YY
puffed out *(noun, adjective)* .... biiwanbiiwan YY
pull *(verb-transitive)* .... buurrma-li YR, YY
   miinma-li YR, GR
pull off *(verb-transitive)* .... baarrama-li YR, YY
pull out *(verb-transitive)* .... buurra-li YR, YY
punty bush *(noun)* .... bandi YY
pup *(noun)* .... waaraal GR
   waayaal YR, YY
pure honey *(noun)* .... gugal YY
purpose *(suffix)* .... -gu² YR, YY, GR
purpose *(verb suffix)* .... -gu³ YR, YY, GR
pus *(noun)* .... mula YR, YY
push *(verb-transitive)* .... yurringga-li YR
push against *(verb-transitive)* .... garranba-li YY
push away *(verb-transitive)* .... dhilay-rri YR, YY
push down *(verb-transitive)* .... bundaama-li YR, YY, GR
put back *(verb-transitive)* .... yuwanma-li YR
put down *(verb-transitive)* .... wiima-li YR, YY, GR
put in order *(verb-transitive)* .... baanda-li YR
put in *(verb-transitive)* .... wa-li YR, YY
put (on self)
   (verb-intransitive) .... wiima-y YR
put out (extinguish)
   (verb-transitive) .... baluburra-li YR, YY
   baluwa-li YY
put out (fire) *(verb-transitive)* .... buudhu-rri YR
put someone to bed
   (verb-transitive) .... dhanduwiyma-li YR
put up *(verb-transitive)* .... mayabi-li YR, YY, GR
   warrayma-li YR, YY, GR
python *(noun)* .... dhuyumanga YR
python (carpet) *(noun)* .... yabaa YR, YY, GR
python (children's) *(noun)* .... dhayaaminyaa YY

Qq

quail (noun)	barrabarruun YR, YY
quandong (noun)	guwadhaa YR, YY, GR
quarrel (noun)	garran YR
quarrel (verb-intransitive)	yayala-y YR, YY
quarrian (noun)	wiraarr GR
	wiyaarr YR, YY
queen native bee (noun)	guniinii YR, YY, GR
question word (question word)	yaama YR, YY, GR
quickly (adverb)	barraay YR, YY, GR
quiet (adjective)	malu YY, GR
	dhabiyaan YR, YY, GR
quiet (be) (verb-intransitive)	dhabi-y YR, YY, GR
quieten (verb-transitive)	binaal bunma-li YR, YY
quietly (adverb)	baluwaa YR, YY
quill (echidna) (noun)	wirayl GR
	wiyayl YR, YY
quinine bark (noun)	gadibundhu YR
quinine tree (noun)	gadibundhu YR, YY
quoll (noun)	bagandi YR, YY, GR

Rr

rabbit (noun)	bina guraarr GR
	yurabirr YR, YY
rag (noun)	bidjaraay YR, YY
ragged (adjective)	gadharrgadharr YR, YY
rain (noun)	gali, yuuruu GR
	yuuyuu YR, YY
rain (verb phrase)	yuuyuu bundaa-gi YY
rain (verb-transitive)	dhama-y YR, YY
rain (fine) (noun)	dhuubaarr YR, YY
rain-making stone (noun)	wuudalay YY
rain (persistent) (noun)	guuyaarrma YY
rainbow (noun)	yuluwirri YR, YY, GR
rainbow bee-eater (noun)	birrubirruu YR, YY
raise (bring up) (verb-transitive)	burrul burranba-li YY
	warrayma-li YR
rake (noun)	girrandhaal YR
ram (noun)	buuldirran YR
randy (adjective)	gayaay[2] YR, YY, GR
rat (bush) (noun)	dhunmidjirr YY
rat (plains) (noun)	wagimal YY
rat (water) (noun)	gumaay YR, YY, GR
rattle (verb-intransitive)	dhirranba-y YR
rattling (adjective)	buwabuwa YY
raven (noun)	waaruu[2] YR, GR
raven (Australian) (noun)	waan[1] YR, YY
raw (adjective)	dhurrin YR, YY
re-growth (noun)	gadjigadji YR
really (particle)	giirr, giirruu YR, YY, GR
really (suffix)	-ban.gaan GR
really (suffix)	-wan.gaan YR, YY
recently (time adverb)	yilaa YR, YY, GR
red (adjective)	guwaymbarra YR, YY, GR
red-backed kingfisher (noun)	dhaadhiirr YR, YY, GR
red-bellied black snake (noun)	galibaay GR
red-browed pardalote (noun)	wiiwambin YY
red-eyed spirit (noun)	wiiyuu YR
red kangaroo (noun)	bawurra YR, YY, GR
	ganuurr GR
red-kneed dotterel (noun)	dhibi YY
red ochre (noun)	guuwarr YR, YY, GR

red-rumped parrot

English	Translation
red-rumped parrot (noun)	barrangga GR
red soil (noun)	gigwidjil YR
	guwaygalaa YR, YY
red-tailed black cockatoo (noun)	biliirr YR, YY, GR
red-tailed phascogale (noun)	marawanda YY
red-winged parrot (noun)	bilay YR, YY, GR
reed (noun)	dhariil GR
reed warbler (clamorous) (noun)	dhuwigalinmal YR, YY
reflection (noun)	nhalawilbayn YR
reflective (adjective)	ngandanganda YY
regurgitate (verb-transitive)	gaawi-li YR, YY, GR
rejoice (verb phrase)	marra gi-gi GR
relaxed (adjective)	dhuurrguu YR
release (verb-transitive)	yanaaynbi-li YR, YY
remember (verb-transitive)	dhiirra-y, winanga-y YR, YY, GR
remove (verb-transitive)	dhuwima-li YR, YY
remove quills (verb-transitive)	wiyayi-li YY
resist (verb-intransitive)	guurrama-li YY
rest (verb-intransitive)	buruwi-y GR
	buuwi-y YR, YY
restless flycatcher (noun)	garaayaa YR, YY
retain (verb-transitive)	garrawa-li YY
return (verb-intransitive)	dharrawu-li YR, GR
	dharrawuluwi-y YR, YY
	dhurraluwi-y YR, YY, GR
	wun.ga-li GR
return (verb-transitive)	yuwanma-li YR
revolve (verb-intransitive)	gayarra-y YR, YY, GR
rib (noun)	dharrarr GR
	nhamun YR, YY, GR
rice (noun)	yarrarr YR
Richard's pipit (noun)	wagaaygaali, wagiwagi YY
riddle (noun)	girribal YR, YY, GR
ride (verb-intransitive)	dhurriya-y YR
	wila-y YR
right, right-handed (adjective)	dhuruyaal GR
	dhuuyaal YR, YY
right around (place adverb)	yalagidhaay YR
right over there (place adverb)	ngaarringaarri YR, GR
ringtail possum (noun)	garrawirr GR
ringneck parrot (noun)	bulunbulun, nhan.garra YR, YY
ripe (adjective)	yiilay YY
ripple (noun)	baynyi YY
	ngamulngamul YR, YY
rise (sun/moon) (verb-intransitive)	galiya-y YR, YY
	dhurra-li[2] YR, YY, GR
river (noun)	bagay YR, GR
	gaawaa YR, YY
river bank (noun)	baga YR, GR
river bank (sloping) (noun)	wanba YR, YY
river bend (noun)	wabu YR, YY, GR
river bug (noun)	babarrngaan YY
river grass (native millet) (noun)	guli YY, GR
river gum flowers (noun)	yarraanbiin YY
river mint (noun)	buuybuuy GR
	ngawingawi YR, YY
river (other side of) (noun)	gandaarr YR, YY, GR
river red gum tree (noun)	yarraan YR, YY, GR
river (straight) (noun)	garragarraan YR
river wattle (noun)	gurrulay YR, YY
river wattle flowers (noun)	gurrulayngayn YR, YY
river's edge (noun)	miimii[2] YR, YY
road (noun)	dhurrabal GR
	yuruun YR, YY, GR
robin (hooded) (noun)	biibin YY
robin redbreast (noun)	guniibuu YR, YY
rocky ground/ridge (noun)	murrila YR, YY
roll (verb-intransitive)	biyuurra-y YR
	wangga-y YY
roll (verb-transitive)	biyuurra-li YR
	wanggama-li YR, YY
roll about/around (verb-intransitive)	biyuurragi-li YR
roll down a bank (verb-intransitive)	dhabirra-y YY
roll up (verb-transitive)	nguwa-li YR, YY
roly-poly spirit (noun)	bindiyaa YY
roost (verb-intransitive)	wana-y YY
root (young kurrajong) (noun)	gaagul YR
rope (noun)	buurr YR, YY, GR
	nhimin GR
	yurrugu YR
rosewood (noun)	bunbarr YR, YY

rosewood fruit *(noun)* .... bunbarrayn YR, YY
rotten *(adjective)* .... gulungguluu YR, YY
　　　　　　　　　　　　　　 nhuwi YR, YY, GR
rough *(adjective)* .... madhamadha YR, YY, GR
round *(adjective)* .... gurru GR
row *(noun)* .... garran YR
rub *(verb-transitive)* .... gaarra-li YR, YY, GR
　　　　　　　　　　　　　　 gamaama-li YR, YY
rubbish *(noun)* .... dhaga YR
　　　　　　　　　　　　　　 gagarr YR, YY
ruby saltbush *(noun)* .... burra YY
rufous whistler *(noun)* .... mulindjal YY, GR
rum *(noun)* .... walanbaa gungan YR
　　　　　　　　　　　　　　 yurraamu YR, YY, GR
run *(verb-intransitive)* .... banaga-y YR, YY, GR

Ss

sack *(verb-transitive)* .... yanaaynbi-li YR
sacred fire *(noun)* .... yanguuwii YR, YY
sacred kingfisher *(noun)* ...... bunduun YR, YY
sacred mountain
　(placename) .... Wubi Wubi YY
sacred stone *(noun)* .... gabarraa YR, YY
sacred things *(noun)* .... buwarr YR
sacred tree *(noun)* .... dhiil[1] YR, YY
sad *(adjective)* .... ganagiil YR
　　　　　　　　　　　　　　 badha GR
　　　　　　　　　　　　　　 gana walingay YY
saddle *(noun)* .... dhaadal YR, YY
salt *(noun)* .... dhal GR
saltbush *(noun)* .... bandiyal YY
saltbush (large) *(noun)* .... binamayaa YR, YY
saltbush (ruby) *(noun)* .... burra YY
saltbush (small) *(noun)* .... nhingil YR, YY, GR
same *(adjective)* .... yaluuyaluu YY
same one *(noun)* .... biyarruu YR, YY
sand *(noun)* .... garaay GR
　　　　　　　　　　　　　　 gayaay[1] YY
　　　　　　　　　　　　　　 gumbugan YR, YY, GR
sand goanna *(noun)* .... biiwii YR, YY
　　　　　　　　　　　　　　 dhulii YR, GR
sandalwood tree *(noun)* ...... garruwi YY, GR
　　　　　　　　　　　　　　 badha YR, YY
sandalwood tree grub
　(noun) .... garruuyal YY
sandfly *(noun)* .... mugiin.gaa YR, YY
sandhill *(noun)* .... garaay dhuyul GR
　　　　　　　　　　　　　　 gayaayaan YY
　　　　　　　　　　　　　　 gumbugan YR, YY, GR
sandhill wattle *(noun)* .... girranbiiyan YY
sate, satisfied *(adjective)* .... yuularaay GR
　　　　　　　　　　　　　　 yuuliyaay YR, YY
sauce *(noun)* .... wirrun YR, YY
saucepan *(noun)* .... ngaymbuwan YR, YY
savage *(adjective)* .... yiiliyanbaa YR, YY
saw *(noun)* .... baladi YR, YY
　　　　　　　　　　　　　　 bul YY
sawdust *(noun)* .... djulu YY
say *(verb-transitive)* .... guwaa-li YR, YY, GR
scab *(noun)* .... giigal YR, YY
scabby *(adjective)* .... giigaliyaay YR, YY

scale

English	Gamilaraay/Yuwaalaraay/Yuwaalayaay
scale (verb-transitive)	giinba-li YR, YY
scales (noun)	giinbal YR, YY, GR
scaly tribe (noun)	giinbaligal YY
scar (noun)	mubirr YY
	yurrun YR, YY, GR
scarf (noun)	gambada YY
school principal (noun)	dhiirralbidi YR
scold (verb-transitive)	yaya-li YR, YY
scoop (verb-transitive)	dhiyarra-li YR, YY
scorpion (noun)	dhula GR
	gunha YR, YY
scrape (verb-transitive)	galaanbi-li YR, YY
	gaynma-li YY
scraper (noun)	gayn YR, YY
scratch (verb-transitive)	mawu-gi YR, YY, GR
scratch (claw mark) (noun)	yulu YY
scrub (noun)	yurrul YR, YY, GR
sea eagle (white-bellied) (noun)	guwinyarri YY
seagull (noun)	giinbaywarraymal YY
	maanggiiwarraywarraymal YR, YY
search for (verb-transitive)	gayarra-gi YR, YY, GR
	ngaawa-y YY
seat (noun)	gulaban YR
secret (noun)	wadhagii YR
secret name (noun)	mudhun YY
section (men's social) (noun)	Gambuu, Yibaay, Gabii, Marrii YR, YY, GR
section (women's social) (noun)	Buudhaa, Yibadhaa, Gabudhaa, Maadhaa YR, YY, GR
sedge (type of) (noun)	barrawan[2] YY
see (verb-transitive)	ngami-li GR
	ngarra-li YR, YY
seed (noun)	dhinggal, yurrul YR
	yiya YY
seed cake (noun)	dharrii YY
seed (grass) (noun)	dhunbarr YR, YY
seed or grass necklace (noun)	dhiiriil GR
self (noun)	burrbiyaan, dhubayn YR
selfish (adjective)	gundhuwundhuu YR, YY
semen (noun)	barabin YR, YY, GR
send (verb-transitive)	warrayma-li YR, YY
	wuurrma-li YY
senior lady (respected elder) (noun)	yinarraa YR, YY
senior man (respected elder) (noun)	dhilaagaa YR, YY
sequentially (adjective, adverb)	mandaymanday
series of steps (sequence) (noun)	manday[2] YR, YY, GR
set (moon/sun) (verb-intransitive)	wuu-gi YR, YY
	gaarri-y YY
	yaarri-y GR
settle down (verb-transitive)	binaal bunma-li YR, YY
seven (adjective)	guulay YR, YY, GR
Seven Sisters (stars) (noun)	miyaymiyaay YR, YY, GR
sew (verb-transitive)	muyawa-li YR, YY
	nhinga-li YY, GR
sexy (adjective)	gayaay[2] YR, YY, GR
shade (noun)	dhadhin[1] YY
shade house (noun)	buuwayamba YY
shadow (noun)	dhadhin[1] YY
shadow (human) (noun)	malawil YR, YY
shadow spirit (noun)	malawil YY
shake (verb-intransitive)	dhirranba-y YR, YY
shake (verb-transitive)	dhirranba-li YR, YY, GR
shake down (verb-transitive)	buwama-li YR, YY
shallow (adjective)	ganaay[2] YR, YY, GR
shallow waterhole (noun)	gilgaay YR
shame (noun)	burriin YR
shame! (exclamation)	barrabandu YR, YY
shameless (adjective)	giyaldhalibaa YR, YY
sharp (adjective)	dhalaybaa YR, YY
	yadhala GR
sharpen (verb-transitive)	barra-li YR, YY, GR
	yadhaba-li GR
sharpening-tools place (placename)	Barrali Mugulbaa YR
shave (verb-transitive)	wiirra-li YR, YY
shave (self) (verb-intransitive)	wiirra-y YR, YY
shaved (adjective)	garragarraa YY
she (doer/doer to) (pronoun)	nguru GR
	nguu[1] YR, YY
sheaf of grass seed (noun)	yaamarra YR, YY
shear (verb-transitive)	wiirra-li YR, YY
shearing handpiece (noun)	bagaay YR
sheep (noun)	dhimba YR, YY, GR

English	Word	Language
sheep intestines (large) (noun)	yaray	GR
sheep intestines (small) (noun)	galinggaa	YR, YY, GR
shell (noun)	waa[1]	YR, YY, GR
shell chest pendant (noun)	waa[1]	YR, YY
shelly log (noun)	dhan.gal	YR, YY
shield (noun)	yiilaman	YR
	burriin	YR, YY, GR
shield (broad) (noun)	burriin	YR, YY, GR
shift (verb-transitive)	dhuurrma-li	YR, YY
shin (noun)	buyu	YR, YY, GR
shine (noun)	guuyal	GR
shine (verb-intransitive)	guuya-li	YR, YY, GR
shingleback lizard (noun)	garrbaali	YR, YY
	manggaay	GR
shiny (adjective)	guuyalaraay	GR
	ngandanganda	YY
shirt (noun)	dhuwadi	YR, YY, GR
shit (noun)	guna	YR, YY, GR
shit (verb-intransitive)	guna-gi	YR
shitty (adjective)	gana garraa	YR
shiver (verb-intransitive)	dhirranba-y	YR
	yii-gi	YY
shoe (noun)	manduwii	YR, YY, GR
	nhangana	GR
shoot (verb-transitive)	dhuudhinma-li	YR
shooting star (noun)	mirii yanan	GR
shop (noun)	garrawal	YR, YY
short (adjective)	buyaduul	YR, YY
	dhambi, dhambidjuul	YR
short cut (noun)	bagaarr	YR
short-necked turtle (noun)	waraba	GR
	wayamba	YR, YY
short of breath (adjective)	buliirral ganaay	YY
shorty (noun)	badjindi	YY
shoulder (noun)	walarr	YR, YY, GR
shoulder blade (noun)	biilaa	YR, YY
	biilara	GR
shout (verb-transitive)	gaga-li	YR, YY, GR
shove (verb-transitive)	garranba-li	YY
shovel (noun)	dhagadhaal	YR
shoveler duck (Australasian) (noun)	dhibayuu	YR, YY, GR
show (verb-transitive)	ngarranma-li	YR, YY
showy (adjective)	dhirradhirra	YY
shrimp (noun)	dhugaalubaa, giidjaa	YR, YY
	mirrindjaa	GR
shrunken (shrivelled) (adjective)	milamilaa	YY
shut (verb-transitive)	muwi-li	GR
shy (adjective)	guyan	YR
sick (adjective)	wiibil	GR
sick (be) (verb-intransitive)	dhaala-gi	YR, YY
	wiibi-li	GR
sick (feel) (verb-intransitive)	dhaala-gi	YR, YY
sickness spirit (noun)	yarayawu	GR
side (noun)	nhirrin	YR, YY, GR
side (location) (suffix)	-gili	YR, YY
sideways (place adverb)	dhaan	YR, YY
silent (adjective)	garaydhalibaa	GR
silly (adjective)	ngarragaa, wamba	YR, YY, GR
	yaambul	YR, GR
silver bream (noun)	gambaal	YR, YY, GR
silver gull (noun)	giinbaywarraymal	YY
	manggiiwarraywarraymal	YR, YY
silver ironbark (noun)	dhiinyaay	YR, YY, GR
silver wattle (noun)	dhaniyaa	YR, YY
similar to (suffix)	-giirr	YR, YY, GR
sinew (noun)	dhunbil, gugirrii	YR, YY
sinew string (noun)	dhunbilyabi	YY
sinewy (adjective)	dhunbiliyaay	YY
sing (verb-transitive)	bawi-li	YR, YY, GR
sing out (verb-transitive)	gaga-li	YR, YY, GR
singe (verb-transitive)	dhinba-li	YY
sip (verb-transitive)	nguuguuba-li	YR
sister (noun)	baawaa	YR, YY, GR
	buurrii, miimi	GR
	bawa[1], gaadhii	YR
sister (older) (noun)	baawaa	YR, YY, GR
	bagaan, dhawurran	YR, GR
	bawa[1]	YR
sister (younger) (noun)	bagaan, bariyan	GR
sister-in-law (noun)	gambaay	YR, YY
sit (verb-intransitive)	ngarri-y	GR
	wila-y	YR
	yilawa-y	YY
sitting emu (noun)	ngurran.gali	YR, YY
six (adjective)	yuli	YR, YY, GR
skeleton spirit (noun)	guwaybuyan	YY

skin

English	Gamilaraay/Yuwaalaraay/Yuwaalayaay
skin (noun)	yulay YR, YY, GR
skin (verb-transitive)	biirra-li YR, YY
skin cracks (noun)	yaydja YR
skinny (adjective)	nharran YY
skip (verb-intransitive)	burrumba-y YR, YY
skip (verb-transitive)	dhangga-li YR
skipping game (noun)	burrumbal YY
sky (noun)	gunagala YR, YY, GR
sky camp (noun)	balima YR, YY
skylark (noun)	mulaydjalbii YY
sleep (noun)	yuwarr YR, YY
sleep (verb-intransitive)	baabi-li GR
	dhanduwi-y YR, YY
sleep (go to) (verb-intransitive)	yuwarra-y YR, YY
sleepy lizard (noun)	wurumal GR
slime (noun)	nhulaan YR, YY
	waylurr, wiiluun YR
slimey (adjective)	nhulaanbil YY
slip (verb-intransitive)	buli-y YR, YY
slippery (adjective)	bulilbulil YY
sloping river bank (noun)	wanba YR, YY
slow worm (noun)	binadhiwuubiyan YR, YY
slowly (adverb)	baluwaa YR, YY, GR
	guraay GR
	guwaaybaa YY
small (adjective)	badjin, dhugaay YR, YY
	bubaay YR
	gaay[2], gaaynmara GR
small (suffix)	-DHuul YR, YY, GR
small berry (noun)	yawurr GR
small brown ant (noun)	wamuwaa YY
small club (noun)	gudhurru GR
small coolamon (noun)	wirri YR, YY
small dragon lizard (noun)	gumawuma YR, YY, GR
small grindstone (noun)	giba YR, YY
small hailstone (noun)	yiyagungawuma YR, YY
small locust (noun)	ngininnginin YR, YY
small mussel (noun)	giinbay GR
	maanggii YR, YY
small pigweed (noun)	yiil YY
small saltbush (noun)	nhingil YR, YY, GR
small sharp things (noun)	binggi YY
small waterhole (noun)	dhanggaal YR, YY
	gilgal YY
smallpox (noun)	buuwirr GR
	dhumadhuma YR, YY
smell (verb-intransitive)	ngawi-y YY
smell (verb-transitive, intransitive)	buwi-y YR, GR
smelly (adjective)	nhuwi YR, YY, GR
smiling (adjective)	dhirrabil YY
smoke (noun)	dhuu YR, GR
	wuyugil YR, YY
smoke (ceremonial) (noun)	wuyugil YR, YY
smoke (ceremonial) (verb-transitive)	wuyugi-li YY
smoke (funeral) (noun)	dhuubaarr YR, YY
smoke tobacco (verb-transitive)	buubi-li YR, YY, GR
smoked (adjective)	dhuumuyu YY
smooth (adjective)	gayn.gayn[1] YY
smooth off (verb-transitive)	gaynma-li YY
snail (noun)	gindjulgarra YR, YY
snail slime/track (noun)	gindjul YR
snake (noun)	dhuru GR
	dhuyu YR, YY
	ngandabaa YR
snake (black) (noun)	ngurray YY, GR
	wuyubuluuy YR, YY
snake (brown) (noun)	warrala YR, YY
snake (brown and yellow) (noun)	babarra YR, YY
snake (fierce) (noun)	wularr YY
snake (grey) (noun)	ngabi YY
	nhiibi GR
snake (king brown) (noun)	ngandabaa YR, YY, GR
snake track (noun)	gay YR, YY
	wayal YR
snake (tree) (noun)	waya[2] YY
snakebean (noun)	wilay YY
sneak (verb-intransitive)	dhila-y YR, YY
sneeze (noun)	giguwi YR, YY, GR
sneeze (verb phrase)	giguwi dhu-rri YR, YY
snore (verb-transitive)	ngurruula-y YR, YY
snot (noun)	mirril YR, YY, GR
snotty gobbles (noun)	baan YR, YY, GR
soak (noun)	girruu YY
soak (verb-transitive)	dhanggima-li YY
soap (noun)	dhuubuu YR, YY, GR
social group (noun)	Bumbira, Magula, Ngara YY
socks (noun)	dhagin YR, YY

English	Translation
soft *(adjective)*	mulamula YR, YY, GR
	mula YR, YY
soft drink *(noun)*	guwiirr gungan YR
soil (baked) *(noun)*	barrin YR, YY
soil (black) *(noun)*	banuwa YR, YY
soil (red) *(noun)*	guwaygalaa YR, YY
soldier bird *(noun)*	dhiidjiinbawaa YR, YY
solid *(adjective)*	walan, walanbaa YR, YY
some *(adjective)*	gulbirr YR, GR
some *(suffix)*	-Waa YR, YY
someone (doer to) *(pronoun)*	ngaanduwaa YR, YY, GR
someone (doer/done to) *(pronoun)*	ngaanawaa YY
	ngaandiyaa YR, YY
someone's *(pronoun)*	ngaannguwaa YR, YY, GR
something *(noun)*	minyagaa YR, YY
somewhere (at) *(place adverb)*	minyaayawaa YR
somewhere (to) *(place adverb)*	minyaarruwaa YR
son *(noun)*	birray YY
	wurrumay GR
son-in-law *(noun)*	badhuul YY
	bambuy GR
son-in-law (woman's daughter's husband) *(noun)*	garrimaay YR, YY, GR
son of Byame *(noun)*	Gindhayndaamuwi YY
song *(noun)*	yugal YR, YY, GR
song (initiation) *(noun)*	burrambuurra YR, YY
song (little) *(noun)*	yugali YY
son's or daughter's child *(noun)*	nhanuwaaydji YR
soon *(time adverb)*	baayan, yilaa YR, YY, GR
soothe *(verb-transitive)*	binaal bunma-li YR, YY
sooty grunter *(noun)*	gambaal YR, YY, GR
sore *(noun, adjective)*	bayn YR, YY, GR
sorry *(adjective)*	gagilbiyal YR
sorry! *(exclamation)*	madja YR, YY, GR
soul *(noun)*	dhuwi YR, YY, GR
sound *(noun)*	dhural YR
soup *(noun)*	wirrun YR, YY
sour *(adjective)*	badha YR, YY, GR
	giyalgil YR
south *(place adverb)*	dhadhin[2] YR
south-west wind *(noun)*	dhurralbuu YR
Southern Cross (stars) *(noun)*	Yarraan YR
sow thistle *(noun)*	dhiinyaan YR, YY
spangled grunter (fish) *(noun)*	babi YY
sparks *(noun)*	dhidhilan GR
	dhuwindhuwi YY
sparks (belah wood) *(noun)*	murrguwidjuwii YR
sparrow *(noun)*	wubu[2] YR
speak *(verb-transitive)*	guwaa-li YR, YY, GR
speak of the devil! *(exclamation)*	galaay YR
spear *(noun)*	bilaarr YR, YY, GR
spear *(verb-transitive)*	dhu-rri YR, YY, GR
spear (emu) *(noun)*	munun YR, YY
spear (fishing) *(noun)*	dhindi YY
spear (jagged) *(noun)*	mirringamu YR, YY, GR
spear thrower (woomera) *(noun)*	wamara YR, YY
speckled *(adjective)*	ngayarray YR
spell *(verb-intransitive)*	buruwi-y GR
	buuwi-y YR, YY
spew *(verb-transitive)*	gaawi-li YR, YY, GR
spicy *(adjective)*	yiiliyiili YR, YY
spider *(noun)*	gayiya YY
spider (huntsman) *(noun)*	gurra YR, GR
spider (trapdoor) *(noun)*	marrgamarrgaay YR, YY, GR
spider web *(noun)*	gayiyabarra YY
spill *(verb-intransitive)*	gaarri-y YR, YY
	yaarri-y GR
spill *(verb-transitive)*	gaarrima-li YR, YY
	yaarrima-li GR
spin *(verb-transitive)*	baayama-li YR, YY
spin (eggs) *(verb-transitive)*	garima-li YR
spine *(noun)*	guriya GR
	guuyaa YR, YY
spirit (any) *(noun)*	wanda YR, YY, GR
spirit (a particular) *(noun)*	Dharramalan, Milaygiin GR
	Munhibarabin YY, GR
	Yulanbay YR
	Yuurrila YY
spirit breath *(noun)*	yawi buliirral YY
spirit (clever man's) *(noun)*	malimali YR, YY
spirit dog *(noun)*	Mirriwuula YR, YY
spirit emu *(noun)*	gawarrgay YR, YY
spirit (evil) *(noun)*	giniirr YR, YY

English	Gamilaraay/Yuwaalaraay/Yuwaalayaay
spirit-haunted stone (noun)	nguruma GR, nguuma² YY
spirit-haunted tree (noun)	mingga YR, YY, GR
spirit holder (noun)	bundurr YY
spirit (human) (noun)	dhubayn YR; dhuwi YR, YY, GR
spirit light (noun)	wii YY
spirit (long-nailed) (noun)	Yuluwaya YR, YY
spirit (man-like) (noun)	murraagu YR, YY
spirit (tree) (noun)	giniybarra YR
spirit (weather) (noun)	wabuwi GR
spirit (whirlwind) (noun)	warrawilbaarru, wilbaarr YR, YY
spirits of the lower world (noun)	yiiliyanbaa wanda YY
spit (noun)	dhubil YY
spit (verb-transitive)	dhubi-li YR, YY, GR
spiteful (adjective)	nhimalnhimal YR, YY
spitfire grub (noun)	maliga YR, YY
splash (noun)	yaarrngan YR, YY
spleen (noun)	marran YR, YY
splinter (noun)	bilgin YR, YY, GR
split (noun)	barra YR, YY
split (verb-intransitive)	baarra-y YR, YY
split (verb-transitive)	baarray-rri YR, YY, GR
split open (adjective)	barrabarraa YY
spoilt child (noun)	yungiirr YR, YY
spoonbill (noun)	maadhaabulaa YY
spotted (adjective)	mundimundi YR, YY, GR
spotted bowerbird (noun)	wiidhaa YR, YY, GR
spotted nightjar (noun)	buugudaguda YR, YY, GR
spotty river gum tree (noun)	yumu YR, YY
spouse (noun)	guliirr YR, YY, GR
spread (verb-transitive)	dhiyaagarra-li, warruma-li GR
spread out (adjective)	waluwarr YY; warru GR
spread out (verb phrase)	waluwarr bunma-li YY
spread out (verb-transitive)	warruma-li GR
spread out to dry (verb-transitive)	guwima-li YY
spring (car) (noun)	gadjul YR
spring (soak) (noun)	girruu YY
spring wind (noun)	yarragaa YR, YY, GR
spur-winged plover (noun)	baaldharradharra YR, YY, GR
spurt (verb-intransitive)	yuuga-y YY
squash (verb-transitive)	bama-li YR, YY
squat (verb-intransitive)	ngadaluwi-y YY
squatter pigeon (noun)	mumumbaay GR
squeeze (verb phrase)	bamba bayama-li YY
stab (verb-transitive)	dhu-rri YR, YY, GR
staggering (adjective)	dhaandhaan YY
staggering drunk (adjective)	dharraadhaandhaan YY
stale (adjective)	murrurwalingay YR, YY
stand (verb-intransitive)	warra-y YR, YY, GR
stand strong (verb-intransitive)	guurrama-li YY
stand up (verb-intransitive)	warra-y YR, YY, GR
stand up (verb-transitive)	warrayma-li YR, YY
standing (adjective)	warrawarra YY
star (noun)	gawubarray YR, YY; mirii GR
star (a particular star) (noun)	gidjirrigaa YY
star (shooting) (noun)	mirii yanan GR
stare (verb phrase)	bamba ngami-li GR; bamba ngarra-li YR, YY
starling (noun)	dhurrubuu YR
stars (string of) (noun)	mandaymanday YY
stay (verb-intransitive)	baabi-li YR, YY, GR; dhanduwi-y YR, YY; wila-y YR, GR; yilawa-y YY
steadily (adverb)	baluwaa YR, YY, GR
steady on! (exclamation)	yaa! YR
steal (verb-transitive)	gaarrama-li GR; manuma-li YR, YY
steep bank (noun)	ngandirr YR, GR; nganggil YY
stick (noun)	dhulu GR; giniy, muyaan YR, YY
stick (verb-intransitive)	mama-y YR
stick (verb-transitive)	mama-li YR, YY, GR
stick (bendy) (noun)	wulbul YY
stick (clever man's) (noun)	wii muyaan YR, YY
stick (digging) (noun)	ganay YR, YY, GR
stick (drawing) (noun)	dhumbaay YR
stick (forked) (noun)	dharran YR, YY
stick horse (noun)	wulbul yaal YR
stick into (verb-transitive)	dhuwi-y YR, YY
stick (yam) (noun)	dhiinbaay YR, YY; ganay YR, YY, GR

English	Gamilaraay/Yuwaalaraay/Yuwaalayaay
sticks (noun)	wugan YR, YY, GR
sticky (adjective)	mamalmamal YY
still (be) (verb-intransitive)	dhabi-y YR, YY, GR
still (continuing) (adverb)	mayabuu YR, YY
stilt (black-winged) (noun)	buyuwaalwaal YY
sting (verb-transitive)	dhu-rri YR, YY, GR
stinking (adjective)	nhuwi YR, YY, GR
stinky (noun)	nhuwiwan YY
stir (verb-transitive)	gayma-li YR, YY
stockman (noun)	bawurra YY
stockwhip (noun)	wulbul YY
stoke (verb-transitive)	wiigunma-li YR
stomach (noun)	mubal YR, YY, GR
stone (noun)	maarama, yarral GR; maayama YR, YY GR; ngurrala YR
stone axe (noun)	birran.gaa YR; gambu YR, YY; yuundu YR, YY, GR
stone (death) (noun)	dhinagarralawaa, wuyugarralawaa YY
stone knife (noun)	magal YR, YY
stone (magic) (noun)	muuliyaay YR, YY
stone (rain-making) (noun)	wuudalay YY
stone (sacred) (noun)	gabarraa YR, YY
stony (adjective)	maayamamayuu YY
stony place (noun)	maayamabaa YY
stool (noun)	gulaay YR
stoop (verb-intransitive)	dhubi-y YR, YY; dhuli-y YR, YY, GR
stop (particle)	garriya² YR, YY, GR
stop (don't do) (particle)	garri-y GR
stop it! (exclamation)	wanagidjay YR, YY
stop (stay) (verb-intransitive)	dhanduwi-y YR, YY; wila-y YR, GR; yilawa-y YY
store (noun)	garrawal YR, YY
store (verb-transitive)	garrawa-li YY
storm (noun)	walawala GR
story (noun)	gaay YR, YY
straight (adjective, adverb)	warragil YR, YY, GR
straight river (noun)	garragarraan YR
straighten up (tidy) (verb-transitive)	baanda-li YR
strange! (exclamation)	ngibaay GR
strange (adjective)	gulguu, wiyaybaa YR, YY; guliyaan YR
stranger (noun)	gandaadhaay YY; wiyaybaa YR, YY
stranger to corroboree (adjective)	muuwi YY
striated pardalote (noun)	wirrwirr YY
string (noun)	buurr YR, YY, GR
string (sinew) (noun)	dhunbilyabi YY
stringybark tree (noun)	gundhi YY
strip off (verb-transitive)	baarrama-li YR, YY
stripe (noun)	bagan YR, YY
stripe (black) (noun)	bilum YR, YY
striped (adjective)	baganbagan YY
striped skink (noun)	baganbi YY
strong (adjective)	dhunbiliyaay YY; gugirriibiyaay, walanbaa YR, YY; warranggal YR, YY, GR
strong (adjective, adverb)	ngaarr GR
stubborn (adjective)	gundhuwundhuu YR, YY
stuck tight (adjective)	garran.garraan YY
stump (tree) (noun)	ngadhul YR, YY, GR
stupid (adjective)	wamba YR, YY, GR
suck, suckle (verb-transitive)	ngamu-gi YR, YY, GR
sucker (tree) (noun)	buugiin YR, YY
sugar (noun)	dhuga YR, YY, GR
sugar ant (noun)	barrawaraay YY
sulky (adjective)	gundhuwundhuu, walingay YR, YY
sulphur-crested cockatoo (noun)	muraay GR; muyaay YR, YY
summer (noun)	yaaybaa YR, YY; yaraaybaa GR
sun (noun)	dhuni, yaay, yayaay YR, YY; yaraay GR
sunbake (verb-intransitive)	wuulaabila-y YR
Sunday school (noun)	dhayaanmaa YR
sunrise (verb phrase)	yaraay dhurra-li GR
supplejack tree (noun)	ganayanay YR, YY
surface (noun)	ngulu GR
surprise (expression of) (exclamation)	nhaan YR
surveyor (noun)	gamidjina YY
swagman (noun)	burriimaan YR
swallow (verb-transitive)	gurruubi-li, wuwi-li YY
swallow (welcome) (noun)	dhunbarra YY

swamp

swamp (belah tree) *(noun)*	murrgugal YR
swamp box *(noun)*	guburruu YR, YY, GR
Swamp Camp *(placename)*	Murrgu Walaay YR
swamp grass *(noun)*	yiindal YY, GR
swamp hen *(noun)*	mayuubiyuu YY
swamp oak *(noun)*	bilaarr, murrgu YR, YY, GR
swamp paperbark *(noun)*	nguu² YR, YY
swan (black) *(noun)*	baayamal YR, YY barayamal, burrunda GR
swap *(verb-transitive)*	ngaambi-li YR
sweat *(noun)*	nguruwi GR nguuwi YR, YY
sweep *(verb-transitive)*	biimba-li YR, YY
sweet *(adjective)*	guwiirr YR
sweet dough *(noun)*	nhaamanhi YR
sweetbread *(noun)*	gulawularr YR
sweetheart *(noun)*	gambaay, guwiirra YR
swell *(verb-intransitive)*	warra-y YR, YY, GR
swelling *(noun)*	mula, wurrun YR, YY
swift (a bird) *(noun)*	biirruun YR, YY
swim *(verb-intransitive)*	gubi-y YR, YY, GR
swim on surface *(verb-intransitive)*	dhangga-y YY
swollen *(adjective)*	wurrun YR, YY
swollen eye *(noun)*	mil warra YY
swoop down *(verb-intransitive)*	wuuli-y YR
sword *(noun)*	garralan GR

Tt

table *(noun)*	man.ga YR
taboo *(noun)*	budun YR gamaal YY wanaal YY, GR
tabooed woman's camp *(noun)*	gayalaay YY
tadpole *(noun)*	nguuluwi YR, YY
tail *(noun)*	dhiil² YR, YY dhun YY, GR
tail (emu) *(noun)*	bubudhala YR, YY
take *(verb-transitive)*	gaa-gi YR, YY, GR
take back *(verb-transitive)*	gaaguwi-y YR, YY
take off (clothes) *(verb-transitive)*	dhuwima-li YY
take out *(verb-transitive)*	dhuma-li GR dhuwima-li YR, YY
talk *(verb phrase)*	gaayaa wana-gi YR
talk (lot of) *(noun)*	burrulaa garay GR
talk (to) *(verb-transitive)*	guwaa-li YR, YY, GR
talkative *(adjective)*	dhalaybidi YR
tall *(adjective)*	guraarr GR guyaarr YR, YY
tangle *(noun)*	yulanbiirr YR
tangle *(verb-transitive)*	yulaanbi-li YR, YY
tangle up *(verb-intransitive)*	gayarra-y YR
tap *(verb-transitive)*	dhu-rri, dhurradhurraba-li YR
tar vine *(noun)*	wudhugaa YR, YY, GR
Tarilarai *(placename)*	Dhariilaraay GR
taste *(verb-intransitive)*	dhadha-y YR, YY
taste *(verb-transitive)*	dhadha-li YR, YY, GR
tasteless *(adjective)*	nhunduu YR, YY, GR
tattletale *(noun)*	dhubayan YY
tawny frogmouth *(noun)*	buluurr YR, YY, GR
tea *(noun)*	dhii garril YR, YY dhii² YR, YY, GR
tea bag *(noun)*	dhii man.garr YR
tea leaves *(noun)*	dhii garril YR, YY
tea-tree *(noun)*	nguu² YR, YY
teach *(verb-transitive)*	dhiirra-li YR ngamilma-li GR
teacher *(noun)*	dhayaanduul YR
teacher *(noun)*	dhiirral YR
teacher of the law *(noun)*	binangarrangarra YY

English	Gamilaraay/Yuwaalaraay/Yuwaalayaay
tear (from crying) (noun)	gali GR
	nguluurr YR, YY
tear, tear off (verb-transitive)	baarrama-li YR, YY
teenage girl (noun)	malagan YR, YY, GR
teeth on edge (adjective)	dhirragal YY
tell (verb-transitive)	buuyawiya-li YY
	guwaa-li YR, YY, GR
tell a lie (verb phrase)	yaal dhanggi-li GR
tell a lie (verb-transitive)	dhanggi-li GR
tell about (verb-transitive)	dhubaanma-li YR, YY, GR
tell off (verb-transitive)	yaya-li YR, YY
temporary waterhole (noun)	gurruway YR
tempting (adjective)	maayndjul YR
ten (adjective)	banay YR, YY, GR
	bulaarruu maa YY
tent (noun)	guwilii YR
Terewah (placename)	Dharrawaawul YR, YY
termite (noun)	baamagaaliyan YY
termite mound (noun)	guwiigaa YR, YY
tern (whiskered) (noun)	budhagalagala YY
testicles (noun)	buu, bugalaa, buugalaa YR, YY
	buru YR, YY, GR
	burugalaa GR
	manday[1] YR
that (demonstrative)	nhama YR, YY, GR
	ngaarrma YR, YY
	nhamali, nguuma[1] YR
that (suffix)	-nha[1] YR, YY
that's enough! (exclamation)	giirrnga YY
that's right! (exclamation)	ngaawawu YR, YY
the (demonstrative)	nhama YR, YY, GR
	nhamali YR
their (more than two people) (pronoun)	ganungu YR, YY, GR
their (two people) (pronoun)	gaalingu YR, YY, GR
then (time adverb)	yalagiirrmawu YR
then (clitic)	-laa YR, YY
	-nga[1] YR, YY
there (demonstrative)	nhama YR, YY, GR
there (place adverb)	ngaarri YR, YY, GR
	ngiirrma GR
	ngiyarrma, nguwama YR, YY
there (close) (place adverb)	marrama YR, YY, GR
therefore (particle)	waama YR, YY
they (more than two people — doer to) (pronoun)	ganugu YR, YY, GR
they (more than two people — doer/done to) (pronoun)	ganunga YR, YY, GR
they (two people — doer to) (pronoun)	gaali YR, YY
	ngurugaali GR
they (two people — doer/done to) (pronoun)	gaalinga YR, YY, GR
thick (adjective)	nhunduwaa YY
thief (noun)	manumadhaay YR, YY
thigh (noun)	dharra YR, YY, GR
	mabun YR, YY
thin (adjective)	bilga YY
	burabura GR
	buyabuya YR, YY
thing (hard) (noun)	walan.gumba YY
think (verb-transitive)	winanga-y YR, YY, GR
thirsty (adjective)	balal YR, YY, GR
	galingin YR, GR
	yarigin YR
this (demonstrative)	nhalay YR, YY, GR
this side (noun)	nguwagili YR, YY
this way (place adverb)	dhaay YR, YY, GR
thistle (milk) (noun)	balamba YR, YY, GR
thistle (sow) (noun)	dhiinyaan YR, YY
thorny (adjective)	bindiyaabiyaay YY
thought (suppose) (particle)	ngadhan.gaa YR
thousand (adjective)	dhawadha YR, YY, GR
thread (noun)	barra YR, YY
three (adjective)	gulibaa YR, YY, GR
throat (noun)	wun.guwi YR, YY, GR
	wuru GR
	wuyu YR, YY
throw (verb-transitive)	waa-li GR
	wana-gi YR, YY
throw at (verb-transitive)	garawi-li GR
	gayawi-li YR, YY
throw out (verb-transitive)	dhilay-rri YR
thug (noun)	bumaldaay YY
thumb (noun)	gunidjarr maa YR, YY
thunder (noun)	dhuluumay YY, GR
	dhuwaarrgaa YR
	murrumay YR, YY, GR
thunder (verb-intransitive)	dhuluuma-y YR, YR
thunder cloud (noun)	dharringarra YR, YY

English *to* Gamilaraay/Yuwaalaraay/Yuwaalayaay Word List

tickle

English	Word
tickle *(verb-transitive)*	gidjigidjiba-li YR, YY
tie up *(verb-transitive)*	yulaa-li YR, YY, GR
	bindaybi-li YR
tight *(adjective)*	garran.garraan YY
Timbumburi Creek *(placename)*	Dhimbambaraay GR
time of *(suffix)*	-Baa YR, YY, GR
time of creation *(noun)*	burruguu YR
tin *(noun)*	nganda YR, YY
tin can *(noun)*	giyaan YR
tin canoe *(noun)*	dhaadharr YR
tin dish *(noun)*	dhindiirr YR, YY
tin mug *(noun)*	gaala YR
tiny *(noun)*	badjindi YY
tip (game) *(noun)*	gubiyalanhay YR
tired *(adjective)*	malu YY, GR
	yinggil YR, YY, GR
tired (very) *(adjective)*	yarrbun YR, YY
to (dative) *(suffix)*	-Ga YR, YY, GR
to and fro *(adverb)*	nganbinganbi YY
to here (place adverb)	dhaay YR, YY, GR
to here (nearby) *(place adverb)*	marragula YR, YY
to the side *(place adverb)*	dhaan YR, YY
to who? *(pronoun)*	ngaanngu, ngaanngunda YR, YY, GR
tobacco *(noun)*	biyaga YR, YY, GR
today *(time adverb)*	yilaadhu GR
toe *(noun)*	dhina GR
toe (big) *(noun)*	gunidjarr baburr GR
toenail *(noun)*	dhina yulu GR
	yulu YR, YY, GR
toes *(noun)*	bambugal GR
toilet *(noun)*	gunagalaa YR, YY, GR
tomahawk *(noun)*	birran.gaa YR
	dhamiyaa, gambu YR, YY
	giirrgal YY
	yuundu YR, YY, GR
tomato (native) *(noun)*	gumi YR, YY, GR
tomorrow *(time adverb)*	ngurrugu YR, GR
tomorrow (near future) *(suffix)*	-ngayi-y YR, YY
tongue *(noun)*	dhalay YR, YY, GR
tonight *(noun)*	yilaa buluuya YY
too *(suffix)*	-bula YR, YY
too right *(particle)*	giirruu YR, YY, GR
tooth *(noun)*	yira GR
	yiya YR, YY
toothless *(adjective)*	yiyadhalibaa YY
top *(noun)*	gabundi YY
	gaburran YR, YY, GR
topknot (bird's) *(noun)*	dhigun YY, GR
topknot pigeon *(noun)*	gulawuliil YR, YY, GR
torn *(adjective)*	gadharrgadharr YR, YY
totem *(noun)*	maa YY
touch *(verb-transitive)*	dhama-li YR, YY, GR
tough *(adjective)*	walan, walanbaa YR, YY
town *(noun)*	gundhilgaa YR
toy club (waddy) *(noun)*	budhal YR, YY
toy roller *(noun)*	wanggal YR, YY
toy spear *(noun)*	widjuwidju YY
track *(verb-transitive)*	yawa-li YR, YY
track (snake) *(noun)*	gay YR, YY
	wayal YR
tracks *(noun)*	dhina YR, YY, GR
trade *(verb-transitive)*	ngaambi-li YR
trample *(verb-transitive)*	ngayu-gi YR, YY
transform *(verb-intransitive)*	gayarra-y YR, YY
trap (bird) *(noun)*	murragal YR, YY
trapdoor spider *(noun)*	marrgamarrgaay YR, YY, GR
tread on *(verb-transitive)*	ngayu-gi YR, YY
tree *(noun)*	dhulu GR
	giniy, muyaan YR, YY
tree bark *(noun)*	bidjal YR, YY
	nganda YR, YY, GR
tree (big) *(noun)*	maalaabidi YR
tree (birthing) *(noun)*	gugurruwan YR, YY
tree branch *(noun)*	bungun, dharra GR
	gugul YY
tree branch game *(noun)*	wulbuldaan YY
tree butt *(noun)*	warran YR, YY, GR
tree (coolabah) *(noun)*	gulabaa YR, YY, GR
tree (dead) *(noun)*	balal giniy, balal muyaan YY
tree dtella *(noun)*	wiibidi YR, YY
tree for storing poison sticks *(noun)*	bugarru YR, YY
tree frog (green) *(noun)*	ngayrrngayrr YR, YY
tree frog (one type) *(noun)*	garrarr YR, YY
tree goanna *(noun)*	guugaarr YR, YY
	mangun.gaali YR, YY, GR
	yurrandaali GR
tree gum *(noun)*	dhani YR, YY

English	Word	Dialect
tree (hollow) (noun)	burran.gul	YR
	ngadhul	YR, YY, GR
tree knot (noun)	buul²	YY
	nhay	YR, YY
tree lizard (noun)	waluubaal	YR, YY, GR
tree martin (noun)	gan.garra	YY
tree root (noun)	warran	YR, YY, GR
tree snake (noun)	waya²	YY
tree spirit (noun)	giniybarra	YR
	maambiyaa	YR, YY
tree stump (noun)	ngadhul	YR, YY, GR
tree sucker (noun)	buugiin	YR, YY
tree (supplejack) (noun)	ganayanay	YR, YY
tree trunk (noun)	warran	YR, YY, GR
tree (unusual) (noun)	giniy walingay	YR, YY
treecreeper (brown) (noun)	bibi	YR, YY
tribe (mythical) (noun)	Murungamildaa	YY
trick (verb-transitive)	dhanggiwa-li	YY
trick (sleight of hand) (noun)	dhanggiway	YR
troublemaker (noun)	dhirridhirri	YY
trough (noun)	walban	YR, YY, GR
trousers (noun)	dharrawurra	YR, YY, GR
true (adjective, adverb)	warragil	YR, YY, GR
true words! (exclamation)	gaay giirruu	YY
truly (particle)	giirr	YR, YY, GR
tucker (noun)	mandha	YR
tune (noun)	dhaalan	YY
turkey (brush) (noun)	wagun	YR, YY, GR
	wirrilaa	YR, GR
turkey bush (noun)	burrgulbiyan	YR, YY
turkey (plains) (noun)	barawaa	YR, GR
	gumbulgaban	YR, YY
turn (verb-transitive)	gayma-li	YR, YY
turn around (verb-intransitive)	gayarra-y	YR, YY, GR
turn into (verb-intransitive)	gayarra-y	YR, YY
turn, turn over (verb-intransitive)	gaya-y	YR, YY
turpentine bush (noun)	muruwaa	YY
turtle (long-necked) (noun)	girrabirrii	YR, YY, GR
	maliyan	YR
turtle (short-necked) (noun)	waraba	GR
	wayamba	YR, YY
twelve apostle bird (noun)	gidjarray	YR, YY
twice (adverb)	bulaarra	GR
twins (noun)	bulaangu	YR, YY
twist (verb-intransitive)	gaya-y	YR, YY
twist (verb-transitive)	gayma-li	YR, YY
	wirra-li	GR
	yabi-li	YY
two (adjective)	bulaarr	YR, YY, GR
two-faced (adjective)	muyumul	YR
two stars (near Southern Cross) (noun)	bulunbulun	YY

Uu

ugly *(adjective)*	gagil ngulu	YR, YY
umbilical cord *(noun)*	ngalirr	YY, GR
umbrella bush *(noun)*	midjirr	YR, YY, GR
uncle *(noun)*	garruu	YR, YY, GR
uncle (father's brother) *(noun)*	yugin	YR, YY
uncle (mother's brother) *(noun)*	garruu	YR, YY, GR
under *(place adverb)*	ngadaa	YR, YY
underneath *(noun)*	ganhaga	YR, YY
understand *(verb-transitive)*	winanga-y	YR, YY, GR
unique *(adjective)*	mamaldhalibaa	YY
unleavened bread *(noun)*	mandhamandha	YR
unmarried *(adjective)*	guliirrdhalibaa	YR, YY, GR
unsweetened *(adjective)*	nhunduu	YR, YY, GR
untidy *(adjective)*	dhurradhurraa	YY
unusual tree *(noun)*	giniy walingay	YR, YY
up *(place adverb)*	ngarribaa	YR, YY, GR
up (be) *(verb-intransitive)*	ma-y	YR
upset *(adjective)*	giligili, bina guwaal	YR
upwards *(place adverb)*	ngarribaali	YR, YY
urinate *(verb-intransitive)*	giili-y	YR, GR
urine *(noun)*	giil	YR, YY, GR
us (more than two people — done to) *(pronoun)*	ngiyaninya	YR, YY, GR
us (two people — done to) *(pronoun)*	ngalinya	YR, YY, GR

Vv

vagina *(noun)*	yanggal	YR, YY, GR
vegetable food *(noun)*	dhuwarr	YR, YY
	yuul	YR, YY, GR
vein *(noun)*	buurraan	YR, YY, GR
velvet potato bush *(noun)*	dhiiburruu	YR, YY
venereal disease *(noun)*	dharrgadharrga	YR
Venus (planet) *(noun)*	Murrudhi Gindamalaa, Maliyan.gaalay	YR, YY
	Nganundi Gindamalaa	GR
verandah *(noun)*	barranda	YR
very *(adverb)*	bamba	YR, YY
very *(suffix)*	-ban.gaan	GR
	-wan.gaan	YR, YY
very deep *(adjective)*	gurrugurru[1]	YY
very flash *(adjective)*	dhirrabuu	YR
very fond *(adjective)*	nhiiyanhiiya	YR
very good *(adjective)*	maayndjul	YR
very heavy *(adjective)*	madhanmadhan	YY
very long ago *(time adverb)*	ngaarribu	GR
very tired *(adjective)*	yarrbun	YR, YY
vomit *(noun)*	gaawil	YR, YY
vomit *(verb-transitive)*	gaawi-li	YR, YY, GR

English	Word	Source
wag (verb-intransitive)	dhirranba-y	YR
wag (verb-transitive)	yuurrambi-li	YR
waist (noun)	bagurr	YR, YY
	gulurr	GR
wait a while! (exclamation)	garriyawu	YR, YY
wait (for) (verb-transitive)	dhurraami-li	YR, YY
wake up (verb-intransitive)	dhirra-li	YR
wake up (verb-transitive)	giirra-li	GR
Walangala (placename)	Walan.gala	YY
walk (verb-intransitive)	yanaa-y, 'naa-y	YR, YY
	yana-y	GR
wallaby (noun)	wan.guy	GR
wallaby (bridled nail-tail) (noun)	mararra	GR
	mayarra	YR, YY
wallaroo (noun)	yulama	GR
wanting (suffix)	-nginda	YR, YY, GR
war (noun)	yiilinhi	GR
warm (adjective)	bulayrr	YR, YY, GR
warm up (verb-intransitive)	guulaabi-y	YR, YR
warrior bush (noun)	gubigala	YY
	wayaarra	YR, YY
wart (noun)	ganagaa	YR
wash (verb-transitive)	wagirrbuma-li	YR, GR
	wagirrma-li	YR, YY
wash (self) (verb-intransitive)	wagirrbuma-y	YR
	wagirrma-y	YY
wasp (noun)	muundhuurr	YR, YY
watch (noun)	yaayngarralgaa	YY
watch (verb phrase)	milu gawaa-y	YY
watch (verb-transitive)	ngami-li	GR
	ngarra-li	YR, YY
watch carefully (verb phrase)	bamba ngarra-li	YR, YY
watchful (adjective)	milgumilgu	YY
water (noun)	gali	GR
	gungan	YR, YY
water bag (noun)	galinmay	YR, YY
	miidja	YY, GR
water bird (noun)	gunambaay	GR
watercourse (overflow channel) (noun)	warrambul	YR, YY, GR
water current (noun)	yarrin	YY
water (deep) (noun)	gaawaa	YR
water drops (noun)	dhulirral	YY
water (full of) (adjective)	galibaraay	GR
water hollow in tree (noun)	gulaagul	YY
water rat (noun)	gumaay	YR, YY, GR
water weed (noun)	buliyaarr	YR, YY
	dhurrulawaa	YR, YY, GR
	dhanggaluwi, gumbi	YR
waterhole (noun)	bilyan	YR, YY
	mayan	GR
waterhole at Gingie (placename)	Gali Gurunha	YR
waterhole name (placename)	Bawa, Bilambulaa, Dhindirrina, Gumbulgabanbaa, Mungungulu	YY
	Milaanbaa, Yulanbiirr	YR
waterhole (shallow) (noun)	gilgaay	YR
waterhole (small) (noun)	dhanggaal	YR, YY
	gilgal	YY
waterhole (temporary) (noun)	gurruway	YR
waterlily (noun)	gabirra, gurragurra	YY
wattle (black) (noun)	dhulan	YR, YY
wattle (brigalow) (noun)	burrii	GR
wattle (golden) (noun)	gulgulay	YY
wattle (gundabluie) (noun)	ngaduwi	YR, YY
wattle (river) (noun)	gurrulay	YR, YY
wattle (sandhill) (noun)	girranbiiyan	YY
wave (noun)	ngamulngamul, yaarrngan	YR, YY
wave (verb-transitive)	yuurrambi-li	YR
wax-lipped orchid (noun)	gurriyaa	YR
wax spout (noun)	mayaarr	YR
we (more than two people — doer/doer to) (pronoun)	ngiyani	YR, YY, GR
we (two people — doer/doer to) (pronoun)	ngali	YR, YY, GR
weak (adjective)	balumbaluu	YY, GR
	gugirriidhalibaa, mula	YR, YY
wear (verb-transitive)	gaa-gi	YR
weather spirit (noun)	wabuwi	GR
wedge-tailed eagle (noun)	maliyan	YR, YY, GR
weebill (bird) (noun)	mindjarru	YR, YY
weed (milky) (noun)	minan	YY

weed

English	Gamilaraay/Yuwaalaraay/Yuwaalayaay
weed (water) *(noun)*	buliyaarr YR, YY
	dhurrulawaa YR, YY, GR
	gumbi YR
weep *(verb-intransitive)*	yu-gi YR, YY, GR
Wee Waa *(placename)*	Wii Waa GR
Wee Warra Plain *(placename)*	Wii Warra YR, YY
Weetalibah *(placename)*	Wiidhalibaa YR, GR
welcome! *(exclamation)*	gulbiyaay YR
welcome swallow *(noun)*	dhunbarra YY
well *(adjective)*	marrabaa GR
well *(adjective, adverb)*	gaba YR, YY, GR
well *(adverb)*	maaru GR
	maayu YR, YY
well *(noun)*	girruu YY
well behaved *(adjective)*	binaal YR, YY, GR
well done! *(exclamation)*	giirr maayu YR, YY
	giirr maaru GR
well (healthy) *(adjective, adverb)*	gaba YR, YY, GR
well known *(adjective)*	gayrriyaay YY
well mannered *(adjective)*	binaal YR, YY, GR
	gaba binaal YR, YY
west (sundown) *(place adverb)*	ngadaa YR, YY
west wind *(noun)*	gigirrgigirr YR, YY
western barred bandicoot *(noun)*	guru GR
	guyu YR, YY
western bloodwood *(noun)*	gawuwildhaa YR
western grey kangaroo *(noun)*	wamburr YY
western grey kangaroo (nickname) *(noun)*	nhuwiwan YY
wet *(adjective)*	galibaraay GR
	gunganbiyaay YR, YY
what? *(question word)*	minya YR, YY, GR
	minyama YR, GR
	ngaan YR
what to do? *(verb phrase)*	galaarr gi-gi YR, YY
what's-a-name *(common expression)*	ngaandingaandi YR
when? *(question word)*	galawu YR, YY
	wirralaa GR
where? *(question word)*	dhalaa GR
where (at)? *(question word)*	minyaaya YR, YY
where (from)? *(question word)*	minyaaya dhaay YR, YY
where (to)? *(question word)*	minyaarru YR, YY
whether *(question word)*	yaamagaa YR, YY
which? *(question word)*	minyaarr YR, YY, GR
whip (stock) *(noun)*	wulbul YY
whirlwind *(noun)*	buulii YR, YY, GR
whirlwind spirit *(noun)*	warrawilbaarru, wilbaarr YR, YY
whiskered tern *(noun)*	budhagalagala YY
whiskers *(noun)*	yarray YR, YY, GR
whisper *(verb-transitive)*	dhayaamba-li YR, YY
	maaya-li YR, YY, GR
whistle *(verb-transitive)*	wiila-y YR, YY, GR
whistling duck *(noun)*	dhibayuu YR, YY, GR
	wululuu YY, GR
whistling kite *(noun)*	biya YY
white *(adjective)*	balaa YY, GR
	bangga YR, YY
	banggabaa YR, YY, GR
white ant *(noun)*	baamagaaliyan YY
white-bellied sea eagle *(noun)*	guwinyarri YY
white-browed woodswallow *(noun)*	dhaluraa YR, YY
white cockatoo *(noun)*	muraay GR
	muyaay YR, YY
white cypress pine *(noun)*	gurraari GR
	gurraay YR, YY
white-faced heron *(noun)*	budhuulgaa, buyudhurrungiili YR, YY
white man *(noun)*	gabaa YR, GR
	wanda YR, YY, GR
white ochre *(noun)*	dhawurraa YR
white paint *(noun)*	bidjaay balaa YY
white pipeclay *(noun)*	bagi YY
white-winged triller *(noun)*	wiigurrun.gurrun YR, YY
white woman *(noun)*	wadjiin YR, YY, GR
whitewood flowers *(noun)*	birraawiin YR, YY
whitewood grub *(noun)*	wungala YR, YY
whitewood tree *(noun)*	birraa YR, YY
who? (doer to) *(pronoun)*	ngaandu YR, YY, GR
who? (doer/done to) *(pronoun)*	ngaana YY
	ngaandi YR, YY, GR
whole *(adjective)*	ganungawu YR, YY
whose? *(pronoun)*	ngaanngu YR, YY, GR
why? *(question word)*	minyadhi YR, YY
why not? *(question word)*	gamilgaa GR
	minyadhi YR, YY
	waalgaa YR

English	Gamilaraay/Yuwaalaraay/Yuwaalayaay
why (what for)? *(question word)*	minyagu YR, YY, GR
wide *(adjective)*	man.gaman.ga YR, YY, GR
	waluwarr YY
	warru GR
widow, widower *(noun)*	gulun YY
widowed *(adjective)*	guliirrdhalibaa YR, YY, GR
wife *(noun)*	dhubaay YR
	guliirr YR, YY, GR
wife's mother's brother *(noun)*	baayna GR
wilga *(noun)*	dhiil¹ YR, YY
Wilkie *(placename)*	Wilgi YY
willy wagtail *(noun)*	dhirridhirri YR, YY, GR
win *(verb-transitive)*	biidjinma-li YR
wind *(noun)*	mayrraa YR, YY, GR
wind (east) *(noun)*	gunyamurr YR, YY
wind gust *(noun)*	buliirral wanda YR, YY
wind (north) *(noun)*	dhurrandhurran, wilaarrdaa YR, YY
wind (south-west) *(noun)*	dhurralbuu YR
wind (spring) *(noun)*	yarragaa YR, YY, GR
wind (west) *(noun)*	gigirrgigirr YR, YY
windbreak *(noun)*	wadhuurr YR, YY, GR
windbreak (grass) *(noun)*	ngana YY
window *(noun)*	barriyay GR
wine *(noun)*	yurraamu YR
wing *(noun)*	bangu YR
	bungun YR, YY, GR
wing noise *(noun)*	maamuu YR
wink *(verb-intransitive)*	milabi-li GR
wink *(verb phrase)*	barraay milu gimbi-li YR
winter *(noun)*	dhandarraa YR, YY, GR
wipe *(verb-transitive)*	gaanba-li YR
wire *(noun)*	waaya YR, YY
wise *(adjective)*	burrul bina GR
witchetty grub *(noun)*	wungala YR, YY
with *(suffix)*	-baraay, -araay GR
	-biyaay, -iyaay YR, YY
with a lot of *(suffix)*	-bil YR, YY, GR
without *(suffix)*	-dhalibaa YR, YY, GR
woma (snake) *(noun)*	mangan YR, YY
woman (Aboriginal) *(noun)*	yinarr, wirringgaa YR, YY, GR
woman (married) *(noun)*	wirringgaa YR, GR
woman (non-marriageable) *(noun)*	ngan.gi, nganbirr YY, GR
woman (old) *(noun)*	dhubaay, nhangi YR maamii, yinarraagalaa YR, YY yambuli GR
woman spirit *(noun)*	yuurri YR
woman (white) *(noun)*	wadjiin YR, YY, GR
woman's armlet *(noun)*	gumil YR, YY
woman's camp *(verb phrase)*	gurruga baabay YY
woman's possum-fur belt *(noun)*	wangal YR, YY
women's social section *(noun)*	Buudhaa, Gabudhaa, Maadhaa, Yibadhaa YR, YY, GR
wonderful! *(exclamation)*	gadhabal GR
won't *(particle)*	waal YR, YY
	gamil GR
wood *(noun)*	wugan YR, YY, GR
wood (dead) *(noun)*	giniy waal YR
wood duck *(noun)*	barrgabarrga YR, YY
wood duck (nickname) *(noun)*	gunambaay GR
wood (heart) *(noun)*	dhuwi GR
woodswallow (black-faced) *(noun)*	biiwanbiiwan YY
woodswallow (white-browed) *(noun)*	dhaluraa YR, YY
wool *(noun)*	dhurrun YR, YY, GR
word *(noun)*	gaay YR, YY
	garay GR
work *(noun)*	waan² YR, YY
worker bee *(noun)*	warrul YR, YY, GR
workplace *(noun)*	warraymbaa YR
worn out *(adjective)*	baramay GR
wound *(noun)*	gun.gan YR
woven bag *(noun)*	waygal YR, YY
wrap up *(verb-transitive)*	marramba-li YR
wrapped *(adjective)*	nguwan.nguwan YY
wrapped (be) *(verb-intransitive)*	marramba-y YR
wren *(noun)*	yundiyundi YY
wrestling game *(noun)*	gumbubudhuu YR, YY
write *(verb phrase)*	mubirr dhu-rri YY
write *(verb-transitive)*	dhu-rri YR
writing *(noun)*	mubirr

Yalaroi

English	Language	Source
Yalaroi (placename)	Yarralaraay	GR
yam (land) (noun)	gugumadharraa	YR, YY
yam (native banana) (noun)	biyarrbirr	YR
	giban	YR, YY
yam (type of) (noun)	gudugaa	YR, YY
	nhaal, warray	GR
yam (water ribbons) (noun)	milaan	YR, YY, GR
yamstick (noun)	dhiinbaay	YR, YY
	ganay	YR, YY, GR
yard (noun)	ngunmal	YY, GR
Yarralduul (placename)	Yarralduul	GR
yarran wattle (noun)	yarran	YR
yell (verb-transitive)	gaga-li	YR, YY, GR
yellow (adjective)	gidjirrgidjirr	YR, YY, GR
	gidjiirr	YR
yellow ochre (noun)	gidjiirr, guwinii	YR
yellow tit (noun)	mindjarru	YR, YY
yellowbelly (noun)	dhagaay	YR, YY, GR
Yeranbah (placename)	Yarranbaa	YY
yes (particle)	ngaa	YR, YY, GR
	yawu	YR, GR
yesterday (time adverb)	gimiyandi	GR
yesterday (suffix)	-ayla-y	YR
yesterday (recent past) (suffix)	-ngayi-y	YR, YY
you (more than two people — doer/doer to) (pronoun)	ngindaay	YR, YY, GR
(suffix)	-ndaay	YR, YY, GR
you (more than two people — done to) (pronoun)	nginaaynya	YR, YY, GR
you (one person — doer/doer to) (pronoun)	nginda	YR, YY, GR
(suffix)	-nda	YR, YY, GR
you (one person — done to) (pronoun)	nginunha	YR, YY, GR
you (two people — doer/doer to) (pronoun)	ngindaali	YR, YY, GR
(suffix)	-ndaali	YR, YY, GR
you (two people — done to) (pronoun)	nginaalinya	YR, YY, GR
young (noun)	bayangurr	YY
young echidna (noun)	nhimaylii	YR, YY
young kurrajong root (noun)	gaagul	YR
young man (noun)	yira murrun	GR
	yiya murrun	YY
young man (fully initiated) (participle)	yiyalgidjaay	YY
young woman (noun)	wirribiiyan	YY
younger brother (noun)	galumaay	YR, YY, GR
younger sister (noun)	bagaan, bariyan	GR
your (more than two people) (pronoun)	nginaayngu	YR, YY, GR
your (one person) (pronoun)	nginu	YR, YY, GR
your (two people) (pronoun)	nginaalingu	YR, YY, GR
youth (initiated) (noun)	guburra	GR
Yuurrila's tree (noun)	mangalaarr	YR, YY
Yuwaalaraay language, tribe (noun)	Yuwaalaraay	YR, YY, GR
Yuwaalayaay language, tribe (noun)	Yuwaalayaay	YR, YY, GR
Yuwaaliyaay language, tribe (noun)	Yuwaalayaay	YR, YY, GR

Gamilaraay/Yuwaalaraay/Yuwaalayaay *to* English
Word List by Topic

People

■ General, including by age and development
(nouns)

baagii	old woman YR
baarrgiin	hermit YR
baayamba	friend, mate YR
barringgu	friend, mate YR
biiwan	orphan (motherless child) YY
birralii	baby, child YR, YY
birraliidjuul	baby YR, YY
birray	boy YR, YY, GR
birraybirraay	boys YR, YY, GR
bulaangu	twins YR, YY
burraay	boy YR
burubiyaay	male YY
buurrabiyaay	boy at initiation YY
buurrbaa	fully initiated man GR
dhaliman	Chinese man YR
dhayn	Aboriginal man, Aboriginal person YR, YY
dhilaagaa	grandfather (father's father), great-uncle (mother's mother's brother), senior man (respected elder) YR, YY
dhiriya	old man GR
dhugaadjuul	little one YR
dhubaay	old woman YR
dhuningarraay	old person YR, YY
dhurriwuudhaay	lover YR, YY
gaay[2]	child GR
gaayli	child GR
gaaynggal	baby GR
gaaynmara	child GR
gabaa	white man YR, GR
gabinya	boy GR
Gamilaraay	Gamilaraay, Kamilaroi, Gamilaroi YR, YY, GR
gandaadhaay	stranger YY
ganduwi	bachelor YR, YY
Garriibarra	orchid country people YY
gawun	orphan (fatherless child) YR, YY
giwiirr	Aboriginal man GR
guburra	initiated youth GR
gulun	widow, widower YY
gunidjaa	orphan (motherless child) YR, YY, GR
gunidjarr	female YR, YY, GR
gunidjarrbaa	female YR, YY, GR
guwiirra	sweetheart YR
maamii	lactating female YR old woman YR, YY
malagan	teenage girl YR, YY, GR
maliyaa	friend, mate YR, YY
mamal	friend, mate YR, YY
mandayaa	male YR, YY, GR
marayrrdhuul	childless woman GR
mari	Aboriginal man, Aboriginal person GR
mayrra	little girl YR, YY
miimii[1]	old woman YR
mil binggarr	Chinese man GR
Mirriyaabarra	lignum country people YY
miyay	girl YR, YY, GR
miyaymiyaay	little girl YR, YY
mudhi	old man, old friend YR, YY
ngaamba	fella, fellow, bloke YY
nhangi	old woman YR
Nhunggabarra	kurrajong country people YY

people

wadjiin	white woman	YR, YY, GR
wamban	baby	YY
wanda	white man	YR, YY, GR
wayamaa	old man	YR, YY, GR
wirribiiyan	young woman	YY
wirringgaa	Aboriginal woman, married woman	YR, GR
wiyaybaa	stranger, foreigner	YR, YY
wuulman	old man	YR
yambuli	old woman	GR
yarraybiyaay	boy at puberty	YY
yinarr	Aboriginal woman	YR, YY, GR
yinarraa	senior lady (respected elder)	YR, YY
yinarraagalaa	old woman	YR, YY
yira murrun	young man	GR
yiya murrun	young man	YY
yiyalgidjaay	fully initiated young man	YY
yumbuy	orphan (fatherless boy)	YR, YY
yuurray	initiated man, Aboriginal man	YR, YY
Yuwaalaraay	Yuwaalaraay tribe	YR, YY, GR
Yuwaalayaay	Yuwaalayaay tribe	YR, YY, GR
Yuwaaliyaay	Yuwaalayaay tribe	YY

■ Descriptions

badha (adjective)	sad	GR
badjindi (noun)	shorty, tiny	YY
balu (adjective)	dead	YR, GR
bana (noun)	cannibal	YY
barranbuu (noun)	boomerang legs (nickname)	YR
bayn (adjective)	sore	YR
biiwanbiiwan (adjective)	boastful, bragging, puffed out	YY
bina guwaal (adjective)	upset, nervous	YR
bina muurr (adjective)	deaf	YR, YY, GR
binaal (adjective)	well behaved, well mannered	YR, YY, GR
binangarrangarra (adjective)	clever, intelligent	YY
buliirral ganaay (adjective)	short of breath	YY
buribara (adjective)	pregnant	YR
burriin (noun)	shame	YR
burrul bina (adjective)	clever, wise	GR
buul (noun)	jealousy	YR, YY, GR
buularaay (adjective)	jealous	GR
buuliyaay (adjective)	jealous	YR, YY
buwabildhalibaa (adjective)	poor	YR
buyu wayawaya (adjective)	bandy legged	YY
buyumadhuul (noun)	glutton	YR
dhalaybidi (adjective)	talkative	YR
dhalaydhalibaa (adjective)	dumb (speechless)	YR, YY
dhandarriyaay (adjective)	grey haired	YR, YY
dharaa (noun)	crowd, big mob	YR
dharraa[2] (adjective)	drunk	YR, YY, GR
dharraadhaandhaan (adjective)	staggering drunk	YY
dharraan.gilaay (adjective)	drunk	YR, YY, GR
dharraawaa (noun)	bigamist	YY
dhaygaliyaay (adjective)	clever	YR, YY
dhaylngulu (adjective)	good-looking	YR
dhigadhiga (adjective)	bold, cheeky	YR
dhiidjalaa (noun)	crawler	YR
dhina (noun)	footprint, tracks	YR, YY, GR
dhirrabil (adjective)	smiling	YY
dhirradhirra (adjective)	flash, showy	YY
dhirragal (adjective)	teeth on edge	YY
dhirridhirri (noun)	nosey person, troublemaker	YY
dhirrindjal (adjective)	numb	YR, YY
dhubayan (noun)	tattletale, dobber	YY
dhuli (adjective)	bent over	YY
dhuningarraay (adjective)	old	YR, YY
dhurrin[2] (adjective)	greedy	YR, YY
dhuruyaal (adjective)	right-handed	GR
dhuurran (adjective)	knowledgeable	YY
dhuuyaal (adjective)	right-handed	YR, YY
gaba binaal (adjective)	peaceful, well mannered	YR, YY
gaba dhaygal (adjective)	clever	YY
gaba guuyay (adjective)	good mood	YR, YY
gaba ngulu (adjective)	good-looking	YR, YY
gadhaa (adjective)	cheeky	YR

people

Gamilaraay/Yuwaalaraay/Yuwaalayaay	English
gagil guuyay *(adjective)*	bad mood YY
gagil ngulu *(adjective)*	ugly YR, YY
galambiirr *(adjective)*	greedy YR
gana garraa *(adjective)*	cranky YR
gana walingay *(adjective)*	sad YY
ganagiil *(adjective)*	sad YR
gandjarra *(noun)*	champion YR
garaydhalibaa *(adjective)*	silent GR
garigari *(adjective)*	afraid, frightened YR, YY, GR
garragarraa *(adjective)*	shaved YY
garran.garraan *(adjective)*	constipated YY
gayaa *(adjective)*	pleased, proud YR, YY
gayaay² *(adjective)*	sexy, randy YR, YY, GR
gayliyaay *(adjective)*	generous, good-hearted, kind YR, YY
gayrr *(noun)*	name YR, YY
gayrriyaay *(adjective)*	named, well known YY
giigaliyaay *(adjective)*	scabby YR, YY
giyal *(adjective)*	afraid, frightened YR, YY, GR
giyaldhalibaa *(adjective)*	shameless, no shame YR, YY
giyalgiyal *(adjective)*	itchy YR, YY
gugan *(noun)*	half-caste YR
guliirraraay *(adjective)*	married GR
guliirrdhalibaa *(adjective)*	unmarried, widowed YR, YY, GR
guliirriyaay *(adjective)*	married YR, YY
guliyaan *(adjective)*	new, strange YR
gundhuwundhuu *(adjective)*	selfish, stubborn, sulky YR, YY
gunhugunhu *(noun)*	cold, cough YR
guuyay *(noun)*	mood, humour YR, YY, GR
guyan *(adjective)*	shy YR
malawil *(noun)*	human shadow YR, YY
manumadhaay *(noun)*	thief YR, YY
mil buluuy *(noun)*	black eye YR
mil guway *(noun)*	bloodshot eye YY
mubalyaal *(adjective)*	pregnant YY, GR
muga *(adjective)*	blind YR, YY, GR
muga bina *(adjective)*	deaf YR, GR
muga wudha *(adjective)*	deaf YY
mugu bina *(adjective)*	deaf YR, YY, GR
mulabiyaay *(adjective)*	kind YR
murrubidi *(adjective)*	lucky YR
muuwi *(adjective)*	stranger to corroboree YY
muyumul *(adjective)*	two-faced YR
ngaarriga *(adjective)*	opposite moiety YY
ngarragaa *(adjective)*	silly, poor (helpless), pitiful YR, YY, GR
nhalawilbayn *(noun)*	reflection YR
nhiiyanhiiya *(adjective)*	very fond YR
nhimalnhimal *(adjective)*	spiteful YR, YY
nhuwiwan *(noun)*	stinky YY
wagibaa dhaygal *(adjective)*	bald YR, YY
walanbaa *(adjective)*	strong YR, YY
walanduurr *(adjective)*	hard-hearted YY
walingay *(adjective)*	lonely, sulky YR, YY
wamba *(adjective)*	eccentric, mad, crazy, stupid, silly YR, YY, GR
waragaal *(adjective)*	left-handed GR
warranggal *(adjective)*	strong, powerful YY
warrayaa *(adjective)*	lost YR, YY
wayagaal *(adjective)*	left-handed YR, YY
wudha muurr *(adjective)*	forgetful YY
wululgal *(noun)*	noisy mob YR, YY
yaambul *(adjective)*	silly, mad YR, GR
yalabiyaay *(adjective)*	not with it YR
yarrbun *(adjective)*	very tired, exhausted YR, YY
yarrbun maa *(adjective)*	clumsy YY
yiili *(adjective)*	angry YR, YY, GR
yiiliyanbaa *(adjective)*	angry, savage YR, YY
yiiliyiiliyan *(noun)*	angry person YY
yinggil *(adjective)*	lazy, tired YR, YY, GR
yiyadhalibaa *(adjective)*	toothless YY
yumbu *(adjective)*	cranky, cry-baby YR
yungiirr *(noun)*	spoilt child, cry-baby YR, YY
yuurray *(noun)*	important man YR, YY
yuwaarran *(adjective)*	broken-hearted YR

people

■ **Family** (nouns)

baagii	grandmother, mother's mother YR, YY
baaman	father's sister, mother's brother's wife, mother's mother's brother's daughter GR
baawaa	sister, older sister YR, YY, GR
baayna	father, wife's mother's brother GR
badhii	grandmother, mother's mother GR
badhuul	son-in-law YY mother-in-law's brother YR, YY
bagaan	younger sister GR older sister YR, GR
bambuy	father-in-law, son-in-law GR
bariyan	younger sister GR
bawa[1]	sister, older sister YR
bawanngaa	granddaughter YR, YY
biila	daddy YY
biiyalaa	father, mother's sister's husband YY
biraman	brother-in-law (sister's husband, wife's brother) GR
birray	son YY
bubaa	father, dad YR, GR
burrul ngambaa	aunt (mother's older sister) YY
buudhan	child (last) YY
buurrii	sister GR
buwadjarr	father YR, YY, GR
buyal	mother-in-law (wife's mother) GR
dhaadhaa	grandfather (mother's father), grandson (daughter's son) YR, YY, GR
dhagaan	cousin, older brother YY brother YR, GR
dhawurran	older sister YR, YY
dhaya	older brother YR, YY, GR
dhiiyaan	family YR
dhilaagaa	great-uncle (mother's mother's brother), grandfather (father's father) YR, YY
dhubaay	wife YR
dhugaaga ngambaa	aunt (mother's younger sister) YY
gaadhii	grandmother (mother's mother), sister YR
galduman	brother YR
galimingaa	grandson YR, YY, GR
galumaay	younger brother YR, YY, GR
gambaay	sweetheart YR sister-in-law YR, YY
gamiyan	aunt (father's sister) YR, YY
garrimaay	grandmother (father's mother) GR mother-in-law (wife's mother), son-in-law (woman's daughter's husband) YR, YY, GR
garruu	father-in-law, uncle, mother's brother YR, YY, GR
gayandaay	brother-in-law YR, YY
giluu	aunt (father's sister) YR, YY
girrinya	daughter-in-law YY
guliirr	spouse, husband, wife YR, YY, GR
gulumaldhaay	foster parent YR, YY
gulun	widow, widower YY
gunidjarr	mother, aunt (mother's sister) YR, YY, GR
gunii	mother, aunt (mother's sister) YR, YY, GR
gunubingaa	nephew (sister's son) YR, YY, GR
gunugayngaa	niece (sister's daughter) YR, YY, GR
maamaa	father's mother YR
mamaay	grandmother (father's mother) GR
maran	ancestors YR, YY
miimi	sister GR
miimii[1]	grandmother YR
miyay	daughter YY
murrambagan	mother's mother's mother YY
nhanuwaaydji	grandchild (son's or daughter's child) YR

people

ngaagii	grandmother (father's mother) YR, YY
ngama	father's sister GR
ngambaa	mother, aunt (mother's sister) YR, YY, GR
ngamurr	daughter GR
nganawayngaa	grandchild (son's child) YY
nganuwaay	potential spouse (for a man) GR
ngarrawidhalba	father-in-law YR
waabi	grandmother (mother's mother), mother's mother's brother GR
waaruu¹	grandson (son's son) GR
walgan	aunt, man's father's sister, mother-in-law (husband's mother) YR, YY
wambanhiiya	cousin YR, YY
wurrumay	son GR
yugin	father, uncle (father's brother) YR, YY

■ Social organisation (nouns)

baanmal	betrothal of babies YY
Bumbira	social group YY
dhii¹	meat (totem) YR, YY, GR
dhinggaa	meat (totem) YR, YY
dhurrun.gal	furry tribe YY
guwaygaliyarr	light blood group YR, YY, GR
guwaymadhan	heavy blood group YR, YY, GR
ngan.gi	non-marriageable (woman) GR
nganbirr	non-marriageable (woman), crosswise, across YY, GR
Ngara	social group YY
Magula	social group YY
Wudhurruu	moiety name YY, GR
Yanguru	moiety name GR
Yanguu	moiety name YY
yarudhagaa	matrilineal totem GR

Men's social sections

Gabii	men's social section YR, YY, GR
Gambuu	men's social section YR, YY, GR
Marrii	men's social section YR, YY, GR
Yibaay	men's social section YR, YY, GR

Women's social sections

Buudhaa	women's social section YR, YY, GR
Gabudhaa	women's social section YR, YY, GR
Maadhaa	women's social section YR, YY, GR
Yibadhaa	women's social section YR, YY, GR

■ Professions, jobs (nouns)

badjin maadha	overseer YR, YY
barran.giiba	boomerang maker YR
bawurra	jackeroo, stockman YY
biliirrman	policeman YY
binangarrangarra	teacher of the law YY
bumaldaay	hit man, thug YY
burriimaan	swagman YR
burrul maadha	boss YR, YY
burrulaabaa	leader YY
dhayaanduul	teacher YR
dhayndalmuu	counsellor, priest YR messenger YR, YY
dhiidhaan	good hunter YR, GR
dhiirral	teacher YR
dhiirralbidi	school principal YR
dhubaay	midwife, nurse YR
dhuurranmay	leader, chief, boss YR, YY, GR
gamidjina	surveyor YY
gandjibal	policeman YR, YY, GR
gayaandhi	peacekeeper YR
gudhuwan	cook YY
maadha	boss, master YR, YY, GR
maawulaaldaanga	policeman YY
maliyan	policeman YR
mandhiigan	initiation guardian YY
midi	missus, mistress YY
murraan.gali	corroboree leader YR, YY
warrgiiba	cook YR, YY
wiringin	Aboriginal doctor, clever man YR, YY, GR
wurrugaa	owner YR
wuumaa	bora messenger YY

people

■ Body parts (nouns)

baa	hip	YY
baburr	foot	YR, YY, GR
bagurr	waist	YR, YY
balandharr	head hair	YY
bambugal	fingers, toes	GR
bana	body	GR
bandji	bottom	YR
baranggal	ankle	YR, YY
bawa²	back (body part)	YR, YY, GR
bigal	navel, bellybutton	GR
bii	chest	YR, YY
biilaa	shoulder blade	YR, YY
biilara	shoulder blade	GR
biirra gawugaa	bald head	GR
bina	ear	YR, YY, GR
bindawu	muscle	GR
biri	chest	GR
biyal	knuckle	GR
buba	biceps	GR
budhi	body hair, pubic hair	YR, YY, GR
bugalaa	testicles, balls	YR, YY
bungun	arm	YR, YY, GR
bura	bone	GR
burrbiyaan	body, self	YR
buru	testicles, balls	YR, YY, GR
burugalaa	testicles, balls	GR
buu	testicles, balls	YR, YY
buugalaa	testicles, balls	YR, YY
buurraan	vein	YR, YY, GR
buya	bone	YR, YY
buyu	lower leg, calf of leg, shin, leg	YR, YY, GR
dhaal	cheek, jaw, jawbone	YR, YY, GR
dhalay	tongue	YR, YY, GR
dhanga	heel	YR, YY, GR
dharra	thigh, leg	YR, YY, GR
dharrarr	rib	GR
dhaygal	head	YR, YY
	head hair	YR, YY, GR
dhiin	elbow	GR
dhina	toe	GR
	foot	YR, YY, GR
dhina yulu	toenail	GR
dhinbirr	knee	YR, YY, GR
dhinggal	foetus	YR
dhinmirr	eyebrow	YY, GR
dhiriya	first finger	GR
dhubayn	body, spirit (human), self	YR
dhun	tail	YY
	penis	YY, GR
dhunbil	sinew	YR, YY
dhurrun	hair	YR, YY, GR
gaban	lung	YR, YY
gana	liver	YR, YY, GR
ganagaa	wart	YR
gawu	brain	YR, YY
gawugaa	head, head hair	GR
gayarr	back of knee	YY
gidjigidji	underarm	YR
gii	gall bladder	YY
	heart	YR, YY, GR
giindjuu	bone marrow	YR
gugirrii	sinew	YR, YY
gulawularr	sweetbread	YR
gulurr	waist	GR
gumay	lip	GR
gumbirri	brain	GR
gumbul	bottom, bum	YR, YY
gunidjarr baburr	big toe	YY, GR
gunidjarr maa	thumb	YR, YY
guriya	backbone, spine	GR
guuyaa	backbone, spine	YR, YY
maa	finger, hand	YR, YY
mabun	thigh	YR, YY
mala	bottom, bum	YR, GR
manday¹	penis, testicles	YR
mandhu	moustache	GR
manga	ear	YR
mara	finger, hand	GR
marran	spleen	YR, YY
mil	eye	YR, YY, GR
mil warra	swollen eye	YY
mila	hip	GR
mubal	stomach, belly, guts	YR, YY, GR
mubirr	scar	YY
mugarr	kidney	YR, YY, GR
murru	bottom, bum	YR, YY, GR
murrundunmali	colon (descending)	GR
muru	nose	GR
muru biruu	nostril	GR
muyu	nose	YR, YY

muyudhaa	nostril YY		buuwirr	smallpox GR
ngaay	mouth YR, YY, GR		dhala	eye dirt (sleep) YR, YY
ngagan	chin YR, YY		dharrgadharrga	venereal disease YR
ngalirr	umbilical cord YY, GR		dhinayal	pins and needles YR
ngamu	breast YR, YY, GR		dhubil	spit YY
ngawurr	ankle YY, GR		dhumadhuma	smallpox YR, YY
ngiirr	eyebrow GR		gaawil	vomit YR, YY
ngubi	chest GR		gagil dhaygal	headache YR
ngudjiin	eyelash YR, YY		galan	blister YY
ngulu	face, forehead YR, YY, GR		gali	tear (from crying) GR
ngunuugaa	elbow YR, YY, GR		giguwi	hiccup YR, YY
nhamun	rib YR, YY, GR			sneeze YR, YY, GR
nhan	back of neck YR, YY, GR		giigal	scab YR, YY
nhirrin	side YR, YY, GR		giil	piss, urine YR, YY, GR
nyii	anus YR, GR		gindjul	diarrhoea YR
nyiinmay	penis head GR		gulu	lump YY
nyiinmaya	foreskin GR		gun.gan	wound YR
walarr	shoulder YR, YY, GR		guna	faeces, shit YR, YY, GR
wamu	fat YR, YY, GR		gunhugunhu	cold, cough YR, YY, GR
wangali	afterbirth GR		guway	blood YR, YY, GR
wirrigaal	navel, bellybutton YR, YY, GR		malagan	menstruation, periods YY
wudha	ear YY, GR		mirril	mucus, snot YR, YY, GR
wun.guwi	Adam's apple, throat YR, YY, GR		mubirr	scar YY initiation scars, cicatrices YR, YY, GR
wuru	neck, throat GR		mula	boil, pus, swelling YR, YY
wuruga	calf of leg GR		ngamu	breastmilk YR, YY, GR
wuyu	neck, throat YR, YY		nguluurr	tear (from crying) YR, YY
yanggal	vagina YR, YY, GR		nguruwi	sweat GR
yarray	beard, whiskers, moustache YR, YY, GR		nguuwi	sweat YR, YY
yili	lip YR, YY, GR		wiiluun	dribble YR
yira	tooth GR		wurrun	swelling YR, YY
yiya	tooth YR, YY		yaydja	skin cracks YR
yulay	skin YR, YY, GR		yurrun	scar YR, YY, GR
yulu	nail, fingernail, toenail YR, YY, GR			
yulumara	fingernail GR			
yuuwirr	armpit YY			

spirits, beings and devils

■ Bodily fluids and products, e.g. blood, milk (nouns)

baburr	footprint YY
bandibandi	diarrhoea YY
barabin	semen YR, YY, GR
bayn	sore YR, YY, GR
buliirral	breath YR, YY, GR
burray	fart YR

Spirits, beings and devils (nouns)

Baayami	Byame, God YR, YY, GR
bagii	bad spirit GR
bindiyaa	roly-poly spirit YY
Birrangulu	Byame's wife YR, YY
Dharramalan	mediator spirit GR
dhinabarra	mythical beings (type of) YY
dhuwi	soul, spirit (human) YR, YY, GR
gaadhaay	ghost YR
Gali Gurunha	creation spirit YR
Ganhanbili	Byame's wife YY

animals

Gamilaraay/Yuwaalaraay/Yuwaalayaay	English
Garriya[1]	crocodile YR, YY
gawarrgay	spirit emu YR, YY
gayandaay	bora spirit YR, YY
Gindhayndaamuwi	son of Byame YY
giniirr	evil spirit YR, YY
giniybarra	tree spirit YR
gudiny	little (hairy) people YY
guuguu	dead relative YR, YY
guuwiyaay	mythological warrior enemies YY, YY
guwaybuyan	skeleton spirit YY
maambiyaa	tree spirit YR, YY
malawil	shadow spirit YY
malimali	person's spirit YR / clever man's spirit YR, YY
Maliyangarr	ancestral eagle man YY
mangalaarr	Yuurrila's tree YR
Milaygiin	spirit GR
Mirriwuula	spirit dog YR, YY
Munhibarabin	spirit YY, GR
murraagu	man-like spirit YR, YY
Murungamildaa	name of a tribe YY
ngarrama	birthplace spirit YR
Nguluyuundu	axe-face spirit YY
nhaagal	bora-ground spirit YY
wabuwi	weather spirit GR
wadhaagudjaaylwan	birth spirit YY
wanda	ghost, spirit YR, YY, GR
warrawilbaarru	whirlwind spirit YR, YY
wiiwiimal	body-snatching spirit YY
wiiyuu	red-eyed spirit YR
wilbaarr	whirlwind spirit YR, YY
winambuu	little (hairy) people YR
Wurrawaadhiyan	battle spirit YR
yanbiyaay	healer's totem YY
yarayawu	sickness spirit GR
yawi	person's spirit YR, YY
yawi buliirral	spirit breath YY
yiiliyanbaa wanda	spirits of the lower world YY
Yulanbay	spirit YR
Yuluwaya	long-nailed spirit YR, YY
yuurri	woman spirit YR
Yuurrila	spirit YY

Animals

■ General, including body parts (nouns)

Word	English
bayangurr	young YY
biibii	cow's paper gut YY
burubiyaay	male YY
dhii[1]	animal YR, YY, GR
dhiil[2]	tail YR, YY
dhun	tail GR
dhurrun	fur, wool, hair YR, YY, GR
gadhuu	echidna ant sack YR
galinggaa	sheep intestines (small) YR, YY, GR
gayadharri	monster, freak YR
gunidjarrbaa	female YR, YY, GR
man.garr	pouch (kangaroo) YR, YY
mandayaa	male YR, YY, GR
marran	spleen YY
mulama	colon YR
ngamawidhalbaa	colon YR
nhalganhalga	cow horn YR, YY, GR
waalwaal	dog's bark YY
wirayl	echidna quill GR
wiyayl	echidna quill YR, YY
yaray	sheep intestines (large) GR
yulu	scratch (claw mark) YY / claw YR, YY, GR

■ Mammals/marsupials (nouns)

Word	English
bagandi	native cat, quoll YR, YY, GR
bagu	gliding possum YR, GR
bandaarr	grey kangaroo YR, YY, GR
barrawan[1]	golden bandicoot YY
bawurra	red kangaroo YR, YY, GR
bibaaya	fruit bat, flying fox YY
bigibila	porcupine, echidna YR, YY, GR
bilba	bilby YR, YY
buubumurr	platypus GR
dharragarra	platypus YR
dhindu	mouse YR
dhuluun.gayaa	bilby YR, YY
dhunmidjirr	bush rat YY
dhurrawaay	kangaroo rat GR
dhurrun.gal	hairy caterpillar YY
gadhuu	male echidna YR
ganuurr	red kangaroo GR

animals

garragali	planigale (rat-like marsupial) YY	buyuma	dog YR
garrawirr	ringtail possum GR	dhimba	sheep YR, YY, GR
gima	marsupial mouse GR	djigin	chicken YR
guba	koala YR	giyarral	cattle, bullock YY
guda	koala YY, GR	maadhaay	dog YR, YY
gumaay	water rat YR, YY, GR	maamii	lactating female YR
gunharr	kangaroo rat YR, YY, GR	milambaraay	cow YR, GR
guru	western barred bandicoot GR	milambiyaay	cow YY
guyu	western barred bandicoot YR, YY	mirri	dog YR, GR
maamii	lactating female YR	nhaniguurr	goat YR, YY, GR
maayn	dingo YR, YY	waaraal	pup GR
mandarray	mouse YY	waayaal	pup YR, YY
mararra	bridled nail-tail wallaby GR	wirribula	goat GR
marawanda	red-tailed phascogale YY	wirrigaali	goat YY
marayn	dingo GR	yarraaman	horse YR, YY, GR
marrawal	porcupine, echidna GR	yurabirr	rabbit YR, YY
mayarra	bridled nail-tail wallaby YR, YY		
milaya	kangaroo rat (bettong) YY		

■ Birds

General, including body parts (nouns)

mudhay	brushtail possum YR, YY, GR	baandjil	mistletoe bird YY
ngarraadhaan	bat YR, YY	banbandhuluwi	crested bellbird YR, YY, GR
nhimaylii	young echidna YR, YY	bangu	wing YR
nhuwiwan	western grey kangaroo (nickname) YY	barawaa	plains turkey, bustard YR, GR
wagimal	plains rat YY	barrabarruun	quail YR, YY
wamburr	western grey kangaroo YY	barriindjiin	peewee, magpie-lark YR, YY, GR
wan.guy	wallaby GR	bibi	brown treecreeper YR, YY
wirayl	echidna quill GR	bidjaaymamal	fairy martin YY
wiyayl	echidna quill YR, YY	biibin	hooded robin YY
wumbala	echidna crop YR	biirruun	swift (a bird) YR, YY
yulama	wallaroo GR	biiwanbiiwan	black-faced woodswallow YY

■ Introduced animals, e.g. horse, cow (nouns)

		bilumbilum	double-barred finch YY
baawul	chicken YR, YY	birrgabirrga	peewee, magpie-lark YR
bibirrgaa	pig YR, YY	birrubirruu	rainbow bee-eater YR, YY
biginini	foal YY	bunduun	sacred kingfisher YR, YY
biguun	pig GR	bungun	wing YR, YY, GR
bina guraarr	rabbit GR	burrugarrbuu	magpie YR, YY, GR
budjigarr	cat YR, YY	buubuurrbu	pied butcherbird YY
bula	bullock GR	buugudaguda	spotted nightjar YR, YY, GR
bulgirran	bull GR	dhaadhiirr	red-backed kingfisher YR, YY, GR
burrgiyan	cat GR	dhadhalurraa	grey-crowned babbler YR, YY
buruma	dog GR	dhaguway	noisy friar bird YR, YY
buuldirran	ram YR	dhaluraa	white-browed woodswallow YR, YY
buumadhayaa	fox YR		

animals

dhamarr	bronzewing pigeon YR, YY, GR	mumumbaay	squatter pigeon GR
dhan.galaadhil	grey shrike-thrush GR	mungin.gagalawaa	pallid cuckoo YR, YY
dhanibanban	dollar bird YY	muru	beak GR
dharruwii	grey shrike-thrush YR, YY	nhanu	bower YR
dhigaraa	bird GR	waagaan	little crow GR
dhigayaa	feathered tribe YY; bird YR, YY	waagiyan	little crow YR, YY
dhigun	bird's topknot YR, YY, GR	waan[1]	crow, Australian raven YR, YY, GR
dhiidjiinbawaa	soldier bird, miner bird YR, YY	waaruu[2]	crow, raven YR, GR
dhiil[2]	tail YR, YY	wagaaygaali	Richard's pipit YY
dhirridhirri	willy wagtail YR, YY, GR	wagiwagi	Richard's pipit YY
dhun	tail YY, GR	wagun	brush turkey YR, YY, GR
dhunbarra	welcome swallow YY	walaay	nest YR, YY, GR
dhunidjuni	Jacky Winter (bird) YR, YY	wiidhaa	spotted bowerbird YR, YY, GR
dhurrubuu	starling, unknown bird YR	wiigurrun.gurrun	white-winged triller YR, YY
dhuwaanbay	channel-billed cuckoo YY	wiiwambin	red-browed pardalote YY
dhuwigalinmal	clamorous reed warbler YR, YY	wiiyuu	chough YR
djiibirrirr	grey-fronted honeyeater YY	wirriil	feather GR
gaarrimay	nest YY	wirrilaa	brush turkey YR, GR
galalu	currawong GR	wirrwirr	striated pardalote YY
galimaramara	flock bronzewing GR	wubu[2]	sparrow YR
gan.garra	tree martin YY	wuruyan	curlew, bush thick-knee GR
garaayaa	restless flycatcher YR, YY	wuuyan	curlew, bush thick-knee YR, YY
garriguwin.guwin	grey butcherbird YY	wuuyuu	chough YR, YY, GR
gawu	egg YR, YY, GR	yadhaarr	feather, down (of birds) YR, YY, GR
gawubaa	egg yolk YR	yulu	claw YR, YY, GR
gidjarray	twelve apostle bird YR, YY	yundiyundi	wren YY
gubadhu	diamond dove YR, YY, GR		
gugurrgaagaa	kookaburra YR, YY, GR		
gulawuliil	topknot pigeon YR, YY, GR		
guluu	butcherbird YY		
gumbulgaban	plains turkey, Australian bustard YR, YY		
gunidjaa	black-faced cuckoo-shrike YR, YY		
guniibuu	robin redbreast YR, YY		
gurabi	curlew, bush thick-knee GR		
gurugun	peaceful dove YR, GR		
guwaaydjiidjii	grey butcherbird YR, YY		
maamuu	wing noise YR		
mandayaa	male YR, YY, GR		
milbay	curlew GR		
mindjarru	yellow tit, weebill (bird) YR, YY		
mugarrabaa	magpie YR, YY		
mulaydjalbii	skylark YY		
mulindjal	rufous whistler YY, GR		

Water birds (nouns)

baaldharradharra	spur-winged plover, masked lapwing YR, YY, GR
baan.giirr	black-tailed native-hen YR, YY
baayamal	black swan YR, YY
bagabagaali	musk duck YR
baluun	great egret YR, YY
barayamal	black swan GR
barrgabarrga	wood duck YR, YY
bilidjuu	black-fronted plover YR, YY
biramba	plover GR
birraala	musk duck YY, GR
birribangga	little pied cormorant YR, YY, GR
budhagalagala	whiskered tern YY
budhanbaa	black duck YR, YY

animals

budhuulgaa	white-faced heron, blue crane YR, YY
bundabul	banded plover YR
burraalga	brolga, native companion YR, YY, GR
burrunda	black swan GR
buuway	grey teal duck YR, YY
buyudhurrungiili	white-faced heron, blue crane YR, YY
buyuwaalwaal	black-winged stilt YY
dhaarrin.gaarrin	nankeen night heron YR, YY
dharrun	nankeen night heron YR, YY, GR
dhawudjarrdalmu	magpie goose GR
dhibayuu	Australasian shoveler duck, whistling duck YR, YY, GR
dhibi	red-kneed dotterel YY
dhiinbin	Australasian grebe, diver (bird) YR, YY, GR
ganandhaal	darter, long-necked shag YY, GR
garraagaa	crane (bird) YR, YY, GR
garrangay	duck YR, YY, GR
giinbaywarraymal	seagull, silver gull YY
gulaanbali	pelican YR
gulayaali	pelican YR, YY, GR
gulguwi	black-tailed native-hen YR, YY, GR
gunambaal	darter, long-necked shag YR
gunambaay	water bird, wood duck (nickname) GR
maadhaabulaa	spoonbill YY
maanggii-warraywarraymal	seagull, silver gull YR, YY
mayuubiyuu	swamp hen YY
murrgumurrgu	ibis YR, YY
wilidhubaay	pink-eared duck YR
wiligabuul	pink-eared duck YY
wululuu	whistling duck YY, GR
wungayawaa	great black cormorant YR, YY
wurungayawaa	great black cormorant GR
yuwagayrr	ibis GR

Parrots (cockatoos, galah, budgerigah) (nouns)

barrangga	ground parrot, red-rumped parrot GR
bilay	red-winged parrot YR, YY, GR
biliirr	red-tailed black cockatoo YR, YY, GR
bulaybulay	blue bonnet (bird) YR, YY
bulunbulun	mulga parrot (ringneck parrot) YR, YY
gaadhal	parrot (feeding) YR
gadharra	corella YY
gagalarrin	pink cockatoo, Major Mitchell cockatoo YR, YY
gidjirrigaa	budgerigar YR, YY, GR
gilaa	galah YR, YY, GR
muraay	white cockatoo, sulphur-crested cockatoo GR
muyaay	white cockatoo, sulphur-crested cockatoo YR, YY
ngaanbanaa	cockatoo (possibly corella) GR
nhan.garra	ringneck parrot YR, YY
wiraarr	cockatiel, quarrian GR
wiyaarr	cockatiel, quarrian YR, YY

Emus

bagabaga	emu chick (striped) YY
barrgay[2]	emu chick YR, YY, GR
bubudhala	emu tail YR, YY
bulawaa	emu pair YR, YY
buubuwin	emu decoy YY
dhinawan	emu YR, YY, GR
gambadhuul	group of emus YR
ganduwi	one male emu YR, YY
ganurran	14 or 15 emus YY
gayaangay	five or six emus YY
gundiirr	emu feather YR, YY
mirrun	emu net YY
ngurran.gali	sitting emu YR, YY
wugalwugal	four emus YY

Birds of prey (eagles, hawks, owls) (nouns)

biya	whistling kite YY
biyaagaarr	brown falcon YR, YY
buluurr	tawny frogmouth YR, YY, GR
guurrguurr	boobook owl YY
guwinyarri	white-bellied sea eagle YY
maliyan	wedge-tailed eagle YR, YY, GR
manggarraan	black kite YR, YY, GR
muurrguu	barking owl YR, YY

animals

wala	Australian (nankeen) kestrel YR, YY
wandhala	eaglehawk GR
wanggii	barn owl YY
wugamaabaydaa	black-breasted kite YR, YY, GR
yirrin	owlet nightjar YR, YY, GR

■ Snakes (nouns)

babarra	brown and yellow snake YR, YY
dhayaaminyaa	Children's python YY
dhuru	snake GR
dhuyu	snake YR, YY
dhuyumanga	python YR
galibaay	red-bellied black snake GR
gay	snake track YR, YY
giinbal	scales YR, YY, GR
giinbaligal	scaly tribe YY
mangan	woma (snake) YR, YY
mundharr	death adder GR
murrubi	death adder YR, YY
ngabi	grey snake YY
ngandabaa	snake YR
	king brown snake YR, YY, GR
ngurray	black snake YY, GR
nhiibi	grey snake GR
warrala	brown snake YR, YY
waya²	tree snake YY
wayal	snake track YR
wularr	fierce snake YY
wuyubuluuy	black snake YR, YY
yabaa	carpet python YR, YY, GR

■ Lizards, goannas (nouns)

baganbi	striped skink YY
balawagarr	bearded dragon, frilled lizard GR
biiwii	sand goanna YR, YY
binadhiwuubiyan	legless lizard, slow worm YR, YY
birriyan	little plains lizard YY
buumayamayal	fly-catcher lizard YR, YY
dhalagal	bearded dragon, frilled lizard GR
dharri	bearded dragon, frilled lizard GR
dhayarr	jew lizard YY
dhulii	sand goanna YR, GR
gadha	little red lizard YY
galgarriirr	black-headed monitor YR, YY
garragarraandi	prickly gecko YR, YY
garrbaali	shingleback lizard YR, YY
giinbal	scales YR, YY, YY, GR
giinbaligal	scaly tribe YY
gulay	goanna eggs YR
gumawuma	small dragon lizard YR, YY, GR
guugaarr	tree goanna YR, YY
manggaay	shingleback lizard GR
mangun.gaali	tree goanna YR, YY, GR
murrawa	lizard (nickname) YR
waluubaal	tree lizard YR, YY, GR
wiibidi	gecko, tree dtella YR, YY
wubun	blue-tongue lizard YR, YY
wurumal	sleepy lizard GR
wuulaa	bearded dragon, frilled lizard YR, YY
yurrandaali	tree goanna GR

■ Turtles (nouns)

girrabirrii	long-necked turtle YR, YY, GR
maliyan	long-necked turtle YR
waraba	short-necked turtle GR
wayamba	short-necked turtle YR, YY

■ Fish (nouns)

babi	spangled grunter (fish) YY
banngala	black bream YR
baraa	perch (unidentified fish) GR
biirrnga	bony bream YR, YY, GR
bin.gal	fish fin YR, YY
dhagaay	golden perch, yellowbelly YR, YY, GR
gambaal	silver bream, sooty grunter YR, YY, GR
gaygay	catfish YR, YY, GR
giinbal	scales YR, YY, GR
giinbaligal	scaly tribe YY
guduu	fish YR
	Murray cod YR, YY, GR
guwiya	fish YR
guya	fish GR
milanhay	eel YR

animals

ngaaluurr	fish	YR, YY
ngandan	type of fish	YY, GR
nguluumanbuu	flat-headed gudgeon	YY
waay	mud catfish	YY
wii	bobby fish	YR, YY
wirraa	fish intestines	YR, YY
yili	gills	YY

■ Frogs (nouns)

baaybal	frog	YR, YY
bulga	crucifix frog	YR, YY
dharran[2]	type of frog	GR
galgalbanaa	burrowing frog	YR, YY
garrarr	tree frog (one type)	YR, YY
giin.gii	frog eggs	YR, YY
gindjurra	frog	GR
ngayrrngayrr	green tree frog	YR, YY
nguuluwi	tadpole	YR, YY
warrungan	bull frog	YY
yurayaa	any frog	GR
yuwayaa	any frog	YR, YY

■ Crustaceans and shell animals (nouns)

dhanggal	large mussel	YR, YY, GR
dhugaalubaa	shrimp	YR, YY
giidjaa	shrimp	YR, YY
giinbay	small mussel	GR
giirray	crayfish	GR
gindjulmaan	crayfish colon	YR
maanggii	small mussel	YR, YY
mirrindjaa	shrimp	GR
muraabi	crayfish claw	YR
ngalaagaa	crab	YR, YY
waa[1]	shell	YR, YY, GR
yin.ga	crayfish	YR, YY

■ Insects and spiders (nouns)

baanduu	horse fly	YR, YY, GR
babarrngaan	river bug	YY
balabalaa	butterfly	YR, YY, GR
banhaayal	house fly, fly	YR, YY
barranbarraan	millipede	YR, YY
biridja	flea	GR
birraa[2]	grub	GR
birrga	bogong moth grub	YR, YY
bulii	flea	YR, YY
buna	fly	YR
bunbun	grasshopper	YR, YY, GR
burruluu	fly	GR
burrun	type of moth	YR, YY
burrunggal	coolabah tree grub	YR, YY
dhanbadhanba	mud hornet	YY
dharrabilay	long-legged insect	YY
dhula	scorpion	GR
dhurrun.gal	hairy caterpillar	YR, YY
dhuyugarral	earthworm	YR, YY
gabuul	mother louse	YR, YY
gambigambi	type of moth	YY
gamugamuu	blowfly, maggot	YR, YY
ganangganaa	type of beetle	YR, YY
garaay	louse nit	GR
gararrngan	caterpillar, grub	GR
garrarana	dragonfly	YR
garruuyal	sandalwood tree grub	YY
gawaruurr wanaayal	blowfly	YY
gawu	insect	YR, YY, GR
gawugalgaa	insects	YY
gayaay[1]	louse nit	YR, YY
gayiya	spider	YY
gayiyabarra	spider web	YY
giiyan	centipede	YY, GR
gindjul	snail slime/track	YR
gindjulgarra	snail	YR, YY
gugun.gugun	policeman fly	YR, YY
gunha	scorpion	YR, YY
gurra	huntsman spider	YR, GR
guurrman	leech	YR, YY, GR
guwaa	hornet	GR
maliga	spitfire grub	YR, YY
marrgamarrgaay	trapdoor spider	YR, YY, GR
mugiin.gaa	sandfly	YR, YY
mungin	mosquito	YR, YY, GR
munhi	louse, lice	YR, YY, GR
murrumanamanaa	dragonfly	YR, YY
muundhuurr	wasp, hornet	YR, YY
ngarrala	large locust	YR, YY, GR
ngininnginin	small locust, cicada	YR, YY
wungala	witchetty grub, whitewood grub	YR, YY
yarraangan	gum tree grub	YR, YY, GR
yuluumaarraa (noun)	bogong moth grub	YY

plants

■ Ants (nouns)

baamagaaliyan	white ant, termite	YY
barrawaraay	sugar ant	YY
bayaarr	greenhead ant	YR, YY
burudha	bull ant	GR
buurrngan	meat ant	YR, YY
buyuga	bull ant	YR, YY
dhuwiyuwiy	black ant	YR, YY
gaalan	type of ant	GR
gabiyan	bull ant	GR
gadhuu	ant nest	YR
ganal	common ant	GR
giidjaa	ant (any, black)	YR, YY, GR
guwiigaa	termite mound	YR, YY
milbaawaay	jumper ant	YR, YY
milbarawaay	jumper ant	GR
muwan	greenhead ant	GR
wamuwaa	small brown ant	YY

■ Bees (nouns)

dhiinaa	brood comb	YR, YY, GR
gugal	pure honey	YY
guligal	bee droppings	YR, YY
guni	native bee	GR
guniinii	queen native bee	YR, YY, GR
mayaarr	bee's wax, wax spout	YR
warangana	bee, honey	YR, YY
warrul	bee's nest, honey, worker bee	YR, YY, GR

Plants

■ Trees and shrubs (nouns)

badha	sandalwood tree, budda tree	YR, YY
bagala	leopardwood tree	YR, YY, GR
bagiluu	cottonbush	YY
balal giniy	dead tree	YY
balal muyaan	dead tree	YY
bambul	native orange tree	YR, YY, GR
bandi	punty bush	YY
bandiyal	saltbush	YY
barigan	nepine	YR
barranbaa	brigalow wattle	YR, YY
barrgay[1]	flowering lignum, lignum fuchsia	YY
bibil	bimble box tree	YR, YY, GR
biibaya	broombush	YR, YY
bilaarr	swamp oak, belah tree	YR, YY, GR
binamayaa	large saltbush	YR, YY
bin.gawin.gal	needlewood tree	YR, YY
birraa[1]	whitewood tree	YR, YY
bulabul	native gooseberry	YY
bulamin	angophora	GR
bulumburr	native tomato	YR, YY
bunbarr	rosewood, bunnary	YR, YY
burra	ruby saltbush	YY
burrgulbiyan	myrtle, turkey bush	YR, YY
burrii	brigalow wattle	GR
dhalan	grasstree	GR
dhalandjaa	fuchsia	YY
dhan.gayan.gan	ironwood	YR, YY
dhaniyaa	silver wattle	YR, YY
dharrday	native mandarine	YY
dharriwa	lemonwood	YR
dhawaarrii	blue crowfoot	YY
dhiil[1]	sacred tree, wilga	YR, YY
dhiinyaay	red ironbark	YR, YY, GR
dhulan	black wattle	YR, YY
dhulu	tree	GR
gaabiin	carbeen	YR, YY, GR
gadibundhu	quinine tree	YR, YY
gadjigadji	re-growth	YR
ganayanay	supplejack tree	YR, YY
garrayarray	native peach	YY
garruwi	sandalwood tree	YY, GR
gawuwildhaa	western bloodwood	YR
gayga	budda pea	YY
gayn.gayn	native lime	YR, YY
gidjiirr	gidgee	YR, YY, GR
gii	blueberry	YY
gilaan.garra	Darling pea	YY
giniy	tree	YR, YY
giniy walingay	unusual tree	YR, YY
girranbiiyan	sandhill wattle	YY
gubigala	currant bush, warrior bush	YY
guburruu	swamp box	YR, YY, GR
gugurruwan	birthing tree	YR, YY
gulabaa	coolabah tree	YR, YY, GR
gulgulay	golden wattle	YY

plants

gundhi	stringybark tree YY	balamba	milk thistle YR, YY, GR
guri	emu apple tree, gruie GR	barrawan²	type of sedge YY
gurraari	white cypress pine GR	bibu	dillon bush YY
gurraay	white cypress pine YR, YY	bilum	melon YR
gurrulay	river wattle YR, YY	bindamula	cactus YR
guwadhaa	quandong YR, YY, GR	bindiyaa	prickly plant YY
guwi	emu apple tree, gruie YR, YY		prickle YR, YY, GR
guwiibirr	nepine YR, YY	buubiyala	blueberry YY
guwiirra	mallee willow YR	buunggal	native potato YR, YY, GR
maalaabidi	big tree YR	buunhu	grass YR, YY
maayaal	myall tree YR, YY, GR	buuybuuy	pennyroyal, river mint GR
maayal	crowfoot GR	dhalayndjaa	native carrot YR
mabu	beefwood tree YR, YY, GR	dhamu	pigweed YR, YY
malga	mulga YR, YY	dhaygalbaarrayn	Darling lily YR, YY
mawurr	mimosa bush YR, YY	dhiiburruu	velvet potato bush YR, YY
midjirr	umbrella bush YR, YY, GR	dhiilguwin	native potato GR
mingga	spirit-haunted tree YR, YY, GR	dhiinyaan	sow thistle YR, YY
mirrii	drooping currant, native cherry YR, YY	dhunbarr	grass seed YR, YY
mirriraa	lignum GR	gaagulu	native banana YR, YY
mirriyaa	lignum YR, YY	gagarr	moss YR, YY
miyaymiyaay	mallee willow YR, YY	galan.galaan	native spinach YR, YY
murrgu	swamp oak, belah tree YR, YY, GR	galuuba	clover YR, YY, GR
muyaan	tree YY	ganalay	plains grass YY
ngaduwi	gundabluie wattle YR, YY	ganhan	pigweed YY
ngamumbirra	native plum YR, YY	garaarr	grass GR
ngarran²	medicine bush (fuchsia) YY	garrii	black orchid YR, YY
ngawil	emu bush YR, YY	giban	native banana yam YR, YY
ngaybaan	nepine GR	gilaan.garra	Darling pea YR
nguu²	swamp paperbark, tea-tree YR, YY	gubiyaay	orchid YY, GR
nhimin	kurrajong tree GR	gudugaa	type of yam YR, YY
nhungga	kurrajong tree YR, YY	gugumadharraa	land yam YR, YY
wayaarra	currant bush, warrior bush YR, YY	guli	river grass (native millet) YY
yarraan	river red gum tree YR, YY, GR	gulimugarr	goat-head burr YR, YY
yarran	yarran wattle YR	gumi	native tomato YR, YY, GR
yiilay	hop bush YR, YY	gurriya	wax-lipped orchid YR
yumu	spotty river gum tree YR, YY	maayal	crowfoot YR, YY
yuurraa	dogwood, eurah YR, YY, GR	madhay	native parsnip YY
		milaan	yam (water ribbons) YR
		milan²	melon YY
		minan	milky weed YY
		mugaadhaa	marthaguy burr YR, YY
		mugiyala	dillon bush YR
		muluumay	type of plant YY
		muruwaa	turpentine bush YY
		ngawingawi	pennyroyal, river mint YR, YY
		ngayuun	camel melon YR, YY
		nhaal	type of yam GR
		nhinay	native melon YR, YY

■ **Vines, ground creepers and grasses** (nouns)

baan	mistletoe, snotty gobbles YR, YY, GR
baaya	hairy melon YY
bagal	plate fungus YY

plants

nhingil	small saltbush	YR, YY, GR
warray	type of yam	GR
warringaay	nut grass	YY
wayway	large oval fungus	YR, YY
wilay	snakebean	YY
wilgi	cane grass	YR, YY
wubu[1]	mushroom	YR, YY
wudhugaa	tar vine	YR, YY, GR
yiil	small pigweed	YY
yiindal	swamp grass	YY, GR

■ Water plants (nouns)

bal	nardoo	YR, YY, GR
buliyaarr	water weed	YR, YY
bunibuni	duckweed	YY
burrarra	bulrush (cumbungi)	YR, YY, GR
dhanggaluwi	water weed	YR
dhariil	reed	GR
dhurrulawaa	water weed	YR, YY, GR
gumbi	water weed	YR
gurragurra	waterlily	YY
milaan	yam (water ribbons)	YY, GR
nhaadhuu	nardoo	YR, YY, GR
nhulaan	slime	YR, YY
waylurr	slime	YR

■ Parts of plants (nouns)

baalaraan	leopardwood flowers	YR, YY
babarrabiin	gidgee flowers	YR, YY
balam	milky fluid	YR
bambulngiyan	native orange tree flowers	YR, YY
bidjal	tree bark	YR, YY
bilgin	splinter, piece, fragment	YR, YY, GR
birraawiin	whitewood flowers	YR, YY
biyarrbirr	native banana yam	YR
bunbarrayn	rosewood fruit	YR, YY
bungun	tree branch	GR
burran.gul	hollow tree	YR
buu[3]	leaf	GR
buugiin	tree sucker	YR, YY
buul[2]	tree knot	YY
dhan.gal	shelly log	YR, YY
dhani	tree gum	YR, YY
dharra	tree branch	GR
dharraa	flaking bark	YY, GR
dharraabiin	manna (on bark)	YY
dharran[1]	forked stick	YR, YY
dhayaarr	bark sheet	YR
dhinggal	seed	YR
dhulu	stick	GR
dhuwarr	vegetable food	YR, YY
dhuwi	heart wood	GR
djulu	sawdust	YY
gaagul	young kurrajong root	YR
gadibundhu	quinine bark	YR
gagilaarriin	carbeen flowers	YY
galariin	coolabah flowers	YR, YY, GR
garril	leaf	YY, GR
giniy	stick	YR, YY
giniy waal	dead wood	YR
girraa	leaf	YR, YY
girran.girraa	leaves	YR, YY
giyiirr	coolabah tree gum	YY
gugul	tree branch	YY
gula	fork in tree	YR, YY
gulaagul	water hollow in tree	YY
guli	river grass (native millet) grain	GR; YY, GR
gun.giyan	manna	YR, YY
gurayn	flower	GR
gurrulayngayn	river wattle flowers	YR, YY
guwiirra	manna	YR
guyayn	flower	YR, YY
mala	fork	YR, GR
mandjaarr	bunch	YR
mawurrngiyan	mimosa bean pods	YY
muramin	kurrajong bark	YY
muyaan	tree branch, stick	YR; YR, YY
ngadhul	hollow tree, tree stump	YR, YY, GR
nganda	tree bark	YR, YY, GR
nhaadhiyaan	log	YR, YY
nhay	tree knot	YR, YY
nhiirruu	burial bark	YY
warran	tree butt, tree trunk, tree root	YR, YY, GR
wiyay	chip	YR, YY
wugan	sticks, wood	YR, YY, GR
wulbul	bendy stick	YY
yaamarra	sheaf of grass seed	YR, YY
yarraanbiin	river gum flowers	YY

228 Gamilaraay/Yuwaalaraay/Yuwaalayaay *to* English Word List by Topic

yawurr	small berry GR	dhiinbaay	yamstick, ceremonial and fighting boomerang YR, YY
yilbin	leaves used for burying YY	dhiiriil	seed or grass necklace GR
yiya	seed YY	dhindi	fishing spear YY
yurrul	seed YR	dhulu	message stick GR
yuuliin	dogwood flowers YY	dhumbaay	drawing stick YR

Material culture

■ 'Traditional' made things (nouns)

baadal	comb YY	dhunbilyabi	sinew string YY
barra	thread, filament YR, YY	dhuurranmay waa	boss shell YY
barran	boomerang YR, YY, GR	gabugaan	hat GR
baya	clothes GR	gabundi	lid, top YY
bayagaa	clothes YR, YY		hat YR, YY, GR
bidjaay	paint YR, YY	galinmay	water bag YR, YY
bidjaay balaa	white paint YY	gambu	stone axe, tomahawk YR, YY
biimbal	broom, brush YY	ganay	yamstick, digging stick YR, YY, GR
bilaarr	spear YR, YY, GR	ganuu	canoe YR
bin.guwi	coolamon YR, YY, GR	garrarana	bullroarer YR
binggi	pin, small sharp things YY	garru	fur cloak YY
birra	axe handle YY	gayandaay	bullroarer YY
birran.gaa	stone axe, tomahawk YR	gayn	scraper YR, YY
bubarraa	fighting boomerang YR, YY	giba	small grindstone YR, YY
budhal	toy club (waddy) YR, YY	gidjiirr	yellow ochre YR
bugu	fighting (big) club YR, YY	giyawaan	kurrajong bark YR, YY
bumal	hitting stick, hitting thing YR, YY	gudhurr	belt GR
bundi	club YR, YY, GR	gudhurru	small club GR
bunduurraa	bark canoe YR, YY	gulagarranba	comeback boomerang YR
bununggaa	armband YY	gulal	headband YR, YY
burriin	broad shield YR, YY, GR cover YY	gulay	net bag YR, YY, GR
burugalaa	ball GR	guliman	coolamon YR
buu²	base YR, YY	gumbilgal	bark container YR, GR
buubuwin	emu decoy YY	gumil	woman's armlet YR, YY
buugalaa	ball YR, YY	gumilaa	possum-fur loincloth YR, YY, GR
buurr	hair-string belt GR string, rope YR, YY, GR	guuwarr	red ochre YR, YY, GR
buuwan	black paint YY	guwinii	yellow ochre YR
buwabil	possessions YR, YY	maadji	feathered stick YY
buwarr	sacred things YR	maang	message stick GR
buwarrgaa	dead person's things YR, YY	magal	stone knife YR, YY
dhabilga	belt GR	man.garr	bag YR, YY, GR
dhawurraa	white ochre YR	manduwii	boot, shoe YR, YY, GR
dhaygaluwi	pillow YR, YY	miidja	water bag YY, GR
dhayurr	large grindstone YR, YY	mirringamu	jagged spear YY, GR
		munun	emu spear YR, YY
		murrula	pointed club YR, YY, GR
		murrumanamanaa	bullroarer YR
		muyu waa	nose bone/shell YY
		nganda	canoe GR
		ngay²	grub hook YR, YY

material culture

ngulugaayrr	headband (plaited) YR, YY, GR	banigan	cup YR
ngunmal	yard, enclosure YY, GR	baril	barrel, bucket GR
nhimin	rope GR	barranda	verandah YR
nhingal	bone needle YY, GR	barriyay	window GR
waa¹	shell chest pendant YR, YY	baya	cloth, clothes GR
wagarraa	bark throwing stick YR	bayagaa	clothes YR, YY
	club (throwing stick) YR, YY	bidjaraay	rag YR, YY
walan.gumba	hard thing YY	biiba	paper YR, YY, GR
wamara	spear thrower (woomera) YR, YY		letter YR
			note (paper money) YY
wambin	breastplate YY	biibabiiba	book YR, YY
wangal	woman's possum-fur belt YR, YY	biligiyaan	billycan YR, YY
wayamaa	old things YR	binggi	nail, needle, pin YY
waygal	woven bag YR, YY	birridul	revolver YR, YY
wayuwaal	man's belt YR, YY	biyaga	tobacco YR, YY, GR
widjuwidju	toy spear YY	budhun	pudding YY
wirrgun	chest protector, breastplate YR, YY	bul	saw YY
		bulanggiin	blanket YR, YY, GR
wirri	small coolamon YR, YY	bumal	hammer YR, YY
wulbul yaal	stick horse YR	burraanban	frying pan YR, YY
yabil	large bark vessel YY	burraaydal	bridle YR, YY
yambiyan	kangaroo tooth ornament YY	burriin	cover YY
		buu²	bucket base YR, YY
yarraadharr	piece of bark YR, YY	buubili	cigarette GR
yiilaman	shield YR	buurr	string, rope YR, YY, GR
yurrugu	rope YR	buuwan	black paint YY
yuundu	stone axe, tomahawk YR, YY, GR	buuwarran	pipe YY
		buwaarr	board YR
		buwabil	possessions YR, YY
		dhaadal	saddle YR, YY

■ 'Introduced' made things (nouns)

		dhaadharr	tin canoe YR
baadhal	bottle YR, YY	dhagadhaal	shovel YR
baadi	paddock YR	dhagin	socks YR, YY
baadjin	poison YR, YY, GR	dhalbin	medicine YR
baaybuu	pipe YR, YY, GR	dhamiyaa	tomahawk YR, YY
babuligaarr	hotel YR, YY	dhani	glue YR
badi	fence YR, YY	dharrawurra	trousers YR, YY
badi ganaay	gate YR	dhayaanmaa	Sunday school YR
badjigal	bicycle YR	dhaygaluwi	pillow YR, YY
bagaay	shearing handpiece YR	dhindiirr	tin dish YR, YY
bagal	plate YY	dhirra mara	fan YR
balaa	clear alcohol YY	dhiyaagarri	bedroll, blanket GR
baladi	saw YR, YY	dhuubuu	soap YR, YY, GR
balanhii	cooler, fridge YR	dhuwadi	shirt YR, YY, GR
banggabaa	clear alcohol, methylated spirits YR	gaala	tin mug, mug, can (tin can) YR
banggul	money YR	gabi	coffee YR
		gabugaan	hat GR

camp, fire and food

Gamilaraay/Yuwaalaraay/Yuwaalayaay	English
gabundi	lid, top YY; hat YR, YY, GR
gadjul	car spring YR
galgandi	flying fox (made of rope/wire) YR
gambada	scarf YY
garralan	sword GR
garrawal	shop, store YR, YY
gaynda	carpenter's plane YY
gayrra	electricity YR
gayrragumbirri	computer YR
giirrgal	tomahawk YY
giniybaal	corner post YR
girrandhaal	rake YR
girrinil	door GR
giyaan	tin can YR
gula	fork (cutlery) YR, YY
gulaay	stool, bench YR
gulaban	seat YR
guliman	dish YR
gum	methylated spirits YR
gumbadhaa	iron, machinery YR, YY
gumbiyaa	horseshoe YR
gunagalaa	toilet YR, YY, GR
gundhi	house YR, YY, GR
gundhilgaa	town YR
guudii	coat YR, YY
guwilii	tent YR
maayama	money YR, YY
mambul	knife YR
manduwii	boot, shoe YR, YY, GR
marrgin	gun YR, YY, GR
marriga	car YR
mugu²	cigarette YR
nganangana	cork YR, YY
nganda	tin YR, YY
ngaymbuwan	saucepan YR, YY
nhaayba	knife YR, YY, GR
nhangana	boot, shoe GR
nhayamban	iron pot GR
nhiigiliirr	necklace YR, YY
waaya	wire YR, YY
walanbaa gungan	rum YR
walban	bucket, trough YR, YY, GR
wanggal	toy roller YR, YY
wayamaa	old things YR
wilbaarr	car, cart YR, YY
wiyayl	pen, pencil YR, YY
wulbul	stockwhip YY
wulbul yiya	cracker on a whip YY
wun.guwi	passage, cattle race YY
yaarrbin	gate post, hitching rail YR
yaayngarralgaa	clock, watch YY
yalaa	jail YR, YY
yanggiidjaa	handkerchief YR, GR
yarral	money (coins) YR, YY, GR
yarrarr	rice YR
yiya	peg YY
yurraamu	wine YR; alcohol GR; rum YR, YY, GR
yuundu	axe YR, YY, GR

Camp, fire and food (nouns)

Gamilaraay/Yuwaalaraay/Yuwaalayaay	English
badha gali	beer YR
bana	lean meat YR, YY, GR
barrin	baked soil YR, YY
bidjiirr	biscuit YR
budidaa	potato YR
bulaawa	flour YR, YY
bundul	banana YR
buri	matches YR, GR
burrumbal	skipping game YY
burugalaa	ball game GR
buugalaa	ball game YR, YY
buuwayamba	bough shed, shade house YY
buuyan	heat YR
dhaadharr	bark hut YR, YY, GR
dhaamba	damper YR, YY
dhaga	mess, rubbish YR
dhal	salt GR
dhanggiway	trick (sleight of hand) YR
dhani	tree gum YY
dharrii	seed cake YY
dhayaarr	bark sheet YR
dhaymaadhi	ground-dwelling animals YY
dhayurr	large grindstone YR, YY
dhidhilan	sparks GR
dhii¹	meat YR, YY, GR
dhii²	tea YR, YY, GR
dhii garril	tea leaves YR, YY
dhii man.garr	tea bag YR
dhiidjuul	piece of meat GR

camp, fire and food

dhiinaa	honeycomb	YR, YY, GR
dhinggaa	meat	YR, YY
dhirrinbaa	bad-weather camp	YR
dhiyaagarra	bed	YR
dhuga	sugar	YR, YY, GR
dhurran.gali	children's game	YR
dhuu	fire, flame	YY
	smoke	YR, GR
dhuuraay	flame, light	GR
dhuuyaay	firestick, flame	YR, YY
dhuwarr	vegetable food	YR, YY
	bread	YR, YY, GR
dhuwindhuwi	sparks	YY
gaarrimay	camp	YY
gabirr	cabbage	YR
gali	water	GR
galindjari	honey drink	YR, YY
galinggaa	sheep intestines (small)	YR, YY, GR
garril budhal	game with toy club	YY
gawu	egg	YR, YY, GR
gawubaa	egg yolk	YR
gayalaay	tabooed woman's camp	YY
giba	small grindstone	YR, YY
giil	beer	YR, YY
giindjuu	bone marrow	YR
girran	ashes	YR, YY, GR
gubiyalanhay	chasings, tip	YR
gugal	pure honey	YY
gumbubudhuu	wrestling game	YR, YY
gundal	bread	GR
gurruga baabay	woman's camp	YY
guwiinbarraan	close to, around a fire	YY
guwiirr widja	cake, biscuit	YR
maadjirr	matches	YR, YY
man.ga	table	YR
mandha	food, tucker	YR
	bread	YR, GR
mandhamandha	unleavened bread	YR
maraay	clear area, camp area	YY
midjul	bone	YR
milgin	milk	YR
mundimundi dhuwarr	brownie (cake)	YY
murrguwidjuwii	belah-wood sparks	YR
ngana	grass windbreak, grass hut	YY
nganda	tin	YR, YY
nhaamanhi	sweet dough	YR
nhigii	coals	YR, YY, GR
nhii	charcoal	YR, YY
waaguu	hide and seek game	YR, YY
wadhuurr	windbreak	YR, YY, GR
walaay	camp, humpy	YR, YY, GR
walaaybaa	home, home country	YR, YY, GR
wanggalay	game with discs and spears, bark discs	YR, YY
warangana	honey	YR, YY
warrul	honey	YR, YY, GR
wayway	little humpy	YR
widja	bread	YR
wii	fire, firewood, light	YR, YY, GR
wiibiyaay	firestick	YR
wiidhaga	bachelor's camp	YR, YY
wiigun	back log	YR
wiimbirru	game with leaf and fire	YY
wiinhii	coals	YR, YY
wirri	plate	YR
wirrun	juice, gravy, soup, sauce	YR, YY
wugan.galgaa	kindling	YR
wulbuldaan	tree branch game	YY
wurranin	cradle	YR
wuyugil	smoke	YR, YY
yaambuwiirr	pretend fight	YR, YY
yaray	sheep intestines (large)	GR
yiyabiyaay	firestick	YR, YY
yuul	food, vegetable food	YR, YY, GR
yuwarr	sleep	YR, YY

Hunting, fishing, gathering, work (nouns)

baayl	axe mark	GR
badi	fish trap	YR, YY
barran	boomerang	YR, YY, GR
bilaarr	spear	YR, YY, GR
birridul	pistol	YR, YY
bugu	fighting (big) club	YR, YY
bundi	club	YR, YY, GR
bunduurraa	bark canoe	YR, YY
burriin	broad shield, shield	YR, YY, GR
buubuwin	emu decoy	YY

water, weather and geography

buurr	fishing line YR, YY, GR	Bariyan Ngama	Pleiades (stars) GR
dhaaliyaay	fish net YR, YY	barrgin	dusk YY
dhiilgulay	bird trap YR, YY	baynyi	ripple YY
dhiilgulaybaa	bird-trapping place YR	bidjaay	mud YR, YY
dhiinbaay	yamstick YR, YY	bilyan	waterhole YR, YY
dhina	footprint, tracks YR, YY, GR	Birraybirraay	Orion's belt (stars) YR, YY, GR
dhindi	fishing spear YY	biruu[2]	hole GR
ganay	yamstick, digging stick YR, YY	biyuu[2]	hole YR, YY
ganuu	canoe YR		cave YR
gay	snake track YR, YY	buliirral wanda	wind gust YR, YY
gudhurru	small club GR	bulunbulun	two stars (near Southern Cross) YY
gulay	fish net GR		
manday[2]	series of steps (sequence) YR, YY, GR	burran	dust storm YY
		burruwi	earthquake YY
marrgin	gun YR, YY, GR		echo YR, YY
mayaarr	bee's wax YR	buulii	whirlwind YR, YY, GR
mirringamu	jagged spear YR, YY, GR	dhadhin[1]	shade, shadow YY
mirrun	emu net YY	dhama-y	
munun	emu spear YR, YY	(verb-transitive)	rain YR, YY
murragal	bird trap YR, YY	dhan.gaay	puddle YR, YY
murrula	pointed club YR, YY, GR	dhandarr	frost, ice YR, YY, GR
nganda	canoe GR	dhandarraa	winter YR, YY, GR
ngay[2]	grub hook YR, YY	dhanggaal	small waterhole, lagoon YR, YY
ngunmal	yard, enclosure YY, GR		
waan[2]	work YR, YY	dhanmurr	burial ground, cemetery YY
wagarraa	club (throwing stick) YR, YY	dharayan	large hailstone GR
wamara	spear thrower (woomera) YR, YY	dharra	creek GR
		dharringarra	thunder cloud YR, YY
wayal	snake track YR	dhawun	earth, ground, dirt GR
wurunggal	peephole YR	dhayan	large hailstone YR, YY
wuu	hook YY	dhaymaarr	earth, ground, dirt, home YR, YY
yalaayn	fishing line YR		
		dhirrin	high ground YY
		dhulirral	water drops YY

Water, weather and geography (nouns)

baaluu	moon YR, YY	dhuluuma-y	
baama	cloud YY	(verb-intransitive)	thunder YR
baayangali	nature YR	dhuluumay	thunder YY, GR
baga	river bank YR, GR	dhun.gayrra	lightning, chain lightning YR, YY
bagaarr	short cut YR		
bagay	creek, river YR, GR	dhuni	sun YR, YY
bagi	white pipeclay YY	dhural	noise, sound YR
balima	place far away YR, YY	dhurrabal	road GR
ban.gul	echo, chopping noise YR, YY, GR	dhurralbuu	south-west wind YR
		dhurrandhurran	north wind YR, YY
bangalaa	dark GR	dhuubaarr	fine rain YR, YY
banuwa	black soil YR, YY	dhuuyaay	light YR, YY
		dhuwaarrgaa	thunder YR
		dhuyul	hill, high ground YR, YY, GR

water, weather and geography

djulu	dirt (debris) YY	Guwaybila	planet Mars YR, YY
gaawaa	deep water YR; river YR, YY	guwaygalaa	red soil YR, YY
gaawal	creek, lagoon YR, YY, GR	guwiigaa	termite mound YR, YY
gaba²	hill, mountain range GR	maarama	stone GR
gagarr	rubbish, leaf litter YR, YY	maayama	stone YR, YY
gali	rain, water GR	maayama yuluwirrigiirr	opal YR, YY
galiya-y (verb-intransitive)	rise (sun/moon) YR, YY	maayamabaa	stony place YY
ganaay¹	opening YR	mabun	gully, creek YR, YY
gandaarr	other side of river YR, YY, GR	Maliyan.gaalay	Morning Star, Venus (planet) YR, YY
garaay	sand GR	mandaymanday	string of stars YY
garaay dhuyul	sandhill GR	mayan	waterhole, creek GR
garra	crack, gap YR, YY, GR	mayrraa	wind YR, YY, GR
garragarraan	straight section of river YR	miimii²	river's edge YR, YY
garran.garra	drought YY	milimili	mud GR
garrul	halo around moon/sun YR	mirii	star GR
gawubarray	star YR, YY	mirii yanan	shooting star GR
gayaay¹	sand YY	Miyaymiyaay	Seven Sisters (stars), Pleiades (stars) YR, YY, GR
gayaayaan	sandhill YY	muran	dark (before dawn) YR, YY
gidjirrigaa	star (a particular star) YY	murrgugal	belah-tree swamp YR
gigirrgigirr	west wind YR, YY	murrila	rocky ground/ridge YR, YY
gigwidjil	red soil YR	Murrudhi Gindamalaa	planet Venus YR, YY
giin.gii	bubble, froth YR, YY	murrumay	lightning, thunder YR, YY, GR
gilay	moon YR, GR	muru	point GR
gilgaay	shallow waterhole YR	muyaay	pointers of Southern Cross YY
gilgal	small waterhole YY	ngaambiyan	give-and-take paddock YR
girraybaa	battle ground YY	ngaay	opening, entrance YR, YY
girruu	well, soak, spring YY	ngamulngamul	ripple, wave YR, YY
gugil	dew YR, YY, GR	ngandirr	steep bank YR, GR
gulaay	log bridge YR, YY	nganggil	steep bank YY
gumbugan	sand, sandhill YR, YY, GR	Nganundi Gindamalaa	planet Venus GR
gunadha	boggy ground YR, YY	ngulawaa	good season YY
gunagala	sky YR, YY, GR	ngulu	point YY, GR
gundaa	cloud YR, YY, GR	ngurrala	stone YR
gundhilgaa	town YR	ngurrambaa	birthplace, family land YR, YY
gungan	water YR, YY	nhalawilbayn	reflection YR
gungurima	halo around moon GR	nhanu	bower YR
gunimaa	mother earth YR	wabu	river bend YR, YY, GR
guniyal	plain, flat GR	wadhi	bush YY
gunu	lime gypsum YY	wadhu	cave YR
gunyamurr	east wind YR, YY	wagi¹	plain, open ground YR, YY
gurru	hole YR, YY, GR	wagibaa	plain, open (treeless) country YR, YY
gurrugaawal	marsh YR		
gurrumayuu	holey country YY		
gurruway	temporary waterhole YR		
guuyaarrma	persistent rain YY		
guwa	fog, mist YR, YY, GR		

› law, ceremony and ritual

Gamilaraay/Yuwaalaraay/Yuwaalayaay	English	Dialects
wagiwagi	plain, open (treeless) country	YR, YY
walan.gumba	hard ground	YY
walanbarruu	claypan	YR, YY
walawala	storm	GR
Wamba (noun)	Canopus (star)	YY
wanba	sloping river bank	YR, YY
warrambul	Milky Way	YR, YY
	watercourse (overflow channel)	YR, YY, GR
warraymbaa	workplace	YR
warruwi	pathway	GR
wawal	echo	GR
wiiluun	slime	YR
wilaarrdaa	north wind	YR, YY
wugawa	flood	YR, YY, GR
wugi	flood peak	YY
wulul	noise	YY
yaarrngan	wave, splash	YR, YY
yaay	sun	YR, YY
yaaybaa	summer	YR, YY
yaraay	sun	GR
yaraay warra-y (phrase)	eclipse of sun	GR
yaraaybaa	summer	GR
Yarraan	Southern Cross (stars)	YR
yarragaa	spring wind	YR, YY, GR
yarral	stone	GR
yarrin	water current	YY
yayaay	sun	YR, YY
yiirriirr	mirage	YR, YY
yiyagungawuma	small hailstone	YR, YY
yuluwirri	rainbow	YY, GR
yurrul	bush, scrub	YR, YY, GR
yuru	cloud	GR
yuruun	road	YR, YY, GR
yuu	dust	YR, YY, GR
yuuruu	rain	GR
yuuyuu	rain	YR, YY
yuuyuu bundaa-gi (phrase)	rain	YY

Law, ceremony and ritual (nouns)

Gamilaraay/Yuwaalaraay/Yuwaalayaay	English	Dialects
Baayami	Byame, God	YR, YY, GR
balima	heaven, sky camp	YR, YY
bigan	law	YY
birru	clever man's stick	YY
biyuu²	grave	YR
budun	taboo	YR
bugarru	tree for storing poison sticks	YR, YY
bugiyaa	poison stick, poison bone	YR
bunbul	little bora ring	YR, YY
bundhabundha	poison	YR, YY
bundurr	spirit holder	YY
	clever man's bag	YR, YY
burrambuurra	initiation song	YR, YY
burruguu	time of creation, dreamtime	YR
Buudhaa	meeting	YR
buurra	initiation ceremony, bora, bora ground, initiation ground	YR, YY, GR
buurrabang	bora ground	YY
buurrabiyaay	boy at initiation	YY
buwarr	sacred things	YR
dhanmurr	burial ground, cemetery	YR, YY
dhawunma	burial ground, cemetery	GR
dhawurraa	white ochre	YR
dhaymaarr	home	YR, YY
dhiil¹	sacred tree, wilga	YR, YY
dhiinbaay	ceremonial boomerang	YR, YY
dhinagarral	poison	YY
dhinagarralawaa	death stone	YY
dhiiyaanmaa	heaven	YR
dhulu	message stick	GR
dhulu buurra	bora message stick	YY
dhunbarran	initiation ground pathway	GR
dhuubaarr	funeral smoke	YR, YY
dhuurranmay	leader, chief, boss	YR
gabarraa	sacred stone	YR, YY
gadhiigurrii	poison stick, poison bone	YY
gamaal	taboo	YY
garrarana	bullroarer	YR
gayandaay	bullroarer	YY
gidjiirr	yellow ochre	YR
ginilgarriya	ceremonial log	YY
girray	battle	YR, YY
girribal	riddle	YR, YY, GR
gumbu	corroboree ground	YR, YY
gunaba	initiation ground	GR

place

gunagala	heaven YR, YY, GR	dhuwi (noun)	inside GR
gurru	grave YR, YY, GR	gaburran (noun)	high place YR
guunay	dirge, funeral song YY		top YR, YY, GR
guuwarr	red ochre YR, YY, GR	gandaarr (noun)	other side of river YR, YY, GR
guwinii	yellow ochre YR	ganhaga (noun)	underneath, below YR, YY
guuyarra	poison bone YR, YY	-gili (suffix)	side (location) YR, YY
maa	totem YY	guwiin (noun, adjective)	close, near YR, YY, GR
maang	message stick GR	guwiinbaa	
manday²	generation level YY	(noun, adjective)	close, near YR, YY, GR
mandhiigan	initiation guardian YY	marrama (place adverb)	there (close) YR, YY, GR
mingga	spirit haunted tree YR, YY, GR	miimii² (noun)	edge YY
mubirr	carving, engraving YR, YY		river's edge YR, YY
	initiation scars, cicatrices YR, YY, GR	milan³ (noun)	close, near YR, GR
		mudhu (noun)	inside YR, YY
murraan.gali	corroboree leader YR, YY	mulandha (noun)	far side GR
murrumanamanaa	bullroarer YR	ngaarri (place adverb)	there, over there YR, YY, GR
muuliyaay	magic stone YR, YY	ngaarribaagili	
ngurrambaa	birthplace, family land YR, YY	(place adverb)	above YR
nguruma	spirit-haunted stone GR	ngaarrima	
nguuma²	spirit-haunted stone YY	(place adverb)	over there YR, YY, GR
nhiirruu	burial bark, coffin YY	ngaarringaarri	
wanaal	taboo, forbidden YY, GR	(place adverb)	right over there YR, GR
wii	spirit light YY	ngadaa (place adverb)	under YR, YY
wii muyaan	clever man's stick YR, YY		down, down there YY, YR GR
wilgu	ceremonial stick YY	ngarraagulay	
wuudalay	rain-making stone YY	(place adverb)	over there (other side) YR
wuurraa	battle YR	ngarribaa	
wuyugarralawaa	death stone YY	(place adverb)	up, high YR, YY, GR
wuyugil	ceremonial smoke YR, YY	ngarrigili (noun)	other side YR, YY, GR
yanguuwii	sacred fire YR, YY	ngayaga (place adverb)	behind YR, YY, GR
yiilinhi	war GR	ngiirrma (place adverb)	there GR
yugal	song YR, YY, GR	ngiyarrma	
		(place adverb)	there YR, YY
		nguwa (place adverb)	here YR, YY, GR
		nguwagili (noun)	this side YR, YY
		nguwalay	

Place

■ General place words

		(place adverb)	here, hereabouts YY
		nguwama	
-Baa (suffix)	place of YR, GR	(place adverb)	there YR, YY
bani (noun)	front YR, YY	nhalay (demonstrative)	here YR, YY, GR
bawadhi (place adverb)	behind GR	nhama (demonstrative)	there YR, YY, GR
bidjun (noun)	middle YR, YY, GR	nhirrin (noun)	side YR, YY, GR
biridji (place adverb)	in front GR	wagi¹ (noun)	outside YR, YY
biruu (noun)	long way GR	wara (noun)	left GR
biyuu (noun)	long way YR, YY	waya (noun)	left YR, YY
burrumbi (noun)	corner YR	wiyalwiyal (adjective)	all over the place YR
dhuruyaal (adjective)	right (not left) GR		
dhuuyaal (adjective)	right (not left) YR, YY		

place

■ **Placenames**

Not all placename derivations are certain

Gamilaraay	English	Source
Baan.giirr	Bangate Station	YR, YY
Baawan	Barwon River	YY, GR
Babarra	Babarra	YR
Badhara Walaay	mountain on Namoi River	GR
Bagala	Bukkulla	GR
Bagaldii	Bugaldie	GR
Bagaybaraay	Boggabri	GR
Bagaybila	Boggabilla	GR
Bagi	Boggy Ridge	YY
Balal	Pallal	GR
Balarangawul	mountain on Namoi River	GR
Baluun	Ballone (place and river)	YY
Baluunbilyan	Bollonbillion	YR, YY
Bana	Bunna	YY
Bandaarraa	Bundarra	GR
Barrali Mugulbaa	sharpening-tools place	YR
Barran	Burren Junction	GR
Barranbaa	location	YR
Bawa	waterhole name	YY
Bayn Gabilaa	Piangobla	YR
Bilambulaa	waterhole name	YY
Biliga	Pilliga	GR
Birraa[1]	Birrah	YY
Biridja	Breeza	GR
Bugayirra	Bokhara River	YY
Buluuy Nhaaybil	Blue Knobby	GR
Bumaay	Boomi	GR
Buman Garriya	location	YY
Burrigala	Brigalow	GR
Burriiwarranha	Brewarrina	YR, YY, GR
Burrul Gungan	Narran Lake	YY
Buruma	Boorooma	GR
Byamee	Baayami	GR
Dhanggalamandjiirr	location	YY
Dhanggaliirr	Dungalear Station	YR
Dhariilaraay	Tarilarai	GR
Dhariilduul	Drilldool	GR
Dharrawaawul	Terewah	YR, YY
Dharrgabala	location	YR
Dharriwaa	Narran Lake	YR
Dhimbambaraay	Timbumburi Creek	GR
Dhindirrina	waterhole name	YY
Dhurrunbandaay	Dirranbandi	YY
Gaawal	Cowal	YY
Gaawalbaa	Cowelba	YY
Gagil	Coghill	GR
Galariinbaraay	Collarenebri	YY, GR
Gali Gurunha	spring at Gingie	YR
Galimandi	Kalmundi	YR
Garra	Gurah	GR
Garrabilaa	location	YY
Garradhuul	location	YY
Garrali	location	YY
Garrawila	Garrawila	GR
Garrawilingaay	Currawillinghi	YR
Garrilgarril	location	YR
Gawubuwan Gunigal	Boobera Lagoon or MacIntyre River	GR
Gigwidjil	Kigwigil	YR
Giiguradjin	Narran Lake	YY
Giin.gii	Gingie	YR
Gilaan.garra	location	YY
Girran.girraa	location	YY
Girrawiin	Girrawheen	YR, YY
Gubiyaandaa	location	YR
Guburruubaa	location	YR
Guduuga	Goodooga	YR, YY
Gugurruwan	Coocoran Lake	YR, YY
Guli	Goolhi	GR
Guligal	Coorigel	YY
Gumbulgabanbaa	location	YR, YY
Gunabarabin	Coonabarabran	GR
Gunambil	Coonamble	GR
Gunidjaa	Gunnedah	GR
Gunu	Goonoo	YY
Gundhimayan	Condamine River	GR
Gunidjaa	Gunnedah	GR
Gunu Gunu	Goonoo Goonoo	GR
Gurrulay	Gurly Station	YY
Guwayda	Gwydir River	GR
Maandhi	lake name	YR
Magarrawayaa	Muckerawa (waterhole)	YY
Malawil	location	YY
Mandiwaa	location	YY
Mangalaalaa	creek name	YR
Marrawal	Murrawal	GR
Milaanbaa	waterhole name	YR
Milduul	Mildool	YR, YY
Mungungulu	waterhole name	YY
Murrgu Walaay	Swamp Camp	YR

direction

Murrumanamanaa	Mirramanar Station	YR
Ngamumbirrabaa	location	YY
Nguluwawul	Nullawa	YY
Nharibaraay	Narrabri	GR
Nharran	Narran River	YY
Nhiinhii	Nee-Nee	YY
Walan.gala	Walangala	YY
Wii Waa	Wee Waa	GR
Wii Warra	Wee Warra Plain	YR, YY
Wiidhalibaa	Weetalibah	YR, GR
Wilgi	Wilkie	YY
Wubi Wubi	name of a sacred mountain	YY
Wularraba	location	YY
Wurrawaadhiyan	location	YR
Yarralaraay	Yalaroi	GR
Yarralduul	Yarralduul	GR
Yarranbaa	Yeranbah	YY
Yulanbiirr	waterhole name	YR
Yuriyuri	location	YR

Direction (place adverbs)

dhaan	sideways, to the side	YR, YY
dhaay	this way, to here	YR, YY, GR
dhadhin²	south	YR
marragula	to here (nearby)	YR, YY
ngaarribiyan	north	YR
ngaarrigulay	over there (that way)	YR, YY, GR
ngaarrimali	over there (that way)	YR
ngadaa	west (sundown)	YR, YY
ngadaali	downwards	YR, YY
ngadaamali	downstream	YR
ngarribaa	east	YR, YY, GR
ngarribaali	upwards	YR, YY
ngiilay	from here	YR, YY, GR
yalagidhaay	right around	YR

Time

-Baa *(suffix)*	time of	YY
baayan *(time adverb)*	soon	YR, YY, GR
baayanbuu *(time adverb)*	immediately	GR
baayandhu *(time adverb)*	later on	YR
barraaywan *(time adverb)*	immediately	YY
buliyaagu *(time adverb)*	morning	YR, YY, GR
bululuwi *(time adverb)*	evening	YR, YY, GR
buluuy *(noun)*	dark, night	YR, YY, GR
buwabiila *(time adverb)*	afterwards	YR
dhuniya *(noun)*	daylight	YR, YY
giibaabu *(time adverb)*	early morning	YR, YY
gimiyandi *(time adverb)*	yesterday	GR
ngaarribu *(time adverb)*	very long ago	GR
ngadaa dhuni *(noun)*	mid-afternoon	YY
ngarran¹ *(noun)*	dawn	YR, YY, GR
ngarribaa bidjunda *(noun)*	midday	YY
ngarribaa dhuni *(noun)*	mid-morning	YY
ngurru *(noun)*	night	GR
ngurrugu *(time adverb)*	tomorrow	YR, GR
yaadha *(noun)*	day	YY
yalagiirrmawu *(time adverb)*	at that time, then	YR
yalagiyu *(time adverb)*	now	YR
yaraadha *(noun)*	day, daytime	GR
yaraay dhurra-li *(phrase)*	sunrise	GR
yilaa *(time adverb)*	recently, soon, directly	YR, YY, GR
yilaa buluuya *(noun)*	tonight	YY
yilaadhu *(time adverb)*	now (immediately), today	GR
yilaalu *(time adverb)*	long time ago, long time later	YR, YY, GR
yilaambiyal *(noun)*	beginning	GR
yilambu *(time adverb)*	long time ago	GR

Language: Words and speaking (nouns)

bilaan	alternative name	YY
burrulaa garay	lot of talk	GR
dhaalan	pronunciation, accent, tune, intonation	YY

dhayaamba-li
    (verb-transitive)......whisper YR, YY
dhulu............................message stick GR
gaay.............................language, message, story, word YR, YY
gaay giirruu
    (common expression)..........true words YY
gaga-li *(verb-transitive)*......call, shout, yell, sing out YR, YY, GR
Gamilaraay.....................Gamilaraay language YR, YY, GR
garay............................word GR
garran...........................quarrel, row YR
gayrr.............................name YR, YY, GR
girribal..........................riddle YR, YY, GR
guwaa-li *(verb-transitive)*...say, tell YR, YY, GR
                                  talk (to), speak (to) YR, YY, GR
maang..........................message stick GR
mubirr..........................mark, writing YY
mudhun.........................secret name YY
ngurrgun........................husky voice YY
wadhagii........................secret YR
wagi² ....lie YR, YY
yaal...............................lie YR, YY, GR
yugal.............................song YR, YY, GR
yugali............................little song YY
Yuwaalaraay....................Yuwaalaraay language YR, YY, GR
Yuwaalayaay...................Yuwaalayaay language YR, YY, GR
Yuwaaliyaay...................Yuwaalayaay language YY

Verbs

■ People

baabi-li *(intransitive)*.........stay YR, YY
baada-li *(transitive)*..........comb (hair) YY
badha-y *(transitive)*..........give a hiding YR
bama-li *(transitive)*..........knead GR
banma-li *(transitive)*.........help GR
barraay milu gimbi-li
    (phrase)......................wink YR
bawi-li *(transitive)*............sing YR, YY, GR
                                  praise GR
biidjinma-li *(transitive)*.......win YR
biimba-li *(transitive)*..........sweep YR, YY

biirra-li *(transitive)*............skin YR, YY
binaal bunma-li
    (transitive)....................quieten, soothe, calm, settle down YR, YY
buganma-li *(transitive)*........prepare GR
bumbaali-y *(intransitive)*.....jump in YR
buubi-li *(transitive)*............blow,
                                  smoke tobacco YR, YY, GR
buurra-li *(transitive)*...........pluck, pull out YR, YY
buuyawiya-li *(transitive)*......tell YY
dhadha-li *(transitive)*.........taste YR, YY, GR
dhadha-y *(intransitive)*........taste YR, YY
dhanduwiyma-li
    (transitive)...................put someone to bed YR
dhan.gurrama-y
    (intransitive)..................dance (make a corroboree) YR
dhanggi-li *(transitive)*.........lie, tell a lie GR
dhanggima-li *(transitive)*.....soak YY
dhanggiwa-li *(transitive)*.....deceive, trick YY
dhawuma-li *(transitive)*......cook in a hole (roast) YR, YY, GR
dhaya-li *(transitive)*............beg GR
                                  ask YR, YY, GR
dhayaamba-li *(transitive)*....whisper YR, YY
dhaygal gaya-y *(phrase)*......headache (head turns) YR
dhiirra-li *(transitive)*...........teach YR
dhiirra-y *(transitive)*...........know, remember YR, YY, GR
dhiyaagarra-li *(transitive)*...prepare a bed YY, GR
dhu-rri *(transitive)*.............poke (with pointed object) YR, YY
                                  spear, stab YR, YY, GR
                                  carve, tap, write YR
dhubaanma-li
    (transitive)....................tell about YR, YY, GR
dhubi-li *(transitive)*............spit YR, YY, GR
dhurra-li¹ *(transitive)*.........make (construct) YR, YY, GR
dhuudhinma-li
    (transitive)....................shoot YR
gaa-gi *(transitive)*.............own, have YR, YY, GR
                                  wear YR
gaarra-y *(intransitive)*.........paint (self) YR, YY, GR
gaarrima-li *(transitive)*........pour YR, YY
gaay gawaa-y *(phrase)*.......mimic, imitate speech YR, YY
gaayaa wana-gi *(phrase)*.....talk YR
gabanma-li *(transitive)*........heal YR

verbs

gadhamayawa-li *(transitive)* .... hide YR, YY
gaga-li *(transitive)* .... call, shout, yell, sing out YR, YY, GR
gana garranba-li *(phrase)* .... contradict YY
gara-li *(transitive)* .... answer GR
garawi-li *(transitive)* .... pelt, throw at GR
garra-li *(transitive)* .... cut YR, YY, GR
gaya-li *(transitive)* .... answer YR, YY
gayawi-li *(transitive)* .... pelt, throw at, point bone, kill YR, YY
gayma-li *(transitive)* .... stir, turn, twist YR, YY
gaynma-li *(transitive)* .... scrape, smooth off, calm YY
gayrrba-li *(transitive)* .... name YR, YY
gidjigidjiba-li *(transitive)* ..... tickle YR, YY
giinba-li *(transitive)* .... scale YR, YY
gimbi-li *(transitive)* .... do, make (construct) YR, YY
gimubi-li *(transitive)* .... do, make (construct) GR
gulagama-li *(transitive)* .... embrace, hold, cuddle YR, YY
guuma-li *(transitive)* .... collect, gather YR
guurrama-li *(transitive)* .... resist, stand strong YY
guwaa-li *(transitive)* .... say, talk (to), speak (to), tell, make (someone do something) YR, YY, GR
guwaala-y *(intransitive)* .... converse (talk to each other) YR
guwiirrnga-li *(transitive)* ...... love (be sweet on) YR
maa buma-y *(phrase)* .... clap hands YR, YY
mara buma-y *(phrase)* .... clap hands GR
maaruma-li *(transitive)* .... fix, heal, make better GR
maaya-li *(transitive)* .... whisper YR, YY, GR
maayama-li *(transitive)* .... make by hand YY
maayuma-li *(transitive)* .... fix, heal, make better YR
maniila-y *(intransitive)* .... hunt, go hunting YR, YY
marama-li *(transitive)* .... make by hand GR
marra gi-gi *(phrase)* .... rejoice, celebrate GR
miinba-y *(transitive)* .... ask for YR, YY
milabi-li *(intransitive)* .... wink GR
mubal dhiyama-li *(phrase)* .... gut YY
mubal dhuwima-li *(phrase)* .... gut YR, YY
mubirr dhu-rri *(phrase)* .... carve, write YY
muurr gi-gi *(phrase)* .... forget YR, YY, GR

muyawa-li *(transitive)* .... sew YR, YY
ngaambi-li *(transitive)* .... trade, swap YR
ngaay gaya-li *(phrase)* .... kiss YR, YY, GR
ngamilma-li *(transitive)* .... teach GR
ngamuma-li *(transitive)* .... milk a cow YR
ngarraga-li *(transitive)* .... feel sorry for someone, pity someone YY
ngarrala-y *(transitive)* .... court YR
ngarri-y *(intransitive)* .... sit GR
ngaydju dhiyama-li *(phrase)* .... hook out (grub) YY
nhamurra-li *(transitive)* .... bury YR, YY
nhinga-li *(transitive)* .... sew YY, GR
nhuunma-li *(transitive)* .... milk a cow YY, GR
nhuwigu buma-li *(phrase)* .... kill (stone dead) YR
nhuyu-gi *(transitive)* .... chastise YR
waa-li *(transitive)* .... throw GR
wagirrbuma-li *(transitive)* ..... wash YR, GR
wagirrbuma-y *(intransitive)* .... wash (self) YR
wagirrma-li *(transitive)* .... wash YR, YY
wagirrma-y *(intransitive)* .... wash (self) YY
walindja-li *(intransitive)* .... be lonely YR
wamba-li *(transitive)* .... carry YR, YY, GR
wana-gi *(transitive)* .... leave YY
                                                    throw, pitch YR, YY
warrayaa yanaa-y *(phrase)* .... be lost YY
warrayma-li *(transitive)* .... build, put up YR, YY, GR
                                                    stand up YR, YY
                                                    raise (bring up) YR
wii wiima-li *(phrase)* .... make a fire, light a fire YR, GR
wiima-li *(transitive)* .... put down YR, YY, GR
wiima-y *(intransitive)* .... put (on self) YR
wiirra-li *(transitive)* .... shave, shear YR, YY
wiirra-y *(intransitive)* .... shave (self) YR, YY
winanga-li *(transitive)* .... hear, listen YR, YY, GR
winanga-y *(transitive)* .... know, remember, think, understand YR, YY, GR
                                                    love YR
wiyayi-li *(transitive)* .... remove quills YY
wulanabi-li *(transitive)* .... light (fire/lamp) YR, YY, GR
wuu-rri *(transitive)* .... give YR, YY, GR
wuuma-li *(transitive)* .... dress someone YY
wuurrma-li *(transitive)* .... send YY
wuyugi-li *(transitive)* .... smoke (ceremonial) YY

verbs

yaal dhanggi-li *(phrase)* ...... lie, tell a lie GR
yaarrima-li *(transitive)* .... pour GR
yaaya-li *(transitive)* .... chop YR, YY
yabi-li *(transitive)* .... twist, plait YY
.... kiss YR, YY
yanaaynbi-li *(transitive)* .... sack YR
yaya-li *(transitive)* .... tell off, scold YR, YY
yayala-y *(intransitive)* .... quarrel YR, YY
yilama-li *(transitive)* .... cook YR, YY
yinabi-li *(transitive)* .... fish, catch fish, catch with instrument YR, YY, GR
yuga-li *(intransitive)* .... celebrate GR
yulu-gi *(intransitive)* .... dance, gamble, play YR, YY, GR
yuulbaarra-y *(intransitive)* .... be astonished YY
yuurrma-y *(intransitive)* .... corroboree, play YR, YY
yuwaya ngarra-li *(phrase)* .... dream YR, YY
yuwaya wiima-li *(phrase)* ..... dream YY

■ Stance and rest

baabi-li *(intransitive)* .... camp, sleep GR
.... stay YR, YY, GR
bayama-y *(intransitive)* .... be caught YR
binda-y *(intransitive)* .... hang YR, YY, GR
buruwi-y *(intransitive)* .... rest, spell, ease up GR
buuwi-y *(intransitive)* .... rest, spell, ease up YR, YY
dhabi-y *(intransitive)* .... be quiet, be still YR, YY, GR
dhanduwi-y *(intransitive)* ..... live YR
.... camp, stop, stay, lie (down), sleep YR, YY
dhinbiya warra-y *(phrase)* .... kneel YR, YY
dhuli-y *(intransitive)* .... lean over YR
dhurraami-li *(transitive)* .... wait (for) YR, YY
dhuwinba-y *(intransitive)* ..... hide (self) YR
guuma-y *(intransitive)* .... hide, plant (self) YY
guurrama-li *(transitive)* .... resist, stand strong YY
ma-y *(intransitive)* .... be on top YR
mama-y *(intransitive)* .... stick YR
nganbi-y *(intransitive)* .... lean YR, YY
ngarri-y *(intransitive)* .... sit GR
nhamurra-y *(intransitive)* ..... be buried YR, YY
wa-y *(intransitive)* .... be in, be inside YR, YY
wana-y *(intransitive)* .... perch, roost YY

warra-y *(intransitive)* .... stand YR, YY, GR
wi-y *(intransitive)* .... lie (inanimate) YR, GR
wila-y *(intransitive)* .... sit YR
.... stay, stop, live YR, GR
wuulaabila-y *(intransitive)* ... sunbake YR
yilawa-y *(intransitive)* .... sit, stay, stop, live YY
yuwarra-y *(intransitive)* .... go to sleep YR, YY

■ Movement: transitive

baayama-li .... spin YR, YY
biyuurra-li .... roll YR
budhu-li .... drive YR, GR
dhama-y .... rain YR, YY
dhanggalma-li .... float YR
dhilay-rri .... push away YR, YY
dhirranba-li .... shake YR, YY, GR
dhiyama-li .... pick up, lift up YR, YY, GR
dhuurrma-li .... shift, drag YR, YY
gaa-gi .... carry YR, GR
.... bring, fetch, take YR, YY, GR
gaaguwi-y .... bring back, take back YR, YY
garima-li .... spin (eggs) YR
gawaa-y .... chase, follow, drive YR, YY
muwi-li .... shut GR
waa-li .... throw GR
wamba-li .... carry YR, YY, GR
wanggama-li .... roll YR, YY
warrayma-li .... send YR, YY
wuurrma-li .... send YY
yuurrambi-li .... wag, wave YR
yuwaba-y .... hunt away, chase away YR, YY
yuwanma-li .... put back, return YR

■ Movement: intransitive

baa-y .... hop, jump YR, YY
baanda-y .... move in a line YY
babaaluma-y .... jump into water (game) YR, YY
banaga-y .... drive YY
.... flow (water) YR, YY
.... run YR, YY, GR
banggadha-y .... float YR, YY
bara-y[1] .... jump GR
bara-y[2] .... fly YR, YY
baragi-y .... fly around, fly in circle YR, YY

verbs

barra-y	fly GR	wila-y	ride YR
biyuugu yanaa-y	avoid YY	wirraa-y	limp, hobble YR, YY, GR
biyuurra-y	roll (self) YR	wun.ga-li	return GR
biyuurragi-y	roll about/around YR	wunga-y	bathe, paddle, dive, duck under YR, YY
buli-y	slip YR, YY		
bumbaali-y	jump in YR	wurunga-y	dive GR
bundaa-gi	fall YR, YY, GR	wuu-gi	go down, set (moon/sun), go into, dress self YR, YY
burrumba-y	skip YR, YY		
buuli-y	blow YR, YY	wuuli-y	swoop down YR
dhabirra-y	roll down a bank YY	yaarri-y	go down, set (moon/sun), spill, drip, leak GR
dhan.gurrama-y	dance (make a corroboree) YR		
		yala-y	follow YR, YY
dhangga-y	float YR / float, swim on surface YY	yana-y	come, go, walk GR
		yanaa-y	come, go, walk YR, YY
dharrawu-li	come back, return YR, GR	yanaawuwi-y	go home, go back YR, YY
dharrawuluwi-y	come back, return YR, YY	yulu-gi	dance YR, YY, GR
dhiinbi-y	dive YR	yuuga-y	gush out, spurt YY
dhila-y	sneak, creep YR, YY	yuurra-gi	move YR
dhirranba-y	shake YR, YY	yuuyuu bundaa-gi	rain YY
dhuba-y	point YR, YY, GR		
dhubi-y	stoop YR, YY	**■ The body**	
dhuli-y	bend down, stoop YR, YY, GR		
dhulirra-li	drip YR, YY, GR	baada-li *(transitive)*	comb (hair) YY
dhurra-li²	come, rise (sun/moon) YR, YY, GR	baaya-li *(transitive)*	bite off, crack between teeth YR
		balu-gi *(intransitive)*	die YR, YY, GR
dhurraluwi-y	come back, return YR, YY, GR	barraay milu gimbi-li *(phrase)*	wink YR
dhurriya-y	ride YR	biiwanma-li *(transitive)*	puff out chest YY
dhuu-rri	crawl YR, YY, GR	buliirra-li *(transitive)*	breathe YR, YY
gaarri-y	go down, set (moon/sun) YY / get down, spill, drip, leak YR, YY	buuba-li *(transitive)*	fart, break wind GR
		buubi-li *(transitive)*	smoke tobacco YR, YY, GR
		buwi-y *(transitive, intransitive)*	smell YR, GR
galiya-y	rise (sun/moon) YR, YY		
garri-y	stop, cease doing GR	dha-li *(transitive)*	eat YR, YY, GR
gaya-y	turn, turn over, twist YR, YY	dhaa-rri *(transitive)*	have sex, make love GR
gayarra-y	tangle up YR / turn around, revolve YR, YY, GR	dhaala-gi *(intransitive)*	feel sick, be sick YR, YY
		dhadha-li *(transitive)*	taste YR, YY, GR
gilgulba-rri	come out, emerge YR, YY	dhadha-y *(intransitive)*	taste YR, YY
gubi-y	swim YR, YY, GR	dhama-li *(transitive)*	feel, touch YR, YY, GR
guwiinba-li	come near YR, YY	dhaygal gaya-y *(phrase)*	headache (head turns) YR
ma-y	be up YR	dhiidja-li *(transitive)*	lick YR, YY
maniila-y	hunt, go hunting YR, YY	dhirra-li *(intransitive)*	wake up, awake YR
'naa-y	go, come, walk YR, YY	dhirranba-y *(intransitive)*	rattle, shiver YR / wag YR
ngadaluwi-y	squat YY		
wangga-y	roll YY	dhu-rri *(transitive)*	have sex, make love YR, YY
warra-y	stand up, get up YR, YY, GR		
warrayaa yanaa-y	be lost YY	dhubi-li *(transitive)*	spit YR, YY, GR
warraynga-y	get up YR		

verbs

gaanga-y *(transitive, intransitive)* .... be born YR, YY
give birth YR, YY, GR
gaawi-li *(transitive)* .... vomit, spew, regurgitate YR, YY, GR
garra-y *(intransitive)* .... choke YR, YY
garrabi-y *(intransitive)* .... be full of food YY
giguwi dhu-rri *(phrase)* .... hiccup YR
sneeze YR, YY
gii-gi *(intransitive)* .... itch YR, YY
giili-y *(intransitive)* .... urinate, piss YR, GR
giiri-gi *(intransitive)* .... itch GR
gindama-y *(intransitive)* .... laugh YR, YY, GR
gudhuwa-y *(intransitive)* .... burn with pain YR
guna-gi *(intransitive)* .... defecate, shit YR
gunhugunhu dhu-rri *(phrase)* .... cough YR, YY, GR
gurra-li *(transitive)* .... consume all YR
gurruubi-li *(transitive)* .... swallow YY
guulaabi-y *(intransitive)* .... warm up YR
maa buma-y *(phrase)* .... clap hands YR, YY
mara buma-y *(phrase)* .... clap hands GR
milu gawaa-y *(phrase)* .... watch YY
mubal muurra-y *(phrase)* ... be full of food YY
ngaay gaya-li *(phrase)* .... kiss YR, YY, GR
ngamu-gi *(transitive)* .... suck, suckle YR, YY, GR
ngarrdanma-li *(transitive)* .. make mouth water YY
ngaru-gi *(transitive)* .... drink GR
ngawi-y *(intransitive)* .... smell YY
ngawu-gi *(transitive)* .... drink YR, YY
ngurruula-y *(intransitive)* .... snore YR, YY
nguuguuba-li *(transitive)* .... chew, sip YR
warra-y *(intransitive)* .... swell YR, YY, GR
wiibi-li *(intransitive)* .... be sick GR
wiila-y *(transitive)* .... whistle YR, YY, GR
wiirra-y *(intransitive)* .... shave (self) YR, YY
wuwi-li *(transitive)* .... swallow YY
yaaga-y *(intransitive)* .... moan YR
yabi-li *(transitive)* .... kiss YR, YY
yii-gi *(intransitive)* .... shiver YY
yu-gi *(intransitive)* .... cry, weep YR, YY, GR

■ Thinking and talking (attention)

bamba ngami-li *(phrase)* .... stare GR
bamba ngarra-li *(phrase)* .... stare, watch carefully YR, YY
banma-li *(transitive)* .... help GR
bawi-li *(transitive)* .... sing YR, YY, GR
praise GR
buuyawiya-li *(transitive)* .... tell YY
dhanggiwa-li *(transitive)* .... deceive, trick YY
dhanggi-li *(transitive)* .... lie, tell a lie GR
dhaya-li *(transitive)* .... ask YR, YY, GR
beg GR
dhayaamba-li *(transitive)* .... whisper YR, YY
dhiirra-li *(transitive)* .... teach YR
dhiirra-y *(transitive)* .... know, remember YR, YY, GR
dhu-rri *(transitive)* .... carve, write YR
dhubaanma-li *(transitive)* ... tell about YR, YY, GR
gaay gawaa-y *(phrase)* .... mimic, imitate speech YR, YY
gaayaa wana-gi *(phrase)* ...... talk YR
gaga-li *(transitive)* .... call, shout, yell, sing out YR, YY, GR
galuma-li *(transitive)* .... care for YR, YY
gana garranba-li *(phrase)* ... contradict YY, YY
gara-li *(transitive)* .... answer GR
gaya-li *(transitive)* .... answer YR, YY
gayarra-gi *(transitive)* .... search for, look for YR, YY, GR
gayrrba-li *(transitive)* .... name YR, YY
gindama-y *(intransitive)* .... laugh YR, YY, GR
girriinba-li *(transitive)* .... make noise YR
gunmi-li *(transitive)* .... look at (greedily) YR
guwaa-li *(transitive)* .... say, tell, talk (to), speak (to), make (someone do something) YR, YY, GR
guwaala-y *(intransitive)* .... converse (talk to each other) YR
guwiirrnga-li *(transitive)* ...... love (be sweet on) YR
maaya-li *(transitive)* .... whisper YR, YY, GR
maniila-y *(intransitive)* .... find, look for YR, YY
marra gi-gi *(phrase)* .... rejoice, celebrate GR
marramarrama-li *(transitive)* .... praise GR
miinba-y *(transitive)* .... ask for YR, YY
milu gawaa-y *(phrase)* .... watch YY
muurr gi-gi *(phrase)* .... forget YR, YY, GR
ngaawa-y *(transitive)* .... find, search for, look for YY
ngami-li *(transitive)* .... look, see, watch GR
ngamilma-li *(transitive)* .... teach GR
ngarra-li *(transitive)* .... look, see, watch YR, YY

verbs

ngarraga-li *(transitive)* .... feel sorry for someone, pity someone YY
ngarrangarra-li *(transitive)* .... mind, look after YR, YY
wanggarra-y *(intransitive)* ... be lost YR
wanggarrama-li *(transitive)* .... lose GR
winanga-li *(transitive)* .... hear, listen YR, YY, GR
winanga-y *(transitive)* .... think, know, understand, remember YR, YY, GR
love YR
wurungga-li *(intransitive)* .... peep (peek) YR
wuumi-li *(intransitive)* .... peep (peek) YR
yaaga-y *(intransitive)* .... moan YR, YY
yaal dhanggi-li *(phrase)* ...... lie, tell a lie GR
yawa-li *(transitive)* .... track YR, YY
yaya-li *(transitive)* .... tell off, scold YR, YY
yayala-y *(intransitive)* .... quarrel YR, YY
yuga-li *(intransitive)* .... celebrate GR
yuulbaarra-y *(intransitive)* .... be astonished YY
yuwaya ngarra-li *(phrase)* .... dream YR, YY
yuwaya wiima-li *(phrase)* .... dream YY

■ Contact and effect

baanda-li *(transitive)* .... straighten up (tidy), put in order YR
baarra-y *(intransitive)* .... burst, crack, split YR, YY
baarrama-li *(transitive)* .... tear, tear off, pull off, strip off YR, YY
baarray-rri *(transitive)* .... burst, crack YR, YY
split YR, YY, GR
baaya-li *(transitive)* .... bite off, crack between teeth YR
chop GR
baaylirrma-li *(transitive)* .... boil YR
badha-y *(transitive)* .... give a hiding YR
baluuma-li *(transitive)* .... kill YY, GR
baluburra-li *(transitive)* .... put out (extinguish) YR, YY
baluwa-li *(transitive)* .... put out (extinguish) YY
bama-li *(transitive)* .... knead GR
squash YR, YY
bamba bayama-li *(phrase)* .... squeeze YY

barra-li *(transitive)* .... sharpen YR, YY, GR
bayama-li *(transitive)* .... catch, hold YR, YY
biimba-li *(transitive)* .... sweep YR, YY
biirra-li *(transitive)* .... skin YR, YY
binaal bunma-li *(transitive)* .... quieten, soothe, calm, settle down YR, YY
bindama-li *(transitive)* .... hang up GR
bindaybi-li *(transitive)* .... tie up YR
hang up YR, YY, GR
buluba-li *(transitive)* .... cover YR, YY
buluba-y *(intransitive)* .... cover (self), be covered YR, YY
bulubama-li *(transitive)* .... cover up YR, YY
buma-li *(transitive)* .... hit, kill YR, YY, GR
buma-y *(intransitive)* .... (be) hit YR
bumala-y *(intransitive)* .... fight YR, GR
bundaama-li *(transitive)* .... knock down YR, YY, GR
push down YR, YY, GR
bunma-li *(transitive)* .... cause (a change) YR, YY, GR
burranba-li *(transitive)* .... cause (a change) YR, YY, GR
burrul burranba-li *(transitive)* .... raise (bring up) YY
buubi-li *(transitive)* .... blow YR, YY, GR
buudhi-rri *(transitive)* .... brush (with leaves) YY
buudhu-rri *(transitive)* .... put fire out YR
buurra-li[1] *(transitive)* .... pluck, pull out YR, YY
buurrma-li *(transitive)* .... pull YR, YY
buwama-li *(transitive)* .... shake down YR, YY
buwawa-li *(transitive)* .... attack YY
buyawila-li *(transitive)* .... make (force) YR
dhanduwiyma-li *(transitive)* .... put someone to bed YR
dhangga-li *(transitive)* .... skip YR
dhanggima-li *(transitive)* .... soak YY
dhawuma-li *(transitive)* .... cook in a hole (roast) YR, YY, GR
dhilay-rri *(transitive)* .... throw out YR
dhinba-li *(transitive)* .... singe YY
dhirranba-li *(transitive)* .... shake YR, YY, GR
dhiyaagarra-li *(transitive)* ... spread GR
prepare a bed YY, GR
dhiyarra-li *(transitive)* .... dip, scoop YR, YY
dhu-rri *(transitive)* .... poke (with pointed object), spear, stab, sting YR, YY, GR
tap YR
dhuma-li *(transitive)* .... open, take out GR

verbs

dhurra-li¹ *(transitive)*	make (construct) YR, YY, GR
dhurraaba-li *(transitive)*	make come out YR
dhurradhurraba-li *(transitive)*	tap YR
dhuudhinma-li *(transitive)*	shoot YR
dhuwi-y *(transitive)*	stick into YR, YY
dhuwima-li *(transitive)*	remove, take out YR, YY; take off (clothes) YY
dhuwinba-li *(transitive)*	hide (plant) YR, YY
gaa-gi *(transitive)*	wear YR
gaanba-li *(transitive)*	wipe YR
gaarra-li *(transitive)*	rub YR, YY, GR
gaarrama-li *(transitive)*	steal GR
gaarrima-li *(transitive)*	spill YR, YY
gabanma-li *(transitive)*	heal YR
gadhamayawa-li *(transitive)*	hide YR, YY
galaanbi-li *(transitive)*	scrape YR, YY
gama-li *(transitive)*	break YR, YY, GR; block (deflect) YR
gama-y *(intransitive)*	break YR, YY
gamaama-li *(transitive)*	rub YR, YY
gandawa-li *(transitive)*	cover GR
ganma-li *(transitive)*	catch, hold GR
garawi-li *(transitive)*	pelt, throw at GR
garra-li *(transitive)*	cut YR, YY, GR
garra-y *(intransitive)*	be cut YR, YY
garranba-li *(transitive)*	push against, shove YY
garungga-y *(intransitive)*	drown YR, YY
garunggama-li *(transitive)*	drown YR
gayawi-li *(transitive)*	pelt, throw at, point bone, kill YR, YY
gayla-y *(intransitive)*	burn, cook YR, YY
gaylama-li *(transitive)*	burn YR, YY
gayma-li *(transitive)*	stir, turn, twist YR, YY
gaynma-li *(transitive)*	calm, scrape, smooth off YY
gidjigidjiba-li *(transitive)*	tickle YR, YY
gigirrma-li *(transitive)*	kick YR, GR
giinba-li *(transitive)*	scale YR, YY
giirra-li *(transitive)*	wake up GR
giiyanma-li *(transitive)*	frighten YR, YY, GR
gimbi-li *(transitive)*	do, make (construct) YR, YY
gimubi-li *(transitive)*	do, make (construct) GR
gudhuwa-li *(transitive)*	burn YR, YY, GR
gudhuwa-y *(intransitive)*	be hot YR, GR; burn, cook YR
gulagama-li *(transitive)*	embrace, hold, cuddle YR, YY
gundaawa-li *(transitive)*	burn (with a lot of flame) YR, YY
gundaawa-y *(intransitive)*	burn (with a lot of flame) YR
guulaabi-y *(intransitive)*	warm up YR
guuma-li *(transitive)*	collect, gather YR
guwima-li *(transitive)*	spread out to dry YY
maaruma-li *(transitive)*	fix, heal, make better GR
maayama-li *(transitive)*	make by hand YY
maayuma-li *(transitive)*	fix, heal, make better YR
mama-li *(transitive)*	stick YR, YY, GR
manuma-li *(transitive)*	steal YR, YY
marama-li *(transitive)*	make by hand GR
marramba-li *(transitive)*	cover up, wrap up YR
marramba-y *(intransitive)*	be wrapped YR
mawu-gi *(transitive)*	dig, scratch YR, YY, GR
mayabi-li *(transitive)*	hang up, put up YR, YY, GR
miinma-li *(transitive)*	pull YR, GR
mubal dhiyama-li *(phrase)*	gut YY
mubal dhuwima-li *(phrase)*	gut YR, YY
mubirr dhu-rri *(phrase)*	carve, write YY
mugi-li *(transitive)*	mix YY
muurra-li *(transitive)*	fill YY
muurra-y *(intransitive)*	fill YY
muyawa-li *(transitive)*	sew YR, YY
muyuwa-li *(transitive)*	duck (in water) YR, YY
ngamuma-li *(transitive)*	milk a cow YR
nganbiyma-li *(transitive)*	lean YR
ngarranma-li *(transitive)*	show YR, YY
ngaydju dhiyama-li *(phrase)*	hook out (grub) YY
ngayu-gi *(transitive)*	tread on, trample YR, YY
nguwa-li *(transitive)*	fold, roll up YR, YY
nhaanma-li *(transitive)*	drop YR, YY
nhamurra-li *(transitive)*	bury YR, YY
nhima-li *(transitive)*	pinch YR, YY, GR
nhinga-li *(transitive)*	sew YY, GR
nhuunma-li *(transitive)*	milk a cow YY, GR
nhuwigu buma-li *(phrase)*	kill (stone dead) YR
nhuyu-gi *(transitive)*	chastise YR
pickima-li *(transitive)*	pick YR

adverbs

wa-li *(transitive)*	put in	YR, YY
wagirrbuma-li *(transitive)*	wash	YR, GR
wagirrbuma-y *(intransitive)*	wash (self)	YR
wagirrma-li *(transitive)*	wash	YR, YY
wagirrma-y *(intransitive)*	wash (self)	YR
waluwarr bunma-li *(phrase)*	make bigger, spread out	YY
wana-gi *(transitive)*	throw, pitch	YR, YY
warrayma-li *(transitive)*	build, put up	YR, YY, GR
	stand up	YR, YY
warruma-li *(transitive)*	spread	GR
wiima-li *(transitive)*	put down	YR, YY, GR
wiirra-li *(transitive)*	shave, shear	YR, YY
wirra-li *(transitive)*	twist	GR
wiya-gi *(transitive)*	cook	GR
wiyayi-li *(transitive)*	remove quills	YY
wubarra-li *(transitive)*	pen up	GR
wula-li *(intransitive)*	blaze	YR, YY, GR
wulanabi-li *(transitive)*	light (fire/lamp)	YR, YY, GR
wuuma-li *(transitive)*	dress someone	YY
wuyugi-li *(transitive)*	smoke (ceremonial)	YY
yaarrima-li *(transitive)*	spill	GR
yaaya-li *(transitive)*	chop	YR, YY
yabi-li *(transitive)*	twist, plait	YY
	kiss	YR, YY
yadhaba-li *(transitive)*	sharpen	GR
yanaaynbi-li *(transitive)*	release, let go	YR, YY
yii-li *(transitive)*	bite	YR, YY, GR
yiili burranba-li *(phrase)*	annoy, make someone angry	YR, YY
yilama-li *(transitive)*	cook	YR, YY
yilama-y *(intransitive)*	cook	YR
yinabi-li *(transitive)*	fish, catch fish, catch with instrument	YR, YY, GR
yubama-li *(transitive)*	make cry	YR, YY
yulaa-li *(transitive)*	knot, tie up	YR, YY, GR
yulaanbi-li *(transitive)*	tangle	YR, YY
yuluurrinma-li *(transitive)*	lose	YR
yurringga-li *(transitive)*	push	YR
yuurraa-li *(transitive)*	cover up	YR
yuurrma-li *(transitive)*	play with	YY
yuuwaanmi-li *(transitive)*	lose	YY

■ Other verbs

balu-gi *(intransitive)*	go out (fire)	YR, YY
burra-li *(intransitive)*	begin	YR
burranba-y *(intransitive)*	become	YR, YY
burrul gi-gi *(phrase)*	grow	YY
dhaarri-y *(intransitive)*	disappear	YR
dhabima-li *(transitive)*	leave alone	YR, YY, GR
dhiirrma-li *(transitive)*	leave alone	YR, YY
dhuluuma-y *(intransitive)*	thunder	YR
dhura-li *(transitive)*	make noise	GR
dhurra-li^2 *(intransitive)*	grow	YR
gaanga-y *(transitive, intransitive)*	lay egg	YR, YY
garrawa-li *(transitive)*	keep, retain, store	YY
gayarra-y *(intransitive)*	turn into, transform	YR, YY
gi-gi *(intransitive)*	going to (do something)	YR, YY
	be, become (get)	YR, YY, GR
	goes to (leads)	YR
gula-li *(transitive)*	bark	YR, YY, GR
guuya-li *(intransitive)*	shine	YR, YY, GR
ngarra-y *(intransitive)*	look	YR, YY
walindja-li *(intransitive)*	be lonely	YR
wana-gi *(transitive)*	leave	YR, YY

Adverbs

badjinbal	gradually	YY
baluwaa	quietly	YR, YY
	slowly, steadily	YR, YY, GR
baluwaal	never	YY
bamba	hard (with force)	YR, YY, GR
	loudly, very	YR, YY
barraay	fast, quickly	YR, YY, GR
bulaarra	twice	GR
dhirra	flash	YR, YY
dhugay	always	YR, YY
gaba^1	all right, correctly; good, well	YR, YY, GR
gabangaarr	nicely	YR
gagil	bad, no good	YR, YY, GR
gamil maaru	badly, carelessly, not right	GR
gibaylandhi	formerly	GR
giidjuugiidjuu	constant	YY
guraay	slowly	GR

describing words (adjectives)

guwaaybaa	slowly	YY
maala	once	GR
maaru	well, carefully	GR
maayu	well, carefully	YR, YY
mandaymanday	sequentially	YY
mayabuu	still (continuing)	YR, YY
miirrmiirr	backwards	YY
ngaarr	hard, strong	GR
ngaliman	almost, nearly	YR, YY
nganangana	floating, buoyant	YR, YY
nganbinganbi	to and fro	YY
nganbirr	crosswise, across	YY, GR
waal maayu	badly, uncarefully, not right	YY
waanda	first	YR
warragil	straight, true	YR, YY, GR
yalagiirrma	like that, in that manner	YR, GR
	because (consequence)	YR
yaliwunga	always	GR
yiyal	just, only	YR, YY, GR

Describing words (adjectives)

badha	bitter, sour	YR, YY, GR
	sad	GR
badjin	small, little	YR, YY
baganbagan	striped	YY
balaa	white	YY, GR
balal	dry, empty, bare, thirsty	YR, YY, GR
baliyaa	cold	YR, YY
balu	dead	YR, YY, GR
balumbaluu	weak	YY, GR
banay	ten	YR, YY, GR
bandu	dirty	YR, YY
bangga	white	YR, YY
banggabaa	white	YR, YY, GR
baramay	worn out	GR
barrabarraa	split open	YY
barran.giirr	new moon	YY
barriga	hundred	YR, YY, GR
bayaal	next	YR
bayn	sore	YR, YY, GR
bidjaaybiyaay	muddy	YY
biganbiyaay	lawful	YY
biirr	one	YR, YY
biiwanbiiwan	boastful, bragging, puffed out	YY
bilabilaa	parallel	YY
bilga	thin, bony	YY
bina guwaal	upset, nervous	YR
bina muurr	deaf	YR, YY, GR
binangarrangarra	clever, intelligent	YY
bindiyaabiyaay	prickly, thorny	YY
biruubaraay	hollow	GR
biyaduul	alone	YR, YY
biyarr	one	YR, YY
biyuubiyaay	hollow	YY
bubaay	small, little	YR
bulaadjal	only two	YY
bulaangaa	pair	YY
bulaarr	two	YR, YY, GR
bulaarrbulaarr	four	YY, GR
bulaarruu maa	ten	YY
bulawulaarr	four	YR
bulayrr	warm	YR, YY, GR
buligaa	four	YR, YY, GR
buliirral ganaay	short of breath	YY
bulilbulil	slippery	YR, YY
buluuy	black, dark	YR, YY, GR
burabura	thin, bony	GR
buribara	pregnant	YR
burranbaa	new	YY
burrul	big, much	YR, YY
burrulaa	many, a lot	YR, YY, GR
burrul bina	clever, wise	GR
buulbuul	knotty, lumpy	YY
buunhuumayuu	grassy	YR, YY
buwabildhalibaa	poor	YY
buwabuwa	loose, rattling	YY
buyabuya	thin, bony	YR, YY
buyaduul	short	YR, YY
buyu wayawaya	bandy-legged	YY
dhaandhaan	staggering	YY
dhaandiyaay	leaning	YR, YY
dhabiyaan	quiet	YR, YY, GR
dhadhaal	grey	YR
dhalaybaa	sharp	YR, YY
dhambi	short	YR
dhambidjuul	short	YR
dhandarriyaay	grey haired	YR, YY
dhan.galan.gaa	covered, disguised	YR
dhan.gurr	lame, crippled	YR, YY, GR
dhawadha	thousand	YR, YY, GR

describing words (adjectives)

dhawunbaraay	dirty GR	ganu	all YR, GR
dhaygaliyaay	clever YR, YY	ganungawu	all, whole YR, YY
dhiriya	old, grey GR	garaydhalibaa	silent GR
dhirrabil	smiling YY	garigari	afraid, frightened YR, YY, GR
dhirrabuu	very flash YR	garragarraa	cut, mown, clipped YY
dhugaay	small, little YR, YY	garran.garraan	constipated, tight, stuck tight YY
dhuli	arched, bowed, bent over YY	garriil	cold GR
dhumbil	full, humped YR	gawarrawarr	green YR, YY, GR
dhunbiliyaay	strong, sinewy YY	gayaa	happy YR, YY, GR pleased, proud YR, YY
dhuningarraay	old YR, YY	gayaay²	sexy, randy YR, YY, GR
dhurradhurraa	untidy, all over the place YY	gayliyaay	generous, good-hearted, kind YR, YY
dhurrin	green (unripe), raw YR, YY		
dhurrin²	greedy YR, YY	gayn.gayn¹	calm, smooth YY
dhurrundhurrun	hairy, furry YY	gidjarri	nervous YR
dhuruyaal	right (not left) GR	gidjiirr	yellow YR
dhuumuyu	blackened, smoked YY	gidjirrgidjirr	yellow YR, YY, GR
dhuurrguu	relaxed YR	gii	bitter YY
dhuuyaal	right (not left) YR, YY	giidjuwaa	green YY
dhuwa	grey YR	giigaliyaay	scabby YR, YY
dhuyuldhuyul	hilly YY	giligili	upset YR
gaay²	small, little GR	giliin	clean YR
gaaynmara	small, little GR	gindarragaa	funny YR
gaba¹	good, well; healthy YR, YY, GR	girrigirri	noisy YR
gaba binaal	peaceful, well mannered YR, YY	giyal	afraid, frightened YR, YY, GR
		giyaldhalibaa	shameless, no shame YR, YY
gaba dhaygal	clever YY	giyalgil	sour YR
gaba ngulu	good-looking YR, YY	giyalgiyal	itchy YR, YY
gababala	better YR, YY	gugirriibiyaay	strong YR, YY
gabanbaa	light (not heavy) YR, YY, GR	gugirriidhalibaa	weak YR, YY
gabangaarr	nicely YR	gulbirr	few YR some YR, GR
gadharrgadharr	torn, ragged YR, YY		
gagan.gagan	many coloured YR, YY	gulguu	strange YR, YY
gagil	bad, no good YR, YY, GR	gulibaa	three YR, YY, GR
gagil ngulu	ugly YR, YY	guliirraraay	married GR
gagilbiyal	sorry YR	guliirrdhalibaa	unmarried, widowed YR, YY, GR
galambiirr	greedy YR		
galay	eight YR, YY, GR	guliirriyaay	married YR, YY
galibaraay	full of water, wet GR	guliyaan	new, strange YR
galingin	thirsty YR, GR	gulungguluu	rotten YR, YY
gamugamuubiyaay	fly-blown YR, YY	gumba	flinty (very hard) YY
gana garraa	cranky YR	gun.gun	afraid, frightened YR, YY
gana walingay	sad YY	gunadha	boggy YY, YY
ganaay¹	open YR	gunagunaa	brown, dirty, disgusting YY
ganaay²	shallow YR, YY, GR	gundhuwundhuu	stubborn YR, YY
ganadhaa	deep YR, YY	gunganbiyaay	wet YR, YY
ganagiil	sad YR	guraarr	long, tall GR
gandjarra	best YR		

describing words (adjectives)

gurru	round	GR
gurrugurru¹	very deep	YY
gurrugurru²	all	YR, YY
gurruubaa	deep	YR, YY, GR
guulay	seven	YR, YY, GR
guuyalaraay	shiny	GR
guwan.guwan	foggy	YR
guwaymbarra	red	YR, YY, GR
guwiirr	sweet	YR
guwin	grey shape/colour	YY
guyaarr	long, tall	YR, YY
guyan	shy	YR
maa	five	YR, YY, GR
maal	one	GR
maayamamayuu	stony	YY
maaydja	free	YR
maayndjul	very good, tempting	YR
madhamadha	knotty, rough, bumpy	YR, YY, GR
madhanbaa	heavy	YR, YY, GR
madhanmadhan	very heavy	YY
malu	quiet, tired	YY, GR
mamaldhalibaa	alone, friendless, unique	YR, YY / YY
mamalmamal	sticky	YY
man.gaman.ga	wide, flat	YR, YY, GR
manbu	flat	YY
mandaymanday	sequentially	YY
marrabaa	good, well	GR
milamilaa	shrunken (shrivelled)	YY
milan¹	one	YR, YY
milanburr	first again	YR, YY
milandjal	only one	YY
milanduul	alone, only one	YY
milgumilgu	alert, watchful	YY
mirraal	nine	YR, YY, GR
mubalyaal	pregnant	YY, GR
muga	blunt / blind	YR, YY / YR, YY, GR
muga bina	deaf	YR, GR
muga wudha	deaf	YY
mugu	blunt	GR
mugu bina	deaf	YR, YY, GR
mula	soft, weak	YR, YY
mulabiyaay	kind	YR
mulamula	soft	YR, YY, GR
mundimundi	spotted	YR, YY, GR
munggal	only	YY, GR
murrubidi	lucky	YR
murrun	alive	YR, YY, GR
murrunbaa	another, other	YR, YY
murrurwalingay	stale	YR, YY
muurr	blunt, full, blocked	YR, YY, GR
ngaarr	hard, strong	GR
ngaaybu	full	YY
nganangana	floating, buoyant	YR, YY
nganbirr	crosswise, across	YY, GR
ngandanganda	shiny, reflective, glittering	YY
ngarragaa	silly, poor (helpless), pitiful	YR, YY, GR
ngayarray	speckled	YR
nguwan.nguwan	folded, wrapped	YY
nharran	skinny	YY
nhiiyanhiiya	very fond	YR
nhulaanbil	slimey	YY
nhunduu	blunt, tasteless, unsweetened	YR, YY, GR
nhunduwaa	thick	YY
nhuubala	new	GR
nhuwi	rotten, smelly, stinking	YR, YY, GR
waawul	narrow	YR, YY
wagi²	pretend, gammon	YR, YY
walan	hard, solid, tough	YR, YY
walanbaa	hard, solid, tough, strong	YR, YY
walingay	out of place	YR, YY
waluwarr	wide, spread out	YY
wamba	mad, crazy, stupid, silly	YR, YY, GR
wamu	fat	YR, YY, GR
waragaal	left	GR
warawara	bent, crooked	GR
warragil	straight, true	YR, YY, GR
warranggal	strong, powerful	YR, YY, GR
warrawarra	standing	YY
warrayaa	lost	YR, YY
warru	wide, spread out	GR
wayagaal	left	YR, YY
wayawaya	bent, crooked	YR, YY
wii	clever	YR, YY
wiibil	sick	GR
wiibiyaay	hot	YY
wirrunbiyaay	juicy	YY
wiwurra	million	YR, YY, GR

Gamilaraay/Yuwaalaraay/Yuwaalayaay *to* English Word List by Topic

question words

wiyal	crooked	YR
wiyaybaa	strange, odd	YR, YY
wubuubiyaay	mouldy	YR, YY
wulan	blazing	YR, YY, GR
wulbuwulbu	flexible, bendy	YY
wurrun	swollen	YR, YY
yaal	pretend, false	YR
yaambul	silly, mad	YR, GR
yadhala	sharp	GR
yaluuyaluu	same, copied	YY
yarigin	thirsty	YR
yarrbun	very tired, exhausted	YR, YY
yiilay	cooked, ripe	YY
yiili	angry	YR, YY, GR
yiiliyanbaa	angry, savage	YR, YY
yiiliyiili	peppery, spicy	YR, YY
yilaan.gaal	fresh, new	YY
yiluwidi	blue	YR
yinggil	lazy, tired	YR, YY, GR
yirrgayn	clear	YR, YY
yiyadhalibaa	toothless	YY
yuli	six	YR, YY, GR
yuularaay	full of food, sated, satisfied	GR
yuuliyaay	full of food, sated, satisfied	YR, YY
yuulngin	hungry	YR, YY, GR
yuumbu	numb	YR

Question words

dhalaa	where?	GR
galaarr	how?	YR, YY
galaarr gi-gi	what to do?	YR, YY
galawu	when?	YR, YY
gamilgaa	why not?	GR
gulaarr	how?	YR, GR
minya	what?	YR, YY, GR
minyaarr	which?	YR, YY, GR
minyaarru	where (to)?	YR, YY
minyaaya	where (at)?	YR, YY
minyaaya dhaay	where (from)?	YR, YY
minyadhi	why?, why not?	YR, YY
minyagu	why (what for)?	YR, YY, GR
minyama	what?	YR, GR
minyangay	how many?	YR, YY, GR
ngaana	who? (doer/done to)	YY
ngaandi	who? (doer/done to)	YR, YY, GR
ngaandu	who? (doer to)	YR, YY, GR
ngaanngu	whose?, to whose?	YR, YY, GR
ngaanngunda	to whom?	YY, GR
ngaanngundi	from who?	YR, YY, GR
waalgaa	why not?	YR
wirralaa	when?	GR
yaama	question word	YR, YY, GR
yaamagaa	whether, if	YR, YY

Other useful words
(exclamations, particles)

baaydjarr (exclamation)	hey!	YR, YY
barrabandu (exclamation)	shame!, oh no!	YR, YY
biyay (exclamation)	enough!	YR
dhalay (exclamation)	finished!, cheeky!	YR
gaabu (exclamation)	hush!	YR
gaay giirruu (exclamation)	true words!	YY
gadhabal (exclamation)	wonderful!	GR
galaay (exclamation)	speak of the devil!	YR
gamil (particle)	no, not, didn't, don't, won't	GR
gamila (particle)	can't, couldn't	GR
gamilu (particle)	before, hold on, not yet	GR
garriya[2] (particle)	don't, stop	YR, YY, GR
garriyawu (exclamation)	wait a while!	YR, YY
giirr (particle)	really, truly	YR, YY, GR
giirr maaru (exclamation)	well done!, good job!	GR
giirr maayu (exclamation)	well done!, good job!	YR, YY
giirrnga (exclamation)	that's enough!	YY
giirruu (particle)	absolutely, too right	YR, YY, GR
gulbiyaay (exclamation)	welcome!	YR
maaya (exclamation)	hey!	YR
maayrr (particle)	no, none	YR, YY
madja (exclamation)	sorry!	YR, YY, GR

madjagurra
  (exclamation) ....oh dear! YR, YY
marayrr *(particle)*...............no, none GR
miyaay *(exclamation)* ....okay! (satisfactory) YR
ngaa *(particle)* ....yes YR, YY, GR
ngaan *(question word)* ......what? YR
ngaawawu
  (exclamation) ....that's right! YR, YY
ngaayaybaay
  (exclamation) ....okay!, all right! YR
ngadhan.gaa
  (particle) ....thought (suppose) YR
ngarragaa
  (exclamation) ....alas!, oh dear! YR, YY, GR
ngibaay *(exclamation)* .....strange! GR
nhaan *(exclamation)* ....expression of surprise YR
nhama dhaay
  (exclamation) ....look out! YR
waa² *(exclamation)* ....expression of praise YR, YY, GR
waal *(particle)*.......................no, not, didn't, don't, won't YR, YY
waala *(particle)* ....can't, couldn't YR, YY
waalu *(particle)* ....before, hold on, not yet YR, YY
waama *(particle)* ....because, therefore YR, YY
wana *(particle)*......................let (something happen) YR, YY, GR
wanaa *(particle)* ....mustn't YY, GR
wanagidjay
  (exclamation) ....stop it! YR, YY
yaa *(exclamation)* ....hey (wake up)!, steady on! YR
yaama *(exclamation)* ....hello, greetings YR, YY, GR
yaambul *(exclamation)* ...pretending! YR, GR
yagaay *(exclamation)* ....hey!, look!, ouch! YR, YY, GR
yalbala *(particle)* ....gammon, pretend YR, YY
yaluu *(particle)* ....again YR, YY, GR
yawu *(particle)*......................yes YR, GR
yii *(exclamation)*...................hey! YR
yiiy *(exclamation)* ....listen! YR
yiyaldu *(particle)* ....furthermore GR

Pronouns

gaali *(pronoun)* ....they (two people — doer to) YR, YY
gaalinga................................they (two people — doer/done to) YR, YY, GR
gaalingu................................their, to them (two people) YR, YY, GR
gaalingunda......................to/at/on them (two people) YR, YY, GR
gaalingundi.......................from them (two people) YR, YY, GR
ganugu.................................they (more than two people — doer to) YR, YY, GR
ganunga...............................they (more than two people — doer/done to) YR, YY, GR
ganungawu.........................everything YR, YY
ganungu...............................their, to them (more than two people) YR, YY, GR
ganungunda......................to/at/on them (more than two people) YR, YY, GR
ganungundi.......................from them (more than two people) YR, YY, GR
gurrugurru²......................everything YR, YY
minyagaa.............................something YR, YY
minyaminyabal................everything GR
minyaminyagaa.............everything YR
-nda *(suffix)* ....you (one person — doer/doer to) YR, YY, GR
-ndaali *(suffix)* ....you (two people — doer/doer to) YR, YY, GR
-ndaay *(suffix)* ....you (more than two people — doer/doer to) YR, YY, GR
ngaana.................................who? (doer/done to) YY
ngaanawaa.........................someone (doer/done to) YY
ngaandi ....who? (doer/done to) YR, YY, GR
ngaandingaandi...............what's-a-name YR
ngaandiyaa.........................someone (doer/done to) YR, YY
ngaandu...............................who? (doer to) YR, YY, GR
ngaanduwaa.......................someone (doer to) YR, YY, GR
ngaanngu............................whose? YR, YY, GR
ngaanngunda...................to who? YR, YY, GR
ngaanngundawaa............to someone YR, GR
ngaanngundi.....................from who? YR, YY, GR
ngaanngundiyaa.............from someone YR, YY, GR
ngaannguwaa....................someone's YR, YY, GR

suffixes

ngali	we (two people — doer/doer to) YR, YY, GR
ngalingu	our, to us (two people) YR, YY, GR
ngalingunda	to/at/on us (two people) YR, YY, GR
ngalingundi	from us (two people) YR, YY, GR
ngalinya	us (two people — done to) YR, YY, GR
nganha	me (done to) YR, YY, GR
nganunda	to/at/on me YR, YY, GR
nganundi	from me YR, YY, GR
ngay[1]	my, to me YR, YY, GR
ngaya	I YR, YY, GR
nginaalingu	to you, your (two people) YR, YY, GR
nginaalingunda	to/at/on you (two people) YR, YY, GR
nginaalingundi	from you (two people) YR, YY, GR
nginaalinya	you (two people — done to) YR, YY, GR
nginaayngu	your, to you (more than two people) YR, YY, GR
nginaayngunda	to/at/on you (more than two people) YR, YY, GR
nginaayngundi	from you (more than two people) YR, YY, GR
nginaaynya	you (more than two people — done to) YR, YY, GR
nginda	you (one person — doer/doer to) YR, YY, GR
ngindaali	you (two people — doer/doer to) YR, YY, GR
ngindaay	you (more than two people — doer/doer to) YR, YY, GR
nginu	your (one person), to you (one person) YR, YY, GR
nginunda	to/at/on you (one person) YR, YY, GR
nginundi	from you (one person) YR, YY, GR
nginunha	you (one person — done to) YR, YY, GR
ngiyani	we (more than two people — doer/doer to) YR, YY, GR
ngiyaningu	our, to us (more than two people) YR, YY, GR
ngiyaningunda	to/at/on us (more than two people) YR, YY, GR
ngiyaningundi	from us (more than two people) YR, YY, GR
ngiyaninya	us (more than two people — done to) YR, YY, GR
nguru	he, she (doer/doer to) GR
ngurugaali	they (two people — doer to) GR
ngurunga	her, him (one person — done to) GR
ngurungu	her(s), his, to her, him GR
ngurungunda	to/at/on him/her GR
ngurungundi	from him/her GR
nguu[1]	he, she (doer/doer to) YR, YY
nguunga	her, him (done to) YR, YY
nguungu	her(s), his, to her, him YR, YY
nguungunda	to/at/on him/her YR, YY
nguungundi	from him/her YR, YY
waal ngaanduwaa	no-one (doer to) YR

Suffixes

-aaba-li	all YR, YY
-araay	with, having GR
-awaa	habitual YR, YY
-Baa	place of, time of YR, YY, GR
-badhaay (clitic)	might (would you) YR, YY
-bala (clitic)	contrast YR, YY
-ban.gaan	very, really GR
-baraay	with, having GR
-barra	people from YR, YY
-bidi	big YR, YY, GR
-bil	covered with, with a lot of YR, YY, GR
-biyaay	with, having YR, YY
-biyal	only, just YR, GR
-Biyan	flower of, fruit of YR, YY
-bula	also, too YR, YY
-dha-y[1]	eating YR, YY, GR
-dha-y[2]	each other (reciprocal -rri class verbs) YR, YY, GR
-dha-y[3]	regular progressive -rri class verbs YR, YY, GR
-dhaan	good at YR, YY, GR

suffixes

-dhalibaa	without, lacking YR, YY, GR	-na	command -rri class verbs YR, YY, GR
-DHi¹	from, because of, circumstance YR, YY, GR	-nda	you (one person — doer/doer to) YR, YY, GR
-dhi²	possessor (family member) YR, YY, GR	-ndaali	you (two people — doer/doer to) YR, YY, GR
-DHuul	one YR, YY / little, small YR, YY, GR	-ndaay¹	you (more than two people — doer/doer to) YR, YY, GR
-Ga	in, at, on, to (dative) YR, YY, GR	-ndaay²	relative -li and -rri class verbs YR, YY, GR
-gaali	group of two YR, YY	-nga¹ *(clitic)*	or YY / now, then YR, YY
-gaalu	pretend YR	-nga²	command -gi class verbs YR, YY, GR
-gal	group, mob YY / many (little things) YR, YY	-ngayi-li	all day, on-going, habitual YR
-galgaa	many YR, YY	-ngayi-y	yesterday (recent past), tomorrow (near future) YR, YY
-gayaluu	inhabitants of, dweller in YY		
-gi	future tense -gi class verbs YR, YY, GR	-ngiili-y	oneself YR, YY
-gi-la-y	regular progressive -gi class verbs YR, YY, GR	-nginda	wanting YR, YY, GR
		-ngindaay	relative -y and -gi class verbs YR, YY, GR
-giirr	like, similar to YR, YY, GR	-nha¹	that YR, YY
-gili	side (location) YR, YY	-nha²	present progressive verb suffix YR, YY, GR
-Gu¹	do with, doer to YR, YY, GR		
-gu²	belonging to, for, movement to, purpose YR, YY, GR	-nhi	past tense -y, -gi and -rri class verbs YR, YY, GR
-gu³	purpose verb suffix YR, YY, GR	-nyi	past tense -y and -gi class verbs (after i) YR, YY, GR
-ili	little (affectionate) YY		
-iyaay	with, having YR, YY	-rraa-y	moving progressive -rri class verbs YR, YY, GR
-la	command -li class verbs YR, YY, GR	-rri	future tense -rri class verbs YR, YY, GR
-la-y	each other (reciprocal -li class verbs) YR, YY, GR	-uwi	back YR, YY, GR
-laa *(clitic)*	then YR, YY	-uwi-y	back verb suffix YR, YY
-laa-y	moving progressive -li class verbs YR, YY, GR	-Waa	some YR, YY
-lda-y	regular progressive -li class verbs YR, YY, GR	-waa-y	moving progressive -y and -gi class verbs YY, GR
-ldaay	relative -li class verbs YR, YY, GR	-Waayaa	don't know YR
		-wan	prominent (big) YR, YY
-li	future tense -li class verbs YR, YY, GR	-wan.gaan	very, really YR, YY
-Vli-y	benefactive -li class verbs YR	-y	future tense -y class verbs YR, YY, GR
-Luu	all possible YR, YY	-y	past tense -li class verbs YR, YY, GR
-ma-li	make (something) happen YR, YY, GR		
-n.giili-y	benefactive -gi class verbs YR, YY, GR	-y-la-y	regular progressive -y class verbs YR, YY, GR

Gamilaraay/Yuwaalaraay/Yuwaalayaay *to* English Word List by Topic

new words

-ya	command -y class verbs YR, YY, GR
-Yaa	either . . . or YR
	must, might YR, YY
-yaa-y	moving progressive -y and -gi class verbs (after -i) YR, YY, GR

New words

badha gali *(noun)*	beer YR
bidjiirr *(noun)*	biscuit YR
dhii man.garr *(noun)*	tea bag YR
gaala *(noun)*	tin mug, mug YR
gabi *(noun)*	coffee YR
gayrra *(noun)*	electricity YR
gayrragumbirri *(noun)*	computer YR
guwiirr gungan *(noun)*	soft drink YR
guwiirr widja *(noun)*	cake, biscuit YR
man.ga *(noun)*	table YR
wirri *(noun)*	plate YR
wiyayl *(noun)*	pen, pencil YR, YY

Numbers

bulaarr *(adjective)*	two YR, YY, GR
buligaa *(adjective)*	four YR, YY, GR
gulibaa *(adjective)*	three YR, YY, GR
maa *(adjective)*	five YR, YY, GR
maal *(adjective)*	one GR
milan *(adjective)*	one YR, YY

■ New numbers

banay *(adjective)*	ten YR, YY, GR
barriga *(adjective)*	hundred YR, YY, GR
dhawadha *(adjective)*	thousand YR, YY, GR
galay *(adjective)*	eight YR, YY, GR
guulay *(adjective)*	seven YR, YY, GR
mirraal *(adjective)*	nine YR, YY, GR
wiwurra *(adjective)*	million YR, YY, GR
yuli *(adjective)*	six YR, YY, GR

The Learner's Guide

Chapter One
Getting Started

This learner's guide is intended for learners of Gamilaraay, Yuwaalaraay and Yuwaalayaay (GY), and for some people it will be the first learner's guide that they have read or used. It is also the first learner's guide of GY which has been written, at least in recent years. It introduces some of the main rules, or grammar, of the language. Mistakes will be found in it, and there may be better ways of explaining things. Further, new rules are being discovered as the original materials are re-examined. Since this is an introductory work, some of the more complex sections of grammar are not covered.

Because there are many common structures in Australian Indigenous languages, learning about these other languages can help in working out the patterns in Gamilaraay, Yuwaalaraay and Yuwaalayaay. Tamsin Donaldson's *Ngiyambaa: The Language of the Wangaaybuwan* (1980) has been particularly useful in providing detail about a closely related language, and has given hints about many rules of GY. So, familiarity with GY sources and familiarity with Australian languages will lead to some new knowledge.

While some new information will be obtained from the original sources, in many other cases the answer to, 'How do you say this?' is simply not there. Somewhere down the track Gamilaraay, Yuwaalaraay and Yuwaalayaay people may decide to expand the grammar to fill in those gaps. They may do so by borrowing rules from other Aboriginal languages or from English.

∎ How to use this learner's guide

If you are new to learning a language it is important to take things slowly, and realise that it is generally only after reading through the material quite a number of times that you will understand most of it. If you want to use the learner's guide to help learn GY then it will help a lot if you can listen to tapes or CDs. (Archival material is listed on pages 14 and 15; other material is available from the language programs listed on page vii.) This helps you get used to the sounds, and also to phrases and sentences. For further information about Gamilaraay, Yuwaalaraay and Yuwaalayaay resources, contact AIATSIS or visit the GY website at www.yuwaalaraay.org.

Grammars divide a language into sections, and it is a good idea to look over the whole section without trying to understand it all — that will come with repetition, revision and re-reading. Most sections contain some basic material and also other material that is more complex. After having a general look at a chapter or section, go back and work on the basic material. Leave the rest of the chapter till later.

These languages are very different from English and take a lot of getting used to, especially for a person who either only speaks English or hasn't had much practice at learning a second language. There is a summary section at the back for when you have the general idea, but need to check out the detail.

Example sentences

There are many example sentences scattered throughout the learner's guide. Remember that words in GY are often made up of several parts (these are known as compound words). To help understand how the word is made up, the parts are separated by a hyphen. In the examples below, the first line is in GY, with the parts of each word separated by hyphens, the second line is in English explaining what each part means, and the third line is an English translation.

Giirr	nhama	maayama	baarra-nhi.
true	the	rock	split-past

The rock split.

In the example below, hyphens once again show parts of words. On some verbs, -y at the end means that the action will take place in the future, and -nhi means that it took place in the past.

banaga-y	banaga-nhi	yinarr-galgaa
run-future	run-past	woman-plural
will run	ran	women

▌Talk it!

If you want to speak the language it helps a lot to actually use it. There are words such as *yaama* 'how are you', *gaba* 'good', *ngarragaa* 'poor thing', *wamba* 'mad', *gamil* 'no', *waal* 'no' and many others that can be used by themselves. You can also learn by using GY and English together: 'That bloke is *wamba*', 'I am going home-*gu* [to home]'. Of course, the sooner you can say complete phrases and sentences in language the better.

▌Abbreviations and source references

A number of abbreviations are used throughout this learner's guide. They are listed below.

- AD Arthur Dodd was interviewed and recorded in the 1970s. Sometimes his initials are followed by a number: AD3319B means that the example is taken from Australian Institute of Aboriginal and Torres Strait Islander Studies archive tape number 3319, side B.
- CW Corinne Williams interviewed Arthur Dodd and Fred Reece in the 1970s and wrote a grammar of Yuwaalaraay.
- FR Fred Reece was also recorded in the 1970s. Sometimes his initials are followed by a number: FR2435B means that the example is taken from Australian Institute of Aboriginal and Torres Strait Islander Studies archive tape number 2435, side B.

JM   Janet Mathews. Janet interviewed Arthur Dodd and Fred Reece.

GR   Gamilaraay

YR   Yuwaalaraay

YY   Yuwaalayaay–Yuwaaliyaay

GY   Gamilaraay/Yuwaalaraay/Yuwaalayaay

Occasionally you will see a box with the following graphic:

These boxes indicate that special attention should be taken, or that you are dealing with sections of the learner's guide where we are still trying to understand the rules. For instance, at this stage the meaning of the suffix -*badhaay* is not well understood, and a better explanation of its use may be found in the future.

▌Simple sentences

Each of the following chapters in the learner's guide section of this book explain the various parts of GY grammar, but to begin with here are some expressions that are simple to learn. You can also build many other expressions using the patterns established here.

If you want to make a simple sentence in GY there are two useful things to note. The first is that GY, and most Aboriginal languages, have some sentences that do not use a verb. When they are translated into English sentences, some form of the present tense of the verb 'to be' (e.g. 'is', 'am', 'are') is used. The second thing to note is that, because of its use of word endings to communicate important information, the word order in GY is generally more flexible than in English.

 The term 'tense', when used about verbs, means the time that the verb is referring to. The most common tenses are present, past and future. Thus, something happening now ('I am well') is present tense, in the future ('I will be well') is future tense and in the past ('I was well') is past tense.

Below are some GY sentences which do not include a verb.

Gaba	*ngaya*.	or	*Ngaya*	*gaba*.
good	I		I	good

I am well.

Giirr	*bayn*	*nhama*	*yinarr*.
True	sore	the	woman

The woman is sore.

| *Birralii* | *nhama* | *ngay.* |
| child | the/that | my/mine |

That is my child./That kid is mine.

| *Gagil* | *ngay* | *dhinggaa.* |
| bad | my | meat |

My meat is bad.

| *Buluuy* | *nhama* | *dhimba.* |
| black | the | sheep |

The sheep is black.

| *Nhuwi* | *nhama* | *dhinggaa.* |
| rotten | the | meat |

The meat is rotten.

One common pattern in GY sentence building is 'adjective–*nhama*–noun'. You can make up many sentences using this pattern. For instance, 'The cup is dirty' would be *Bandu* (dirty) *nhama* (the) *banigan* (cup). Another common pattern is 'adjective–pronoun', as in 'I am happy' *Gayaa* (happy) *ngaya* (I). Looking at these two simple sentences, can you now say 'I am dirty' in GY? Easy!

You can also ask and answer simple questions. In the example below, *minya* means 'what', *nhama* means 'that' and *gilaa* means 'galah'.

| *Minya* | *nhama?* | | *Gilaa* | *nhama.* |
| what | that | | galah | that |

What is that?   That is a galah.

You can also make negative sentences (remember *waal* is Yuwaalaraay for 'no' and *gamil* is Gamilaraay for 'no').

| *Waal/Gamil* | *yinggil* | *ngaya.* |
| no | tired | I |

I am not tired.

An important part of GY is the word endings that it uses. These word endings, called suffixes, add meaning to words (and tell us lots of information). One of the simplest suffixes is *-gu*. By adding *-gu* to a word, a GY speaker can tell us that something belongs to someone, who something is for, and other information such as purpose and movement. (Suffixes are dealt with extensively in the following chapter.) Look at the examples below:

Getting started

i. *-gu* meaning 'of, belonging to'

| *Barran* | *mari-gu.* |
| boomerang | man-of |

The (Aboriginal) man's boomerang.

| *Yulay* | *bandaarr-gu.* |
| skin | grey kangaroo-of |

The grey kangaroo's skin.

You can now say things like:

| *Gabundi bubaa-gu.* | *Bayagaa ngambaa-gu.* |
| Dad's hat | Mum's clothes |

ii. *-gu* meaning 'for'

| *Dhinggaa* | *nhalay* | *dhaadhaa-gu.* |
| meat | this | grandfather-for |

This meat is for grandfather.

Can you say 'This money (*banggul*) is for Bill.'?

iii. *-gu* meaning 'purpose'

| *Ngaya* | *yana-y* | *dhinggaa-gu.* |
| I | go-future | meat-for (purpose) |

I will go for meat.

iv. *-gu* meaning 'movement to'

| *Banaga-y* | *ngaya* | *gundhi-gu.* |
| run-future | I | house-to |

I will run to the house.

Getting started

In many instances there is not one GY word which corresponds to an English word, or one English word which corresponds to a GY word.

In particular the English verb 'is' (or other forms of this verb such as 'am', 'are', 'was', 'were' and so on) is translated by a number of GY verbs. In GY 'is' can be translated by *gi-gi* (be, become) but often by *dhanduwi-y* (lie), *wila-y* (sit) and *warra-y* (strand), and by other words such as *yanaa-y/yana-y* (walk). This is shown in the following examples:

The story of the galah and the frilled lizard concludes with 'and so the lizard is covered in prickles and the galah has a red chest.' In Yuwaalaraay this was:

Bindiyaay-biyaay	*yanaa-y-la-nha*	*nhama wuulaa.*
prickle-with	walk-y-regular-present	the frilled lizard

The frilled lizard was walking about with prickles.

Yalagirrma	*nhama-nha*	*gilaa*	*yanaa-y-la-nha*	*guwaymbara*	*bii.*
therefore	there-?	galah	walk-y-regular-present	red	chest

So the galah is walking about, red chested.

Yanaa-y (walk, go) is used in place of English 'is' in the following:

Giirruu	*ngaama*	*bandu*	*birralii-djuul*	*yanaa-y-la-nha.*
really	there	dirty	child-little/one	walk-y-regular-present

[Which in standard English is something like:] That kid is (always) dirty.

Another verb used to translate 'is' is *dhanduwi-y* (lie, sleep), for example, 'The snake is under the stone.'

Wa-y-la-nha (be in) is found a number of times, including in 'There is a nest in the fork of a tree' and 'The spear is sticking into the man.'

Wi-y-la-nha (lie) is used to translate 'The water was on the ground.'

The verb *warra-y* (stand) is used to translate the following example from Fred Reece:

Minya-gu-nha	*warra-y-la-nha.*
what-purpose-there?	stand-*y*-regular-present

What are you waiting for? (literally: What are you standing there for?)

Ma-y-la-nha (be up) is used to translate 'There is a possum in the tree.'

Wila-y (sit) is commonly used to translate 'lives' (I live in Moree). Another example of *wila-y* is:

| | Ngiyani | | yuulngindi | | wila-y-la-nhi. |
| | we | | hungry | | sit-y-regular-past |

We were all starving.

This is not an exhaustive treatment of translation, but does point out some of the more common areas where care needs to be taken, it shows that 'good' translation into GY will require familiarity with the sources and with patterns common in Aboriginal languages.

Congratulations! You are now familiar with the structure of simple GY sentences, and can now say lots of things in GY by combining simple words with a suffix. Now go back and revise the sounds of GY (in the introduction to the dictionary) and re-read this section before going on to the next chapter.

Chapter Two
Suffixes (word endings)

What is a suffix?

Suffixes are added to the ends of words to provide extra information or meaning. We use them all the time in English. By adding different endings to the word 'cook' you can make 'cooks', 'cooker', 'cooking' and — with a bit of imagination — 'cookable'.

Suffixes are very common in GY, and are used with verbs in the same way as English. But GY also uses suffixes where English uses words such as 'to', 'at', 'from', 'with', 'without' and others. The suffixes considered in this chapter are mainly attached to nouns and adjectives, but some can be attached to verbs or other types of words. Note that some suffixes cannot be attached to pronouns.

With suffixes you need to get used to two things. The first thing you need to get used to is the affect or *meaning* of the suffix. Most suffixes can have more than one purpose or meaning. The other thing you will need to get used to is that the pronunciation and spelling of some suffixes can change — that is, the *form* of the suffix changes — depending on what word the suffix is attached to. This will be explained below.

 Suffixes can be grouped together in different categories which help describe what the suffix does. Both non-technical names and some technical names for these different categories are given in this section. Note that because suffixes can have lots of different purposes and meanings you need to be careful not to take the non-technical names or descriptions given to suffixes too literally. This is clearest in the case of the suffix *-DHi*, which is used for much more than its non-technical label, 'source' (which tells us that *-DHi* indicates the source of an object or action). Linguists therefore try to use the technical names which are more general, and aren't as closely linked to a single meaning.

Some common GY suffixes

The following suffixes are among the most commonly used in GY. To become proficient in GY it is important that you learn to recognise and understand them. Each of the suffixes in the table below is explained later. (In the table below, only the main translations and technical category names are given.)

Suffixes (word endings)

Suffix	Translation	Technical names (cases)
-Ga	at, in, on (something)	locative, dative
-DHi	from, at, (because) of	source, circumstantial
-Gu	doer.to, do with	ergative, instrumental
-gu	of (owner), to (somewhere), for	genitive, purposive, allative

Note that when a suffix is written with capital letters (as in -*Ga* above) it means that the form the suffix takes, that is, its spelling and pronunciation, changes depending on the sound at the end of the word it is attached to.

-*Ga*: 'at', 'in', or 'on (something)' (locative/dative)

The main use of this suffix is to do with being at or near a place. So it sometimes translates to the English words 'in' and 'on', as in '**in** the water' or '**on** the road'. It is also used with non-place words, such as '**in** the evening'. This suffix is sometimes translated as 'near' or 'beside', and is used for 'talking **to** someone'.

Note that this suffix is occasionally used for 'giving **to**', but this is usually translated by the 'of' suffix, described later. It is not used for 'going **to**', as this is done by the -*gu* (owner of) suffix.

This suffix takes different forms depending on the end of the word to which it is attached. The different usual forms are given below, and some exceptions are listed at the end of the chapter.

The basic form of this suffix is -*ga*, and this occurs after words ending in *a* and *u*. However, when words end in any other letters the suffix takes a different form. See how the suffix changes in the examples below:

i. Words ending in *a* and *u* (take basic form, -*ga*)

ngambaa-ga   in, on or around mum

garruu-ga   in, on or around uncle

ii. Words ending in *n* (take -*da* form)

maliyan-da   in, on or around the wedge-tailed eagle

iii. Words ending in *l* or *y* (take -*a* form)

birray-a   in, on or around the boy

dhanggal-a   in, on or around the mussel

Gamilaraay/Yuwaalaraay/Yuwaalayaay Learner's Guide

Suffixes (word endings)

iv. Words ending in *y* (the suffix form depends on the language)
   birray-a (YR, YY)   in, on or around the boy
   birray-dha (GR)   in, on or around the boy

v. Words ending in *i* (the suffix form depends on the language)
   wii-dja (YR, YY)   in, on or around the fire
   wii-dha (GR)   in, on or around the fire

vi. Words ending in *rr* (the suffix form depends on the language)
   bandaa-ya (YR, YY)   in, on or around the grey kangaroo
   bandaarr-a (GR)   in, on or around the grey kangaroo

Note the different forms the suffix takes in the examples below:

| *Guwaa-la* | *dhayn-**da**/mari-**dha***. |
| talk-command | man-at |

Talk to the man.

| *Buluuy-**a*** | *ngaya* | *banaga-y*. |
| black-at | I | run-future |

I will run in the dark.

| *Yinarr* | *nhama* | *yarraaman-**da***. |
| woman | the | horse-at |

The woman is on the horse.

Word ending	Suffix form	Example
a or *u*	-ga	*ngambaa-ga* 'on mum'
i	-dja (YR, YY)	*wii-dja* 'on the fire'
i	-dha (GR)	*wii-dha* 'on the fire'
n	-da	*yarraaman-da* 'on the horse'
l	-a	*mubal-a* 'on the 'stomach/belly''
y	-a (YR, YY)	*birray-a* 'on the boy'
y	-dha (GR)	*birray-dha* 'on the boy'
rr: delete *rr* and add *ya*	-ya (YR, YY)	*bandaa-ya* 'on the grey kangaroo'
rr	-a (GR)	*bandaarr-a* 'on the grey kangaroo'

-DHi: 'from', 'at', '(because) of' (source, circumstantial)

This suffix is used for a range of meanings, with the common idea that something is the source or origin. The range of meanings include movement from somewhere (away *from* the river), the source of some material (the letter is *from* grandma), and something that caused fear (afraid *of* the dog). There are a further set of meanings which will be examined later.

Like the 'in, at, on, to' *(-Ga)* suffix, the 'from' *(-DHi)* suffix changes in form depending on the last letter of the word it is attached to. However, the *-DHi* suffix always has a final *-i*. The standard forms of the *-DHi* suffix in YR/YY are given below.

Word ending	Suffix form	Example
a or u	-dhi	dhimba-dhi 'from the sheep'
n	-di	baan-di 'from the mistletoe'
i or y	-dji (YR, YY)	wii-dji 'from the fire', miyay-dji 'from the girl'
i or y	-dhi (GR)	wii-dhi 'from the fire' miyay-dhi 'from the girl'
l or rr	-i	bandaarr-i 'from the kangaroo', dhanggal-i 'from the mussel'

Several YR/YY example sentences are set out below.

| *Dhigayaa* | *bara-y* | *birralii-dji.* |
| bird | fly-future | child-from |

The bird will fly away from the child.

| *Nhama* | *dhinggaa* | *dhimba-dhi.* |
| the | meat | sheep-from |

That meat is from the sheep.

| *Manuma-li* | *walaay-dji* | *ngay.* |
| steal-future | camp-from | my |

(He) will steal from my camp.

| *Giyal* | *ngaya* | *buulii-dji.* |
| afraid | I | whirlwind-from |

I am afraid of the whirlwind.

Suffixes (word endings)

Other meanings of -DHi

This is a good example of an area where further work is needed. The suffix *-DHi* is used in many other instances where a common explanation has not been found. By looking at them closely, and also by looking at other languages, it may be possible to find a consistent definition, but that may take some time. This is not an area of the grammar to try to learn now, but is simply intended to provide some background information. For the time being here are a few examples of other uses of this suffix.

On one of the recordings there is a description of how to cook an emu, including putting hot stones in the emu's stomach to cook it:

| *mubal-**i*** | *wa-li* |
| stomach-**?from** | put in-future |

(You'll) put them in the stomach.

Other examples of this suffix include:

| *galiya-nhi* | *ngaya* | *muyaan-**di***. |
| climb-past | I | tree-?from |

I climbed a tree.

| *Buma-y* | *ngaya* | *dhaygal-**i***. |
| hit-past | I | head-?from |

I hit him on the head.

Donaldson (1980) gives a discussion of the *-DHi* source suffix in that language, and there are some parallels with GY.

-Gu: 'doer.to', 'with' (ergative, instrumental)

The first use of the *-Gu* suffix discussed is 'doer.to', or what is technically called the ergative suffix. The previous two suffixes (to, at, in, from) took ideas that are common in English, and showed how in English they are expressed by prepositions (words that go in front), but how in GY they are expressed by suffixes.

The *-Gu* suffix is different in that it has no equivalent in English. In English sentences the word order shows what is acting and what is being acted on. Thus, 'The echidna will bite the mouse' is different to 'The mouse will bite the echidna.' The thing **doing the action** (the **doer.to**) comes before the verb, and the one **being acted on** (the **done.to**) comes after the verb.

In GY, and most other Aboriginal languages, the same job is done differently. The thing or person **acting on something else** has a suffix attached. The basic form of the suffix in GY is *-gu*, as in *bigibila-gu*.

Consider the following GY sentences, all of which mean 'The echidna will eat the ants' (*bigibila* means 'echidna, porcupine', *buurrngan* 'meat ant' and *dha-li* 'will eat'):

Bigibila-gu buurrngan dha-li.   *Bigibila-gu dha-li buurrngan.*
Buurrngan bigibila-gu dha-li.   *Buurrngan dha-li bigibila-gu.*
Dha-li bigibila-gu buurrngan.   *Dha-li buurrngan bigibila-gu.*

The first sentence is the most common form, but all are quite correct. This variety allows many differences in emphasis, as putting a word first in a sentence gives it emphasis.

It can take a while to get used to the *-Gu* suffix, so the more you can read of GY the quicker you will get used to it.

Like the other suffixes looked at so far, the *-Gu* suffix can take different forms. The good news is that it is exactly like the suffix *-Ga*, except that the vowel is *u* instead of *a*.

Word ending	Suffix form	Example
a or *u*	-gu	*ngambaa-gu* 'mother'
i	-dju (YR, YY)	*baagii-dju* 'grandmother'
i	-dhu (GR)	*mari-dhu* 'person'
n	-du	*yarraaman-du* 'horse'
l	-u	*gulawuliil-u* 'crested pigeon'
y	-u (YR, YY)	*miyay-u* 'the girl'
y	-dhu (GR)	*miyay-dhu* 'the girl'
rr delete *rr* and add	-yu (YR, YY)	*bandaa-yu* '(grey) kangaroo'
rr	-u (GR)	*bandaarr-u* '(grey) kangaroo'

Below are some further YR/YY sentences.

| *Birray-u* | *dhinggaa* | *dha-li.* |
| boy-doer.to | meat | eat-future |

The boy will eat the meat.

| *Dhimba* | *dhaadhaa-gu* | *buma-li.* |
| sheep | grandfather-doer.to | hit-future |

Grandfather will hit the sheep.

| *Giirr* | *bandaarr* | *bubaa-gu* | *bayama-li.* |
| truly | kangaroo | father-doer.to | catch-future |

Father will catch a kangaroo.

| *Birralii* | *nhama* | *wagirrma-li* | *guni-dju.* |
| child | the | wash-future | mum-doer.to |

Mum will wash the child.

Gamilaraay/Yuwaalaraay/Yuwaalayaay Learner's Guide

Suffixes (word endings)

The use of the doer.to (ergative) suffix is a very important part of learning to use GY. The examples given above involve verbs where there is a doer.to and a done.to: the **echidna** will eat the **ants**.

However, the ergative suffix in GY is also used with many verbs where the done.to is generally not mentioned. Such verbs include the GY words for 'talk', 'sing', 'urinate', 'cough', 'vomit' and others. There is, in some way, a done.to. After all, you talk words, sing songs, pass urine and vomit vomit. Verbs which require the use of the ergative suffix on the noun are called transitive verbs and are clearly labelled as such in word lists and dictionaries.

Verbs where the doer does not have the doer.to (ergative) suffix are called intransitive. They include verbs such as 'walk', 'run', sleep' and 'fly'. For these verbs there is no done.to at all. In English you can use the same word transitively and intransitively: 'I will walk', and 'I will walk the dog'. You cannot use the same word to do these two jobs in GY. (There are in fact a few instances where you can, but they are rare.) In older word lists some verbs were incorrectly labelled as intransitive.

The second use of the *-Gu* suffix is as the instrumental suffix, which indicates what is used to do something, and is often translated into English as 'with'. The instrumental suffix has exactly the same form as the doer.to (ergative) suffix above, so you do not need to learn new forms, simply a new use for forms already learnt.

Here are two sentences that illustrate the instrumental use of *-Gu*:

| *Bigibila* | | *ngaya* | | *buma-y* | | ***yuundu-gu***. |
| porcupine | | I | | hit-past | | stone.axe-instrument |

I hit the echidna **with the stone axe**.

| *Bigibila* | | *ngaya* | | *buma-y* | | ***barran-du***. |
| porcupine | | I | | hit-past | | boomerang-instrument |

I hit the echidna **with the boomerang**.

-gu: '(owner) of', 'to (somewhere), for' (genitive, allative, purposive)

The last suffix to be looked at in this section has been mentioned earlier. Remember, it only has one form, *-gu*, but has a range of meanings.

i. belonging to

| *Barran* | | *mari-gu*. |
| boomerang | | man-of |

The (Aboriginal) man's boomerang.

| *Bubaa* | | *miyay-gu*. |
| father | | girl-of |

The girl's father.

ii. for

| Dhinggaa | nhalay | dhaadhaa-gu.
| meat | this | grandfather-for

This meat is for grandfather.

iii. purpose

| Ngaya | yana-y | dhinggaa-gu.
| I | go-future | meat-for (purpose)

I will go for meat.

| Ngaya | yanaa-y | gundhi-gu | dha-li-gu.
| I | go-future | house-to | eat-future-purpose

I will go to the house to eat.

The sentence above illustrates how this suffix can be attached to verbs as well as nouns.

iv. movement to

| Banaga-y | ngaya | gundhi-gu.
| run-future | I | house-to

I will run to the house.

Irregular suffix forms: a few notes

 **Note:** Skip the following section if this is the first time you have read through the learner's guide. The information on irregular suffix forms is quite complex and is based on incomplete research. It might be confusing, so go back, revise and become familiar with the common suffixes.

There are a number of variations on common suffix forms which have been identified in the recordings of GY speakers. What follows are some common variations.

i. The ergative suffix -*Gu* takes the form -*dhu* after the word *minya*, 'what?'
ii. The suffix -*Ga* sometimes takes the form -*dha* after words ending in -*aay*. Both *yaay* and *yayaay* mean 'sun' (YR/YY), and *yaa-dha* and *yayaay-dha* are used for 'in the sun'. Also *walaay* is 'camp' and both *walaa-dha* and *walaay-dha* are used for 'in/at the camp'.

iii. There are also some instances where a number of forms are given for the same meaning. Sometimes the informants seem to change their minds — on one occasion Fred Reece uses *buwadjarr-u* then *buwadjarr-gu* for 'giving to father'. This may simply be a case of him correcting himself, but it may also indicate that a number of forms can be used for the same meaning.

iv. The *-DHi* (from) suffix can take a variety of forms when words end in *rr*, with *yinarr-i* and *yina-yi* (or *yina-y*) found for 'from the woman'.

v. Fred Reece is recorded as using *gaarrimay* for 'camp', and *gaarrimawu* for 'to the camp' where, according to the rules above, it would be *gaarrimay-gu*.

vi. The Gamilaraay forms are based on very limited materials, and they may be revised in the future.

What has been given in the main part of this chapter contains most of what is known about the forms and meanings of these suffixes, but there are some exceptions, and some areas where more can be learnt. It is also true that as the use of a language declines the speakers often simplify the forms and uses of suffixes.

▌Suffixes and noun phrases

One type of noun phrase is a noun and any associated adjectives. For example, *burrul bigibila* 'big echidna' is a noun phrase. Often, when using the suffixes outlined above, the suffix is used on both words, so:

| Burrul-u | bigibila-gu | buurrngan | dha-li. |
| big-doer.to | echidna-doer.to | meat.ant | eat-future |

The big echidna will eat the ants.

But note, the suffixes are always used on both noun and adjective if the two are separated by other words. It is common to find sentences such as:

| Bigibila-gu | buurrngan | dha-li, | burrul-u. |
| echidna-doer.to | meat.ant | eat-future, | big-doer.to |

The echidna will eat the ants, the big one.

It is clear in this sentence that *burrul* refers to *bigibila* because they both have the same suffix, *-Gu*.

▌Some other suffixes

Some of the suffixes below have very clear meanings and uses. It is relatively easy for you to use these. There are others whose meaning and use are a lot less clear. They are included here for your information, and so that you can interpret texts, but it is not recommended that you use them until your language skills develop. In the table below are the suffixes which are dealt with in this section.

Suffix	Basic use
-gal, -galgaa	plural
-DHuul	little, just, one
-bidi	big
-Baraay, -Biyaay	having, with
-bil	having a lot of
-dhalibaa	without
-Baa	place of, time of
-gaali	two
-nginda	wanting
-giirr	like (similar to)
-bula	also
-wan.gaan, -ban.gaan	very
-gaalu	pretend

-gal, -galgaa (plural)

The plural does not need to be shown in GY, or in most Aboriginal languages. Often it is obvious if the discussion is about one or more things, either from the situation people are in (you can see what is being discussed), or from other words (in *burrulaa bandaarr* 'a lot of kangaroos' the *burrulaa* tells you that there is more than one kangaroo).

When the plural is shown it has two forms. The first, *-gal*, can be added to 'young things' such as *birralii* 'child', thus forming *birralii-gal* 'children'. Of around 200 occurrences of *-gal* in the recordings, all are on *birralii* except one on *birray* 'boy'. The second, *-galgaa,* can be added to 'adult things', such as *yinarr* 'woman' to make *yinarr-galgaa* 'women'. Thus, if you need to show the plural, use *-galgaa* except when referring to children.

A rarer (and so far unexplained) instance of *-galgaa* is to make *buunhu* 'grass' into *buunhu-galgaa* 'long grass'. A further use of *-gal* is shown by group names. One part of the Yuwaalaraay classification system divides living creatures into *dhurrun-gal* (i.e. fur-*gal* 'furry creatures'), *giinbal-i-gal* (scale-*gal* 'scaly creatures' such as fish and snakes) and *dhigayaa* 'birds'. However, these words are fairly rare; the main uses of these suffixes is clear.

These two suffixes, and all suffixes relating to size or number, are often followed by other suffixes. An example of *-galgaa* followed by another suffix is:

| *Dhayn-galgaa-gu* | *bamba* | *dha-y.* |
| man-plural-doer.to | to with.energy | eat-past |

The men ate a lot.

Suffixes (word endings)

-DHuul (little, just, one)

The *-DHuul* suffix has a number of meanings. It often means 'small' as in *birralii-djuul* 'baby' (small child), but at other times it seems to mean 'one' as in *dhayn-duul* 'one man (only)' or 'just' as in *yinarr-duul* 'young woman' (just arrived at womanhood).

The form this suffix takes also changes depending on the word it follows. After words ending in *-i* or *-y* it changes to *-djuul*, and after words ending in *-n*, *-l*, (and perhaps after *-rr*) to *-duul*.

An example of *-DHuul* followed by another suffix is given below.

| Giirr | buyabuya-dhuul-u | burrulaa | dhuu | garra-y. (FR2435B) |
| true | skinny-one-doer.to | a.lot | fire(wood) | cut-past |

The skinny bloke cut a lot of firewood.

-bidi (big)

This suffix only has one form, *-bidi*. It is most commonly attached to the adjective *burrul* 'big' in order to give *burrul-bidi* 'great big'. Another example of *-bidi* attached to an adjective is:

| Wamu-bidi | nhama | milan | dhayn. (FR2435B) |
| fat-big | the | one | Aboriginal man |

Big fat fellow.

It is also attached to nouns, for instance:

maayama-bidi	big stone
maalaa-bidi	big tree (in fact *maalaa* rarely occurs without *-bidi*)
nhan-bidi	big neck
gumbul-bidi	big bottom
guduu-bidi	big cod
yili-bidi	big lips
dhalay-bidi	big tongue (used to mean 'talkative')

-Baraay (GR), *-Biyaay* (YR/YY) (having, with)

The Gamilaraay form of this suffix is *-Baraay* and in Yuwaalaraay it is *-Biyaay*. In both languages the initial *b* is dropped after word final *rr* and *l*, and the suffixes are *-araay* or *-iyaay*. The basic meaning of the suffix is 'with', and various uses are illustrated below. It is common in names.

| Kamilaroi/Gamilaroi | *Gamil-araay* | 'no-having', or the name of the group and language |
| Yuwaalaraay/Yuularoi | *Yuwaal-araay* | 'no-having', or the name of the group and language |

| Collarenebri (a town) | *galariin-baraay* | 'gum blossoms-having', place of gum tree blossoms |
| Boggabri (a town) | *bagaay-baraay* | 'creeks-having', place of creeks |

The following examples further illustrate uses of these suffixes.

| *Nhama* | *yilawa-nhi* | *barran-biyaay.* |
| that | sit-past | boomerang-with |

He sat with a boomerang.

| *Buwadjarr-iyaay* | *ngali* | *yanaa-nhi.* |
| father-with | we.two | go-past |

We went with father.

| *Maayama-biyaay* | *nhama* | *dhaymaarr.* |
| stone-with | the | ground |

That ground is stony.

| *Giirruu* | *guyaarraala* | *dhaygal* | *yarray-biyaay.* |
| true-very | long | head/hair | beard-with |

He's got long hair and a beard.

-bil (having a lot of)

This suffix has only one form, *-bil*. One meaning is 'having a lot of' but at times it seems to be more like 'covered with'. An example of its use is:

| *Dhaymaarr-bil* | *ngay* | *ngaay.* |
| earth-with lots | my | mouth |

My mouth is full of dirt.

Arthur Dodd says that the place name Coonamble is *guna-m-bil*. The *-m* may be a sign that the word is Ngiyambaa or Wiradjuri.

-dhalibaa (without)

This is a common suffix. Occasionally, the start of the suffix changes after word final *-i* (see *wii-djalibaa* below), but as this is uncommon, it is simplest to always write it as *-dhalibaa*. An example of its use is:

| *Buunhu-dhalibaa* | *dhaymaarr* |
| grass-without | ground |

There's no grass on the ground

An apparently abbreviated form of the suffix occurs in the word *guni-djaa*, meaning both an orphan and a black-faced cuckoo-shrike (a grey bird with a black face, like an orphan mourning). This might possibly be the origin of the place name Gunnedah. The suffix also occurs in the name *wii-dhalibaa* 'fire-without', which in English is the place-name Weetalibah or Wytaliba. There is some evidence that *dhalibaa* can be used as a word as well as a suffix.

-Baa (place of, time of)

This suffix takes the form *-aa* after word final *rr* (i.e. *-rr-aa*). It is most commonly translated to 'time of' or 'place of', but its meaning is actually wider than that — a similar suffix in Wangaaybuwan is called a domain suffix. The word *walaay* means 'camp', in the sense of 'humpy', and *walaay-baa* seems to mean 'camping ground'. Other uses of the suffix are to form *yaay-baa* 'summer' from *yaay* 'sun', and *dhandarr-aa* 'winter' from *dhandarr* 'ice, frost'.

-gaali (two)

There is a very rare pronoun, *gaali*, meaning 'they (two people)', which should not be confused with this suffix. The suffix is also uncommon.

Arthur Dodd (3219A) says the following, without giving a translation. The meaning of *-gaali* is probably 'two'.

Ngaama	bulaarr,	bubaay-gaali	buma-la-nhi.
that	two,	little(ones)-two	hit-each.other-past

The two little ones were fighting, the pair of little ones was fighting.

-nginda (wanting)

This suffix occasionally occurs as *-ngin* and *-ngindi*, without any obvious change in meaning, and can be pronounced *nyinda* after words ending in *i* or *y*. It translates several English words such as 'want', 'need' and 'like'. The suffix is attached to both nouns and verbs.

Minya-nginda-nda?

what-wanting-you(one)

What do you want?

(Note: *-nda* is a shortened form of *nginda* 'you'.)

Dhinggaa-nginda	ngaya.
meat-wanting	I

I want meat.

Yanaa-y-nginda	ngaya.
go-future-wanting	I

I want to go.

The form *-ngin* occurs in *yuulngin* 'hungry' (*yuul* is not used by itself in the recordings, only as *yuul-ngin* and *yuul-dhalibaa*), while the word *yuulngindi* 'hungry' is relatively uncommon.

-giirr (like, similar to)

This suffix only has one form, *-giirr*. Its meaning is clear from the examples below. It is currently relatively common in Walgett and Lightning Ridge in expressions such as, 'She swims fish-*giirr*' (pronounced 'gear') meaning she swims like a fish, or *mari-giirr* 'like an Aboriginal person'. Those using it often do not realise its origin. The *-giirr* suffix is attached to nouns.

Giirruu	*nguu*	*banaga-nhi*	*dhinawan-giirr.*
true	he	run-past	emu-like

He ran like an emu.

Yuluwirri-giirr	*maayama.*
Rainbow-like	stone

Opal.

-wan.gaan (YR/YY), *-ban.gaan* (GR) (very)

This relatively uncommon suffix, *-wan-gaan* in YR/YY and *-ban.gaan* in GR, translates as 'very'. See the examples below.

Gunadha-wan.gaan	*nhama*	*dhaymaarr.*
boggy-very	the	ground

The ground (was) very boggy.

There is some evidence that *wan.gaan* and *ban.gaan* can be a word as well as a suffix. It is likely that *-wan* by itself is also a suffix, meaning something like 'prominent' (as in *dhina-wan* 'emu', prominent foot); however, it is rare. The suffix *-wan.gaan* can also follow other suffixes. Arthur Dodd (AD3219B) uses the phrase *wamu-bidi-wan.gaan*, which must mean something like 'great big fat'.

-gaalu (pretend)

This suffix is rarely found, but its use is illustrated below.

Giirr	*ngaama*	*birralii-gal*	*yulu-gi-la-nhi*	*ngaama*	*walaay-gaalu.*
true	there	child-plural	play-*gi*-regular-past	there	camp-pretend

The children were playing (in) a pretend (cubby) house.

A *yarraaman-gaalu* 'horse-pretend' is a toy horse.

Suffixes (word endings)

-bula (also)

This suffix has a similar form to the adjective *bulaarr* (two). It is generally used when there is a similarity between two events. There are indications that -*bula*, unlike the suffixes discussed so far, can follow pronouns.

| Yinarr | gi-yaa-nha | yuurrma-y-bula. (FR2435B) |
| woman | going-to | dance-future-also |

The women are going to dance too.

| Yina-yu-bula-nga | nhama | ngurruula-waa-nha. (FR2436A) |
| woman-doer.to-also-now | the | snore-progressive-present |

The women are even snoring now.

■ Knowledge suffixes

These suffixes all have something to do with knowledge. For instance, the regular translation of one suffix is 'I don't know' and another suffix means that something is uncertain and is translated as 'might', 'might be' or 'must have'. There is some clear information about these suffixes, but also room for further investigation.

-Waa (some)

This suffix has been found in the forms -*waa*, -*yaa*, -*aa* and -*gaa*. The common form is -*waa*, while -*yaa* occurs after word final *i*, -*aa* after word final *rr*, *l* and *y*, and -*gaa* is the form after *minya* 'what' and *yaama* (a greeting).

-*Waa* is attached to question words and question pronouns, and indicates that the identity of the person or thing is unknown, or of no particular interest. It is like the 'some' in English 'someone', 'somebody', 'somewhere', 'somehow' and 'sometime'. It is occasionally translated as 'I don't know'.

| Ngaandu-waa | ngalingu | bigibila | manuma-y. (FR2438A) |
| who(doer.to)-some | our(two) | porcupine | steal-past |

Somebody stole our porcupine.

| Minya-gu-waa | nhama | wanda | dhaay | yanaa-nhi. (FR2439A) |
| what-purpose-some | the | white.man | to.here | come-past |

That white man came here for something.

| Ngarraagula | minyaarru-waa | 'naa-ya. (AD2833B) |
| over-there | where.to-some | go-command |

Go somewhere else, over there.

>  *Ngaandi* is 'who' and *ngaandi-yaa* is 'someone'. *Gulaarr* is 'how', and *gulaarr-aa* means something like 'somehow'. There is also a form *galaarr-aa*, which may be a variant of *gulaarr-aa* and is used in sentences such as, 'I don't know how (they are going to get on for water)'. *Yaama* is a word which changes statements into questions, and *yaama-gaa* seems to be 'whether'.

-Yaa (chance, probable, maybe)

This word part occurs frequently as *-yaa*, and as *-aa* after word final *y*, *rr*, and probably in other circumstances. It is a clitic (see overleaf), generally attached to the first word of a phrase or sentence. It is translated in a number of ways, such as 'must' and 'probably'. There is much about it that remains unclear.

Corinne Williams asked Arthur Dodd to translate 'What did the boy eat the kangaroo for?' He did not translate, but replied:

| *Yuulngindi-yaa* | *gi-ngindaay.* (AD3998B)
| hungry-probable | get-relative

When he got hungry, I suppose.

Other examples of this clitic include:

| *Waal-yaa* | *ngay* | *guliirr* | *dharrawuluwi-y.* (FR1853A)
| not-probable | my | spouse | come back-will

I don't think my missus going to come home.

It is also used for 'either . . . or', by attaching *-yaa* to the alternatives.

| *Nhama-yaa* | *birralii-gal-u,* | *manuma-y,* | *maadhaay-u-yaa*
| that-chance | child-plural-doer.to | steal-past | dog-doer.to-chance
 | *dha-y.* (AD3220A)
 | eat-past

That kid must have taken it, or the dog ate it.

-Yaa is often attached to *-badhaay* 'might', as in:

| *Mangun.gaali-badhaay-aa-nda* | *ngarra-li*
| goanna-might-probable-you | see-future

You might see a goanna.

Suffixes (word endings)

-Waayaa (don't know)

This suffix takes the form -*yaayaa* after word final *i* and -*aayaa* after word final *y* and *rr*. After *minya* 'what' it takes the form -*gaayaa*. It is almost always translated as 'I don't know.' Like -*Waa*, it is only attached to question words.

| *Minyaarru-waayaa* | *ngaama* | *yarraaman* | *yanaa-nhi* (AD5129) |
| where.to-don't.know | that | horse | go-past |

They didn't know where it had gone.

| *Ngaandu-waayaa* (AD5054A)
| who (doer.to)-don't.know

I don't know who it is.

| *Minyaaya-waayaa* (AD5055)
| where.at-don't.know

Anywhere.

| *Minya-gaayaa*
| what-don't.know

I don't know what it is.

▌Clitics

It is important to distinguish between suffixes and clitics. Suffixes relate directly to the word they are attached to. So *yinarr-galgaa* gives you information about the women — there is more than one of them. However, clitics are generally attached to the first word of a sentence or phrase and may not be directly related to the word they are attached to. The example sentences for -*bala* show how it can be attached to different words.

-bala (contrast)

A simple definition covering the various uses of -*bala* has not yet been written. Perhaps the best so far is 'contrast'. The contrast can be with other things, with what was before, or with what you would expect. It is used for comparisons and can also mean a change in subject. At other times it means something like 'unexpectedly'.

| *Burrul-bala* | *ngaya,* | *nginda-bala* | *bubaay.* |
| big-contrast | I, | you(one)-contrast | small |

I am bigger than you.

Notice the position of -*bala* in the following example, where the word order changes, but not the meaning of the sentence.

Burrul-bala ngaya, bubaay-bala nginda.

I am bigger than you.

When a comparison of two things is not made -*bala* is often translated as a comparative adjective like 'better', as in:

| *Gaba-bala* | *ngay* | *barran*. |
| good-contrast | my | boomerang |

But my boomerang is better.

The following example, from Arthur Dodd (AD3994A), is from the story of the emu and the brolga. The brolga has killed most of her children, but the emu merely pretended to kill her own children. Brolga says:

Giirr	*ngaya*	*buma-y*	*birralii*	*ngay,*	*nginda-bala*	*nhama-nga*
true	I	kill-past	kid(s)	my,	you-contrast	those-then?
	burrulaa	*birralii-biyaay*.				
	many	kid(s)-having				

I killed my kids, but you have still got a lot.

Not all uses of -*bala* are as easily explained. If you have a computer and a copy of the transcripts of the Arthur Dodd and Fred Reece recordings, then a great way to see how this (and other) suffixes are used is to use the 'find' function to look at actual uses of -*bala*.

-*badhaay* (might, would you?)

This clitic is used hundreds of times by Arthur Dodd, but only a few times by Fred Reece and others. In many cases there is no apparent meaning for -*badhaay*. It might be similar to 'well' or 'might', which people say at the beginning of a sentence such as, 'Well, I might go to the shop.'

| *Buma-li-badhaay* | *ngaya* | *nginunha*. |
| hit-future-might | I | you (done.to) |

I might hit you.

| *Yanaa-ya-badhaay*. |
| go-command-might |

Would you go away.

This is gentler than the simple command *Yanaa-ya!* 'Go!'.

 The following section contains suffixes and clitics that you may meet, but which need further work to determine their exact meanings and contexts.

Suffixes (word endings)

-laa (then)

This is a poorly understood word part of GY which is probably a clitic. It occurs frequently in the recordings. In many cases *-laa* occurs with verbs in future tense ('will . . . ') and behaves like a shortened form of *yilaa* 'then'. It is often attached to the first word of the sentence or phrase, or the second if the first word is a particle such as *giirr* or *waal*. There may also be a *-la* suffix/clitic.

	Giirr		*ngaya-laa*		*maniila-y*. (AD2833A)
	true		I-then		hunt-future

I'll go out hunting.

	Yilaa		*ngaya-laa*		*dhurra-l-uwi-y*.
	then		I-then		come-l-back-future

I will come back then.

	Yanaa-waa-nha		*ngaya,*		*waal*		*ngaya-laa*		*dhurra-l-uwi-y*. (FR1853B)
	go-ing-present		I,		not		I-then		come-*l*-back-future

I am going and not coming back again.

However, in some cases the meaning is not obvious.

	Giirr		*ngaya-laa*		*dhaay*		*dhurra-laa-nha*		*gundugurranbun*. (AD5052)
	true		I-laa		to here		come-moving-present		

I come from Collarenebri.

-nga (now, then)

Like *-laa* this is common in the tapes and is generally attached to the first or second word of a phrase. It is likely to be a clitic, with a meaning to do with time, such as 'then'. An indication of this meaning is that it often occurs in narratives where one action happens, then another, then another. An example from the recordings is:

	Giirr-nga		*ngaya*		*yuuliyaay*		*gi-nyi*. (FR1850B)
	true-now		I		food-with		get-past

I'm full now.

-nha (that, there)

One meaning for *-nha* seems to be as a shortened form of *nhama* 'that'. The situation is complicated because the sounds *-nha* and *-nga* are difficult to distinguish on the recordings. There are some parallels between words like *nhama-nha* and the Aboriginal English expressions 'that-there' and 'this-here'. At this stage it seems justifiable to use *-nha* as an equivalent to *nhama*, but there may well be many other uses.

| *Giirr* | *ngaya* | *nhama-nha* | *wii* | *buubi-lda-nha.* (AD3996A)
| true | I | that-there/now | fire | blow-regular-present

I am putting out the fire.

In one recording Arthur Dodd talks about a horse that won't run, and says:

| *Buma-la-badhaay* | *nhama,* | *barraay-nha/nga* | *banaga-y.* (AD3996A)
| hit-command-might | that | fast-that/then | run-will

You hit him then he'll go.

-barra (people from)

This is a common suffix in a number of languages. It is attached to the name of a characteristic feature of a place, and forms a word which generally means 'the people of that place'. The suffix occurs a small number of times in GY sources. The people on the Narran River near Goodooga are the *nhungga-barra* 'the kurrajong tree people', presumably because the kurrajong tree was a distinctive feature of that area.

Other possible suffixes

It is possible that further suffixes will be defined as analysis of recordings and written records continues.

One example is the ending sometimes recorded as *-luu/-buu/-wuu/-uu*. The records contain a series of words with suffixes, all of which include *-uu* (or perhaps occasionally *-u*), with some common meaning to do with 'all' or 'totally'. A Wangaaybuwan suffix, *-buu* 'all possible', seems related to this GY suffix. This suffix may also be related to the inclusive/exclusive pronoun distinction discussed in the next chapter. So a clear form and meaning are still to be arrived at.

Below are some of the examples from the records which indicate the existence of the *-luu/-buu/-wuu/-uu* suffix.

| *Giirr* | *ganunga-wu* | *bagay-gu* | *yanaa-nhi.* (AD5130)
| true | they-all | river-to | go-past

They, all of them, went to the river.

| *Ngali-luu* | *gi-yaa-nha* | *buma-li,* | *nginaaynya.* (AD3997B)
| we(two)-all | going to | kill-future | you-many

The two of us will kill all of you.

| *Bulaarr-uu-ndaali* | *wamba.* (FR2438A)
| two-all-you(two) | mad

You're both mad.

Suffixes (word endings)

Other pairs of words which point to the existence of the suffix include:

ngiyani	we
ngiyani-luu	all of us
giirr	truly
giirruu	absolutely
dhirra	flash
dhirra-buu	real flash

There are several other possible suffixes that have been recorded. The word *guyaarr* means long, but the form *guyaarr-aala* has been recorded, which seems to mean 'very long'. The word *gunadha* 'boggy ground' suggests that *-dha* might also be a suffix, attached to *guna* 'faeces'. The suffix *-wan* 'prominent' occurs in a number of words such as *dhina-wan* 'emu' (in which *dhina* is 'foot', and so the emu's name may come from its 'big foot'). Similarly, in the bird name *bii-wan-bii-wan* 'black-faced woodswallow', *bii* means 'chest' and the name may come from the bird's habit of fluffing out its feathers. It is an example of a rare suffix and one that was generally found in names and not actively used.

The *-u/-uu* time suffix is another poorly understood GY suffix. Even the length of the vowel is fairly questionable. Its existence is based on examples such as the ones that follow, but again it needs further work.

The word *waal* means 'no' or 'not' and is obviously related to *waaluu/waalu* 'not yet', which has a time meaning. Its use is shown in the excerpt from the recordings below.

	Waaluu		*ngaama*		*ngaya*		*ngarra-y,*		*minyaaya-waayaa*		*ngaama,*
	not-yet		that		I		see-past		where at-don't know		that
	dhayn-duul				*gi-nyi.* (AD3219B)						
	man-one				get-past						

I haven't seen him yet, I don't know where he got to.

| | *Guyaarraala-gu* | | *ngaama* | | *dhaygal-u,* | | *waalu* | | *guduu* | | *dha-lda-nha.* (AD3219B) |
| | long-doer.to | | that | | man-doer.to | | not-yet | | cod | | eat-ing-present |

The long-haired man hasn't eaten his fish yet. (JM)

| | *Barraay* | | *dhuwima-la,* | | *waaluu-nha* | | *garungga-waa-ndaay.* (AD3998B) |
| | fast | | pull out-command, | | not.yet-that | | drown-ing-relative |

Pull him out of the water before he drowns.

There are a number of words which are translated 'blossom, fruit or manna of'. These words often incorporate the name of the tree or plant, and there is some similarity in their endings. This indicates that the words include a possible suffix, *-(b)iyan* — 'blossom of, fruit of', but the form is uncertain. Some examples are:

fruit/blossom	English	what the fruit/blossom is on
birraawiin	whitewood blossom	*birraa* — whitewood tree
dharraabiin	manna on bark	*dharraa* — flaking bark
yarraanbiin	gum blossom	*yarraan* — river red gum
bambulngiyan	bumble tree blossom	*bambul* — bumble tree
bunbarriyan	rosewood fruit	*bunbarr* — rosewood
gurrulayngiyan	river wattle blossom	*gurrulay* — river wattle

Finally, the following sentence (from Arthur Dodds; AD8184) is an example of multiple suffixes and clitics on a noun. The sentence is from the story of a time before people had fire, and so had to eat their meat raw.

Ngiyani-luu-badhaay-bala | *dhurrin,* | *dhurrin* | *gaa-g-uwi-la-nha,*
we-all-might-contrast | raw | raw | bring-*g*-back-continuous-present

| *wii-dhalibaa.*
| fire-without

We all bring home raw goanna, kangaroo, crayfish, and emu (but pelican, who has five, cooks her meat).

Congratulations! This chapter has contained lots of information, much of it new for the first-time language learner. Don't expect to understand or remember everything straight away, this will only come with time and practice. But remember that you now have an understanding of the sounds of GY, simple sentence structure and the use of suffixes. This is a good time to review what you've learnt so far before beginning the chapters on pronouns and verbs.

Chapter Three
Pronouns

Pronouns in English are words such as 'I', 'you', 'we', 'our', 'my', 'us', 'them', 'her', 'he' and 'their'. They don't actually name the thing they stand for, as a noun does, but are used to replace those nouns. Pronouns are grouped into three broad groups: first person, second person and third person. First person is the term used to describe the person or people doing the talking (I, we, us). Second person is the person or people being talked to (you, your). Third person is the person or people (or sometimes thing) being talked about (he, her, them, it).

One of the most noticeable differences between GY and English is the use in GY of the dual pronoun. Thus, between first person singular ('I') and first person plural ('we') is first person dual ('we: just two people'). Between second person singular and second person plural is second person dual ('you: two people'). And between third person singular and plural is third person dual ('they: two people').

 As with other chapters there is a range of material here, beginning with simpler ideas, then some more complex ones and some areas where the analysis of GY is incomplete. It might be best just to look at the easier material the first time through and skim the rest of the chapter.

Look at the table below, showing the basic English pronouns.

English pronouns

	subject doer/doer.to	object done.to	'of' genitive	'to, at, on' dative
1st person singular	I	me	my, mine	at me, to me
1st person plural	we	us	our, ours	at us, to us
2nd person singular	you	you	your, yours	at you, to you
2nd person plural	you	you	your, yours	at you, to you
3rd person singular	he, she, it	him, her, it	his, hers, its	at him, her, it
3rd person plural	they	them	their, theirs	at them, to them

Now look at the GY pronoun table.

GY pronoun table

	Pronoun	doer doer.to	done.to	'of' genitive	'to, at, on' dative	'from' source	
1st person	Singular	*ngaya* I	*nganha* me	*ngay* my/mine	*nganunda* to, at, on me	*nganundi* from me	**speaker**
	Dual (two people)	*ngali* we (two)	*ngalinya* us (two)	*ngalingu* our, ours	*ngalingunda* to, at, on us	*ngalingundi* from us	
	Plural (more than two)	*ngiyani* we	*ngiyaninya* us	*ngiyaningu* our, ours	*ngiyaningunda* to, at, on us	*ngiyaningundi* from us	
2nd person	Singular	*nginda* you	*nginunha* you	*nginu* your, yours	*nginunda* to, at, on you	*nginundi* from you	**spoken to**
	Dual (two people)	*ngindaali* you (two)	*nginaalinya* you (two)	*nginaalingu* your, yours	*nginaalingunda* to, at, on you	*nginaalingundi* from you	
	Plural (more than two)	*ngindaay* you	*nginaaynya* you	*nginaayngu* your, yours	*nginaayngunda* to, at, on you	*ngiyaningundi* from you	
3rd person	Singular (YR/YY) Singular (GR)	*nguu* *nguru* he, she	*nguuna (?)* *ngurunga (?)* her, him	*nguungu* *ngurungu* his, her, hers	*nguungunda* *ngurungunda* to, at, her/him	*nguungundi* *ngurungundi* from him, her	**spoken about**

	Pronoun	doer.to	doer, done.to	'of' genitive	'to, at, on' dative	'from' source	
3rd person	Dual (two people)	*gaali* they	*gaalinga (?)* they, them	*gaalingu* their	*gaalingunda* to, at them	*gaalingundi* from them	**spoken about**
	Plural (more than two)	*ganugu* they	*ganunga* they, them	*ganungu* their	*ganungunda* to, at them	*ganungundi* from them	

The first thing you will notice is that there appear to be a lot more pronouns in GY than in English. Instead of six rows there are nine, due to the addition of the three dual pronoun rows. You will also notice that the table is broken into two parts; this is fully explained overleaf.

The part you need to master is knowing which pronoun to use and when to use it. Look carefully at the GY pronoun table again, but don't be put off by the large number of rows and columns. Each row refers to a similar person, people or things. If you look at the right-hand-side of the table you will see that the nine rows have also been put into three broad groups (speaker, spoken to, spoken about). On the left-hand side of the table those labels are 'first person', 'second person' and 'third person'.

Pronouns

To decide which row to use, **firstly ask** yourself whether the pronoun is referring to:

First person (speaker); or

Second person (spoken to); or

Third person (spoken about).

Then ask whether those referred to are:

One person/thing (singular); or

Two people/things (dual); or

Three or more people/things (plural).

In order to explain which pronoun to use, we will go across row 1 (first person singular) and look at each column. (The rules for the columns apply whether you are using first, second or third person, singular, dual or plural.)

All of row 1 is about one person doing the talking: I, me, my etc. The word *ngaya* in row 1 column 1 means 'I' and is used in sentences such as:

| *Yinggil* | *ngaya.*
| tired | I

I am tired.

| *Ngaya* | *banaga-y.*
| I | run-future

I will run.

| *Dhinggaa* | *ngaya* | *dha-li.*
| meat | I | eat-future

I will eat the meat.

Note *ngaya* is used with both the transitive verb 'eat' and the intransitive verb 'run'.

In row 1, column 2 the word *nganha*, meaning 'me', is used when I am the 'done.to'. Thus:

| *Dhindu-gu* | *nganha* | *yii-li.*
| mouse-doer.to | me | bite-future

The mouse will bite me.

In row 1, column 3 the word *ngay*, meaning 'my' or 'mine', is used as follows:

Bigibila	*ngay*.
porcupine	my

My echidna.

Ngay	*nhama*.
my	that

That is mine.

As well as indicating ownership, *ngay* is also used for 'giving to' me:

Ngambaa-gu	*ngay*	*dhinggaa*	*wuu-rri*.
mother-doer.to	my	meat	give-future

Mother will give **me** the meat (i.e. give it **to me**).

The dative pronoun *nganunda*, in row 1, column 4, means 'to me', 'at me' or 'on me'. This pronoun has the same use as nouns to which the *-Ga* suffix ('at', in', 'on') has been added.

Ngambaa-gu	*nganunda*	*guwaa-li*.
mother-doer.to	me-at	talk-future

Mother will talk **to me**.

Burrulaa	*mungin*	*nganunda*.
many	mosquito	me-on

Lots of mosquitoes **on me**.

The pronoun *nganundi* in row 1, column 5, means 'from me' and has the same use as nouns to which the *-DHi* (source) suffix has been added.

Yarraaman	*banaga-y*	*nganundi*.
horse	run-future	me-from

The horse will run away **from me**.

Gugurrgaagaa-gu	*gindama-nhi*	*nganundi*.
kookaburra	laugh-past	me-from

The kookaburra laughed **at me**.

Bigibila	*nhama*	*giyal*	*nganundi*.
echidna	that	afraid	me-from

The echidna is frightened **of me**.

Now go down to row 2. If 'we' refers to two people, then use the dual pronoun *ngali* 'we (two people)'. If 'we' refers to more than two people, the correct pronoun for 'we' is found in row 3: *ngiyani*.

Now move down to the last two rows — third person dual and plural. In the first seven rows you will notice that column 1 is 'doer' and 'doer.to', and that column 2 is 'done.to'; but rows 8 and 9 follow an ergative pattern, that is, one in which the 'doer' and 'done.to' are the same, but the 'doer.to' is different.

Ngindaali banaga-y.   You (two) will run.

The verb is intransitive, so the doer pronoun is used.

Ngindaali dhinggaa dha-li.   You (two) will eat the meat.

The verb is transitive, so the doer.to pronoun is used.

Buyuma-gu nginaalinya dhama-li.   The dog will touch you. (two)

'you' is done to, so the done.to pronoun is used.

For rows eight and nine this pattern changes. The first column is only the doer.to.

Ganugu dhinggaa dha-li.   They will eat the meat.

and the second column is the doer and done.to.

Ganunga banaga-y.   They will run.
Buyuma-gu ganunga dhama-li.   The dog will touch them.

This last arrangement is the same as that applying to ordinary nouns in GY. The doer.to has the special suffix ending in *u*.

Yina-yu dhinggaa dha-li.   The woman will eat the meat.

but the doer, and done.to have no suffix, and are the same.

Yinarr banaga-y.   The woman will run.
Ngaya yinarr ngarra-li.   I will see the woman.

So remember! Who is the **doer**, who is the **doer.to** and who is the **done.to**? They have been bolded in the examples below:

i. **doer**: **I** walk, **the bird** flies, **someone** fell (the verb is intransitive)

ii. **doer.to**: **I** ate the bread, **the bird** saw the worm, **someone** talked. There is usually (but not always a **done.to**). The verb here is transitive.

iii. **done.to**: The ant bit **me**, Mary saw **the bird**, the car hit **someone**.

You need to be careful to know which of these three — 'doer', 'doer.to', or 'done.to' — is being talked about in order to get the right pronoun.

Here is one further example of how to use the pronoun chart. If you want to say 'The sheep will run away from us (two)' then you need the first person (us), dual (two people) and from/source column. The sentence is:

Dhimba	nhama	ngalingundi	banaga-y.
Sheep	that	from us two	run-will

The sheep will run away from us (two).

Try to look at lots of examples of this in the various resources available.

 Give yourself lots of time to learn the pronouns, and just take a few at a time. If you can see the patterns there is a lot less to learn.

Note that the historical materials have many examples of most of the pronoun forms in the tables. However, some of the forms in the seventh and eight rows (third person singular and dual) are very rare, or have not in fact been found and are conjectured forms. Also the pronoun *nguunga/ngurunga* is rarely if ever used, and the word *nhama*, 'that', is usually used instead in sentences like:

Giirr	maadhaay-u	nhama	yii-li.
true	dog-doer.to	that(one)	bite-future

The dog will bite him.

Bound pronouns

Bound pronouns are shortened forms of pronouns that are attached to other words. They occur in many Aboriginal languages. There are three common bound pronouns in GY, though some Aboriginal languages have many more. The common bound GY forms are shown in the table below, with the full pronouns.

English pronoun	Full GY form	Bound GY form
you (one)	*nginda*	*-nda*
you (two)	*ngindaali*	*-ndaali*
you (three or more)	*ngindaay*	*-ndaay*

These bound pronouns can only be used when 'you' is the 'doer' or 'doer.to', not when it is the 'done.to'. They mostly occur attached to the first word of a phrase or sentence, or attached to question words and negatives. For example:

| *Yaama-nda* | *banaga-y?* |
| question-you | run-future |

Will you (one) run?

The following example from a recording of Arthur Dodd (3219A) shows both the full and bound pronouns being used:

| *Ngindaali,* | *garriya-ndaali* | *buma-la-ya,* | *yaluu,* |
| you(two) | don't-you(two) | hit-each.other-command, | again, |

| *minya-ngin-ndaali* | *buma-la-y-la-nha?* |
| what-wanting-you(two) | hit-each.other-y-regular |

Don't fight no more, what you two fighting over?

Somewhat similar is the suffix *-nha*, which seems to be an abbreviated version of *nhama*, 'that'.

Question pronouns

The following table contains question pronouns which refer to people. Remember that there is a separate word, *minya* 'what?', for referring to things.

doer.to	doer, done.to	genitive	dative	source
ngaandu who	*ngaandi* YR, GR *ngaana* YY whom, who	*ngaanngu* whose	*ngaanngunda* on, at, to who	*ngaanngundi* from who

There are five question pronouns (with a sixth, *ngaana*, as an alternative for *ngaandi*). The columns above follow the same pattern as for the dual and plural third person pronouns. The first column is the doer.to only. The second is both doer and done.to.

Ngaandu dhinggaa dha-y?	Who ate the meat?
Ngaandi yulu-gi?	Who will dance?
Ngaandi nginda ngarra-y?	Who did you see?
Ngaanngu nhama birralii?	Whose child is that?
Ngaanngunda nguu widja wuu-rri?	Who will she give the bread to?
Ngaanngundi nginda banaga-nhi?	Who did you run away from?

 Now go back and revise before proceeding with the rest of this chapter!

Inclusive–exclusive and related topics

Please note that this area of GY grammar needs further work. It requires more investigation of the original sources, and comparison with related languages.

If one says in English 'We will go', it is not made clear whether the person or people being spoken to are included, whether they are part of the 'we' who will go. However, in some Aboriginal languages a distinction can be made between these different uses of 'we'. Inclusive means that 'we' **includes** the person spoken to, whereas exclusive means that 'we' **excludes** the person spoken to.

It is not clear if GY had a widespread and common distinction between inclusive and exclusive. What is clear is that there are expressions such as the following in the historical sources. The first example is inclusive, as it does include the one spoken to. The second example is exclusive as it does not include the one spoken to:

| *Ngali-nginda* | *yanaa-y.* |
| we (two)-you (one) | go-will |

You and I will go.

| *Ngali-dhayn* | *yanaa-y.*
| we (two)-the man | go-will

The man and I will go.

The previously discussed suffix *-luu/-buu/-wuu* 'all, totally' (see page 281) also occurs with pronouns, and may be related to inclusive and exclusive use.

▎Zero pronouns

A 'zero' pronoun is a way of saying that a statement can leave out pronouns where one would normally expect to find them. The sentence:

| *Giirr* | *buma-y.*
| Indeed | hit-past

can be translated as 'He did hit it', even though there are no words in GY for 'he' and 'it'. The same statement could be said:

| *Giirr* | *nhama* | *nguu* | *buma-y.*
| Indeed | that | he/she | hit-past

It is not clear when the first form of the sentence can be used.

▎Determiners/demonstratives and place words

The material in this section is quite complicated and not well understood; you may want to read it at a later stage.

This section treats a group of GY words which are translated by English words such as 'the', 'that', 'this', 'here', 'there', 'this way', 'over there' and 'downwards'. While this group of words requires some further work, many things are clear.

The words can translate at least three groups of English words. Determiners are words such as 'the' and 'that' which indicate that the identity of what you are talking about is known. ('He is at the pub' means that you know which pub it is.) Demonstratives are words such as 'this' and that'. They are used when pointing out something. Place and direction words are words and phrases such as 'here', 'there', 'over there', 'this way', 'up there' and many more.

These GY words can also be used as linking words, and in that case are often not translated into English. These words are treated as one group because a number of the words fit into more than one of the above categories, and there are many similarities between the words.

These words form an extensive, but incompletely understood, area of GY. Mathews, in his 1902 grammar of Yuwaalayaay, says, 'The demonstratives are many and diverse and can be declined for number and case.' But then, in his material on Gamilaraay, says:

> [I]n all the expressions illustrating the several grammatical cases in Kamilaroi . . . the demonstrative pronouns are purposely omitted, for the two-fold object of saving space and avoiding confusion by introducing any more words than the sentence really required. For example, where I have given '*Murridu mindere kauai*' (man at padamelon threw), would be expressed by the black fellow: 'This man-in-front at yonder-on-left padamelon threw,' or as the subject might require. (1903, p 268)

Thus, while Matthews pointed out the complexity of the system of demonstratives and related words, he did not point out details about these words. As Williams (1980) says: 'Yuwaalaraay appears to have had a very complex set of demonstratives (place and direction words, and words like 'this, that'). It has not been possible to define the underlying principles in any satisfactory way.' The material below is a very preliminary stage in such an analysis.

Determiners/demonstratives

In this section we deal with a number of words that are primarily used as determiners and demonstratives.

i. nhama

The word *nhama* is one of the most common GY words, being found over 600 times on the recordings. The word *ngaama* is slightly less common. So far no difference in meaning has been found between *nhama* and *ngaama*. They are currently treated as identical in meaning. The form *ngama* also occurs and seems to also have the same meaning.

They are generally translated as 'that' or 'the' and occasionally as 'there'. They often occur with a noun, but are also used as an independent word. As independent words they can at times be translated as third person pronouns such as 'it', 'her' and 'them.' Examples of their use are given below. Before words beginning in *b* (and especially before the clitic *-bala*) *nhama/ngaama* is often said *nham/ngaam* (e.g. *nham-bala*).

| *Gaba* | *nhama* | *yinarr*. |
| good | that | woman |

That woman is good.

| *Dhaay* | *gaa-nga* | *nhama* | *dhuu*. (FR1988A) |
| to.here | bring-command | that | fire(wood) |

Bring me that bit of (fire)wood.

| *Giirr* | *ngaama* | *nguu* | *wii-n-barraan-da* | *dhanduwi-y-la-nha*. |
| true | that | he | fire-*n*-around-place | sleep-*y*-regular-present |

He is lying down by the fire.

Nhama/ngaama also occurs frequently with suffixes such as *-nga*, *-nha* and *-laa* and in a phrase with *dhaay*.

| Yina-yu | nhama-nga | buurra-laa-nha | dhinawan. (FR2435B)
| woman-doer.to | there-now | pluck-moving-present | emu

The women are plucking the emu now.

| Giirr | nhama-nha, | nhaadhiyaan, | dhuurrma-laa-nha, | burrul | nhaadhiyaan.
| true | that-there? | log | roll-moving-present | big | log

He's got that big log there, rolling it. (AD2833B)

| Balu-nhi | ngaama-nga, | giibaabu.
| die-past | that-then? | early.morning

He died yesterday in the morning.

The phrase *nhama-dhaay!* is common in current use. It means 'watch out!', but literally means 'that/there-to.here'.

There are also a number of forms similar to *nhama/ngaama* which have the same translation. The most common of these are *nguuma*, *nguumu(u)* and *ngaamu*. It may be that these other forms are somehow related to functions such as 'doer', 'doer.to' etc., but again, they await further investigation.

ii. ngaarrma

At present no difference has been found between the meaning of *ngaarrma* and *nhama/ngaama*. This word is not as common as *nhama/ngaama*. However, its similarity to *ngaarri* and *ngaarrima* below are hints that it may have a distinctive use or meaning. The quality of the recordings and of the listener's ears means that the distinction between *ngaama* and *ngaarrma* is not always clear.

iii. nhalay

The word *nhalay* is used as 'this' and 'here'. It is less common than *nhama/ngaama*, occurring about 80 times on the recordings. There is also a word, *nhali*, which is probably a variant pronunciation of *nhalay*. The meaning of *nhalay* seems to be that the object or place is nearby and usually visible. At times it is used in contrast with *nhama* 'that' and other words. Examples of its use include:

| Dhinggaa | nhalay.
| meat | here

Here's a bit of meat.

| ... *nhalay-bala* | *ngay* | *bilaarr.* (AD3217B)
| ... this-contrast | my | spear

... but this spear is mine.

| *Ngaarrima* | *bandaarr,* | *burrul-bidi,* | *nhalay-bala* | *bubaay-djuul.* (AD3217B)
| over.there | kangaroo | big-big | this-contrast | little-one

That's a big kangaroo over there, this is a little fellow.

| *nhama maa* | that hand
| *nhalay maa* | this hand

Place/direction words

Australian languages often include different sets of information in place words. This information can include the following:

- How far away the thing is. The distance can refer to the distance from the speaker or the distance from the listener. Sometimes there are separate words for near, middle distance and far.
- Whether the thing is visible or not.
- Whether the listener knows which place is being referred to.
- Whether the word is about a direction or a place. (In English 'over there' can refer to a direction or to a place.)
- Whether it is 'at', 'to' or 'from' a place.

Many of the GY words discussed here are compounds, in other words they are made up of a number of elements called morphemes. There are quite a number of examples of similar words where no difference in meaning has been found (for example, *nhama/ngaama* above). It may be that there are two or more words with the same meaning, but it may also be that distinguishing features have yet to be found.

Place/direction words are often compounds.

i. dhaay

The basic meaning of the word *dhaay* is 'to me', 'to the person speaking'. A typical use is:

| *Dhaay* | *wuu-na.*
| to.here | give-command

Give it here. (Give it to me.)

Pronouns

It also occurs in phrases with other place words, including question words such as:

| Minyaaya | dhaay?
| where.at | to.here

Where from?

ii. ngiilay, ngiima

The word *ngiilay* appears about ten times on recordings and is consistently translated to 'from here', as in:

| Yanaa-ya | ngiilay.
| go-command | from.here

Go away from here.

The form *ngiima* is probably related to *ngiilay*. Its meaning is not clear, but occurs a few times in expressions such as:

| Yanaa-ya | ngiima | wii-n-barraan-di.
| go-command | ?? | fire-*n*-around-from

Get away from that fire.

However, at other times it is possible that *ngiima* and *ngiyama* (below) are confused in transcriptions.

iii. ngaarri

The word *ngaarri*, and compounds including it, are fairly common on the archival recordings. Below is a list of the main occurrences.

ngaarri	generally translated as 'over there'
ngaarri-ma	'over there', sometimes referring to something visible
ngaarri-ma-li	'over there' (this meaning is not further specified)
ngaarri-gulay/gula	'over there', may be referring to a direction, and not generally visible; this also occurs in the phrase *ngaarrigulay ngarraagulay* 'this way and that' or 'all over'
ngaarri-gili	'other side', e.g. of a river; this is often followed by the suffixes *-dja* 'at', *-gu* 'to' or *-dhi* 'from'
ngaarringaarri	'right over there'

Some of the suffixes above are common, and found in many other place and direction words. There are indications of their meanings, but not enough is understood to confidently define all of them. However, *-gili* 'side of' is an exception, with a clear meaning.

iv. ngarraa

The morpheme *ngarraa* occurs around twelve times, mostly as *ngarraagulay/ ngarraagula*. These seem to be variant forms with no difference in meaning. The translations available do not make the meaning specific, but it often involves a contrast such as 'other side' ('. . . the spear came out **the other side**', '. . . wait for me **somewhere else**', '. . . he jumped this way and **that**').

At times it is translated as 'further away', and there is an unexplained form, *ngarraa-gu*.

v. nguwa

This morpheme occurs in the recordings around ten times each in two main compound forms. These are *nguwa-lay* 'here, hereabouts' and *nguwa-ma*. *Nguwa-lay* seems to indicate a larger area than *nhalay* 'here'. It is used in sentences such as 'There are no kangaroos here (*nguwalay*)' and 'Don't fish here.'

There is no indication of the precise use of *nguwa-ma* 'there'. It seems similar in use to *ngiyama* below.

vi. marra

This word occurs as *marra* 'there' and *marra-ma* and *marra-gula*, both of which mean 'over there'. It seems likely that this word is used to refer to things that are visible (e.g. 'That's his house over there').

vii. ngarri

The word element or morpheme *ngarri-* occurs in words to do with 'up' or 'on top'. It has, at times, been heard as *ngaarri-*. It occurs in:

ngarri-baa	'on top'
ngarri-baa-li	'upwards'

viii. ngadaa

The word *ngadaa* is found as a word and in compounds. It occurs as:

ngadaa	the word is used to mean 'going down' when diving, clouds being 'low'; it is also translated as 'underneath'; it is also probably used as 'west' (i.e. where the sun goes down)
ngadaa dhaay	'from the west'
ngadaa-li	'downwards'
ngadaa-ma-li	'downstream'
ngadaa-gili	'downstream' (possibly 'the other side of the bend in the river')

Place word suffixes

There are a number of suffixes which occur regularly in the above words. The meaning of one, *-gili* 'side', is clear, but the others are less clear.

-baa	This possibly means 'up' (as in *ngarri-baa* 'on top').
-li	This may be a directional suffix, as in *ngarri-baa-li* 'upwards' and *ngadaa-li* 'downwards'.
-ma	This may mean 'known' or 'visible'. It is possible that *nhama* and *ngaama* are in fact compounds, but at present there is no analysis of their components.
-gulay/-gula	These may or may not be variants, and seem related to direction, but no clear description of their use has been found.

There are various other combinations of these suffixes, such as *-ma-lay*, *-ma-li*, *-ba-li* and *-baa-lay*. If the variation in place/demonstrative words is as extensive as Mathews stated, then there is still a lot to learn and define about this area of GY grammar.

Linking words

The heading 'linking words' is used because that seems to be the main use of the words below. In English, time words are often used as linking words in narratives such as, 'He climbed the wall, **then** he saw the princess, **then** he . . .'. It seems that in GY, and probably other Aboriginal languages, such linking words are typically place words rather than time words. This may be the reason some Aboriginal Englishes frequently use expressions such as 'this-here' and 'that-there', they are patterns that people have carried on from their original languages.

These linking words are easily left out of sentences without destroying their meaning. The English example sentence above could just as easily read, 'He climbed the wall, he saw the princess, he . . .'.

Because the words are, in some ways, optional, and because they are so difficult to translate and analyse, it is understandable that people studying the language did not describe them well. Below are some of the GY linking words. It is likely that some of these words have other uses, and that other words from the previous sections are also used as linking words at times.

The words *ngiyarrma* and *ngiyama* occur around 50 times in the recordings and no difference has been found in their meaning. Williams (1980) writes *ngiyarrma* as *nhirrma*. They typically occur in the second part of a sentence, as shown in:

Giirr | *ngaya* | *ngay* | *bilaarr* | *gaa-waa-nhi,* | *ngiyarrma* | *dhu-dha-y-gu*
true | I | my | spear | take-moving-past | there | pierce-regular-*y*-purpose

| *ngaya* | *guduu,* | *bilaa-yu.*
| I | cod | spear-with

I used to take my spear, to spear the cod there.

| *Dhuwinba-nhi* | *ngaya,* | *ngiyarrma,* | *yurrul-a* | *ngaya* | *dhuwinba-nhi.*
| hide-past | I | there | bush-place | I | hide-past

I hid in the bushes.

More rarely it occurs in a sentence with one verb:

| *Giirr* | *ngaama* | *nguu,* | *bagala,* | *ngiyama* | *nguu-nga* | *garra-y,*
| true | that | she | leopardwood | there | she-then? | cut-past

   | *garra-y* | *ngaama* | *yulay.* (AD)
   | cut-past | that | skin

She cut that-there leopardwood there, she cut that skin (bark).

The first and third examples above show *ngiyarrma/ngiyama* being translated by the Aboriginal English 'there'/'that.there'.

There are a number of words which are probably related to *ngiyarrma*, including *ngiyarrima, ngiyarru-ma, ngiyarruu, ngiyarri* and *ngiyarr-gili-dja-dhaay*.

Chapter Four
Verbs

■ What is a verb?

A verb can be described as a 'doing word' (such as 'walk', 'eat', 'be', 'smile'). Another way of describing verbs is by pointing out any special parts that can be added to them. In English, verbs can have parts such as '-ing' attached ('run' becomes 'running', 'walk' 'walking and 'be' 'being') or they can have 'will' in front of them ('will run', 'will walk', 'will be').

GY verbs are made up of a stem and at least one ending, or suffix. GY verbs can have many different suffixes attached to them. In the first part of this chapter simple stems, the most common suffixes and the four verb classes will be considered. The second part of this chapter will look at less common suffixes.

■ Simple verb stems, simple verb endings

We will begin by looking at some actual verbs, and then point out the patterns in them. The first verb to be considered is *banaga-y* 'will run'. It is used in both GR and YR/YY.

The word part *banaga-* is called the stem. It does not change and is present whenever this verb is used. The word part *-y* is the ending, or suffix, and it indicates that the action is going to take place in the future (i.e. 'will run'). It can be replaced by two other simple endings. These are *-nhi*, indicating that the action took place in the past, and *-ya*, indicating that the word is a command. So *banaga-nhi* means 'ran' and *banaga-ya* means 'run!'.

The word for walk or go is *yanaa-y* in YR/YY and *yana-y* in GR. The same three endings are used with *yanaa-/yana-* as with *banaga-*. So *yanaa-y/yana-y* means 'will walk/go' (future tense), *yanaa-nhi/yana-nhi* means 'walked' or 'went' (past tense) and *yanaa-ya/yana-ya* means 'walk!', 'go!' (command).

■ Transitive and intransitive verbs

It is important to note whether a verb is intransitive (Int) or transitive (Tr). This distinction is very important in Aboriginal languages, much more so than in English. You need to be aware of it all the time.

As a rough guide, transitive verbs are usually about **doing to** something, e.g. 'eat the meat', 'cut the bread'. Intransitive verbs are about just **doing**, e.g. 'walk', 'sleep' etc. All verbs are clearly labelled as transitive or intransitive in the body of the dictionary (see pages 269–70).

Verb classes

Over 400 GY verbs have been recorded. As mentioned above they all have a stem, a part which does not change. These verb stems are divided into four groups depending upon the suffixes they use to indicate tense. In the above example we looked at *banaga-y* 'will run' and *yanaa-y/yana-y* 'will talk'. These are called *-y* class verbs because the future tense is indicated by the suffix *-y*. There are three other future tense suffixes: *-li*, *-rri* and *-gi*. The verbs that use these future tense suffixes are therefore classed as *-li* class, *-rri* class or *-gi* class verbs. (There is an alternative system which calls these verb classes *y*, *l*, *ng* and *rr*.)

The following table shows the three simple endings for the four verb classes:

Class	Future	Past	Command
-li class	*-li*	*-y*	*-la*
-y class	*-y*	*-nhi* (but *-nyi* after *i*)	*-ya*
-gi class	*-gi*	*-nhi* (but *-nyi* after *i*)	*-nga*
-rri class	*-rri*	*-nhi*	*-na*

-li class verbs

The class names tells you that the future tense of these verbs ends in *-li*. The *-li* class is the largest GY verb class, and most *-li* class verbs are transitive. The GY word for talk is *guwaa-li*. The three simple endings for *-li* class verbs are *-li* (future tense), *-y* (past tense) and *-la* (command). Thus, the forms are *guwaa-li* **will** talk', *guwaa-y* 'talk**ed**' and *guwaa-la* 'talk!'.

There is one exception. Sometimes, when the verb stem ends in a single *a*, two past endings (*-y* and *-ay*) may occur. So the past tense of *gama-li* 'will break' can be either *gama-y* or *gama-ay*. In this learner's guide only the common form, *gama-y*, is used.
Some example sentences containing *-li* class endings are given below.

| *Maadhaay-u* | *dhinggaa* | *dha-li*. |
| dog-doer.to | meat | eat-future |

The dog will eat the meat.

| *Yaama* | *ngindaali* | *dhinggaa* | *yilama-y?* |
| question | you(two) | meat | cook-past |

Did you two cook the meat?

| *Bayama-la* | *nhama* | *bandaarr!* |
| catch-command | that | kangaroo(grey) |

Catch that kangaroo!

-y class verbs

Verbs whose future tense form ends with a -y are called -y class verbs. This is a large group of verbs in GY. Some examples are: *baa-y* (YR/YY), *bara-y* (GR) meaning 'hop' or 'jump'; *bara-y* (YR/YY)/*barra-y* (GR) meaning 'fly'; *wunga-y* (YR/YY), *wurunga-y* (GR) meaning 'dive', 'play around in the water'; and *gubi-y* meaning 'swim'.

Note that *banaga-y*, as well as being the future form of the verb, is also the citation form. Thus, if you asked a GY speaker, 'What is the word for "run"?' the answer given would be *banaga-y*. The future form is the normal citation form for all GY verbs, whatever their class.

Below are more examples of the -y class verb endings:

-y class stem	Future	Past	Command
wila-	*wila-y* 'will sit'	*wila-nhi* 'sat'	*wila-ya!* 'sit!'
warra-	*warra-y* 'will stand' (Int)	*warra-nhi* 'stood'	*warra-ya!* 'stand!'
gaarri-	*gaarri-y* 'will spill' (Int)	*gaarri-nyi* 'spilt'	*gaarri-ya!* 'spill!'
gubi-	*gubi-y* 'will swim'	*gubi-nyi* 'swam'	*gubi-ya!* 'swim!'

There is a slight difference when the stem ends in *i*. The past tense is shown by the ending *-nyi* rather than *-nhi* (see *gubi-nyi* above).

-gi class verbs

This is a relatively small group of about twenty verbs. The three simple endings for this verb group are *-gi* (future), *-nhi* (past) and *-nga* (command). When attached to the verb stem *gaa-* 'bring', the result is *gaa-gi* **'will** bring', *gaa-nhi* **'brought'** and *gaa-nga!* 'bring!'.

-rri class verbs

This is the smallest group of verbs. The three simple endings are *-rri* (future), *-nhi* (past) and *-na* (command). When attached to the verb stem *wuu-* 'give', the result is *wuu-rri* **'will** give', *wuu-nhi* 'gave' and *wuu-na* 'give!'.

| Nhama | dhinggaa | ngay | wuu-na!
| the | meat | my | give-command

Give me that meat!

Some comments on verb classes

Many Aboriginal languages have verb classes similar to the GY classes, though the number of classes varies considerably. There is often something like the *-li* and *-y* class, with the *-li* class mainly transitive and the *-y* class intransitive.

To get used to the class of verbs try to read a lot of sentences, and make up some of your own. There are many sentences in the body of the dictionary. Below are a few example sentences for you to study.

Birralii bundaa-nhi.	The child fell.
Mirri-dju nhama gungan ngaru-nhi.	The dog drank the water.
Ngali mudhay-gu yanaa-nhi.	We went for possums.
Birralii mirri-dji banaga-nhi.	The child ran away from the dog.
Dhinggaa ngay wuu-na!	Give me meat!
Yaama birray yu-nhi?	Did the boy cry?
Yaama yulu-gi ngindaali?	Will you (two) dance?
Banaga-ya school-gu!	Run to school!
Ngaya yana-nhi town-gu.	I went to town.
Ngaya yana-nhi town-dhi.	I came from town.

▌Progressive endings

So far we have looked at the simplest verb endings. The next most common forms are called progressive endings. Look at the verbs in the following sentences:

*Dhinawan banaga-**waa**-nhi.*	The emu was running.
*Dhinawan banaga-**y-la**-nhi.*	The emu used to run.
*Dhinawan warra-**y-la**-nhi.*	The emu was standing.

There are two suffixes (*-waa-* and *-y-la-*) for *-y* class verbs, which have some similarity in meaning. They are both called progressive suffixes because they both indicate that the action is ongoing.

Initially it was thought that there was no difference in meaning. However, more and more differences have been noted, and it is to be expected that more will be learnt about these suffixes. The main differences are that the *-waa-* suffix, and the corresponding forms in other classes, indicate movement or change ('is running', 'was crawling', 'is going to sleep', 'is dying'), whereas the *-y-la-* suffix, and the corresponding forms in other classes, indicate regular action ('runs', 'crawls', 'sleeps') or action which does not involve movement ('is sleeping', 'is standing').

The progressive suffixes for all verb classes are set out in the table below. To build verbs with progressive suffixes, take the verb stem, then add *either* a moving suffix *or* a regular suffix (but not both), then place the appropriate final suffix on the end. The suffixes similar to *-waa-* are *-laa-* and *-rraa-*. Note that all these contain *aa*. Those similar to *-y-la-* are *-gi-la-*, *-lda-* and *-dha-*. Note that all these have a single *a*.

Verbs

Verb class	Moving	Regular	Final suffixes
-li class	-laa-	-lda- (-la-)	-y, -nha, -nhi, -ya
-y class	-waa- (-yaa-)	-y-la-	-y, -nha, -nhi, -ya
-gi class	-waa- (-yaa-)	-gi-la-	-y, -nha, -nhi, -ya
-rri class	-rraa-	-dha-	-y, -nha, -nhi, -ya

Note that the *-waa-* ending is *-yaa-* after stems ending with *i*. Thus *gubi-yaa-nha* means 'is swimming'.

Both these suffixes create new, *-y* class stems (e.g. *banaga-waa-* and *banaga-y-la-*) to which a final suffix must be added. The final suffixes are the same as those for *-y* class verbs, except that there is a fourth suffix. The extra suffix is present tense and is shown below, as are the other tenses.

i. moving forms of *banaga-y* 'run'

banaga-waa-y	will be running	future moving (continuous)
banaga-waa-nha	is running	present moving (continuous)
banaga-waa-nhi	was running	past moving (continuous)
banaga-waa-ya	keep running!	moving (continuous) command

ii. regular forms of *banaga-y* 'run'

banaga-y-la-y	will run (regularly)	future regular
banaga-y-la-nha	runs	present regular
banaga-y-la-nhi	used to run	past regular
banaga-y-la-ya	keep running!	regular command

Verbs such as *yanaa-y* 'walk', *banaga-y* 'run', *bundaa-gi* 'fall', *dhuu-rri* 'crawl' and *bara-y* 'fly' usually use the moving suffix. If you are walking or crawling or flying you must be moving along, as it were. However, they can also use the regular suffix to show that an action happens frequently. Thus:

dhuu-rri	'crawl' has the progressive forms:
dhuu-rraa-nha	'is crawling'
dhuu-dha-nha	could be used in phrases like 'always crawls'

gaa-gi	'bring', 'carry' has the progressive forms:
gaa-waa-nha	which is used in phrases such as 'She is bringing the meat'
gaa-gi-la-nha	which is used in phrases such as, 'He carries a spear' and, 'They have children'
dhurra-li	is 'come' and it is most common as:
dhurra-laa-nha	'someone is coming', 'the sun is rising' but also occurs as
dhurra-lda-nha	'the crow comes here for water' or 'feathers grow on the bird'

The next three examples show very clearly the differences between regular and moving suffixes.

dha-li	is 'eat' and it often occurs as:
dha-lda-nha	'is eating (but not moving around)'

However, on two occasions it occurs on the recordings as:

dha-laa-nha	'is eating, while walking along'

yii-li	is 'bite', and it often occurs as:
yii-lda-nha	'is biting'

However, on one occasion it occurs on the recordings as:

yii-laa-nhi	'was biting', referring to a dog that bit a boy while, or straight after, chasing him

baa-y	is 'hop', and the most common form is:
baa-waa-nha	'is hopping' (which involves moving along)

But when the verb is used about a fish hopping about in the bottom of a boat, or a man jumping up and down on the spot, the verb is

baa-y-la-nha	'is hopping' (up and down on the one spot)

Verbs such as *yilawa-y* 'sit', *warra-y* 'stand', *dhanduwi-y* 'sleep' and *wila-y* 'sit, live' are about actions that involve staying in the one spot. You would therefore expect them to use the regular suffix, since that is the one used when there is no moving along. And in fact they do use the regular suffix in the vast majority of cases:

Birralii	*yilawa-y-la-nha.*
child	sit-regular-present

The child is sitting.

| *Minyaaya-nda* | *wila-y-la-nha?*
| where.at-you (one) | live-regular-present

Where do you live?

There are, however, exceptions. In a recorded example, a child was riding in a bag on its mother's back and so was both sitting *and* moving. So a sitting verb is used with a moving suffix. Arthur Dodd said:

| *Giirr* | *ngaama* | *biirralii-djuul,* | *maayu* | *wila-waa-nhi,* | *gulay-a,*
| true | the | child-little | well | sit-moving-past | bag-place

| *ngambaa-ngun-da nguungu* | *bawa-ga.*
| mother-s-place his/her | back-place

The child had a good ride on his mother's back.

The moving suffix is also used if there is a change happening. The verb *balu-gi* means 'die', and the only progressive suffix used on *balu-gi* is *-waa-*, the moving (and change) suffix:

| *Giirr* | *nhama* | *wii* | *balu-waa-nha.*
| true | the | fire | die-moving-present

The fire is dying/going out.

In summary, the forms of progressive suffixes are given above, and their meanings. They are followed by the three *-y* class endings plus a present tense ending, *-nha*. That is, when there is a progressive suffix there are four possible final endings for the verb. At other times there are three possible final endings for the verb.

So, after *banaga-waa-* and *banaga-y-la-* the choices are *-y*, *-nha*, *-nhi* and *-ya*. And after *banaga-* the choices are *-y*, *-nhi* and *-ya*. Further examples of these suffixes are:

-y class

| *Giirr* | *ngaya* | *maayu* | *dhanduwi-y-la-nha.*
| true | I | well | sleep-*y*-regular-present

I always sleep well.

| *Giirr* | *ngaama* | *birralii-djuul,* | *galiya-waa-nha,* | *maayama-ga.*
| true | the | child-little | climb-moving-present | rock-place

The child is climbing on the rock.

-li class

| *Ngaandi-yaa* | *dhaay* | *dhurra-laa-nha.* |
| who-indefinite | to here | come-moving-present |

Someone is coming here.

| *Dhaygal* | *dhurra-laa-nha.* |
| hair | come-moving-present |

(Your) hair is growing.

| *Bayagaa* | *nguungu* | *ngaya* | *wagirrma-lda-nhi.* (FR2436B) |
| clothes | his | I | wash-regular-past |

I used to wash his clothes.

The second example above shows that the present descriptions of the suffixes do not fully explain all their uses.

-gi class

| *Maadhaay* | *ngay* | *balu-waa-nha.* (FR1853) |
| dog | my | die-moving-present |

My dog is dying.

| *Gaawaa-dhi* | *nguu* | *gungan* | *ngawu-gi-la-nha.* (FR1853) |
| river-from | he | water | drink-regular-present |

He drinks at the river.

A particularly important verb in *-gi* class is *gi-gi* 'be, become'. The past tense form, *gi-nyi*, is used to describe things which have recently changed. It also commonly occurs in its progressive forms as *gi-yaa-nha/gi-yaa-nhi*, and in its regular form as *gi-gi-la-nha/gi-gi-la-nhi*.

| *Yuulngin* | *ngaya* | *gi-nyi.* |
| hungry | I | be-past |

I am hungry. (I got hungry.)

Verbs

Notice the difference in the following:

Burrul	*nhama*	*buruma.*
big	the	dog

That dog is fat (and has been for a while).

Burrul	*nhama*	*buruma*	*gi-nyi.*
big	the	dog	be-past

That dog has got fat.

The progressive form, *gi-yaa-nha*, has two main translations, 'getting' and 'going to':

Giirr	*ngarran*	*gi-yaa-nha.* (AD5052)
true	visible/light?	be-moving-present (going to)

It's getting daylight.

Bayn	*ngaya*	*gi-yaa-nha.*
sore	I	be-progressive-present

I am getting sick.

Wila-y	*ngaya*	*gi-yaa-nha.* (AD3997B)
sit-future	I	be-moving-present

I am going to sit down now.

The regular form, on the other hand, generally refers to something that is or was staying the same:

Minya-nginda-nda	*gi-gi-la-nha?*
what-wanting-you	be-gi-regular-present

What do you want?

Buyuma	*ngay*	*ngama*	*garigari*	*gi-gi-la-nha.*
dog	my	that/there	afraid	be-*gi*-regular-present

My dog is frightened (of yours).

In sentences such as the last one, Fred Reece generally uses *gi-la-nha*, whereas Arthur Dodd uses *gi-gi-la-nha*. The latter form, *gi-gi-la-nha*, is recommended as it is the more regular form.

***-rri* class**

| *Gaba* | *gi-la-ya* | *yina-ya,* | *burrulaa* | *dhuwarr* | *wuu-dha-ya.*
| good | be-regular-command | woman-at | lot | bread | give-regular-command

Be good to those women and give them plenty of bread. (FR2437A)

| *Garriya* | *ngaarrima-lay* | *dhuu-rraa-ya.* (AD5056)
| don't | there-? | crawl-moving-command

Don't crawl there.

| *Giirr* | *nhama* | *birralii* | *dhuu-rraa-nha.* (FR1989A)
| true | the | child | crawl-moving-present

He's just starting to crawl, crawl along

Some of the above work on progressive suffixes is subject to revision, but it reflects the current state of knowledge in GY.

 The following section on verbs contains material that is very different from English and other European languages. It's a good idea at this point to go back and revise what you learnt in the earlier part of this chapter before proceeding.

Complex stems

This section is about combining a number of parts to make a new, longer verb stem. It may take a bit of getting used to. However, there are words in English which are also made up of many parts, and we use them easily once we are used to them. Consider, for example, 're-in-vigor-at-ion'.

Complex GY verb stems are made up of a number of parts. They always begin with a simple verb stem — such as *banaga-* 'run' — then one or more suffixes are added, sometimes with fillers (see box). The final part is one of the *-li* or *-y* class endings shown earlier in this chapter.

Fillers. Sometimes a suffix with one meaning takes a number of slightly different forms. For example the verb suffix meaning 'back' is *-wuwi-y* after *-y* class stems, *-luwi-y* after *-li* class stems, *-rruwi-y* after *-rri* class stems, and sometimes *-guwi-y* after *-gi* class stems. This can become confusingly complex and so it is easier to describe this suffix as simply *-uwi-y* rather than the four variations above. The part at the front — the 'filler' or 'class marker', can be treated seperately. Each class has a different filler, or fillers, which occurs with many suffixes:

verb class	filler
-li class	l
-y class	w/y*
-rri class	rr
-gi class	g/w/ng

*The *-y* class filler is *y* before some suffixes. For other suffixes it is *w* when the verb stem ends in *a*, and *y* when the verb stem ends in *i*. These fillers are also called class markers.

The following four examples are complex forms based on *banaga-y* 'run'.

i. By adding the suffix *-waa-nha* the progressive-present tense is made, and so *banaga-waa-nha* means '**is** running'.

ii. The suffix *-uwi-y* after a verb means 'back', and so *banaga-w-uwi-* is a complex stem meaning 'run back'. However, it still needs a tense ending. After *-uwi-* the tense endings are the *-y* class endings. These can be simple (*-y* for future tense, *-nyi* past and *-ya* command) or progressive (*-y-la-* or *-waa-*). So *banaga-w-uwi-nyi* means 'ran back' and *banaga-w-uwi-yaa-nha* means 'is running back'.

iii. The suffix *-aaba-li* is a suffix meaning 'all', and it takes *-li* class endings (in which *-li* is future tense, *-y* past and *-la* command). So *banaga-w-aaba-li* means 'will all run'.

iv. On occasions more than one suffix is added, so:

| *Banaga-w-uwi-y-aaba-lda-nhi.*

| run-*w*-back-*y*-all-regular-past

(They) were all running back.

Verb stem-forming suffixes

There are many GY verb suffixes, and these can be thought of as forming new stems to which the simple and progressive suffixes above can then be added. Some of these suffixes are well understood. There are others about which we have a moderate amount of information and others again where there is very little information — they are not included in this introductory learner's guide.

In the section below, you will see three different groups of verb stem–forming suffixes. The first group is suffixes about 'who is involved?'. The next group — 'common' and 'less common' suffixes — have a variety of functions. The third group is time suffixes.

1. The 'who is involved?' suffixes

i. *-la-y*

This suffix is usually translated as 'each other' in English. The rules for forming a new stem are to add *-la-y* to *-li* class verbs and *-dha-y* to *-rri* class verbs. The rules for *-y* class and *-gi* class are not known. Examples of the suffix include:

Giirruu	nhama	gagil	birralii-gal	nhima-la-y-la-nha.
true	the	bad	child-plural	pinch-each.other-y-regular-present

The bad children are pinching each other.

 Note! The original verb *nhima-li* is transitive and *-li* class, but the 'new' verb *nhima-la-y* is intransitive and *-y* class.

Ngindaali	garriya	buma-la-ya	yaluu! (AD3218B)
you (two)	don't	hit-each.other-command	again

Don't fight no more!

Sometimes GY reciprocal verbs are used to translate English verbs which are not explicitly reciprocal. For instance, *buma-la-y* 'hit each other' translates as 'fight' and *guwaa-la-y* 'talk to each other' translates 'talk', as in sentences such as, 'The people were talking (to each other).'

ii. *-ngiili-y*

This suffix is used when the action is done.to oneself. The change of verb class (discussed below) also conveys this idea. This again changes the verb from transitive to intransitive. To form the new stem:

-li, *-gi* class	verb stem + *ngiili-y*
-rri class	verb stem + *rr* + *ngiili-y*
-y class	not known

Verbs

| *Buma-ngiili-nyi* | *ngaya.*
| hit-oneself-past | I

I hit myself.

| *Garriya* | *bilaa-yu* | *dhu-rr-ngiili-ya!*
| don't | spear-using | pierce-*rr*-oneself-command

Don't spear yourself!

iii. *-aaba-li*

This suffix adds the meaning 'all' to the doer or done.to. The suffix operates ergatively. If the verb is intransitive, it is all the doer. If the verb is transitive, it is all the done.to. The verb stays transitive or intransitive. The rules for forming a new stem are:

-li, -y, -rri class   verb stem + class marker (*l, w/y, rr*) + *aaba-li* (see p 312 for information about class marker)
-gi class   verb stem + *w-aaba-li*

| *Maadhaay-u* | *buya* | *ngaama* | *dhuwima-l-aaba-y.*
| dog-doer.to | bone | the | pull.out-*l*-all-past

The dog dug up all the bones (i.e. all the **done.to**, since the verb is transitive).

| *Dhaay* | *nganunda* | *yanaa-w-aaba-la.*
| to.here | to-me | come-*w*-all-command

Come to me all of you (i.e. all the **doers**, since the verb is intransitive).

| *Nhama* | *ngaya* | *bubaay* | *giniy* | *gama-l-aaba-li.*
| the | I | little | stick | break-*l*-all-future

I will break the stick all up (i.e. all the **done.to**).

iv. *-n.giili-y*, V-*li-y*

This suffix is used to show that the action is done 'for someone's benefit'. The 'V' indicates that the preceding vowel is lengthened. The rules for forming a new stem are:

-li class   verb stem + vowel lengthened + *-li-y*
-gi class   verb stem + *-n.giili-y*
-rri class   verb stem + *rr* + *-n.giili-y*

Examples of this suffix are given below.

| *Giirr* | *ngaya* | *nginu* | *yilama-a-li-nyi* | *nhama,* | *dha-li-gu-nda.*
| true | I | your | cook-a-benefit-past | that | eat-future-purpose-you (one)

I cooked that for you to eat.

| Gaa-n.giili-ya | ngay.
| bring-benefit-command | my

Bring (it) for me.

2. Other verb suffixes

The following suffixes are common, and rules for their use are fairly well understood.

i. -uwi-y

This is a common suffix, usually on movement and giving verbs. It adds the meaning 'back', as in 'give it back' or 'come back'. The rules for forming a new stem are:

-li, -y, -rri class   verb stem + class marker (l, w/y, rr) + -uwi-y

-gi class   wana-w-uwi-y 'throw back', gaa-g-uwi-y 'bring back'

(Note: The -uwi-y suffix is only found on the two -gi class verbs shown above.)

| Wuu-rr-uwi-ya | nhama | ngay | bilaarr!
| give-rr-back-command | that | my | spear

Give my spear back to me!

| Giirr | ngaya-laa | yanaa-w-uwi-y.
| true | I-laa[later?] | come-w-back-future

I will come back (to see you).

Yanaa-w-uwi-y 'will go back' is often translated as 'will go home'.

ii. -ma-li

This suffix is common and has a number of uses. The rules for forming a new stem are:

-y class   verb stem + y + -ma-li

-gi class   verb stem + -ma-li

The suffix makes a transitive verb from an intransitive one. The verb *bundaa-gi*, which means 'fall', is intransitive, but *bundaa-ma-li* 'make fall' is transitive. Also, *warra-y* means 'stand' but *warra-y-ma-li* has various translations including 'build' and 'stand' (transitive).

| Giirruu | nhama | dhayn-duul | nganha | bundaa-ma-y.
| true-very | the | man-one | me | fall-make-past

That man made me fall over.

| *Dhuyul-i* | *gi-yaa-nha* | *ngaya* | *dhaadharr* | *warra-y-ma-li.* (FR1987A)
| hill-from | going.to | I | bark(shelter) | stand-*y*-make-future

I am going to pitch my humpy on that high knob.

The ending *-ma-li* is also used to change English verbs into GY. Thus, *gigima-li* is 'kick', *wagirrma-li* is 'wash' and also *pickima-li* 'pick' was recorded once. The rule is to change the English verb into the GY sound system (so that 'kick' becomes *gig*), add *i* (or sometimes *-irr*) and then add *-ma-li*.

The suffix cannot be used to translate expressions such as 'I made him go'. It seems that *-ma-li* 'make' cannot be used where someone is being told or forced to do something, that is, where the person has some choice. In these cases the verb *guwaa-li* 'tell' is used. There are possibly many more sub-rules like this that have not been found.

The suffixes which follow are less common. Often their meaning is not fully understood. It is likely that more such suffixes will be defined as the language is further investigated.

iii. -bama-li

This is a causative suffix. It is found on *yu-gi* 'cry' and forms *yu-bama-li* 'make cry'. The form *-bama-li* is also found on a small number of other words. An example of *yu-bama-li* is given below:

| *Giirr* | *nhama* | *birralii-djuul-u* | *bubaay-djuul* | *yu-bama-y.*
| true | the | child-little-doer.to | little-one | cry-make-past

The child made the little one cry.

iv. -bi-li

This suffix adds the meaning 'let', and is also quite rare. Its use is most clearly illustrated by the verbs *yanaa-y*, 'go', and *yanaayn-bi-li*, 'let go'.

There is also the pair of words *binda-y*, 'hang', (Int) and *bindaybi-li*, 'hang' (Tr). These two indicate that there may be another meaning for *-bi-li*, and at least two sets of rules for using it (with and without the *n*).

v. -dha-y

Two verb suffixes with the form *-dha-y* have already been introduced, both for *-rri* class verbs — the regular progressive suffix and the reciprocal suffix, though the status of the second is uncertain. A further use is that when *-dha-y* is added to a verb stem it indicates that the action of the main verb is somehow associated with eating. For example, *buma-dha-y* means 'hit after eating' ('hit-*dha*-past').

vi. -mi-y

This is not recorded in recent information, but Ridley (1875) called it the 'ironic imperative'. On page nine he records the word *gowaalmia*, meaning 'speak, if you can, or if you dare'. In the current spelling system (as used in this learner's guide and dictionary), the word for 'speak' is *guwaa-li*, so *gowaalmia* would now be spelt *guwaa-l-mi-ya*.

3. Time suffixes

So far we have seen the simple future, non-future and progressive endings. There are many other endings to show the time of the action. Full information on all of these endings is not available, and they are not all that common in recent material. It may be that they were more common in earlier use, but were declining in their frequency of usage. It is also quite possible that some other similar forms have been lost. These suffixes appear vague to people who are used to talking more precisely about time. Since they do not often correspond exactly to something in current English it can be harder to use them.

The suffixes are given below, with a definition and some example sentences.

i. *-ngayi-y*

This suffix indicates the recent past or the near future. It is added to the verb stem and forms a *-y* class verb. The rules for forming a new stem are:

-li, -y, -rri class   verb stem + class marker (*l, y, rr*) + *-ngayi-y*

-gi class   verb stem + *-ngayi-y*

| Giirr | ngiyani | yanaa-y | wunga-y-ngayi-y. |
| true | we | go-future | swim-*y*-near-future |

We are going swimming tomorrow.

| Giirr | ngaya | gi-yaa-nha | wana-ngayi-y. |
| true | I | going.to | throw-near-future |

I will throw it tomorrow.

| Giirr | ngaya | dha-l-ngayi-nyi | ngaama | dhinggaa. |
| true | I | eat-*l*-near-past | the | meat |

I ate the meat early in the morning.

| Giirr | ngaya | galiya-y-ngayi-nyi. |
| true | I | climb-*y*-near-past |

I climbed (it) yesterday.

When Arthur Dodd and Fred Reece were asked for the words for 'yesterday' and 'tomorrow' they replied, 'There are no words'. It seems likely that GY used the verb form as the usual way of conveying that information, and not time words, as English does.

Verbs

ii. -mayaa-y
This suffix means that something happened a long time ago (though it is also sometimes used for 'yesterday'). The rules for forming a new stem are:

verb stem + class marker (*l, y, ng* or *rr*) + -*mayaa-y*

-*gi* class verb stem + -*ngayi-li*

| Giirr | maadhaay-u | gula-l-mayaa-nhi.
| true | dog-doer.to | bark-*l*-long.time-past

The dog barked long ago.

| Giirr | nhama | nguu | bilaa-yu | dhu-rr-mayaa-nhi.
| true | the | he/she | spear-using | pierce-*rr*-long.time-past

He speared it long ago.

iii. -ngaya-li
This suffix roughly means 'all day', and describes something which is on-going or habitual. The rules for forming a new stem are:

verb stem + class marker + -*ngaya-li*

-*gi* class verb stem + -*ngaya-li*

| Giirruu | birralii-djuul | bamba | yu-ngaya-lda-nhi.
| true.very | child-little | hard | cry-all.day-regular-past

The child cried hard all day.

| Bubaay-djuul, | birralii | bundaa-ngaya-laa-nha, | waalu | maayu
| little-one | child | fall-all.day-moving-present | not.yet | well

  | yanaa-y-la-nha.
  | walk-*y*-regular-present

The baby falls over all the time, he can't walk properly (yet).

iv. -ayla-y
There are not many examples of this suffix, meaning 'before' or 'yesterday', and it needs more analysis. However, the rules for forming a new stem are:

verb stem + class marker + -*ayla* + -*y*, -*nha*, -*nhi* or -*ya* (it takes the 'progressive' tense ending)

| Giirr | nguu | nhama | bandaarr | bilaa-yu dhu-rr-ayla-nhi.
| true | he/she | the | kangaroo | spear-using pierce-*rr*-before-past

He speared that kangaroo yesterday.

| Giirr | birralii-djuul | yu-ng-ayla-nhi.
| true | child-little | cry-*ng*-before-past

The child was crying before.

Change of verb class

This process involves verbs that are basically -*li* class, and which then change to -*y* class in some circumstances. Look at the following examples of the verb *gama-li* 'will break' (transitive), adapted from Arthur Dodd (AD5058):

| Giirr | ngaya | ngaama | maayama | gama-li. (*l* class)
| true | I | the | rock | break-future

I will break the rock.

| Giirr | ngaama | maayama | gama-y. (*y* class)
| true | the | rock | break-future

The rock will break.

In the first sentence the verb is -*li* class and transitive (there is a breaker and a broken). However, in the second sentence the verb is -*y* class and intransitive (there is no 'break-er'). The usual verb for 'break' is *gama-li* (transitive). The following sentence from Fred Reece (FR1849B) also shows the -*y* class form:

| Buyu | gama-nhi.
| leg | break-past

He broke his leg.

In this case *gama-nhi* is the past tense of a -*y* class verb.

> This last example shows the -*y* class verb being used with a reflexive meaning (i.e. to do to oneself), though it is not clear how this use is different from the -*ngiili-y* reflexive forms given above.
>
> The change of verb class generally changes a transitive verb to an intransitive one. The new verb can be a simple intransitive (the stick **broke**) or it can be reflexive (I broke **my** leg). This area needs further work as there is more to find out and explain. There are many examples of the change of verb class in the body of the dictionary.

Relative verb endings

This is a different type of suffix. It is used when a verb is in a subsidiary or secondary clause. Consider the English sentences below. The main verb is in normal letters, the secondary clause and verb are in italics:

I was happy *when I won Lotto*.

He saw the man *who was carrying the fish*.

The woman *that I know* will come soon.

This is the girl *you gave the bread to*.

The main clause can be used by itself and it still makes sense. 'I was happy', 'The woman will come soon' and so on, but this is not true of the secondary or relative clause. The secondary clause, e.g. 'when I won Lotto', makes no sense if used by itself. Often secondary or relative clauses in English start with words such as 'who', 'which', 'when' and 'that'.

Different languages have different rules for relative clauses, and different ways of showing which is the relative clause. The rules for GY have not been fully analysed, but the verb in a GY relative clause has a special ending, called the relative ending, and these endings are shown below.

Verb class	Relativised verb
-li class	stem + *-ndaay*, stem + *-ldaay*
-y class	stem + *-ngindaay*
-gi class	stem + *-ngindaay*
-rri class	stem + *-ndaay*

Verbs which already have a progressive suffix add *-ndaay* (e.g. *banaga-waa-ndaay*). The examples below show some of the uses of relative endings.

| *Bandaa-yu* | *ngiyarrma* | *ngaama* | *buunhu* | *dha-***ldaay**, | *balu-nhi*.
| kangaroo | there | the | grass | eat-relative | die

The kangaroo **which** ate the grass died.

| *Buyu* | *ngay* | *bayn,* | *maadhaay-u* | *ngaama* | *yii-***ldaay**.
| leg | my | sore | dog-doer.to | that | bite-relative

My leg is sore **because** the dog bit it.

| *Giirr* | *nhama-la* | *dhayn-duul* | *dhanduwi-y,* | *dhurra-lda-***ndaay**.
| true | the-*la*? | Aboriginal.man-one | sleep-future | come-regular-relative

The man will lie down **when** he comes (home).

| *Dhaala-gi* | *gi-yaa-nha* | *nginda,* | *dhinggaa* | *nginda* | *dha-ldaay*. |
| be.sick-will | going.to | you (one) | meat | you (one) | eat-relative |

If you eat the meat you'll be sick.

-gu ('for', with a command)

A reminder about *-gu*. We have already seen *-gu* used as a suffix on nouns. It is also used as a suffix on verbs with the meaning 'for' (purpose). It is also used when verbs follow a command word, as in 'I told you to go'.

In purpose sentences ('I made the fire to cook the emu') and command sentences ('I told you to run away'), *-gu* is placed on the end of a verb in future-tense form.

| *Giirr* | *ngaya* | *wii* | *wiima-y,* | *dhinawan* | *yilama-li-gu.* |
| true | I | fire | put.down-past, | emu | cook-future-purpose |

I made the fire to cook the emu.

| *Wadjiin-du* | *nganha* | *guwaa-y* | *bawi-li-gu.* (FR2439A) |
| white.woman-doer.to | me | tell-past | sing-future-purpose |

The white woman asked me to sing.

 In the Wangaaybuwan language there are more verb suffixes than in GY. This indicates that there may have been other suffixes in GY which have not been recorded. The *-dha-y* 'eating' suffix above is one that has recently been rediscovered in GY, and others may be found in the future.

Chapter Five
Questions, Negatives, Time

■ Questions

The simplest way of asking a question is by changing the tone of your voice at the end of a sentence. In a statement the tone goes down at the end, and in a question the tone rises. You can say *yinggil nginda* 'tired you' as a statement, 'You are tired', or as a question, 'Are you tired?'

Questions can also be asked using the many specific question words, most of which are covered in this section.

Yaama?

Yaama is the general question word that turns a statement into a question which can be answered yes or no. *Yaama*, and other question words, are placed at the beginning of the sentence. *Yaama* is also used these days as a greeting, meaning something like, 'How are you? How's it going?'. It seems likely that this use developed following contact with non-Aboriginal people, and that originally it was only a question word.

| *Yinggil* | *nginda.* |
| tired | you (one) |

You (one) are tired.

| *Yaama* | *yinggil* | *nginda?* |
| question | tired | you (one) |

Are you (one) tired?

Note how word order can be used to change the emphasis in GY questions. From the statement *Yinarr nhama banaga-waa-nha*, 'The woman is running', two questions can be used, with clear differences in meaning:

| *Yaama nhama yinarr banaga-waa-nha?* | Is the **woman** running? (or somebody else running?) |
| *Yaama banaga-waa-nha nhama yinarr?* | Is the woman **running**? (or is she doing something else?) |

The answer or response often begins with *giirr* 'true', or *gamil/waal* 'no':

Giirr banaga-waa-nha. She **is** running. (No pronoun is needed.)

Gamil/waal nhama yinarr banaga-waa-nha. The woman is not running. (It is not the woman who is running.)

Minya? and similar forms

Minya, and words which incorporate *minya*, are very common question words. Once again, these words are generally the first in the sentences.

i. *Minya?* (what?)

| *Minya* | *nhama?* |
| what | that |

What is that?

| *Minya* | *nginda* | *gimbi-li?* |
| what | you | do-future |

What will you do?

ii. *Minyaarr?* (which?)

An example of the use of this word is illustrated below.

| *Minyaarr* | *wanda?* |
| which | white.man |

Which white man?

iii. *Minyaaya?* (where at?)

There are two YR/YY question words which are almost certainly derived from *minyaarr* 'which?'. They both translate to the English 'where?', but have different meanings. Thus, *minyaaya* means 'where at?' and *minyaarru* (see below) means 'where to?'.

| *Minyaaya* | *gungan?* (FR1850B) |
| where.at | water |

Where is the water?

iv. *Minyaarru* (where to?)

| *Minyaarru* | *nginda* | *yanaa-waa-nha?* (AD3998A) |
| where.to | you (one) | go-moving-present |

Where are you going?

v. *Dhalaa?* (where? GR)

There is only one GR word listed for 'Where?' and it probably means 'Where at?'

vi. *Minyaaya-dhaay?* (where from?)

This is a combination of *minyaaya* and *dhaay* 'to.here'. The word *dhaay* is often used in combination with other place words.

Minyaaya	dhaay	nhama	dhinawan	yanaa-nhi?
where.at	to.here	that	emu	come-past

Where did that emu come from?

vii. *Minyangay?* (how many? or how much?)

Minyangay	birralii	nginu? (JS1852)
how.many	child	your (one)

How many children have you?

viii. *Minya-gu?* (what for?, why?)

This question word consists of *minya?*, 'what?', and *-gu*, the purpose suffix. It literally means 'for what purpose?'.

Minya-gu	nginda	nganha	buma-y? (FR1852B)
what-purpose	you (one)	me	hit-past

What did you hit me for?

Minya-gu	dhaay-nda	yanaa-waa-nhi? (AD3219B)
what-purpose	to.here-you (one)	go-moving-past

What were you coming here for?

ix. *Minya-dhi?* (what from?, why?)

This uncommon word consists of *minya?*, 'what?', and *-dhi*, the source suffix. It literally means 'what from?' or 'because of what?'.

Minya-dhi	garigari	nginda?
what-from	frightened	you (one)

What are you frightened of?

Minya-dhi is also recorded, rarely, as 'why not?'. The word *minya* also occurs in a number of other forms, which are quite rare and not fully analysed.

Questions, negatives, time

▌Other question words

These words are listed with their simple meaning and examples given.

i. *Gulaarr?* (how?)
Note that there is a variant form of this word: *galaarr*.

Gulaarr-nda	*bundaa-nhi*	*muyaan-di?* (FR2435B)
how-you (one)	fall-past	tree-from

How did you fall out of the tree?

Gulaarr	*nhama*	*birralii-djuul*	*garungga-nhi?* (AD3998A)
how	the	child-one/little	drown-past

How did that kid get drowned?

ii. *Galawu?* (when?)

Galawu	*ngindaali*	*dhaay*	*yanaa-nhi?*
when	you (two)	to.here	come-past

When did you come here?

iii. *Warilaa?* (when?)
A small number of older sources have listed *warilaa* as the GR word for 'when?', but these sources have different versions and are quite difficult to decipher.

iv. *-ma* (a possible question suffix)
The suffix *-ma* occurs a number of times on question words, and also on other words. In his section on question words, Ridley (1875, p 7) has the entry '... *aandi?* — who? (hence the verb "*anduma*", "tell who")'.

In the YR/YY recordings this question ending occurs as *minya-ma* (*minya?* 'what?'), *minyanga-ma* (*minyangay?* 'how many?') and *minya-gu-ma* (*minya-gu?* 'what for?'). The addition of *-ma* does not seem to add anything to the way the word is translated. However, it is generally used where a direct question is being asked of someone. At this stage the best guess about *-ma* is that it means something like 'the person being spoken to knows the answer'.

Question pronouns

There are a number of question pronouns ('who?', 'whose?' etc.) discussed in chapter three.

Negatives

English negatives are words such as 'no' and 'not', words which include 'no' and 'not' (e.g. 'can't', 'won't') and related words such as 'never', 'none' and so on. There are a number of GY negatives.

i. *Gamil, waal* (no, not)

These are the simplest negatives in GY. These can translate to 'no' when it is a one-word statement, but are not used to directly translate expressions such as 'no water'. (For that expression, see *marayrr* and *maayrr* below.) *Gamil* and *waal* also translate 'not', which is used with verbs. Examples of their use are given below.

As mentioned earlier, the names of the languages come from their words for 'no', these being *gamil* (GR) and *waal* (YR/YY). It is likely that *waal* is a shortened version of *yuwaal*.

Yaama-nda	*budjigarr*	*ngarra-y?*	*Waal!, Gamil!*
question-you (one)	cat	see-past	
Did you see the cat?			No!

Yaama	*dhinggaa*	*nguwalay?*	*Waal, maayrr dhinggaa.* (YR/YY)
question	meat	here	*Gamil, marayrr dhinggaa.* (GR)
Is there any meat?			No, no meat.

Gamil/waal	*banaga-nhi*	*ngaya.*
no	run-past	I

I did not run.

Waal	*ngaya*	*gi-yaa-nha*	*nhama*	*dhinggaa*	*dha-li.* (AD3998B)
not	I	going.to	the	meat	eat-future

I am not going to eat any of that meat.

Waal,	*waal,*	*biya-duul*	*ngaya.* (AD5056)
no	no	one-only	I

No, no, I am on my own.

(This is an extract from the story of *maliyan*, the wedge-tailed eagle, and *wiidhaa*, the bowerbird.)

Waal	*gimbi-la.*
no(t)	do/make-command

Don't do it.

Words such as 'no-one' or 'nowhere' are probably translated by *waal* and *gamil* in combination with other words. Thus, *waal ngaandi-yaa* (literally 'not anyone') can mean 'no-one' and *waal minyaaya-waa* (literally 'not somewhere') can mean 'nowhere'. However, this area of GY grammar may be revised after further investigation.

In the following sentence *waal* is used to translate 'never':

Waal	nhama	balal	gi-gi-la-nha. (AD3998B)
not	that	dry	get-*gi*-regular-present

That water never gets dry.

The next two sets of negatives are derived from *gamil* and *waal*.

ii. *gamila* and *waala* (can't)
These words are clearly based on the simple negative. They are mostly, but not always, followed by the regular progressive forms of the verb.

Waala	nguuma	gaay	guwaa-lda-nha. (AD3998B)
can't	he/she	word	say-regular-present

He can't talk.

iii. *waalu* and *gamilu* (not yet)
Waalu means 'not yet', and like many time words ends in *u*. The word *gamilu*, its GR equivalent, has not been recorded in the historical materials available and so, at this stage, is a presumed form. *Waalu* can be used as a one-word statement. Fred Reece, in FR1851B, says, '. . . *waalu* means "hold on, wait"'. Another example is:

Waalu	gimbi-la	dhuu. (FR1989A)
not.yet	make-command	fire

Don't make the fire yet.

iv. *garriya* (don't)
This negative is used only with commands, and is stronger than *gamil* or *waal* (which can also be used with command verbs). By itself it means 'don't!'. In the first example below *banaga-ya* is the command 'run!', but there are two ways of saying 'Don't run' in each language.

Waal banaga-ya. (YR/YY)	Don't run.
Gamil banaga-ya. (GR)	Don't run.
Garriya banaga-ya! (GR and YR/YY)	Don't run! (stronger)

Garriya	gaay	guwaa-la! (FR2435B)
don't	word	say-command

Stop talking!

Questions, negatives, time

v. *garriyawu* (wait a while!)
This word is used as an exclamation and is derived from *garriya* 'don't' and a time suffix. It is similar to *waalu* above, but presumably stronger, since *garriya* is stronger than *waal*.

vi. *maayrr* (YR/YY), *marayrr* (GR) (none)
These words negate nouns. The YR/YY word is sometimes pronounced *maarr*. They are used in phrases and sentences such as *maayrr gungan* 'no water' and:

| Maayrr | ngiyaningu | dhinggaa | walaay-dja (AD3998A) |
| none | we(more than two).of | meat | camp-at |

We haven't got any meat in the camp.

They may also be used to translate 'nothing'.

Time words

There are quite a number of time words recorded in GY, but many of them have not been fully defined. For instance, both *yilaa* and *yilaal* have been recorded and it is not clear if these are two forms of one word or have different meanings. Many time words end in *u* (*waalu* 'not yet', *giibaabu* 'early in the morning', *yilaalu* 'long time' and others). However, it is not clear if this *u* is a suffix with a common meaning. Some time words in the dictionary are based on just a few written examples and their form and meaning are to some extent speculative. For instance, *gimiyandi* is listed as 'yesterday', but the form of the word is uncertain, and its rare occurrence means that the meaning is also not certain. The word *ngurrugu*, 'tomorrow', is more common, but still fairly rare, and is at times translated as 'morning'. There are also verb suffixes which are used to indicate that the action was done 'yesterday' or 'tomorrow', meaning that there was less need for time nouns.

A few of the more common time words are given below. There are other time words including *giibaabu* 'early in the morning', *bululuwi* 'evening', *baayandhu* 'later on', *baayanbu* 'immediately' and more.

i. *yilaa* (now — little while ago, soon)
This is generally placed at the beginning of a sentence or phrase. As with the English 'now', *yilaa* can mean 'at the present', 'a little while ago' or 'in a little while'. The English sentences, 'He came just now', 'I am walking now' and 'I will go now' show how 'now' can refer to past, present and future.

 It is currently believed that *yilaal* is a variant form with the same meaning as *yilaa*, but this is open to further investigation. There is often the suffix *-laa* attached to words following *yilaa*. The meaning or function of that suffix has not been determined.

| *Yilaa* | *ngali* | *yanaa-y*. (FR1851B)
| now | we (two) | go-future

We'll go directly (the two of us).

| *Yilaa* | *ngaya-laa* | *yilama-li,* | *waal-bala* | *yalagiyu*. (AD3220B)
| now | I-(?then) | cook-future | not-contrast | now

I'll cook it later, not now.

ii. *yilaalu* (long time ago/in the future)

This word generally occurs at the beginning of the sentence or phrase. It is clearly related to *yilaa* and is generally translated as 'long ago'. However, it means 'in a long time' when it is used with a future tense verb.

| *Yilaalu* | *ngay' [ngaya]* | *yanaa-nhi.* (AD3394B)
| long.time | I | go-past

I went a long time ago.

| *Giirr* | *maadhaay-u,* | *yilaalu* | *gula-lda-nhi.* (AD5057)
| true | dog-doer.to | long.time | bark-continuous-past

The dog barked a long time ago.

| *Yilaalu* | *ngaya* | *dhurra-l-uwi-y.*
| in a long time | I | come-*l*-back-future

I'll come back later on.

iii. *yalagiyu* (now)

While *yilaa* is used more to mean 'in a little while', *yalagiyu* is closer to 'right now, immediately'. Some recorded examples of *yalagiyu* include:

| *Giirruu-nha,* | *yalagiyu* | *nguu,* | *ngaarrma* | *bilaarr,* | *maayu* | *gimbi-lda-nha.* (AD3220A)
| true-that? | now | he | the? | spear | well | make-regular-present

Right now he is making a spear.

| *Yilaa* | *ngaya-laa* | *yilama-li,* | *waal-bala* | *yalagiyu*. (AD3220A)
| soon | I-(?then) | cook-future | not-contrast | now

I'll cook it later.

| *Giirr* | *ngaya* | *yanaa-waa-nha* | *yalagiyu*. (AD 3994B)
| true | I | go-moving-present | now

I am going now.

Chapter Six
Sentences and Particles

▌Language rules for sentences

There are many different rules which apply to languages. The simplest are rules which apply to individual words. In English, for instance, the plural of 'cat' is 'cats', or the past tense of 'cook' is 'cooked'. Then there are rules which apply to groups of words, such as the rule that, in English, the adjective goes before the noun.

There are also rules for sentences. The usual word order in English is as in the sentence 'I ate the meat'. The doer is first, the verb second followed by the done.to. However, this can be varied to 'That meat, I ate it' or 'The meat was eaten by me'. At an even larger scale there are rules about how to organise a sequence of sentences.

To add to the complexity, there are different rules in different situations. There are formal rules for the way people talk at work or on the television news, and less formal rules when at home or with friends.

The simple word-only rules (as opposed to the bigger structural rules) are relatively easy to formulate, but the larger and more complex the part of a language that you are working with, the harder it is to formulate and apply the rules. So while a lot is known about the rules for words in GY, a lot less is known about the rules for sentences and larger parts of language. (While the sources do contain lots of narrative material there is almost nothing on other types of language use, such as greetings, conversational GY or jokes.) What follows is information based on what is known about some of the broader structural rules of GY. This is a preliminary analysis.

Word order

A prominent feature of GY, and of many other Aboriginal languages, is that the word order in phrases and sentences can be changed much more freely than in English without altering the basic meaning. This gives great scope to change emphasis. In general, that which comes early in the sentence or phrase is being emphasised.

Fred Reece often points out the variable word order. In his recording 1848A, in the AIATSIS archive, he says:

> *Gugurrwaan-da burrulaa gungan*, 'There's a lot of water in the Corcoran.' And you can change word order back-the-front, and it means the same: *Burrulaa gungan Gugurrwaan-da*.

He also says, in his recording 1987B, that the following two sentences both mean 'A white man dug a deep hole there':

Sentences and particles

Ganadhaa	nhama	dhaymaarr	mawu-nhi	wanda-gu.
deep	the	ground	dig-past	white.man-doer.to

Wanda-gu	nhama	ganadhaa	biyuu	mawu-nhi.
white.man-doer.to	the	deep	hole	dig-past

With questions, the thing being asked about would generally come after the *yaama*. The question, 'Did the boy eat the meat?' can be about the doer (**who** ate the meat), the action (**what** was done) or the thing eaten (**what** was eaten). It can be asked a number of ways in GY:

Yaama	nhama	birray-u	dhinggaa	dha-y?
question	the	boy-doer.to	meat	eat-past

Did the boy do it? (or someone else)

| Yaama dhinggaa nhama birray-u dha-y?

| Did he eat the meat? (or something else)

| Yaama dha-y nhama birray-u dhinggaa?

| Did he eat it? (or do something else to it)

The most common word order in sentences is **doer** then **done.to** then the **verb**, as in:

Giirr	nhama	birray-u	dhinggaa	dha-y.
true	the	boy-doer.to	meat	eat-past

The boy ate the meat.

In GY there are often parts at the beginning or end of a sentence which tell something about the participants in the action. In the example below, the object (the done-to) is placed after a pause at the end of the sentence:

Yurrul-a-nha	gandjibal-u	gaa-waa-nha,	gulibaa
bush-at-the	policeman-doer.to	take-moving-present	three

| dhayn.

| Aboriginal.man

The policeman is taking three men back to the scrub.

In GY it is rare for two adjectives to be placed together. While in English a number of adjectives can be used together (**two big red noisy** cars), in GY one adjective is usually placed next to the noun (rarely two) and other adjectives are placed at the end of the phrase. In the following sentence *burrul-bidi* is before the noun (*mangun.gaali* 'goanna') and *wamu* at the end of the sentence, after a pause. On tape 8185 Arthur Dodd says:

| Giirr | ngay | ngaama | gulii-yu | burrul-bidi | mangun.gaali | bayama-y,
| true | my | that | partner-doer.to | big-big | tree.goanna | catch-past
| wamu.
| fat

My husband had caught (two) big fat goannas.

There is still much to learn about GY word order rules. A good way to get a feel for them is to read and listen to lots of spoken GY on the recordings and to read the available transcripts.

■ Sentences: joining parts, style

This is a complex area of GY which still requires lots of work. There are a number of linking words or suffixes which are used to form a connection between phrases and sentences. The word *yilaa* 'then' and the suffixes *-laa* and *-nga* (which may also mean 'then') are used in narrative speech, as in 'this happened, **then** that'. The following sentence shows one use of *-nga*:

Guway-u | nhama | gaarra-la, | yulay, | dhinawan-gu, | ngiyama-nga
blood-with | that | rub-command | skin | emu-of | there-then
| ngiyani | gurru-ga | wa-li.
| we | hole-place | put.in-future

Rub that with blood, the skin, of the emu, and we'll shove him in the hole then.

The sentence also shows the use of a place word, *ngiyama* 'there'. This is also used as a linking word, and place words are frequently used like this, but this part of GY is not well analysed. The following sentences show *yilaa* being used to link sentences:

| Giirr | nhama-laa | burrulaa | bandaarr, | gungan-gu, | dhaay,
| true | the-(?then) | many | kangaroo | water-to | to.here
| baa-waa-nhi | yilaa ganunga | baa-w-uwi-y.
| hop-moving-past | then they | hop-*w*-back-future

The kangaroos were coming here for water, then they will hop back (to where they came from).

When there is a change in subject, or other important contrast between two sentences or phrases, *-bala* 'contrast' is used.

| Maniila-y | ngaya | gi-yaa-nha, | ngindaay-bala | nguwalay
| hunt-future | I | going.to, | you(more than two)-contrast | here
| yilawa-ya | gaarrimay-a (FR2438A)
| sit-command | camp-at

I'm going hunting, you can all stop in the camp.

Other particles

There are some words that do not fit neatly into the main word categories of noun, verb, adjective and adverb. Some of these are called particles, and some GY particles are given below. In general particles only have a limited set of suffixes attached to them. Because some particles are used to emphasise a particular point, or to add a flavour to a sentence, the use of these particles can be a matter of personal style.

i. giirr (true, really)

This is a very common word which occurs as a one-word statement, to emphasise another word or as the first word of a sentence. *Giirr* by itself means 'right' or 'true'. It also occurs in expressions such as *giirr gaba* 'too right', 'that's right', 'true'. However, the most common occurrence of *giirr* is at the beginning of a sentence where it points out that the speaker is asserting that the sentence is true.

| Giirr | ngaya | wuu-nhi | nguungunda | dhinggaa. (FR1988B)
| true | I | give-past | him.at | meat

I *did* give him some meat.

| Giirr | ngaya | guwaa-y, | giirr.
| true | I | say-past | true

I *did* tell, I *did*.

Giirr also occurs with suffixes, such as *giirr-badhaay* — which is sometimes translated as 'might' — but at other times its meaning is not clear. However, *giirr-badhaay-aa* is almost always translated as 'might'.

| Giirr-badhaay-aa | ngaya | ngarra-li | dhayn, | gaawaa-ga. (AD5055)
| true-*badhaay*-chance | I | see-future | man | river-place

I might see a man at the river.

Giirr-yaa (true-chance) also occurs. Its meaning is not obviously different from *giirr-badhaay-aa*, as shown by the next sentence.

| Giirr-yaa | nguungu | dhinggaa. (AD3218A)
| true-chance | his/her | meat

He might have some meat.

ii. *giirruu* (absolutely, too right)

This particle is made up of *giirr* + *-uu* (all, totally). It has sometimes been written as *girru*. It is used like *giirr*, but its meaning is stronger, as shown in:

Giirruu	*dhalaybaa.* (AD3217B)
absolutely	sharp

Terrible sharp.

iii. *wana* (let)

This word is often associated with a verb in its future tense form and is translated as 'let'. It is probably related to *wana-gi* 'throw', 'leave' and to *wanagidjay* 'stop it'.

Wana	*ganugu,*	*barran*	*gaa-gi,*	*budhal,*	*bundi,*
let	they-doer.to	boomerang	take-future	toy club	club

minyaminyagaa	*nhama,*	*wana*	*gaa-gi.* (AD3217B)
everything	that	let	take-future

Let them take all that *bundis* and boomerangs and nullanullas.

Wana	*ganunga-wu*	*yuurrma-y.* (FR2437A)
let	they-all?	dance/play-future

Let them play.

iv. *yaluu* (again)

This is a common particle which has sometimes been written *yalu*. In many cases *yaluu* means 'again', as in the next two example sentences.

Ngarragaa-dhuul	*birralii*	*warra-nhi,*	*bundaa-nhi*	*yaluu.* (FR2437B)
poor.thing-little	child	stand-past	fall-past	again

The little boy got up and fell down again.

Yaluu	*ngaya*	*ngaama*	*nhaadhiyaan-da*	*baa-nhi.* (AD5056)
again	I	there	log-place	hop-past

I jumped back up on the log. (CW)

In the following example the meaning of *yaluu* is not clear:

Yaluu	*ngaya*	*gi-yaa-nha*	*wagirrbuma-y.* (AD5054A)
again	I	going.to	wash(intransitive)-future

I'll wash myself.

v. *yiyal* 'just'

The word *yiyal* 'just' is relatively common. In the old records it is often written *yeal*, and on the recordings it is often heard as *yal*, with one syllable only. There is an expression common in current GY — *yal-bala* or *yala-bala* — which is translated as 'gammon' or 'pretend'. This may be related to *yiyal*. A number of words which begin with *yal*, such as *yalagirrma* and *yalagiyu*, may also be related to *yiyal*. The meaning and use of *yiyal* is well illustrated by the following:

	Yiyal		nginda		bilaa-yu		dhu-nhi. (AD8185)
	just		you (one)		spear-instrument		pierce-past

This translates the italicised section: Why didn't you kill him? *You only just speared him* and left him there.

	Yilawa-nhi		ngali,		gaawaa-ga,		milanduul		yiyal		ngali
	sit-past		we (two)		river-at		one-only		just		we (two)

	bayama-y		dhagaay. (FR2436A)
	catch-past		yellowbelly

We sat for a long time, fishing and we only caught one little yellowbelly.

vi. *ngadhan.gaa* (suppose)

This particle occurs a number of times and is translated as 'I thought that'.

	Giirr		ngaama,		ngadhan.gaa		nguu		ngaama		guduu		bayama-y. (AD5131)
	true		that		I.thought		she		the		cod		catch-past

I thought she caught a fish.

	Giirruu		ngaya,		ngadhan.gaa		ngaama		ngaandi-yaa,		dhaay		yanaa-waa-nhi.
	true-all		I		thought		there		someone		to.here		come-moving-past

I thought the men were coming.

There may well be other particles to be defined or found. One possibility is *waama/wama*. Its meaning is not certain but it seems to mean something like 'because', 'as a result', 'therefore'.

▌Reduplication

There are a number of processes in GY for forming new words from existing words. The only one that is described here is 'reduplication'. This is the term for doubling up a word or part of a word. The new word has a new, but related, meaning. This process is common in Aboriginal languages, but the effect varies. Mostly words with two syllables are reduplicated, as in all the examples which follow.

Below are some rules which apply to most examples of reduplication, but some exceptions to these rules have been found. When reduplication is used with nouns it forms an adjective associated with the noun. The association is not always obvious. The noun *buya* (YR/YY)/*bura* (GR) means 'bone', and *buyabuya*/*burabura* means 'thin' or 'bony'. Similarly, *waya* (YR/YY)/*wara* (GR) means 'left' or 'left handed', and *wayawaya*/*warawara* means 'crooked'. When longer words are reduplicated often only the first two syllables are repeated. So from *banaga-y* 'run' comes *banabanaga-y*, which means something like 'sort of run' or 'jog'.

Reduplication of verbs seems to change the meaning to 'more or less'. The most common GY example of verb reduplication is the formation of *ngarrangarra-li* 'keep an eye on', 'look after' from *ngarra-li* 'see', 'look at':

| *Maayu-nga* | *ngaya* | *ngarrangarra-lda-nhi.* (FR2436B)
| well-then | I | looking.after-regular-past

I was looking after him properly.

| *Nguwa-badhaay-bala* | *nginda,* | *walaay* | *ngarrangarra-lda-y,*
| here-might-contrast | you (one) | camp | look.after-regular-future
  | *ngaya-bala* | *yanaa-y.* (AD3218B)
  | I-contrast | go-future

You stop here look after the camp while I go away.

There are other uses of reduplication. In only a few cases reduplication forms a plural, e.g. *girran.girraa* 'leaves'. The singular form is *girraa* but that is very rarely found. A related pattern is seen in *minyagaa* 'something', *minyaminyagaa* 'everything'. Here, reduplication forms a 'universal' (all, every) rather than a plural.

With the information in this learner's guide and the words in the dictionary you will be able to understand and say many things in Gamilaraay and Yuwaalaraay. While the dictionary section contains almost all the available information on words, the learner's guide is more of an introduction to the grammar. There is more known in some areas of the grammar than others. There are also many aspects of GY grammar which are still being investigated. As language revival continues, the grammar of GY will continue to be discovered and developed. There will eventually be fewer blanks when the question is asked, 'How do you say . . . ?'

Appendixes

1. Glossary of terms

This glossary does not set out to be a complete list of grammatical terms, or to give the full range of meanings, but rather to give some main ideas.

ablative case	a word in the ablative case indicates 'movement from', the 'place from' or related meanings (*gaawaa-dhi* 'from the river').
adjective	words, such as 'big', 'small' and 'happy', which describe a person, place, feeling or thing. Adjectives are generally attached to a noun. Some analyses of GY do not distinguish between adjectives and nouns.
adverb	tells how, when or where something happens, such as the English 'quickly', 'slowly' or 'often'. This is also something of a catch-all category for words that do not fit neatly elsewhere.
allative case	a word in the allative case shows 'movement to' or 'towards', as in 'she ran **to** the river'.
bound pronoun	is an abbreviated form of a pronoun that is a suffix on another word.
case	refers to the role of a noun or pronoun in a sentence or phrase (e.g. who is the doer or doer.to, done.to or owner). In English, case is generally shown by prepositions or by the position of the word in the sentence. In GY many cases are shown by suffixes.
clitic	GY clitics are a little like suffixes as they are attached to the ends of words. However, unlike suffixes they do not give information about the specific word to which they are attached. Rather, they are used to say something about a whole phrase within a sentence.
consonant	sounds which are not vowels. In GY these are represented by the letters *l, m, n, r, rr, ng*, etc. (Note that *w* and *y* are sometimes called semi-vowels.)
dative case	a case which indicates 'giving to', or related meanings, as in *dhimba-gu* 'to the sheep'.
demonstrative	words such as 'this' and 'that'. GY has a large range of demonstratives.
dual	words (often pronouns) that refer to two things, such as *ngindaali* 'you (two people)'.
ergative case	indicates the cause or agent of an action (the 'doer.to'), that is, the subject of a transitive verb. *Dhimba-gu dha-y* 'The sheep ate'.

exclamation	short statements of response, protest or surprise, such as 'yes', 'no', 'quick!', 'oh dear!' 'hell!'.
genitive case	see 'possessive case'.
grammar	a description of the rules of a language. This includes how words are adapted (e.g. suffixes), how they are put together to make sentences and other features of the language.
idiom	an expression whose meaning cannot be worked out from the meaning of individual words, such as *dhalay-bidi* 'big tongue', meaning a talkative person.
instrumental case	if something is done using a particular object, then that object is the 'instrument' of the action and takes the instrumental case.
locative case	a word in the locative case refers to where something happened, the 'place at', e.g. **on** the table.
morpheme	a bit of word that has a meaning. The following words are divided into morphemes: like, like-s, like-ness, like-ness-es, un-like, like-d.
negative	words such as 'no', 'not', 'none', 'never'.
noun	words which denote the names of things, such as 'house', 'girl', 'idea', 'car', 'kangaroo'.
number	in this context, refers to how many people or things are being talked about. Special terms for pronouns include singular (one person), dual (two people only) or plural (three or more people).
particle	words such as *giirr* 'truly' and *gamil* 'no', which often have a special place in the sentence and to which most suffixes cannot be attached. This word class is not clearly defined.
plural	in English, plural means 'more than one (thing or person)'. GY has dual pronouns, so plural pronouns refer to 'three or more (things or people)'. It is not clear if this dual/plural distinction was always maintained with nouns.
possessive case	a case which shows the ownership of a thing. In English we use apostrophes (e.g. the cat's whiskers, the book's jacket) or the word 'of' (the father of the bride).
pronoun	words that can be replaced by or refer to a noun. Examples are 'he', 'she' and 'my'. These examples are also called personal pronouns.
purposive case	a case which shows the reason something is done, as in 'they went **to get** wood', 'this is **for** grandma'.
reduplication	repetition of all or part of a word to create a new word with a related meaning, such as *buyabuya* 'thin', 'bony'.
simple sentence	is a set of words that expresses one idea. 'He is coming.' 'Dad cooked the tea.' 'Where are the kids?' 'I don't know.'
singular	one thing or person. See also number, dual and plural.
stem	the basic part of a word, to which suffixes may be attached.
stress	refers to the fact that some parts of words are said with greater emphasis than others (to**day**, **in**sect).
suffix	a word ending which tells you something about the word to which it is attached. In English, the ending -ly on the word 'bright' gives us 'bright-ly'; the ending -er creates 'sleeper'. In GY, nouns suffixes can indicate case, number and other concepts.

syllable	an individual sound part of a word containing a vowel. Examples of two-syllable words in English are 'ri-ver' and 'ca-stle'. The word 'ju-ven-ile' is a three-syllable word. In GY each syllable begins with a consonant and contains one vowel, e.g. *ga-ba* 'good', *biirr-nga* 'bony bream'.
tense	the way in which a verb is changed to indicate whether an action or event is taking place now (present tense), has already taken place (past tense) or will take place some time in the future (future tense).
verb	'doing' words, and words to do with a state of being — such as 'sit' or 'sleep' — and words such as 'think' and 'know'. Most present tense English verbs have the '-ing' ending attached to them: 'eat-ing', 'look-ing', 'die-ing'.
verb class	a group of verbs that has the same pattern of suffixes (that is, tense suffixes). There are four verb classes in GY.
vowel	a speech sound made with the mouth fairly open and with no major block to air flow, such as *a, aa, i, ii, u, uu*. (Note that *w* and *y* are sometimes called semi-vowels.)

Appendixes

2. Summaries

The following summaries are designed for checking details when you already understand the main concepts. It is important that you check the fuller explanations to make sure that you are using the information in the summaries correctly.

2.1. Suffixes

Main case suffixes

The four main case suffixes in GY are reproduced in the table below.

Word ending	-Ga (locative/place)	-Gu (ergative/ instrumental)	-Dhi (source)	-gu (possessive 'of', 'to', 'for')
-a, -aa	-ga	-gu	-dhi	-gu
-i, -ii (YR/YY)	-dja	-dju	-dji	-gu
-i, -ii (GR)	-dha	-dhu	-dhi	-gu
-u, -uu	-ga	-gu	-dhi	-gu
-n	-da	-du	-di	-gu
-l	-a	-u	-i	-gu
-rr (YR/YY)	delete rr and add -ya	rr and add -yu	keep rr and add -i	-gu
-rr (GR)	-a	-u	-i	-gu
-y (YR/YY)	-a	-u	-dji	-gu
-y (GR)	-dha	-dhu	-dhi	-gu

Other suffixes

-galgaa	plural
-gal	plural on 'child'
-DHuul	little, just, one
-bidi	big
-Baraay, -Biyaay	having, with (*-araay, -iyaay*)
-bil	having a lot of
-dhalibaa	without
-nginda	wanting
-giirr	like
-Baa	place of, time of
-bula	also
-gaali	two
-wan.gaan (YR/YY)	very
-ban.gaan (GR)	very
-gaalu	pretend

Clitics

-bala	contrast
-badhaay	might, would you?
-laa	then
-nga	now, then

Knowledge suffixes/clitics

-Waa	some
-Yaa	maybe, chance
-Waayaa	don't know

2.2. Pronouns

Prounouns

	Doer.to	Done.to	Genitive	Dative	Source
First person					
Singular	*ngaya*	*nganha*	*ngay*	*nganunda*	*nganundi*
Dual	*ngali*	*ngalinya*	*ngalingu*	*ngalingunda*	*ngalingundi*
Plural	*ngiyani*	*ngiyaninya*	*ngiyaningu*	*ngiyaningunda*	*ngiyaningundi*
Second person					
Singular	*nginda*	*nginunha*	*nginu*	*nginunda*	*nginundi*
Dual	*ngindaali*	*nginaalinya*	*nginaalingu*	*nginaalingunda*	*nginaalingundi*
Plural	*ngindaay*	*nginaaynya*	*nginaayngu*	*nginaayngunda*	*nginaayngundi*
Third person					
GR singular	*nguru*	*ngurunga**	*ngurungu*	*ngurungunda*	*ngurungundi*
YR/YY singular	*nguu*	*nguunga**	*nguungu*	*nguungunda*	*nguungundi*

Prounouns

	Doer.to	Doer, done.to	Genitive	Dative	Source
Third person					
Dual	*gaali*	*gaalinga**	*gaalingu**	*gaalingunda*	*gaalingundi*
Plural	*ganugu*	*ganunga*	*ganungu*	*ganungunda*	*ganungundi*

* hypothesised forms

Question pronouns

'Doer.to'	Doer, done.to	Genitive	Dative	Source
ngaandu	*ngaandi* YR, GR *ngaana* YY	*ngaanngu*	*ngaanngunda*	*ngaanngundi*

Suffixed pronouns

Suffixed form	Full form	Meaning
-nda	*nginda*	you (one) doer, doer.to
-ndaali	*ngindaali*	you (two) doer, doer.to
-ndaay	*ngindaay*	you (more than two) doer, doer.to
-nha *	*nhama*	that one, he, she, it, they

2.3 Verb endings

Simple tenses

	Future tense	Past tense	Command
-li class	-li	-y, (-ay)	-la
-y class	-y	-nhi (-nyi after i-)	-ya
-gi class	-gi	-nhi (-nyi after i-)	-nga
-rri class	-rri	-nhi	-na

Progressive forms

	Moving	Regular	Final suffixes
-li class	-laa-	-lda-	-y –nha –nhi -ya
-y class	-waa- (-yaa-)	-y-la-	-y –nha –nhi -ya
-gi class	-waa- (-yaa-)	-gi-la-	-y –nha –nhi -ya
-rri class	-rraa-	-dha-	-y –nha –nhi -ya

Suffixes about who is involved

Suffix	Meaning	Technical name
-la-y	each other	reciprocal
-ngiili-y	oneself	reflexive
-aaba-li	all	completive
-n.giili-y, *V-li-y	benefit	benefactive

*V = lengthen the final vowel of the stem

Time suffixes

Suffix	When did action happen?
-ngayi-y	recent past, near future (this forms a -y class verb)
-mayaa-y	distant past (sometimes 'yesterday')
-ngayi-li	'all day', on-going, habitual (this forms a -li class verb)
-ayla-y	'before', 'yesterday'

Other suffixes

Suffix	Meaning	Technical name
-uwi-y	'back'	
-ma-li	causes something	causative

Relative verb endings
(used in cases such as 'the woman who', or 'which', 'when', 'that', 'if', 'because')

Verb class	Suffix
-li class	-ndaay, -ldaay
-y class	-ngindaay
-gi class	-ngindaay
-rri class	-ndaay

Other verb features

-li class to -y class change
This change turns a transitive verb into an intransitive verb. The intransitive verb is used as a reflexive verb and in other ways.